# Tourism and Hospitality Marketing

# Tourism and Hospitality Marketing

## A Global Perspective

**Simon Hudson**

Los Angeles • London • New Delhi • Singapore

First published 2008

Apart from any fair dealing for the purposes of research or
private study, or criticism or review, as permitted under
the Copyright, Designs and Patents Act, 1988, this publication
may be reproduced, stored or transmitted in any form, or
by any means, only with the prior permission in writing of
the publishers, or in the case of reprographic reproduction,
in accordance with the terms of licenses issued by the
Copyright Licensing Agency. Enquiries concerning
reproduction outside those terms should be sent to
the publishers.

SAGE Publications Ltd
1 Oliver's Yard
55 City Road
London EC1Y 1SP

SAGE Publications Inc.
2455 Teller Road
Thousand Oaks, California 91320

SAGE Publications India Pvt Ltd
B 1/I 1 Mohan Cooperative Industrial Area
Mathura Road
New Delhi 110 044

SAGE Publications Asia-Pacific Pte Ltd
33 Pekin Street #02-01
Far East Square
Singapore 048763

**Library of Congress Control Number: 2007930777**

**British Library Cataloguing in Publication data**

A catalogue record for this book is available from the British Library

ISBN 978-1-4129-4686-5
ISBN 978-1-4129-4687-2 (pbk)

Typeset by C&M Digitals (P) Ltd., Chennai, India
Printed and bound in Great Britain by TJ International Ltd, Padstow, Cornwall
Printed on paper from sustainable resources

# CONTENTS

# PREFACE

The strong and sustained rise of tourism over the past 50 years is one of the most remarkable phenomena of our time. The number of international arrivals has risen from 25 million in 1950 to 842 million in 2006. While this represents an annual growth rate of about 7 per cent over more than half a century, the receipts generated by these tourists has increased nearly twice as fast. This growth rate for tourism far outstrips the world economy as a whole, and tourism now represents a quarter of all exports of services. In 2005 employment in the travel and tourism economy comprised over 200 million jobs or 8.2 per cent of total employment.

Alongside the growth of the tourism industry, tourism education has expanded rapidly over the last few decades, reflecting the growing recognition of tourism (and the travel and hospitality industries that serve it) as one of the world's most significant economic, social and environmental forces. Tourism education and training has been developed at various levels, ranging from highly vocational courses to higher research degrees. The growth reflects the widely held belief that one of the major challenges the industry faces is to recruit, develop and retain employees and managers who have appropriate educational backgrounds.

For most tourism and hospitality courses, tourism marketing is a required module or core subject, yet despite this obvious interest there are few recent texts that deal with tourism and hospitality marketing on a global scale. Marketing is a subject of vital concern in tourism because it is the principal management influence that can be brought to bear on the size and behaviour of this major global market. The main sectors of the tourism industry – travel organizers, destination organizations, transportation and various product suppliers – combine to manage visitors' demands through a range of marketing influences.

Tourism marketing also has an important and increasing international dimension. In our globalizing world, people, places and countries are increasingly interdependent. Countries once considered inaccessible to Western tourists because of geographical, cultural and political barriers are now not only becoming accessible – their very remoteness makes them an attractive choice for travel today. This globalization of tourism has cultural, political and economic dimensions, and these are important considerations for tourism marketers.

This very readable text makes it suitable for use in both educational and professional contexts. There are 78 up-to-date case studies from all over the world, covering all sectors of the tourism and hospitality industry. The majority of cases have been developed via personal visits and in-depth interviews conducted by the author. They examine the marketing of diverse tourism products, such as sport and adventure tourism, nostalgia tourism, space tourism, wine tourism and educational tourism, and have been carefully selected so as to be of specific interest to students. Some readers will be fascinated to learn how Canadian Mountain Holidays sells 7,000 heli-skiing trips a year with no advertising; why educational tourism is attracting an increasing number of students; why tourists are keen to volunteer whilst on holiday; how the backpacker is getting older and richer; how destinations are promoting experiences rather than products; and how a new hotel chain is promoting itself in a virtual world.

As well as offering numerous examples, the book provides comprehensive coverage of essential marketing principles, such as developing a marketing plan, understanding consumer behaviour, doing marketing research, and implementing the marketing mix. The text also includes sections on contemporary marketing issues such as integrated marketing communications, internet marketing, responsible marketing, and internal marketing.

*Tourism and Hospitality Marketing: A Global Perspective* begins, in Chapter 1, with an introduction to tourism and hospitality marketing in general, which discusses the definition and role of marketing and its importance in tourism. A synopsis of services marketing theory highlights the unique characteristics of services and introduces important service marketing models, such as the services marketing triangle and the services marketing mix. The chapter then focuses on tourism worldwide and analyses the key players in the tourism industry. The remainder of the chapter examines the marketing environment's microenvironmental and macroenvironmental forces, and the ways in which they affect an organization's ability to serve its customers.

Chapter 2 considers behavioural trends in tourism by reviewing tourism motivational studies, examining typologies of tourists and discussing the external factors that influence consumer behaviour. The chapter includes a section devoted to organizational buying behaviour, and an analysis of the current trends in consumer behaviour that are affecting tourism marketing today.

Successful marketing in tourism and hospitality requires careful planning and execution. Chapter 3, which focuses on the development of a marketing plan in the tourism and hospitality industry, discusses the eight key steps in the marketing planning process. Practical examples from various sectors of the tourism industry are also provided.

Chapter 4, on marketing research in tourism and hospitality, begins with a description of the type of applied research conducted in tourism, which is followed by a discussion of the various stages in the research process. The chapter then describes the various methodologies available to researchers and discusses the relative merits of primary and secondary research. The next part of the chapter looks at sampling and highlights five common research problems. The final section discusses effective use of research in decision-making.

Chapter 5 begins by introducing the peculiarities of the tourism product and the idea that tourism and hospitality products are a group of selected components or elements brought together in a 'bundle' to satisfy needs and wants. The chapter includes sections on the different product levels, product planning, the product life cycle model, and the positioning strategies available to organizations in the tourism and hospitality fields. An in-depth analysis of branding in tourism is supported by a case study about the growth of chefs as brands. The final sections of the chapter discuss the concepts of packaging and new product development.

Chapter 6, on pricing, begins by looking at the impact that various corporate objectives have on pricing, the key factors determining a company's pricing decisions, and the contribution of economics to pricing. The basic approaches to pricing are then described, followed by an important discussion on yield management. The difference between strategic pricing and tactical pricing is then explained, and the final section of the chapter looks at the specific characteristics of the tourism and hospitality industry that affect pricing policy.

Chapter 7 examines the various ways of distributing a tourism and hospitality product. It begins by looking at the nature and types of distribution channels and the different functions of a distribution system. It dicusses the key intermediaries involved in the tourism distribution system, and then considers the issues of channel conflict and organization. Finally, it examines the process of designing a company's distribution system and ensuring the effective execution of the distribution strategy.

The next three chapters explore the various marketing communications methods used by tourism and hospitality providers. Chapter 8 begins with an introduction that explains the role and types of promotion tools used in tourism and hospitality, and a section on the communications process follows. The chapter then discusses the rise of integrated marketing communications – the recognition that advertising can no longer be crafted and executed in isolation from other promotional mix elements. The communication techniques of advertising and sales promotion are then considered.

Chapter 9 begins by focusing on the roles and functions of public relations, and the main public relations techniques used in tourism and hospitality. Personal selling is the subject of the following section, which discusses the roles and objectives of personal selling, the sales process, and the roles of a sales manager. Next, the key advantages of direct marketing are discussed, as are the major direct marketing tools. The chapter concludes with a section on word-of-mouth communication, an important but often misunderstood form of promotion in tourism.

Chapter 10 examines a fast-growing area of tourism and hospitality marketing: direct internet marketing. The chapter discusses the six ways in which the internet is being used by the tourism and hospitality industry: direct e-marketing, advertising, distribution and sales, providing information, customer service and relationship marketing, and marketing research.

Chapter 11 begins by defining internal marketing and describing the four key steps in the internal marketing process. The next section, on service quality, includes segments on the 'gaps model' of service quality, methods of measuring service quality, and behavioural consequences of service quality. The third section discusses loyalty and relationship marketing. Various customer retention strategies are introduced, as are the benefits of relationship marketing to both company and customer. The final part of the chapter discusses service recovery and offers guidelines for tracking and handling complaints.

Chapter 12 considers both the opportunities and challenges inherent in the marketing of destinations. It begins by discussing the principles of destination marketing and by defining, characterizing and classifying destinations. A small section also examines the scope of visitor attractions. A summary of the objectives and benefits of destination marketing is followed by a more in-depth look at the role of destination marketing organizations (DMOs). The next two sections focus on destination branding and destination promotion. Finally, the chapter looks at the marketing of two particularly important sectors: events and conferences, and all-inclusive resorts.

Chapter 13 is concerned with contemporary tourism marketing issues and looks towards the future. An analysis of tourism marketing trends is followed by a discussion about tourism marketing in the experiential economy. The next two sections examine responsible marketing and cause-related marketing of tourism. The final two sections look at the marketing of sport and adventure tourism, and marketing tourism in times of crisis.

## Pedagogical Features

The objective of all chapters in this text is to cover the basic tourism and hospitality theories well while omitting unnecessary detail. Careful selection of topics, appropriate depth of coverage, and concise writing help to achieve this objective. Current examples from all types and sizes of tourism and hospitality businesses are used in the text discussion.

Each chapter contains the following pedagogical features:

**Opening Vignette**
These stories have been designed to draw students into the chapter by presenting a real-life example that is carefully linked to the material covered in the chapter.

**Objectives**
Objectives are provided at the beginning of each chapter to identify the major areas and points covered and to guide the learning process.

**Introduction**
An introductory section summarizes and lays the foundation for the material to be covered in that chapter.

**Chapter Summary**
A summary that distils the main points of the chapter. This synopsis serves as a quick review of important topics covered and as a helpful study guide.

**Key Terms**
Throughout each chapter, key terms appear in **bold** in the text and have corresponding definitions in boxes. A list of these, including page numbers, appears at the end of each chapter, making it easy for students to check their understanding of important terms.

**Discussion Questions and Exercises**
Each chapter ends with discussion questions that provide students with an opportunity to review how well they have learned the material.

**Case Study**
Each chapter contains an up-to-date and relevant case study. As a collection, these studies cover a variety of tourism and hospitality sectors and regions. Designed to foster critical thinking, the case studies illustrate actual business scenarios that stress several concepts found in the chapter. End-of-case questions encourage students to spot issues, analyse facts and solve problems.

**Websites**
Web addresses of companies discussed in the chapter are provided for students who wish to explore topics presented in the text further.

**Endnotes**
Bibliographical references for sources cited within each chapter are provided in a numbered end-of-chapter list.

**Special Interest Boxes**
Boxed features in each chapter help students to connect principles to practice more easily. Two types of feature boxes are interspersed throughout the text:

1. **Global Spotlights**
   Global Spotlights (one per chapter) highlight achievements of successful individuals or organizations in the tourism and hospitality industry. They were chosen for their expertise in specific areas related to the chapter material.
2. **Snapshots**
   Snapshots (three per chapter) provide shorter examples of tourism and hospitality marketing in practice. These are used to illustrate a particular concept or theoretical principle.

## Website support

This rich web resource to accompany the first edition of *Marketing for Tourism and Hospitality: A Global Perspective* provides resources for both the instructor and the student. The Student site includes true/false and multiple-choice questions, internet exercises, PowerPoint slides, career information and more. The instructor site includes the Instructor's Manual/Test Bank, incorporating answers to discussion questions and exercises, case study questions and a test bank, and PowerPoint slides.

## Acknowledgments

I am grateful to the many individuals who helped to make *Tourism and Hospitality Marketing: A Global Perspective* a reality. In particular, I would like to thank Anne Summers and Delia Alfonso from Sage, my wife Louise for her editorial assistance, and my secretary Joyce Twizell for all her help with the tables and diagrams.

This book has also benefited tremendously from the people in the tourism industry who took the time to talk to me and to provide me with valuable material. Those people are too numerous to list, but I thank them all. Finally, I am indebted to the reviewers who took the time to review the manuscript so professionally.

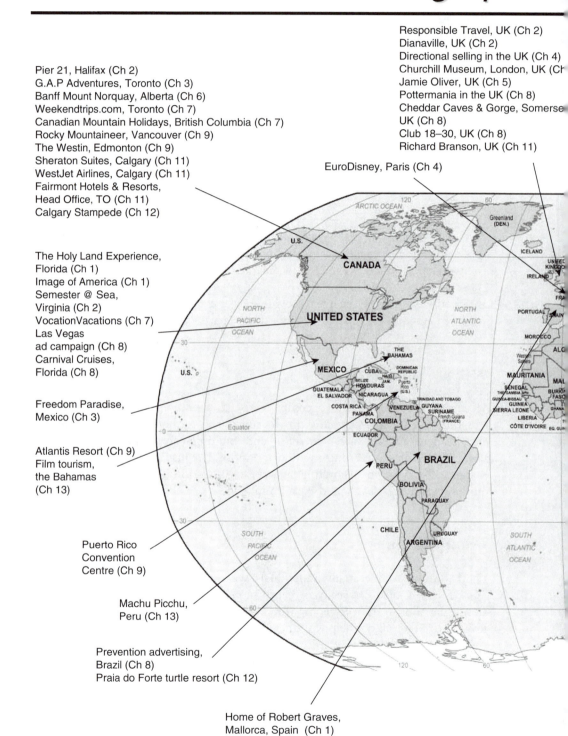

Pier 21, Halifax (Ch 2)
G.A.P Adventures, Toronto (Ch 3)
Banff Mount Norquay, Alberta (Ch 6)
Weekendtrips.com, Toronto (Ch 7)
Canadian Mountain Holidays, British Columbia (Ch 7)
Rocky Mountaineer, Vancouver (Ch 9)
The Westin, Edmonton (Ch 9)
Sheraton Suites, Calgary (Ch 11)
WestJet Airlines, Calgary (Ch 11)
Fairmont Hotels & Resorts,
Head Office, TO (Ch 11)
Calgary Stampede (Ch 12)

The Holy Land Experience,
Florida (Ch 1)
Image of America (Ch 1)
Semester @ Sea,
Virginia (Ch 2)
VocationVacations (Ch 7)
Las Vegas
ad campaign (Ch 8)
Carnival Cruises,
Florida (Ch 8)

Freedom Paradise,
Mexico (Ch 3)

Atlantis Resort (Ch 9)
Film tourism,
the Bahamas
(Ch 13)

Puerto Rico
Convention
Centre (Ch 9)

Machu Picchu,
Peru (Ch 13)

Prevention advertising,
Brazil (Ch 8)
Praia do Forte turtle resort (Ch 12)

Home of Robert Graves,
Mallorca, Spain  (Ch 1)

Responsible Travel, UK (Ch 2)
Dianaville, UK (Ch 2)
Directional selling in the UK (Ch 4)
Churchill Museum, London, UK (Ch )
Jamie Oliver, UK (Ch 5)
Pottermania in the UK (Ch 8)
Cheddar Caves & Gorge, Somerse
UK (Ch 8)
Club 18–30, UK (Ch 8)
Richard Branson, UK (Ch 11)

EuroDisney, Paris (Ch 4)

# ndex of Cases

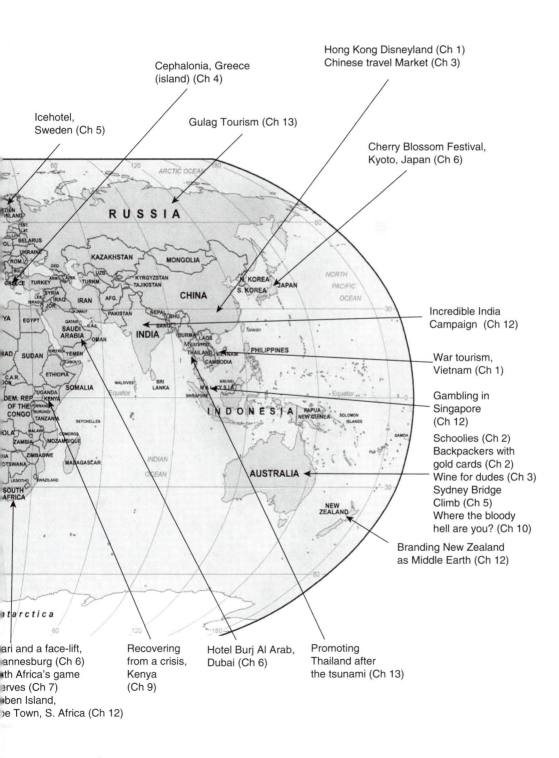

Icehotel,
Sweden (Ch 5)

Cephalonia, Greece
(island) (Ch 4)

Gulag Tourism (Ch 13)

Hong Kong Disneyland (Ch 1)
Chinese travel Market (Ch 3)

Cherry Blossom Festival,
Kyoto, Japan (Ch 6)

Incredible India
Campaign (Ch 12)

War tourism,
Vietnam (Ch 1)

Gambling in
Singapore
(Ch 12)

Schoolies (Ch 2)
Backpackers with
gold cards (Ch 2)
Wine for dudes (Ch 3)
Sydney Bridge
Climb (Ch 5)
Where the bloody
hell are you? (Ch 10)

Branding New Zealand
as Middle Earth (Ch 12)

ari and a face-lift,
annesburg (Ch 6)
th Africa's game
erves (Ch 7)
ben Island,
e Town, S. Africa (Ch 12)

Recovering
from a crisis,
Kenya
(Ch 9)

Hotel Burj Al Arab,
Dubai (Ch 6)

Promoting
Thailand after
the tsunami (Ch 13)

# 1

# THE GLOBAL TOURISM MARKETING ENVIRONMENT

## Disney Expands Global Empire to Hong Kong

Despite financial and cultural difficulties in Paris, Disney expanded its global empire to Hong Kong, opening its fifth theme park in the fall of 2005. The Hong Kong government offered financial incentives to encourage Disney to the island as part of its marketing strategy to boost tourism and assuage business fears about the return of the island to China from its former UK control. The government invested around HK$22.45 billion, providing 90 per cent of the investment as well as providing the site on Lantau Island, formerly a semi-rural paradise inhabited by fishermen and Buddhist monks. According to its promotional website, the partnership will inject HK$148 billion into the island's economy over the next 40 years and create 18,000 jobs.

Hong Kong Disneyland is Disney's first step in challenging the Chinese market and there are tentative plans to expand to the mainland, with a focus on Shanghai. However, there have been some hitches. Hong Kong residents (anglicized after a hundred years of British rule and education) have been outraged by mainland Chinese visitors walking barefoot, smoking in non-smoking areas, and urinating in public. There have also been food poisoning issues as well as fish farm claims to settle in relation to toxic construction damage to fish stocks. Another unforeseen problem was the overwhelming success of a discount-ticket promotion in 2006 which, in conjunction with the Chinese Lunar New Year, led to huge numbers of mainland families being turned away at the gates despite having valid tickets. Shark-fin soup served at the park has also caused an animal rights outcry. Critics point out Disney's hypocrisy in promoting nature in films such as *Finding Nemo* and, at the same time, condoning the wholesale annual slaughter of millions of sharks for their fins and wasting the rest of the meat.

A billboard in Hong Kong announces the opening of Hong Kong Disneyland

Inside the park Disney has been forced to make dozens of changes to make the experience more understandable to Chinese visitors, many of whom have seemed more confused than amused during visits. The 'Jungle Cruise' attraction, for example, has separate queues for three languages, so that riders can hear the narration in their native tongue. But Mandarin speakers were regularly hopping into the often-shorter English line, eager to get to the front faster – only to be perplexed by the English-speaking guide. There are now three separate signs to make it clear to guests that there is no point in moving to a different queue. The addition of Mandarin speakers to the park's staff as guides has been accompanied by new Mandarin reading materials and subtitles added to shows like 'Festival of the Lion King' and the 'Golden Mickeys', because Disney noticed that audiences were missing their cues to laugh or applaud. 'The subtitles are very helpful,' said Lu Ming, a 34-year-old finance worker from Zhe Jiang province who was at the park recently with her husband as part of a tour group. However, she expressed a common complaint: 'The park is too small, even smaller than the parks in our province. We have all sorts of theme parks at home so there is really nothing more exciting here.'

Ocean Park with its 28-year history of education, entertainment and animal conservation (notably, two giant pandas) is Disney's competition in Hong Kong. It attracts three million visitors a year and the entrance fee is nearly half the price of the new Disneyland. Overseas, Disney is, of course, competing against itself. The more established and larger branches in the US, Europe and Japan have between 44 and 65 attractions at their sites, whereas Hong Kong can only boast 22 at the moment, making the cost per item the highest. However, the Hong Kong government has already allocated US$2.9 billion for future expansion to provide more attractions and satisfy local opinion and tourist needs.

Michael Eisner, CEO of the Walt Disney Co. during construction, claimed that the 'turbulence' caused by the project helped create a better product. 'Life is turbulence. Life isn't only Disneyesque. Disneyesque is the end result of trying to do it better,' he asserted. He also explained that although Asia has never been a 'castle-oriented environment' and did not really know the Disney product, Hong Kong Disneyland would become over time one of Disney's biggest properties, with about 40 per cent of the customer demographic being Chinese because of their love of family entertainment.

*Sources*: Foreman, W. (9 December 2005) 'Life not always "Disneyesque"', *Globe & Mail*, B8; Hutchinson, B. (23 October 2004) 'The next Hong Kong', *National Post*, P11; Anon. (24 May 2005). 'Disneyland in hot water over plan to serve shark's fin soup', *National Post*, A13; Marr, M. and Fowler, G.A. (12 June 2006) 'Chinese lessons for Disney at Hong Kong Disneyland: park officials learn a lot from their past mistakes', *Wall Street Journal*, B1.

## OBJECTIVES

On completion of this chapter, you should understand:

▶ what is meant by tourism and hospitality marketing;

▶ the unique challenges of services marketing;

▶ who the key players are in the global tourism industry; and

▶ the various macroenvironmental forces shaping the tourism industry worldwide.

## Introduction

The Opening Vignette is an example of an aggressive, risk-taking global adventure in the tourism industry. By understanding and adapting to a changing environment, Disney has become the largest theme park company in the world, but it is clear from this case that success depends on a clear understanding of the changing tourism marketing environment. This book begins with a chapter dedicated to the current global tourism marketing environment. The chapter starts with an introduction to tourism and hospitality marketing in general, by discussing the definition and role of marketing and its importance in international tourism. A synopsis of services marketing theory highlights the unique characteristics of services and introduces important service marketing models, such as the services marketing triangle and the services marketing mix. The remainder of the chapter examines the major environmental forces that affect an organization's ability to serve its customers.

Tourism is a powerful economic force providing employment, foreign exchange, income and tax revenue. The **tourism market** reflects the demands of consumers for a very wide range of travel and hospitality products, and it is widely claimed that this total market is now being serviced by the world's largest industry. Players in this industry are increasingly operating in a global environment, where people, places and countries are increasingly interdependent. Countries once considered inaccessible to Western tourists because of geographical, cultural and political barriers are now not only becoming accessible – their very remoteness makes them an attractive choice for travel today. An example is Tibet, one of the most impoverished parts of the world, where the opening of a new Chinese railway in 2006 across the Himalayas is expected to double tourist revenue, with more than a million people a year predicted to use the line.

---

**TOURISM MARKET**
a market that reflects the demands of consumers for a very wide range of travel and hospitality products

---

The globalization of tourism has cultural, political and economic dimensions. Cultural globalization is characterized by cultural homogenization as Western consumption and lifestyle patterns spread throughout the world, a process facilitated by the flow of travellers from the West to the developing world. Travel also enhances friendships between peoples and facilitates cultural exchange. Political globalization involves the undermining of the roles and importance of nation states as borders are opened up to free trade and investment. Economic globalization has both positive and negative effects. On the one hand, it could be argued that a key aspect of economic globalization has been the increasing power in the hands of a small number of travel organizations, leading to oligopolistic control in the industry. On the other hand, tourism brings with it economic rewards and opportunities for host communities in particular, which benefit from foreign exchange and enhanced livelihood options. The Opening Vignette shows how the Hong Kong government offered financial incentives to encourage Disney to the island as part of its marketing strategy to boost tourism and therefore benefit the island's economy.

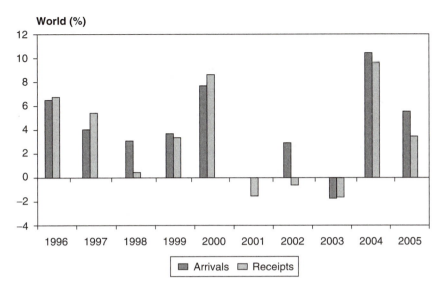

**Figure 1.1**   International Tourist Arrivals and Receipts (per cent change)

*Source: United Nations World Tourism Organization News* (2006), Issue 3, p. 4.

There are many examples in tourism and hospitality industries of companies operating in a global environment. Disney of course is one, but another is the Hard Rock brand, a favourite on tourists' T-shirts the world over. The chain was founded by music-lovers Isaac Tigrett and Peter Morton with one London restaurant in 1971, and in 2006 included 124 cafes in more than 40 countries. Hard Rock International, now owned by the Seminole Tribe of Florida, had worldwide sales in 2005 of US$493 million and profit of US$65 million (Allen, 2006).[1] Between them, the rock'n'roll diners, which carry the motto 'Love All, Serve All', own the world's most comprehensive collection of rock memorabilia. The collection has grown from Pete Townsend's and Eric Clapton's guitars, donated during the 1970s, to include the doors of the Beatle's Abbey Road recording studios and one of Madonna's trademark bustiers.

The increased globalization of tourism is reflected in the statistics related to the industry. The number of international arrivals rose from 25 million in 1950 to 842 million in 2006. While this represents an annual growth rate of nearly 7 per cent over more than half a century, the receipts generated by these tourists have increased nearly twice as fast. In 2005, income, excluding air tickets and revenue from domestic tourism, reached US$682 billion. Including air tickets, the figure is more than $800 billion (UNWTO, 2006).[2] Figure 1.1 shows the percentage change in international tourist arrivals and tourist receipts between 1996 and 2005. Africa has proved to be one of the strongest tourism markets, with most of its destination countries showing consistently higher than average increases in both arrivals and receipts. Between 2000 and 2005, international arrivals to Africa soared from 28 million to 40 million, and receipts doubled from US$10.5 billion to $21.3 billion.

This growth rate for tourism far outstrips the world economy as a whole, and tourism now represents a quarter of all exports of services. In 2005 employment in the travel and tourism economy comprised over 200 million jobs or 8.2 per cent of total employment. The United

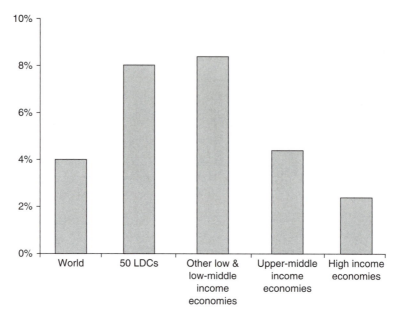

**Figure 1.2** Annual Growth in International Tourist Arrivals 1990–2005 (%)

*Source: United Nations World Tourism Organization News* (2006), Issue 3, p. 5.

Nations World Tourism Organization's (UNWTO) Tourism 2020 Vision forecasts that international arrivals will reach over 1.56 billion by the year 2020. Of these, 1.18 billion will be intra-regional and 377 million will be long-haul travellers.[3] The top three receiving regions are expected to be Europe, East Asia and the Pacific, and the Americas, followed by Africa, the Middle East and South Asia.

The impact of tourism goes far beyond enrichment in purely economic terms, helping to benefit the environment and culture and the fight to reduce poverty. Over the past decade, the annual growth rate of tourists to developing countries was higher than the world average, with 326 million arrivals generating US$205 billion in revenue. Figure 1.2 indicates the annual growth in international tourism arrivals between 1990 and 2005 in different parts of the world. In 2005, arrivals to least developing countries (LCDs) were up 48 per cent compared with the world as a whole. Tourism can serve as a foothold for the development of a market economy where small and medium-sized enterprises can expand and flourish. And in poor rural areas, it often constitutes the only alternative to subsistence farming, which is in decline. In Rwanda, Africa, for example, tourism has become the country's third largest source of foreign income after tea and coffee exports, taking in over £6 million in 2005. Rwanda is targeting £50 million in foreign earnings by 2010.

Big emerging markets (BEMs) like Brazil, India, Turkey and Vietnam also see the potential of tourism as a powerful economic force. The Snapshot below shows how the Vietnam National Administration of Tourism (VNAT) has been actively encouraging war tourism as part of its marketing plan. VNAT forecasts US$11.8 billion tourism earnings by 2010 based on 3.5 million international tourist arrivals plus around 25 million domestic tourists.

Vietnam's economy and infrastructure were in a shambles after 20 years of socialism and years of war, but this country of over 70 million people is poised for significant growth.

## Snapshot

### War as a tourism attraction in Vietnam

War tourism has been around for hundreds of years. Admiral Lord Nelson's battleship, *HMS Victory,* has long been a tourist attraction drawing millions of visitors to Portsmouth, England. Heroes from the American Civil War have likewise been venerated in the US with statues, artifacts, memorials and re-enactments of their battles, attracting tourists in their thousands. The eerie reminders of World War II atrocities at Belsen and Auschwitz are still major tourism destinations as well as the city of Hiroshima in Japan. However, it is only more recently that tourism marketers in Vietnam have identified the cultural value of their war-ravaged country in terms of an attraction and focus for overseas visitors.

Having suffered more than 30 years of war (first with France, then with the US, and finally civil war), Vietnam has since its 1987 economic reform policy, *doi moi,* been engaged in renovation and rebuilding. The reforms promote open-door policies and a free market economy. Since the establishment of the Vietnam National Administration of Tourism (VNAT), war tourism has been actively encouraged and targeted as part of a government and private sector marketing plan. VNAT is focusing on increasing state management of tourism, strategic planning and forecasting, human resource training, and the easing of formalities within the industry. The intention is to attract overseas investment and develop tourism as a dominant foreign exchange earner for Vietnam.

War in Vietnam led to the deaths of more than three million inhabitants along with 75,000 French and 59,000 US soldiers. The environmental, social, political and economic repercussions of this devastation still persist. VNAT predicts that two million Vietnamese immigrants will revisit their native country as tourists from the 80 different countries where they now live. Former American soldiers also seek the 'closure' of revisiting the scenes of their nightmares in order to 'remember the fallen', come to terms with the past and also to participate in a more positive future for Vietnam. Already there are several non-profit organizations and tour companies in the US providing tailor-made trips to these former scenes of battle.

The challenges of authenticity and sensitivity in war tourism underline many other fundamental problems for tourism development in Vietnam. There is poor infrastructure with low-standard roads and inadequate transport links between the north and south of the country. The system of business laws and policies is inadequate and confusing, undermining investors' confidence. Safety is another tourist concern as petty crime is prolific in the cities and exacerbated at night by poor or non-existent street lighting in some areas. Skilled workers and qualified management personnel are often lacking. However, Vietnam is geographically ripe for mass tourism. Three-quarters of the mainly agricultural country is tropical forest and wild mountains and 3,200 kilometres of coastline is home to 125 mostly unspoilt beaches. The climate is mainly hot, humid and dry although there are tropical monsoons from May to October. There is a huge variety of historic sites, French colonial architecture, diverse traditions, thriving northern tribal hill culture and also the wartime heritage whereby anything relating to the conflict with the US and its allies is an important component of tourism marketing.

A major war tourism attraction in Vietnam is the Cu Chi Tunnels, 40 miles from Ho Chi Minh City (formerly Saigon). Cu Chi was made famous during the Vietnam wars for its extensive network of underground tunnels spanning almost 200 kilometres. The tunnels were first used by the Viet Minh to hide from the French in the 1940s, then later became hideouts, living quarters and sniper bases for the Viet Cong, who at one point had even tunnelled under the Mekong Delta headquarters of the US Army's 25th Division. Guerillas and villagers often lived underground for months, surviving on tapioca and breathing with the help of an elaborate ventilation system that also served to direct cooking smoke away from the inhabited areas. From these hiding places, the Viet Cong were often able to make sneak attacks on their enemies, often within the US garrison. The American soldiers made every effort to destroy them, trying manpower, firepower, bombs, dogs and even gas, but ultimately failed.

Today, short sections of the tunnel cobweb are open to the public and, on request, tourists can explore even further into the narrow, dark, dusty and bat-filled tunnels. These have been enlarged for the western frame, but some, just 30 inches in diameter, were originally only accessible to the diminutive Vietnamese 'tunnel rats'. The dirt, heat and claustrophobic confines can be relived by tourists now as they fumble their way through, bent double or on hands and knees just for a few hundred metres. The area is circled by bomb craters, testament to the 500,000 tonnes of bombs dropped in the area. Such bombing often collapsed the upper tunnels, killing all inhabitants.

A diverse number of tourist facilities now support the tunnel tours, with lectures, propaganda videos from the 1960s, shooting ranges, gift shops featuring rice wine with cobras and scorpions inside the bottles as well as necklaces of silver bullets, and refreshments all established in an education/entertainment format. Visitors are shown vicious mantraps made of sharpened bamboo spikes concealed by foliage-covered trapdoors. There are gun-totting mannequins dressed in guerilla warfare jungle gear both above ground in the forest and below in the tunnel rooms. This commodification of war relics, sites and memorabilia could be seen as trivialization of suffering and death, whereby history is replaced by a heritage industry presenting a somewhat false view of the past. Alternatively, it could be applauded for its exploitation of the past to help create a prosperous future for hitherto poverty-stricken populations as well as providing a grim reminder of past mistakes for future generations to learn from. Certainly, the Cu Chi tunnels are a vivid testament to the ingenuity and perseverance that eventually helped the Vietnamese win the war.

*Sources*: Becker, K. (4 December 2003) 'Monuments to successful soldiers', *National Post*, PT3; Aramberri, J., and Ai Dao, T.T. (2005) 'Vietnam for the Vietnamese'. *Tourism Recreation Research*, Rhetoric and Image Creation, 30(2).

## The Influence of Marketing on Tourism

### Marketing

**Marketing** has been defined as 'the process of planning and executing the conception, pricing, promotion, and distribution of ideas, goods, and services to create exchanges that satisfy individual (customer) and organizational objectives (Kotler, 1984)'.[4] The marketing concept is a business philosophy that defines marketing as a process intended to find, satisfy, and retain customers while the business makes a profit. Central to both these definitions is the role of the customer and the customer's relationship to the product, whether that product is goods, a service, or an idea. The tourism and hospitality sector, like other service sectors, involves a combination of tangible and intangible products. A hotel is a mixture of goods (beds, food, telephone, and communication systems) that are linked with a range of services (front desk, housekeeping, room service, finance, and accounting). A tourist attraction such as a national park is a combination of facilities (hotels, shops, visitor centres) situated within a physical attraction (the mountains, forests, or rivers, for example), offering a range of services (guided tours, interpretation, education, etc.). This whole package of tangible and intangible products is perceived by the tourist as an experience, and represents the core of the tourism product.

---

**MARKETING**
the process of planning and executing the conception, pricing, promotion, and distribution of ideas, goods, and services to create exchanges that satisfy individual (customer) and organizational objectives

---

## International Marketing

**International marketing** is defined as 'the business activities designed to plan, price, promote and direct the flow of a company's goods and services to consumers in more than one country for profit' (Cateora and Graham, 2005).[5] The important difference between this definition and the one given earlier is that international marketing activities take place in more than one country. The uniqueness of foreign marketing comes from the range of unfamiliar problems and the variety of strategies necessary to cope with different levels of uncertainty encountered in foreign markets. The Opening Vignette highlighted some of the challenges Disney encountered when the company moved into Hong Kong, and the marketing strategies they employed to overcome these challenges.

---

**INTERNATIONAL MARKETING**
the business activities designed to plan, price, promote and direct the flow of a company's goods and services to consumers in more than one country for profit

---

Figure 1.3 illustrates the environment of an international marketer. The inner circle depicts the domestic controllable elements that constitute a marketer's decision area, such as product, price, promotion, distribution and research decisions. The second circle encompasses those environmental elements at home that have some effect on foreign-operation decisions, and the outer circles represent the elements of the foreign environment for each of the foreign markets in which the marketer operates. As the outer circles illustrate, every foreign market in which

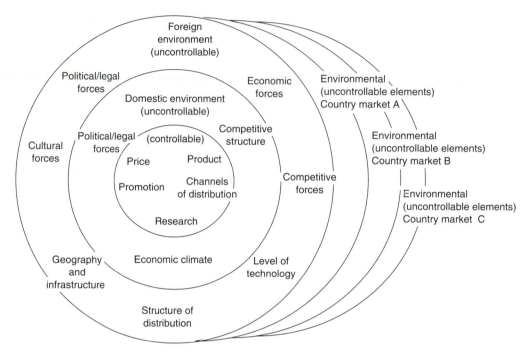

**Figure 1.3**   The International Marketing Task

*Source*: Cateora, P. R. and Graham, J. L. (2005) *International Marketing*. New York: McGraw-Hill Irwin, p. 10. Reproduced with permission of the McGraw-Hill Companies.

the company operates can present separate problems involving certain uncontrollable elements. Examples of uncontrollables include political instability, economic climate, cultural problems, and the level of technology. To adjust and adapt a marketing programme to foreign markets, marketers must be able to interpret effectively the influence and impact of each of the uncontrollable elements on the marketing plan for each foreign market in which they hope to do business. The Opening Vignette illustrates how Disney's management was insensitive to cultural differences in Hong Kong, and therefore experienced some teething problems. More market research and better environmental scanning would have helped make some of the hiccups at least foreseeable, if not entirely controllable.

Key obstacles facing international marketers are not limited to environmental issues. Just as important are difficulties associated with the marketer's own self-reference criteria (SRC) and ethnocentrism. SRC is an unconscious reference to one's own cultural values, experiences, and knowledge as a basis for decisions. Closely connected is ethnocentrism, which is the notion that one's own culture or company knows best how to do things. Both limit the international marketer's ability to understand and adapt to differences prevalent in foreign markets. A global awareness and sensitivity are the solutions to these problems. In recent years, Americans have been accused of ethnocentrism, and this has led to the country developing a poor image overseas. This in turn has adversely affected tourism to the country. The Snapshot below looks at the efforts the country is taking to overcome this problem.

## Snapshot

### Repairing the Image of America

A 2006 poll conducted by Washington-based Pew Research found that George Bush's six years in office have so damaged the image of the US that people worldwide see Washington as a bigger threat to world peace than Tehran. Another 2006 study by RT Strategies found that the US is the world's most unfriendly country for international travellers, mainly due to rude immigration officials and long delays in processing visas. The US image for most of the 20th century was relatively positive, being regularly identified with democracy, human rights and openness. However, the Pew survey, carried out annually, shows a continued decline in support for the US since 1999. This decline in image has had a knock-on effect on America's travel and tourism industry. Total inbound international arrivals dropped from 51.2 million in 2000 to 41.2 million in 2003 – a 20 per cent decrease. A 12 per cent recovery in 2004, due to favourable exchange rates for visitors, changed the declining trend somewhat, but also led to industry and governmental fears that future fluctuations in currency could reduce numbers again unless something was done about the 'ugly American' image.

The image issue became paramount in tackling a massive decline in worldwide tourism market share. In order to try and tempt back both business and tourist travellers, the tourism industry partnered with government to launch an aggressive and highly competitive marketing campaign to revive US figures. Visa, passport and security procedures were targeted to make international visitors feel more welcome. With wait times of up to 100 days for some visitors just to secure their interview for a visa, the travel industry campaigned for additional staffing and facilities in order to reduce these times and improve customer service training.

President Bush himself appeared in his first ever advertising campaign promoting US tourism in 2001, as part of a US$20 million initiative organized by Marriott International under the auspices of the Travel Industry Association of America (TIA), to revive tourism in the wake of 9/11. By 2006 both the TIA and the Travel Business Roundtable supported the establishment of a Presidential Advisory Council on Travel and Tourism to promote the US at the major travel destinations in the world. The aims of this federal advisory committee would include fostering tourism policy development and co-ordination within the federal government; demonstrating how effective tourism policy can be implemented; raising awareness of the economic importance of travel and tourism; and developing appropriate benchmarks to measure tourism policy success.

The not-for-profit Business for Diplomatic Action (BDA) launched a project in May 2003 to beautify the time-worn image of the 'ugly American' by promoting an attitude adjustment among American business executives travelling abroad. Its 2006 *World Citizens Guide* includes advice on speaking quietly and more slowly, being more sensitive in word choice, listening to others rather than talking over them, dressing well to meet the higher grooming standards of the host country and keeping one's own religion to oneself. Part of the problem is that too few Americans actually want to experience a different culture. US residents make only 28 million visits abroad each year (compared to 68 million made by the British who have a fifth of the population). On average, an American makes a foreign trip just once every 11 years.

The BDA also delivered its message via pamphlets to more than fifty US businesses including American Airlines, Loews Hotels and Novell. Surveys had revealed that international opinion was against the American personality as well as foreign policy issues. According to Carl Eggspuehler, BDA's executive director, Americans used to be admired for their way of life but this was no longer the case, and dislike of American values and personality traits was undermining business interests abroad as well as marketing efforts in the US tourism industry at home. In polls conducted in more than 100 countries after 9/11 by the advertising conglomerate DDB Worldwide, the words 'arrogant', 'loud' and 'uninterested in the world' were universally applied to Americans. More importantly, it was revealed in the survey that Americans appeared not to 'respect' other cultures.

In 2004 the BDA started with the creation of a student version of the behavioural guide that went out to 200,000 study-abroad participants. The overwhelming response to this led to the 2006 business travellers' version as well as another programme for schoolchildren. Although there is no official governmental connection, BDA chairman Keith Reinhard met with Undersecretary of State Karen Hughes, who supported the BDA's efforts in her key role to improve the USA's standing abroad. The Travel Industry Association of America (TIA) also supported the initiative as part of its drive to improve the international image of Americans.

*Sources*: Clark, J. (28 April 2006) 'That "ugly American" image is getting a makeover guide', *USA Today*, 9D; Price, M. (2006) 'Industry issues and trends: America's image abroad', *The Power of Travel 2006*, 8–11; MacAskill, Ewen. (15 June 2006) 'US seen as a bigger threat to peace than Iran, worldwide poll suggests', *The Guardian*, 8; Anon (21 November 2006) 'It's the stars and gripes as travelers rate US world's unfriendliest country', *National Post*, A12.

## Tourism Marketing

Marketing is a subject of vital concern in tourism because it is the principal management influence that can be brought to bear on the size and behaviour of this major global market. Figure 1.4 shows the vital linkages between demand and supply in tourism, which are fundamental to an understanding of the role of marketing. The figure shows the relationship between market demand, generated in areas of origin, and product supply, mainly at visitor destinations. In particular, the model shows how the main sectors of the tourism industry – travel organizers, destination organizations, transportation, various product suppliers – combine to manage visitors' demands through a range of marketing influences.

The marketing mix is in the centre of the diagram, and it is discussed in detail in this book. However, it is important to note that the influence of this marketing activity is likely to vary according to visitors' interests and circumstances. For example, domestic visitors travelling by car to stay with friends or relatives may not be influenced by destination marketing in any way, whereas first-time buyers of package tours to exotic destinations may find that almost every aspect of their trip is influenced by the marketing decisions of the tour operator they choose. In between these two examples, a business traveller will select his or her own destination according to business requirements, but may be influenced as to which airline or hotel he or she selects.

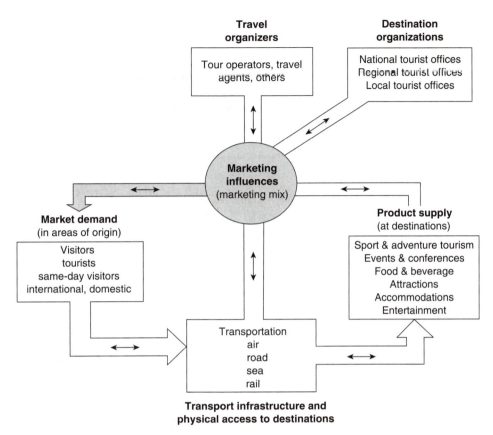

**Figure 1.4** The systematic links between demand and supply: the influence of marketing

*Source*: Middleton, V. T. C. and Clarke, J. (2001) *Marketing in Travel and Tourism*. Oxford: Butterworth-Heinemann.

Knowledge of the customer, and all that it implies for management decisions, is generally referred to as consumer or marketing orientation. A detailed understanding of consumer characteristics and buying behaviour is central to the activities of marketing managers, and therefore consumer behaviour is the topic of Chapter 2.

## Marketing Services

The tourism and hospitality sector incorporates both goods and services. Goods are easier to measure, test, and evaluate, while services provide a greater challenge. Service products are commonly distinguished from goods products by the four unique characteristics listed here.

1. **Intangibility** Service products cannot be tasted, felt, seen, heard or smelt. Prior to boarding a plane, airline passengers have nothing but an airline ticket and a promise of safe delivery to their destination. To reduce uncertainty caused by service intangibility, buyers look for tangible evidence that will provide information and confidence about the service.
2. **Inseparability** For many services, the product cannot be created or delivered without the customer's presence. The food in a restaurant may be outstanding, but if the server has a poor attitude or provides inattentive service, customers will not enjoy the overall restaurant experience. In the same way, other customers can affect the experience in service settings.
3. **Heterogeneity** Service delivery quality depends on who provides the services. The same person can deliver differing levels of service, with a marked difference in tolerance and friendliness as the day wears on. Lack of consistency is a major factor in customer dissatisfaction.
4. **Perishability** Services cannot be stored. Empty airline seats, hotel rooms, daily ski passes, restaurant covers – all these services cannot be sold the next day. If services are to maximize revenue, they must manage capacity and demand since they cannot carry forward unsold inventory.

The Opening Vignette showed how Disney was affected by the inseparability characteristic of services, with Hong Kong residents being outraged by mainland Chinese visitors walking barefoot, smoking in non-smoking areas, and urinating in public. Also, in an attempt to overcome the perishability of its offerings, Disney used a discount-ticket promotion, but this was too popular and led to huge numbers of mainland families being turned away at the gates despite having valid tickets.

Several models and frameworks have been developed to assist in making services marketing and management decisions at both the strategic and implementation levels. Two of these will now be discussed: the services marketing triangle and the services marketing mix. Both of these frameworks address the challenges inherent in services, and each of them can be used to assess and guide strategies, as well as provide a roadmap for implementation planning.

## The Services Marketing Triangle

The **services marketing triangle** (see Figure 1.5) shows the three interlinked groups that work together to develop, promote, and deliver services. These key players – the company, the customers, and the providers – are labelled on the points of the triangle. Between these three points there are three types of marketing that must be successfully carried out for a service to succeed: external, interactive, and internal marketing. For all services, especially for

---

**SERVICES MARKETING TRIANGLE**
a model that illustrates the three interlinking groups that work together to develop, promote, and deliver services: the company, the customer, and the provider

**Figure 1.5**  The services marketing triangle

*Source*: Zeithaml, V. A. and Bitner, M. J. (2000) *Services Marketing: Integrating Customer Focus across the Firm*. New York: McGraw-Hill, p. 16. Reproduced with permission of the McGraw-Hill Companies.

tourism and hospitality services, all three types of marketing activities are essential for building and maintaining relationships. Through its external marketing efforts, a company makes promises to its customers regarding what they can expect and how it can be delivered. Traditional marketing activities (such as those discussed in Chapters 8, 9, and 10) facilitate this type of marketing, but for services, other factors such as the servicescape and the process itself help to establish customer expectations.

Keeping promises, or interactive marketing, is the second kind of marketing activity captured by the triangle. Interactive marketing occurs in the 'moment of truth' when the customer interacts with the organization and the service is produced and consumed. From the customer's point of view, the most vivid impression of service occurs in the service encounter or the moment of truth. It is in these encounters that customers receive a snapshot of the organization's service quality, and each encounter contributes to the customer's overall satisfaction and willingness to do business with the organization again.

Finally, internal marketing takes place through the enabling of promises. Promises are easy to make, but unless providers are recruited, trained, provided with tools and appropriate internal systems, and rewarded for good service, the promises may not be kept. Internal marketing is discussed in more depth in Chapter 11.

## The Marketing Mix for Services

Another way to begin addressing the challenges of services marketing is to think creatively about the **services marketing mix**, through an expanded marketing mix for services. The

---

**SERVICES MARKETING MIX**
the original four Ps of the marketing mix – product, place, promotion, and price – plus the people, the physical evidence, and the process

**Table 1.1** Expanded Marketing Mix For Services

| Traditional 4 Ps of Marketing | *Product* | *Place* | *Promotion* | *Price* |
|---|---|---|---|---|
| | Physical good features | Channel type | Promotion blend | Flexibility |
| | Quality level | Exposure | Salespeople | Price level |
| | Accessories | Intermediaries | Number | Terms |
| | Packaging | Outlet locations | Selection | Differentiation |
| | Warranties | Transportation | Training | Discounts |
| | Product lines | Storage | Incentives | Allowances |
| | Branding | Managing channels | | |
| | | | Advertising | |
| | | | Targets | |
| | | | Media types | |
| | | | Types of ads | |
| | | | Copy thrust | |
| | | | Sales promotion | |
| | | | Publicity | |

| Traditional 3 Ps of Services Marketing | *People* | *Physical evidence* | *Process* |
|---|---|---|---|
| | Employees | Facility design | Flow of activities |
| | Recruiting | Equipment | Standardized |
| | Training | Signage | Customized |
| | Motivation | Employee dress | Number of steps |
| | Rewards | | Simple |
| | Teamwork | Other tangibles | Complex |
| | | Reports | |
| | Customers | Business cards | Customer involvement |
| | Education | Statements | |
| | Training | Guarantees | |

*Source*: Booms, B. H. and Bitner, M. J. (1981) 'Marketing strategies and organizational structures for service firms'. In J. H. Donnelly and W. R. George (eds). *Marketing Services*. Chicago: American Marketing Association, pp. 47–51.

marketing mix may be defined as 'the mixture of controllable marketing variables that the firm uses to pursue the sought level of sales in the target market' (Kotler, 1984).[6] The original four Ps of the marketing mix, introduced by McCarthy (1981),[7] are product, place, promotion, and price. Because services are usually produced and consumed simultaneously, customers are often part of the service production process. Also, because services are intangible, customers will often be looking for any tangible cue to help them understand the nature of the service experience. These facts have led service marketers to conclude that they can use additional variables to communicate with and satisfy their customers. Acknowledgement of the importance of these additional variables has led service marketers to adopt the concept of an expanded marketing mix for services, shown in Table 1.1. In addition to the traditional four Ps, the services marketing mix includes people, physical evidence, and process.

The people element includes all human actors who play a part in service delivery and thus influence the buyer's perceptions – namely the firm's personnel, the customer, and other customers in the service environment. The physical evidence is the environment in which the service is delivered and where the firm and customer interact, and any tangible components that facilitate performance or communication of the service. Table 1.1 gives some examples of tangible evidence or cues used by service organizations. Finally, the process is the actual procedures, mechanisms, and flow of activities by which the service is delivered. The three new marketing mix elements are included in the marketing mix as separate elements because they are within the control of the firm, and any or all of them may influence customers' initial decision to purchase a service, their level of satisfaction and their repurchase decisions. The traditional elements as well as the new marketing mix elements are explored in depth in later chapters.

## Key Players in the Global Tourism Industry

The key players in the tourism industry are outlined in Figure 1.6. They include private and non-profit sector services, public sector services, suppliers (transportation, accommodations, food and beverage services, attractions, and events and conferences), intermediaries, and the customers (tourists/travellers) themselves. Each will be discussed in turn below.

### Private and Non-profit Sector Services

The private and non-profit sector includes tourism industry associations such as travel agency or tour operator associations, financial and banking services, educational institutions, the media and insurance services.

### Public Sector Services

Public sector involvement often comes in the form of national, regional or destination management or marketing organizations. Under the umbrella of each provincial tourism organization, there are a number of public, quasi-public and independent organizations, which work independently and in co-operation with others to create more attractive tourism products. At a state or provincial level, marketing agencies spend millions of dollars promoting tourism. Their marketing programmes target both individual travellers and travel trade intermediaries. Often they enter into co-operative marketing with suppliers, carriers, intermediaries, and other destination marketing organizations. Chapter 12, on destination marketing, explores these issues in more detail.

### Transportation

A good transportation infrastructure is crucial for the tourism industry to thrive in any country. In India for example, tourism growth has been hampered for many years by the

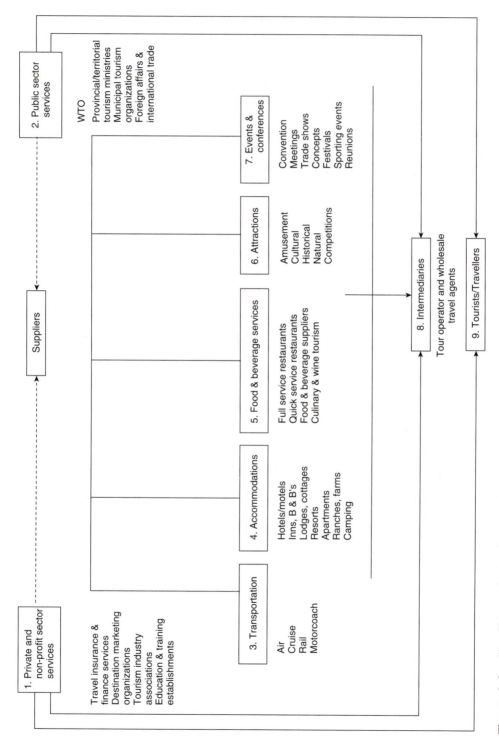

**Figure 1.6** Key Players in the Tourism Industry

nation's poor infrastructure. However, in 2000 India began the Golden Quadrilateral Project. This endeavour connects the top four metros of India by a four-lane highway, connecting Srinagar to Kanyakumari and Silcher to Saurashtra. The project has had a very positive impact on tourism, particularly domestic tourism. As mentioned above, a new railway connecting China to Tibet is expected to double tourism revenue in Tibet. Until the first train made its way over the mountains in July 2006, the passage to Tibet involved a back-breaking bus journey or a flight still beyond the reach of many Chinese tourists.

*The Airline Industry*
Despite the impacts of high-profile terrorism acts and natural disasters over the last decade, the world's airlines are experiencing increasing demand. Rising economic growth is spurring travel demand in Asia and Europe, where airlines were expected to be profitable in 2006 (Suga, 2006).[8] North American carriers meanwhile were expected to have lost US$4.5 million in 2006 as several major US airlines restructured under Chapter 11 bankruptcy protection. Airline deregulation around the world has led to the development of no-frills, low-cost airlines, operating mainly out of secondary airports. A Snapshot in Chapter 6 ('Low-cost Airlines Take to the Air') focuses on this development. There is also a trend in airlines towards 'bigger and better'. Airbus's new 560-tonne jet, the A380, carries up to 800 passengers and has become the world's biggest commercial airliner. After the demise of Concorde, which epitomized speed and luxury, the new superjumbos have redirected the industry towards size, facilities and economies of scale.

Airports are spending millions in adapting their facilities to handle the new-style outsize jets. Heathrow, expected to become the leading hub for the A380 with 10 million more passengers each year predicted by 2016, is investing more than US$840 million over the next decade to handle the aircraft. Airports in Paris, Amsterdam, Washington and Hong Kong are also catering for the A380. Airports play a vital role in keeping the tourism sector growing in many countries. In Thailand, for example, the government has recently opened a new US$3 billion airport. The building is the world's single largest airport terminal building, according to Thailand's airport authority, and will have an initial capacity to serve 45 million passengers annually. Thailand estimates international tourist arrivals at 13.8 million for 2006, creating $13 billion in revenue, and expects to double that to $26 billion over the next five years (Promyamyai, 2006).[9]

*The Cruise Industry*
This US$40 billion industry has been growing for many years, with more than 12 million people around the globe taking a cruise each year. Cruises will continue to be one of the fastest-growing segments in the tourism industry. Bigger and better-equipped ships are being built in order to provide more varied facilities for different age-groups and cultures, and also to appeal to wider income brackets. Since 1998, when 223 cruise ships carried ten million passengers, the industry has grown by an average of ten per cent annually.

Traditionally, cruises were the preserve of the rich and famous who travelled in luxury with no financial or time restraints on such vessels as the *Lusitania* and the *Queen Elizabeth 2*. Nowadays, bigger ships can improve company profits, since economies of scale in purchasing and operating expenses reduce overhead costs. Thus cruise lines with the latest 3,000-passenger mega-ships can offer all-inclusive fares for about $100 per person per day, less than half the cost on most small ships and comparable to resorts on shore.

*Railways*

With the rising cost of fuel around the world, many countries are turning to the railways to solve their transportation problems. In mainland Western Europe and Japan for example, governments have invested massive sums in dedicated high-speed lines and trains offering city-to-city services at speeds in excess of 200 kmph. Even the British Conservative party recently put forward high-speed trains as a solution to current environmental concerns and as a means of boosting the country's economy. Major new projects are also planned in many other countries, including China and the US. A high-speed network is being developed in South Africa to be ready in time for the 2010 Soccer World Cup.

Luxury train travel is another important component of the transportation sector. According to international travel agents, Canada offers the best experience in the world. Royal Canadian Pacific won the world's leading luxury train award at the 2006 World Travel Award ceremony, held in the Turks and Caicos Islands. The other nominees were the Blue Train (South Africa), the Eastern and Orient Express (Asia), Pride of Africa-Rovos Rail (Africa), Palace on Wheels (India) and the Venice Simplon Orient Express (Europe). At the same ceremony, Eurostar was named the world's leading rail service, beating Via Rail, Amtrak, SNCF, Die Bahn and Rail Europe.

## Accommodations

The accommodation sector consists of a great variety of accommodation facilities to meet the consumers' needs. Among these, the subsector of hotels is the most important, and hotel chains are particularly significant in large cities. In London and Paris for example, their share of bed capacity amounts to 50 per cent. An example of the global nature of the hotel sector is the Hilton group. Hilton has nearly 2,800 hotels in 80 countries and has plans to spread its traditional US brands such as Conrad, Doubletree, Embassy Suites, Hampton Inn and Hilton Garden to other parts of the world. Aiming for growth of 7 per cent a year across the group, Hilton is focusing its main international expansion on China, India and Eastern Europe for the high-demand mid-price market (Blitzin, 2006).[10] Hilton will tailor the brand for different parts of the world, for example increasing the food and beverage offering in India to attract Western travellers.

Other types of accommodation, such as lodgings, bed and breakfast, tourist residences, holiday dwellings, timeshare apartments and campsites, are showing considerable growth. In the US, one of the country's largest privately held companies, Utah-based Flying J, is transforming the highway hospitality and service business. Targeting mainly long-haul drivers, the company operates about 180 travel plazas in America for truckers, RV owners and the public. The plazas feature showers, a lounge, laundry facilities, internet, phone and banking services. The company has recently expanded into Canada, with plans for 15 plazas built in partnership with Shell Canada at a cost of CDN$200 million.

## Food and Beverage Services

Another important supplier to the tourism industry is the food and beverage sector. Worldwide statistics on the size of this sector are hard to come by, but there is considerable growth in developing countries. For example, the food and beverage sector in China and India grew by 20 per cent and 9 per cent respectively in 2005. A fair share of that growth can be attributed to multinational corporations expanding into those countries. An example is Starbucks. At the end of August 2006, Starbucks had 12,142 stores around the world, about 70 per cent of them in the US. The company's target is 30,000 stores globally, and Chairman Howard Schultz is aiming to open more in areas where the company remains under-represented, including parts of the US, China and India. Starbucks was expecting to have 2,400 new stores in 2007, opening on average six new stores a day.[11]

## Attractions

As with other sectors of the tourism industry, attractions are increasingly polarized between a few large attractions and thousands of small and micro-sized enterprises. An example of a new, small attraction is the home of writer Robert Graves, recently opened on the Spanish island of Majorca, and profiled in the Snapshot below. Within the range of visitor management techniques available to attractions, marketing is increasingly seen as fundamental to success. It is recognized as the best way of generating revenue to contribute to the cost of operation and maintenance of the resource base, to develop and sustain satisfying products, to create value for money, and to influence the volume and seasonality patterns of site visits.

Tourist attractions can be classified as natural or human-made, and increasingly consumers are attracted to attractions that provide entertainment. For example, throughout the world, 253 million people visited theme parks in 2005, up 2.2 per cent from 2004. No fewer than 176 million attended the most popular parks in North America, in part due to investments made by the big players like Disney and Six Flags. However, the growth in the industry is expected to come outside of the US, particularly in China and India, where the middle classes are growing rapidly and are undersupplied with entertainment opportunities. Theme parks are forecast to grow 3.7 per cent in the US between 2005 and 2009, whereas revenues will grow 5 per cent in Europe, the Middle East and Africa, and 5.7 per cent in the Asia/Pacific region (Cetron, 2006).[12]

## Snapshot

### Opening the Home of Robert Graves

In a tourism environment where the 'bucket and spade brigade' has prevailed since the 1960s, it was rather surprising when the government of the Balearic Islands announced it would spend €2.5 million to turn the Majorcan house of poet and Nobel Prize winner, Robert Graves, into a tourist attraction for the public. With over ten million tourists annually, Majorca had until then been famed for its beaches and resorts and ability to cram as many (mainly European) tourists as possible into small beachside towns, whose overcrowded beachfronts are sandwiched between the sea and high rise hotels and apartment blocks.

Cultural tourism does not usually go hand in hand with mass beach tourism but the tiny, mountain village of Deya, hugging the dramatic coastline between the bustling port of Soller and the beautiful architectural hillside haven of Valldemossa, stands to attract possibly more tourists than it can accommodate. Recently improved major highways in Majorca are already over-used, with traffic jams even in low season, so the narrow, winding roads around Deya will be sorely stretched. The village is on the western side of the island in an area designated for environmental protection, so road-widening may become a controversial conservationist issue in the future.

Robert Graves lived on the island from 1929 till his death at the age of 90 in 1985, when he was buried in the tiny Deya cemetery. He left the island during the Spanish Civil War and returned in 1946 to find his house, Canellun, unscathed. During his self-imposed exile at the house, he wrote many of his most famous works, including *I, Claudius, The White Goddess* and *The Greek Myths*. But until July 2006, the only landmark in his honour was his modest grave site in a tiny churchyard, listed in most tourist guides. 'You'd be surprised how many people leave little notes on the grave, but everyone wanted to see the house where he lived,' said his son William, who has been in charge of refurbishment, which aimed to preserve the atmosphere in the family home.

The house tour (priced at €5) includes a fifteen-minute video, screened in a theatre set up in the garage, which features readings by Robert Graves himself. It is also available in various languages although Graves can only be heard in the English version. William Graves said it recreates the spirit of the house as it looked in the 1940s when his father was most productive. 'This is a house, not a museum,' he explained. Visitors can admire his office, the old printing press he used to publish poems, and the amphitheatre where his children would perform plays. There is also a display of photos, books and the newspaper clippings that erroneously announced his death in World War I.

Naturally, during Graves' long life span, the house was often frequented by other famous personalities, which will also be a pull for tourists. Gertrude Stein first advised him to move there, and American writer Laura Riding accompanied him in 1929 when they first rented and then bought the house. Ava Gardner was one of his most spectacular guests but Alec Guinness, Peter Ustinov and Gabriel Garcia Marquez also visited the poet. Kingsley Amis, artist Gustave Dore, Santiago Rusinol, Alastair Reid, Anais Nin, Carmen Riera and Allan Silitoe were other illustrious visitors.

*Sources*: Ihnenfeldt, H. (2006) 'A Review of Deya and the Graves Myth', promotional material for Graves tours; Anon. (21 May 2006) 'Graves house to be opened to public', *Majorca Daily Bulletin*, Daily Home News, 3; Fuchs, D. (1 July 2006) 'Mallorca opens Graves' home as museum', *The Guardian*, 19.

## Events and Conferences

Events and conferences often play a key role in bringing business and leisure travellers to destinations. These events can vary from conventions and exhibitions for the business market to huge sporting events like the Olympics or the soccer World Cup, which attract millions of sport tourists. From the destination's perspective, event tourism is the development and marketing of events to obtain economic and community benefits. To the consumer, it is travel for the purpose of participating in or viewing an event. The marketing of events and conferences is discussed more fully in Chapter 12.

## Intermediaries

The key intermediary players in the tourism industry are tour operators and wholesalers, destination marketing companies, travel agents, travel specialists, and web-based intermediaries (a detailed analysis of intermediaries can be found in Chapter 7). Both tour operators and wholesalers are organizations that offer packaged vacation tours to the general public. These packages can include everything from transportation, accommodation and activities, to entertainment, meals and drinks. Destination marketing companies (DMCs) are private sector companies that also act as inbound tour operators. Travel agents are the most widely used marketing intermediaries in the tourism industry, but the emergence of new and cheaper distribution tools such as the internet has placed the future role of travel agents in doubt. This is explored in more depth in Chapter 10.

## The Tourists

The final key player in the tourism industry is the tourist. As mentioned above, international tourist arrivals reached an all-time record of 808 million in 2005. The majority of arrivals corresponded to trips for the purpose of leisure, recreation and holidays (52 per cent), whilst business travel accounted for about 16 per cent. A further 24 per cent covered travel for other motives, such as visiting friends and relatives (VFR), religious purposes, and health treatment. For the remaining 8 per cent of arrivals the purpose of visit has not been specified. Chapter 2 will focus on the tourist in more detail.

## Influences on the Tourism Marketing Environment

### Microenvironment

The marketing environment is made up of a microenvironment and a macroenvironment. The **microenvironment** consists of forces close to the organization that can affect its ability to serve its customers: the organization itself, marketing channel firms, customer markets, and a broad range of stakeholders or publics (see Figure 1.7). For a tourism marketer, these factors will affect the degree of success in attracting target markets, so it is important to understand their importance. This book discusses most of these components in detail: customers in Chapter 2, competitors in Chapter 3, intermediaries in Chapter 7, and the

---

**MICROENVIRONMENT**
forces close to the organization that can affect its ability to serve its customers: the organization itself, marketing channel firms, customer markets, and a broad range of stakeholders or publics

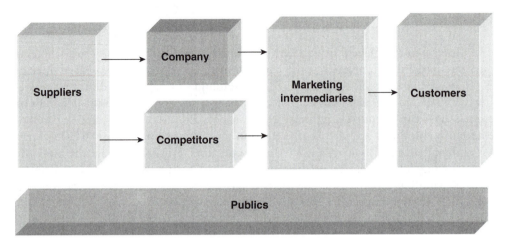

**Figure 1.7** Major components of the company's microenvironment

various publics in Chapter 9. However, it is important to acknowledge the influence that the company and its suppliers will have on achieving marketing objectives.

Marketing managers need to work closely with other departments in the company, as all of these departments will have some impact on the success of marketing plans. Every tourism organization will differ as to how many departments it has and what they are called. However, finance is normally responsible for finding and using the funds required to carry out marketing plans, accounting has to measure revenues and costs in order to evaluate marketing objectives, and human resources will be crucial in supporting a service marketing culture (see Chapter 11). Suppliers also have an important role to play in supporting marketing objectives. Suppliers are firms and individuals that provide the resources needed by the company to produce its goods and services. Marketing management must pay close attention to trends and developments affecting suppliers, and to changes in supply availability and supply costs. At a micro level, hotels and exhibition centres contract with restaurant companies to supply food and beverage services. In turn, these restaurants will have their own favoured suppliers of produce. On a macro basis, tourist destinations will need suppliers in the form of airlines, hotels, restaurants, ground operations, meeting facilities, and entertainment.

## Macroenvironment

The **macroenvironment** comprises the larger societal forces that affect the entire microenvironment, and this will shape opportunities and pose threats. The macroenvironment consists of the eight major forces shown in Figure 1.8, and tourism businesses need to take into consideration the fact that they operate in a competitive national and international environment.

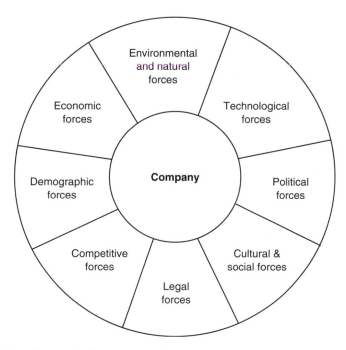

**Figure 1.8**    Major forces in the company's macroenvironment

Although an organization cannot control many of these external factors, they should never be allowed to come as a total surprise. A planned response to potential environmental issues allows for a balanced, thoughtful reaction – a process often referred to as 'environmental scanning'. Chapter 13 looks in more detail at how some tourism organizations have responded to environmental influences outside of their control.

---

**MACROENVIRONMENT**
the larger societal forces that affect the microenvironment: competitive, demographic, economic, environmental and natural, technological, political, cultural and social, and legal forces

---

*Competitive Forces*
Being aware of who the competition is, knowing what their strengths and weaknesses are, and anticipating what they may do are important aspects of understanding the macroenvironment. The marketing concept states that to be successful, a company must satisfy the needs and wants of consumers better than its competitors. Furthermore, competitive advantage is now widely accepted as being of central importance to the success of organizations, regions, and countries. As we enter the third millennium, the world of tourism is becoming increasingly competitive. Although competition occurs between hotels, airlines, tour operators, travel agents, and other tourism services, this inter-enterprise competition is dependent upon and

derived from the choices tourists make between alternative destinations. Competition therefore centres on the destination. Countries, states, regions and cities now take their role as tourist destinations very seriously, committing considerable effort and funds toward enhancing their touristic image and attractiveness. As a consequence, destination competitiveness has become a significant part of tourism literature, and evaluation of the competitiveness of tourism destinations is increasingly being recognized as an important tool in the strategic positioning and marketing analysis of destinations.

As a result of globalization, a growing number of countries are aware of the importance of tourism to their economies, as was mentioned at the beginning of this chapter. These countries have therefore increasingly targeted international tourism markets, augmenting their investment in marketing to attract international visitors and increase foreign earnings. For example, competition is intensifying to grab a larger share of the expected growth in outbound travel from China. The World Tourism Organization expects that by the year 2020, China will become one of the world's major outbound tourism markets, generating globally 100 million tourists, or 6.2 per cent of the world total. Competitive product, price, and quality, as well as access to and delivery of tourism goods and services will be the major success factors in attracting new Chinese outbound tourists and encouraging repeat travellers in the next decade and beyond.

*Demographic Forces*

**Demographics** are statistics that describe the observable characteristics of individuals, including our physical traits, such as gender, race, age, and height; our economic traits, such as income, savings, and net worth; our occupation-related traits, including education; our location-related traits; and our family-related traits, such as marital status and number and age of children. According to David Foot, author of *Boom, Bust & Echo* (2000), demographics explain about two-thirds of everything.[13] For example, the dramatic increase in popularity of golf over the last 25 years is explained by golf's popularity among aging baby boomers who are entering a stage of life that enables them to spend more time on the golf course.

---

**DEMOGRAPHICS**
statistics that describe the observable characteristics of individuals

---

In fact, the single most notable demographic trend in many countries is the aging population. The over-50 segment, sometimes referred to as the maturing or greying market, constitutes nearly 30 per cent of many western countries, and this market has a keen interest in travel and leisure services. Other demographic trends affecting the marketing of tourism worldwide include the relatively slow population growth, the continued increase in education and service sector employment, increasing ethnic diversity, the demise of the traditional family, and the geographic mobility of the population. In addition to understanding general demographic trends, marketers must recognize demographic groupings that may turn out to be market segments because of their enormous size, similar socioeconomic characteristics, or shared values. Such segments are discussed in Chapter 3.

*Economic Forces*

**Economic forces** in the environment are those that affect consumer purchasing power and spending patterns. Total purchasing power depends on current income, prices, savings and credit, so marketers must be aware of major economic trends in income and of changing consumer spending patterns. For example, newly rich Russians, Indians and Chinese and a wider rise in disposable income are expected to boost the luxury goods market over the next decade. As a consequence, the luxury travel market will grow considerably. The market is already a lucrative one. In 2005, Virtuoso, a network of over 6,000 travel consultants that specialize in the luxury travel segment, booked more than US$4.2 billion in travel for their clients.

---

**ECONOMIC FORCES**
those forces that affect consumer purchasing power and spending patterns

---

Price changes and exchange rates can also have a significant impact on tourism. A snapshot in Chapter 4 ('Measuring the Impact of *Captain Corelli's Mandolin* on Tourism in Cephalonia') shows how price increases in Cephalonia, as a result of the island's increased popularity following the *Captain Corelli* movie, led to dissatisfaction amongst both locals and prospective tourists. In 2006, Moscow replaced Tokyo as the world's most expensive city, and this will undoubtedly impact on visitors to the city. New York city remains the most expensive city in North America with currency appreciation being the main cause, although price increases in fuel and certain consumer goods have also contributed.

*Environmental and Natural Forces*

The last four decades have witnessed a dramatic increase in environmental consciousness worldwide. Media attention given to the greenhouse effect, acid rain, oil spills, ocean pollution, tropical deforestation and other topics has raised public awareness, which has had an impact on the tourism industry. International leisure travellers are increasingly motivated by the quality of destination landscapes, in terms of environmental health and the diversity and integrity of natural and cultural resources. Studies of German and US travel markets indicate that environmental considerations are now a significant element of travellers' destination-choosing process, down to – in the case of the Germans – the environmental programmes operated by individual hotels (Ayala, 1996).[14]

The growing concern amongst consumers for the protection of the environment has clearly attracted the attention of companies seeking to profit from environmentally sound marketing practices. Surveys have shown that consumers are more likely to choose one brand over another if they believe the brand will help the environment, and environmental quality is a prevailing issue in making travel-related decisions. This has led to the 'greening' of attractions, hotels, and even resorts, and to an increase in the number of environmentally friendly tourism products. An increasing emphasis is also being placed upon evaluating the likely environmental impacts of any tourism development, with environmental audits, environmental impact analysis, and carrying capacity issues being taken more seriously. A recent report from the UK (2005) suggested that there are a growing number of concerned individuals in Britain who have begun to turn away from international travel because of its environmental price.[15]

Finally, uncontrollable natural forces can have a negative impact on the tourism industry. For example, the South Asian tsunami of 2004, due to the number of victims among foreign visitors and among workers of the tourism sector, constitutes the greatest catastrophe ever recorded in the history of tourism (see Case Study in Chapter 13). Before the tsunami, tourism was at an all-time high in many of the affected countries. A two-year cease-fire between the Sri Lankan government and the Tamil Tigers had helped produce an 11 per cent increase in the number of tourists. Thailand was continuing its strong growth with a 20 per cent rise from the previous year. Even Bali, which was unaffected by the tsunami, had seen an almost complete recuperation of tourism revenues, to the level they were at prior to the Al-Qaeda bombings in October 2002. The tsunami devastated tourism in many of these countries. Due to its magnitude and repercussions the disaster took on a global scale, reflecting the worldwide reach tourism has today.

*Technological Forces*
The most dramatic force shaping the future of tourism and hospitality is technology. The accelerated rate of technological advancement has forced tourism organizations to adapt their products accordingly, particularly in terms of how they develop, price, distribute, and promote their products. Technology facilitates the continual development of new systems and features that improve the tourism product. It has allowed for extra security in hotels and resorts, thanks to security systems and safety designs. It has also created new entertainment options for travellers, such as in-room movies and video games. Increasingly, hotels and even airplanes are offering internet services to cater to the technological needs of today's consumer.

The internet fits the theoretical marketing principle in the travel industry because it allows suppliers to set up direct links of communication with their customers. Travellers are turning in increasing numbers to the internet to help them plan and book their travel (see Chapter 10 for more on this subject). Technology is also beginning to have an impact on consumer research, as tourism organizations realize the potential of database management and the value of relationship marketing. Databases of customer profiles and customer behaviour are the basis for effective direct marketing. In tourism, the collection and analysis of data streams that now flow continuously through distribution channels and booking systems provide the modern information base for strategic and operational decisions of large organizations. The rate of technological change as databases connect and interact indicates that the speed and quality of information flows will be further enhanced in the coming decade.

*Political Forces*
Marketing decisions are strongly affected by developments in the political environment. This environment is made up of government agencies and pressure groups that influence and limit the activities of various organizations and individuals in society. Government policies can have far-reaching implications for the tourism industry. For example, the nation of Myanmar (formerly called Burma) receives very few tourists because of the turbulent political situation in the country. The Case Study at the end of this chapter explores these issues in more depth. In Fiji, tourism is often influenced by political forces. A military coup in December 2006 – the country's fourth in 20 years – had a negative impact on tourism arrivals.

Terrorism can also have a devastating impact on tourism around the world. Since 11 September 2001 there have been more than 3,000 major terrorist attacks worldwide, most of which have impacted on the tourism industry. The media attention given to these attacks is usually enough to persuade many international travellers to reconsider their vacation plans. The terrorists themselves target tourism destinations in order to force governments to rethink and abandon specific policies, or to deny governments the commercial and economic benefits of tourism. The response by governments and the private sector to the impact of terrorism on tourism is given more attention in Chapter 13.

Political actions can also have a positive impact on tourism. In some parts of the world, the relaxing of political barriers is making areas more accessible to tourists. An example is Mongolia, where Soviet influence smothered Mongolia's cultural traditions and closed off outside access until recently. But now, adventurous Westerners are exploring central Asia's vast wilderness of grasslands, deserts, and alpine terrain.

### Cultural and Social Forces

Marketing's consumer focus relies on an understanding of who the markets are, what motivates them, and how to appeal to them. Understanding the cultural environment is thus crucial for marketing decision-making. This **cultural environment** includes institutions and other forces that affect society's basic values, perceptions, preferences, and behaviours. Cultural values influence consumer behaviour, and marketers tend to concentrate on dominant cultural values or core values. A grouping technique that is used to track trends in cultural values is psychographics, which determines how people spend their time and resources (activities), what they consider important (interests and values), and what they think of themselves and the world around them (opinions). Psychographics is discussed more fully in Chapter 2. Core values are slow and difficult to change, but secondary values are less permanent and can sometimes be influenced by marketers.

---

**CULTURAL ENVIRONMENT**
institutions and other forces that affect society's basic values, perceptions, preferences, and behaviours

---

Many major cultural trends affect the tourism industry, and the final section of Chapter 2 focuses on ten key trends or demands in consumer behaviour that are influencing tourism and hospitality marketing today. These include the demand for security and safety, convenience and speed, and spiritual enlightenment. The Global Spotlight below is an example of an attraction that has responded to these changing attitudes to travel. After 11 September 2001, US tourists began taking shorter vacations, and were apprehensive about leaving their home country. Due to time constraints and job insecurity, tourists also preferred shorter vacations to the traditional two-week stays. These factors obviously make domestic vacation facilities more attractive and the Holy Land Experience in Florida has been developed as a response to these demands.

# Global Spotlight

## The Holy Land Experience

The Holy Land Experience theme park in Orlando, Florida, is just one of a series of religious entertainments in the US, bringing the spiritual world and corporeal amusement together. Alongside biblical movies such as *The Passion* and the new Kentucky-based Creation Museum, both religious tourists and entertainment seekers are being invited to experience religion outside of the more conventional settings of church and temple. The park was opened in 2001 to capitalize not only on the tens of millions of tourists who flock to nearby Disney World every year, but also to take advantage of the growing Christian market in the US. The market for Christian products – including books, movies and music – is worth $8.5 billion a year, and may be even larger for services.

The emergence of a distinctly Christian market in the US has paralleled a political and cultural coming out. In George W. Bush, Americans had their first born-again President. Mr. Bush, who often speaks in overtly religious language, told a group of Conservatives in 2006 that the US is in the midst of a 'Third Awakening' of religious fervour, not unlike the periods 1730–60 and 1800–30. 'After 9/11, people are beginning to realize that life isn't just fun and games,' says Dan Hayden, executive director of the 15-acre theme park. 'They are looking for meaning that knowledge of God brings.' At Holy Land, the quest for knowledge comes in the form of re-enactments of the crucifixion, plus scale models of Jerusalem, Herod's Temple and Christ's tomb. The destination now draws more than 200,000 visitors a year. 'We thought that if we put flesh and blood on biblical stories, it would be a way to capture the interest of people,' Hayden explained.

For the past two decades, Gallup polls in the US have shown that around 45 per cent of Americans believe that God created man sometime within the past 10,000 years. The not-for-profit evangelical Christian ministry, Zion's Hope, capitalized on this pool of potential believers by building the $18.4 million theme park in conjunction with ITEC entertainment in 15 acres of prime real estate near Universal Studios and Walt Disney World in Orlando. In counterpoint to its rival parks, Holy Land Experience does not offer rides. However, it does provide 100 authentically clad actors recreating biblical episodes in Israel circa 1450 BC to AD 66 in an educational, inspirational, theatrical and historical environment. Even camel hoofprints are noticeable on dusty Jerusalem streets (but apparently actual camels were considered unnecessary to the staged authenticity). The Holy Land Web site (www.holylandexperience.com) outlines its agenda: '(our) singular purpose is to provide answers to life's most important questions: "Where did I come from? Why am I here? Where am I going? What is life really all about?"' Perhaps the visitors contemplate these questions whilst munching on Goliath Burgers and Centurion Salad in the site's many refreshment facilities.

Alongside more frivolous attractions such as Calvary's Garden Tomb, the Qumran Dead Sea Caves and the Temple of The Great King, the theme park houses a separate $14 million Scriptorium, a museum and archive for serious religious scholars, with the largest private collection of biblical texts and artifacts in the US.

With Las Vegas providing the US tourist with mini experiences of Paris, Venice, Egypt and New York all conveniently along the same street, the Holy Land Experience is doing much the same thing for Christianity by saving tourists the anxieties and expense of foreign pilgrimage. Unlike Vegas, however, the Holy Land Experience does not seem to have targeted its customer very distinctly. Its doors are open to religious scholars, general theme park fanciers, spiritually lost pilgrims and anyone who happens to be in Orlando to experience its vacation product range. However, they do cater for children, with a KidVentura area where children can meet biblical characters and scale a rock-climbing wall. One dramatic presentation portrays the biblical account of Jesus greeting the children. The audience's reaction to the actors tends to vary: 'Some of the children run and jump into my arms, but others are shy,' said Steve Bleiler, a Methodist at the Baptist Church in Orlando, who is one of the cast members who portray Jesus.

*Sources*: Alford, H. (2005) 'It's a surreal world after all', *Travel + Leisure*. 111–15; McKenna, B. (25 September 2006) 'The prophet motive: US faithful form rich market', *Globe & Mail*, B1; Holloway, L. (1 June 2006) 'Orlando's Holy Land experience theme park offers guests a living museum feel with dramas, exhibits', *Alabama Baptist Online*. www.thealabamabaptist.org.

### Legal Forces

The tourism industry has witnessed an increase in legislation and regulation that affects business, normally enacted to protect companies and consumers from unfair business practices. Government regulation also aims to protect society's interests against unrestricted business behaviour, as profitable business activity does not always improve the quality of life within a society. Hence the regulations in many parts of the world that restrict smoking in restaurants and hotels. In fact, government agencies have become involved in the regulation of everything from food-handling practices in restaurants to fire codes for hotels. Travellers are seen as good sources of revenue by politicians, as witnessed by the increasing number of cities, states or provinces that are implementing hotel taxes.

Most countries have laws that permit governments to restrict foreign trade when such trade could adversely affect the economy of the country, or when such trade is in conflict with foreign policy. There are laws about the level of foreign investment permitted and the amount of money that can be transferred out of the country, and immigration laws affect the transfer of staff internationally from one multinational property to another. All laws have an impact on investment and development in the tourism industry. More specifically, laws regarding landing taxes for aircraft, health regulations, gaming licenses, and visa and entry permits all affect the tourism industry in one way or another.

An example of how legislation has affected the tourism industry comes from Israel, where the law prohibits gambling. However, the Israeli government recently gave the go-ahead for 'flying casinos' – specially fitted planes that give gamblers a four-hour spin in the air. By leaving Israeli airspace, the planes will get around the country's gambling ban. Three flights a day are run by an Icelandic airline. The project, a private initiative of Israeli investors and financiers from abroad, is expected to generate about US$50 million a year in revenue for Israel.

---

### Chapter Summary

Service products are commonly distinguished from goods products by four unique characteristics: intangibility, inseparability, heterogeneity, and perishability.

The services marketing triangle shows the three interlinked groups that work together to develop, promote, and deliver services. These key players are the company, the customers, and the providers. The triangle also suggests that three types of marketing must be successfully carried out for a service to succeed: external, interactive, and internal marketing.

The expanded marketing mix for services includes the traditional four Ps – product, price, place, and promotion – as well as the more recently added people, physical evidence, and process.

The key players in the tourism industry are private and non-profit sector services, public sector services, suppliers (transportation, accommodation, food and beverage services, attractions, events and conferences, and sport and adventure tourism), intermediaries, and the customers (tourist/travellers) themselves.

The marketing environment is made up of a microenvironment and a macroenvironment. The microenvironment consists of forces close to the organization that can affect its ability to serve its customers: the organization itself, marketing channel firms, customer markets, and a broad range of stakeholders or publics.

The macroenvironment comprises the larger societal forces that affect the entire microenvironment and shape opportunities and pose threats. The macroenvironment consists of eight major forces: competitive, demographic, economic, environmental and natural, technological, political, cultural and social, and legal.

---

## Key Terms

cultural environment, p. 29
demographics, p. 26
economic forces, p. 27
international marketing, p. 9
macroenvironment, p. 25
marketing, p. 9
microenvironment, p. 23
services marketing mix, p. 15
services marketing triangle, p. 14
tourism market, p. 4

## Discussion Questions and Exercises

1. Why do managers in tourism and hospitality need to understand the services marketing triangle and the services marketing mix?
2. Choose one key player in the tourism industry and suggest how it should deal with the unique characteristics of services listed on page 14. For example, how do airlines overcome the perishability of their product?
3. Which of the key players in the tourism industry outlined in Figure 1.6 are more vulnerable to external influences such as terrorist attacks and tsunamis?
4. Choose one of the transport sectors discussed in the chapter (airlines, cruises, railways, or motorcoach operators) and update the material presented in the text. How is this sector performing in today's environment?
5. What are the key challenges facing the global tourism and hospitality industry today? Which of these are controllable and which are uncontrollable?

## The Influence of Politics on Tourism: The Case of Myanmar

Tourists contemplating a visit to any country with a history of human rights abuses are confronted with a similar ethical dilemma: keep yourself and your tourist dollars away, or go and bear witness, facilitate the exchange of ideas and support local businesses. Visitors to Myanmar are faced with such a dilemma and some profound political and ideological decision-making. Tourism marketing strategies in Myanmar have focused on a picturesque and idyllic landscape, imbued with spirituality as a consequence of its Buddhist traditions, and inhabited by peaceful people whose traditional culture has been preserved. However, this image of a country at peace denies the harsh realities that underlie such representations, and Myanmar has been referred to as the 'land of fear'. Under allegations of human rights abuse, the generals running the country spend about 40 per cent of the county's budget on the military, while most of the people live in poverty and disease. The Burmese health system is ranked 190th out of 190 countries by the World Health Organization. Aung San Suu Kyi, leader of the elected Democratic Party and winner of the Nobel Peace Prize in 1991, remains under house arrest, whilst over 1,800 political prisoners are held in jail.

Tourism to Myanmar has been both promoted and deterred. On one side, the State Peace and Development Council (SPDC), the ruling elite, opens its arms to foreign visitors. For over 25 years, tourism has been accepted as an industry of potential importance and a major foreign exchange generator. In 1990 a Tourism Law recognized tourism as a significant economic activity and ended the state monopoly, allowing local and foreign private operators to run hotels, transport businesses, and tour guiding services. A Hotel and Tourism Law in 1993 affirmed

**Case Study**

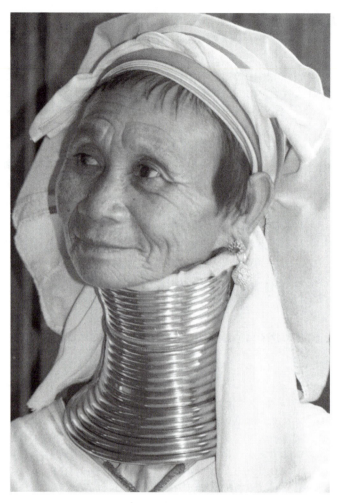

A woman from the Padaung tribe in Myanmar poses for tourism

official support, setting out objectives related to the growth of the hotel and tourism sector. Myanmar's cultural heritage and scenic beauty were to be exploited, maximizing employment opportunities, while fostering international friendship and understanding. In short, the SPDC saw tourism as an opportunity to disseminate a favourable picture of Myanmar to the rest of the world.

But the high-speed growth in tourism infrastructure did not come without a price. It caused mass upheaval, with millions of labourers required to erect the suitable tourism infrastructure, and to restore cultural sites as tourist attractions (often crudely, according to archeologists and conservationists). Tourism development was directly linked to human rights violations, and there were reports in the 1990s of the government conscripting labour to complete infrastructure and tourism projects. People were also displaced from their homes to make way for tourism. For example, tribes such as the Padaung, also known as 'long necks' (pictured above), have been relocated and exploited for tourism purposes. Whether the peoples of these ethnic groups object to their cultural identities being commodified for tourism purposes is not a concern of the SPDC.

In reaction, many groups, both inside and outside Myanmar, have opposed tourism, including Suu Kyi and her party. They have urged travellers to refrain from visiting Myanmar until there is a political transition to democracy. In 2002 she said, 'Burma will always be here, and when it is democratic it will be a place that I think tourists will enjoy visiting with no qualms and guilty feelings.' Her anti-tourism campaign has proved to be successful, with travellers and their dollars staying away. Whilst tourism has expanded rapidly in neighbouring Asian countries, Myanmar still receives relatively few visitors. In 2005, 660,000 tourists visited Myanmar, compared to neighbouring Thailand, which attracted more than ten million.

Non-government organizations that support Myanmar's pro-democracy movement are also raising the call to world travellers, urging them to avoid travel to Myanmar and thus prevent the SPDC from obtaining the hard currency and global legitimacy it needs to survive. These NGOs stress that tourism fosters an illusion of peace and regularity while providing foreign exchange to pay for arms which strengthen the military. It thus fortifies the regime whose members may benefit personally and politically from any increase in arrivals. The Burma Campaign UK – which refers to the country by its former name – has lined up politicians and celebrities to back the 'I'm not going' campaign. In February 2005 Tony Blair, the British prime minister, joined such stars as Susan Sarandon and Ian McKellen in pledging not to vacation in Myanmar and urging others to do the same.

However, there are some outside analysts that believe tourism should be encouraged in Myanmar, despite the political situation. The opportunities to engage in cross-cultural communication form the basis of the ethical arguments put forward. These protagonists argue that tourism can break down barriers and accelerate economic progress which improves the lives of local people; that tourism provides a rare channel of communication for the Burmese, it provides jobs and it allows foreigners to learn about the culture; and that travel enhances friendships between peoples and facilitates cultural and political exchange. In the case of repressive countries such as Myanmar, it may also allow visitors to bear witness to local conditions. Such arguments fall under the umbrella of 'citizen diplomacy' – the cross-national interactions between people of different cultures that can have a positive impact on society.

To conclude, the recent fortunes of Myanmar's tourism are clearly tied to various manifestations of its politics. The instability of the military regime has been a deterrent to travel, and unattractive images of its leaders, associations of political repression and arguments that tourism is partly responsible for human rights abuses represent strong disincentives in certain markets. The features and actions of Myanmar's government seem to have hindered tourism and prevented the country from realizing its potential as a popular tourism destination. Until the underlying political tensions are resolved and new policies put in place leading to improvements both in realities and perceptions, Myanmar's tourism industry is unlikely to thrive.

*Sources*: Hudson, S (2007) 'To go or not to go? Ethical perspectives on tourism in an "Outpost of tyranny"', *Journal of Business Ethics*, 76(4), 385–96.

**Case Study**

## Questions

1. Explain how political factors have influenced the growth of tourism in Myanmar.
2. Do some research and find out what the political situation in Myanmar is today.
3. Do you think boycotting tourism in Myanmar will have any effect on government policies in the country?
4. Give examples from other countries around the world where politics is having a negative impact on tourism.
5. Apart from political factors, what other environmental factors are influencing tourism in Myanmar?

## Websites

| | |
|---|---|
| www.hongkongdisneyland.com | Hong Kong Disneyland |
| www.holylandexperience.com | The Holy Land Experience |
| www.fundaciorobertgraves.org | Robert Graves |
| www.cruising.org | Cruise Lines International Association |
| www.world-tourism.org | World Tourism Organization |
| www.myanmar-tourism.com | Myanmar Tourism Promotion Board |
| www.businessfordiplomaticaction.org | 2006 World Citizens Guide |

## References

1 Allen, K. (5 July 2006) 'Rank may roll Hard Rock off its wagon', *The Guardian*, 25.
2 United Nations World Tourism Organization. (2006) 'Tourism is a socioeconomic driver', *UNWTO News*, 3, 4–5.
3 World Tourism Organization. (2003) *Tourism highlights*. Retrieved 14 April 2003 from http://www.world-tourism.org.
4 Kotler, P. (1984) *Marketing management: Analysis, Planning, Implementation and Control* (8th ed.). Upper Saddle River, NJ: Prentice Hall. 92.
5 Cateora, P.R. and Graham, J.L. (2005) *International Marketing*. New York: McGraw-Hill Irwin.
6 Kotler, P. (1984) *Marketing management: Analysis, Planning, Implementation and Control* (8th ed.). Upper Saddle River, NJ: Prentice Hall. 92.
7 McCarthy, E. J. (1981) *Basic Marketing, a Managerial Approach* (7th ed.). Georgetown, ON: Irwin.
8 Suga, M. (1 September 2006) 'Rising travel demand lifts world's airlines', *National Post*, FP3.
9 Promyamyai, T. (27 September 2006) 'Thais hope new airport eclipses coup', *The Globe and Mail*, R8.
10 Blitzin, R. (15 September 2006) 'Hilton set to make move', *Financial Post*, FP8.
11 Anon. (20 September 2006) 'Starbucks raises the bar on national, global expansion plans', *Financial Post*, FP4.
12 Cetron, M. (2006) 'Seven trends directly affecting theme parks', *Hospitality Sales & Marketing Association International*, 23(1).
13 Foot, D. (2000) *Boom, Bust & Echo: Profiting from the Demographic Shift in the 21st Century*. Toronto: MacFarlane Walter & Ross, 313.
14 Ayala, H. (1996) 'Resort ecotourism: a paradigm for the 21st century', *Cornell Hotel and Restaurant Administration Quarterly*, 37(5), 1–9.
15 Anon. (16 May 2005) 'Global studies', *Globe and Mail*, A12.

# 2

# CONSUMER BEHAVIOUR

## Vacations from the Heart: Traveller Philanthropy

In all regions of the world, a new source of international development aid called 'traveller philanthropy' is evolving. Civic-minded travellers and travel businesses are giving time, talent and financial resources to further the well-being of the places they visit. Traveller philanthropy is described as 'the process of visitors choosing to give money (or other help) to assist the conservation or management of places they visit'. The phenomenon is expected to grow exponentially, benefiting from trends in giving, travel and globalization.

Philanthropic initiatives have a number of benefits. Destinations obviously benefit from increased funds for conservation; lack of money to sustain tourism destinations is a growing problem worldwide. Travellers themselves also benefit. Travel provides the rare opportunity to witness first hand the beauty and fragility of other societies, cultures, and natural systems. Such experiences generate strong philanthropic impulses. The majority of travellers agree that their travel experience is better when the destination preserves its natural, historical and cultural sites and attractions.

Tourism organizations also benefit from traveller philanthropy. It has been shown to offer a number of strategic benefits to corporations, including brand differentiation, enhanced image, higher sales and increased brand loyalty. Travellers exhibit a high degree of commitment to travel that protects the local environment, engages visitors in the local culture, and returns benefits to the community. Previous research shows that travel companies can gain competitive advantage by adopting ethical policies.

Scores of travellers' philanthropy programmes now exist across the globe, representing every sector of the travel and tourism industry. In many of the programmes, a foundation has been created that channels donations and

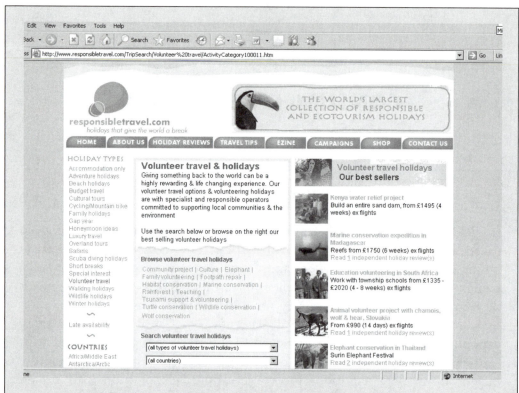

Responsibletravel.com web page describing volunteer travel holidays

charitable funds to address environmental and social needs. An example is the Yasawa Island chain of Fiji, where resort owners have created the Yasawas Community Foundation, which channels charitable funds to village chiefs to address many social needs. The foundation typically receives US$23,000 to $35,000 annually in donations from guests who are primarily American.

How guests are asked to contribute to these philanthropic efforts varies. For the Galapagos Conservation Fund created by Lindblad Expeditions, guests are provided with a direct solicitation envelope the night before landing, and offered a discount coupon of US$250 on future Lindblad excursions in return for charitable contributions of $250 or more. Since 1997, guests have contributed close to $1 million. The New Orleans Metropolitan Convention and Visitors Bureau enlist large convention groups to forgo dessert and donate the saved money to local non-profits. Some operators send out newsletters to clients once they have returned home, and these often have details about projects the tourists could support.

Many schemes exist whereby the travel company makes a 'per booking' contribution on behalf of their customers. For example, Sunvil Africa brought together 19 operators in 2002 who committed to donating £50 per person booking a trip to Zambia or Malawi. Alternatively, a travel company might include an optional additional item on invoices that is then donated to support work in the destination country. Gambian Expeditions, for example, match donations by clients with equal or greater contributions to assist schools in the Gambia.

Other schemes ask travellers (or corporations) to make quite significant payments to support a very specific project or activity. The name of the sponsor may then be linked to the project. The gift may be in the form of a one-off payment, or a pledge to give support over a number of years. Another method is to invite visitors to join a club that supports a conservation cause. Payment is usually by annual subscription. Typical examples are 'Friends' schemes for national parks. Merchandizing is another form of philanthropic giving. Visitors are invited to purchase specific items where it is indicated that a percentage of the purchase price will be passed on by the retailer or manufacturer to support a conservation cause.

Finally, a growing form of traveller philanthropy comes in the form of what has been labelled 'voluntourism', whereby travellers contribute time and effort to philanthropic initiatives. Visitors may get involved in practical tasks, such as restoring old buildings or wildlife habitats, or undertake research. Activities may take place for a few hours, like an organized beach cleaning, or form the basis of a complete working eco-tourism package holiday. One company that specializes in offering this type of package is responsibletravel.com. Based in the UK, Justin Francis and Harold Goodwin co-founded responsibletravel.com in April 2001. The idea was to create a place for tourists to find and book holidays from tour companies that were committed to more responsible travel. They originally launched with 20 holidays from just 4 tour companies that met their criteria. Since then they have turned away far more tour companies than they have accepted, but at the end of 2006 had over 2000 holidays from 220 tour companies. The web page above gives some examples of the type of volunteer holidays the company offers.

*Sources:* CESD. (2004) 'Travellers' philanthropy. Centre on Ecotourism and Sustainable Development', retrieved from www.ecotourismCESD.org; Goodwin, H. (2004) 'Visitor payback in the outbound UK tourism industry', retrieved from www.responsibletourismpartnership.org; Tearfund. (2000) 'A tearful guide to tourism: don't forget your ethics', London: Tearfund.

---

### OBJECTIVES

On completion of this chapter, you should understand:

▶ the importance of consumer behaviour within tourism marketing;

▶ the major factors influencing consumer behaviour;

▶ some of the typologies of tourist roles;

▶ the underlying principles of organizational buying behaviour; and

▶ some of the trends in consumer behaviour influencing tourism marketing today.

---

## Introduction

The opening vignette is an excellent example of changing behavioural patterns among tourists – in this case the increasing desire of tourists to give time, talent and financial resources to further the well-being of the places they visit. This chapter looks at behavioural trends in tourism, and begins by reviewing the factors that influence consumer behaviour. The second part of the chapter focuses on typologies of tourists, and the third examines the external factors that influence consumer behaviour. The fourth section looks at the stages in the buying process. This is followed by a section devoted to organizational buying behaviour, as tourism marketers need to understand both the decision-making criteria used and the process of decision-making that groups and organizations go through in buying tourism services. The final section looks in depth at some of the trends in consumer behaviour affecting tourism marketing today.

The cornerstone of marketing theory is the satisfaction of the consumer. Therefore, the marketer needs to understand three related aspects of **consumer behaviour analysis**: consumer motivations, consumer typologies, and the consumer purchasing process.

---

**CONSUMER BEHAVIOUR ANALYSIS**
the study of why people buy the products they do and how they make decisions

---

Most tourism and hospitality organizations have an imperfect picture of their customer, and few monitor patterns of consumer behaviour at a level of detail necessary to remain competitive. Many organizations consider that they are sufficiently close to their visitors and therefore do not commit resources to more formal consumer studies. Others are constrained by limited marketing budgets and by the fact that researching consumer motivation and the buying process can be a time-consuming and difficult procedure. In fact, most organizations rely almost entirely on the scanning of secondary consumer data, combined with management observation and judgment. However, in

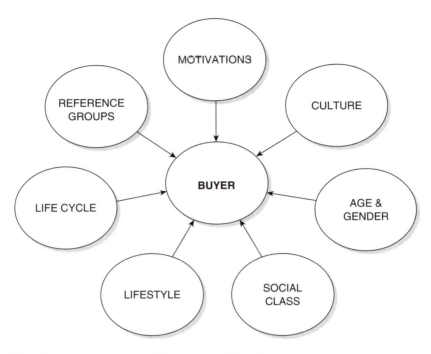

**Figure 2.1** Factors Influencing Consumer Behaviour

a rapidly changing environment, conclusions drawn from secondary data can be out of date in no time. Consumer patterns recorded in 2008, for example, will most likely have changed by the year 2015, but many companies might still be using this type of information as a benchmark.

## Factors Influencing Consumer Behaviour

Figure 2.1 shows the seven key factors that influence a consumer's behaviour. Motivation is often seen as a major determinant of consumer behaviour, but cultural, personal, and social influences will also have an important effect on consumer purchases. Each of the influences in Figure 2.1 will be discussed here in turn.

### Motivations

**Motivations** are inner drives that cause people to take action to satisfy their needs. Understanding consumer motivation is one of the most effective ways of gaining competitive differential advantage. Understanding the key triggers that lead to the purchase of a tourism or hospitality product, such as a visit to an attraction or a hotel booking, is recognized as one of the main factors in the success of competitive organizations. Central to most content theories of motivation is the concept of need. **Needs** are seen as the forces that arouse motivated behaviour, and it is assumed that, to understand human motivation, it is necessary to discover what needs

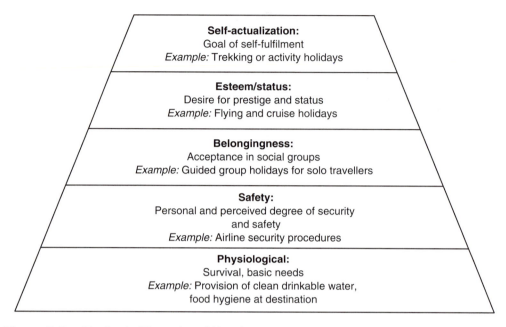

**Figure 2.2** Maslow's Hierarchy of Needs

*Source*: Maslow, A. H. (1943) 'A theory of human motivation', *Psychological Review*, 50, 370–396.

people have and how they can be fulfilled. Maslow, in 1943, was the first to attempt to do this with his needs hierarchy theory, now the best-known of all motivation theories (see Figure 2.2).

---

**MOTIVATIONS**
inner drives that people have that cause them to take action to satisfy their needs

---

**NEEDS**
the gaps between what customers have and what they would like to have, seen as the force that arouses motivated behaviour

---

Maslow's theory is that human needs are arranged in a hierarchy, from the most pressing to the least pressing; these needs, in order of importance, are physiological needs, safety needs, social needs, esteem needs, and self-actualization needs. One of the main reasons for the popularity of **Maslow's hierarchy of needs** is its simplicity. A person tries to satisfy their most important need first. When that need is satisfied, it will stop being a motivator, and the person will then try to satisfy the next most important need. It could be argued that traveller philanthropy, as described in the Opening Vignette, is an outcome of the modern consumer seeking to satisfy self-actualization needs, since all the other needs in Maslow's hierarchy have been met.

Attempts to explain tourist motivation have agreed with Maslow's hierarchy. Mills and Morrison (1985), for example, see travel as a need or want satisfier, and show how Maslow's hierarchy ties in with travel motivations and travel literature.[1] Similarly, tourism motivators as described by Dann (1977) can be linked to Maslow's list of needs. He argues that there are basically two factors in a decision to travel: the push factors and the pull factors.[2] The push factors are those that make you want to travel, and the pull factors are those that affect where you go. Crompton (1979) agrees with Dann as far as the idea of push and pull motives are concerned. He identifies nine motives, seven classified as sociopsychological or push motives, and two classified as cultural or pull motives. The push motives are escape from a perceived mundane environment; exploration and evaluation of self; relaxation, prestige, and regression; enhancement of kinship relationships; and facilitation of social interaction. The pull motives are novelty and education.[3]

Krippendorf (1987), in an enlightening book on tourism, sees a thread running through all these theories of tourism motivation. First, travel is motivated by 'going away from' rather than 'going toward' something; second, travellers' motives and behaviour are markedly self-oriented. The author classifies these theories into eight explanations of travel: recuperation and regeneration, compensation and social integration, escape, communication, freedom and self-determination, self-realization, happiness, and broadening the mind.[4]

Other factors influencing motivation and purchase include learning, beliefs and attitudes, and perception. **Learning** refers to the way in which visitors receive and interpret a variety of stimuli. People gain experience through taking holidays, by listening to others, and from a variety of other sources. From these experiences a consumer will develop a mental inventory of expectations about places – a catalogue of good and bad holiday experiences. These form the basis of learned criteria that will be recalled when selecting future holidays and destinations.

---

**LEARNING**
the way in which visitors receive and interpret a variety of stimuli

---

**Beliefs** refer to the thoughts that people have about most aspects of their life. As far as tourism is concerned, consumers will have beliefs about companies, products, and services, including tourism offerings and destinations. Such thoughts can be positive, such as trust or confidence in a certain hotel or tour guide, or negative, such as a feeling about lack of security on airlines, or fear of injury on the ski slopes.

---

**BELIEFS**
the thoughts that people have about most aspects of their life

---

**Attitudes** are more difficult to change, as they are ingrained feelings about various factors of an experience. Many people have a negative attitude towards flying, so airlines are attempting to convert non-flyers into flyers by holding special flying educational days to combat their fear. Similarly, theme parks hold seminars on combating the fear of rollercoaster rides – a session one psychologist described as helping people cope with their 'weaker self'.[5]

---

**ATTITUDES**
ingrained feelings about various factors of an experience

---

Finally, **perception** is an overall mind-picture of the world, shaped by information that people filter and then retrieve. Thus, perception is inextricably bound to the concepts of bias and distortion. People choose to interpret different stimuli in different ways, ignoring some factors while enhancing others. This is known as selective perception. People often perceive tourism offerings in a way that compliments their self-image. In this way tourism products are viewed as bundles of benefits that are personal to the consumer. It is, however, through the technical factors (which are called 'significative stimuli') that the marketer can seek to change perceptions.

---

**PERCEPTION**
an overall mind-picture of the world, shaped by information that people filter and then retrieve

---

Marketers sometimes use a technique known as **perceptual mapping** to identify the relationship between the level of perceived importance of certain aspects of a product or destination on the part of the tourist and the actual performance on the part of the supplier.

---

**PERCEPTUAL MAPPING**
technique used to identify the relationship between the level of perceived importance of certain aspects of a product on the part of the tourist and the actual performance on the part of the supplier

---

Figure 2.3 shows how the Czech Republic was perceived by visitors relative to seven other destinations (Orth and Tureckova, 2004).[6] The x-axis was labelled according to the polarity between traditional and modern, with traditional representing the negative and modern the positive. Germany, the Czech Republic and Hungary are representatives of the traditional hemisphere while France, Austria, Italy and Spain represent the modern destination. The second dimension (y-axis) measures the difference between education and brain versus relaxation and body. Accordingly, vacationers consider the destinations below the x-axis to

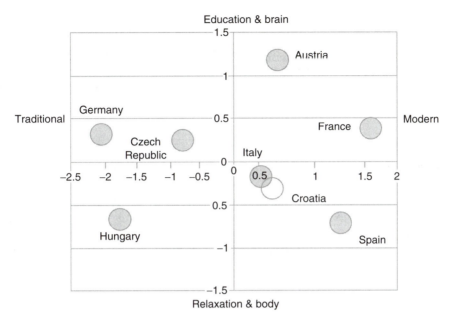

**Figure 2.3** Perceptual Map Showing Czech Republic's Competitive Position among Eight International Vacation Destinations.

be more suitable for sunbathing and relaxing (Spain, Croatia, Hungary and Italy) while countries closer to the positive pole have more cultural interest (Austria, France, the Czech Republic and Germany). According to visitors, Italy and Croatia have strong similarities.

**Consumer attitudes** are a consumer's enduring favourable or unfavourable cognitive evaluations, emotional feelings, and action tendencies toward some object or idea. As these attitudes and perceptions evolve, travel industry organizations must try to stay ahead without venturing too far off course. Some changes are evident years in advance – for example, few failed to anticipate the impact that aging baby boomers would have on the industry. Others changes, however, are unforeseeable. After 11 September 2001, many in the hospitality industry had to adapt strategies quickly to suit customers whose perceptions and needs changed literally overnight. Destinations began to focus on the geographic demographic of the driver market.

---

**CONSUMER ATTITUDES**

a consumer's enduring favourable or unfavourable cognitive evaluations, emotional feelings, and action tendencies toward some object or idea

---

Restaurants, too, have had to adapt to changing needs. Ed Michalski, president of Management Insight, a hospitality consulting firm, says that, 'For some, comfort food had a new appeal, while for others, suddenly it seemed the time to try something new and be more adventurous' (Sutherland, 2002).[7] Michalski also says that people are increasingly demanding high-quality ingredients, service and presentation, whether they are eating pork chops or prime rib. 'There's so much access to information about fine foods, with the popularity of food magazines, the food channel and cooking shows on television, that people are much more knowledgeable than they used to be, and restaurants have to upgrade their products and services.'

## Culture

The second key factor from Figure 2.1 that influences a consumer's behaviour is culture. **Culture** can be defined as the norms, beliefs and rituals that are unique to each person. These different factors influence how we live, communicate, and think about certain things; culture can also dictate how a person will act in a certain situation. In terms of self-image and the satisfaction of underlying tensions, most people seek to satisfy their desires in a way that fits societal norms. For example, it is acceptable to be a green consumer, but sex tourism is viewed disparagingly. Awareness of cultural shifts is equally important. For example, smokers are increasingly being prohibited from smoking in social places, especially on transport carriers and in restaurants.

---

**CULTURE**
the norms, beliefs and rituals that are unique to each person

---

A complete and thorough appreciation of the origins (geography, history, political economy, technology, and social institutions) and elements (cultural values, rituals, symbols, beliefs, and ways of thinking) of culture may well be the single most important goal for a marketer in the preparation of international marketing plans and strategies (Cateora and Graham, 2005).[8] One of the most accepted theories in cross-cultural and marketing research was developed by Gert Hofstede (1980).[9] He defined culture as 'the collective mental programming of the people in an environment', and stated that 'culture is not a characteristic of individuals; it encompasses a number of people who were conditioned by the same education and life experience'. It was mentioned in the opening chapter that cultural globalization is characterized by cultural homogenization as Western consumption and lifestyle patterns spread throughout the world, a process facilitated by the flow of travellers from the West to the developing world. However, it is still critical for tourism marketers to have an understanding of different cultures. For example, Korea has one of the most homogenous populations in the world with few cultural or racial variations, and virtually no ethnic minorities. In Myanmar, on the other hand, there are an estimated 135 ethnic minority groups with over 100 languages and dialects spoken in the country.

Other aspects of culture that are appropriate to motivational studies include languages, societal practices, institutions, and subcultures. The transmission of culture is primarily through the spoken and written word, but also through symbolic gestures, including the ways in which people expect to be greeted by others. Cultural practices include how we divide the day and our attitudes toward opening hours for shops or restaurants.

Institutions, such as the church, the media, and educational systems will affect cultural patterns. The church, for example, seeks to retain a special day for worship and hence is reluctant to sanction secularization of this day, often in opposition to the promoters of tourism. Finally, most societies comprise a number of subcultures that exhibit variations of behaviour as a result of ethnic or regional differentiation.

## Age and Gender

As mentioned later in Chapter 3, a traditional way of segmenting markets has been by age. For example, many travel suppliers are today targeting the growing senior market. This market is both lucrative and unique because it is less tied to seasonal travel, involves longer trips, and is not wedded to midweek or weekend travel, so it can boost occupancy rates for business and leisure travel operators. For the senior market, too, perceived value is much more important than price. After people retire, they may stay loyal to brand names they know best, but the price points will have to be suitable to a retirement income. Disney's recent push to attract visitors in their fifties and sixties is a good indicator that the baby boomer bandwagon is picking up momentum, as the majority of the population in North America starts sliding down the wrong side of middle age. Some believe that this will result in a decline in the number of family restaurants and quick-food services, as these were products demanded by the baby boomers who are now aging.

In some societies gender can influence consumer behaviour in terms of the roles men and women are expected to play. Gender segmentation has long been used in marketing clothing, hairdressing, cosmetics, and magazines. But more recently it has been applied to tourism and hospitality products and services. For example, the number of women travelling for work purposes has been growing steadily for two decades, and vocal women travellers have influenced the introduction of better-lit parking garages, higher-quality soaps and lotions in hotel bathrooms, and improved room-service fare. Travel industry experts say that women travellers are more demanding and discerning than their male counterparts. Their main concerns are safety and security, followed by comfort and convenience.

## Social Class

Social class is still considered to be one of the most important external factors influencing consumer behaviour. **Social class** is the position one occupies within society, and it is determined by such factors as income, wealth, education, occupation, family prestige, value of home and neighbourhood. Social class is closely linked to the existence of social institutions. The role and status positions found within a society are influenced by the dictates of social institutions. The caste system in India is one such institution. The election of a low-caste person – formally called an 'untouchable' – as president made international news because it was such a departure from traditional Indian culture. Decades ago, touching or even glancing at an untouchable was considered enough to defile a Hindu of high status. Even though the caste system has been outlawed, it remains a visible part of the culture in India, and it is difficult for people to move out of the class into which they were born.

In the West, it is easier for people to move into social classes that differ from their families'. However, most developed countries still have a class system consisting of upper, middle, and lower classes. In the UK for example, the middle class has been expanding and is forecast to overtake the working class by 2020 as the largest social group. A report published by the Future Foundation in 2006, titled *Middle Britain*, found that 43 per cent of Britons say they are middle class, a figure that is rising (Brean, 2006).[10] Unfortunately, that does not mean social inequality is on the decline – quite the opposite. By 2000, the gap between rich and poor was the highest it had ever been, and it continues to widen.

Marketers assume that people in one class buy different goods and services and for different reasons than people in other classes. As a rule, the higher the level of disposable income people have, the more likely they are to travel, and premium income earners tend to be those people who have studied at a higher educational level. The Snapshot below shows how the backpacking segment has changed over the years, due to rising income and a higher disposable income amongst young people.

---

**SOCIAL CLASS**

the position one occupies within society, determined by such factors as income, wealth, education, occupation, family prestige, value of home and neighbourhood

---

## Snapshot

### Backpackers with Gold Cards

Few modern social developments are more significant and less appreciated than the rise of backpacker travel. The tens of thousands of young Australians, Germans, Britons, Americans, and others who wander the globe, flitting from Goa to Costa Rica, from Thailand to Tasmania, are building what may be the only example of a truly global community. Nobody has an accurate way of guessing the size of the backpacker market, but the growth of the Lonely Planet brand offers an approximation. The first Lonely Planet guidebook was stapled together on an Australian kitchen table in the early 1970s; 30 years later, the company publishes more than 600 destination guides from all over the world.

Although the majority of backpackers are still aged between 18 and 25, and use inexpensive, communally oriented accommodations like hostels, there is evidence that the traditional backpacker profile is changing. John Hughes, a British expatriate who runs a website for backpackers in Asia, says that young people taking breaks in schooling, and those seeking temporary employment and learning opportunities abroad, have largely replaced the travellers of old who wandered footloose and fancy-free as far and long as their money would take them. And there are some older ones who come back drawn by fond memories of their younger backpacking days. 'It seems to me that a lot of backpackers have plastic in their back pockets whereas they didn't before,' says Hughes. 'They're better organized and getting more packaged.'

Hostel owners are also saying they are seeing a marked increase in the number of backpackers in their thirties and forties. As people marry later, make more money earlier, and switch careers more often, many are tapping into savings to have an extended adventure before going back to the grind. Moreover, companies that value their employees are bowing to their workers' wanderlust by granting travel sabbaticals. These travel patterns are being catered for by specialized guidebooks that increasingly give more expensive options to an older market. Backpacker destinations are also attracting growing numbers of Koreans, Taiwanese and Hong Kong citizens, and a vast potential market is seen in China and India. An example of a more sophisticated backpacking package comes from Vietnam. Ho Chi Minh City-based Linh Nam Travel Co. has a 79-day tour of Vietnam with an itinerary of 8,000 kilometres through 59 cities and provinces nationwide. The programme runs twice a year and tourists can chose to stay in hotels of one to three stars, or take a home-stay.

'Flashpackers' is the name often given to those who prefer nice hotels to the backpacker's dormitory. They not only boast an adventurous spirit but enjoy the safety net of a healthy bank balance when the going gets tough. 'The twentysomething flashpacker accounts for around 20 per cent of our overall bookings,' says Nikki Davies, marketing manager for Trailfinders, a backpacking specialist in the UK. According to Dan Linstead, editor of *Wanderlust*, the adventure travel magazine, the advent of the young flashpacker is down to the blurring of distinctions between suitcase and backpacking holidays. 'Conventional backpacking territories have broken down,' he says. 'While travellers are still booking independent flights and exploring adventurous locations, they prefer to stay in upmarket hotels.' The reason for this, according to Lonstead, is that today's twentysomething travellers are used to far higher standards of living than their predecessors on the original hippy trail. 'A flashpacker pays in money rather than time,' he says, 'condensing what a backpacker spends in a year into a two- or three-week break.'

These trends have brought new tensions to the adventure of the backpacker trail. Younger, more traditional backpackers say the sense of community they cherish in hostels is being lost as the richer backpackers use the accommodation only to sleep. 'These new backpackers can take away from the communal aspect of what these backpacker hostels started out as,' complains Lauren Roberts, manager of Whale House Backpackers in Hout Bay, near Cape Town. Traditional backpackers, she says, use hostels as one-stop social outlets – inexpensive places to sleep and meet travellers from around the world to share adventures and travelling tips. But older backpackers often rent cars and flash credit cards to ditch the hostel and fellow tourists for (in this case) white-linen wine-tasting evenings in Cape Town's excellent wine regions. 'The double rooms people are building defeat the object of the backpackers; the dorm rooms get people talking to each other,' she said. 'It's sort of a fight in the industry now. You can lose the whole concept of the hostel.'

*Sources*: Winston, A. (13 August 2006). 'The flash pack', *The Independent on Sunday: The Compact Traveller,* 15; Anon. (25 September 2002) 'Backpackers lift an economy', *The Vancouver Sun,* A15; Cousineau, A. (2 November 2002) 'Backpackers really do have more fun', *Calgary Herald,* TS04; Daley, B. (29 September 1999) 'Slumming it, with a gold card', *National Post,* B9; Gray, D. (27 July 2002) 'The new backpacker: less scruffy and stinky, more moneyed and packaged', *Times–Colonist.* Victoria, B.C., D2.

## Lifestyle

Marketers are increasingly segmenting their markets by consumer lifestyles. **Lifestyle analysis** examines the way people allocate time, energy and money. Lifestyle analysis tends to exclude demographic traits, so researchers in marketing have combined demographic and psychological variables into a concept called 'psychographics'. **Psychographic analysis** attempts to measure people's activities, interests and opinions. By profiling the way groups of people live, it is possible to predict their travel motivations and purchases.

> **LIFESTYLE ANALYSIS**
> examines the way people allocate time, energy and money

> **PSYCHOGRAPHIC ANALYSIS**
> attempts to measure people's activities, interests and opinions

One of the best-known categorizations in this area is the **VALS**™ System. The VALS framework divides the US population into different lifestyle groups, defined according to psychological factors that correlate with purchase behaviour. As can be seen in Figure 2.4, VALS distinguishes between eight psychographic groups: innovators, thinkers, achievers, experiencers, believers, strivers, makers, and survivors. Members of each group have different psychological profiles and maintain different lifestyles. The position of a person in the VALS framework depends on the person's primary motivations (ideas, achievement or self-expression) and resources including income, education, self-confidence, health, eagerness to buy and energy level. The VALS tool can be used to help businesses develop and execute more effective strategies. For example, a cruise company in the US used VALS to identify and understand which consumers were most interested in its specialized tours. By designing direct mail to appeal to targeted consumers and mailing to key ZIP codes, the cruise line increased reservations by 400 per cent.

> **VALS**™
> a typology framework that divides the population into eight lifestyle groups, defined according to factors such as self-image, aspirations, values and products used

## Life Cycle

The concept of the **family life cycle** – the stages through which families might pass as they mature – is based on the premise that when people live together, their way of life changes. Single people are likely to behave differently from couples, and if couples subsequently have children, their lifestyle changes more radically, as do their levels of financial and other commitment. Many authors have applied the **life cycle model** to tourism, suggesting that travel patterns and destinations vary as people move through their life cycle (Pearce, 1993).[11] The model works well when investigating the traditional nuclear family composed of two parents

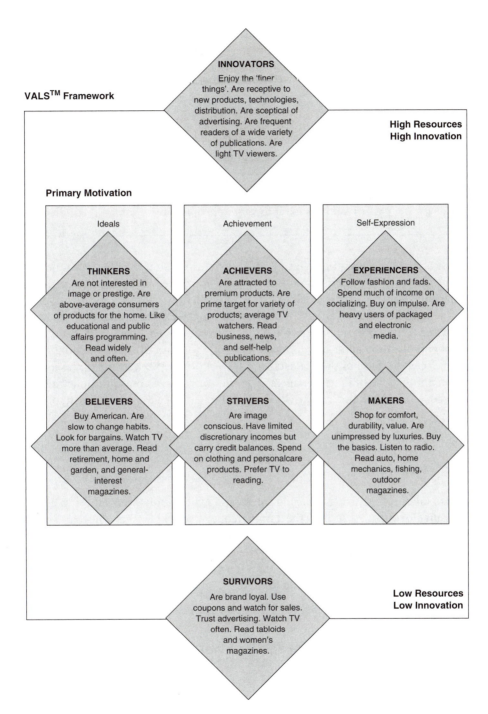

**Figure 2.4**   The VALS™ Typology Framework

and one or more children. It does not, however, purport to represent the increasing proportion of households that do not fall into this pattern, such as single-parent families, extended family networks, and those who remain single throughout their life.

---

**FAMILY LIFE CYCLE**
the stages through which families might pass as they mature

---

**LIFE CYCLE MODEL**
suggests that travel patterns and destinations vary as people move through their life cycle

---

Tourists may also change their behaviour patterns over time, so if the life cycle model is used to predict behaviour, then trends in consumer behaviour need to be monitored. For example, the Snapshot 'Backpackers with Gold Cards' showed how backpackers are no longer just young people aged between 18 and 25. They have been joined by an older and wealthier segment of backpackers who are changing the structure of the backpacker market. The Case Study at the end of this chapter is a good example of a tourism product – Schoolies Week – that has developed because of the life cycle model. Schoolies Week is one of the few 'rites of passage' remaining to Australian teenagers. The rites of passage concept implies a transition from adolescence to adulthood, an activity designed to enhance the development of a distinct self identity.

## Reference Groups

Learning also takes place through sharing values and expectations with others in a variety of social **reference groups**, including the family, college, workplace or church. This brings exposure to a normative set of values, i.e., those that set a tone as to how we should behave morally in society. For example, experienced travellers, who have been exposed to other cultures and to people who are less fortunate than they, are influencing the new trend of volunteer tourism highlighted in the Opening Vignette.

---

**REFERENCE GROUPS**
groups that have a direct (face-to-face) or indirect influence on a person's attitude or behaviour

---

The United Nations World Tourism Organization (UNWTO) has noticed that there is 'an increasing tendency among contemporary travel consumers to view travel as a means for enhancing the quality of their own lives by building on a philosophy of doing well while doing something good for society'.[12] The UNWTO and other tourism organizations that monitor trends in the travel industry say it is precisely the growing number of well-heeled, well-educated older travellers – people who are indeed concerned with 'doing something good for society' – that has been driving the demand for such developing niche markets as educational tourism, ecotours, agritourism, and cultural tourism. Travellers can take a 'volunteer vacation' and give their time and expertise to help in projects in developing countries. These trips aren't free, but they're often cheaper than conventional tours.

## Typologies of Tourists

The discussion so far has been about the variables that influence tourist behaviour. But many tourism researchers have tried to explain tourist behaviour by developing typologies of the tourists themselves. The tourist motivation model proposed by Stanley Plog (1974) is one of the most widely cited.[13] According to Plog, travellers may be classified as allocentrics or psychocentrics. Travellers who are more **allocentric** are thought to prefer exotic destinations, unstructured vacations rather than packaged tours, and more involvement with local cultures. **Psychocentrics**, on the other hand, are thought to prefer familiar destinations, packaged tours, and 'touristy' areas. Later, Plog changed these labels to more 'reader-friendly' terms; specifically, psychocentrics became **dependables**, and allocentrics **venturers**. Figure 2.5 presents a visual picture of the old and new concepts, as applied to a normal population curve. Plog found that the majority of the population was neither allocentric nor psychocentric, but 'midcentric' – somewhere in the middle. It has been argued, however, that Plog's theory is difficult to apply, as tourists will travel with different motivations on different occasions. There are many holidaymakers who will take a winter break in an allocentric destination, but will then take their main summer holiday in a psychocentric destination.

---

**ALLOCENTRICS**
travellers who prefer exotic destinations, unstructured vacations rather than packaged tours, and more involvement with local cultures

---

**PSYCHOCENTRICS**
travellers who prefer familiar destinations, packaged tours, and 'touristy' areas

---

Other tourism researchers have developed different typologies. Most are based on empirical data obtained from questionnaires and/or personal interviews. Cohen's typology (1972) – one of the first – proposed four classifications of tourists: (1) the organized mass tourist, highly dependent on the 'environmental bubble', who purchases all-inclusive tours or package holidays; (2) the individual mass tourist, who is more autonomous and free than those in the previous group; (3) the explorer, who seeks new areas but would sometimes opt to step

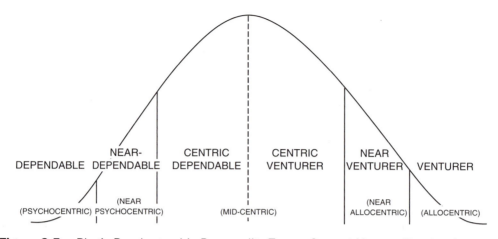

**Figure 2.5**  Plog's Psychographic Personality Types: Current Versus (Previous)

*Sources*: Plog, S.C. (1974) 'Why destination areas rise and fall in popularity', *Cornell Hotel and Restaurant Quarterly*, 14(4), 55–58; Plog, S.C. (2002) 'The power of psychogaphics and the concept of venturesomeness', *Journal of Travel Research*, 40, 244–251. Copyright Cornell University. All rights reserved. Used by permission.

back into comfortable accommodation, etc.; and (4) the drifter, who avoids any kind of 'tourist establishment'.[14] The Snapshot on Adventurer Annie below takes a tongue-in-cheek look at the typology of modern-day 'explorer'.

## Snapshot

### Adventurer Annie

Adventurer Annie gets around. In the last few years she's been heli-skiing in the Rockies, watched killer whales off the coast of British Columbia, climbed Everest, kayaked around Greenland, bungee-jumped in Queenstown, and been on a 'Survivor Tour' in Thailand. In between, she is busy making big bucks in the city, trading stocks, and planning her trips. Next year she is off on a wildlife safari in Tanzania, hiking up Kilimanjaro and rafting down the Zambezi. But Annie doesn't do any of this on a budget, and wouldn't compromise on comfort. Annie is part of a new breed of adventure tourists that many in the outdoor recreation business are referring to as 'Bobos': bourgeois bohemians. They are looking for an escape to nature from their stressed-out urban lives, but they want the experience without the hassle of hauling a lot of gear into the back-country, sleeping on lumpy ground, or hunting for kindling to cook smoky, second-rate meals.

So who is Annie? She's 45 years old and hence classified as a baby boomer. She is fit, well educated, and is interested in novelty, escape and authentic experiences. These days, she and her friends are opting for more physically challenging and 'adrenalin-driven' activities. She is also rich monetarily but poor in time, and so wants to squeeze as much experience into as short a time as possible. What makes Annie tick? She is certainly motivated by the thrill and challenge of learning, and by the experience of nature and the environment. She is also health conscious and has realized that her travel experiences are a terrific stress reliever and make her more productive at work. However, she is also motivated by the physical and symbolic capital she can accumulate by purchasing these adventure tourism holidays.

She holds regular dinner parties in between her trips to let all her friends and family know where she has been and where she is going next. In return for being fed, guests have to gaze with awe and murmur appreciatively as Annie serves up a slide show for a main course and a portfolio of digital photos for dessert. Occasionally Annie gets too busy at work to get away for an adventure experience. Fortunately there is a new 'dirt spray' on the market that she can use to discolor her SUV. She wouldn't want friends thinking she was becoming a suburban bore.

Adventure tourism is one of the fastest-growing segments of the tourism industry (growing 10–15 per cent annually) and it is the experiential engagement that distinguishes it from other types of tourism. In the past, adventure was associated with uncertainty of outcome; any outdoor recreation that was *planned* could not be an adventure. Yet today this is precisely how adventure tourism is marketed. There exists, therefore, something of a paradox whereby the more detailed, planned and logistically smooth an adventure tourist itinerary becomes, the more removed the experience is from the notion of adventure. Much as Annie would like to think she is engaging in a dangerous, unplanned adventure, in reality she is so dependent on her guides that if she was left to her own devices, she would kill herself within an hour!

As for the future, it is likely that Annie will continue her adventure tourism activities but will go from being a Bobo to a GRAMPIE – that is, someone who is 'growing old, retired and moneyed, in good physical and emotional health'. It is estimated that by 2040, over half the population in the developed world will be over 50. This means there will be more people in good health with a more informed global perspective – more GRAMPIES – and thus more adventure tourists. The only change for Annie will be that her adventures will be softer, and she will be supported by an increasing number of masseuses, chiropractors and physiotherapists.

## The Buying Process

Before discussing the buying process, it is important to recognize that various buying situations will have an influence on this process. First of all, consumers are likely to display various levels of commitment, depending on the nature of the purchase. It has been suggested that there are three such levels (Howard and Sheth, 1969):[15]

1. **Extended problem solving**: In this situation, such as the decision to take a long-haul holiday, the consumer is likely to have a deep level of commitment, to make a detailed search for information, and to make an extensive comparison of the alternatives.
2. **Limited problem solving**: In this situation, the consumer will have some degree of knowledge or experience already, but many factors will be taken for granted and the information search will be far more limited. A second holiday at a favorite skiing destination may be purchased in this way.
3. **Habitual problem solving**; This is a repeat purchase of a tried and tested short break or day excursion, which requires little or no evaluation. The purchase is made primarily on the basis of a previous satisfactory experience and a good understanding of the destination or brand name of the tourism or hospitality offering.

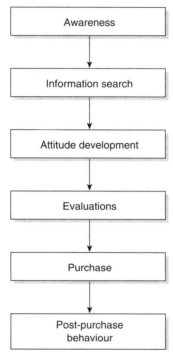

**Figure 2.6** The Consumer Buying Process

Given the variation in decision-making styles, it is difficult to propose just one universal decision-making process for travellers. Depending on the project, Decrop and Snelders (2005) suggest that six types of vacationers can be described: habitual, rational, hedonic, opportunistic, constrained and adaptable.[16] These typologies were based on a study of Belgian travellers, but the authors believe that these six types could be found in different parts of the world.

Role adoption will also influence the buying process, and it is proposed that there are five roles (Engel, Blackwell and Miniard, 1990):[17]

1. **Initiator**: the person who starts the purchasing process and who gathers information;
2. **Influencer**: a person or persons who expresses preferences in choice or selection of information – this can be a group of friends, relatives, or a partner;
3. **Decider**: the person who has the financial control and possibly the authority within a group of people to make the purchase;
4. **Buyer**: the person who actually makes the purchase, visits the travel agent, and obtains the tickets, etc.; and
5. **User**: the person or persons who consumes the purchase and actually goes on the trip.

The consumer buying process for tourism is often regarded as similar to that for other products and services. The assumption is that a consumer moves through a number of stages leading up to a purchase. Figure 2.6 outlines these stages.

The process begins with **awareness**, a stage that may be initiated by promotional efforts, by word of mouth, or through an informational search such as an online search. The next stage involves the buyer **obtaining more information**, and as suggested previously, there are likely to be various levels of commitment depending on the nature of the purchase. Recent surveys show that the internet plays a major role when travellers research and book travel (see Chapter 10). This information search will result in the **formation of an attitude**, perhaps reinforcing an existing attitude or bringing about a change on the part of the buyer. At the **evaluation** stage, the buyer will make more detailed comparisons. For example, a consumer may consider a number of destinations and will choose based on criteria such as price, recommendation, convenience or convention. Subject to time and financial constraints, the consumer will then make the **purchase**. The majority of travellers prefer to book their vacations months in advance, but an increasing number of consumers are booking their trips on the spur of the moment, a phenomenon facilitated by the growth of the internet.

The purchase is followed by the final stage of the buying process, **post-purchase behaviour**. If the experience is satisfactory, the visitor may purchase the same type of holiday in the future. Often the importance of this stage is underestimated, but several studies have examined the association between service quality and more specific behavioural intentions, and there is a positive and significant relationship between customers' perceptions of service quality and their willingness to recommend the company or destination to others (Zeithaml et al., 1996).[18]

## Organizational Buyer Behaviour

### Decision-making for Organizations

Tourism marketers need to understand both the decision criteria used and the decision-making process undergone by groups and organizations in buying tourism services. The process is likely to be quite different for group buyers, and there can be many individuals or groups involved in making decisions for the conference market. These include the users, influencers, deciders and buyers. It has been argued that in order to close a sale within a business-to-business market, the supplier has to identify and satisfy all stakeholders in the decision-making unit.

A marketer will also need to understand the buying phases for organizations. The conference market, for example, follows a pattern of group decision-making, and the 'buy phase' has been described as follows: problem recognition, general need description, product specification, supplier search, proposal solution, supplier selection, order routine specification, and performance review (Radburn, 1997).[19] These buy phases sometimes take a long period of time, depending on the size of the conference or the complexity of arrangements, with lead times of two or three years in some instances and longer ones for mega-events such as the World Cup soccer tournament.

The process is also affected by the nature of the purchase, as it can be a new purchase, a modified re-buy, or a straight re-buy. A new purchase involves a high degree of risk, as the client is buying a facility or service for the first time. A modified re-buy is less risky, as the client has bought a service offering before, perhaps at another hotel or conference centre within the group, but now seeks to modify the purchase. This might mean a new venue or new specifications for service levels. The straight re-buy is the least risky purchase situation, as it involves, for example, re-ordering a service at the same venue.

Having identified the key decision-makers and phases in the purchase process, the marketer must then establish which criteria these decision-makers have used to differentiate between suppliers. Webster and Wind suggest that four main factors influence the decision-making criteria of organizational buyers: environmental, organizational, interpersonal, and individual (Webster and Wind, 1972).[20] These factors are constantly changing, so it is essential to re-evaluate market trends frequently.

## The Behaviour of Business Travellers

The behaviour of business travellers is significantly different from that of leisure travellers. In fact, according to experts, executives do not see travel as a perk but rather as another source of stress (Cohen, 2000).[21] They feel that they have no proper balance between home and work life, and that this causes problems in their relationships with partners and children. And it is not just the business traveller who suffers. One study found that people whose spouses travel frequently on business suffer more mental health problems than those whose partners remain at home (Tong, 2002).[22] Short, frequent trips away from home have a worse effect on people than longer, less frequent trips. The study recommended that workers travel no more than 90 days a year and that companies allow employees to refuse too many trips; it also suggested video-conferencing and flexible work arrangements as substitutes for travel. Unfortunately, few businesses pay attention to the damaging effect travel can have on their employees. The paradox is that travel costs the company money, and much business travel has been made redundant by modern communication technologies such as telephone- and video-conferencing.

Airlines spend a lot of time and money trying to understand the needs of their business travellers. As the demographic gets wider for this group (as it has been doing for the last decade), zeroing in on which services and programmes would most appeal is becoming more difficult. The group is not necessarily unified in terms of age, dress, or tastes, or in terms of what its members want to do or have in business class. Whether a flight is inbound for business or outbound for home makes a difference to what a customer expects, and the key for airlines is to offer their customers the ability to work or play. Work-related technology – laptop power plugs and in-air phones – are obligatory for any airline interested in attracting the business traveller. For passengers' downtime, not much has changed: movies, food and drink remain required staples. The selection in the last category has become much broader, due in part to the fact that 30 to 40 per cent of frequent business passengers are women, and women don't always want a beer or a soft drink. One factor that is consistent among all passengers, however, is the need for space, and airlines are always looking for ways to increase personal space for passengers. Space is an equally important service consideration on the ground. It is standard to isolate first or business class passengers from those flying economy with special lounges and facilities devoted to their needs. Computer hook-ups, boardrooms, and entertainment centres are now standard requirements.

## Global Trends in Consumer Behaviour

As mentioned in Chapter 1, many major cultural trends affect the tourism industry, and the final section of Chapter 2 focuses on ten key trends or demands in consumer behaviour that are influencing tourism and hospitality marketing today.

### Learning and Enrichment

One of the major trends in tourism today is the desire of the tourist to have a learning experience as part of the vacation. Educational travel has boomed over the past few decades. A recent survey found that half of North American travellers want to visit art, architectural or historic sites on vacations, while one third would like to learn a new skill or activity. Of course, the desire for self-improvement is nothing new. Young gentlemen of the 18th and 19th centuries who set out on the Grand Tour were looking for a dose of classical culture spiced with some pleasant debauchery as part of the package. But putting the label 'educational' on vacation trips is becoming increasingly popular these days.

Today's travellers are seeking experiences that provide them with greater insight, increased understanding, and a personal connection to the people and places they visit. Rather than choose their vacation by the destination, many are first determining the experiences they want, and then choosing the destination where these experiences are located. **Learning and enrichment travel** refers to vacations that provide opportunities for authentic, hands-on, or interactive learning experiences, featuring themes such as adventure, agriculture, anthropology, archaeology, arts, culture, cuisine, education, forestry, gardening, language, maritime culture, mining, nature, science, spirituality, sports, wine and wildlife – to name just a few!

---

**LEARNING AND ENRICHMENT TRAVEL**
vacations that provide opportunities for authentic, hands-on, or interactive learning experiences

---

L'Oceanografic in Valencia, Europe's largest marine park, is an example of a tourism attraction whose goal is to educate as well as entertain. The US$200 million project opened in 2003 and has 42 million litres of saltwater holding 45,000 fish and marine mammals, comprising 500 species. There is even an aquarium of the senses, where visually handicapped visitors can acquaint themselves with the size and shape of life-size models of fish and crustaceans. This hands-on approach is a common theme throughout Valencia's City of Arts and Sciences. The Global Spotlight on Semester at Sea, below, provides a closer look at a unique educational experience.

# Global Spotlight

## Semester At Sea

Educational tourism is not a recent innovation. It has its roots in the Grand Tour, a term first applied in England over 300 years ago. This type of travel was seen as the best means of teaching wealthy young men about culture, taste, geography, art and general worldliness in preparation for careers in the military, government and civil services. Nowadays, more than 150,000 American college students go on their own international travels every year in the form of study-abroad programmes. One of the most varied of such educational opportunities is provided by Semester At Sea which twice annually takes around 650 students around the world in a 100-day semester, visiting ten different countries in a fusion of education and travel.

For more than 40 years, over 40,000 students from the US and abroad have experienced Semester At Sea programmes, studying four credit courses from a comprehensive international curriculum. The Institute for Shipboard Education, a non-profit organization, has been administering these programmes since 1975 in conjunction with various US universities. The actual concept was inaugurated in 1926 with the University World Cruise which later became the University of the Seven Seas, then World Campus Afloat and finally, with the help of the late C. Y. Tung (founder of the Orient Overseas Container Line), Semester At Sea.

Students, staff and faculty from all over the world work, socialize, study, and travel together during a 100-day spring or fall semester or the 65-day summer programme. Spring trips usually proceed eastwards around the world and fall tours head west, with the shorter summer trips concentrating on Asia or Latin America. The focus is on non-Western cultures with developing economies and diverse political and cultural systems. A multi-disciplinary overview of the areas and issues encountered during the voyage is provided by a mandatory upper-level geography course. Called Global Studies, this draws upon the experience and expertise of the whole faculty as well as specialized inter-port lecturers who provide a more personal insight into their nations' histories, cultures and customs.

The author of this book, Simon Hudson, was a professor on Semester at Sea during the Spring 2006 Voyage. 'It really was a fulfilling experience,' he said. 'I could never normally afford to travel around the world for four months with my family (the cost for a 109-day cruise with Crystal Cruises is around US$57,000), so this was the perfect opportunity to combine travel with work in an affordable fashion. My two boys just loved every minute and have not stopped talking about the experience. Interestingly, tourism had not been taught on the ship in previous voyages, and yet it seemed like an obvious choice for such a venture. I ended up with three full classes (about 36 students in each class) and a wonderfully eclectic group of students. For me, the most memorable countries we visited were Myanmar, India and South Africa, but every port offered a distinctive adventure.'

It's not just undergraduates who are learning about the world on these trips. A small contingent of 'Senior Passengers' also pays to circumnavigate the world, joining in with classes, Community College activities, clubs, Global Studies and lectures on board. They form part of the extended family on the ship, acting as surrogate 'parents' and 'grandparents' for the younger generations. Students, too, volunteer as 'Big Brothers' and 'Big Sisters' for the school-age kids on board – children of faculty and staff are also educated while travelling around the world with their parents.

Subjects include anthropology, biological studies, business, economics, music, geology, philosophy and theatre arts among many others. Students with every major can apply and there are also grants available for those who qualify for financial aid. Fieldwork, which accounts for 20 per cent of the hours needed for course credits, is geared to each specific interest as well as different budgets. Day trips might include a tea ceremony in Japan or a candomble ceremony in Brazil; overnight travel could take students to sites of significant cultural, historical or political interest such as the Great Wall of China or Angkor Wat in Cambodia.

Other field experiences concentrate more on the local people and active involvement in the countries visited. Students and faculty can learn about local customs during a home-stay with a Japanese or Indian family. There are overnight trips to 'untouchable' villages where students work, eat and sleep as the locals do. There are also opportunities to meet university students in each country during welcome receptions, sports competitions and lectures.

The ship, M V *Explorer,* includes all the luxuries of a regular cruise ship with the academic atmosphere and rules of a normal land-based campus. Thus there is a fully equipped library and computer room as well as a gym and a health centre.

At a basic cost of around US$16,000 per 100-day voyage, Semester At Sea is by no means cheap for students. But when you factor in the opportunity to visit ten different countries for about five days apiece, on top of the potential to obtain 12 course credits during a regular school semester, it is not particularly expensive. However, students also need money for in-country travel, books and general spending. As the promotional brochure says: 'Semester At Sea costs more than the average semester at college. But, if you consider that you will earn a semester of academic credit and add a dimension to your undergraduate education that will pay dividends throughout your life, it will be the investment of a lifetime.'

Such international educational tourism is in keeping with the current trend towards globalization, where, through trade, countries are increasingly interdependent and the marketplace is global in scope. Semester At Sea's mission statement echoes this trend: 'Humankind's pursuit of knowledge has been intricately linked to ships and the sea. From early civilizations to the modern era, the exploration of distant lands, the exchange of ideas and commodities, and the search for knowledge have occurred in this manner.' It goes on to define its commitment to combining academic excellence with challenging experiential programming in order to remain at the forefront of global education.

*Sources*: Personal communication with Lauren Heinz, associate director of communications, Semester At Sea, March 2007; Semester At Sea Media Kit, retrieved from www.semesteratsea.com, April 2007.

## Ethical Products

In the last few decades, responsible tourism has emerged as a significant trend in the Western world, as wider consumer market trends towards lifestyle marketing and ethical consumption have spread to tourism. Tourism organizations are beginning to realize that promoting their ethical stance can be good business as it potentially enhances a company's profits, management effectiveness, public image and employee relations. In a recent survey, 26 per cent of people aged 33–44 said they increasingly used their purchasing power to reward ethically, socially, and environmentally aware companies (Hickman, 2006).[23] International leisure travellers are increasingly motivated to select a destination for the quality of its environmental health and the diversity and integrity of its natural and cultural resources. Studies of German and US travel markets indicate that environmental considerations are now a significant aspect of travellers' destination-choosing process, down to – in the case of the Germans – the environmental programmes operated by individual hotels. Certainly in the United States, the growth in special-interest, nature-oriented travel reflects an increasing concern for the environment. A recent study also showed that approximately 80 per cent of American travellers believe it is important that hotels take steps to preserve and protect the environment. According to the study, 70 per cent are willing to pay as much as US$150 more for a two-week stay in a hotel that has a 'responsible environmental attitude', and 55 per cent are more likely to book a hotel that purports to be environmentally friendly.[24]

Even restaurants are taking the green route. Chanterelle Country Inn, on the Cabot Trail in Cape Breton, Nova Scotia, Canada offers a 'green environment' and 'Cape Breton fresh' cuisine. Besides recycling and precycling, the inn uses only organic and fragrance-free facial, bath, and laundry soaps, as well as cleaning products; linens and bedding of natural fibres; and solar power for water and space heating. Its water comes from a deep well fed by a spring. All dishes are prepared in the restaurant's own kitchens, using organic and locally produced ingredients. Its dining room also stocks organically grown wines.

## Nostalgia

According to author Charles Leadbeater, we are in the middle of a nostalgia boom. The more rapidly people are propelled into an uncertain future, the more they yearn for the imagined security of the past. 'Globalization promotes a yearning for local roots and identities. Our immersion in the digital and virtual world creates a demand for tactile and tangible skills at home: cooking, gardening, and decorating. The growth of individualism makes us yearn for a time when we imagined that we lived in real communities, with a sense of shared memory and moral commitment,' says Leadbeater (2002).[25]

The outcome is an increase in nostalgia tourism, and the Snapshot below shows how two nostalgia tourism attractions – Pier 21 in Canada and Dianaville in the UK – are capitalizing on this trend.

## Snapshot

### Longing for the Way We Were: Nostalgia Tourism

From films to music, from cars to architecture, we are using new technology to return us to the past, to deliver better versions of old experiences. Not only have we become more interested in history, but the scale, richness, and diversity of the history we are interested in has also expanded enormously in the past 30 years. History used to be about stately homes, battles, and kings and queens. Now it can be about everything from pencils to maple syrup, from toys to matches, from kitchens to bricks. Nostalgia tourism allows people to revisit the past, enabling them to come to terms with tragic historical events in order to put them into perspective, obtain closure, as well as keep good memories alive. Two examples of nostalgia tourism attractions are Pier 21 in Canada and Dianaville in the UK.

A National Historic Site located in Halifax, Nova Scotia, Pier 21 is a unique tourism facility that offers the visitor the opportunity to understand the difficult early immigration process that many people had to endure. Winner of a national award for being the Best New Attraction in 2001, Pier 21 operates as a learning facility and an informational and experiential tourism destination, and presents an in-depth look at what over one million people went through to make a new life in a new country. It also provides a place to honour the members of Canada's armed forces who served in World War II.

First operational in 1928, Pier 21 was the immigrant gateway to Canada until its closure in 1971. When ships arrived, immigrants would begin the final process leading to their new lives. No more than 250 people at once would disembark and be led to the Assembly Room. From there, they filed into the Examination Room for a medical exam and an immigration interview. If successful, they could then take trains to their final destination. During World War II, Pier 21 also operated as the departure point for the troops who sailed to Europe to engage in battle. Today, the Wall of Service, located on the World War II Deck, stands as a tribute to members of the Canadian military who fought to safeguard the freedoms enjoyed by so many. In 1999, Pier 21 reopened to honour the contributions of immigrants to the building of Canada and to acknowledge the sacrifice of Canadian troops. Today, it operates as a non-profit society and offers a variety of services to special interest groups, visitors, and the local community.

Britain's Dianaville commemorates the life of Princess Diana, whose tragic death in 1997 inspired national and international mourning. Thousands flocked to the Crowther Gates of Kensington Palace to leave flowers, messages and other mementos immediately after the news of her death. This is still a well-visited, symbolic spot for Diana fans, since it was from Kensington Palace that her funeral cortege left for Westminster Abbey. After the tragedy, Diana's brother, Earl Spencer, opened up the family estate at Althorp House in rural Northamptonshire, England, so that visitors could see Diana's island grave, visit the museum displaying memorabilia from her youth and adulthood and pay tribute to the internationally influential princess. Within six dedicated rooms, tourists can visit a permanent exhibition of the life and work she undertook, see the famous bridal gown, view relics from her childhood and schooling, and find information about the Diana, Princess of Wales' Memorial Fund. The estate has seen success since it first opened in 1998. Dianaville, with its souvenir shop and café, has become a pilgrimage destination; thousands of grief-stricken mourners, often whole families, from all over the world have made the journey. Tickets run at around £5 for children, £8 for seniors and £10 for adults.

*Sources*: Leadbeater, C. (6–7 July 2002) 'Longing for the way we were', *Financial Times Weekend*, IV; Lowrie, M. (1998) 'Visitors flock to Diana museum on first day', CNN. Retrieved from www.cnn.com; Pier 21 promotional printed material; Pier 21 Education Kit; Pier 21 website: www.pier21.ca.

## Health Consciousness

A more health-conscious society is often attributed to the influence of the baby boomer. Patterson has examined the demographic characteristics of baby boomers and their growing interest in active tourism as they age (Patterson, 2002).[26] Baby boomers are generally healthier, financially better off, better educated, and more interested in novelty, escape, and authentic experiences than were previous cohorts of older people. Many baby boomers and senior adult groups are consequently opting for more physically challenging and 'adrenalin-driven' activities. The demographics of the baby-boom bulge are also having an impact on the health and wellness industry. Health and wellness centres are springing up in many tourism destinations, although spa tourism is not a new phenomenon. One of the oldest spa towns in history is Arima Onsen, just north of Kobe in Japan. Arima has a 1400-year history and has attracted such luminaries as Shōgun Hideyosho Toyotomi, tea ceremony master Sen-no-Rikyu, and in recent times, novelist Jun'ichiro Tanizaki. Tucked in a valley at the foot of the Rokkō mountains, the Onsen area is compact with about 30 ryokan and hotels. Arima's waters – kinsen (rusty red) and ginseng (transparent) – work together against gastrointestinal diseases, women's disorders, neuralgia and skin problems. Long ago, people who came to bathe in the spas of Arima used a walking stick when they came, and, on returning home, would throw the stick in the river. Even today, there is a bridge called 'Tsuesute Bridge' (Tsuesute means to throw away one's walking stick).

Tourists are also looking to eat healthier foods on vacation. Interestingly, in 2005 Scottish & Newcastle, which makes Fosters and Kronenbourg lagers, became the first brewer in the world to put general health warnings on beer bottles. The company said the initiative, similar to health warnings on cigarette packets, was just a part of being a responsible company, whereas critics argue that it was introducing the warnings as a way of avoiding potential lawsuits that could blame drink companies for health problems (Dennis, 2004).[27] Either way, the move is responding to growing consumer pressures for a healthier lifestyle and for socially responsible companies, as mentioned previously.

## Customization

Requests for customized and personalized vacations are also rising sharply, and both agents and traditional tour operators are changing their businesses to meet that demand. In addition to booking air and hotel reservations, agents and outfitters today are arranging customized wine tastings, visits to artisan workshops, and private after-hour tours of the British crown jewels and the Vatican. Even at companies like Butterfield & Robinson and Abercrombie & Kent – both of which have been primarily associated with pre-arranged tours – requests for customized trips are increasing. Kristina Rundquist, spokesperson for the American Society of Travel Agents, says that there are two parallel trends now: people who want personalized service and those who want highly specialized trips: 'Many tourists have precious little time for vacations, so they like to make sure they get exactly what they want, whether it's a boutique hotel or a special kind of restaurant. They need someone who will listen and cater to their needs.' (Whitlock, 2001)[28]

An example of such customization can be found in Jamaica. During a stint as guest relations manager with the Holiday Inn in Montego Bay, Diana McIntyre-Pike (only 21 years old at the time) noticed there was nothing of the real Jamaica to be found at the hotel. 'Even the so-called "native show" had nothing to do with us. It was limbo dancing and fire dancing,' she says. After studying hotel management in Germany, Diana returned to Jamaica and, in 1997, launched the Countrystyle Institute. She had two goals: to give visitors a real experience of Jamaican life, and to get tourism dollars to areas where unemployment rates are high. Her seven-day all-inclusive tours cost about US$1600, including airfare, food, accommodation and entertainment. She customizes her vacations for her clients, depending on whether they have an interest in cooking, playing cricket or golfing. Guest speakers visit to tell groups about the local economy, politics and food. 'What was drawing people to the Sandals and the SuperClubs was that they could pay one rate and get an experience,' she says. 'Now I'm offering the same thing but with a chance to see the real Jamaica.' (Cornell, 2005)[29]

## Convenience and Speed

The increasing desire for convenience and speed is having a great impact on various sectors of the tourism industry. In the restaurant sector, drive-through sales are on the rise; in transportation, self check-in terminals are increasingly popular; and in accommodation, business travellers are seeking convenient rooms for shorter stays. An example of the latter is the new hotel concept introduced recently at Heathrow and Gatwick airports in the UK. Owing much to Japanese 'capsule hotels', Yotel cabins are a cross between a hotel and a first-class airline seat. Each self-contained cabin has a double rotating bed, and facilities include an ensuite bathroom with shower, a flat-screen television and a pull-down desk. The first phase of cabins cost about £80 for an overnight stay, with the option of paying less for shorter periods, offering the opportunity to stretch out and freshen up even on a short stopover. The company has plans to extend the concept into central London to compete with similar accommodation concepts such as Stelios Hakiloannou's EasyHotel.

Theme parks are also responding to the desire for convenience and speed. At both Universal's Orlando theme parks (Islands of Adventure and Universal Studios) visitors can get priority access to all rides and attractions at no extra cost. In front of each attraction is a Universal Express Kiosk with a computer touch screen. Guests insert their park ticket or pass and choose from a selection of times to return later in the day. The distribution centre prints out a Universal Express Pass with the attraction name and return time, and guests can use this later to proceed directly inside, bypassing the usual queues. The Universal Express Plus programme, as it is called, allows customers to create their own schedule and maximize their Universal Orlando experience.

## The Unpredictable

An increasing number of tourists are seeking experiences that have a sense of unpredictability. For example, during the October 2004 earthquake activity of Mount St. Helens, Washington captured worldwide attention as the volcano came back to life, spewing clouds of steam and ash. Thousands of tourists travelled to the area, determined to catch a close-up glimpse of North America's most active volcano. Local hotels, restaurants and souvenir shops all enjoyed brisk business from tourists and the onslaught of the media. One expedition outfit offered helicopter rides over the volcano for US$100 per person. Similarly, in Canada in 2003, firefighters battling British Columbia's forest fires said 'fire tourists' in Kelowna were making it increasingly difficult for firefighters to do their job. Tourists were travelling to suburbs to view the 200 homes destroyed by the fires and venturing into the woods to see the still-raging fires first hand (Skelton, 2003).[30]

Tour operators are beginning to cater to this new type of tourist. LIVE Travel in the UK specializes in tours to countries in the midst of warfare. In 1997 Philip Haines became the youngest person to have visited all 193 sovereign countries, including a trip to off-limits Iraq. He now offers packages to Iraq, Afghanistan and Iran, Vietnam and Cambodia, Bali, East Timor, Bolivia and more. The company even had a trip to see the aftermath of Hurricane Katrina. Many of the destinations on LIVE's itinerary have strict warnings issued by the US State Department against non-essential travel.

## Spiritual Enlightenment

The desire for spiritual enlightenment on a vacation has led to a boom in religious tourism (see the Global Spotlight on 'The Holy Land Experience' in Chapter 1). Even monks are cashing in on this growing trend. Monasteries and temples provide the perfect backdrop for peaceful periods of meditation, prayer and reflection for world-weary businessmen and women. Often set in beautiful scenery, more religious institutions are jumping on the tourism bandwagon and opening their facilities for one- to three-day stays. Southern Koreans, for example, have around 36 different Buddhist temples to choose from for their retreats from everyday life. While the food can be very basic (vegetarian and lots of rice gruel), the peace and tranquillity is priceless. Haein Temple, a World Heritage site, is in the idyllic Kaya Mountains and offers two-day stays for approximately US$60 per night. Tourists have to don monkish robes, pray and meditate with the real monks, eat together and even have lessons in calligraphy before an early bedtime of 9.30 pm. Wake-up call each day is 3.30 am and the day kicks off with an hour of silent meditation. Guests enjoy tours around the beautiful grounds and the hermitages after breakfast.

The notion of combining religion and tourism is also gaining momentum in other countries, notably Japan, where the Wakayama region is attracting day trippers from Kyoto and

Nara. Visitors can also stay overnight in rooms ranging from simple to luxurious. With views of the Pacific from ancient forest trails, tourists learn about Shinto and Buddhist theory by day. By night, accompanying their vegetarian meals served by the monks, guests can also enjoy sake and beer. In Utah, Trappist-Cistercian monks are offering up to three-day trips for males only at their Huntsville Monastery. Women are allowed to stay in the guest house, when available. The Catholic monks lead prayer, reading and hiking; and counselling is also offered.

## Service Quality

Service quality has been increasingly identified as a key factor in differentiating service products and building a competitive advantage in tourism. The process by which customers evaluate a purchase, thereby determining satisfaction and likelihood of repurchase, is important to all marketers, but especially to services marketers because, unlike their manufacturing counterparts, they have fewer objective measures of quality by which to judge their production. Many researchers believe that an outgrowth of service quality is customer satisfaction. Satisfying customers has always been a key component of the tourism industry, but never before has it been so critical. With increased competition, and with more discerning, experienced consumers, knowing how to win and keep customers is the single most important business skill that anyone can learn. Customer satisfaction and loyalty are the keys to long-term profitability, and keeping the customer happy is everybody's business. Becoming customer-centred and exceeding customer expectations are requirements for business success. Chapter 11 gives examples of individuals or companies that have succeeded in the tourism industry by being customer-focused.

## Experiences

According to Pine and Gilmore, today's consumer desires what the service industry is calling **experiences**, which occur when a company intentionally uses services as the stage, and goods as props, to engage individual customers in a way that creates a memorable event. More and more travel organizations are responding by explicitly designing and promoting such events. As services, like goods before them, increasingly become commodified, experiences have emerged as the next step in the 'progression of economic value'. From now on, cutting-edge companies – whether they sell to consumers or businesses – will find that the next competitive battleground lies in staging experiences (Pine and Gilmore, 1998).[31]

---

**EXPERIENCE**
occurs when a company intentionally uses services as the stage, and goods as props, to engage individual customers in a way that creates a memorable event

---

An experience is not an amorphous construct; it is as real an offering as any service, good, or commodity. In today's service economy, many companies simply wrap experiences around their traditional offerings to sell them better. To realize the full benefit of staging experiences, however, businesses must deliberately design engaging experiences that command a fee. Commodities are fungible, goods tangible, services intangible, and experiences memorable. Buyers of experiences value what the company reveals over a period of time. While traditional economic offerings – commodities, goods, and services – are external to the buyer, experiences are inherently personal, existing only in the mind of an individual who has been engaged on an emotional, physical, intellectual, or even spiritual level. Thus, no two people can have the same experience, because each experience derives from the interaction between the staged event (like a theatrical play) and the individual's state of mind.

Experiences have always been at the heart of the entertainment business – a fact that Walt Disney and the company he founded have creatively exploited. But today the concept of selling an entertainment experience is taking root in businesses far removed from theatres and amusement parks. At theme restaurants such as the Hard Rock Cafe, Planet Hollywood and the House of Blues, the food is just a prop for what is known as 'eatertainment'. And stores such as Niketown, Cabella's and Recreational Equipment Incorporated draw consumers in by offering fun activities, fascinating displays, and promotional events (sometimes labelled 'shoppertainment' or 'entertailing'). But experiences are not exclusively about entertainment; companies stage an experience whenever they engage customers in a personal, memorable way. For example, WestJet and Southwest airlines go beyond the function of transporting people from point A to point B, and compete on the basis of providing an experience. The companies use the base service (the travel itself) as the stage for a distinctive en route experience – one that attempts to transform air travel into a respite from the traveller's normally frenetic life (see the Snapshot on WestJet in Chapter 11). Other tourism experiences that engage consumers in a personal, memorable way have been highlighted in this chapter, and include Semester At Sea, volunteer tourism packages, Pier 21 and Dianaville.

## Chapter Summary

Understanding the consumer's needs and buying process is the foundation of successful marketing. By understanding the buyer's decision-making process, the various participants in the buying procedure, and the major influences on buying behaviour, marketers can acquire many clues about how to meet buyer needs. The key factors that influence consumer behaviour are motivation, culture, age and gender, social class, lifestyle, life cycle, and reference groups.

It has been suggested that there are three levels of buying commitment, which are dependent on the nature of the purchase: extended problem solving, limited problem solving and habitual problem solving. It is also proposed that there are five buying roles: initiator, influencer, decider, buyer and user. A consumer moves through a number of stages leading up to purchase: awareness, information gathering, formation of an attitude, evaluation, purchase and post-purchase.

A marketer will also need to understand the buying phases for organizations. The conference market, for example, follows a pattern of group decision-making, and the 'buy phase' has been described as follows: problem recognition, general need description, product specification, supplier search, proposal solution, supplier selection, order routine specification and performance review.

The behaviour of business travellers is significantly different from that of leisure travellers. For example, business travellers do not see travel as a perk but rather as another source of stress. Hence some sectors of the tourism industry, such as airlines, are spending considerable effort trying to understand the needs of their business travellers.

There are a range of trends or demands in consumer behaviour that are influencing tourism and hospitality marketing today. These include the desire for learning and enrichment travel, concern for the environment, a more health-conscious society, the desire for spiritual enlightenment, requests for customized and personalized vacations, the increasing desire for convenience and speed, and the desire for experiences.

## Key Terms

allocentrics, p. 53
attitudes, p. 44
beliefs, p. 43
consumer attitudes, p. 45
consumer behaviour analysis, p. 40
culture, p. 46
experience, p. 67
family life cycle, p. 52
learning, p. 43
learning and enrichment travel, p. 59
life cycle model, p. 52
lifestyle analysis, p. 50
motivations, p. 42
needs, p. 42
perception, p. 44
perceptual mapping, p. 44
psychocentrics, p. 53
psychographic analysis, p. 50
reference groups, p. 52
social class, p. 48
VALS™, p. 50

## Discussion Questions and Exercises

1. Using the Snapshot on backpackers, and all the material on consumer behaviour in this chapter, create a profile of a typical backpacker. How is he or she different in behaviour from other types of travellers, such as the packaged or the business traveller?
2. Where would you place the backpacker on Plog's continuum? What are likely to be the popular backpacker destinations of the future? Are there some destinations that are not capitalizing on this market?
3. Why is the post-purchase behaviour stage included in most models of the buying process?
4. Consider the trends in consumer behaviour discussed at the end of the chapter. Can you think of any other trends that have emerged since this book was published?
5. Discuss the roles that each member of the family plays in the decision-making process when choosing a holiday. Is there any evidence that children play an influential role?

**Case Study**

### Rites of Passage: Schoolies Week in Queensland, Australia

Schoolies Week is actually a month-long graduation festival celebrated by Year 12 school leavers from all over Australia. It takes place after the Year 12 Leaving Certificate, between mid-November and mid-December. The event is predominantly held on Queensland's Gold Coast, but alternative destinations include Byron Bay, Sunshine Coast, Airlie Beach, Magnetic Island and Lorne on the Great Ocean Road in Victoria. Traditionally there are separate Schoolies Weeks for Queensland and New South Wales/Victorian Year 12s on the Gold Coast, so that at each one, students party with their peers. It is estimated that between 30,000 and 35,000 school leavers take part in the event every year, generating over AUS$60 million for Queensland's economy.

Schoolies Week is one of the few 'rites of passage' remaining for Australian teenagers. The rites of passage concept implies a transition from adolescence to adulthood, an activity designed to enhance the development of a distinct self-identity. Such a transition can be seen as a basic human development stage characterized by a postponement of the taking up of adult responsibilities, a desire for novel and varied activities, interest in risk-taking and experimentation, and a desire to spend time socializing with peers.

At one time, the rites of passage of young adults in Australia took the form of debutante balls. However, the popularity of the debutante ball fell due to a number

Schoolies in Lorne, Victoria, enjoying the beach

of social and economic changes in the '60s and '70s. These included a rise in the number of high school leavers associated with the baby boom after World War II, a stronger emphasis on higher education by governments in Australia, and an increasingly liberal and permissive social climate. These social changes, coupled with free tertiary education introduced in 1974, and a lowering of the legal drinking age from 21 to 18 years of age, resulted in a large number of students not immediately occupied in seeking work after completing Year 12 and who were more likely to experiment with previously 'forbidden' activities.

Schoolies Week is often the first holiday these students go on without their families, and their youth creates special needs. The festival affects Schoolies themselves, residents, other tourists and tourism operators and businesses; it is therefore not surprising that Schoolies Week has become a contentious issue. Each year it is associated with numerous reports of crimes by and against Schoolies, and the activities of Schoolies, including drunk and disorderly behaviour, have affected the image of Queensland's Gold Coast as a family destination.

When the Gold Coast developed as the original primary location of Schoolies Week in the late 1970s and 1980s it was not an organized or commercial event. Instead it was a spontaneous group activity over an extended period that developed through a process of communication and diffusion into a cultural event – part of the youth 'rites of passage'. Commercialization of Schoolies Week began in the late 1980s, as companies like Breakfree Holidays focused on the Schoolies market. In the 1990s, the Gold Coast City Council (GCCC) became active in the planning and management of the festival (in part because of negative publicity caused by drunken Schoolies), and so Schoolies Week developed into a much more organized event. Commercial forces have since guided the evolution of Schoolies into a carefully choreographed event, sponsored by big companies and decorated by a flourishing line in merchandising. The Queensland Government has even provided a text messaging information service whereby registered Schoolies can agree to have their details passed on to third parties. The festival has also become a focus for State Education, Health and Police Departments who provide educational material about Schoolies Week in schools across Queensland. One particular problem associated with the festival is predatory sexual behaviour by older males. Incidents of violence associated with the festival are also believed to have been perpetrated by older non-school leavers.

Today, a number of tour operators cater to the Schoolies Week market, including Schoolies.com who claim to be the market leader for Schoolies travel arrangements. In their promotional material the company promises qualified and licensed security guards on all 'Schoolies' properties, individual Photo ID building entry passes, supervised no-alcohol Schoolies-only dance parties, as well as a 24-hour helpline throughout the Schoolies month. For other tourism businesses, particularly budget accommodation, Schoolies Week occurs in a traditional low occupancy period and so counters the negative impacts of seasonality. However, the Queensland Gold Coast is a popular holiday destination for a large, and diverse, number of domestic and international travellers. Managing and developing quality standards for such heterogeneous visitors can be a challenge for the destinations concerned.

*Sources*: Scott, N. (2006) 'Management of tourism: Confirmation to whose standards?' in Prideaux, B., Moscardo, G. and Laws, E. (eds). *Managing Tourism and Hospitality Services: Theory and International Applications.* London: CAB International, pp 54–61; Moscardo, G. (2006) 'Backpackers and other young travellers to the Great Barrier Reef: An exploration of changes in characteristics and behaviours over time', *Tourism Recreation Research*, 31(3): 29–37.

## Questions

1. Account for the growth in Schoolies Week in Queensland.
2. Does the increasing management and control of Schoolies Week challenge the reason for its existence as a 'rite of passage'?
3. What are the advantages and disadvantages of Schoolies Week for tourism operators in Queensland?
4. How should destination managers in Queensland deal with the challenge of pleasing both Schoolies and other tourists?
5. Can you think of other tourism products that have been developed in response to changes in the consumer life cycle?

## Web Sites

| | |
|---|---|
| www.voluntourism.org | Information on Volunteer Tourism |
| www.responsibletavel.com | Responsibletravel.com website |
| www.astanet.com | American Society of Travel Agents |
| www.letacanada.com | The Learning & Enrichment Travel Alliance |
| www.ntaonline.com | National Tour Association |
| www.pier21.ns.ca | Pier 21 (Nova Scotia) |
| www.disney.go.com | Walt Disney World |
| www.semesteratsea.com | Semester At Sea |
| www.templestay/korea.com | Temples in Korea |
| www.landofvalencia | Valencia's tourist office |
| www.czech.cz | Official Czech Republic Destination website |
| www.countrystylecommunitytourism.com | Countrystyle Community Tours |

## References

1 Mills, A. S. and Morrison, A. M. (1985) *The Tourism System: An Introductory Text*. Englewood Cliffs, NJ: Prentice-Hall.

2 Dann, G. (1977) 'Anomie, ego-enhancement and tourism', *Annals of Tourism Research*, 4, 184–194.

3 Crompton, J. L. (1979) 'Why people go on pleasure vacation', *Annals of Tourism Research*, 6(4), 408–424.

4 Krippendorf, J. (1987) *The Holidaymakers*. London: Heinemann.

5 Anon. (13 May 2004) 'Theme park roller coaster seminar helps people cope with their "weaker self"', *National Post*, A14.

6 Orth, U.R. and Tureckova, J. (2004) 'Segmenting the tourism market using perceptual and attitudinal mapping', *Agricultural Economics*, 48(1), 36–48.

7 Sutherland, S. (May 2002) 'Hospitality trends', *Alberta Venture*, 49–53.

8 Cateora, P.R. and Graham, J. L. (2005) *International Marketing*. New York: McGraw-Hill Irwin, 119.

9 Hofstede, G. (1980) 'Motivation, leadership, and organization: do American theories apply abroad?' *Organizational Dynamics*, 9, 42–63; Hofstede, G. (1983) 'National cultures in four dimensions: a research based theory of cultural differences among nations', *International Studies of Management & Organization*, 13, 46–75.

10 Brean, J. (21 October 2006) 'Where suburbia was born', *National Post*, A14.

11 Pearce, P. L. (1993) 'Fundamentals of tourist motivation', in D. Pearce and W. Butler (eds), *Tourism and Research: Critiques and Challenges*. London: Routledge, 113–134.

12 Anon. (2 February 2002) 'Mature travelers and volunteer holidays', *The Edmonton Journal*, K2.

13 Plog, S. C. (1974) 'Why destination areas rise and fall in popularity', *Cornell Hotel and Restaurant Quarterly*, 14(4), 55–58; Plog, S.C. (2002) 'The power of psychogaphics and the concept of venturesomeness', *Journal of Travel Research*, 40, 244–251.

14 Cohen, E. (1972) 'Toward a sociology of international tourism', *Social Research*, 39(1), 164–182.

15 Howard, J. A. and Sheth, J. N. (1969) *The Theory of Buying Behavior*. New York: Wiley.

16 Decrop, A. and Snelders, D. (2005) 'A grounded typology of vacation decision-making', *Tourism Management*, 26(2), 121–132.

17 Engel, J. F., Blackwell, R. D. and Miniard, P. W. (1990) *Consumer Behavior*. Orlando, FL: Dryden.

18 Zeithaml, V. A., Berry, L. L. and Parasuraman, A. (1996) 'The behavioral consequences of service quality', *Journal of Marketing*, 60, 31–46.

19 Radburn, D. (1997) 'Organizational buyer behavior', in L. Lumsdon (ed.), *Tourism Marketing*. London: Thomson Business Press, 52–63.

20  Webster, F. and Wind, Y. (1972) *Organizational Buying Behavior*. Englewood Cliffs, NJ: Prentice Hall.

21  Cohen, A. (31 January 2000) 'Business takes all the fun out of travel', *National Post*, C17.

22  Tong, T. (8 March 2002) 'Business travelers' spouses pay psychological price', *National Post*, A1.

23  Hickman, M. (29 May 2006) 'How ethical shopping is making business go green', *The Independent*, 2.

24  Anon. (2002) 'Americans going green?' *Tourism*, 6(8), 12.

25  Leadbeater, C. (6–7 July 2002) 'Longing for the way we were', *Financial Times Weekend*, IV.

26  Patterson, I. (2002) 'Baby boomers and adventure tourism: The importance of marketing the leisure experience', *World Leisure*, 2, 4–10.

27  Dennis, G. (18 October 2004) 'Brewer to put health warnings on beer bottles', *National Post*, A11.

28  Whitlock, S. (September 2001) 'The world on a platter', *Travel + Leisure*, 176–178.

29  Cornell, C. (26 February 2005) 'The culture is included. New packaged vacations', *National Post*, WP11.

30  Skelton, C. (2003) 'Fire tourists get in the way', *National Post*, September 2, A5.

31  Pine, B. J. II and Gilmore, J. H. (1998) 'Welcome to the experience economy', *Harvard Business Review*, 76(4), 97–108.

# 3

# DEVELOPING A MARKETING PLAN

## An Adventure with Bruce Poon Tip

In 1990, Bruce Poon Tip withdrew every last penny in his bank account to open his own travel company specializing in taking tourists to emerging countries in Central and South America. Due to the risky nature of the travel industry at that time, caused by the persistent Gulf War, the banks were unwilling to lend him any money. Poon Tip would not be discouraged and, as a result, he stretched the limit of his credit card to follow his vision. Today, G.A.P Adventures is one of the largest adventure companies in the world. At 21, Poon Tip found his G.A.P concept when he travelled in Thailand for $10 a day and stayed with the hill tribes. 'It wasn't my first visit, but it was my most genuine,' says Poon Tip, who has consulted on *Survivor*. 'That was when I knew others would want authentic travel experiences.' Just as baby boomers were maturing and realizing the detrimental effects of their hedonistic youth, Poon Tip positioned his company as a vehicle to do some good while travelling via environmentally friendly, experience- and adventure-oriented tourism.

Born in Trinidad, Poon Tip runs his company based on his ethical commitment to developing mutually beneficial international relationships, incorporating values and respect for local cultures, and promoting ecotourism. His $100 million business, which sells 1000 different trips to 100 destinations through its many offices worldwide, does more to promote sustainable tourism than any other company in the business.

Toronto-based G.A.P Adventures and Bruce Poon Tip himself have been recognized by many organizations as leaders in business practices and leadership. In 2006, Poon Tip won Entrepreneur of the Year in Canada for the second time at the 13th Annual Ernst & Young Entrepreneur of the Year Awards. In addition to receiving an award as one of Canada's top 40 Canadians Under 40, Poon Tip has also been honoured as one of Canada's top five entrepreneurs by *Canadian Business* and as one of Canada's 100 leaders of tomorrow. Poon Tip also received the Global Traders Leadership award from the government

Bruce Poon Tip, G.A.P. Adventures

for his groundbreaking ideas in exporting services. He has spearheaded a postgraduate diploma programme for Humber College on Ecotourism and Adventure Travel; recently, he was asked by the World Bank and UNESCO to be on a team visiting the People's Republic of China to lecture on sustainable development. In January 2002, Poon Tip was the only Canadian operator invited to attend the United Nations' launch of the Year of Ecotourism in New York.

In 2005 and 2006, G.A.P was selected as one of Canada's Best Managed Companies as well as Canada's Top 100 Employers and one of the Top 10 Employers for Young People. The company's enthusiasm for the product is instrumental, too, in creating customer and staff loyalty. Poon Tip explains: 'We are a company of travellers and our employees share a true passion for the industry. We are a work hard/play hard company that is dedicated to our entrepreneurial spirit.'

In a world where people are living longer and staying fit and healthier later in life, the company is targeting those who are 'young at heart'. For 'adventure with a bit of comfort', G.A.P offers the traveller small group excursions throughout South and Central America, Africa, Asia, North America and Europe, plus expeditions to the Antarctic, the Arctic and the Panama Canal onboard the ship M/S *Explorer*. With a slant towards wildlife, culture, history and the environment, these expeditions are putting leisure and entertainment in an educational package rather than offering the indulgence of typical cruise holidays. G.A.P uses small-scale lodging and local transportation. The company also supports locally owned businesses and incorporates community-based ecotourism projects into the majority of tours.

Newspaper advertising focuses attention on the company's differentiation within the travel industry. No glossy photos of perfect hotels or idyllic beaches, but instead, pictures of indigenous people and text that says 'our impact is low and sustainable tourism is at the forefront of our agenda'. Instead of listing resorts, the ads promote adventures in every corner of the globe for the 'New Traveller' in small groups. Accommodation is advertised not as a star rating, but as 'local' and 'full of character', with activities described as 'unique and off the beaten track'. This innovative targeting stresses the company's authenticity and experience-based, cultural tourism.

Poon Tip believes that ecotourism does not have to be small scale. 'Most people say ecotourism means "leave only footprints"', he says. 'I disagree with that. I think that we've got to get those 10,000 people off the cruise ships and into 200 small groups. I think that tourists can leave behind a huge impact.' To that end, Poon Tip has worked with the World Bank to help impoverished villages finance tourist lodges and teach communities to profit through tourism. Six communities in Bolivia, for example, now sustain themselves through such initiatives, which helps reduce their dependence on logging and the drug trade. This aspect of G.A.P's philosophy puts the company into the cause-related tourism category as well as making a stand against typical profit-oriented tourism operations. G.A.P Adventures was recently included in Conde Nast Traveller's 12th annual Green List. Top candidates are chosen for their commitment to environmental initiatives, contributions to local communities and quality of guest experience.

Despite the obvious advantages to ecotourism, which brings sustainable prosperity to locals as well as cultural exchanges between the travellers and the inhabitants, there are detractors to this concept. Some think that ecotourists travel on low budgets (and Poon Tip emphasizes good value for the traveller's dollar in the company's advertising) and contribute less to local economies. However, Poon Tip contends that ecotourists generally stay longer than five-star hotel guests and that the money they spend goes directly to the community, rather than into the coffers of a Western-run hotel chain.

*Sources*: Baginski, M. (2002) 'GC acquisition fills large G.A.P', retrieved from www.canadatourism.com/en/ctc/ctx/ctxnews/search/newsbydateform.cfm; G.A.P Adventures website: www.gapadventures.com; B. Poon Tip, personal communication, 15 December 2006; Anon. (26 May 2005) 'Travel for the fifty plus', *Travelweek*, 16.

## OBJECTIVES

On completion of this chapter, you should understand:

▸ the eight key steps in the marketing planning process;

▸ the importance of the corporate connection;

▸ analysis and forecasting;

▸ setting goals and objectives;

▸ targeting and positioning;

▸ tactics and action plans; and

▸ how marketing planning is conducted in various sectors of the tourism industry.

## Introduction

The Opening Vignette highlights the importance of successful positioning and planning in today's marketing environment. Through careful planning, G.A.P Adventures has become one of the largest adventure companies in the world. In its principles, marketing planning is no more than a logical thought process in which all businesses should engage. It is an application of common sense, relevant to a small bed and breakfast as it is to an international airline. However, not all companies do follow a marketing plan, as can be seen in the end of chapter Case Study on Roots Air.

The term **marketing plan** is widely used to mean a short-term plan for two years or less. This chapter is devoted to the development of such plans. A **strategic marketing plan**, on the other hand, is different, as it covers three or more years. A marketing plan serves a number

---

**STRATEGIC MARKETING PLAN**
a written plan for an organization covering a period of three or more years into the future

---

**MARKETING PLAN**
a written, short-term plan that details how an organization will use its marketing mix to achieve its marketing objectives

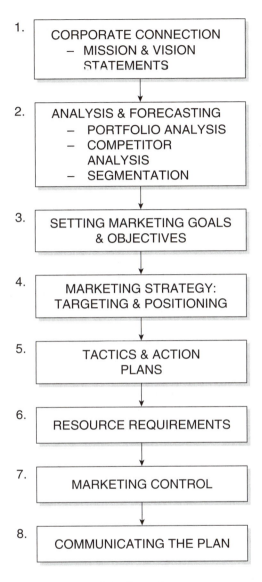

**Figure 3.1**   Marketing Planning: An Eight-Step Process

of purposes within any tourism organization. It provides a road map for all future marketing activities of the firm; it ensures that marketing activities are aligned with the corporate strategic plan; it forces marketing managers to review and think through all steps in the marketing process objectively; it assists in the budgeting process to match resources with marketing objectives; and it creates a process to monitor actual against expected results.

A systematic marketing planning process consists of eight logical steps, as outlined in Figure 3.1. For the strategic marketing plan, the first four stages may be more detailed, but any short-term marketing plan should also include an assessment of these steps. Each step feeds into the next one. A marketing plan is not a stand-alone tool, so the first stage is examining the goals and objectives of the organization as a whole and then developing a marketing plan that will support the company's mission statement, corporate philosophy, and corporate goals. Once the corporate connection has been clarified, the next stage is defining the current situation, reviewing the effectiveness of current activities, and identifying opportunities. This is the 'analysis and forecasting' stage. The third stage is concerned with defining marketing goals and objectives derived logically from the previous stages of the planning process.

At the fourth stage, target markets should be selected from the previously developed list of available segments, and once the market has been segmented and a target market identified, the next step is positioning. Market positioning is ultimately how the consumer perceives the good or service in a given market, and is used to achieve a sustainable competitive advantage over competitors. The fifth stage involves selecting and developing a series of strategies that effectively bring about the required results. This part of the plan shows how the organization intends to use the 7 Ps. The marketing plan needs to address the resources required to support the strategies and meet the objectives, and resource requirements are the focus of the plan's sixth stage. The seventh stage is concerned with marketing control and how objectives will be achieved in the required time, using the funds and resources requested. Finally, at the eighth stage, the plan should be communicated both internally and externally to achieve maximum impact. Most marketing plans will contain an **executive summary** of the whole, and this should be no more than a few pages in length. A good approach is to sum up each section and present them in the order in which they appear.

---

**EXECUTIVE SUMMARY**
a few pages, usually positioned at the beginning of the marketing plan, that sum up the plan's main sections

---

The role played by each section of the marketing plan will now be discussed in more detail.

## The Corporate Connection

A good marketing plan begins with the fact that the only purpose of marketing is to support the enterprise. Marketing planning should therefore reflect the goals and objectives of the organization as a whole. The mission or vision statement reflects the organization's philosophy, and the goals and objectives as set out in the business plan become the basis of planning for all departments. Marketing's responsibilities in relation to the corporate vision are usually outlined in one or more separate marketing-specific documents.

**Goals** can be defined in terms such as sales growth, increased profitability and market leadership, whereas **objectives** are the activities that will accomplish the goals. A vision statement usually answers the question, 'What do we want to be?', whilst the **mission statement** will answer the question, 'What business are we in?' Whereas the vision describes where the organization wants to be in some future time, the mission is a broader statement about an organization's business and scope, goods or services, markets served and overall philosophy.

---

**GOALS**

the primary aims of the organization

---

**OBJECTIVES**

the specific aims that managers accomplish to attain organizational goals

---

**MISSION STATEMENT**

a brief simple phrase or sentence that summarizes the organization's direction and communicates its ethos to internal and external audiences. It also answers the question, 'What business are we in?'

---

Vision and mission statements can vary. G.A.P Adventures (see the Opening Vignette) has the following mission statement that focuses on service: 'Our priority is to satisfy every customer, every time, through outstanding, personalized service! We are dedicated to the customer experience and are constantly evaluating how we can improve this experience.' Cheddar Caves & Gorge in the UK (see Chapter 8), however, has a mission statement based on social values and sustainability: 'To make the Caves accessible to visitors in a way which increases visitor awareness of their value, while responding to the social needs of our visitors and protecting the natural environment for future generations.'

## Analysis and Forecasting

The next stage of the marketing plan is defining the current situation. It is essential that each component of the business be reviewed in order to ensure that resources can be allocated efficiently. Several models exist for reviewing effectiveness and identifying opportunities but those proven by time and practical application across a range of industries include portfolio analysis, competitor analysis, segmentation analysis, SWOT (strengths, weaknesses, opportunities and threats) analysis, and forecasting.

## Portfolio Analysis

**Portfolio analysis** first became popular in the 1960s, when many organizations sought to improve their profitability by diversifying their activities so as not to keep all their eggs in one basket. The **Boston Consulting Group (BCG) model** was one of the most popular approaches to evaluating a very diverse group of goods and services, based on long-term planning and economic forecasts. The model adopts the view that every product of an organization can be plotted on a two-by-two matrix to identify those offering high potential and those that are drains on the organization's resources.

---

**PORTFOLIO ANALYSIS**

an approach to evaluating a very diverse group of goods and services, based on long-term planning and economic forecasts

---

**BOSTON CONSULTING GROUP (BCG) MODEL**

a technique designed to show the performance of an individual product in relation to its major competitors and the rate of growth in its market

---

In **Figure 3.2**, the horizontal axis represents market share, and the vertical axis represents anticipated market growth. High market share means that a business is a leader in that good or service; low market share indicates that either the marketplace is heavily competitive or a good or service has not had widespread market acceptance. A good or service can then take up one of four theoretical positions within the model. A **cash cow** is a product that generates cash and turnover, but has limited long-term prospects. The company in Figure 3.2 operates two cash-cow businesses. A **dog** provides neither cash flow nor long-term opportunities and does not hold great promise for improved performance. In the illustration, the company has three dogs.

---

**MARKET SHARE**

the percentage relationship of an organization's sales to total industry sales

---

**CASH COW**

a product that generates a high volume of income in relation to the cost of maintaining its market share

---

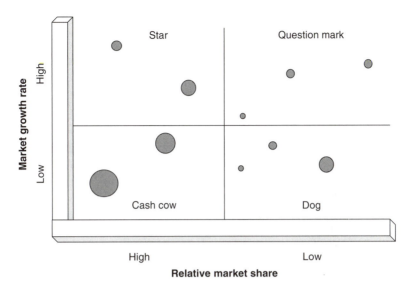

**Figure 3.2**  The Boston Consulting Group (BCG) Model

Adapted from: Hedley, B. (1977) 'Strategy and the "Business Portfolio"', *Long Range Planning*, 10(1), 9–15.

---

**DOG**
a product that provides neither cash flow nor long-term opportunities and does not hold great promise for improved performance

---

**Stars** are products that have a dominant share of a fast-growing market. Although they may not generate a large amount of cash at present, they have potential for high returns in the future. **Question marks** are fairly speculative products that have high-risk potential. They may be profitable, but because they hold a small market share, they may be vulnerable to competition. Goods or services go through the product life cycle, which can affect where they are positioned within the BCG model. A new product may be in the 'question mark' cell; as it becomes successful it moves into the 'star' category, and then moves on to become a 'cash cow' before starting to decline and becoming a 'dog'.

---

**STARS**
products that have a dominant share of a fast-growing market

---

> **QUESTION MARKS**
> fairly speculative products that have high-risk potential. They may be profitable, but because they hold a small market share, they may be vulnerable to competition

A good example of a tourism product that has taken up all four positions in the BCG model is the Concorde jet airplane (see the Opening Vignette in Chapter 5). Beginning as a question mark, the delta-winged marvel, a product of 1960s technology and optimism, quickly became a star as business executives and famous stars asserted their status by happily spending thousands of dollars to save a few hours' travelling time. The product soon became a cash cow, and more than 2.5 million passengers flew on British Airways' Concordes after they entered service in 1976. However, filling the 100 seats on a Concorde became increasingly difficult, and between 2000 and 2003, Concorde could be classified as a dog. In April 2003 it was announced that the supersonic airline run by British Airways and Air France would be retired that year because of slumping ticket sales.

As part of a portfolio analysis, an organization should assess each good and service in terms of its position on the product life cycle. This concept is discussed in Chapter 5.

## Competitor Analysis

Information on the number and type of competitors, their relative market shares, the things they do well and things they do badly all assist in the planning process. **Competitor analysis** also highlights market trends and the level of loyalty of consumers. Competitors can be divided into four broad categories: **direct competitors** offer similar goods and services to the same consumer at a similar price; **product category competitors** make the same product or class of products; **general competitors** provide the same service; and **budget competitors** compete for the same consumer dollars. In addition to the existing competition, there is also the threat of potential competition in the form of new entrants (Porter, 1980).[1]

> **COMPETITOR ANALYSIS**
> a review of competitors that allows the organization to identify and highlight the market trends and the level of loyalty of consumers

> **DIRECT COMPETITORS**
> companies that offer similar goods and services to the same consumer at a similar price

> **PRODUCT CATEGORY COMPETITORS**
> companies that produce the same product or class of products

> **GENERAL COMPETITORS**
> companies that provide the same service

> **BUDGET COMPETITORS**
> companies that compete for the same consumer dollars

In China recently, a number of new foreign entrants has led to a very competitive hotel sector, particularly in the budget inn category. Ambitious players like US-based Wyndham Worldwide Corp's Super 8 chain entered China in 2004, and by 2006 had 33 hotels. It plans to increase that to 110 hotels by 2009. Local players in this sector, like Home Inns & Hotels Management Inc., and Jinjiang International, are also expanding aggressively. The Snapshot later in this chapter describes how other organizations are planning for the growing Chinese travel market.

Michael Porter (1980) suggests that there are only three generic strategies for dealing with competition: low-cost leadership, differentiation, and focus.[2] **Low-cost leadership** is the simplest and most effective strategy, but it requires large resources and strong management to sustain. A low-cost leadership strategy is used when a firm sets out to become the low-cost producer in its industry. Low-cost producers typically sell a standard, or no-frills, product and place considerable emphasis on reaping scale or absolute cost advantages from all sources. It may be short lived, as it is easy for competitors to match a low price in an attempt to drive off the challenge. The low-cost airlines that are springing up all over the world are examples of companies following such a strategy. These airlines are profiled in Chapter 6.

> **LOW-COST LEADERSHIP**
> the simplest and most effective strategy for dealing with competition, but one requiring large resources and strong management to sustain. It may be short lived, as it is easy for competitors to match a low price in an attempt to drive off the challenge

**Differentiation** is a strategy that consists of an innovative technological breakthrough, which can take competitors a long time to imitate. A competitive advantage can be gained with a product that is newer, better and/or faster. The improvement can be in performance, durability, reliability, or service features. Airbus's new 560-tonne jet, the A380, carries up to 800 passengers and has differentiated itself from competitors by becoming the world's biggest commercial airliner.

> **DIFFERENTIATION**
>
> a strategy that consists of an innovative technological breakthrough, which can take competitors a long time to imitate. A competitive advantage can be gained with a product that is newer, better, and/or faster

A **focus** strategy concentrates on designing a good or service to meet the needs of one segment of the market better than the competition does. Bruce Poon Tip from G.A.P Adventures (see Opening Vignette) follows such a strategy in the adventure tourism business.

> **FOCUS**
>
> a strategy that concentrates on designing a good or service to meet the needs of one segment of the market better than the competition does

All three of these generic strategies are based on the organization's creation of a unique position for itself, which distinguishes its offerings from those of its competitors by price, product features, or the way in which it serves the needs of a particular segment. This process, known as 'positioning', is discussed later in this chapter. The Global Spotlight below shows how a Mexican resort is differentiating itself from other all-inclusive resorts by targeting the overweight tourist.

## Global Spotlight

### Targeting the Overweight: Size-friendly Vacations at Freedom Paradise

'Live Large – Live Free, At Any Size, At Any Age' is Freedom Paradise's motto. Dutchman Jurriaan Klink opened the 'size-friendly' resort in the Mexican Riviera in June 2003 after observing that overweight holidaymakers did not seem comfortable in traditional resorts, and discovering that no other specific facilities existed for this growing niche market – despite the fact that an estimated 61 per cent of the US adult population is considered overweight by the Centres for Disease Control.

The former Cancun hotel manager spent three years researching the plus-size community to determine both needs and concerns. With over 300 million obese people worldwide, and, in particular, over 60 per cent of his target American customers overweight, the market was ripe. Klink, along with General Director Julio Rincon was amazed that no one else had tapped into this lucrative niche and set about developing the resort from two existing bankrupt hotels. The project was kept secret while US$2 million of renovations were completed at the Riviera Maya site, near Tulum, Mexico, about 70 miles south of Cancun. Its close proximity to the US was paramount in choosing the site, as Americans were to be the key target market for the 112-room resort.

In order to cater for the needs of the larger consumer, walls were ripped out and doorways were widened; constricting bath tubs were removed and bathrooms were reconstructed with benches in the showers and hand-held nozzles; furniture was custom-designed with larger sizes in mind. Dining chairs, for example, are twice the standard 26-inch size and without restricting arms. The king-sized beds were reinforced to encourage uninhibited romance. Sturdy wooden, four-foot wide loungers plus thick benches with tree trunk legs were produced for poolside comfort and gradual inclines with grab bars were added to the pools, rather than flimsy ladders. In the hibiscus- and palm-filled gardens, wider and flatter walking spaces were created. Three restaurants were also added to the existing two, featuring different themes: Mexican, Italian, international, a steak-house and a Hawaiian-style seafood room. Menus were created with healthy eating as well as plentiful, good quality food in mind, all of which is included in the resort tariff.

A large mural in the reception area depicts the 'King and Queen of Paradise', a large couple feasting on a picnic rug in a beautiful tropical setting, designed to make larger visitors feel welcome. Staff are hired in all sizes and given sensitivity training by psychologist and human resources director Martha Bueno, who emphasizes that size acceptance goes beyond physical accommodations. Klink's creed is that oversized people should not 'postpone their lives' because of their size, always putting off fun until they manage to lose weight. All resort activities, including snorkelling, scuba diving, beach volleyball, fishing and sailing, have been customized to be safe and comfortable for the guests. There are also cultural tours to nearby ruins and beauty spots plus a wellness centre that promotes yoga, meditation and Tai Chi without pressurizing weight loss programmes. A children's club, bird-feeding, flower and astrology workshops are also featured. Pricing ranges from US$125 to $195 per person per night depending on season and based on double occupancy.

Klink gained huge media attention prior to opening his innovative resort, resulting in a flood of potential plus-size customer inquiries. With a plethora of TV and newspaper articles and features, even negative publicity such as crude jokes made by late night television show hosts did not deter people from making reservations. Bookings could be made directly or through tour wholesalers and travel agencies. Travel agent orientation trips were also arranged to enlighten sales forces about the differentiation of the product and to help them assess and advertise the new concept. Cross-promotions were also eventually established with fashionable, plus-size clothing company, Lane Bryant and Figure magazine. Competitions were set up with the two partners, offering an all-expenses-paid holiday at Freedom Paradise for the winners. Figure magazine also featured articles and ads for the resort. These partnerships enabled Freedom Paradise to reach target market customer databases for further promotions.

Klink intends to open more size-friendly resorts in North America if the market permits. He is concerned that some oversized individuals who have already been put off travelling because of hardship and mental and physical discomfort will not easily be convinced to try another beach vacation. However, brand awareness was created quickly for the first resort due to its uniqueness as well as its humanitarian aspects. Says Klink, 'From a business standpoint, this is a smart idea. From a humanity standpoint, it's really beautiful.'

*Sources*: Kadane, L. (23 October 2004). 'Size-friendly vacations a growing trend', *Calgary Herald*, Travel, H1–H2; Davidson, P. (10 June 2003) 'Freedom Paradise resort picks a target market', retrieved from www.peterthink.blogs.com; Savage, B. (2004) 'The queen of paradise', *Alberta Views*, 36–37; Sullivan, K. (21 July 2003) 'Having XXL fun in Mexico sun', *Washington Post*, retrieved from www.mindfully.org.

## Segmentation Analysis

**Segmentation analysis** refers to the way in which organizations identify and categorize customers into groups defined by similar characteristics and similar needs or desires. The Global Spotlight above showed how the owner of Freedom Paradise spent three years researching the plus-size community to determine both the needs and concerns of his target market. The concept of segmentation is widely adopted in tourism marketing, as few companies in the industry attempt to appeal to an entire market. The core advantage of segmentation is that customers will be more satisfied with the product because it has been designed with their needs in mind. Their social needs are also satisfied because they will be mixing with people like themselves and avoiding incompatible types. If an organization knows exactly which segments it wishes to reach, it can select the media most likely to be read, heard, or seen by those consumers, and so spend less on general mass-market advertising. If it knows the lifestyles and attitudes of that segment and the benefits they are seeking from the product, the advertising message can be made more persuasive. Figure 3.3 is an example of segmentation in the tour operating sector of Europe. It shows the major European customer travel segments, their characteristics, and the tour operators that serve each segment.

---

**SEGMENTATION ANALYSIS**
the practice of dividing total markets up into groups on the basis of similar characteristics

---

The criteria used most often by tourism and hospitality suppliers to segment the market are as follows:

1. Demographic segmentation uses the primary variables of age, gender, family life cycle, and ethnicity to segment the markets. Club 18–30, for example, uses age and lifestyle stage variables to attract young singles interested in a vibrant night life (see Case Study in Chapter 8).
2. Psychographic segmentation divides buyers into different groups based on social class, lifestyle and personality characteristics. Psychographics and lifestyle segmentation are based on personality traits, attitudes, motivations, and activities, and are discussed in more detail in Chapter 2. People in the same demographic group can have very different psychographic profiles.
3. Geographic segmentation is the division of markets according to geographical boundaries, such as countries, provinces/states, regions, cities, or neighbourhoods. In the past, for most

destination marketing organizations (DMOs), market segmentation was often limited to under-standing the more lucrative international tourist market. However, since the terrorist attacks of 11 September 2001, destination marketers have recognized the significance of local and provin-cial residents and the impact that they have on tourism receipts (Hudson and Ritchie, 2002).[3]

4. Benefit segmentation divides customers based on the benefits they desire, such as education, entertainment, luxury, or low cost. Customers weigh different features of a service, and these are evaluated to form the basis of benefit segmentation. Customers of Freedom Paradise (see Global Spotlight above) would value benefits such as large walking spaces and large dinner portions, whereas for most sport tourists these services would be irrelevant.

5. Behaviour segmentation divides the market into groups based on the various types of buying behaviour. Common bases include usage rate (light, medium, and heavy), user status (former users, non-users, potential users, first-time users, and regular users of a product), loyalty status (many people stay in five-star hotels as much for the status it con-fers on them as for the additional comfort), buyer-readiness stage, and occasions. On spe-cial occasions, people are prepared to pay more for special treatment, so many restaurants now have deals for children's birthday parties, while hotels and cruise lines have special honeymoon suites.

| | Mainstream Budget | Mainstream Good Value | Mainstream Premium | Specialists |
|---|---|---|---|---|
| Characteristics | *Increasing margin* → | | | |
| | *Decreasing price sensitivity* → | | | |
| | • Price more important than destination<br>• Very competitive | • Major segment<br>• Intense price competition | • 4 & 5-star hotels<br>• More dynamic packaging | • High value to customer<br>• High brand affinity<br>• High customer loyalty |
| Challenges | • Economies of scale<br>• Efficiency in sales<br>• Simplicity | • Domination of sales channels<br>• Economies of scale<br>• Capacity management<br>• Simplicity, low complexity | • Value proposition vs. mainstream segment<br>• Customer loyalty<br>• Sales management | • Differentiation of offer<br>• Marketing and sales optimization<br>• Synergies in 'production' |
| Examples | • 72Fly<br>• Sunstart<br>• Neckermann<br>• Preisknueller | • My Travel<br>• First Choice<br>• Neckermann Reisen<br>• Tjaereborg | • Kuoni<br>• Airtours<br>• Meier's Weltreisen | • The Cruise Store<br>• Neilson<br>• Dr Tigges<br>• Manta Reisen |

**Figure 3.3** Major European Customer Travel Segments

In sum, the heart of any marketing plan is careful analysis of available market segments and the selection of the appropriate target markets. A common mistake within tourism and hospitality is the selection of inappropriate segments. The Opening Vignette in Chapter 8 mentions how Las Vegas tried unsuccessfully to rebrand itself as a family destination, providing pirate- and circus-themed hotels, funfairs, rides, amusement and games arcades, and animal attractions. They have since reverted to attracting more appropriate market segments, with the help of their 'What Happens in Vegas, Stays in Vegas' advertising campaign. When developing a marketing plan, marketers can gather information concerning market segments from two sources. Internal data can be analysed by looking at business cards, guest registrations, credit card receipts, customer surveys, direct observations and staff perceptions. External data can be gathered from published industry information, marketing research, or by making guesstimates after talking with competitors, vendors, and others in the industry.

Market segmentation is a dynamic process because customer trends are not static. It is thus important to carry out regular – preferably continuous – tracking studies to monitor changes happening in the market. One of the most recent trends in tourism and hospitality has been a 'demassification' of the market, in which a greater number of niche markets are replacing the mass ones of the past (Crawford-Welch, 1991).[4] As a result, **niche marketing** is increasing, whereby products are tailored to meet the needs and wants of narrowly defined geographic, demographic, or psychographic segments. The Snapshot below highlights how an Australian wine tourism company has successfully targeted the Generation X market.

---

**NICHE MARKETING**
the tailoring of products to meet the needs and wants of narrowly defined geographic, demographic, or psychographic segments

---

## Snapshot

### Wine for Dudes

Wine tourism is hot. Nearly five million people who travel in Australia visit a winery, generating over AUS\$4.6 billion in tourism expenditure. These wine tourists are generally over 45 years old and travel as couples. But how about wine tourism for Generation X? Generation X, also known as the Baby Busters, were born between 1965 and 1979. Now adults, they grew up with television and have been described as independent-minded and somewhat cynical. They are concerned with their physical health (they grew up during the AIDS outbreak) and financial future (they suffered the most from the dot.com bust).

Until a few years ago, wine tours targeted at this generation were almost non-existent. Then Cathy Willcock came along and set up Wine for Dudes. Willcock was no novice to the wine industry. Her parents owned a hobby vineyard when she was young, and she had spent time after university working in an Italian winery and for a London-based food and beverage company. When she returned to Australia, she moved to Western Australia's Margaret River region, home to over 90 vineyards. 'I realized Generation X were being neglected. I couldn't understand why because this age group have got cash, their eyes are wide open and they like drinking', she said. 'I know this cynical generation. All they want is a no-bull attitude. I could see this niche emerging.' So she set up Wine for Dudes, providing a number of different wine tours styled for a younger market, taking out on average 40–50 people a week.

It took Willcock nearly two years to write the business plan and she brought her brother on board as an investor to help her keep an eye on the finances. 'That's what he is good at. I knew my downfall was in number crunching and finance', she said. Business was brisk right from the beginning, helped along by a feature on one of Australia's largest travel shows. The locality was also a helping feature, and Willcock has been impressed with the amount of community support. 'A lot of the winemakers here are supportive of me pitching wine tours to the Generation X market because traditionally it has been a hard one for them to market to.'

Willcock, named South West Young Business Achiever for the second year in a row in 2005, says that running the wine tours is a pretty simple business. 'We're trying to pull back the restraints from people enjoying wine. People think they can't enjoy wine unless they know about it and that's not true.' One of the ways Wine for Dudes helps people overcome their nervousness about wine-tasting is by letting them blend up their own wines. 'It gives them confidence in their own palette and what they like and don't like.' In 2007, Wine for Dudes' tours, promising to 'demystify wine and wine culture in a refreshing, intimidation-free environment' were selling at about AUS$55. The tours were available seven days a week and included lunch at a winery, pick up and drop off, wine tastings all day and a tour in a working winery. The company also produces its own brand of 'Wine for Dudes' wine, including a shiraz cabernet merlot and a chard sem sauv blend. 'It's well priced at $14 a bottle, and easy drinking, available at any local restaurant with any kind of street cred!' said manager John O'Connor.

*Source*: Martin, R. (30 December 2005). 'Tasting Success', retrieved from www.abc.net.au; O'Connor, J. (12 April 2007) Manager for Wine for Dudes, personal communication.

## SWOT Analysis

SWOT is an acronym for strengths, weaknesses, opportunities and threats. A **SWOT analysis** provides scope for an organization to list all its strengths (those things it does best and its positive product features) and its weaknesses (problems that affect its success). These factors are always internally focused. For hotels and visitor attractions, location may be a major strength, or the strength may lie in the skills of certain staff members. Strength may also lie in historical artifacts or architectural style, or having a particularly favourable consumer image. Once identified, strengths are the basis of corporate positions and can be promoted to potential customers, enhanced through product augmentation, or developed within a strategic framework. In the Snapshot profiling Four Seasons in this chapter, several strengths of the Four Seasons Hotels and Resorts can be identified, including their reputation, brand equity and global positioning.

Weaknesses, ranging from aging products and declining markets to surly customer contact staff, must also be identified. Once identified, they may be subject to management action designed to minimize their impact or to remove them where possible. Weaknesses and strengths are often matters of perception rather than 'fact', and may be recognized only through consumer research. Again, using Four Seasons as an example, weaknesses could include not being diversified enough and therefore being vulnerable to negative external environmental impacts.

Opportunities are events that can affect a business, either through its reaction to external forces or through its addressing of its own weaknesses. An opportunity identified recently by Four Seasons Hotels and Resorts is in private charters and general cruises, a move that may improve the group's weakness of not being diversified enough.

Threats are those elements, both internal and external, that could have a serious detrimental effect on a business. After 11 September 2001, the subsequent downturn in the economy had a devastating impact on tourism and by the end of 2002, Four Seasons had not recovered. The subsequent Iraq war and concerns about sudden acute respiratory syndrome (SARS) led to a huge number of cancelled trips to North America and to thousands of dollars in lost tourism revenue for all hotels, including Four Seasons.

---

**SWOT ANALYSIS**
a technique that provides scope for an organization to list all its strengths, weaknesses, opportunities, and threats

---

A SWOT analysis is usually best undertaken early in the planning process, and in large organizations a SWOT is often carried out for each division. For example, a convention hotel would conduct a SWOT on the property as a whole, but might also undertake a separate exercise for the functions area, restaurants, retail outlets and recreation facilities. To enhance their own foresight and bring to bear an independent, fresh vision, it is common practice in large market-oriented businesses for managers to commission consultants to carry out regular audits of all aspects of their business, including a SWOT analysis.

## Forecasting

Because information is never perfect and the future is always unknown, no one right conclusion can ever be drawn from the evidence gathered in the SWOT process. As a result, forecasting becomes an important stage in the planning process to support a SWOT. **Forecasting** is market research based but future oriented, and it relies on expectations, vision, judgement, and projections for factors such as sales volume and revenue trends, consumer profiles, product profiles, price trends, and trends in the external environment. The Snapshot below provides forecasts for the growing Chinese travel market based on reports by several market research companies. Because the future for tourism and hospitality products is subject to volatile, unpredictable factors and competitors' decisions, the goal of forecasting is not accuracy but careful and continuous assessment of probabilities and options, with a focus on future choices. Forecasting recognizes that most marketing-mix expenditure is invested months ahead of targeted revenue flows. Since marketing planning is focused on future revenue achievement, it is necessarily dependent upon skill, judgement, foresight and realism in the forecasting process.

> **FORECASTING**
> a market research–based but future-oriented process that relies on expectations, vision, judgement, and projections for factors such as sales volume and revenue trends, consumer profiles, product profiles, price trends, and trends in the external environment

There are two main sets of forecasting techniques: qualitative and quantitative. Qualitative techniques are those that seek to estimate future levels of demand, based on detailed subjective analysis. They include sales staff estimates, senior management opinions and buyers' intention surveys. Two more sophisticated qualitative techniques are the Delphi technique and scenario planning. The Delphi technique involves obtaining expert opinions about the future prospects for a particular market without the experts actually meeting or necessarily knowing at any stage the composition of the panel. Long-term scenario planning is undertaken by larger organizations such as hotel or airline companies. This is a systematic attempt to predict the composition of the future market environment in 10–25 years' time, and the likely impacts on the company.

Quantitative techniques rely on analysis of past and current data. In some instances this implies the simple projecting of future demand in terms of past trends; in other instances, unravelling causal determinants needs to be considered. A number of well-tested methods are used, but most require a degree of statistical ability. Time-series (non-causal) techniques involve the forecasting of future demand on the basis of past trends. Causal methods attempt to show, by using regression analysis, how some measure of tourism demand is influenced by selected variables other than time. Finally, computer simulations are becoming more popular – trend-curve analysis and multiple regressions are combined mathematically to generate a computer model that simulates tourism demand.

## Snapshot

### Planning for the Growing Chinese Travel Market

According to many reports, China's tourism industry holds massive potential. Due to the rising levels of affluence, particularly among the expanding middle class, the number of outbound tourists from China grew nearly 50 per cent in 2004 to reach 28.85 million. In the same year, 15 European countries were granted Approved Destination Status (ADS) by China, which is predicted to lead to a sharp increase in the number of Chinese nationals visiting the continent. At the end of 2005, the number of countries granted ADS by China was over 90. It is predicted that China's outbound sector will grow 20 per cent annually. According to the Economic Intelligence Unit, the number of Chinese travellers is forecast to rise to 49 million by 2008, 60 million by 2010 and 100 million by 2015. At that point, China will be the world's biggest source of outbound tourism.

Chinese travellers are somewhat conservative in their travel behaviours. Most travel with tour groups, making the trip as comfortable as possible. Not until they have embarked on multiple trips do they shun the tour group and take on more individual travel itineraries. A recent study of Chinese travellers by Synovate Hong Kong showed that they were technologically up to date, with most owning computers, mobile phones and MP3 players. Sightseeing, visiting friends and relatives and shopping were the main purposes for leisure travel and the average leisure visit lasted about five days. The study also showed the need for international hotels to build brand loyalty in the Chinese market. Very few hotels obtained an overwhelming percentage of unaided awareness amongst Chinese travellers. Synovate suggests that the best way to build such loyalty amongst the younger generation of future Chinese travellers may be through the internet.

According to a survey by Goldman Sachs Global Investment Research, Chinese travellers spend twice as much on luxury items abroad as they do at home. In the short term, Hong Kong is likely to attract most of this spending by mainland tourists due to its proximity and attractive prices. However, Europe, particularly France and Italy, will lure an increasing number of Chinese tourists in the future. 'Travelling overseas has already become the hot new lifestyle choice for modern Chinese,' said Willie Fung, senior vice president and general manager, Greater China, for Mastercard International. From research, his firm has concluded that the Chinese regard travel overseas as a way of expressing pride in their achievements, improvements and social status, and proving that they are indeed becoming 'world travellers'.

In anticipation of the influx of Chinese tourists, tourism industry leaders are carving into their marketing budgets in order to capture a share of the market. NYC and Company, for example, employs a multi-pronged approach to the Chinese market. The bureau participated in the China International Travel Mart for the first time in 2005, but earlier sent sales missions to Shanghai and Beijing to meet with tour operators, airlines, government, and trade organizations. Additional components of the programme include relationship building with both US and Chinese news media, and cultivating the large Chinese population in New York City. The bureau has also added Chinese language pages to its website and provides market intelligence and educational seminars for its members. A specialist in Asia tourism development was brought on board to address the market in 2001.

*Sources*: Alberta Economic Development. (15 April 2005) 'Tourism trends', *Tourism Issues*; In:Fact, Synovate Research. (29 September 2005) 'Study shows Chinese travelers are a market force to be reckoned with', *Business Wire*.

## Setting Marketing Goals and Objectives

Goals are the primary aims of the organization, and objectives the specific aims that managers try to accomplish to achieve organizational goals. Goals can be defined in terms of sales growth, increased profitability, and market leadership. Objectives are the activities that will accomplish the goals. For example, the goal of sales growth for a hotel could be reached via the objectives of a 20 per cent increase in accommodation sales and a 30 per cent increase in food and beverage sales. The goal of increased profitability could be translated into objectives of a 15 per cent increase in profits across the board, and a goal of market leadership could be translated into objectives for each city in which a hotel chain operates. The Case Study at the end of this chapter shows that the goals of the new airline Roots Air were too ambitious, and the company had unrealistic expectations.

Marketing objectives at the tactical level derive logically from the previous stages of the planning process.

To be effective and actionable in practice, Middleton and Clarke (2001) assert that tactical marketing objectives must be:

1. integrated with long-term corporate goals and strategy;
2. precise and quantified in terms of sales volume, sales revenue, or market share;
3. specific in terms of which products and which segments they apply to;
4. specific in terms of the time period in which they are to be achieved;
5. realistic and aggressive in terms of market trends (revealed in the situation analysis) and in relation to budgets available;
6. agreed and endorsed by the managers responsible for the programmes of activity designed to achieve results; and
7. measurable directly or indirectly.[5]

If these criteria are not fully met, the objectives will be less than adequate for achieving the success of the business, and the marketing programmes will be harder to specify and evaluate. The more thorough the previous stages of the marketing plan, the easier the task of specifying precise objectives. To ensure profitability and to remain competitive in today's marketplace, it has become necessary to establish several sub-objectives. For instance, a 1,000-room hotel will undoubtedly have two broad objectives: average occupancy and average room rate. By themselves, these objectives do not serve as sufficient guides for developing marketing strategies. A set of sub-objectives might therefore include occupancy per period of time, the average room rate by type of room, and annual sales by each salesperson. Each marketing support area needs to be guided by a set of sub-objectives. This includes areas such as advertising, promotion, public relations, market research and sales. It is important to acknowledge that objectives may not always be profit-based. The main objective for Cheddar Caves & Gorge, for example, is to protect the fragile environment rather than to make money (see Chapter 8).

## Marketing Strategy: Targeting and Positioning

### Targeting

No area of the marketing plan surpasses the selection of **target markets** in importance. If inappropriate markets are selected, marketing resources will be wasted, as was the case for Roots Air in the end of chapter Case Study. High-level expenditures on advertising or sales will not compensate for misdirected marketing effort. Target markets should be selected from a previously developed list of available segments. These include segments currently served by the organization and newly recognized markets. A target market is simply the segment at which the organization aims its marketing message. Implicitly, the non-profitable customers should be given less attention. A target market generally has four characteristics. It should comprise groups of people or businesses that are well defined, identifiable and accessible; members should have common characteristics; they should have a networking system so that they can readily refer the organization to one another; and they should have common needs and similar reasons to purchase the product or service. The target market for Wine for Dudes (Generation X) fulfils these characteristics (see Snapshot above)

---

**TARGET MARKET**
a clearly defined group of customers whose needs the company plans to satisfy

---

The family market is a popular target market for many tourism organizations. Family travel is growing as more parents are choosing to share travel experiences with their children. Club Med is a good example. Once known for its ability to cater to young singles, it now has more than 60 family-friendly holiday villages worldwide. Adventure tours for families are also on the increase. A family-oriented, 13-day tour of South Africa offered by Explore is one example. Other tour operators are choosing to target the baby boomers. This sector, born between 1947 and 1966, generates the highest travel volume in North America, and is a very attractive market for the tourism and hospitality industry. Two other target markets growing in attractiveness for the tourism industry are the gay market and the senior market.

The gay tourism market offers enormous growth for the tourism industry. The British Tourist Authority's (BTA) campaign to attract gay and lesbian travellers from the United States is evidenced by the launch of the 2002 edition of its gay travel guide, as well as by new strategies for building a market niche that it says has already produced 'gratifying' results. The decision to begin targeting gay and lesbian travellers from the United States was made in 1997. The BTA has subsequently expanded the campaign, with the introduction of a larger travel guide and a dedicated gay and lesbian website.[6]

## Positioning

Once the market has been segmented and a target market identified, the next step in the marketing plan is positioning. **Positioning** is a communications strategy that is a natural follow-through from market segmentation and target marketing. Market positioning is ultimately how the consumer perceives the product or service in a given market, and is used to achieve a sustainable advantage over competitors. The Snapshot below on Four Seasons Hotels and Resorts is an excellent example of distinctive positioning leading to global competitive success. Best Western recently changed its positioning strategy in China in the hope of going beyond its traditional image as a purveyor of budget hotels. In 2006, the Phoenix-based chain scrapped plans to build a network of 100 three-star hotels in China by 2007. Instead, it plans to triple the number of its four- and five-star hotels in the country to 60 by 2009 (Fong, 2006).[7]

---

**POSITIONING**
establishing an image for a product or service in relation to others in the marketplace

---

Three steps are necessary to develop an effective position in the target market segment: product differentiation; prioritizing and selecting the competitive advantage; and communicating and delivering the position.

*Step One: Product Differentiation*

**Product differentiation**, a phrase coined by Michael Porter, describes a technique that enables organizations to gain competitive advantage by offering a product that has features not offered by its competitors. Product differentiation can give companies a competitive edge and competitive advantages, which offer greater value to the consumer by providing benefits that justify a higher price. These advantages can be established through product attributes, features, services, level of quality, style and image, and price range. The key elements will shape how the consumer perceives the product. Physical attribute differentiation is achieved by enhancing or creating an image in the consumer's mind through tangible evidence. For example, Quality Inn offers a very simple physical appearance, communicating a clean, safe, cheap place to sleep. Fairmont Hotels & Resorts, on the other hand, combines an elaborate exterior with a luxurious interior to inspire feelings of comfort, relaxation, and prestige.

---

**PRODUCT DIFFERENTIATION**

a technique that enables organizations to gain competitive advantage by offering a product that has features not offered by its competitors

---

Service differentiation is an increasingly important way of gaining competitive advantage. The process by which customers evaluate a purchase, thereby determining satisfaction and likelihood of repurchase, is important to all marketers, but especially to services marketers because, unlike their manufacturing counterparts, they have fewer objective measures of quality by which to judge their production (Zeithaml et al., 1988).[8] Several studies have examined the association between service quality and more specific behavioural intentions, and there is a positive and significant relationship between customers' perceptions of service quality and their willingness to recommend the company or destination (Zeithaml et al., 1996).[9] Likewise, research on service quality and retaining customers suggests that willingness to purchase again declines considerably once services are rated below good (Gale, 1992).[10]

*Step Two: Prioritizing and Selecting the Competitive Advantage*

Positioning is much like a ranking system, and an organization must decide where it wants to be in the hierarchy. Some companies have an image of high quality, service, and price; others, of being low budget. Neither image is better or worse. However, once the position is established, it is very difficult to change it in the consumer's mind. Therefore, companies must be very cautious in selecting the most effective combination of competitive advantages to promote.

It is important to promote not only one benefit to the target market, but to develop a **unique selling proposition (USP)**, a feature of a product that is so unique that it distinguishes the product from all other products. The goal of a USP is for a company to establish itself as the number one provider of a specific attribute in the mind of the target market. The attribute chosen should be desired and highly valued by target consumers. If the marketing mix elements build the brand and help it to connect with the customer year after year, the total personality of the brand, rather than the trivial product differences, will decide its ultimate position in the market. Although it is difficult in the tourism industry to find an effective USP in such a competitive and free market, it is essential to offer something new, as Freedom Paradise in Mexico has done. Package holidays tend to offer similar deals, with only minor differences. Therefore, it is important for a company to create a new good, service, or benefit that can be offered to consumers by that company alone. An example of a company offering a unique transportation service to tourists is TucTuc Ltd in the UK. The company imports motorized rickshaws from Delhi to Brighton, England. Owner Dominic Ponniah says ,'I guess they're so popular because they have a certain romance and because, running on natural gas, they're environmentally sound.'[11]

---

**UNIQUE SELLING PROPOSITION (USP)**
a feature of a product that is so unique that it distinguishes the product from all other products

---

*Step Three: Communicating and Delivering the Position*
The final goal of an organization in the positioning process is to build and maintain a consistent positioning strategy. The overall aim of tourism providers is to attract attention from potential customers and to delight them with product offerings that cannot be beaten by competitors. Programmes and slogans that support the organization's position must be continuously developed and promoted in order to establish and maintain the organization's desired position in the consumer's mind. Quality, frequency, and exposure in the media will determine how successful the positioning strategy will be.

Tourism and hospitality providers try to differentiate their products by using **branding**, a method of establishing a distinctive identity for a product based on competitive differentiation from other products. Branded products are those whose name conjures up certain images – preferably positive ones – in consumers' minds. These images may relate to fashion, value, prestige, quality, or reliability. Image is an important element of customer perception. If a hotel chain has an image of quality, staying at the hotel will provide benefits to business customers who want to project a successful image to their clients or colleagues. Some brands are recognized for their reliability. It is comforting for many travellers, for example, to know that a Best Western property will meet certain standards, and that selecting one will be a reliable choice, even if the traveller is unfamiliar with the specific property or region. Hotels, in particular, brand specific properties within their group to identify different categories of product. (See Chapter 5 for a more detailed discussion of branding.)

---

**BRANDING**
a method of establishing a distinctive identity for a product based on competitive differentiation from other products

---

## Snapshot

### Positioning 'Four' Success: Four Seasons Hotels and Resorts

Toronto-based Four Seasons Hotels and Resorts is an excellent example of distinctive positioning leading to global competitive success. In 2006 Four Seasons was operating 73 luxury hotels and resorts in 31 countries around the world, turning over more than US$290 million a year. It wins awards at an unprecedented level in industry publications as the leading player in the luxury hotel and resort business worldwide. Ten or more of its hotels routinely make lists of the top 100 hotels in the world, and the company often appears on the *Fortune* list of best places to work. Its revenue per available room (RevPAR) in the highly competitive US market is more than 30 per cent higher than that of its closest chain competitor, Ritz-Carlton. Countries and cities around the world encourage Four Seasons to build hotels in their jurisdiction because the presence of a Four Seasons signals a high-quality location.

The success of the company has been derived from making an integrated set of choices that are highly distinctive from those of competitors. Its goal was to develop a brand name synonymous with an unparalleled customer experience, and to meet these aspirations it chose to focus exclusively on serving high-end travellers. This is in direct contrast to large competitors such as Hyatt, Marriott, Hilton and Westin, all of which compete across the spectrum of hotel classes, thereby struggling to establish consistent high-end service and branding.

Using high prices as a means of positioning, Four Seasons hotels raise their prices when competitors come near them. Even when September 11, 2001, and the SARS outbreak of 2003 led to increased costs and lower occupancy levels, Four Seasons decided to maintain its room rates despite moves by competitors to slash prices. CEO Isadore Sharp believes the room rates are easily justified. 'It isn't what you might call a discretionary expense, as most luxury items are,' he says. 'We provide a service. When travellers can rely on prompt room service, their suit being properly pressed, and their messages actually reaching them,' says Sharp, 'they realize this is a great value.'

Another key early strategic choice for Four Seasons was to pursue a truly global strategy by developing an ever-growing portfolio of hotels and resorts in key destinations around the world. This distinguished Four Seasons from the bulk of smaller high-end competitors. The final key strategy was to specialize as a hotel manager, not a developer and owner. This was a distinct choice in the industry until Marriott divided its business into hotel ownership and hotel management companies. Because its business model means Four Seasons doesn't own most of its hotels, the capital risk is low, and the company boasts a sound balance sheet. Indeed, even in punishing economic cycles, the brand remains highly valued by investors – unusual for a place that often charges three or four times the price of a typical Sheraton.

Because the Four Seasons strategy is unique and is ensconced in an activity system that would force competitors to make unacceptable trade-offs, its competitors have been disinclined to imitate Four Seasons, despite its obvious success. The result is a Canadian global leader with attractive growth prospects for the future.

*Sources*: 'The unseen precondition of long-term success', presentation by Isadore Sharp at the World Tourism Education & Research Center's Air Canada Distinguished Lecture Series, University of Calgary, Calgary, AB. Thursday, 27 April 2000.

## Tactics and Action Plans

Although no single strategy will be suitable for all organizations, marketing planning provides the opportunity to understand the operating environment and to choose options that will meet the organization's goals and objectives. Planning involves selecting and developing a series of strategies that effectively bring about the required results.

Among the types of strategies that can be considered are:

1. making good investment decisions. Selecting the best, most effective use of financial resources is crucial. This will include reviewing the product's life cycle and doing a portfolio analysis;
2. diversifying. While it is important to ensure that resources are allocated to those markets showing the best potential yields, the possibility of disruptions to markets must also be taken into account. Diversification can provide an important cushion;
3. planning for the long term. Tourism marketing campaigns can have long lead times. The cumulative effect of promotions may take a while to produce measurable results. Building effectiveness over time is just as important as generating instant results;
4. seizing new opportunities. Being aware of consumer trends, fads, fashions, and attitudinal shifts will also help an organization to identify opportunities. Being flexible enough to respond to market developments will give an organization a strong competitive edge;
5. developing strategic partnerships. It is important to identify customers, suppliers, and competitors with whom it is possible to develop an enhanced working relationship. Strategic alliances offer the opportunity to increase profits for all participants.

### Applying the Marketing Mix

Marketing strategies are designed as the vehicle to achieve marketing objectives. In turn, marketing tactics are tools to support strategies. Action programmes comprise a mix of marketing activities that are undertaken to influence and motivate buyers to choose targeted volumes of particular products. This part of the marketing plan shows how the organization intends to use the 7 Ps introduced in Chapter 1. Table 3.1 shows the activities that should be included in this section of the marketing plan. The third column lists the chapters in this book where these topics are covered in detail. A marketing mix programme or marketing campaign expresses exactly what activities will take place in support of each identified product/market subgroup on a week-by-week basis. The Case Study at the end of the chapter discusses how Roots Air implemented a major advertising campaign to win new customers, with a jazzy website, large banners inside and outside major airports, and moody, black-and-white print ads in major daily newspapers. However, the airline did not forge a clear marketing message – one of the reasons it eventually failed.

## Resource Requirements

The marketing plan needs to address the resources required to support the marketing strategies and meet the objectives. Such resources include personnel, equipment and space, budgets, intra-organizational support, research, consultation and training. A common error in writing a marketing plan is developing strategies that may well be highly workable, but for

**Table 3.1** Specific Strategies Included in the Action Plan

| Strategies | Marketing Mix Elements (Ps) | Chapter |
|---|---|---|
| Product strategies | Product | 5 |
| | Physical evidence | |
| | Process | |
| Pricing strategies | Price | 6 |
| Distribution strategies | Place | 7 |
| Advertising strategies | Promotion | 8 |
| Sales promotion and merchandising strategies | Promotion | 8 |
| Public relations strategies | Promotion | 9 |
| Sales strategies | Promotion | 9 |
| Direct marketing strategies | Promotion | 9 |
| Internet marketing strategies | Place | 10 |
| | Promotion | |
| Internal marketing strategies (personnel, managing service quality, etc.) | People | 11 |
| | Process | |

which there is insufficient support. Generally, the most costly and difficult resource needed to ensure the success of marketing/sales strategies in tourism and hospitality businesses is personnel. Management commonly views the addition of personnel as unnecessary, impractical or unwise, given budgetary restrictions.

Of prime importance in analysing resource requirements is the budget. Setting a budget that provides the marketing department with sufficient resources to deliver its plan is essential. However, in most organizations, various departments compete for funds, and it is not always easy to convince management that the marketing budget should have a priority claim on limited funds. Although this is less of an issue in commercially oriented organizations, it can be a major problem in arts and entertainment organizations and non-profit groups. The idea of spending money on marketing (which is frequently not viewed as a core activity) at the expense of collections, maintenance, acquisitions, or expanding performance programmes is often a very contentious issue.

## Marketing Control

The penultimate step in the planning process is to ensure that objectives will be achieved in the required time, using the funds and resources requested. In order to measure effectiveness, evaluation programmes have to be put in place, and regular monitoring needs to occur. There is little value in preparing a one-year marketing plan and including an evaluation methodology that commences toward the end of the operating year. This will not allow enough time to identify potential problems or initiate remedial action.

Because objectives have been set in quantifiable terms, regular reviews of sales forecasts and quotas, assessments of expenditure against budget, and data collection and analysis will provide guidance on how well objectives are being met. If a problem arises, contingency plans can be activated. Effective contingency plans are considered long before emergencies or problems arise. Reacting under pressure is rarely as effective as preplanning. If, as part of the original process, alternatives are considered, it is more likely that they will be successful. The most important reason for insisting on precision in setting objectives is to make it possible to measure results. Such results for a tourism business might be flow of bookings against planned capacity, enquiry and sales response related to any advertising, customer awareness of advertising messages measured by research surveys, sales response to any price discounts and sales promotions, sales response to any merchandising efforts by travel agents, consumer use of websites and flow of bookings achieved, and customer satisfaction measurements.

Most marketing plans are written to cover a one-year action plan in detail, with references made to the longer term – traditionally three years and five years. While the corporate goals may be longer term (often as long as ten or 20 years), the actual objectives are usually defined in terms of a much shorter time frame. Some organizations base their marketing plans on their funding cycles. Some art organizations or government departments on three-year funding cycles prepare business and marketing plans that cover the full funding period. Even these, however, stress the importance of regular reviews, and re-evaluate their action plan sections on a 12-month basis.

## Communicating the Plan

Involving as many staff members as possible in the process of setting objectives and drawing up plans that communicate well is an important aspect of motivating staff at all levels and securing enthusiastic participation in the implementation process. This involvement is a subject of increasing attention in many tourism and hospitality organizations (Middleton and Clarke, 2001).[12] It is especially important for service businesses, in which so many staff members have direct contact with customers on the premises. It is a good idea to time the stages in marketing planning so that managers and as many staff as possible in all departments can take some part in initiating or commenting on draft objectives and plans. Motivation can be damaged if objectives are continuously changed or if there is no opportunity to debate their practicality in operation. While marketing planning is conducted primarily to achieve more efficient business decisions, its secondary benefit is to provide a means of internal participation and communication, vital in creating and sustaining a high level of organizational morale.

Marketing plans must be sold to many people. Internally, these include members of the marketing and sales department, vendors and advertising agencies, and top management. Marketing plans are also important in communicating with stakeholders outside the company. Approaching banks or other investors – for example, in tourism projects funded by government sources – invariably requires a business plan in which marketing is a primary component. Where money is granted, evidence of results will be required through a formal evaluation process. In terms of presenting the report, many readers, both inside and outside the organization, will be impatient and will want the conclusions immediately. The executive summary is therefore a key section of the report. Indeed, it can be assumed that some staff – and perhaps senior executives and board members – will read only the executive summary. In general, an executive summary should be between two and six pages. It should avoid the use of jargon, and it should highlight the key objectives and action aspects of the plan and budget, leaving the analysis of current situations and detailed market analyses for the main document.

---

## Chapter Summary

A marketing plan serves a number of purposes within any tourism organization: it provides a road map for all marketing activities of the firm for the future; it ensures that marketing activities are in agreement with the corporate strategic plan; it forces marketing managers to review and think objectively through all steps in the marketing process; it assists in the budgeting process to match resources with marketing objectives; and it creates a process to monitor actual against expected results.

There are eight logical steps in a systematic marketing planning process:

1. Corporate connection. Marketing planning should reflect the goals and objectives of the organization as a whole.
2. Analysis and forecasting. This includes portfolio analysis, competitor analysis, segmentation analysis, and SWOT analysis. Forecasting becomes an important stage in the planning process to support a SWOT.
3. Setting marketing goals and objectives. Goals are the primary aims of the organization, and objectives are the specific aims that managers accomplish to achieve organizational goals.
4. Marketing strategy: targeting and positioning. Target markets should be selected from the previously developed list of available segments. Positioning is a natural follow-through from market segmentation and target marketing.
5. Tactics and action plans. This part of the marketing plan shows how the organization intends to use the 7 Ps.
6. Resource requirements. The marketing plan needs to address the resources required to support the strategies and meet the objectives.
7. Marketing control. This step in the planning process is to ensure that objectives will be achieved in the required time, using the funds and resources requested.
8. Communicating the plan. This is an important aspect of motivating staff at all levels and securing participation in the implementation process.

---

## Key Terms

Boston Consulting Group (BCG) model p. 82
branding p. 98
budget competitors p. 85
cash cow p. 82
competitor analysis p. 84
differentiation, p. 86

## Discussion Questions and Exercises ?

1. Examine the mission statement for a local tourism or hospitality organization. Does it reflect the 'smart' rule described in this chapter? If not, try to redefine the statement.
2. Choose a large tourism or hospitality enterprise in your country and apply the BCG matrix to the various products and services on offer. Does the organization have a balanced portfolio?
3. Four Seasons has achieved success through distinctive positioning. Think of another three examples of tourism organizations that have clearly understood the significance of positioning. Describe their target markets.
4. It is suggested in this chapter that competitors can be divided into four broad categories. Take an example from the tourism industry in your country (a hotel chain perhaps) and list its competitors under the four categories.

5.  The chapter highlights a number of target markets growing in attractiveness for the tourism industry. Segment the tourists that your region attracts. Are there any segments of the travel market that are not being targeted? Why not?

6.  Go out and find a marketing plan from a tourism organization in your area. Does it follow the eight steps of the planning process outlined in this chapter? How is it different?

## The Failure of Roots Air

The story of Roots Air began early in 2000, with a cryptic voicemail message from Ted Shetzen, the man behind Roots Air, to Leo Desrochers, the chief operating officer of Skyservice Airlines Inc., a Toronto-based charter carrier that mostly ferried travellers south in the winter. Mr Desrochers's acquaintance with Mr Shetzen went way back, to the days when both worked at Air Canada. Shetzen's message was brief and to the point, saying only, 'It's time.'

From those two words emerged a plan to steal away a small portion of Air Canada's most profitable customers – business flyers – by enticing them with celebrity pitchmen and promises of great food, plush lounges, and excellent service, all at lower prices. A main attraction of the new venture was its branding agreement with Roots, the clothing empire founded by Michael Budman and Don Green. Roots invested $5 million for the right to put its name on the carrier and design the uniforms, lounges, and other promotional items. Trading on the trendy image of the apparel retailer, the timing of the new airline seemed encouraging. The merger of Air Canada and Canadian Airlines was not going well, and there was reason to believe there were a lot of disgruntled travellers looking for an alternative.

A key element of the Roots Air strategy was to use brand-new A320 and A330 aircraft but exploit Skyservice's existing infrastructure to operate at low cost. 'We basically saw an opportunity to carve a place out for ourselves in the business market, not with high expectations of market share, not competing with Air Canada everywhere, but enough to allow us an adequate return on capital,' recalled Desrochers. Roots had two service tiers: gold and silver. Gold included luxury items such as leather-covered seats, whereas silver service was tailored for the more price-sensitive business traveller. In March 2001, a Roots silver-class fare was about $800 one way from Vancouver to Toronto. Air Canada's fare was almost $2,000 for the same journey.

As well as targeting the business traveller, Roots Air was looking to attract consumers who wanted to associate themselves with the cachet of the retailer, Roots Canada. But apart from outfitting its cabin staff and baggage personnel in the hip

**Case Study**

Roots Air – A short history

designs that have made Roots famous from Hollywood to the Olympics, Roots Air did not forge a clear marketing message. A major advertising campaign by Grey Worldwide of Toronto touted the Roots Air image with a jazzy website, large banners inside and outside major airports, and print ads in major daily newspapers. The agency tried to entice customers and executives and travel agents with moody, black-and-white photos unconventional for the airline industry. This led to further criticisms that the Roots message was unclear.

As far as public relations were concerned, Michael Budman and Don Green, co-founders of the Roots apparel phenomenon, were conspicuously absent in the airline's development phase, choosing not to play the Richard Branson role of playful, ubiquitous promoters – probably the only chance Roots Air had of making an impression on jaded air travellers. If they deferred to Russell Payson, CEO of Skyservice, it was perhaps with the knowledge that the Roots owners' previous non-retail fling with a Roots hotel in Colorado in the early 1990s was a flop.

But in general, the goals of the new airline were too ambitious. An offering circular was sent out in June 2000, by Research Capital Corp., to raise $35 million to fund the venture. It included a pro forma statement showing that Skyservice's revenue would increase to $548.3 million from $228.9 million in the first year of Roots Air's operation, starting with four planes and adding two more by the end of the year. By comparison, WestJet, arguably Canada's most successful airline ever, took five years to attain those numbers, reaching them only in 2000 after it had grown to 22 aircraft. 'The expectations were not realistic, particularly for a start-up airline in its first year of operations,' says Kobus Dietzsch, who worked in marketing planning and analysis in Roots Air. 'A more realistic expectation would have been for $175 million in revenue the first year'.

Other assumptions made at the outset were also dubious. For example, the plan was based on a 50/50 mix of business and leisure customers, whereas 20 per cent business class is considered good by most industry standards. In estimating traffic, the original plan was premised on having 71 per cent of its silver and 78 per cent of its gold business seats filled during August, a time when such traffic tapers off. 'The real problem was that we had too many business-class seats on airplanes,' says Russel Payson, president of Skyservice.

Confusion was rampant within Skyservice leading up to and beyond its first Roots Air flight on 26 March 2001. 'Despite the excitement of launching a new airline, there is a feeling of being overwhelmed by the enormity of the task and compressed timeline,' said a consultant's study done by Marketing Matters for Skyservice in mid-January. Even basic scheduling decisions raised intractable problems. The airline did not know 11 days before 26 March whether or not it would be flying Calgary–Toronto on the first day. The flight was ultimately cancelled. Only one interline agreement (despite plans for many more) with other carriers to receive and hand off passengers was signed by the launch date. Even that deal with Air Tahiti fell apart after Roots Air announced on the first day that it would not fly to Los Angeles, where it was to connect with the Pacific Island carrier. This further hurt earnings projections, since initial expectations were that a significant portion of revenue would come from arrangements with other airlines. Desrochers states that it was difficult to negotiate such agreements because potential partners wanted to see Roots Air up and running before signing.

Perhaps the biggest fiasco came on launch day, when the carrier was forced to cancel two of its inaugural flights because one of its planes had not arrived on time. Compounding the problem was a mistaken entry in the travel agent computer reservation system, showing Roots Air operating a 316-seat Airbus A330 when in fact the plane was a 120-seat A320. As a result, the aircraft was oversold and Roots' Mr Budman and his guests found themselves bumped.

Other problems ran deeper, and included internal disorganization and in-fighting between the low-end charter side of Skyservice, which operated the Roots Air scheduled flights, and the Roots Air people who aimed to be high end. Skyservice operational people began referring derogatorily to those in the Roots Air marketing arm as the 'hangar people' because they were holed up in a different building. Cultural differences also had a negative effect on the advertising, which was crucial to attracting customers and of prime importance to the Roots clothing partners, for whom marketing has always been fundamental. Mark Stoiber, creative director of the Roots Air account at Grey Advertising says, 'With two very different cultures coming together, understandably there was tension and the stakes were very high. Is it a price-driven thing or a style-driven thing?'

One month after launching, it was clear that a host of assumptions on which Roots Air had been based were incorrect. It was now clear that Air Canada did in fact have

*Case Study*

a hammerlock on corporate Canada, and business traffic was not materializing. Calgary passengers in particular were not as disaffected with Air Canada as had been believed, and the Roots Air brand was not resonating with the public as expected. Finally, the Roots Air's service aspirations were being thwarted by the charter mentality of Skyservice. Promising more legroom, shorter line-ups, better food, and real china in the promotional material, the airline found that it just could not deliver on promises.

There were simply too few passengers to sustain the business. During its short life, Roots Air flew on average less than 60 per cent full. While some flights had 80 per cent loads, others were much worse, such as the Calgary–Toronto run on 3 May 2001, the day the airline announced it would shut, when the 120-seat plane had only five people on board. The low loads overturned the economics of the operation, with the result that Roots Air lost money on virtually every flight. Payson says the carrier was losing $1 million a week, a significant expense for a company the size of Skyservice, which had revenue of about $110 million in the fiscal year ending April 30, 2000. In the end, having lost about $7.5. million, Skyservice opted for a deal with Air Canada that called for shutting down Roots Air on 4 May 2001, and for the two to collaborate on running a new low-cost carrier. The low-cost plan fell apart, but the deal allowed for an orderly closure with no passengers left stranded and no creditors left unpaid.

*Sources*: Bramham, D. (27 March 2001) 'Roots Air: not quite flight of fancy', *Vancouver Sun*, F1; Fitzpatrick, P. (31 January 2002) 'Up, up … and down: Roots, a short history', *Financial Post*, 1, 14; Laucius, J. (5 May 2001) 'Roots air couldn't compete with frequent fights', *Ottawa Citizen*, D1.

## Questions

1. What went wrong with Roots Air? Were there elements of the marketing plan outlined in this chapter that did not receive sufficient attention?
2. What can new start-up airlines learn from the experiences of Roots Air?
3. The text lists the criteria used most often by tourism and hospitality suppliers to segment the market. What particular segments was Roots Air trying to attract and what methods did it use to segment the market? Was it successful?
4. The Roots brand has never travelled very far beyond its established position in leisure apparel. Why do you think that is?

## Websites

| | |
|---|---|
| www.gapadventures.com | G.A.P. Adventures |
| www.fourseasons.com | Four Seasons Hotels and Resorts |
| www.freedomparadise.com | Freedom Paradise |
| www. winefordudes.com | Wine For Dudes |

# References

1 Porter, M. E. (1980) *Competitive Strategy: Techniques for Analyzing Industry and Competitors.* New York: Free Press, 4.

2 Porter, M. E. (1980) *Competitive Strategy: Techniques for Analyzing Industry and Competitors.* New York: Free Press, 4.

3 Hudson, S. and Ritchie, J. R. B. (2002) 'Understanding the domestic market using cluster analysis: A case study of the marketing efforts of Travel Alberta', *Journal of Vacation Marketing*, 8(3), 263–276.

4 Crawford-Welch, S. (1991) 'Marketing hospitality in the 21st Century', *International Journal of Contemporary Hospitality Management*, 3(3), 21–27.

5 Middleton, V. T. C. and Clarke, J. (2001) *Marketing in Travel and Tourism.* Oxford: Butterworth-Heinemann, 209.

6 BTA launches 2002 edition of gay and lesbian campaign (2002). Canadian Tourism Commission press release, retrieved from www.canadatourism.com/en/ctc/ctx/ctxnews/search/newsbydateform.cfm.

7 Fong, M. (23 November 2006) 'Best Western strategy in China goes upscale', *Globe & Mail*, B19.

8 Zeithaml, V. A., Berry, L. L. and Parasuraman, A. (1988) 'Communication and control processes in the delivery of service quality', *Journal of Marketing*, 52, 35–48.

9 Zeithaml, V. A., Berry, L. L. and Parasuraman, A. (1996) 'The behavioral consequences of service quality', *Journal of Marketing*, 60, 31–46.

10 Gale, B. (1992) 'Monitoring customer satisfaction and market-perceived quality', *American Marketing Association Worth Repeating Series*, No. 922CSO 1. Chicago: American Marketing Association.

11 Anon. (29 July 2006) 'Where I'd rather be', *Guardian Travel*, 2.

12 Middleton, V. T. C. and Clarke, J. (2001) *Marketing in Travel and Tourism.* Oxford: Butterworth-Heinemann, 213.

# 4

# MARKETING RESEARCH

## Mystery Shopping Uncovers Directional Selling in the UK

Travel agents represent a major communication channel for British travellers. Between 60 and 70 per cent of inclusive tours are sold through travel agents, where vertically integrated tour operators (those that control the distribution channel) are the dominant retailers. In 2000, the distribution of inclusive tours came under close government scrutiny, and after a thorough investigation, the Monopolies & Mergers Commission (MMC) came to the conclusion that the vertical integration of tour operators, charter airlines and major travel agents did not affect consumer choice adversely. One practice that was of some concern to the MMC was 'directional selling', which they defined as 'the sale or attempted sale by a vertically integrated travel agent of the foreign package holidays of its linked tour operator, in preference to the holidays of other operators'.

Despite the findings of the MMC, independent operators and consumer groups continued to claim that directional selling existed and that the practice was of detriment to consumer choice. The author of this book undertook a study to determine the extent of directional selling in the UK and this was achieved using mystery shoppers. Mystery shopping, the name given to participant observation in the commercial sector, has become a mainstream market research technique. For this project, mystery shoppers were used to test travel agent recommendations across the country, with the largest three 'linked' travel agency chains coming under investigation. Fifty-two agencies from Lunn Poly (owned by Thomson), Going Places (Airtours) and Thomas Cook or Carlson (Thomas Cook) were sampled. A mixture of actual visits (36) and telephone calls (120) were used to get an insight into what happens when potential holidaymakers call, or walk into a travel agent to book a holiday.

'Shoppers' (students in this case) chosen to carry out the research had to match a customer profile that was appropriate for the scenario they were being asked to act out. Shoppers were trained, through role-plays, to adopt a neutral rather than an aggressive or defensive approach in the encounter with agents. The training of

A Thomas Cook travel agency in the UK

data collection skills focused on identifying the elements of the service to be observed as well as the retention and recording of the information. For example researchers had to record how forcibly the agent tried to 'switch sell' on a five-point scale, and then comment on the tactics employed by the agent.

Taken as a whole, of the 156 travel agents approached, 95 (60 per cent) clearly employed directional selling tactics. However, only nine of the Thomson-owned agencies, Lunn Poly, attempted to steer the researchers towards the Thomson products. So aside from Thomson, 86 of the other 104 agencies (82 per cent) owned by Airtours and Thomas Cook, gave biased advice. Of Going Places agencies, 90 per cent pushed the Airtours brand, whilst 75 per cent of agencies owned by Thomas Cook tried to sell their own brands, the largest being JMC Holidays. The results confirmed the significance of travel agent recommendations in the decision-making process and suggested that customers entering a travel agent linked to Airtours and Thomas Cook were likely to receive biased recommendations, and a distinct lack of choice. This means that these travel agents are much more likely to put the interests of large tour operators before the interests of consumers. Ultimately this policy could mean a consumer ending up on a package holiday unsuited to their needs; it is also anti-competitive for the industry. Supporters of directional selling (and some have argued that it makes eminent business sense to control the chain of supply) suggest that the real issue is whether the consumer is being led to believe they are getting the best independent advice to suit their holiday needs. The mystery shoppers used for this piece of research did not believe they were receiving such advice, other than from the Lunn Poly agents.

*Source*: Hudson, S., Snaith, T., Miller, G.A. and Hudson, P. (2001) 'Distribution channels in the travel industry: using mystery shoppers to understand the influence of travel agency recommendations', *Journal of Travel Research*, 40 (2), 148–154.

## OBJECTIVES

On completion of this chapter, you should understand:

▶ what is meant by marketing research;

▶ the types of applied marketing research employed in the tourism industry;

▶ the key stages in the marketing research process;

▶ the relative merits of the various methodologies available to researchers; and

▶ how marketing research can be used for effective decision-making.

## Introduction

The Opening Vignette is a real-life example of a research project undertaken using a qualitative technique called mystery shopping. This technique is one of many discussed in this chapter, which focuses on marketing research in tourism and hospitality. It begins with an introduction to marketing research, its definition, and its role in the tourism and hospitality industry. A description of the type of applied research conducted in tourism is followed by a focus on the various stages in the research process. A section then describes the various methodologies available to researchers and discusses the relative merits of primary versus secondary research. The next part of the chapter looks at sampling, and five common research problems are then highlighted. Finally, the effective use of research in decision-making is discussed.

Research should form the basis of an ongoing system for gathering data about a company, its products and its markets. Often, managers, in the course of their everyday duties, gather intelligence informally and subconsciously by observing, listening to discussions, talking to colleagues in the industry, and reading trade journals and papers. Valuable as this process is, it should be supported by more formal procedures carried out in a systematic and scientific manner. The way in which an organization gathers, uses, and disseminates its research in the marketing context is generally referred to as the **marketing information system (MIS)**. The success of an MIS depends on the quality of the information, its accuracy and relevance, and the way it is collected, interpreted, and applied. A key component of the MIS is the marketing research process.

---

**MARKETING INFORMATION SYSTEM (MIS)**
the way in which an organization gathers, uses, and disseminates its research in the marketing context

---

Researchers and managers seldom address the question of what constitutes marketing research. To complicate the issue further, the terms 'market research' and 'marketing research' are often used interchangeably, sometimes within the same document. Gerhold (1993)[1] asserts that there is no difference between the two terms and that they can both be defined as 'any scientific effort to understand and measure markets or improve marketing performance'. Kinnear et al. (1993)[2] distinguish between the two terms, arguing that the focus of market research is on the analysis of markets, whereas marketing research extends the role and character of research and emphasizes the contact between researchers and the marketing management process. This chapter adopts the term **marketing research** exclusively, defining it as the systematic and objective search for and analysis of information relevant to the identification and solution of any problem in the field of marketing (Green et al., 1988).[3]

---

**MARKETING RESEARCH**
the systematic and objective search for and analysis of information relevant to the identification and solution of any problem in the field of marketing

---

According to McIntosh et al. (1995), there are six reasons for conducting tourism and hospitality research:

1. to identify, describe, and solve problems in order to increase the efficiencies of day-to-day tourism operations;
2. to keep tourism and hospitality firms in touch with trends, changes, predictions, etc. related to their markets;
3. to reduce the waste produced by tourists and tourist organizations;
4. to develop new areas of profit by finding new products, services, markets, etc.;
5. to help promote sales in situations where research findings are of interest to the public; and
6. to develop goodwill, as the public thinks well of firms that are doing research in order to meet consumers' needs.[4]

Unfortunately, in tourism and hospitality many smaller organizations feel that 'real' marketing research is a costly and time-consuming luxury only available to large companies that have professional research staff, sophisticated computers, and almost unlimited budgets. Other organizations see marketing research as something to be undertaken when a major event is about to occur – the introduction of a new product, the acquisition of a new property, or a change in target markets. Its value at these junctures is recognized, but its ability to contribute to an organization's success on a day-to-day basis is often overlooked. Another common problem in the tourism industry is that organizations are not making full use of the information that already exists, which can easily be accessed. Disney was guilty of this when it developed its Paris theme park (see Global Spotlight). Sometimes information is available and studies are done, but the results are either ignored or not fully considered in the final decision-making process. This lack of attention happens when the information is not in accord with the prevailing view of management or when the information has not been properly analysed and clearly presented.

## Applied Research in Tourism and Hospitality

Most marketing research is classified as applied research, which is undertaken to answer specific questions. It differs from pure research (done by scientists at universities or by government authorities), which is aimed at the discovery of new information. Applied research in tourism and hospitality can be grouped into eight categories: research on consumers; research on products and services; research on pricing; research on place and distribution; research on promotion; research on competition; research on the operating environment; and research on a destination. Table 4.1 lists some of the typical research programmes undertaken within these categories. Already in this book, examples have been given for research on consumers ('Freedom Paradise' and 'Backpackers with Gold Cards'), research on competition (G.A.P Adventures), research on the operating environment ('Planning for the Growing Chinese Market'), and research on place and distribution (Opening Vignette on Mystery Shopping). Further on in this book, you will find examples for the other programmes of research in Table 4.1: research on products and services (Case Study on measuring service quality at the end of this chapter); research on pricing (the Opening Vignette on Space Tourism in Chapter 6); research on promotion (Opening Vignette on Second Life in Chapter 13); and research on a destination (Opening Vignette on Las Vegas in Chapter 8).

**Consumer research** is one type of applied research, and cases in this chapter look at consumer studies in food services (see Snapshot on food research), consumer research (or the lack of) conducted by EuroDisney (see Global Spotlight), and a consumer behavioural study by Carton Donofrio Partners Inc. (see Snapshot below, 'Global Study Finds Travellers' Needs Not Being Met by the Travel Industry'). A word of caution about consumer research. Often consumers will tell researchers what they think they want to hear, or what the respondents want to believe about themselves. Food psychologists, for example, tell us that people drink more than a third more fruit juice when they pour it into a short, wide glass instead of a tall, long one, and that people will eat more of a product if it comes in a bigger package. People will

**Table 4.1**  Applied Research in Tourism and Hospitality

| 1. **Research on consumers** | 2. **Research on products and services** |
|---|---|
| • Identifying existing markets <br> • Identifying potential markets <br> • Identifying lapsed consumers <br> • Testing customer loyalty <br> • Developing detailed consumer profiles <br> • Identifying general trends in demographics and psychographics <br> • Identifying changes in attitudes and behaviour patterns (generally) <br> • Identifying changes in attitudes and behaviour patterns (product specific) | • Measuring attitudes towards existing products or services <br> • Identifying potential new products which may be at the end of their product life cycle <br> • Identifying products that are considered acceptable substitutes/alternatives <br> • Evaluating competitors' products <br> • Evaluating consumer attitudes towards décor, presentation and packaging <br> • Evaluating consumer attitudes about combinations of products and services (bundles of product attributes) |
| 3. **Research on pricing** | 4. **Research on place and distribution** |
| • Identifying attitudes towards prices <br> • Testing attitudes towards packages and individual pricing <br> • Identifying costs <br> • Identifying costing policies of competitors <br> • Testing alternative pricing strategies <br> • Testing payment processes (credit cards, electronic funds transfer, etc.) | • Identifying attitudes towards location <br> • Identifying attitudes towards buildings/premises <br> • Identifying attitudes on virtual sites <br> • Identifying potential demand for product or services at other locations <br> • Identifying co-operative opportunities for distribution of information or services |
| 5. **Research on promotion** | 6. **Research on our competition** |
| • Testing and comparing media options <br> • Testing alternative messages <br> • Testing competitor's messages and their effectiveness <br> • Testing new communications options (internet, email, web pages) <br> • Identifying co-operative opportunities <br> • Measuring advertising and promotion effectiveness | • Measuring awareness <br> • Measuring usage <br> • Identifying levels of customer loyalty <br> • Identifying competitors' strengths and weaknesses <br> • Identifying specific competitive advantages (locations, suppliers, etc.) <br> • Identifying co-operative opportunities |
| 7. **Research on the operating environment** | 8. **Research on a destination** |
| • Economic trends <br> • Social trends <br> • Environmental issues <br> • Political climate and trends <br> • Technological development and their impact | • Measuring residents' attitudes <br> • Benchmarking <br> • Measuring customer loyalty <br> • Identifying tourism activities <br> • Identifying spending patterns <br> • Branding research |

report that a breakfast bar tastes worse if the package describes it as containing soy, even if it contains no soy, and that Black Forest Double-Chocolate Cake tastes better than Chocolate Cake, even when the cakes are identical (Burkeman, 2006).[5] A decade ago, consumers told researchers that they wanted healthier fast-food options. Burger chains around the world responded by offering salads and fruit and fresh juices. Wendy's added a fresh-fruit bowl to its menu; two years later they killed it, blaming a lack of demand. 'We listened to consumers who said they wanted to eat fresh fruit but apparently they lied,' a Wendy's spokesman said. Recent times have seen the launch of a rash of products that the fast-food industry calls 'indulgent offerings' – foods marketed specifically on the basis of how much meat and cheese they contain and how few annoying vegetables they contain.

---

**CONSUMER RESEARCH**
one type of applied research that focuses on the consumer

---

Another important type of applied research is **competitor intelligence**. If a company wants to keep track of competition, it requires a clear understanding of who the competition is, as well as knowledge of how the company is doing in comparison to the competitors. Competitor intelligence is available through a variety of sources, including competitors' annual reports, local tourism authorities and state tourism departments, magazine articles, speeches, media releases, brochures, and advertisements. It is important, too, to recognize what is meant by 'the competition' – see Chapter 3 for a discussion of four broad categories of competition. As previously noted, information about the number and type of competitors, their relative market shares, the things they do well, and the things they do badly will assist in the planning process. A review of the competition will also highlight market trends and the level of loyalty of consumers.

---

**COMPETITOR INTELLIGENCE**
keeping track of competition by having a clear understanding of who the competition is and knowing how the company is doing in comparison to the competitors

---

While some information is willingly shared, to get a true picture of how the competition is doing, a firm often needs to undertake research. The form of this research varies from business to business. For a tourist attraction or food operation, it could be as simple as counting the number of cars in the parking lot at various times, or actually going into the facility to see how busy it is. For a hotel, it might mean checking room availability at particular times or watching for advertisements of special offers and discounts. For tour operators, it may involve counting the number of competing coaches at major destinations and collecting tour brochures and schedules. Participant observation is also often used to9 gather competitor intelligence. For example, executives of airlines might travel with competitors, or hotel managers might check in to competitor hotels. These are effective ways of gathering valuable knowledge for research purposes.

## Snapshot

### Global Study Finds Travellers' Needs Not Being Met by the Travel Industry

In 2002, a team of anthropologists in Tokyo, London, Israel, New York, Los Angeles, Chicago, Orlando and Las Vegas gathered data from a global sample of travellers and identified basic needs that were not being met by the travel industry. These findings were used to locate and understand points within the travel experience where industries such as hotels, rental car companies, attractions and cruises could better meet the needs of their customers. The report, published by Carton Donofrio Partners Inc., views 'travel' as a brand. The collaborative nature of the travel industry makes it unique in that consumers come into contact with numerous products, services, and people each time they travel. The study examines the sum of all these interactions, which is one 'travel' brand experience.

More specifically, the researchers found that consumers see travel as a process; they plan their trip, travel via some mode of transport (air, train, ship, car), stay at their destination for a time, then pass back through the same mode to get home. They found that if one part of the process is in distress, the whole process suffers. The study concludes that this travel process is powered by three variables – the three needs that travellers seek to fulfil. The most basic is that of **control** over their travel experience. People also demand a consistent level of **service** throughout the whole process. And ultimately, people want an experience that brings them the **joy** of travel. The needs of control, service, and joy must be satisfied throughout the planning, mode of transport, and destination stages.

Figure 4.1 illustrates the differences between the ideal travel brand experience and that of today. The ideal model begins with a high level of control during the planning stage. Travellers, especially leisure travellers, slowly relinquish control as they move through their travel brand process. By the time they reach the destination, they want to turn a good deal of control over to someone else, whether it's to the leisure resort or the business lodging chain. They want things taken care of **for** them, not **by** them. Ideally, the service level remains consistent through every step of the travel brand experience. Travellers expect at least a satisfactory level of service at each stage of their trip. The joy level rises from planning to a peak at the destination. In today's experience, however, these fundamental travel needs are often not being satisfied. The major source of this distress is the mode of transport and people cannot easily plan their trip or truly enjoy their destination because of that disruption. Thus, needs are met minimally at this stage and this in turn lowers the level of satisfaction throughout the whole process.

The Carton Donofrio study suggests that the travel industry should focus on needs – on satisfying control, service, and joy – to balance today's travel brand experience. In sum, it found that travel is no longer a fluid process, but is now broken up by anxieties that leave many consumers re-evaluating their reasons for travel. Companies who, by the nature of their business, are able to touch a traveller only at one point in his or her experience should look to expand their influence to span many other segments. By doing so, they will be recognized for increasing the level of customer service in unique ways that go beyond traditional measures and outside their usual boundaries.

*Source*: Carton Donofrio Partners Inc. (13 May 2002). 'Global study on travel examines consumer behaviors', retrieved from http://cartondonofrio.com/study.cfm.

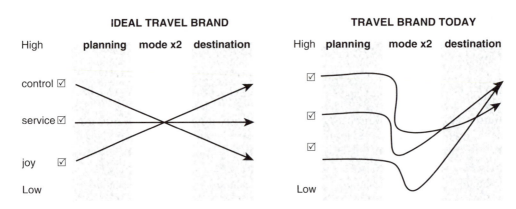

**Figure 4.1**   The Ideal Travel Brand and the Travel Brand Today

## Stages in the Research Process

In undertaking research, there are a number of steps that should be followed, as outlined in Figure 4.2.

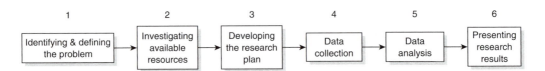

**Figure 4.2**   Stages in the Research Process

### Identifying and Defining the Problem

Before beginning the task of gathering information, it is first necessary to identify the problem for which research is required. This step is crucial to ensure that any information collected is relevant. As well as formulating an aim, specific research questions (objectives) should be stipulated at the outset. These objectives will determine the type of information required.

There are three types of objectives for a marketing research project:

1. exploratory, to gather information that will help define the problem and suggest hypotheses;
2. descriptive, to describe the size and composition of the market; and
3. causal, to test hypotheses about cause-and-effect relationships.

### Investigating Available Sources

There is little point in embarking upon a research programme involving the collection of primary data if that information is already available. Seeking out available information involves a search of internal data generated and recorded by the organization as well as an examination of secondary sources. Such information should then be assessed to establish the extent to which the research questions can be tackled using this information alone.

## Developing the Research Plan

Specific information should be determined from the research objectives. Research objectives must be translated into specific information needs. Two types of data may be used to meet the manager's information needs: **secondary data**, consisting of information that already exists somewhere, having been collected for another purpose, and **primary data**, consisting of information collected for the specific purpose at hand.

---

**SECONDARY DATA**
information that already exists somewhere, having been collected for another purpose

---

**PRIMARY DATA**
information collected for the specific purpose at hand

---

## Data Collection

Upon development of a research plan, data should be collected using the method(s) selected. The data collection phase of the marketing research process is generally the most expensive and the one most frequently subject to error. Great care should be taken to avoid bias, which, if introduced, could render results meaningless. This is a particular problem associated with interview and observation methods.

## Data Analysis

The collected data must be processed and analysed to extract important information and findings. The methods used and the type of information collected will determine the analysis needed. Raw data taken from questionnaires, in-depth interviews, checklists, etc. need to be recorded, analysed, and interpreted. Researchers are constantly searching for similarities and differences, for groupings, patterns, and items of particular significance. Commonly used statistical packages among tourism researchers are SPSS (Statistical Package for the Social Sciences), MINITAB, and NCSS (Number Cruncher Statistical System). These packages are continually being monitored, reviewed and updated to reflect the process of continuous evolution in computer software.

Presenting Research Results

Information needs to be tabulated and interpreted, so that recommendations can be made regarding an appropriate course of action. This will almost certainly involve the presentation of a report that summarizes the results of the research, which enables the management of the organization to make decisions based on the newly acquired information.

## Research Methodology

The increased importance of tourism management decision-making has caused more attention to be focused on the theories and methodologies of the tourism research process. A recurrent theme has emerged in travel research literature concerning the appropriateness of specific types of tourism research and certain methodological applications.

There are several approaches to collecting data, but two key decisions that have to be made are as follows:

1. **Primary versus secondary data**. In planning a research project, it is sensible to consider whether it is worth going to the expense of collecting new information (primary data, where the researcher is the primary user) or whether existing data (secondary data, where the researcher is the secondary user) will be sufficient. In practice, it may be necessary to collect both types of information. The various types of primary and secondary research are explored later in this chapter.
2. **Qualitative versus quantitative research. Qualitative research** methods and techniques give rise to qualitative (subjective) information, whereas **quantitative research** is research to which numerical (empirical) estimates can be attached. There has been much debate recently about appropriate methods for leisure research, with some authors arguing for extended use of qualitative research over quantitative research. In tourism research, quantitative and qualitative research approaches seem to co-exist without the apparent rivalry seen in leisure studies. It is possible for research to be conducted entirely quantitatively, entirely qualitatively, or using a mixture of both. In fact, it is common for large-scale quantitative research to be planned on the basis of prior exploratory qualitative studies.

---

**QUALITATIVE RESEARCH**
research methods and techniques that use and give rise to qualitative (subjective) information

---

**QUANTITATIVE RESEARCH**
research to which numerical (empirical) estimates can be attached

**Table 4.2**  Qualitative Versus Quantitative Research

| Comparison Dimension | Qualitative Research | Quantitative Research |
| --- | --- | --- |
| Types of questions | Probing | Limited probing |
| Sample Size | Small | Large |
| Information per respondent | Much | Varies |
| Administration | Interviewer with special skills required | Fewer special skills required |
| Types of analysis | Subjective, interpretive | Statistical, summarizing |
| Hardware | Tape recorders, projection devices, video equipment, pictures | Questionnaires, computers, printouts |
| Ability to replicate | Low | High |
| Training of the researcher | Psychology, sociology, social psychology, consumer behaviour marketing, marketing research | Statistics, decision models, decision support systems, computer programming, research marketing |
| Types of research | Exploratory | Descriptive or causal |

*Source*: McDaniel, C. D., Jr. and Gates, R. (1993) *Contemporary Marketing Research*. Minneapolis–St. Paul, MN: West, 126.

The distinction between the two methods is indicated in Table 4.2. Both research methods possess distinct limitations and weaknesses, but both also have redeeming characteristics. The choice between the two must be determined by the situation in which research takes place, not by some misguided search for rigour simply for its own sake. The Snapshot below describes how both qualitative and quantitative research methods are used in the food service industry depending on the research objectives.

## Snapshot

### Research in the Food Service Industry

Research in the food service industry is a subject that has received minimal attention in the literature on tourism. In a recent article, Johns and Pine (2002) reviewed the literature related to consumer studies in food service, organizing it into four sections representing different schools of research (see Table 4.3). 'Survey research' includes studies of consumers as groups, while the work reviewed under 'experimental research' involves test situations in which different factors have been manipulated. Studies under 'economics and geography' represent alternative quantitative approaches to consumer research. Under 'sociology and anthropology' is included a range of qualitative research that provides complementary insights into the restaurant experience.

Most quantitative studies in food service consumer research are concerned with some aspect of segmentation, i.e. characterizing segments, identifying needs, or positioning specific offerings relative to specific segments. A large amount of work in this field has established a coherent structure linking restaurant attributes to repeat business. Many studies use

**Table 4.3** Summary of the Four Areas of Food Service Consumer Research

| Area | Practical Focus | Methods Used | Theoretical Focus | Examples of Authors |
|---|---|---|---|---|
| Survey research | Segmentation Targeting Positioning | Geo-demographic, attitude, and behavioural-based surveys Modelling | Attribute theory Expectancy-disconfirmation Repeat business | Capps (1994) Binkley (1998) |
| Experimental research | Customer preferences | Control of specific variables | Factors affecting food preference | Bruner (1990) Love (1995) Birch et al. (1984) |
| Economics and geography | Spatial and socio-economic location | Analysis of secondary data | Population flow and behaviour | Holm et al. (1995) Smith (1985) |
| Sociology and anthropology | Individual experience Wider social context | In-depth interview Observation Literature review | Power relations Social impacts Semiotics | Jamal (1996) Finkelstein (1989) |

expectancy-disconfirmation theory (how well actual performance confirms or disconfirms expectations) and the relationship between the quality of the offering and likelihood of repeat business has been demonstrated using sophisticated multivariate techniques.

The experimental research tradition regards eating out as a function of the food itself and the situation in which it is eaten. Surprisingly, the physical surroundings in which food is eaten have been given comparatively little attention, despite offering very attractive targets for experiment. The effects of image, colour and music were extensively investigated in retail settings in the 1960s and 1970s. More recently, it has been claimed that McDonald's uses colour and image to manage the behaviour of patrons. Taste experiments have shown that the time of day, and also the speed of a meal, affect taste perceptions, and social context experiments reveal that the amount people eat increases with the number of people in a group.

Economic reports of the restaurant business appear frequently in the trade periodicals, but are generally limited in scope, are descriptive rather than analytical, and quickly become outdated. National statistics are offered by government publications in many countries, and deeper analyses of national data occasionally find their way into more permanent literature. No serious attention seems to have been paid to forecasting or to assessing the contribution of the restaurant business to local or national economies. Similarly, the geography of eating out seems to be a neglected area of research, apart from some work by Smith who analyzed restaurant location patterns in relation to geographical issues, such as the distribution of populations.

Social and anthropological studies have the potential to enrich consumer research in the food service industry by casting light on the individual experience that underlies consumer responses. Most studies have been more concerned with the societal effects of the industry, but a few researchers have used semiotics and discourse analysis to access consumers' deeper meanings. This approach may represent a way to understand perceptions of restaurant experiences.

In general, Johns and Pine see a need for studies to seek new techniques and to exchange ideas and perspectives between disciplines – particularly as many of the articles reviewed have been published outside the usual hospitality management journals. The eclectic approach of the review contributes in some measure to this process.

*Source*: Johns, N. and Pine, R. (2002) 'Consumer behavior in the food service industry: a review', *International Journal of Hospitality Management*, 21(2), 119–134.

## Secondary Research

Secondary data is data that already exists for an established purpose, and secondary research is also referred to as documents and desk research. It includes information collected from internal sources such as occupancy rates, sales figures, attendance figures, types of services sold, etc. In-house surveys can also be valuable sources of data. Data can be collected from external sources as well. Government agencies such as Visit Britain, The Australian Tourism Commission (ATC) or the Canadian Tourism Commission (CTC) compile statistics on visitor arrivals, how much they spend, where they are coming from, etc. As well as generating a considerable amount of statistical data at the macro level, government is also responsible for a number of tourism-related publications (*Tourism*, a journal published monthly by the CTC, is one example). Hotels, travel agents, tour operators and airlines all have associated trade bodies that compile information on their members and the market. The study that measured the impact of *Captain Corelli's Mandolin* on tourism in Cephalonia (see Snapshot below) used airport statistics to gauge the impact of the film on visitor arrivals.

The trade press can also provide a regular supply of information. Popular travel trade publications in various countries include *Travel Weekly* in the UK, *Tourism* in Canada and *Travel Trade* in the US. Research journals, periodicals, and special reports can be useful sources of information, as can conference papers, speeches and annual reports. A veritable explosion of new journals has been introduced as the outlet for academic publication of research in hospitality and tourism. A recent inventory, while neither exhaustive nor exclusive, yielded a count of 69, as listed in Table 4.4.

Searching the internet, while sometimes a time-consuming process, can also reveal other potential sources of information, as can chat groups and online newsletters. It is worth noting, however, that the accuracy of such information is not guaranteed, so checking the reliability of the source is important.

Collecting secondary data is more cost effective than acquiring the information from scratch. It may still be necessary to identify major gaps and fill them in by undertaking the required research, but using and incorporating information that already exists can save significant amounts of time and money. However, the major disadvantage of secondary data is that it does not always meet the specific requirements or objectives of a research project. Because it hasn't been collected specifically to address the problem being studied, it may not include everything that would be useful. Research from government reports may not break regional tourism statistics into precisely the units that are required, or it may have categories different from those that are really desired.

**Table 4.4**    An Inventory of Tourism and Hospitality Publications

| General Interest | Tourism | Food Service |
| --- | --- | --- |
| The Cornell Hotel & Restaurant Administration Quarterly | Annals of Tourism Research | Journal of Restaurant & Foodservice Marketing |
| International Journal of Hospitality Management | ACTA Turistica | Journal of Nutrition, Recipe and Menu Development |
| Journal of Hospitality and Tourism Research | Asia Pacific Journal of Tourism Research | Journal of College and University Foodservice |
| FIU Hospitality Review | Current Issues in Tourism | Journal of Foodservice Systems |
| Int'l Journal of Contemporary Hospitality Management | Event Tourism | Journal of Agricultural & Food Information |
| Journal of Quality Assurance in Hospitality & Tourism | Information Technology & Tourism | Journal of Nutrition for the Elderly |
| The Journal of Applied Hospitality Management | International Journal of Tourism Research | Journal of the American Dietetic Association |
| Australian Journal of Hospitality Management | Journal of Convention & Exhibition Management | NACUFS Journal (National Association of College & University Foodservices) |
| The Consortium Journal: Journal of HBCU | Journal of Ecotourism | School Foodservice Research Review |
| International Journal of Hospitality and Tourism Administration | Journal of Sports Tourism | Journal of Food Production Management |
| Praxis - The Journal of Applied Hospitality Management | Journal of Sustainable Tourism | Journal of Food Products Marketing |
| ANATOLIA | Journal of Travel Research | Journal of Foodservice Business Research |
| | Journal of Travel & Tourism Research | Journal of Culinary Science |
| Scandinavian Journal of Hospitality and Tourism | Journal of Vacation Marketing | |
| Tourism and Hospitality Research | Pacific Tourism Review | |
| Journal of Hospitality & Leisure for the Elderly | Teoros International | |
| Journal of Convention & Exhibition Management | Tourism Analysis | |
| Journal of Hospitality & Leisure Marketing | TOURISM: An International Interdisciplinary Journal | |
| Journal of Tourism and Hospitality Education | The Tourist Review | |
| Hotel & Motel Management | Tourism, Culture & Communication | |
| International Journal of Hospitality Information Technology | | |
| Journal of Gambling Studies | Tourism Economics | |
| Journal of Hospitality Financial Management | Tourism Geographies | |

**Table 4.4**  *(Continued)*

| General Interest | Tourism | Food Service |
|---|---|---|
| | Tourism Management | |
| | Tourism Recreation Research | |
| | Tourism Today | |
| | Tourismus Journal | |
| | Tourist Studies | |
| | Travel & Tourism Analyst | |
| | Journal of Teaching in Travel & Tourism | |
| | Journal of Human Resources in Hospitality & Tourism | |
| | Journal of Travel & Tourism Marketing | |
| | Journal of Tourism Studies | |
| | Tourism Intelligence Quarterly | |
| | Papers de Turisme | |

## Snapshot

### Measuring the Impact of *Captain Corelli's Mandolin* on Tourism in Cephalonia

Measuring the impact of a film on tourism is no easy task, but some destinations (like New Zealand after *Lord of the Rings*) have made attempts to quantify the effect that a film can have on visitor numbers. This study, undertaken by the author of this book, was an effort to measure the impact of *Captain Corelli's Mandolin* on tourism in the Greek island of Cephalonia. The film (based on a book by Louis de Bernières) was made over four months between May and September 2000 and many people came to watch the filming. Publicity shots featuring the two main stars (Nicolas Cage and Penelope Cruz) were flashed around the world, raising the island's profile considerably. The couple allegedly had an affair, generating even more publicity, and a local woman still advertises her apartment as the location for their rendezvous. Unfortunately, after filming, the set was destroyed and very little remains to remind visitors of the film.

When the film was released the following year, tourism numbers rose significantly with film tourists flocking to the island, especially from the UK. Spiros Galiatsatos, president of the Hotel Association of Cephalonia said at the time, 'The film is a good love story and it shows the weather, the culture, the people and locally produced goods such as Cephalonia meat pie. Everyone who has seen the film will expect to find us to be friendly and warm people.' Table 4.5 shows the number of arrivals according to airport statistics. In the year of filming (2000), visitor numbers to Cephalonia rose by 14 per cent, and in 2001 the island experienced a 16 per cent increase in charter traffic from over 137,000 to nearly 160,000. Numbers rose 6 per cent the following year; in 2003, arrivals remained the same. In 2004, visitor numbers fell nearly 9 per cent to 154,822. The rise in numbers from Britain immediately following the film was even more significant, with 2001 seeing a 22 per cent increase on the previous year to 143,063, and

**Table 4.5** Visitor Arrivals to Cephalonia, 1999–2004

| Origin of arrivals | 1999 | 2000 | 2001 | 2002 | 2003 | 2004 |
|---|---|---|---|---|---|---|
| Austria | 2998 | 2453 | 3186 | 2823 | 2314 | 2260 |
| Czech Republic | 2221 | 2608 | 2310 | 1781 | 4651 | 4348 |
| Germany | 1664 | 1008 | 1050 | 942 | 742 | – |
| Ireland | – | – | – | – | 2860 | 3212 |
| Italy | – | – | – | – | 132 | – |
| Netherlands | 1062 | 1479 | 1210 | 1059 | 1050 | 797 |
| Slovenia | 563 | 600 | 712 | 756 | 690 | 744 |
| Sweden | 3909 | 4589 | 4271 | 2863 | 1762 | – |
| Denmark | 1418 | 3174 | 1964 | – | – | – |
| Norway | – | 1558 | 1397 | – | – | – |
| Finland | 1766 | 2470 | – | – | – | – |
| United Kingdom | 104412 | 117375 | 143063 | 157171 | 154782 | 143461 |
| **Increase/Decrease** | – | **+12.4%** | **+22%** | **+10%** | **(1.52%)** | **(7.31%)** |
| Other | – | – | – | 1328 | – | – |
| **TOTAL** | **120013** | **137314** | **159163** | **168723** | **168983** | **154822** |
| **Increase/Decrease** | | **+14%** | **+16%** | **+6%** | **+0.15%** | **(8.88%)** |

a huge 37 per cent increase on numbers before filming took place. In 2002 numbers rose about 10 per cent, but then declined slightly in 2003. In 2004 UK visitor numbers fell another 7.3 per cent to 143,461, back to similar numbers for 2001.

In order to attribute the increase in tourism arrivals to the exposure that the book and film gave Cephalonia, it is important to examine the numbers in relation to arrivals for Greece as a whole. A comparison of Table 4.5 and Table 4.6 shows that in the year of the filming (2000), arrivals to Cephalonia from the UK increased by slightly less than for Greece overall. However, in 2001 there was a 16 per cent increase to Cephalonia compared to a 7.3 per cent increase to Greece. During that year, visitor numbers from the UK to Greece overall rose by 5.8 per cent compared to a 21 per cent increase in UK visitors to Cephalonia. In 2002, cuts in capacity were made by many of the big tour operators on the larger islands of Corfu, Zante, Crete and Rhodes; overall visitor numbers to Greece fell 0.8 per cent, and from the UK numbers rose just 1.7 per cent. Cephalonia, on the other hand, continued to do well, showing a 6 per cent increase in overall tourist numbers, and an increase of nearly 10 per cent from the UK. These statistics would seem to suggest that *Captain Correlli's Mandolin* had a significant effect on tourism arrivals for Cephalonia, particularly from the UK.

**Table 4.6** Arrivals to Greece (millions)

| | 1999 | 2000 | 2001 | 2002 | 2003 |
|---|---|---|---|---|---|
| UK Arrivals to Greece | 2.433 | 2.772 | 2.916 | 2.966 | 2.988 |
| **Increase/Decrease** | | **+14%** | **+5.8%** | **+1.7%** | **(.74)%** |
| Total Arrivals to Greece | 12.164 | 13.095 | 14.033 | 13.917 | 13.886 |
| **Increase/Decrease** | | **+7.6%** | **+7.3%** | **(0.8)%** | **(.22)%** |

*Source*: Hudson, S. and Ritchie, J.R.B. (2006) 'Film tourism and destination marketing: the case of *Captain Corelli's Mandolin*', *Journal of Vacation Marketing*, 12(3), 209–221.

## Primary Research

### Qualitative Research Techniques

The term 'qualitative' is used to describe research methods and techniques that use and give rise to subjective rather than empirical information. In general, the approach is to collect a great amount of 'rich' information from relatively few people. Potential purposes of qualitative research include developing hypotheses concerning relevant behaviour and attitudes; identifying the full range of issues, views and attitudes that should be pursued in large-scale research; and understanding how a buying decision is made. Qualitative research can be used in unstructured and structured situations.

### Unstructured Situations

Participative observation falls into this category, in which a tourism field researcher may adopt one of four different roles. The first is the 'complete participant', where the researcher becomes a genuine participant, and the second is the 'participant as observer', where researchers reveal their intentions. Third, 'observers as participants', also reveal themselves as researchers, and will participate in the normal social process, but make no pretence of being participants. The fourth type, 'the complete observer', simply observes without being involved. Just as Procter & Gamble researchers spend hours doing 'shop-alongs' in retail outlets to understand their customers, so do Las Vegas conduct 'tag-alongs' to observe the behaviour of visitors to the city (see Opening Vignette in Chapter 8).

Mystery shopping, the name given to participant observation in the commercial sector, has become a common market research technique in tourism and hospitality, and the Opening Vignette describes a mystery shopping research exercise to test travel agent recommendations in the UK. In the services context, mystery shopping provides information about the service experience as it unfolds, and helps to develop a richer knowledge of the experiential nature of services. One example of such a study is that by Boote and Mathews (1999), who were employed by Whitbread PLC to develop guidelines for the siting of middle-market restaurant outlets.[6] Part of their research involved participant observation of customers at lunchtime and in the evenings, so as to identify whether the actual clientele matched the intended market segment. Table 4.7 summarizes the various advantages and disadvantages of using this method of participative observation.

### Structured Situations

Qualitative research also permits more structured situations in which the researcher can play a more proactive role, although that role is more facilitative than directive. At the initial stages of tourism research, it may be necessary to follow up a conversation, and, if the research is intended to generate quantitative data, to develop items for scales to be used on a questionnaire. Hence, there is a need to identify clearly the constructs that inform the attitudes toward specific destinations, behaviours, or experiences that are being surveyed. One effective method of identifying these constructs is the **repertory grid technique**, which requires respondents to select from a group of three items. In this research process, the question posed to respondents is along the lines of 'looking at three destinations, which one do you think is different and why?' The object is to elicit the basis of comparison.

**Table 4.7** Advantages and Disadvantages of Covert Participative Observation or Mystery Shopping

| Advantages | Disadvantages |
|---|---|
| Offers deep insights into feelings and motivations behind service/practice (Palmer, 2000) | Raises ethical issues by observing people without their knowledge (Jorgenesen, 1989) |
| Experience is natural and not contrived for the sake of the observer (Boote and Mathews, 1999) | Based on assumptions that need to be made explicit and addressed (Savage, 2000) |
| Serves as a management tool for improving standards in customer service by providing actionable recommendations (Erstad, 1998; Cramp, 1994) | Information collected may be biased as a result of arbitrary or careless selection of observation periods, or the observers' own prejudices (Smith, 1995) |
| Ideal for investigating services (Crano and Brewer, 1986; Grove and Fisk, 1992) | In the long term, advantages for improving customer service can wear off if not integrated with other measures of service delivery process (Wilson, 1998) |
| Serves as a management tool for enhancing human resource management (Erstad, 1998) | Can be very costly and time–consuming (Grove and Fisk, 1992) |

The constructs underlying an attitude can be revealed in other ways, one of which is the use of **projection techniques**. These may be called 'what if?' techniques, as they get subjects to respond to hypothetical, or projected, situations. For example, subjects might be asked to indicate how they would spend a particular sum of money if given a free choice, or how they would spend additional leisure time if it were made available. Another projection technique is to show respondents a picture or cartoon representing a particular situation, and ask them to state what they think is actually happening or what one cartoon character is saying to another. The concept behind many of these projection techniques is that respondents tend to give socially acceptable answers in normal interviews, whereas if they answer for another character, they are able to project the unacceptable feelings that they may actually be experiencing. The techniques are based on Freudian psychoanalysis, which posits that anxiety is easily dealt with by the ego if it is projected and attributed to some external part of the respondent's world (Ryan, 1995).[7]

---

**REPERTORY GRID TECHNIQUE**
structured research technique that requires respondents to select from a group of three items

---

**PROJECTION TECHNIQUES**
called 'what if?' techniques, as they get subjects to respond to hypothetical, or projected, situations

The idea of interviewing groups of people together rather than individually is becoming increasingly popular in market research. In a **focus group**, the interviewer becomes the facilitator of a discussion rather than an interviewer as such, in order to obtain representative views of a wider population. A focus group is usually fairly homogeneous in nature and comprises eight to ten people. It is important that those selected have little experience of working in a focus group, as the researcher needs to obtain views representative of a wider population, not from expert 'opinion givers' who are used to the dynamics of such a group.

---

**FOCUS GROUP**

type of research in which the researcher acts as a facilitator to obtain views representative of a wider population; usually comprises eight to ten people

---

Ryan believes that the advantages of using focus groups for obtaining views arise from the social dynamics of the group, which he categorizes as being:

1. **synergism**. A wider range of ideas can result from a cumulative group effect, as opposed to individual interviews;
2. **snowballing**. One comment can elicit a whole range of additional confirmatory or modifying statements;
3. **security**. Focus groups can generate a social ease, reducing the insecurity or defensiveness that often arise in an interview situation;
4. **spontaneity**. It is likely that focus groups will elicit more spontaneous views; and
5. **stimulation**. The members of the group can stimulate each other to participate in group discussion.[8]

Focus groups are commonly used in commercial research, especially in the development and monitoring of advertising campaigns. They are beginning to be widely used in the world of tourism, and are often used for obtaining feedback on holiday brochures. Groups are asked to respond to the layout, pictures, text and typeface of brochures, to help companies find those that appeal most to various market niches.

**Virtual focus groups** are also becoming more common. Online 'chat' sessions, in which one to dozens of pre-recruited respondents type in responses to a guided online discussion, can be used effectively to bring together participants from virtually anywhere to discuss a client issue, activities and experiences, or provide feedback on products. While virtual focus groups cannot always replace in-person interviews, the time- and cost-saving benefits of such groups make them a very useful tool for researchers – especially for gathering website feedback from participants when they are using the internet.

---

**VIRTUAL FOCUS GROUPS**

online 'chat' sessions, in which one to dozens of pre-recruited respondents type in responses to a guided online discussion

---

**In-depth interviews** tend to be used for three main reasons. Firstly, they are used in situations where the limited number of subjects renders quantitative methods inappropriate. Secondly, they are used when information obtained from each subject is expected to vary considerably, i.e. when the question of 'what percentage of respondents said what' is not relevant. Thirdly, in-depth interviews can be used to explore a topic as a preliminary stage in planning a more formal questionnaire-based survey.

---

**IN-DEPTH INTERVIEW**
a qualitative research technique in which an interviewer will meet an interviewee for about 45 minutes to one hour

---

Interviews can be structured, unstructured, or a combination of the two. The unstructured interview differs from a conversation in the sense that both parties are aware of an agenda of question and answer. The structured interview involves a number of skills on the part of the researcher. For example, questionnaire-drafting skills, such as determining the sequence of questions and their precise content, are key. Other required skills are the interpersonal skills involved in conversation and being able to 'lead' the interviewee. Also, the researcher must develop the skills of recording responses accurately; very often, interviews are taped and a word-for-word transcription is prepared.

There are various ways of going about the analysis of interview transcripts, but it is imperative that the researcher returns to the terms of reference and statement of objectives and begins to evaluate the information gathered in relation to the questions posed. Recently, a variety of computer packages have become available to analyse interview transcripts.

### Quantitative Research Techniques

Traditionally, most consumer research studies have been based on questions identified in market decision-making, to be posed to random samples of existing or potential customers. The Case Study at the end of this chapter is typical of such research. This study found that many services were not meeting customer expectations. These findings are quantifiable dimensions that can be used for future decision-making. This is quantitative research, meaning a study to which numerical estimates can be attached. Quantitative research is usually based on 'structured' questionnaires, in which every respondent is asked the same questions. Because the range of possible answers is printed on questionnaires, variations to suit individual respondents are not possible.

However, quantitative data can also be collected via observations, as in the Opening Vignette. Some researchers believe that this is one of the most effective ways to gain knowledge about consumers. Tracking studies, for example, are used in museums, galleries and tourist attractions to monitor people's activities. These provide information on what people do, the amount of time they spend on various activities, and the order in which they do things. Other types of observation include counting the number of people in a dining room at various times of the day, counting the number of cars in the parking lot, counting the number of people entering a casino, and even seeing which way people move through a museum or an art gallery.

### The Questionnaire or Survey Method

A review of the methods used in collecting tourism and hospitality research data shows that the questionnaire technique or survey method is the most frequently used. The survey method includes factual surveys, opinion surveys, or interpretive surveys, all of which can be conducted by personal interview, telephone, mail, or by electronic means.

**Factual surveys** are by far the most beneficial. 'When you are on holiday, what activities do you engage in?' is a question to which respondents should be able to give an accurate response. In an **opinion survey**, the respondent is asked to express an opinion or make an evaluation or appraisal. In **interpretive surveys**, the respondent acts as an interpreter as well as a reporter. Subjects are asked why they chose a certain course of action – why they chose a particular package, for example. While respondents can reply accurately to 'what' questions, they often have difficulty replying to 'why' questions. Therefore, while interpretive research may give a researcher a feel for consumer behaviour, the usefulness of the results tends to be limited.

---

**FACTUAL SURVEY**
the respondent is asked to state certain facts, such as age or number of children

---

**OPINION SURVEY**
the respondent is asked to express an opinion or make an evaluation or appraisal

---

**INTERPRETIVE SURVEY**
the respondent acts as an interpreter as well as a reporter

---

Personal interviews tend to be much more flexible than either mail or telephone surveys because the interviewer can adapt to the situation and the respondent; therefore, much more information can be obtained. A major limitation of the personal interview method, however, is its relatively high cost. An interview takes a considerable amount of time, and there is always the possibility of personal interviewer bias. Telephone surveys are conducted much more rapidly and at less cost; however, these interviews tend to be less flexible, and they also have to be brief. Computer-assisted telephone interviewing using random dialling is very popular in North America. Mail surveys involve mailing the questionnaire to carefully selected sample respondents and requesting them to return them completed. Advantages are that a large geographical area can be covered, respondents can fill out the survey at their own convenience, and personal interview bias is absent. The greatest problems with mail surveys are the lack of good lists and lack of adequate response.

Finally, a relatively new way of conducting research is the use of electronic surveys that ask consumers questions and immediately record and tabulate the results. Computer-type electronic equipment might be placed in a hotel lobby, mall, or other high-traffic location (for example, Whistler Resort collects data from its skiers using electronic devices placed up and down the main street). Alternatively, respondents may be asked to complete a survey online. Internet-based survey methodology is gaining increasing popularity (see Chapter 10 for information related to online research).

*Questionnaire Design*

The value of a survey questionnaire depends on its design. As there are so many ways in which a questionnaire can be formulated it is difficult to develop a set of rules for doing so. Each one is unique. Consequently, the design of questionnaires has been referred to as an art that is influenced by the researcher's knowledge of the population, the subject matter, common sense, experience and pilot work.

According to Crouch (1986), questionnaires have four main purposes:[9]

1. to collect relevant data. When drafting each question, the researcher should always ask, 'What use will the answers be?' This relates back to the definition and purpose of the research, but also tests whether the question is phrased so as to produce the desired information.
2. to make data comparable. The wording of the questions and alternative answers should be clear and not open to more than one interpretation. The language employed should be simple so that it can be understood by all respondents. Sentences should be kept short and to the point. Carrying out a pilot survey on a small sample is useful for detecting any ambiguities.
3. to minimize bias. The phrasing of questions can bias the response given. For example, if a question begins with, 'You don't think, do you…?', a negative response is likely to be given, and if a question begins with, 'Shouldn't something be done about…?', a positive response is the likely outcome. Care should be taken to avoid wording questions that lead respondents to feel that one answer will be regarded as more acceptable than others.
4. to motivate the respondent. The respondent must be made to feel that answering the question will be interesting, useful and not time consuming. If the questionnaire is too long, this can be demoralizing for the interviewer and respondent, thus affecting both refusal rates and the quality of the data. The survey should begin with interesting questions, not with requests for personal details like, 'How much do you earn?' These questions can be placed at the end of the questionnaire.

Traditionally, travel research has been conducted in-house, which is a reflection of both narrow profit margins and an ignorance of the benefits that skilled independent researchers can offer. The result has been a proliferation of amateurishly designed questionnaires, many of which can be found in hotel rooms or which are given to tourists on charter planes on the return journey home. There is also a tendency to distribute questionnaires to as many clients as possible, without worrying too much about what percentage will respond and whether there will be any built-in response bias among respondents. Furthermore, there has been very little research on the validity or accuracy of questionnaire data used in leisure and tourism studies. One study found that in a survey of tennis participation, respondents exaggerated their level of participation by as much as 100 per cent. This suggests that the researcher and the user of research results should always bear in mind the nature and source of the data. Questionnaire surveys rely on information from respondents, and what respondents say depends on their own powers of recall, on their honesty, and, fundamentally, on the questions asked of them.

The Global Spotlight below highlights how EuroDisney failed to ask the right questions before opening the French theme park. Researchers failed to collect relevant data and simply didn't understand the needs of both domestic tourists and those travelling from other parts of Europe.

## Global Spotlight

### Lack of Research Contributes to EuroDisney Disaster

After the resounding success of Disney's first foreign expansion in Tokyo, where the US theme park was transplanted in its entirety, the Paris experiment was initially an unprecedented disaster – partly due to ethno-centrism, partly due to insufficient cultural research and partly to competition and adverse world economic conditions.

EuroDisney first opened in April 1992, right in the middle of a European recession which had been burgeoning since the end of the 1980s. Disney underestimated the economic results of this for tourists, aiming prices too high for both hotel accommodation and holiday packages. It had been banking on averages of three-day stays, whereas in reality Europeans were more likely to consider the theme park a one-day experience. Disney had projected it would attract 11 million visitors, generating over US$100 million in its first year in Paris. By summer 1994, however, it had lost more than $900 million since opening. Visitor numbers were drastically down and so was spending on related purchases. This less than enthusiastic response to what French people saw as 'American imperialism' was due to a litany of errors in research, planning and implementation. One of the first problems was lack of sufficient understanding of the customer.

Early advertising campaigns, which focused on 'glitz' and 'size' rather than the variety of rides and attractions, were unsuccessful in persuading visits by the French, initially predicted to make up 50 per cent of the attendance figures. After the first year, a park services consulting firm summed the problem up as a widespread scorn for American fairytale characters in a land that already had its own cartoon favourites, such as Asterix, saying, 'The French see EuroDisney as American imperialism – plastics at its worst.' Right from the outset, Paris theatre director Ariane Mnouchkine had slated the theme park as a 'cultural Chernobyl'.

When researchers tried to understand why tourists were not visiting during the summer of 1992, they discovered that due to the combination of transatlantic airfare wars, currency movements and domestic economic recession, it was actually cheaper to go to Disney World in Orlando than on an equivalent trip to Paris. Why would tourists flock to the new, smaller park when they could just as easily go to the home of Disney with all its other facilities, plus guaranteed sunshine and beautiful beaches – and why did researchers not consider this? Moreover, the Gulf War put the brakes on travel during 1991, and in 1992 the Olympics in Barcelona was heavy competition for the beleaguered Paris park.

There were many other miscalculations in the early stages of the Paris project. The original ban on alcohol at the park had to be lifted due to public demand, as no self-respecting French person could contemplate lunch without a glass of wine. Personal grooming rules also had to be bent to accommodate staff demands; pets had to be accommodated as the French routinely take dogs and even cats on their road holidays. Other errors were made in the way visitors could book their Disney vacations. Reservations started out as direct bookings made by telephone or by internet. This alienated British tourists who usually book holidays via travel agencies. Disney also expected European tourists to change their travel habits for their park. Traditionally, French tourists travel in August during a one-month vacation period, when factories and offices shut down; the British take two weeks sometime between the end of July and the first week of September. Disney predicted erroneously that both nationalities would take their children out of school for shorter periods outside the main vacation.

The biggest changes in the fortunes of EuroDisney came after the appointment in 1993 of a Frenchman, Philippe Bourguignon, as CEO. He took over financial negotiations and implemented wide-ranging improvements in marketing. In particular, he changed marketing tactics to separate national identities throughout Europe. Individual marketing offices were opened in several capital cities in order to tailor campaigns to each national identity, taking into account cultural expectations. He also inaugurated price cuts, reducing park admission by 20 per cent and cutting hotel room rates by some 30 per cent.

Bourguignon spearheaded special promotional rates for the most inclement winter months. And he focused attention on an authentic Disney day out rather than on longer-stay packages. In October 1994 the park's name was changed to Disneyland Paris to help focus on the American aspects of the experience, rather than the European. Lessons were learnt regarding food, weather fluctuations, language facilities, and continental cultural variations. Small details reflected attempts to get things right the second time around, such as providing covered seating to take into account the rainfall, and a wider selection of different ethnic foods.

Sources: Roberts, K. (8 August 2004) 'Less a sleeping beauty, more a rude awakening at EuroDisney', *The Independent on Sunday*, Business, 6; Amine, L.S. (2006) 'The not-so-wonderful world of EuroDisney – things are better now at Paris Disneyland', *International Marketing*, 620–623.

**Benchmarking** is essentially a management technique that allows companies to compare how well they are performing relative to their competitors. To date, the application of benchmarking within tourism and hospitality industries has been confined mainly to hotels (Kozak and Rimmington, 1999).[10] Benchmarking initiatives might include collecting guest satisfaction scores. For Sheraton Hotels and Resorts, measuring guest satisfaction is a crucial part of marketing research, and plays an important role in internal marketing. Guest satisfaction scores (GSS) are closely monitored by the research group, and results are shared with all hotels and all employees. To measure satisfaction, Sheraton Hotels has commissioned NFO Worldwide Group to send out a questionnaire to every customer who stays in a Sheraton property in North America.

---

**BENCHMARKING**

a management technique that allows companies to compare how well they are performing relative to their competitors

---

## Sampling

Because of the expenses associated with research, marketing managers often find themselves grappling with the question of how many people must be surveyed in order to obtain accurate responses. It is almost impossible – and not very cost effective – to interview every product user or potential product user. Therefore, a company's decisions are based on the opinions and reactions of a sample of the population.

The sample selection process is as follows:

1. **Defining the population**. The first stage in the sampling process is specification of the target population.
2. **Specifying the sample frame**. This is a specification of the listing, directory, or roster from which the sample will be chosen.
3. **Selecting the sampling method**. The researcher has to decide whether a probability or non-probability approach will be applied to draw the sample, and exactly how the sample members will be selected. There is a wide range of both probability and non-probability sampling methods. The key difference between the two is that in probability sampling, a statistical evaluation of sampling error can be undertaken; such an assessment is not possible for samples drawn by non-probabilistic methods. Therefore the more accurate form of sampling is the probability method, in which each unit of the population has a known, but not necessarily an equal, chance of selection. Techniques subsumed within this method are simple, random, systematic, stratified, cluster, multi-phase, and area sampling.
4. **Determining sample size**. The selection of sample size has received considerable attention from critics of tourism research. Baker et al. (1994) suggest that there are two basic approaches for the tourism researcher interested in accountability and efficiency: required size per cell and the traditional statistical model.[11] The required size per cell approach requires approximately 30 responses for each demographic cell of data. For example, two genders, four ethnic groups, and four age groups would require a sample

size of 960 ($2 \times 4 \times 4 \times 30$). The traditional statistical model is based on a management specification of allowable error (e), the level of confidence in the sampling process (z), and the variance in the population (@). The sampling size is thus expressed as: $n = z@/e$. One important aspect of the traditional statistical method of sample size determination is that the sample must be randomly selected; every member of the population of interest must have a known chance of being selected. This is a key to eliminating systematic bias. Another important point is that if questionnaire respondents are all basically alike, a small sample size is required, no matter how large the population. This is often a fundamentally difficult concept for researchers and managers alike to accept. Sample size is not a function of population size: it is a function of population variance. Large-scale data collection is very costly, and quite often not needed.

5. **Drawing the sample and collecting the data**. The final stage in the sampling process is the implementation stage, in which the sample is chosen and surveyed.

The sampling procedure adopted will have a direct impact on the validity of the results, so if the survey is to be the principal tool for data collection, careful consideration must be given to the technique employed and the sample size chosen.

## Common Research Errors

There are many potential pitfalls in conducting research; the most common four errors are discussed here.

### Not Including Enough Qualitative Information

Most surveys reported in trade magazines provide descriptive information. For example, an American Express survey of business people in 2002 reported that business travellers were using more online booking tools to make travel arrangements. However, to use this information, tourism suppliers and intermediaries need to know specifically what online tools these business travellers are using, what they believe is an effective website, how long they stay online per transaction, etc. All these questions could be asked in face-to-face interviews or in focus groups with business travellers.

### An Improper Use of Sophisticated Statistical Analysis

It is possible for a multitude of errors to creep into the research process if collection, tabulation, and analysis are not done properly. In today's environment, tabulation is likely to take place on the computer; a number of excellent packages are available for this purpose. However, statistical conclusions must be interpreted in terms of the best action or policy for the organization to follow. This reduction of the interpretation to recommendations is one of the most difficult tasks in the research process.

## Failure to Have a Sample That Is Representative of the Population

A sample is a segment of the population selected to represent the population as a whole. Ideally, the sample should be representative, so that the researcher can make accurate estimates of the thoughts and behaviours of the wider population. In the end-of-chapter Case Study, the objective was to measure the service quality perceived by skiers, and the sample of skiers was drawn from the population of bookings taken for the upcoming winter season. A representative sample was chosen in terms of accommodation types and resorts in order to increase both the reliability and validity of the research programme.

## Problems with Interpretation

In many cases, results from research can be interpreted the wrong way. The end-of-chapter Case Study shows how managers can interpret the results in different ways. The results showed that there was no statistical difference between the four measurements of service quality and therefore one could assume any of them could be used to measure satisfaction. Such a finding would enable managers to employ the most straightforward test of satisfaction, so there would be justification in measuring performance only. But although the perceptions format offers the most predictive power – a finding that has consistently emerged in the literature – it offers little diagnostic potential and, indeed, may result in inappropriate priorities being established.

## Effective Use of Marketing Research in Decision-making

There is little doubt that in an industry as dynamic and expansive as tourism, research must play a critical role in its development. Not only should research be undertaken by every organization, whether large or small, to assist in the task of practical decision-making at a strategic level, but it should also be acknowledged as important at the academic level for its shedding of valuable light on the development of tourism on a global basis. For research to be worthwhile, it has to be acted upon. A good example of a company successfully using the results of marketing research is the Marriott Corporation (Lovelock and Wirtz, 2007).[12] When they were designing a new chain of hotels for business travellers (which eventually became known as Courtyard by Marriott) they sampled 601 consumers using a sophisticated technique known as conjoint analysis, which asks respondents to make trade-offs between different groupings of attributes. The objective was to determine which mix of attributes at specific prices offers them the highest degree of utility, so they were asked to indicate on a five-point scale how likely they were to stay at a hotel with certain features, given a specific room price per night. Features included room fixtures, food-related services, leisure facilities and other services.

The research yielded detailed guidelines for the selection of almost 200 features and service elements, representing those attributes that provided the highest utility for the customers in the target segments, at prices they were willing to pay. After testing the concept under real-world conditions, the company subsequently developed a large chain that filled a gap in the market with a product that represented the best balance between the price customers were prepared to pay and the physical and service features they most desired.

Research is never an exact science, but it can reduce the margins of error to which hunches on their own are subject. The feasibility study, for example, is an essential prerequisite to any new project, whether it is the launch of a new company, the introduction of a new logo, or the development of a new product. The Opening Vignette in Chapter 13 provides an interesting example of a hotel company conducting research online to test a new prototype hotel concept.

Above all, the success of research will be contingent on three conditions:

1. sufficient resources must be allocated to do the job properly, both in terms of time and money;
2. managers must be willing to believe the results of the research when they become available, even if they conflict with the management's own preconceived views;
3. the results should be used. All too frequently, research is commissioned in order to avoid making an immediate decision. Expensively commissioned research is then left to gather dust in a drawer instead of being used to enable managers to make better decisions on the future direction of the company.

---

## Chapter Summary

The way in which an organization gathers, uses and disseminates its research in the marketing context is generally referred to as the Marketing Information System (MIS). A key component of the MIS is the marketing research process: the systematic and objective search for and analysis of information relevant to the identification and solution of any problem in the field of marketing.

In undertaking research, these steps should be followed: identify and define the problem; investigate available sources; develop the research plan; collect data; analyse data; and present research results. There are several approaches to collecting data, but two key decisions that have to be made are whether to use primary or secondary data and whether to use qualitative or quantitative research. The sample selection process is as follows: define the population; specify the sample frame; select the sampling method; determine sample size; draw the sample and collect the data. There are many potential pitfalls in conducting research. The most common four errors are not including enough qualitative information; an improper use of sophisticated statistical analysis; failure to have a sample that is representative of the population; and problems with interpretation. The success of research will be contingent on three conditions: sufficient resources must be allocated to do the job properly, both in terms of time and money; managers must be willing to believe the results of the research when they become available; and the results should be used.

## Key Terms

benchmarking, p. 135
competitor intelligence, p. 116
consumer research, p. 116
factual survey, p. 131
focus group, p. 129
in-depth interview, p. 130
interpretive survey, p. 131
marketing information system (MIS), p. 113
marketing research, p. 113
opinion survey, p. 131
primary data, p. 119
projection techniques, p. 128
qualitative research, p. 120
quantitative research, p. 120
repertory grid technique, p. 128
secondary data, p. 119
virtual focus groups, p. 129

## Discussion Questions and Exercises

1. Do some research and find an example of a local tourism or hospitality organization that has recently published research results. How have they used the results for decision-making?
2. If you owned a high-class restaurant and wanted to improve the level of service offered by your staff, how could observational research help you accomplish your goal?
3. How does secondary data differ from primary data, and what are the main sources of tourism secondary data in your country?
4. Differentiate between qualitative and quantitative research and give specific examples of how each could be used by a hotel.
5. How would a tour operator go about collecting competitor intelligence on the success of tours in the Far East?
6. As marketing research manager for a large destination-marketing organization, how might you use focus groups to collect information?

## How was the Skiing? Finding the Best Way to Measure Service Quality

Service quality in the tourism industry receives increasing attention in the literature and yet confusion still exists as to which measure offers the greatest validity. The two main research instruments are Importance Performance Analysis (IPA) and SERVQUAL. IPA is a procedure that shows the relative **importance** of various attributes, and the **performance** of the firm, product or destination under study in providing these attributes. **SERVQUAL**, on the other hand, focuses on the notion of perceived quality and is based on the difference between consumers' expectations and perceptions of service. However, both measures have been questioned and some researchers have suggested a better measure of service quality is one that multiplies SERVQUAL by importance, or one that measures just performance (SERVPERF). This case reports on a research project that assessed these four main methods of measuring customer service quality.

The data was obtained in co-operation with a ski tour operator who was interested in measuring the service quality it provided to its skiers. Since the focus of the study was on aspects of the package holiday that were within direct control, or at least, zone of influence of the tour operator, a team of managers from seven different departments – operations, overseas, product, reservations and agency sales, customer services, marketing and purchasing – was asked to brainstorm each individual aspect of the holiday that the

Skiers and Boarders at Lake Louise, Canada

**Table 4.8** Comparisons Between Expectation and Performance in Holiday Dimensions (SERVQUAL)

| Dimensions of the Holiday | Expectations | | Performance | | Pair-Wise t-test | |
|---|---|---|---|---|---|---|
| Experience | Mean | Std Dev | Mean | Std Dev | t-value | p-value |
| 1. Brochure | 4.254 | .438 | 3.742 | .575 | -10.88 | .000 |
| 2. Waiting to go | 4.144 | .427 | 3.640 | .715 | -9.35 | .000 |
| 3. Journey | 3.849 | .428 | 3.358 | .464 | -12.20 | .000 |
| 4. Meeting the Rep | 4.082 | .515 | 3.894 | .811 | -2.80 | .006 |
| 5. Transfer to Accommodation | 3.811 | .563 | 3.471 | .759 | -4.93 | .000 |
| 6. Arrival at Accommodation | 3.767 | .521 | 3.582 | .871 | -2.46 | .015 |
| 7. Accommodation | 3.994 | .416 | 3.645 | .719 | -5.86 | .000 |
| 8. Welcome | 4.053 | .442 | 3.700 | .882 | -4.95 | .000 |
| 9. Resort Activities | 4.009 | .472 | 3.634 | .600 | -7.11 | .000 |
| 10. Skiing/Snowboarding | 4.230 | .493 | 4.208 | .538 | -.43 | .666 |
| 11. Company Magazine | 3.250 | .938 | 2.963 | 1.443 | -2.38 | .018 |
| 12. Departure | 3.954 | .484 | 3.784 | .830 | -2.41 | .017 |
| 13. Transfer to Airport | 4.120 | .584 | 3.912 | .919 | -2.59 | .011 |

customer might experience with the company. The resulting 146 elements were divided into 13 different dimensions reflecting various aspects of the holiday experience, from receiving the holiday brochure through to contact with company after returning home (see Table 4.8).

One month before they went on holiday, customers were asked to complete a first questionnaire asking them:

1. **What is important to you?** This asked respondents to rate, on a five-point Likert scale (ranging from extremely important to not at all important), 146 elements of their holiday. These elements represented the complete service delivery chain and included the usefulness of the brochure, getting to the airport, flights, representative, resort, accommodation and contacts with the tour operator at home.
2. **What are your expectations?** Respondents were then asked to rate, on a five-point Likert scale (ranging from definitely expected to definitely not expected), the same 146 elements of their holiday. In a second questionnaire *towards the end* of their holiday, respondents were asked:
3. **How did you find it?** This questionnaire asked respondents to rate, on a five-point Likert scale (ranging from strongly agree to strongly disagree), the same elements of their holiday as measured in points 1 and 2 above.

The sample was drawn from the bookings taken for the upcoming winter season. Customers from all over the UK were asked in writing if they would like to participate in the panel and offered a £100 travellers' cheque for participating. A total of 250 people were asked to participate in the study and the response rate was 88 per cent. When the respondents had completed the questionnaires, a service quality score was calculated for each question, using the following four formulas:

**Case Study**

1.   *Performance (P) minus Importance (I)*
2.   *Performance (P) minus Expectations (E)*
3.   *Performance (P) minus Expectations (E) multiplied by Importance (I)*
4.   *Performance (P) only*

Data was analysed and a service quality score was calculated for each dimension of the holiday experience. Table 4.8 compares the mean scores for expectations and performance (SERVQUAL), and the results clearly show a negative service gap in all dimensions. To analyse IPA, a two-dimensional action grid was plotted (see Figure 4.3), where importance values form the vertical axis, while performance values form the horizontal axis. Figure 4.3 identifies where each of the 13 dimensions fall in terms of the four quadrants. Significantly, the largest number of dimensions (eight) fell into the 'Concentrate Here' (quadrant A) area of the action grid. Respondents rated these attributes high in importance but low in performance. These dimensions were the brochure; waiting to go; meeting the rep; transfer to accommodation; accommodation; resort activities; departure; and transfer to the airport.

Service quality scores were then calculated whereby the SERVQUAL gap was multiplied by importance. Finally the results of performance only (SERVPERF) were analysed in order to compare with the other three formulas. Table 4.9 shows how each service quality dimension ranks according to the four models. It is interesting to note that factoring in importance actually makes little difference to the SERVQUAL rankings (the ranking of only four dimensions changes). The results of calculating performance only (SERVPERF) appear to produce very different rankings to the IPA, most noticeably for the

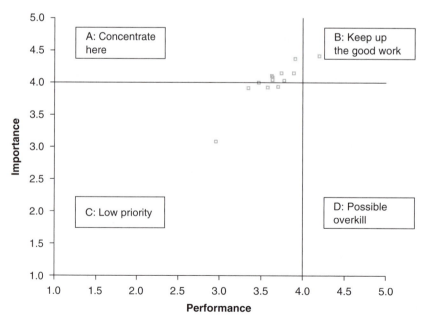

**Figure 4.3**   Importance-Performance Grid with Ratings for Holiday Dimensions

**Table 4.9**    Ranking Service Quality Dimensions According to the Four Models (1 = top service quality score; 13 = lowest service quality score)

| Ranking | SERVQUAL (P-E) | IPA (P-I) | SERVQUAL X Importance (P-E)(I) | SERVPERF P only |
|---|---|---|---|---|
| 1 | Skiing/ snowboarding | Company magazine | Skiing/ snowboarding | Skiing/snowboarding |
| 2 | Departure | Skiing/ snowboarding | Departure | Transfer to airport |
| 3 | Arrival at accommodation | Welcome | Arrival at accommodation | Meeting the rep |
| 4 | Meeting the rep | Meeting the rep | Transfer to airport | Departure |
| 5 | Transfer to airport | Departure | Meeting the rep | Brochure |
| 6 | Company magazine | Arrival at accommodation | Company magazine | Welcome |
| 7 | Transfer to accommodation | Accommodation | Transfer to accommodation | Waiting to go |
| 8 | Accommodation | Brochure | Welcome | Accommodation |
| 9 | Welcome | Transfer to airport | Accommodation | Resort activities |
| 10 | Resort activities | Waiting to go | Resort activities | Arrival at accommodation |
| 11 | Journey | Resort Activities | Journey | Transfer to accommodation |
| 12 | Waiting to go | Transfer to accommodation | Waiting to go | Journey |
| 13 | Brochure | Journey | Brochure | Company magazine |

company magazine, which is ranked highest using IPA, but lowest using SERVPERF. Similarly, SERVPERF and SERVQUAL formulas produce differing ranks for each of the dimensions, although respondents show a reasonably high level of satisfaction with the overall level of performance. Yet, despite the many differences in rankings, the dimension skiing/snowboarding is ranked in the top two by all four tests, while the journey is ranked in the bottom three by all the tests.

As would be expected, SERVQUAL and IPA produced different rankings for each of the holiday dimensions. According to SERVQUAL, the largest gaps can be found in the brochure, waiting to go and the journey. Customers ranked the skiing, the departure arrangements and the arrival at accommodation as the top three in service quality. IPA, on the other hand, suggested that the biggest service quality problems were to be found in the journey, transfer to accommodation and resort activities, with the smallest gaps being for the magazine, the skiing and the welcome. Despite some differences in ranking, further statistical analysis revealed no significant differences between the four methodologies used for calculating service quality.

## Questions

1. What do these results suggest? Is there a best way to measure service quality?
2. What are the managerial implications of this research?
3. Should anything be done about the company magazine?
4. What are the limitations of this research?

*Source*: Hudson, S., Hudson, P. and Miller, G.A. (2004) 'The measurement of service quality in the UK tour operating sector: A methodological comparison', *Journal of Travel Research*, 42(3), 305–312.

## Websites

www.sheraton.com — Sheraton Hotels and Resorts
www.sheratonsuites.com — Sheraton Suites Calgary Eau Claire
www.cartondonofrio.com — Carton Donofrio Partners Inc.
www.ionian-islands.com/kefalonia — Destination website for Cephalonia
www.disneylandparis.com — Disneyland Resort Paris

## References

1  Gerhold, P. (1993) 'Defining marketing (or is it market?) research', *Marketing Research*, 5(Fall), 6–7.
2  Kinnear, T., Taylor, J., Johnson, L. and Armstrong, R. (1993) *Australian Marketing Research*. Sydney, Australia: McGraw-Hill.
3  Green, P., Tull, D. and Albaum, A. (1988) *Research for Marketing Decisions*. Englewood Cliffs, NJ: Prentice-Hall.
4  McIntosh, R.W., Goeldner, C.R. and Ritchie, J.R.B. (1995). *Tourism: Principles, Practices, Philosophies*. New York: Wiley.
5  Burkeman, O. (23 August 2006) 'Extreme dining', *The Guardian*, 6–9.
6  Boote, J. and Mathews, A. (1999) 'Saying is one thing; doing is another: the role of observation in marketing research', *Qualitative Market Research: An International Journal*, 2(1), 15–21.
7  Ryan, C. (1995) *Researching Tourist Satisfaction: Issues, Concepts, Problems*. London: Routledge.
8  Ibid.
9  Crouch, S. (1986) *Marketing Research for Managers*. London: Heinemann.
10  Kozak, M. and Rimmington, M. (1999) 'Measuring tourist destination competitiveness: conceptual considerations and empirical findings', *Hospitality Management*, 18, 273–283.
11  Baker, K.J., Hozier, G.C., Jr. and Rogers, R.D. (1994) 'Marketing research theory and methodology and the tourism industry: a nontechnical discussion', *Journal of Travel Research*, 32(3), 3–7.
12  Lovelock and Wirtz (2007, 6th Edition) Services Marketing. New York: Prentice Hall.

# 5

# THE TOURISM AND HOSPITALITY PRODUCT

## Concorde: A Journey Through the Product Life Cycle

At a cost of US$12,000 per round trip, passengers used to be able to travel at supersonic Mach 2 speed, in the company of superstars and royalty, from London to New York in less than 3 ½ hours. Since the demise of Concorde in 2003, however, emphasis has been on size rather than speed and on low-cost aviation rather than premium pricing.

After 27 years, the legendary needle-nosed, delta-winged product of 1960s technology was finally grounded and the 14-strong fleet donated to museums around the world. The end of this supersonic aviation era was caused by a combination of soaring repair costs, declining global economy, rising fuel costs, confidence failure after a tragic crash in Paris in 2000 which killed 113 and the resultant downturn in bookings.

Concorde was first launched, amidst both acclaim and criticism, in Toulouse, France in March 1969. It broke the sound barrier for the first time in October the same year. Eight years later, the first commercial flights began from London and Paris to New York. After that, only 20 models were built despite initial overseas orders for 200, because of high fuel and maintenance costs and noise protests from the environmental lobby.

By building Concorde, with its famous Rolls-Royce Snecma Olympus 593 engines (the most powerful jet engines in commercial use), Europe gambled on speed. It also targeted wealthy passengers, indulging stars of music and film, diplomats and top businessmen, with the finest champagne and caviar during their trans-Atlantic crossings. At the same time, having failed to make their own reliable supersonic rival, the Americans opted for size, which, in the long term, has proved to be the winner.

From the outset, Concorde differentiated itself in its appearance (both beautiful and useful), its high pricing, its unmatched speed and its luxury. Appealing to the rich and famous, it featured in the media constantly

Concorde differentiated itself in its appearance

throughout its 27-year reign. Pop star Phil Collins performed for the Live Aid concert in London in 1985, then jumped on the Concorde and resumed his globally televised act in Philadelphia a few hours later. Allying itself with such larger-than-life characters, whose lives are assiduously followed in all the glossy media magazines, Concorde became a household name synonymous with prosperity, fame and technological innovation.

Concorde's death knoll was presaged by a fatal crash in Paris in 2000, which led to all planes being withdrawn for 15 months to be refitted at a cost in excess of US$36 million. Subsequently, Concorde was unable to lure back passengers in sufficient numbers.

Aviation today is being taken over by slower, roomier, steadier aircraft. The latest jet on the runway is the Airbus 380, a double-decker for 555 passengers, with sleeper cabins, crew quarters and business centres.

*Sources*: Wallace, B. (24 October 2003) 'Concorde era on final approach', *Calgary Herald*, A3; Stokes, D. (10 October 2003) 'Farewell Concorde and thanks for the pearl caviar spoon', *National Post*, A5; Bertin, O. (11 April 2003) 'The Concorde: first the boom, now the bust', *Globe and Mail*, A1 & A9; Fitzgerald, J. (2 October 2003) 'Thrill Seekers Pack Concorde', *Globe and Mail*, A7; Webster, B. (10 April 2003) 'Concorde may be retired by year-end', *Calgary Herald*, A17.

## Introduction

The Opening Vignette provides a classic example of the journey of one tourism product – Concorde – through the product life cycle, one of the most basic product analysis tools. This chapter begins by introducing the peculiarities of the tourism product and the idea that **tourism and hospitality products** are a selected group of components or elements brought together in a 'bundle' to satisfy needs and wants. The next section looks at the three levels of tourism products – the core product, the tangible product, and the augmented product – and these product levels are then applied to theme parks. Product planning is the focus of the next section, which begins by describing the five basic market/product options, and then discusses the usefulness of a features/benefits analysis. A critique of the product life cycle model is then followed by a discussion of various positioning strategies available to organizations in the tourism and hospitality fields. An in-depth analysis of branding in tourism is supported by a case discussing the growth of chefs as brands. The next section gives attention to the concept of packaging, and the final part of the chapter looks at new product development and the various theoretical stages a company can follow in developing a new product or service.

> **TOURISM AND HOSPITALITY PRODUCTS**
> a group of selected components or elements brought together in a 'bundle' to satisfy needs and wants

Product decisions, with all their implications for the management of tourism and hospitality operations, influence not only the marketing mix, but also a firm's long-term growth strategy and its policies for investment and human resources. Product specifications largely determine the corporate image and branding an organization is able to create in the minds of its existing and prospective customers (Middleton and Clarke, 2001).[1] Tourism constitutes such a wide span of products that it has to be considered in terms of sectors rather than as a single industry, as discussed in Chapter 1. These sectors include accommodations, attractions, transportation, travel organizers and destination organizations, among others (see Figure 1.6). This diversity is matched by an even greater diversity of component features specific to each tourism product sector, which need to be considered and managed in providing individual products for particular markets. The conceptualization of tourism and hospitality products as a group of selected components or elements brought together in a 'bundle' to satisfy needs and wants is a vital image for marketing managers.

From the standpoint of a potential customer considering any form of tourist visit, the product may be defined as a bundle or package of tangible and intangible components, based on activity at a destination. The package is perceived by the tourist as an experience that is available for a price. There are five main components in the overall product: destination attractions and environment; destination facilities and services; accessibility of the destination; images of the destination; and price (ibid).[2] Although these components are combined and integrated in the visitor's overall experience, they are capable of extensive and more or less independent variation over time. Intrawest, for example, has transformed the natural environment in North America and created popular purpose-built tourist winter destinations (see end-of-chapter Case Study). But it is in the promotional field of images and perceptions that some of the most interesting planned changes occur, and these are based on marketing decisions (see Chapter 12 for examples).

## Product Levels

For many years, marketing theory has differentiated between three levels of product offering. The three levels can be seen as a continuum, with the product's most basic benefit at one end, and a range of add-on benefits, not directly related to the product's essential purpose, at the opposite end.

These three levels are:

1. **core product**: the basic need function served by the generic product. In the Opening Vignette the core product for Concorde was transportation;
2. **tangible product**: these are the specific features and benefits residing in the product itself – styling, quality, brand name, design, etc. Concorde differentiated itself in its appearance with its legendary needle-nose and unusual delta-wings;
3. **augmented product**: the add-ons that are extrinsic to the product itself but may influence the decision to purchase. Augmented features may include credit terms, after-sales guarantees, car parking, etc. For Concorde, add-ons included the finest champagne and caviar served during trans-Atlantic crossings.

---

**CORE PRODUCT**
the basic need function served by the generic product

---

> **TANGIBLE PRODUCT**
> the specific features and benefits residing in the product itself   styling, quality, brand name, design, etc.

> **AUGMENTED PRODUCT**
> the add-ons that are extrinsic to the product itself but may influence the decision to purchase

Although these levels were defined with manufactured products in mind, they do apply, with modifications, to tourism and hospitality goods and services. For example, Swarbrooke has applied the three levels to theme parks (see Figure 5.1).

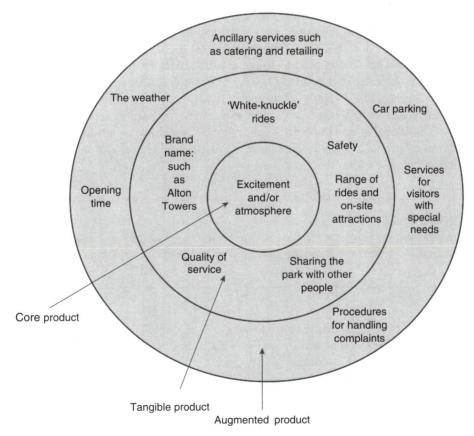

**Figure 5.1**   The Three Levels of Product – Example of a Theme Park

*Source*: Swarbrooke, J. (1995) *The Development and Management of Visitor Attractions*. Oxford: Butterworth-Heinemann.

Conceptualizing the product in these three areas allows the tourism marketer to appraise the comparative advantages and consumer appeal of his or her product versus those of others. In a highly competitive market, it is unlikely that any supplier will have an advantage in terms of its core benefits, and differentiation is instead likely to reside in the second and third levels. For example, most theme parks offer excitement and thrills for consumers, but will compete with each other in the variety and quality of rides, or the quality of the surrounding environment.

## Physical Evidence and the Servicescape

An important part of the augmented product is the physical environment. Because many tourism and hospitality services are intangible, customers often rely on tangible cues, or physical evidence, to evaluate the service before its purchase and to assess their satisfaction with the service during and after consumption. As explained in Chapter 1, the physical evidence is the environment in which the service is delivered and in which the firm and customer interact, and any tangible components that facilitate performance or communication of the service. The physical facility is often referred to as the **servicescape**, and is very important for tourism and hospitality products such as hotels, restaurants and theme parks, which are dominated by experience attributes. Disney, for example, effectively uses the servicescape to excite its customers. The brightly coloured displays, the music, the rides, and the costumed characters all reinforce the feelings of fun and excitement that Disney seeks to generate in its customers. The Global Spotlight on Sweden's Icehotel shows how important the servicescape is for accommodations. In this case, the hotel is made entirely of ice and snow, and provides a unique experience for tourists.

---

**SERVICESCAPE**

the environment in which the service is delivered and in which the firm and customer interact, and any tangible components that facilitate performance or communication of the service

---

General elements of physical evidence are shown in Table 5.1. They include all aspects of the organization's servicescape that affect customers, including both exterior attributes (such as parking and landscape) and interior attributes (such as design, layout, equipment and décor). Signage is also part of the physical evidence; in 2007, Beijing attempted to stamp out embarrassingly bad English on bilingual signs in the run-up to the 2008 Olympics. The municipal government issued translation guidelines for signs in hotels, shopping malls, public transport and tourist attractions. At the time, the Park of Ethnic Minorities was identified as 'Racist Park', while the emergency exits at Beijing's international airport read, 'No entry on peacetime'.

Consumer researchers know that the design of the servicescape can influence customer choices, expectations, satisfaction and other behaviours. Retailers know that customers are

**Table 5.1**   Elements of Physical Evidence

| Servicescape facility exterior | Servicescape facility interior | Other tangibles |
|---|---|---|
| Parking | Layout | Uniforms |
| Landscape | Equipment | Business cards |
| Signage | Signage | Stationery |
| Exterior design | Air temperature | Invoices |
| | Interior design | Brochures |
| | Lighting | Web pages |
| | | Employee dress |

influenced by smell, décor, music and layout. Arby's, a fast-food chain in North America, uses the servicescape to position its restaurants as a step above other quick-service outlets. With carpeted floors, cushioned seating and a décor 'superior' to other fast-food chains, the company asserts that the interior ambience of Arby's outlets contributes to attracting diners. Design of work environments can also affect employees' productivity, motivation and satisfaction. The challenge in many tourism and hospitality settings is to design the physical space in a way that supports the needs and preferences of customers and employees simultaneously.

Employees and customers in service firms respond to their physical surroundings in three ways – cognitively, emotionally, and physiologically – and these responses influence their behaviours in that environment. First, the perceived servicescape may elicit *cognitive* responses, including people's beliefs about a place and their beliefs about the people and products found there. For example, a consumer study found that a travel agent's office décor affected customer understanding of the travel agent's behaviour (Bitner, 1990).[3] In addition to influencing cognitions, the perceived servicescape may elicit *emotional* responses that in turn influence behaviours. The colours, décor, music, and other elements of the atmosphere can have an unexplained and sometimes subconscious affect on the moods of people in the place. According to Russell et al. (1981), servicescapes that are both pleasant and arousing are 'exciting', while those that are pleasant and non-arousing, or sleepy, are 'relaxing'. Unpleasant servicescapes that are arousing are 'distressing', while unpleasant, sleepy servicescapes are 'gloomy'.[4] Finally, the servicescape may affect people in purely *physiological* ways. Noise that is too loud may cause physical discomfort, the temperature of a room may cause people to shiver or perspire, the air quality may make it difficult to breathe, and the glare of lighting may decrease ability to see and may cause physical pain. All of these physical responses will influence whether people remain in and enjoy a particular environment. In 2004, a Vancouver-based company, Enhanced Air Technologies, developed Commercaire pheromone, a synthetic compound that mimics the maternal sense of comfort piped to children when they are crying or unhappy. Filtered into a store, the odourless substance is meant to relax customers so they stay longer and buy more (Brieger, 2004).[5] The firm claims retailers can expect revenue growth of between 9 per cent and 20 per cent when using the product. While Enhanced Air's sales-stimulating pheromone may be a first, there is a long history of retailers using fake sawdust or fresh bread smells to foster favourable emotions in patrons.

In Chapter 2, the discussion of consumer trends pointed out that today's consumer desires experiences, and more and more businesses are responding by explicitly designing experiences with themed servicescapes. At themed restaurants such as the Hard Rock Café, Planet Hollywood or the Rainforest Café, the food is just a prop for what's known as 'eatertainment'. Retailers are also creating themes that tie merchandising presentations together in a staged experience. A popular tourist attraction in Las Vegas is the Forum, a mall that displays its distinctive theme – an ancient Roman marketplace – in every detail. The Simon DeBartolo Group, which developed the mall, disperses this motif through a panoply of architectural effects. These include marble floors, stark white pillars, 'outdoor' cafes, living trees, flowing fountains – and even a painted blue sky with fluffy white clouds that yield regularly to simulated storm, complete with lighting and thunder. Every mall entrance and every storefront is an elaborate Roman replica. Hourly, inside the main entrance, statues of Julius Caesar and other Roman luminaries come to life and speak. 'Hail, Caesar!' is a frequent cry, and Roman centurions periodically march through on their way to the adjacent Caesar's Palace casino.

Despite the increased emphasis on the servicescape in designing experiences, companies that fail to provide consistently engaging experiences, overprice their experiences relative to the value perceived, or overbuild their capacity to stage them will see pressure on demand, pricing, or both. The Rainforest Café and Planet Hollywood have both encountered trouble because they have failed to refresh their experiences. Guests find nothing different from one visit to the next. Disney, on the other hand, avoids staleness by frequently adding new attractions and even whole parks, such as the Animal Kingdom in 1998 and California Adventure in 2001. The latter US$1.4 billion project, which also included construction of a first-class hotel, was designed to accommodate 30,000 people a day, to add to the 70,000 visitors that come to Disneyland across the street. Covering 55 acres, California Adventure is a high-energy park, celebrating the dreams of the many Americans who came to California and reflecting the highlights and the pop culture of the state today. It features attractions a little wilder and a lot more grown up than the original Disneyland. These attractions are situated in three themed areas: Paradise Pier, Golden State and Hollywood Pictures Backlot.

The Snapshot below about the new Churchill Museum in London shows how designers of a museum have used technology to enhance the servicescape, creating an interactive educational experience for visitors.

## Snapshot

### The Greatest Briton Ever: The New Churchill Museum in London

'*A benchmark for personality museums in the twenty-first century.*'

Forty years after his death, and shortly after being named the greatest Briton ever in a 2002 BBC Poll, the World War II leader – as well as renowned journalist, author, artist, soldier and even bricklayer – has finally been immortalized in his own museum in the historic Cabinet War Rooms in the basement of the Treasury building in London's Whitehall.

Her Majesty Queen Elizabeth II, who was present at Sir Winston Churchill's state funeral, opened the world's first major museum dedicated to his life in February 2005. The Cabinet

War Rooms had already been preserved in their 1945 state and also extended at a cost of £8 million with the assistance of a major grant from the National Heritage Memorial Fund. The further £6 million needed for the adjacent Churchill Museum's high-tech facilities was provided through donations from private individuals and trusts in the UK and USA. The whole project took over ten years to come to fruition.

The ten-year project, spearheaded by Phil Reed, now director of the new exhibition, celebrates the achievements of the wartime icon in a 850-square metre facility combining cutting-edge technology, rare and significant historical objects, and thousands of images, film and sound recordings to chronicle Churchill's 90-year life. With no-holds-barred realism, visitors can follow the successes and controversies, highs and lows, and joys and sorrows of the pre-eminent and multi-talented writer, historian, soldier and politician.

One ground-breaking feature of the museum is a unique electronic 'Lifeline' table that allows visitors to journey through his extraordinary life. The 18-metre-long Lifeline is a computerized filing cabinet with a virtual file containing items relating to each year, and in many cases each month and day, of Churchill's career. Touching the strip at the edge of the Lifeline brings up contextual data, documents, films, photographs and even sound tracks that relate to his life while providing historical context. The Lifeline includes 4,600 pages, 200,000 words, 100 documents, 1,150 images and 206 animations.

Exhibit designers Casson Mann, are proud of their technological and interactive advances, calling it 'a 21st-century museum about a 20th-century giant'. Designers of the British Galleries at the Victoria & Albert Museum in London, Casson Mann are exhibition, museum and interior designers. Their specialty is thoughtful and expert communication. They communicate through all the senses by telling interesting stories in intelligent spaces. They aim, through design, to make people feel wanted and comfortable so that they can do what they came to do. This might be to look at art, take in information, to entertain the children, or to have a discussion, to learn, concentrate or relax.

Promotional materials dub the museum 'a benchmark for personality museums in the twenty-first century' and as such it also celebrates Churchill's unique quirks, with items of clothing such as his signature red siren suit, iconic spotted bow tie, school reports, love letters and the ransom note for his escape from a South African prisoner-of-war camp. Such personal artifacts have been lent or given by the Churchill family and private individuals and benefactors from around the world.

*Sources*: Renzetti, E. (2 March 2005) 'In a Bunker with Churchill', *Globe & Mail*, Travel, T1 & T4; Churchill Museum and Cabinet War Rooms Press Pack.

## Product Planning

### Product Mix

The most basic decisions a tourism organization has to make are what business it is in and what product mix is appropriate to it. The **product mix** is the portfolio of products that an organization offers to one market or several.

---

**PRODUCT MIX**
the portfolio of products that an organization offers to one market or several

---

According to Seaton and Bennett (1996), five basic market/product options exist:[6]

1. several markets with multi-product mixes for each (e.g., mass tour operators that offer a wide range of multi-destination packages to a variety of market segments);
2. several markets with a single product for each (e.g., airlines with a product for business and economy class travellers);
3. several markets with a single product for all (e.g., a national tourist organization promoting a country);
4. single market with a multi-product mix (e.g., a specialist tour operator with a range of cultural tours aimed at a wealthy, educated market); and
5. single market with a single product (e.g., a heli-skiing operator targeting the very rich).

The decision as to which product mix option to adopt depends upon many factors, including the strength and value of consumer demand in the different markets, the level of competition in each market, and the distinctive competence of the organization to service the markets adequately. The starting point in product analysis and planning is thus an analysis of the consumer and competitive offerings in relation to the goals and product capacity of the tourism organization. The most successful products emerge when the marketing planning steps outlined in Chapter 3 are followed. Portfolio and SWOT analysis are discussed there; another useful method of analysing the tourism product is by considering its features and benefits. **Features** consist of the objective attributes of a tourism product; **benefits** are the rewards the product gives the consumer. The difference between the two is shown in Table 5.2. Hong Kong International Airport was recently named the world's best airport in a survey of over 50,000 frequent travellers.[7] Part of the reason is the features of the airport and the benefits they offer passengers. As well as shops that sell everything from rare white tea to cell phones, there are free plasma televisions to watch, a children's play area, wireless broadband, internet cafés, a prayer room, a pharmacy, nap rooms, a beauty salon, shower facilities, a medical centre (complete with on-site vaccinations and x-ray machines) and displays from Hong Kong museums.

---

**FEATURES**
the objective attributes of a tourism product

---

**BENEFITS**
the rewards the product gives the consumer

---

**Table 5.2**  Features and Benefits Analysis for Tourism and Hospitality Products

| Tourism Product Item | Product Feature | Consumer Benefit |
| --- | --- | --- |
| Low-cost airline | Low service | Low-cost travel |
| Purpose-built ski resort | All lifts near hotel rooms | Ski in, ski out facility |
| Museum | Interactive facilities to learn | An entertaining place |
| River adventure tour | Quality kayaks and rafts | Reconnecting with nature |
| 5-star hotel | Quality beds | Comfort, a good night's sleep |

## Product Life Cycle

One of the most basic product analysis tools is the **product life cycle (PLC) analysis** (see Figure 5.2), the Opening Vignette described the journey of Concorde through this life cycle. Plotting products or services to identify what stage they are at in their PLC is a valuable way of reviewing a product's past and current position and making predictions about its future. As part of a portfolio analysis (see Chapter 3), an organization should access each good and service in terms of its position in the product life cycle. *Product development* begins when the company finds and develops a new product idea. The Snapshot later in this chapter about the Sydney BridgeClimb describes how its founder conceived the idea nine years before it was put into action. The *introduction* phase is a period of slow sales and low profits because of the investment required for product introduction. The new Churchill Museum in London (see Snapshot above) could be considered to be in this phase. The *growth* phase is characterized by increasing market acceptance and substantial improvement in profits. This is the case for the Sydney BridgeClimb, as it now takes tourists on the climb 12 hours a day, 363 days a year. The *maturity* phase is a period of slow sales marked by high profits, as the product is well entrenched in the marketplace and has an acceptable market share. An example would be Sweden's Icehotel (see Global Spotlight). However, when sales begin to drop because competitors are moving into the marketplace, the product enters the *decline* stage. Profits and market share decline, and major costs may be involved in redeveloping, refurbishing, or maintaining the product. This is the case for many small ski resorts around the world (see Case Study at the end of the chapter).

---

**PRODUCT LIFE CYCLE (PLC) ANALYSIS**
a way of plotting products or services to identify what stage they are at in their life cycle; a valuable way of reviewing a product's past and current position and making predictions about its future

---

Using the PLC concept to develop marketing strategy can be difficult. Strategy is both a cause and a result of the PLC. At the introduction stage, promotion spending is likely to be high in

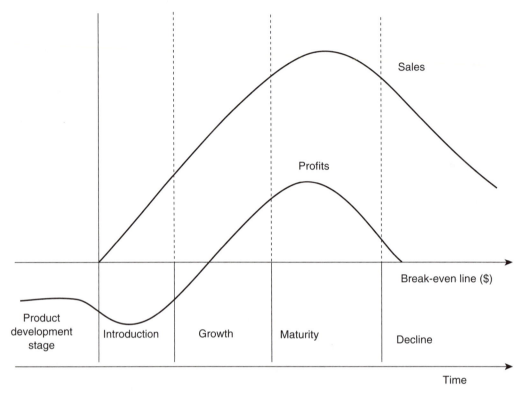

**Figure 5.2**  Sales and Profits Over the Product's Life from Inception to Demise

order to inform consumers about the new product and encourage them to buy it. A company will focus on selling to buyers who are ready to buy, usually higher-income groups. Prices tend to be on the high side because of low output, production problems, high promotion costs and other expenses. At the growth stage, the early adopters will continue to buy, and later buyers will start following their lead, encouraged by favourable word of mouth. Competitors will enter the market, attracted by the opportunity for profit, and they will introduce more product features that will expand the market. In the growth stage, the organization faces a trade-off between high market share and high current profit. By investing heavily in product improvement, promotion and distribution, it can capture a dominant position. But it sacrifices maximum current profit in the hope of making this up in the next stage.

When sales start to slow down, the product will enter the maturity stage; this lasts longer than the previous two stages and poses stronger challenges to marketing management. Most products or services are in this stage, and it is a phase that is characterized by heavy competition. The only way to increase sales is to lure customers away from competition, and so price wars and heavy advertising are common. At this stage, an aggressive product manager will seek to increase consumption by modifying markets and/or products. The product manager may also try to improve sales by changing one or more of the marketing mix elements.

In the decline stage, some firms will withdraw from the market. Those that remain may reduce the number of their product offerings or the number of market segments they are targeting. They may also reduce the promotion budget, and prices. For each declining product, management must decide whether to maintain, harvest, or drop it.

However, the PLC is not as simple as it sounds in theory, and according to Mercer (1992), 'its supposed universal applicability is largely a myth'.[8] The study of the PLC pattern for a particular product has to take into account the market the product is in. For example, if a product is showing no growth or decline, it may still be very successful if the market as a whole is in decline. Another complication of the PLC is that a product that is in overall decline may be losing its customers from one market segment but increasing appeal or holding steady with another. Ski areas, for example, have been very successful in attracting an increasing number of snowboarders over the past decade, despite a drop in the number of downhill skiers. In addition, although the PLC concept is neat on paper, it is often difficult to determine what particular stage a product is at. Finally, even assuming that a product's life cycle position can be determined, it may not be obvious what action should be taken.

Despite these problems, the PLC is a valuable concept, since it forces the organization to analyse trends for its product in relation to the overall market and the segments within it, in order to assess future marketing requirements. Ski areas have adapted to the growth in snowboarders (referred to above) by changing the products they offer; most successful ski areas these days have designated areas for snowboarders (see end-of-chapter Case Study). A related concept for analysing destinations is that of the tourism area life cycle, which is discussed in Chapter 12.

## Positioning

**Positioning** is the bedrock of product management. Chapter 3 introduces the concept as the natural follow-through of market segmentation and market targeting, and highlights the three steps necessary to develop an effective position in the target market segment. The objective of positioning is to create a distinctive place in the minds of potential customers. Positioning in tourism should evoke images of a destination or product in the customer's mind – images that differentiate the product from the competition and also convey that it can satisfy their needs and wants. Effective positioning should direct all the marketing functions of a business. Advertising and promotions, as well as decisions on price, product and distribution channels must all be consistent with positioning goals. Often, these marketing functions will be driven by a **positioning statement**, which is a phrase that reflects the image the organization wants to create. The positioning statement for the Churchill Museum, for example (see Snapshot), is: 'A benchmark for personality museums in the twenty-first century'. This statement encapsulates what the Museum stands for, the essence of what the museum does, and how it stands out from competitors.

---

**POSITIONING**
establishing an image for a product or service in relation to others in the marketplace

---

**POSITIONING STATEMENT**
a phrase that reflects the image an organization wants to create

---

There is an endless number of positioning strategies, and selection of the appropriate approach is vital to the success of a tourism organization.

Burke and Resnick (1991) have identified four key positioning strategies that are not mutually exclusive and may therefore be used individually or in combination:

1. positioning relative to target market (e.g. business travellers, families with children under ten, etc.);
2. positioning by price and quality (e.g. a premium product such as the Concorde);
3. positioning relative to a product class (e.g. a tour operator positioning its products within a winter sports tourism category); and
4. positioning relative to competitors (e.g. the Hertz Rental Car campaign 'We try harder', which drew attention to the fact that Hertz was not market leader but would work harder to catch up with its competitors).[9]

Boutique hotels use a combination of these positioning strategies to succeed in the very competitive hotel market. Loosely defined as small, specialized accommodations, mainly in prime city locations, boutique hotels offer high standards of service, style and comfort which suit the corporate jet-setter. The main challenge for boutiques is how to keep ahead in such a fiercely competitive market. Ian Schrager, owner of the Sanderson and St Martin's Lane hotels in London, has managed to stay ahead of the game by attracting a celebrity clientele and introducing luxurious spas at his properties. In Spain, Sorat Hotels and Sol Melia have tried to differentiate themselves by emphasizing the quality of their personal service, while the UK group Hotel du Vin has made its name with the high standard of food on offer at its stylish bistros (Goff, 2003).[10] The Global Spotlight below is an example of an unusual tourism product that has positioned itself as a unique, one-off hotel; one that has been rebuilt every year since 1990.

## Global Spotlight

### The Coolest Place in Town: Sweden's Icehotel

Icehotel, the world's first and biggest hotel made entirely of ice and snow, was created in 1990, and is situated in the village of Jukkasjärvi, 200 kilometres north of the Arctic Circle in Sweden. The company that runs Icehotel has been a tourist operator in the region since the 1970s, and for many years the focus was on the summer season and the outdoor experiences offered by the land of the midnight sun. During the dark winters the river was frozen and the people of the small village of Jukkasjärvi went into hibernation.

But at the end of the 1980s it was decided to turn things around. Instead of viewing the dark and cold winter as a disadvantage, the unique elements of the Arctic were to be exploited as an asset. In 1990 the French ice artist Jannot Derit was invited to have the opening of his exhibition in a specially built igloo on the frozen Torne River. The 60-square metre building, named Arctic Hall, attracted many curious visitors to the area. One night a group of foreign guests, equipped with reindeer hides and sleeping bags, decided it would be a good idea to use the cylindrical-shaped igloo as accommodation. The following morning the brave group raved about the unique sensation of sleeping in an igloo. Hence, the concept of Icehotel was born, and today Icehotel is world-famous for its unique concept and its fantastic works of art.

The Icehotel has been rebuilt every year since 1990, and what started off as a 60-square metre igloo has grown to an almost 5,000-square metre hotel, using more than 30,000 tons of snow and 4,000 tons of ice. Snow cannons help to form the snow over arched steel sections. The ice pillars are then put in place to give extra strength to the self-supporting snow arches. In March, ice is harvested from the River Torne with the help of tractors and special ice saws. The blocks are then stored and used to build the hotel in the winter.

The hotel is never more than six months old, because in summer it melts. As a result, the exact number of rooms varies, but during the winter of 2004/2005 it had 85. The hotel also has a reception, hall of pillars, ice art exhibition, cinema, and a church. About 14,000 guests a year spend the night in the hotel, with over 40,000 day visitors walking through the reindeer-skin covered doors. In April, the entire hotel literally trickles into the Torne River, to be resurrected during November and December the following winter, with a new architecture and new works of art. So visitors can experience a new Icehotel every year.

The temperature in the Icehotel varies between −4 and −9 degrees centigrade, depending on the temperature outside, which can dip to −40. At night, guests are supplied with a specially made sleeping bag, and are given a talk on 'how to survive in the Icehotel'. For some, this may mean sampling the wonderfully coloured cocktails served in ice glasses at the Absolut Ice Bar. Others may want to try the food at the Icehotel Restaurant which serves Laplandic gourmet food on plates of ice from the Torne River. During the daytime there are plenty of activities for visitors such as snowmobiling, dog-sledding, moose safaris and ice sculpting. Visitors can also attend concerts in an open-air venue inspired by Shakespeare's Globe Theatre in London. The 520-person theatre is a marvel of ice engineering, carefully crafted by technicians in just three weeks. However, staying at the Icehotel doesn't come cheap. A deluxe suite costs about 6,000SKr a night (£440).

*Sources*: www.icehotel.com; Thorne, P. (1 October 2005) 'Snow Traveller', *The Independent*, 6.

## Branding

The practice of **branding** was developed in the field of packaged goods, as a method of establishing a distinctive identity for a product based on competitive differentiation from other products. Branding was commonly achieved through naming, trademarking, packaging, product design and promotion. Successful branding gave a unique identity to what might otherwise have been a generic product. This identity produced a consistent image in the consumer's mind, which facilitated recognition and quality assurance. In the 19th century, products such as Beecham's Pills, Cadbury's Chocolate and Eno's Salts were early users of branding. These days, the market in packaged goods is dominated by brands, and in the last few decades branding has also been widely recognized in services marketing. A 'brand', in the modern marketing sense, offers the consumer relevant added value – a superior proposition that is distinctive from competitors' and that imparts meaning above and beyond the product's functional aspects. There is even a Museum of Brands in London, where visitors can view 10,000 consumer products covering 200 years of packaging, branding and advertising.

> **BRANDING**
> a method of establishing a distinctive identity for a product based on competitive differentiation from other products

Branding offers a solution to some of the problems in services marketing discussed in Chapter 1 – in particular those of consistency and product standardization. Branding can be a way of unifying services, which is why it has been particularly developed in hotel marketing. Research shows that nearly 90 per cent of bookings are made with branded hotel chains, and nine out of ten consumers can distinguish between chains, franchise operators and independents (Gilpin, 1994).[11]

For large hotel companies that have a wide variety of properties, grouping them into brands can:

1. unify them into more easily recognizable smaller groups;
2. enable each branded group to be targeted at defined market segments; and
3. enable product delivery, including human resource management, to be focused on creating a specific set of benefits for a specific market.

North America has over 200 hotel brands competing for business, and many hotel chains offer a family of sub-brands or endorsed brands. For example, Hilton Hotels Corporation, Intercontinental and Starwood each has seven sub-brands, while Marriott International has 12 (as well as the Ritz-Carlton chain which, to protect its exclusive image, is not normally identified for marketing purposes as part of the Marriott Group) (Lovelock and Wortz, 2007).[12] For a multi-brand strategy to succeed, each brand must promise a distinctive value proposition, targeted at a different customer segment. There are even branded hotel floors in some hotels. American Express and the Sheraton Vancouver Wall Centre Hotel have partnered to open a floor dedicated to business accommodations for American Express credit card holders. Located on the 27th floor, the 'American Express Club Floor' features a private lounge with business service centre, direct access to boardrooms and fitness facilities, dedicated front-desk check-in and a late 4.00 p.m. check-out. According to officials, guests using the club floor pay the same price for their room as Amex's negotiated standard room rate and benefit from a host of value-added services and amenities. These include complimentary continental breakfast, all-day coffee and tea, evening hors d'oeuvres, international and local newspapers, and 24 hour room service.

In the past, branding was often seen mainly as a matter of promotion and of creating the right image through advertising and publicity. But marketing managers now recognize that successful branding involves the integrated deployment of product design, pricing policies, distribution selection and promotion. The case for branding is stronger for tourism products that offer the possibility for differentiation in several areas of the marketing mix. This is why branding has been particularly successful in hotel and restaurant marketing. Branding of restaurants, hotels and airlines developed extensively in the United States during the 1980s and 1990s, and companies in the rest of the world are following suit. The momentum is driven mainly by large organizations that recognize that, to remain competitive, they need to offer several products to different markets instead of relying upon a monolithic presence in one main one.

Apart from the advantages already mentioned, Middleton and Clarke (2001) suggest that branding in tourism offers other specific advantages:[13]

1. it helps reduce medium- and long-term vulnerability to the unforeseen external events that so beset the tourism industry. Recovery time after an event such as a terrorist attack or a natural disaster is likely to be shorter for a well-established brand;
2. it reduces risk for the consumer at the point of purchase by signalling the expected quality and performance of an intangible product. It offers either an implicit or explicit guarantee to the consumer;
3. it facilitates accurate marketing segmentation by attracting some consumer segments and repelling others. For an inseparable product, onsite segment compatibility is an important marketing issue;
4. it provides the focus for the integration of stakeholder effort, especially for the employees of an organization or the individual tourism providers of a destination brand; and
5. it is a strategic weapon for long-range planning in tourism, as can be seen in the Snapshot on Four Seasons in Chapter 3.

It should be recognized that a competitive brand is a live asset and not a fixture, and therefore its value may depreciate over time if starved of investment and marketing and management skill. Brand decay may begin if a brand is over-stretched into new products that damage its essence, or following a merger or takeover. Marketers sometimes use the term **brandicide** to describe the process of taking a well-known brand and extending it into a new area that will 'kill' the brand. Companies are increasingly attempting to stretch their proven expertise into new areas. Walt Disney Inc., for example, has recently entered the produce business. Disney's cartoon characters are popping up on fruit and vegetable packaging across the US, as growers clinch licensing deals with entertainment companies hungry to cultivate positive images among health-conscious parents and children. The Snapshot below describes how chefs – some of the most successful and fastest-growing consumer brands today – are stretching their brand names into a number of different areas.

---

**BRANDICIDE**
the process of taking a well-known brand and extending it into a new area that will 'kill' the brand

A combination of factors has made companies more eager than ever to stretch their brands further and more boldly. Advances in technology have reduced barriers to entry in new sectors. Companies have developed stronger and more knowledgeable relationships with customers, and the cost and difficulty of developing new brands is encouraging companies to exploit the brands they already have. But there can be a cost to leveraging brand equity. If a brand loses credibility in one sector, this tainted sector can contaminate everything else that bears the brand's name. So brandicide should be avoided.

The Case Study on Richard Branson in Chapter 11 shows how over the past 25 years, Branson has diversified his Virgin brand into a far-reaching empire, encompassing mobile phone services, a rail service and even wedding dresses, as well as his original record label and discount airline. The Snapshot below takes a look at the Jamie Oliver brand, and how, albeit on a smaller scale than Branson the celebrity chef has used his name to promote cookbooks, cookware, healthy school lunches, supermarkets, restaurants, and, of course, television shows.

## Snapshot

### Chefs as Brands: The Case of Jamie Oliver

Some of the most successful and fastest-growing consumer brands today are chefs. Chefs used to be limited to working in the back of restaurants and creating great meals that consumers loved to eat. Since the 1990s, they have moved to the forefront, becoming brands in their own right. Many chefs today have their names attached to multiple product lines and have a stake in a wealth of restaurants and businesses. They are a new breed of chef – one that understands how powerful a brand name can be in the marketplace. And they are following popular marketing theory, which states that if you find a product that works, you should create brand extensions from it.

One celebrity chef has differentiated himself drastically from all the others. Jamie Oliver, one of Britain's most loved TV personalities since his teenage debut as the 'Naked Chef', is a prime example of branding success as well as innovative positioning. Traditionally, chefs were equated with the stereotype of older, portly or balding men (and the equivalent women) who appealed to an older demographic. Oliver, however, gives male chefs a fresh, youthful, hip spin, appealing to young people with his casual clothes and no-nonsense cooking style. Moreover, he has aligned himself with underprivileged youth and also with schoolchildren through his television reality shows, and has even affected British politics with his successful campaign for healthy, government-funded school lunches.

From his early 'Naked Chef' bachelor image, Oliver has developed his brand alongside his personal life. Since marrying and having two children, he has portrayed the image of the devoted family man and extended this to his professional life by taking on the job of improving nutrition throughout Britain amongst children. In 2004 he used his celebrity status to launch a nationwide Feed Me Better campaign along with a documentary TV series called *Jamie's School Dinners*, which was aired in early 2005. His Feed Me Better petition secured over 72,000 signatures, became front-page news and inspired Tony Blair's government to respond with a vote-catching 'children's manifesto' as well as a substantial increase in funding for school meals. He also launched a set of Feed Me Better starter information packages for schools. Now he is expanding the campaign in the US. In 2006 British Education Secretary Alan Johnson said the Children's Food Bill, passed as a result of Oliver's lobbying, was aimed at improving school pupils' nutrition and undoing decades of neglect.

Oliver understands how powerful his name can be both in the marketplace and in society. His brand expansion is not only making him very wealthy but also furthering his altruistic approach to national and international healthy eating. He called his reform efforts 'one of the biggest food revolutions England has ever seen', explaining that, having achieved so much personally, he had two choices: 'I could go two ways at this point. I could give back or I could be greedy.' His chic restaurant, Fifteen London, combines his business acumen with his humanitarian tendencies. It is the result of another television show, in which he took a group of down-and-out youngsters and turned them into able kitchen staff. He has repeated this theme in Holland, too, at Fifteen Amsterdam.

The internet is also furthering the successful branding of celebrity chefs like Oliver. The medium brings chefs a wide-reaching sales channel that they couldn't find elsewhere. Oliver's website provides all the same marketing components traditionally found in direct marketing. There are electronic updates of his shows and events plus information on recipes, new cookbook launch dates, and links to distributors of the Tefal cookware he sponsors. The site also serves as a customer service and relationship marketing tool, furthering brand loyalty. Fans can share ideas and information with him and with each other via an interactive messaging forum.

How far can you extend a chef's name as a brand without committing the ultimate brandicide? Jamie Oliver sensibly refused to pose naked for Nestle and Coca Cola ad campaigns, both of which would have compromised his healthy eating ethos. He has, amid some media criticism, agreed to promote the pro-organic British supermarket, Sainsburys, which he considers more in line with his business principles. Oliver receives an estimated £1 million a year for his Sainsbury advertisements.

For celebrity chefs – as for many consumer products – marketing is all about connecting with an audience. 'These celebrity chefs are so hot because they are so touchable,' says industry publicist Lisa Ekus. 'Consumers can see them, taste their food, feel like they are really getting something from them. That intimacy is invaluable when it comes to marketing. It allows them to turn themselves into successful brands.'

*Sources*: Cohen, A. (December 2001) 'Look who's cooking now', *Sales & Marketing Management*, 152(12), 30–36; Turner, C. (31 March 2003) 'Edible peep show', *The Globe and Mail*, R3; Fernand, D. (2 April 2006) 'School meals revolution hits home', *The Sunday Times*, Focus; Eckler, R. (29 November 2004) 'Bloody good', *National Post*, B12; Renzetti, E. (22 March 2005) 'St. Jamie serves up a cafeteria food fight', *Globe and Mail*, R1 & R3; Fletcher, V. (20 May 2006) 'Junk food ban is lesson in health', *Daily Express*, 17.

## Packaging

In the tourism and hospitality industry, **packaging** is the process of combining two or more related and complementary offerings into a single-price offering. A package may include a wide variety of services, such as lodging, meals, entrance fees for attractions, entertainment, transportation costs, guide services, or other similar activities. Travel packages have become increasingly popular over the years. They are attractive because they benefit both the consumer and participating businesses by providing convenience and value to the consumer and added revenue for businesses. An example of a package holiday is one on offer from Arctic Experience, a UK tour operator. In 2007, the operator was selling a three-night trip to the Icehotel in Sweden (see Global Spotlight) on a bed and breakfast basis for just over £1000 for a single person. This price included return flights from London.

---

**PACKAGING**
the process of combining two or more related and complementary offerings into a single-price offering

---

Packaging provides several customer benefits, including:

1.  easier budgeting for trips: the customer pays at one time and has a good idea of the trip's total cost;
2.  increased convenience, which saves time and prevents aggravation;
3.  greater economy, as the cost to the customer is usually more economical than purchasing the package components individually;
4.  the opportunity to experience previously unfamiliar activities and attractions; and
5.  the opportunity to design components of a package for specialized interests.

For tourism operations, packages are attractive for the following reasons:

1.  they can improve profitability by allowing businesses to price at a premium by adding special good and services;
2.  they can streamline business patterns. Packaging during low demand periods may add attractive features to the service or product, thus generating additional business;
3.  they allow joint marketing opportunities, which can in turn reduce promotional costs;
4.  they can be an effective tool for tailoring tourism products for specific target markets.

The tourism industry is becoming increasingly sophisticated and innovative with its packaging. The Snapshot on weekendtrips.com in Chapter 7 is an example of the growing number of companies catering to the demand for short-break tourism experiences sold via the internet. Others are catering for the more sophisticated backpacker market (see Snapshot in Chapter 2). For example, Ho Chi Minh City-based Linh Nam Travel Co. has a 79-day tour of Vietnam with an itinerary of 8,000 kilometres through 59 cities and provinces nationwide. The programme runs twice a year and tourists can choose to stay at hotels of one to three stars or take a home-stay. Others are packaging holidays for the growing interest in wildlife tourism amongst older, more affluent tourists. Churchill, Manitoba in Canada, for example, attracts 2,500 tourists a year who take trips in tundra buggies to see wildlife, primarily polar bears, but also ptarmigan, Arctic fox, Arctic hare, snowy owls and lemmings. Tour packages range from CDN$2,200 to $7,000 for two nights including accommodation and transportation to and from Winnipeg. A 2004 study found that 75 per cent of Churchill's visitors were American, and about 15 per cent were from abroad, primarily Japan, Germany and France. About 10 per cent of visitors were Canadian (Redekop, 2004).[14]

## New Product Development

According to the *Los Angeles Times*, 700 new products are introduced every day.[15] Many of them fail, and many new ideas take years before becoming a reality. The BridgeClimb in Sydney is a prime example of the latter, and the Snapshot below explains how it took nine years for the idea to become reality. Safety concerns and other issues kept the unique tourism product on hold for nearly a decade.

Developing new products is different from maintaining existing ones, and planning for both kinds of product will differ according to whether the products are targeted at existing markets or new ones. According to Holloway and Plant[16], a company has four alternatives when developing new products.

### Market Penetration

Firstly, the company can follow a **market penetration** strategy by modifying an existing product for the current market. Improvements to an existing product can transform it, so that prospective purchasers view it as a genuinely new product. The case study at the end of the chapter highlights a number of ways in which ski resorts are modifying their service offerings to provide new experiences for their customers.

---

**MARKET PENETRATION**
modifying an existing product for the current market

---

### Market Development

The second strategy, **market development**, calls for identifying and developing new markets for current products. If an existing product is launched to a new market that is unfamiliar with it, that product is also, for all intents and purposes, a new product. When Banff Mount Norquay in Canada introduced hourly tickets, they attracted a new market of skiers – locals who would not normally ski due to lack of time (see Chapter 6).

---

**MARKET DEVELOPMENT**
identifying and developing new markets for current products

---

## Product Development

The third strategy, **product development**, involves developing a genuinely new product to be sold to existing customers. Over the last few years, fast-food companies have developed new healthier products for existing customers. Subway, for example, has positioned itself as a healthy fast-food alternative, turning its low-fat, low-calorie food into a marketing coup. When the company learned that Jared Fogel, a once 425-pound (193 kg) college student, lost 245 pounds (111 kg) on a diet consisting of Subway turkey and veggie subs, Fogel was recruited to endorse Subway products in numerous (successful) promotions. The Snapshot below on Sydney BridgeClimb is an example of a genuinely new product sold to tourists visiting the Australian city.

---

**PRODUCT DEVELOPMENT**
developing a genuinely new product to be sold to existing customers

---

## Diversification

**Diversification** growth makes sense when good opportunities can be found outside the present business. Three types of diversification can be considered. Firstly, the company can seek new products that have technological or marketing synergies with existing product lines, even though the product may appeal to a new class of customers (concentric diversification). Secondly, the company may search for new products that could appeal to its current target market (horizontal diversification). Finally, the company can seek new businesses that have no relationship with the company's current technology, products or markets (conglomerate diversification). An example of diversification comes from Four Seasons, the hotel company that moved into new territory in 2003 with the launch of a luxury catamaran cruise in the Maldives.

---

**DIVERSIFICATION**
seeking opportunities outside the present business

---

## Snapshot

### Sydney BridgeClimb

In 1989, Paul Cave was involved in organizing a climb over the arch of Sydney Harbour Bridge as part of an international business convention. It was such a success that the dream of allowing all people to climb the bridge was born. Few could imagine the awesome challenge that this concept presented to BridgeClimb's founder and chairman. Cave's dream was to involve years of dealing with state and local government bodies, community groups and hundreds of experts on everything from safety and logistics to media, heritage and conservation issues. There were occasions when Cave was the only one who refused to let go of the dream. His vision, commitment, persistence and entrepreneurial skills were fundamental to BridgeClimb's creation.

Nine years later, on October 1, 1998, BridgeClimb was officially launched, and by August 2006 it had sold over 1,750,000 tickets, 360,000 gift certificates, and had become a major tourist attraction in Australia. It is estimated that BridgeClimb is a US$8,000-per-hour business that runs 12 hours a day, 363 days a year. The company takes small groups to the summit of the bridge, 134 metres (400 feet) above sea level. The experience offers climbers the chance to walk over catwalks and climb ladders and stairs while trained ClimbLeaders provide a full commentary on the history of Sydney and its harbour bridge. With the choice of climbing at dawn, day, twilight or night, climbers are rewarded with spectacular 360 degree views of one of most beautiful harbours in the world.

Climber origins are 28 per cent locals, 17 per cent domestic visitors and 55 per cent international visitors, and it is estimated that over 1,700 couples have become engaged whilst on the BridgeClimb. Celebrities such as Will Smith, Matt Damon, Nicole Kidman, Kylie Minogue, Justin Timberlake and Cameron Diaz have all made the climb. Safety is BridgeClimb's number one priority. All climbers are breath-tested (and must register under 0.05 per cent blood alcohol level), and sign a medical declaration form to satisfy BridgeClimb's terms and conditions. No personal items are permitted on the bridge, and climbers have to pass through a metal detector.

BridgeClimb has won a number of awards, which recognize the impact the company has had on the tourism industry since commencing. These include the 'Major Tourist Attraction' category at the New South Wales Tourism Awards for Business Excellence which it has won four times. Cave himself won an Ernst & Young 'National Entrepreneur of the Year' award in 2001, and the Australian Export Heroes award in 2002/3. Paul Cave was not new to business.In 1974, following a career in marketing for B & D Roll-A-Door, he founded and created Amber group aged 29. Amber became Australia's largest tile and paving retailer, with 17 outlets. In 1996, 22 years later, he sold his 100 per cent interest in Amber to staff, via a management buy-out.

The Sydney Harbour Bridge is particularly special to Cave because his father-in-law, then just a teenager, purchased the first rail ticket ever sold to the public for crossing the bridge on March 20, 1932 – ticket number 0001 from Milson's Point to Wynyard Station. Having inherited this rail ticket (just one item from his 5,000-piece Sydney Harbour Bridge memorabilia collection), he will never forget its significance, or indeed that of the journey it has taken him on.

*Sources*: Karlgaard, R. (2 October 2005) 'A can-do-country', *Forbes*, 176(6), 37; Mediakit retrieved from www.bridgeclimb.com on 9 April 2007.

## Approaches to New Product Development

A company must develop new products to survive. New products can be obtained through acquisition or through new product development (NPD). There is a reasonably established approach to NPD, but Scheuing and Johnson (1989) have proposed a model for new service development (NSD), based on a review of other models and research into 66 US-based service firms.[17] The model has 15 steps and four main stages.

The first stage (steps 1–3) of NSD focuses on how new ideas are generated and developed. The development process must begin with a precise formulation of objectives and strategy. A well-designed strategy drives and directs the entire innovation effort and imbues it with effectiveness and efficiency. The second step is for companies to ensure that they have organized or structured their plan in such a way as to enable innovation to take place. In large companies, this may involve setting up a research and development (R & D) department. The third step consists of idea generation and screening. New ideas can be drawn from external sources, or be generated internally through consultation and brainstorming. Often the most powerful idea source is customer feedback.

The idea generation and development stage of NSD is followed by the second stage – the 'go/no-go' stage – comprising four steps (steps 4–7) that enable the company to decide whether or not it will proceed with the new development. Concept development requires that the surviving ideas be expanded into fully fledged concepts, especially if there is a significant service element. Concept testing is a research technique designed to evaluate whether a prospective user understands the idea of the proposed good or service, reacts favourably to it, and feels it provides benefits that answer unmet needs. The sixth step, business analysis, should represent a comprehensive investigation into the business implications of each concept. The project authorization step occurs when top management commits corporate resources to the implementation of a new idea. In an industry such as tourism, which consists of many small organizations, it is likely that 90 per cent of companies have just one person or department to authorize all innovative projects (Jones et al., 1997).[18]

Once the go-ahead has been given, the third stage of NSD – test design – is reached, in which detailed design and implementation of the innovation is carried out (steps 8–11). At this point, the new concept is converted into an operational entity. This requires design and testing. For a service, this activity should involve both the input of prospective users and the active co-operation of the operations personnel who will ultimately be delivering the service. It may also be necessary to design new production processes or develop new equipment. This stage also includes marketing design and testing. To complete the test design phase, all employees should be familiarized with the nature and operational details of the new service. For instance, research into flight catering has showed that 91 per cent of airlines engage in personnel training, whereas only 68 per cent of food manufacturers do so (Jones, 1995).[19]

The final stage of NSD is the evaluation of the new innovation, comprising four steps (steps 12–15). *Service testing* should be used to determine potential customer acceptance of the new service, while a pilot run ensures its smooth functioning. Chapter 4 described how the Marriott Corporation designed a new chain of hotels for business travellers – Courtyard by Marriott – but tested the concept under real-world conditions before subsequently developing the large chain that filled a gap in the market.

The next step, *test marketing*, examines the saleability of the new service, and a field test should be carried out with a limited sample of customers. With the delivery system and marketing in place and with the service thoroughly tested, the company should next initiate the full-scale *launch*, introducing the service product to the entire market area. Different sectors tend to evaluate their new services/products in slightly different ways. For instance, fast-food operators use market surveys, whereas food service contractors rely more on after-sales customer feedback. The final step, *post-launch review*, should be aimed at determining whether the strategic objectives were achieved or whether further adjustments are needed.

Sheuing and Johnson suggest that firms should not rigidly follow this model but instead consider it as a framework from which to select those activities they deem necessary for a specific development. In fact, research studies have shown that tourism organizations do not follow a systematic NSD process (Jones et al., 1997).[20] It has been suggested that the systematic and formal approach to innovation is likely to be adopted only when one of the following is true: new products with major process impact are developed; a number of interrelated innovations are being developed simultaneously; product life cycles are long; competitors are unlikely to enter the market with a similar product or service; the new product is protected by license or patent; or the innovation is original or 'new to the world' (Jones et al., 1997).[21] The tourism and hospitality market clearly has few of these characteristics. Innovation is likely to follow a shorter, simplified development process when minor modifications are made to existing products or services; there is no license protection; the 'new' product is largely a copy of a competitor's product; innovation is not part of a major change programme; and competitors are actively innovating.

An organization creates internal conditions that either foster or hinder innovation. Often, these are strongly influenced by the external environment. Conditions that may encourage a systematic but rigid approach to innovation are a bureaucratic culture, mature marketplace, the involvement of external consultants, and formal research and development departments. Conditions that encourage a dynamic and flexible approach to innovation are the following: growing supply chain integration; an organizational culture founded on innovation; industry association sponsorship; creative and entrepreneurial leadership; and deregulated markets. These conditions are likely to be more typical of organizations in tourism and hospitality, as there are many small, highly entrepreneurial firms, such as weekendtrips.com (see Snapshot in Chapter 7), operating in a largely deregulated marketplace. However, large companies can also encourage innovation. Virgin, profiled in Chapter 11 for example, has always been innovative, largely because of the entrepreneurial leadership of Richard Branson. His entrepreneurship has always led him to take on challenges, risks and new projects, which he calls 'brand stretching'.

## Chapter Summary

Tourism and hospitality products are a group of selected components or elements brought together in a 'bundle' to satisfy needs and wants. There are three levels of tourism products: the core product, the tangible product, and the augmented product. An important part of the augmented product is the physical environment – often referred to as the 'servicescape'. This is very important for tourism and hospitality products such as hotels, restaurants and theme parks, which are dominated by experience attributes.

The product mix is the portfolio of products that an organization offers to one market or several. Another product analysis tool is the product life cycle (PLC); an organization

*(Continued)*

*(Continued)*

should assess each product and service in terms of its position on the product life cycle. The final product planning tool is positioning, its purpose being to create a distinctive place in the minds of potential customers.

Branding has developed in the field of packaged goods as a method of establishing a distinctive identity for a product based on competitive differentiation from other products. The case for branding is stronger for tourism products that offer the possibility for differentiation in several areas of the marketing mix. This is why branding has been particularly successful in hotel and restaurant marketing.

In the tourism and hospitality industry, packaging is the process of combining two or more related and complementary offerings into a single-price offering. Packaging provides several customer benefits, including easier budgeting for trips; increased convenience; greater economy; the opportunity to experience previously unfamiliar activities and attractions; and the opportunity to design components of a package for specialized interests.

Developing new products is different from maintaining existing ones, and planning for both kinds of product will differ according to whether the products are targeted at existing markets or new ones. Holloway and Plant suggest that a company has four alternatives in developing new products: market penetration, market development, product development, and diversification.

## Key Terms

## Discussion Questions and Exercises

1. Apart from the illustrations provided in this chapter, give some examples of businesses that are responding to consumer desires for experiences. How are they using the servicescape to deliver these experiences?

2. Think of a particular tourism or hospitality organization in which you believe physical evidence is particularly important in communicating with and satisfying customers. What information would you give to the manager of that organization to convince him or her of the importance of physical evidence in the organization's marketing strategy?

3. Re-read the Snapshot on the Churchill Museum. Apply the three levels of product to the museum. Where would you place the attraction on the product life cycle (PLC), and how are the managers trying to position the museum? How important is the servicescape for the museum?

4. It has been suggested that companies can commit 'brandicide' by stretching a well-known brand too far. Think of a brand that has done this. What was it that killed it off? Take a tourism brand you are familiar with and keep stretching it. How far can you go?

5. Holloway and Plant suggest that a company has four alternatives in developing new products: market penetration, market development, product development, and diversification. Think of an example (not already given in the text) of each strategy use in the tourism industry.

6. Why is it that many research studies have found that services rarely follow the new service development (NSD) steps suggested by Scheuing and Johnson (1989)?

## Creating an Alpine Winter Experience

*' To create memories for our guests and staff as the best mountain and resort experience... again and again.'*

This is the mission statement of Vancouver-based Intrawest – perhaps the most successful ski resort company in the world. Its success has been achieved by developing resort destinations as opposed to ski resorts. 'Experience' is a word used liberally by Intrawest in its marketing materials and by its staff. 'Disney does an incredible job of delivering a terrific experience – they provide a consistent experience and that's what we strive for,' says James Askew, former director of marketing and sales for the Pacific Northwest region of Intrawest. According to Askew, people are looking for an overall vacation experience when they go skiing, a holiday that offers more than skiing down

The resort village at Whistler, Canada

the mountain. So to meet the demands of ever-fussier, more sophisticated winter enthusiasts, and to entice guests to stay longer, Intrawest offers a slew of services besides skiing. The resort village is at the core of this formula, and for Intrawest the most important ingredient of this has been the real estate at the base of the mountain. Such convenient access to the slopes attracts more guests and fuels further commercial development, creating a bustling off-slope atmosphere.

Intrawest is not alone in revolutionizing the ski industry. Other resorts have followed suit, with property development and management becoming an important part of the ski business. For the operators, the most desirable visitors are what the trade calls 'destination skiers', the longer-stay tourists. Resort operators are increasingly banking on these visitors to fill hotels, townhouses and condominiums in the valleys below the slopes. The operators benefit not only from selling townhouses and condos, but also by helping the new owners rent their properties to visitors. Destination skiers tend to spend more, and it has been suggested that to defeat seasonality, destinations should focus on yield, rather than volume. In the Banff region of Canada, for example, the ski areas have been aggressively targeting European skiers over the last few decades. Although these destination skiers represent only 50 per cent of Banff's tourist market, they account for nearly 80 per cent of tourism expenditures.

There are many ingredients that combine to create a memorable alpine winter experience, but successful mountain operators appear to have followed one or more of three strategies to enhance the service experience: **product diversification, product improvement,** or **product differentiation**. Two factors are driving the diversification of winter sports. Firstly, winter resorts are losing customers. An analysis of market trends in North America and Europe suggests that an increasing proportion of those who take winter sports holidays on a regular basis do not ski at all. Secondly, even avid skiers are typically skiing less. On average they are somewhat older, and new high-speed lifts enable a skier to attain his/her physical stamina quotient much more quickly. As a result, winter resorts have realized that they have to offer more activities, both on-snow and off-snow. The more progressive resorts are now treating skiing as a form of entertainment by establishing more off-slope diversions. They are expanding the range of activities they offer to include ice-skating, snow-scooting, sledging and dog-sledging, ice-driving, paragliding, snowmobiling and tubing (the increasingly popular activity of sliding down the slope on the inner tube of a truck tyre). Many resorts – Verbier in Switzerland is an example – are also looking to enhance the efficiency, quality and profitability of their restaurants and shops.

Mountain resorts have to evolve and improve continually to meet the new demands of the consumer. The ski-runs and related lift systems clearly represent a prime attraction and therefore have long been the object of continuous improvements. For example, the process of linking ski areas has now become commonplace in France, following the initial lead given by resorts such as Tignes and Val d'Isere, which combined to form 'Espace Killy'; and Courchevel, Meribel, les Menuires and Val Thorens, which created the 'Trois Vallées'. With these changes, skiing areas have been expanded to higher altitudes, giving better snow conditions, increasing resorts' capacities and extending their season. The customer service experience can also be enhanced by the training of instructors and guides, and by offering authentic and natural experiences.

A third strategy taken by ski areas to enhance the service experience is differentiation. Despite the trend towards large resort alpine villages, there is a future for the small, independently owned resorts with comparatively shallow pockets. Some local hills are often more accessible, making them perfect for day trips, especially when they are close to large urban areas. Lake Louise and Sunshine, for example, are based in a national park and cannot offer all the amenities of a bustling alpine village. However, the relative tranquillity and beauty of the preserved environment sets them apart from other more developed resorts. Smaller resorts can also differentiate in other respects. Crested Butte in Colorado, for example, is attempting to differentiate on customer service, and believes its small size is a selling point. 'You don't have to be a huge mega-resort to offer a good ski vacation,' says Tim Mueller, the resort owner. Tamarack, also in Colorado, is positioning itself as a 'boutique' resort, limiting the number of skiers and boarders to 3,500 a day, despite capacity to accommodate 7,000. The idea is to create a private resort, with a focus on yield rather than volume, catering for a more discerning customer. 'This is not just a ski resort,' says owner Jean-Pierre Boespflug, 'but a unique place where homeowners, guests, and the public can take advantage of all there is to do here. We can send you into the wilderness, biking, skiing, golfing or boating.'

**Case Study**

**Case Study**

What is the future for the alpine winter experience? In most parts of the world, the ski industry has stagnated, with many resorts facing severe financial difficulties. If resorts are not to face inevitable decline, adaptation is essential. The trend to use winter sports as almost a 'loss leader' to bring in revenue from base operations continues to be the dominant financial model for resort operations. All the signs suggest that successful resorts of the next decades will be custom designed to meet the needs of every type of winter sports lover.

*Sources*: Hudson, S. (2000) *Snow Business: A Study of the International Ski Industry*. London: The Continuum International Publishing Group; Kadane, L. (30 November 2001) 'Lasting resort', *Calgary Herald*, SS1; Meyers, C. (February 2004) 'Crested Butte on the brink', *Ski*, 69–73. Hudson, S. (2006) 'Creating memorable alpine winter experiences', in Weiermair, K. and Brunner-Sperdin, A. (eds) *Erlebnisinszenierung im Tourismus*. Berlin: Erich Schmidt Verlag, pp 137–152.

## Questions

1. The text suggests that companies that fail to provide consistently engaging experiences, overprice their experiences relative to the value perceived, or overbuild their capacity to stage them will see pressure on demand, pricing, or both. How can ski resorts avoid these pitfalls?
2. With reference to Holloway and Plant's new product development options, what strategies have ski resorts followed in order to attract visitors?
3. Take a look at Intrawest's website. Is it continuing to develop resort destinations or has it changed its strategy?
4. Take a look at the marketing strategies of a ski resort near you. Is the resort following any of the three strategies mentioned in order to enhance the service experience?

## Websites

| | |
|---|---|
| www.disney.com | Disney |
| www.vegas.com/shopping/forumshops | The Forum, Las Vegas |
| www.tourtrends.com/customtours | Tour Trends |
| www.weekendtrips.com | Weekendtrips.com |
| www.churchillmuseum.iwm.org.uk | The Churchill Museum |
| www.fourseasons/maldives | Four Seasons Catamaran |
| www.museumofbrands | The Museum of Brands in London |
| www.bridgeclimb.com | Sydney Harbour BridgeClimb |
| www.arctic-experience.co.uk | Arctic Experience |
| www.jamieoliver.com | Jamie Oliver's website |
| www.intrawest.com | Intrawest |

# References

1  Middleton, V. T. C. and Clarke, J. (2001) *Marketing in Travel and Tourism*. Oxford: Butterworth-Heinemann.

2  Ibid.

3  Bitner, M. J. (1990) 'Evaluating service encounters', *Journal of Marketing*, 54(April), 69–82.

4  Russell, J. A., Ward, L. M. and Pratt, G. (1981) 'An affective quality attributed to environments', *Environment and Behavior*, 13(3), 259–288.

5  Brieger, P. (14 July 2004) 'The whiff of a shopping spree', *Financial Post*, 1 & 10.

6  Seaton, A. V. and Bennett, M. M. (1996) *Marketing Tourism Products: Concepts, Issues, Cases*. Thomson Business Press.

7  Anon. (7 May 2005) 'Enough perks to make you hope for another flight delay', *National Post*, FW4.

8  Mercer, D. (1992) *Marketing*. Oxford: Blackwell, 295.

9  Burke, J. F. and Resnick, B. P. (1991) *Marketing and Selling the Travel Product*. Cincinnati, OH: South-Western.

10  Goff, S. (3 February 2003) 'The advantages of being small, intimate and secure', *Financial Times*, IV.

11  Gilpin, S. (5–7 April 1994) 'Branding in the hotel industry. Where are we now?' Paper presented at the CHME Conference, Napier University, Edinburgh, April 5–7.

12  Lovelock and Wirtz (2007) Services Marketing 6th edition. New York: Prentice Hall.

13  Middleton, V. T. C. and Clarke, J. (2001) *Marketing in Travel and Tourism*. Oxford: Butterworth-Heinemann.

14  Redekop, B. (24 April 2004) 'Bear facts about tourism', *National Post*, FT4.

15  Anon. (3 January 2005) 'What's new', *Globe & Mail*, A8.

16  Holloway, J. C. and Plant, R. V. (1992) *Marketing for Tourism*. London. Pitman, 73.

17  Scheuing, E. E. and Johnson, E. M. (1989) 'A proposed model for new service development', *The Journal of Services Marketing*, 3(2), 25–34.

18  Jones, P., Hudson, S. and Costis, P. (1997) 'New product development in the UK tour-operating industry', *Progress in Tourism and Hospitality Research*, 3(4), 283–294.

19  Jones, P. (1995) 'Innovation in flight catering', in P. Jones and M. Kipps (eds), *Flight Catering*. London: Longman, 163–175.

20  Jones, P., Hudson, S. and Costis, P. (1997) 'New product development in the UK tour-operating industry', *Progress in Tourism and Hospitality Research*, 3(4), 283–294; Easingwood, C. J. (1986) 'New product development for service companies', *Journal of Product Innovation Management*, 3(3), 296–312.

21  Jones, P., Hudson, S. and Costis, P. (1997) 'New product development in the UK tour-operating industry', *Progress in Tourism and Hospitality Research*, 3(4), 283–294.

# 6

# PRICING

## Space Tourism: Priced Out of This World

Since 2001, when American millionaire Dennis Tito became the first space tourist, paying around US$20 million for a week's trip, space tourism is gradually becoming a viable commercial industry. Virgin's Richard Branson is spearheading the private enterprise movement towards making space trips a reality via Virgin Galactic Airways, founded in 1991. A million would-be passengers are estimated to be ready and willing to pay for such cutting-edge tourism experiences.

Branson plans to start offering sub-orbital space flights as early as 2008 and 40,000 people are already registered. Around 100 of them reputedly paid the full US$200,000 up front to become 'astronauts' during their three-hour flights, at 4,000 kilometres per hour, with a maximum of half an hour actually spent in space. 'We priced the tickets to give us enough money to get off the ground, as well as to start looking into orbital flights, hotels in space, hopefully a hotel on the moon,' said Branson. He first became interested in the project in the 1980s when he was outraged at a quote for US$25 million to accompany Russian astronauts on a space voyage. He and various family members planned to be aboard the first Virgin Galactic flight.

Branson is not the only contender in the race to make commercial space flights routine. In 2006 Space Adventures Ltd announced plans to build a US$265 million spaceport in the United Arab Emirates. Spacecraft for sub-orbital flights built by a Russian company were expected to be ready before 2008. Three telecommunications entrepreneurs (Hamid Ansari, his wife Anshousheh and brother Amir), from Texas, decided to back Space Adventures in this challenge to Branson's plans. The United Arab Emirates government also invested in the project to the tune of US$30 million.

Branson and Virgin have the advantage of brand recognition, connections, resources and 20 years of airline experience. In 2005 Virgin Galactic announced an agreement with New Mexico for a state-built $225 million spaceport at Las Cruces near the White Sands Missile Range. Construction at Las Cruces was

Space adventures is just one company seeking to make commercial space flights routine

hoped to start in 2007, depending on approval from environmental and aviation authorities. Virgin would have a 20-year lease on the facility with annual payments of $1 million for the first five years, rising to cover the cost of the project by the end of the lease. New Mexico's steady climate, free airspace, low population density and high altitude were all factors in choosing the site; factors which would also significantly reduce the cost of the space flight programme.

Surveys by the space industry show that at least half of Americans would like to see the Earth from space – if they could afford it. In fact, demand for space travel is fairly elastic; in willingness-to-pay surveys, demand increases significantly when the price falls. By 2015, competition within the fledgling industry could cut prices to around $15,000 per head. And the Space Frontier Foundation, an industry group, is aiming even lower, at about $5,000. In 2006 Space Adventures was already offering various space-related experiences at cheaper rates. Simulated lunar gravity flights could take passengers on parabolic rides, climbing and diving, giving a few minutes of weightlessness, for about $4,000. Florida-based Zero Gravity offers similar experiences, marketed as the world's largest rollercoaster rides, all available through travel agents. For those who would rather watch than experience such hair-raising rides, Planetspace was cashing in on voyeurism by providing paid public viewing of Canadian Arrow experiments at the Georgian Bay base in Ontario.

At the 55th Annual International Astronautical Congress in Vancouver in 2004, Prof. Haym Benaroya, a scientist from Rutgers University in New Jersey, presented a paper entitled 'Doing Business On the Moon', describing a lunar landscape dotted with resorts and amusement parks. Benaroya noted that Hilton Hospitality Inc., owner of the Hilton hotel chain, had also jumped on the space tourism bandwagon, commissioning an architectural study of a surface lunar hotel. It seems that space tourism will soon become a reality.

*Sources*: Hutchinson, B. (10 August 2004) 'Booking dreams at Moon Hotel', *National Post*, A3; Branson, R. (August 2005) 'My final frontier', *National Post Business*, 33; Otis, P. (2004) 'Please have your boarding pass ready at the launch pad', *Business Week*, 3903, 130-131; Wattie, C. (22 June 2004) 'US pilot makes space history', *National Post*, A11; Schwartz, John. (2 February 2006) 'More enter race to offer space tours', *The New York Times*.

## OBJECTIVES

On completion of this chapter, you should understand:

▶ the key factors determining pricing decisions;

▶ the contribution of economics to pricing;

▶ the specific characteristics of the tourism and hospitality industry that affect pricing policy;

▶ the key approaches that companies take toward pricing in tourism;

▶ how prices are calculated for new products;

▶ yield management as it applies to tourism; and

▶ the difference between strategic pricing and tactical pricing in tourism.

## Introduction

The Opening Vignette looks at the pricing of space tourism, and in particular the willingness to pay and the elasticity of demand for this new tourism product. These concepts are two of many pricing theories discussed in this chapter, which begins by looking at the impact of various corporate objectives on pricing. These objectives may be profit maximization, target rate of return, market share, survival, or growth. Even if these objectives are not explicit, they can have a significant impact on pricing. The second section highlights the key factors determining pricing decisions. As well as marketing objectives, these include costs, other mix variables, channel member expectations, buyer perceptions, competition, and legal and regulatory restrictions.

The third part of the chapter focuses on the contribution of economics to pricing. This includes a discussion of the interaction between supply and demand, and the importance of elasticity of demand. Generally, companies position their product employing one of three basic approaches to pricing: premium pricing, value-for-money pricing, and undercut pricing. These are examined here, using hotels as examples. The next main section discusses the basic approaches to pricing itself, which fall into three general categories: cost-based methods, demand-based methods, and competition-oriented pricing. Pricing strategies for new products are the subject of the next part of the chapter, which discusses prestige pricing, market skimming, and penetration pricing. Other pricing techniques are then examined, followed by a discussion of yield management. The difference between strategic pricing and tactical pricing is then explained, and the final section of the chapter looks at the specific characteristics of the tourism and hospitality industry that affect pricing policy.

Pricing is crucial to the successful marketing of any product or service, but it is often the least understood of the marketing mix elements. The prices that an organization charges for its products must strike a balance between gaining acceptance with the target market and making profit for the organizations. Even in not-for-profit organizations, the pricing of products and services is the key to encouraging consumption. The pricing element of the marketing mix is unique in that it is the only one that directly affects an organization's revenues, and hence its profits. The fields of finance and economics have much to contribute in setting prices, but on their own perhaps do not lead to the best pricing decisions. Other marketing mix decisions often interact with pricing decisions. Product quality (both real and perceived) needs to be considered in light of price. Knowledge of the **price–quality trade-off** compels decision-makers to recognize that consumers might accept a higher cost for a better quality of product. Similarly, with regard to brand image – often the consequence of marketing communications decisions – lesser-known brands might command lower prices. Finally, pricing decisions must take into account the needs of the distributor. Distributors will sell a product only if they will obtain a certain profit margin.

---

**PRICE–QUALITY TRADE-OFF**
acceptance of the higher cost of a better quality of product

---

As with other elements in the marketing mix, pricing should be treated as a tool to achieve corporate and marketing objectives. If the target market has been clearly identified, and a decision has been made about where a product is to be positioned, then pricing will become easier to determine. Companies choosing to position their products in the mass market and to enter a field with many competitors will need to adopt a very careful pricing policy. Those seeking to appeal to niche markets, like Space Adventures in the Opening Vignette, may have

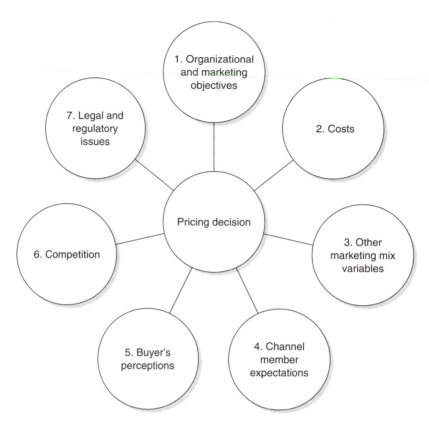

**Figure 6.1** Factors Affecting Pricing Decisions

*Source*: Dibb, S., Simkin, L., Pride, W.M. and Ferrell, O.C. (1994) *Marketing: Concepts and Strategies* (2nd edn). London: Houghton-Mifflin.

slightly more price flexibility, since they have fewer competitors and perhaps more points of difference between their products and others in the niche.

## Factors Determining Pricing Decisions

Whatever the strategy of the organization, clear pricing objectives should be established before price levels are set. The key factors determining pricing decisions are shown in Figure 6.1. They are as follows.

### Organizational and Marketing Objectives

The most common objectives are **profit maximization**, **target rate of return**, **market share**, and survival. However, for some organizations, such as national parks or museums, objectives are not only commercial in their nature, and pricing decisions are made for societal reasons. This may involve raising entry fees to reduce the social and environmental impacts of increasing numbers of visitors, as in the case of Machu Picchu in Peru (see Global Spotlight in Chapter 13), or lowering fees to encourage more access. Other objectives may include being perceived as offering outstanding value for money, or being the brand leader in the marketplace. The first may be reflected in lower prices, whereas the second goal could lead to high prices in the long term.

---

**PROFIT MAXIMIZATION**
corporate objective that causes managers in organizations to make decisions in such a way as to maximize profits

---

**TARGET RATE OF RETURN**
corporate objective that aims to achieve a particular return on the assets employed in an organization

---

**MARKET SHARE**
the percentage relationship of an organization's sales to total industry sales

---

## Costs

The setting of prices should incorporate a calculation of how much it costs the organization to produce the product or service. If the company is profit-oriented, a margin will be added to the cost price to derive the selling price. An organization could also decide to sell below cost for a period of time, which is often referred to as a tactical price reduction, discussed later in this chapter. The Snapshot 'Low-Cost Airlines Take to the Air' looks at the low-cost airlines that are springing up all over the world. These airlines are able to compete by offering low prices.

## Other Marketing Mix Variables

Pricing decisions always have an interaction with the other elements of the marketing mix. Consider the example of Canadian Mountain Holidays (CMH), which sells expensive heli-skiing holidays (see the Case Study in Chapter 7). The high price of this product must be reflected in other elements of the marketing mix. A high level of personal service is included as part of the promotional package, and the quality of the lodges must meet the expectations that the high price has generated in the minds of the customers. Distribution of the holidays takes place via an exclusive channel system of overseas agents, reflecting the high-quality image and resulting high price.

## Channel Member Expectations

A marketer must consider the intermediaries in the distribution channel when pricing a product or service. Travel agents, for example, will expect to earn commissions for their efforts. However, some stakeholders in the travel industry, such as airlines, car rental companies and international hotel chains, have been quick to grasp the potential of marketing and selling their services online. They have recognized an opportunity to bypass agents and sell their basic products and services directly to the customer. Increasingly, package holiday tour operators are also including direct sales via the internet in their sales strategy, thus bypassing the travel agent.

## Buyer Perceptions

The prices set for travel products and services must reflect customers' perceptions in the target market. The key is whether customers perceive that the price they have paid represents good value for money and matches their quality expectations. In tourism and hospitality, consumers expect a high level of service and special features if a high price is being charged. For example, after paying CDN$9,000, a CMH heli-skier can expect lodges to contain a fully stocked bar, a sauna and jacuzzi, and even a resident qualified massage therapist.

## Competition

In competitive markets, organizations will be trying to win customers from competitors in two ways. Price competition involves offering the product or service at a lower price than that charged by competitors. In a very competitive marketplace, organizations are likely to resort to intense price competition to sell goods and services. Non-price competition, on the other hand, is concerned with trying to increase market share or sales by leaving the price unchanged, but persuading target customers that the product is superior to that offered by the competition. Such a strategy is more typical in oligopolistic markets, in which there are few competitors. It is important for tourism organizations, including destinations, to monitor the prices charged by competitors. A study of holiday costs in three different countries in 2006 found that the UK was considerably more expensive that Spain or the US for the same tourism services (Ungoed-Thomas, 2006).[1]

## Legal and Regulatory Issues

There may be legal and regulatory restrictions that control the ways in which an organization fixes prices. For example, Robben Island in Cape Town (see Opening Vignette in Chapter 12), which is subsidized by the government, may be put under pressure to keep prices low to encourage people to visit. Legal restrictions are often placed on the practice of price fixing and collusion. Additionally, there are a number of organizations, quasi-governmental and

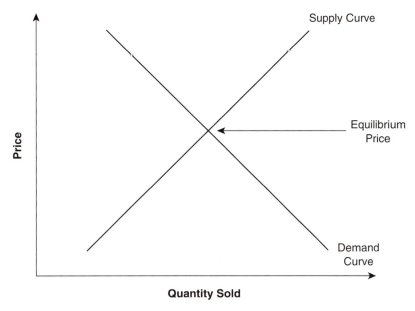

**Figure 6.2**   The Interaction of Supply and Demand

industrial, that exercise some influence on pricing policies and strategies, a fact that marketing managers must bear in mind.

## Contributions of Economics to Pricing

Economists contend that producers of a commodity are more likely to provide that commodity if the price for it in the marketplace is high. This is coupled with the suggestion that buyers are likely to purchase more of the commodity if prices are low. From this comes the idea that the quantity produced and consumed and the price acceptable to each party will be in equilibrium at some point. This is shown in Figure 6.2.

Unfortunately, this simplistic model is unlikely to be useful as a mathematical way of determining prices because it assumes that certain conditions need to be present for the process to occur. One of these is the assumption that consumers have perfect knowledge, and know all the prices from all the producers. Although the use of the internet is increasing, the likelihood of such wide consumer knowledge is small in the travel industry. However, although the model may not help pricing decisions in a mathematical or graphical way, the concept is not completely redundant. For instance, if a tourism organization has a feeling that the market is undersupplied, it may tend to increase prices. This happened in Las Vegas between 2003 and 2008, when hoteliers were able to charge premium room rates due to high demand. Similarly, if buyers sense that the market is oversupplied, they may try to negotiate lower prices – as happened in the hotel market

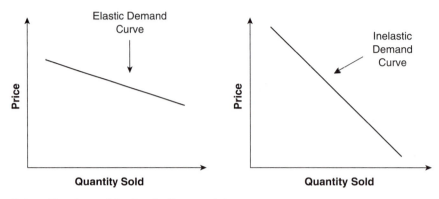

**Figure 6.3**   Elastic and Inelastic Demand Curves

after terrorist attacks, the war in Iraq, and the outbreak of severe acute respiratory syndrome (SARS).

## Elasticity of Demand

The raising and lowering of prices generally has an effect on the level of sales. The analysis of buyers' reactions to price change employs the concept of the **elasticity of demand**. This is represented by the formula:

$$\text{Price elasticity of demand} = \frac{\%\ \text{change in quantity demanded}}{\%\ \text{change in price}}$$

If demand increases in line with price cuts then the product or service is said to be elastic. But if demand remains relatively unaltered by price changes, the product or service is said to be inelastic. In the tourism and hospitality industry, many products are elastic – as prices fall, demand increases. However, there are many occasions when this is not true. Business travel is often inelastic, and popularity or fashion may render a destination or restaurant inelastic. In the Snapshot below, demand for the Burj Al Hotel in Dubai would seem to be inelastic. The hotel can charge very high prices, as business travellers are willing to pay for such luxury. Figure 6.3 shows two demand curves – for an elastic and an inelastic product. As with knowledge of the state of supply and demand, managers are not often in a position to know mathematically the value of elasticity for a product. They may not have access to all price and quantity data, or the service may be new and there may therefore be no historical data from which to derive the slope of the demand curve.

---

**ELASTICITY OF DEMAND**
the sensitivity of customer demand to changes in the prices of services

---

Price elasticity can be affected by a number of factors, including the customer's perception of the uniqueness of the product, the availability and awareness of substitutes, and how the consumer budgets. For example, a leisure traveller buying a holiday for personal use will have one perspective on price value; if the same person uses a company charge account, he or she may have another set of values. If consumers are purchasing something for someone else to use, they may be prepared to spend more – or less – than they would spend on themselves. Price elasticity of demand gives management a statistical method to measure whether or not the organization's prices are too high or low. In setting prices, a company will want to know what levels of demand it is likely to experience at different prices. This can be done in two ways.

The first method is often called **willingness-to-pay (WTP) assessment**. The Opening Vignette suggested that demand for space travel is fairly elastic; in willingness-to-pay surveys, demand increases significantly when the price falls. The difficulty with this is that what people say they will do does not always translate into actual behaviour when the product is launched. A second way of assessing demand at different prices is **test marketing**, although it is difficult to control all the factors apart from price that will influence consumer decisions in different areas.

---

**WILLINGNESS-TO-PAY (WTP) ASSESSMENT**
asking potential customers what they would be willing to pay for the product

---

**TEST MARKETING**
a limited introduction of a product or service to test public reactions

---

## Snapshot

### Pricing for the Luxury Market: Burj Al Arab Hotel, Dubai

The United Arab Emirates may not be the first destination on many travellers' wish lists, but Dubai's draw is undeniable. Described variously as the Gold City, the Artificial City and the billionaire's playground, Dubai has been slowly shifting its attention away from energy over the years and into finance, commerce, transportation and tourism. In short, Dubai is cash rich and resource poor, interested in doing business with the world and with money to pay for it. Construction has been more or less non-stop in Dubai over the last few decades, with a number of high-class hotels built to cater for the growing number of tourists. The sail-shaped Burj Al Hotel is one such development.

Boasting seven stars, the Burj Al Hotel caters to the millionaires and billionaires of the world with its luxurious and spectacular facilities. It provides exclusivity, security and privacy – for celebrities in particular but also for international businessmen – for a high price tag: US$600 for a basic room per night and US$8,000 for the Royal Suite. Voyeurs can also nose around the hotel's decadent public areas for $25, refundable against any purchase in the lavish bars, restaurants or gift shops.

Working on the premise that people are willing to pay more for luxury, for the quality of service and for the setting, the hotel was opened in 1999 on a man-made island 280 metres offshore, reached by a causeway across which guests are shuttled in Rolls Royces. Each of the 202 rooms has a 42-inch plasma TV, Versace sheets on canopied beds, and is set on two floors connected by a spiral staircase. Every floor has its own check-in desk plus private elevators for the Royal Suites, ensuring both privacy and security. Butlers are available for guests' every need and they enter suites via separate entrances to guarantee the least disruption to the visitor. The two-bedroom Royal Suites are decorated in marble and gold, have revolving beds, private cinema, and dressing rooms larger than average hotel rooms.

No expense was spared on the hotel's design or its rococo furnishings fit for a sheik's palace. It is shaped like a ship's sail soaring over 341 metres high, making it the tallest hotel in the world. The lobby is a massive atrium, stretching several hundred feet up, making it one of the largest in the world. Gold pilasters and enormous aquariums surround the escalators. On the 17th floor, a British artist has an exhibition, sponsored by British Aerospace and Lockheed, where he sells his paintings of local flora and fauna for $30,000 apiece.

Restaurant facilities are equally luxurious, in particular the sealife-encircled Al Mahara Seafood Restaurant, reached by a short submarine from the lobby. The Skyview Restaurant, 200 metres above the Arabian Gulf, is reached by an express panoramic lift that travels at six metres per second. During the day, only hotel residents can use the facilities but the restaurants are open to outside diners by night. Bills can soar into thousands of dollars but the average cost is between US$200 and $500 for two people.

*Sources*: Dalrymple, T. (6 May 2002) 'Gulf de Luxe – Luxury Hotel in Dubai', *National Review*; Fannin, R. (May 2005). 'Desert luxury; a burgeoning oasis, Dubai is the new 'in' place for the vacationing CEO', *The Chief Executive*.

## Pricing and Positioning

Generally, companies use pricing as part of their positioning of a product, employing one of three strategic approaches: premium pricing, value-for-money pricing, and undercut pricing (Dickman, 1999).[2]

### Premium Pricing

In **premium pricing**, a decision is made to set prices above market price, to reflect either the image of quality or the unique status of the product. The product may be new, or it may have unique features not shared by competitors, such as the Burj Al Hotel in Dubai (see Snapshot). Also, the company itself may have such a strong reputation that the brand image alone is sufficient to merit a premium price. The Four Seasons Hotel chain follows this strategy in setting prices. Promoted as upscale, full-service hotels, Four Seasons will, on occasion, raise prices to the highest level in the area. Others may use premium pricing in order to generate publicity. In 2005 the Hotel Jerome in Aspen started offering a ten-night holiday package that included unlimited ski tickets, private lessons, on-call masseuses, a chauffeur and a Maybach car that guests could get to keep. The price tag was US$1 million.[3] Not to be outdone, The Marquis Los Cabos hotel in Baja California created a three-night stay with private jet and golf with Jack Nicklaus for US$7 million.

---

**PREMIUM PRICING**

setting prices above market price, to reflect either the image of quality or the unique status of the product

---

## Value-for-Money Pricing

In **value-for-money pricing**, the intention is to charge medium prices and emphasize that the product represents excellent value for money at this price. Organizations with well-established reputations for service generally do well with such a pricing strategy. According to *Travel & Leisure* magazine, guests staying at properties in the Fairmont Hotels & Resorts collection are consistently maximizing the value of their dollar by receiving exceptional service, unique offerings, and renowned hospitality at an affordable price. For many 'medical tourists', having surgery in a foreign country represents excellent value for money, given the exorbitant costs of medical care in developed countries, and the comparative ease and affordability nowadays of international travel. The Case Study at the end of this chapter explores this phenomenon in more detail.

---

**VALUE-FOR-MONEY PRICING**

charging medium prices and emphasizing that the product represents excellent value for money at this price

---

## Undercut Pricing

Sometimes called 'cheap value' pricing, the objective in **undercut pricing** is to undercut the competition by setting lower prices, and the lower price is used as a trigger for immediate purchasing. Entrants into the low-cost airline segment use this tactic (see Snapshot below). Unit profits are low, but satisfactory overall profits are achieved through high turnover. This strategy is often used by organizations seeking a foot in or rapid expansion into a new market. EasyCruise, the cruise line owned by Sir Stelios Haji-Ioannou, follows such a pricing strategy. Launched in 2005, EasyCruises (there are two of them now) sail around the hotspots of the French and Italian Rivieras. Instead of emphasizing the shipboard experience (his are bare-bones cruise ships with just a bed, a shower unit and a toilet in the cabins) Stelios makes the ports the main attraction. It is part of his strategy to attract a younger demographic – tourists in their twenties or thirties who might usually avoid a week-long cruise. Sailing happens in the early morning for six hours or less, so that passengers can go on land, have a night of fun, then sleep it off in their cabins. Nightly rates are around £20 per person; the earlier one books, the lower the rate.

---

**UNDERCUT PRICING**

setting prices lower than the competition and using the price as a trigger to purchase immediately

---

Any of these policies can be seen as 'fair-pricing' policies. A fair price can be defined as one that the customer is happy to pay while the company achieves a satisfactory level of profit. Thus a premium-pricing policy is acceptable, provided that the customer receives the benefits appropriate to the price. Only when companies are able to force up prices against the consumers' will, such as in the case of monopolies, can it be said that fair pricing is inoperative. A **monopoly** is a supply situation in which there is only one seller.

---

**MONOPOLY**
a supply situation in which there is only one seller

---

## Snapshot

### Low-cost Airlines Take to the Air

'No frills' is the latest term buzzing around the airline industry, and cut-price companies such as Ryanair are taking it to the extreme. The Dublin-based airline, the second biggest international carrier in the world, is spearheading the move towards very basic, cheap continental travel with no complimentary food and beverage services, very low luggage allowances, tight cabin space, high charges for excess baggage, and other surcharges for extras, such as wheelchair service. Also, cut-price flights often use smaller, secondary airports, sometimes situated far from city centres (Ryanair frequently uses Stansted instead of Heathrow). There are also compensation limitations if flights are delayed: passengers may not be eligible for food and accommodation since most cut-price airlines are not part of the EU's Passenger Service Commitment.

Despite the disadvantages and potential discomforts of cheap travel, price is the bottom line and passengers vie for seats sometimes offered as low as $25 for one-way European flights. This only covers the flight taxes and service charges, so basically the seats are free. There are about 60 low-price airlines within Europe, including Geneva-based Flybaboo. Many have recently failed in this volatile, cut-throat market – such as JetGreen, Duo, JetMagic, V Bird and Volareweb.com – leaving customers somewhat insecure, with no guarantees for advance reservations.

Similar price-cutting is also happening throughout India, Asia and the Middle East. SpiceJet, an Indian low-fare airline, competes with Kingfisher Airlines Ltd. and Air Deccan for the lucrative domestic market. Within India, with its increasingly prosperous emerging middle class, there has been a shift from train travel to the quicker and more efficient air travel. Air travel demand is expected to rise 25 per cent per year until 2010, with up to 100 million people choosing air over travel by land, thanks to low fares and also improved in-flight amenities and service. This is partly due to government deregulation but also to the fierce competition between airlines, which has transformed the industry, with its original reputation for poor service, to an efficient and comfortable option. Low-cost air travel is mainly distributed via the internet in India. SpiceJet sells about 70 per cent of its seats on the internet and also reduces its overheads by utilizing its aircraft for a full 12 hours per day as well as aiming to fill up each flight with at least 80–90 per cent loads.

In Southeast Asia, likewise, a fierce price war erupted in the budget airline market during 2004, in sharp contrast to the high-price flights traditionally offered in the region. To gain market share and capture public attention, low-cost carriers offered one-way tickets from Singapore to popular destinations such as Bangkok for less than US$1 each. The lowest price was 59 cents, which Tiger Airways offered for one-way tickets to three different Thai destinations. In retaliation Thai Air Asia offered a 29-cent ticket to Bangkok, delighting consumers who would normally pay around US$250 return for Singapore to Bangkok. In the Middle East, the air transportation sector is becoming increasingly segmented, as new start-up airlines emerge to challenge the incumbent Middle Eastern carrier Emirates for a share of the global aviation pie. Low-cost carriers, like Air Arabia and Jazeera Airways, launched in 2003 and 2005 respectively, were prompted by the success of low-cost pioneers in North America and Europe, as well as the opportunity to offer a wide choice of prices and options on intra-regional flights compared to legacy rivals.

In 2006, Brazilian carrier Varig offered free tickets for domestic flights in an effort to win back flyers after financial problems resulted in cancellations and stranded clients. However, most of these media-hitting promotions are short lived. Ryanair's Chief Executive, Michael O'Leary, is looking to push the boundaries in a bid to replace airfares with inflight gambling. He has introduced gambling services via passengers' mobile phones or Blackberries, using a payment system that debits a passenger's credit card before the plane lands. In 2005 subsidiary services such as car hire, hotels, travel insurance and in-flight sales accounted for around 20 per cent of Ryanair's £950 million turnover, and O'Leary predicts that non-ticket revenues could rise dramatically with the introduction of more in-flight entertainment.

*Sources*: Park, K. (12 March 2006) 'Flying high on low costs', *The Hindu Business Line*, 11; Hutchinson, B. (5 November 2005) 'Citizens discover joys of air travel', *Financial Post*, FP1; Harrison, M. (3 November 2005) 'Onboard gambling may lead to free flights on Ryanair', *The Independent*, 13.

## Basic Approaches to Pricing

Organizations involved in the marketing of tourism, leisure and hospitality products use different methods of calculation to set prices. Pricing methods fall into three main categories:

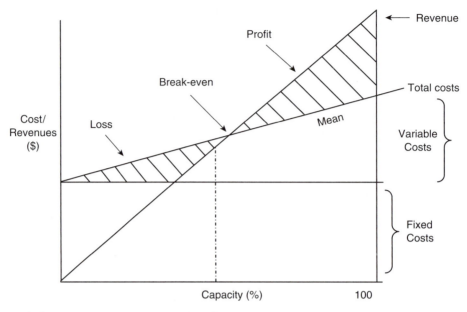

**Figure 6.4**  The Break-even Point for a Hypothetical Hotel

## Cost-based Methods

**Cost-based pricing** – the addition of a certain monetary amount or percentage to the actual or estimated costs of a service to arrive at a final price – draws heavily on the accounting discipline of costing. To use this method, it is necessary to understand the differences in the nature of costs. At the simplest level, costs can be split into two types. **Fixed costs** are costs that do not vary with the amount of the service provided. Hence, a hotelier has the fixed cost of owning the hotel to bear, whether or not rooms are occupied. **Variable costs**, on the other hand, are those that increase as more of a service is provided. For example, the energy and cleaning costs of a hotel will increase as more guests occupy the rooms. These two cost elements can be combined with revenue – which should increase as more of the service is sold – to give a picture of when an operation becomes profitable. Known as **break-even analysis** or cost/profit/volume (CPV) analysis, the interaction of these elements can be shown graphically. Figure 6.4 shows the break-even point for a hypothetical hotel that has high fixed costs.

---

**COST-BASED PRICING**
adding a certain monetary amount or percentage to the actual or estimated costs of a service to arrive at a final price

---

---

**FIXED COSTS**

costs that do not vary with the amount of the service provided

---

**VARIABLE COSTS**

costs that increase as more of a service is provided

---

**BREAK-EVEN ANALYSIS**

a pricing technique that considers fixed and variable costs, customer volumes, and profit margins

---

Having established the cost of doing business, the simplest approach to pricing is to add a standard mark-up to the cost of the product, known as **cost-plus pricing**. A restaurant manager might decide that all wines will be marked up by 100 per cent and all food dishes will be marked up by 60 per cent. For example, a bottle of wine purchased at £12 will be sold for £24, and a steak dinner that costs £10 (including both fixed and variable costs) will be sold for £16. Clearly, this approach to pricing takes little account of market forces, and while costs do have to be covered in the long run, policies have to respond to changing market conditions and what the market will bear. However, the concept of marginal costing, which attempts to identify the cost of one or more unit of a product, is an important one in cost-plus pricing, since it offers the marketing manager a flexible tool for pricing. For example, in the case of an airline ticket for a flight across Europe, the additional cost of carrying one more passenger is extremely small: an added meal, a minute addition to fuel, etc. Therefore, once break-even is achieved, it becomes very attractive to price the 'marginal seats' (any remaining seats over the number that have to be sold to break even) at a price that will attract market demand from those unwilling to pay regular fares. This is the tactic used by many of the low-cost airlines (see Snapshot above).

---

**COST-PLUS PRICING**

adding a standard mark-up to the cost of the product to reach the price charged

---

## Demand-based Methods

Sometimes called **buyer-based pricing** (or **sensitivity pricing**), techniques in the demand-based category share the feature of giving major consideration to the consumer. These methods allow for high prices when the demand is high and for lower prices when the demand is low, regardless of the cost of the product. Such pricing is common for accommodation in the popular holiday beach resorts of Europe, where hotels tend to be more expensive in summer than in winter due to higher demand. Demand-based pricing allows an organization to charge higher prices and therefore to make higher profits as long as the buyers value the products above the cost price. Segmentation is often used to price travel and tourism products, using time (see the Global Spotlight on Banff Mount Norquay) and age (children usually pay less for tourism services and attractions), for example, as the basis for segmenting the market.

---

**BUYER-BASED PRICING (SENSITIVITY PRICING)**
allows for high prices when the demand is high and for lower prices when the demand is low, regardless of the cost of the product

---

Deeper understanding of the way consumers perceive prices can lead to **psychological pricing**. This usually manifests itself as prices that avoid barriers. For example, a £1,000 holiday may seem psychologically cheaper if offered at £999. Similarly, in order to present a simplified choice of product to the consumer, **price lining** – pre-establishing price lines (levels) that the company feels confident will attract customers – may be employed. For example, a whale-watching trip may be priced at £75 but may not include lunch. The same trip including lunch might be priced at £100 – even though lunch can be provided at a low cost, the £25 is added to make the offer clearly distinct. As long as consumers perceive the gap as representing a clear difference of price and quality, they should accept the distinction. The mistake to avoid is to price many products with marginal differences and prices, as this may lead to consumer confusion.

---

**PSYCHOLOGICAL PRICING**
using slightly lower prices to give consumers the perception of added value

---

**PRICE LINING**
pre-establishing price lines (levels) that the company feels confident will attract customers

---

One customer-driven pricing strategy that has increased in popularity due to the internet is the reverse auction. Travel e-tailers, such as Priceline.com (see Global Spotlight in Chapter 10), Hotwire.com, and Lowestfare.com, act as intermediaries between prospective buyers, who request quotations for a product or service, and multiple suppliers who quote the best price they are willing to offer. Buyers can then review the offers and select the supplier that best meets their needs. Different business models underlie these services.

While some are provided free to end users, most e-tailers either receive a commission from the supplier or do not pass on the whole savings. Others charge a fixed fee or one based on a percentage of the savings. Another important type of demand-based pricing, particularly in organizational buying, is **negotiating**, a technique used to establish prices when at least two parties are involved who have a conflict of interest with respect to the product. Hotel space, exhibition services and transport seats are all examples of tourism and hospitality products that are often block-booked by buyers, be they tour operators or specialist buyers.

---

**NEGOTIATING**

a technique used to establish prices when at least two parties are involved who have a conflict of interest with respect to the product

---

## Competition-oriented

In **competition-oriented** pricing, an organization fixes prices in relation to competitors' prices; this is also called **going-rate pricing**. This method offers the advantage of giving the organization the opportunity to increase sales or market share, but it is a dangerous approach, as it does not focus on either costs or the consumer. The arguments in its favour are that the industry will have developed prices that are acceptable to the market-place, and that there is little to be gained by offering different prices (so-called 'industry wisdom'). The counter-argument is that there may be the opportunity to offer different prices (and therefore possibly to achieve better profits) that the majority of the industry has ignored.

---

**COMPETITION-ORIENTED PRICING (GOING-RATE PRICING)**

technique in which an organization fixes prices in relation to competitors' prices

---

Some companies use competitors' prices as a target to be undercut. Those adopting this approach will need to be sure of their cost structures compared to those of others. The danger is that competitors may have supply links that give them a cost advantage, or have some kind of 'hold' on customers, such as a strong loyalty scheme. In this case, prices charged may not be a true indication of either costs or price sensitivity. Generally, undercutting is a difficult position to sustain if the price cutter does not have lower costs in the long term. It may also lead to price wars. The Snapshot on the low-cost airlines above described how in Southeast Asia, a fierce price war erupted in the budget airline market during 2004, in sharp contrast to the high-price flights traditionally an offer. Some airlines may be competition-oriented to the extent that they use prices to try to drive out competition, perhaps to give themselves a long-term monopoly. Airlines have also been accused of price-fixing in the past. For example, in 2006, several airlines including British Airways, American and United, were at the centre of a criminal investigation into alleged price-fixing on long-haul passenger flights across the Atlantic (Teather et al., 2006).[4]

## Pricing Strategies for New Products

At the core of pricing is the consumer's perception of price in relation to quality and value for money. This perception can be influenced by the way in which a company charges for its services. When a new product enters the market, it is vital to obtain market share and create the desired image for the product in the consumer's eyes. New products face unique problems. If the product is truly new – something never before available in the marketplace, like the BridgeClimb featured in Chapter 5 – it will be extremely difficult for consumers to develop a sense of what price is appropriate. If there are no similar products with which to compare it, they may either undervalue the innovation or perhaps overvalue it. Detailed research on price sensitivity, clearly outlining the unique features of the new product and researching the best way to communicate this information to consumers, will be important.

Three strategies commonly used for the introduction of new products are prestige pricing, market skimming and penetration pricing.

### Prestige Pricing

**Prestige pricing** sets prices high to position a product at the upper or luxury end of the market. For example, tourism and hospitality operators that wish to be seen as top-end operators or establishments must enter the market with high prices to reflect this quality image. The product itself will need to deliver this quality level (in terms of décor, menu, locations, fittings, etc.) A coach company introducing a new luxury vehicle with airline-style seats, individual light and air-conditioning controls, panoramic windows, onboard catering, and amenities can price the transportation as a prestige product. If consumers value these attributes, they will pay the additional premium price. The Hotel Burj Al Arab in Dubai follows such a strategy (see Snapshot above).

---

**PRESTIGE PRICING**
setting prices high to position a product at the upper or luxury end of the market

---

### Market Skimming

This policy of 'skimming the cream' calls for setting high prices at the launch stage and progressively lowering them as the product becomes better established and progresses through its life cycle. **Market skimming** takes advantage of the fact that most products are in high demand in the early stage of the life cycle, when they are novel or unique or when supplies are limited. Demand can be managed by setting very high prices initially to attract those prepared to meet them, and gradually reducing the price to meet different market segments' price elasticities. The particular value of this policy is that it provides a high inflow of funds to the company when the marketing costs are highest. Operators in the space tourism market are currently following this strategy (see Opening Vignette). If the product anticipates a very short life cycle – as in the case of major events such as the World Cup football tournament – and organizing and marketing costs must be recovered quickly, market skimming is a sensible policy to pursue.

> **MARKET SKIMMING**
> a policy of 'skimming the cream' that calls for setting high prices at the launch stage and progressively lowering them as the product becomes better established

## Penetration Pricing

This strategy is the opposite of market skimming, as prices are set at a very low initial level. If an organization is trying to achieve maximum distribution for the product in the initial stages, it will probably price at a lower level to obtain maximum sales and market share. This method is commonly used in the marketing of fast-moving consumer goods, when rapid distribution-stocking is essential to the success of the product. If the market is price sensitive (such as in the fast-food sector), **penetration pricing** is an efficient way to gain a quick foothold. The intention is to set low prices only until this market share has been established and then to raise prices gradually to market levels. EasyCruise, mentioned earlier, penetrated the cruise market with very low prices for its first ship, and then with their second, EasyCruiseTwo, raised prices, justified by a more up-market restaurant and bar.

> **PENETRATION PRICING**
> setting prices at a lower level initially to get maximum sales and market share; used when an organization is trying to get maximum distribution for the product or service in the initial stages

## Other Pricing Techniques

### Promotional

**Promotional pricing** is used by companies when they temporarily sell products below their normal list price (or rack rate). This is often done to introduce new or revamped products.

Promotional pricing is used in the restaurant sector in these situations. The assumption is that consumers will buy other items at normal price levels along with the promotionally priced items. Promotional pricing is often used in conjunction with product-bundle pricing (see below).

---

**PROMOTIONAL PRICING**
temporarily selling products below their normal list price (or rack rate)

---

## Product-bundle Pricing

When a company groups several of its products together to promote them as a package, it is using **product-bundle pricing**. An example would be a hotel offering a weekend special that includes a room, dinner in a restaurant, valet parking, room-service breakfast, and late check-out for a set price. In some cases the package will include products that customers might not normally buy (such as the valet parking); this is often done to improve usage during slow periods. Package tours are a popular type of product bundling. Wholesalers package airfare, ground transport, accommodation, sightseeing tours and admission to attractions, and because of their bulk purchases they can negotiate significant discounts. These companies can then offer packages to customers that work out to be considerably cheaper than buying the individual components separately. Bundling therefore offers cost advantages to the company as well as convenience to the consumer. Banff Mount Norquay, featured in the Global Spotlight below, often bundles together a lift ticket with accommodation in a nearby hotel.

---

**PRODUCT-BUNDLE PRICING**
grouping together a company's products to promote them as a package

---

## Price Spread and Price Points

Organizations in tourism and hospitality try to offer a **price spread** – a range of products that will suit the budget of all target markets. A holiday park, for example, may offer campsites with tents, standard cabins, en suite cabins and family units, each different from the other in terms of size, location, types of fittings and furnishings. Table 6.1 shows the range of prices offered by Banff Mount Norquay, the ski resort profiled in the Global Spotlight on page 198. The range of prices that an organization can set is virtually unlimited. However, research in the restaurant sector has suggested that if the price spread is too wide, consumers will tend to order from among the lower-priced items (Carmin and Norku 1990).[5]

**Table 6.1**   Banff Mount Norquay Lift Ticket Prices, 2006–2007

**Regular Tickets (not upgradeable)**

| Categories | Adult 18+ | Youth/Student | Child 6–12 | Senior 55+ |
|---|---|---|---|---|
| Full-day | 49.00 | 39.00 | 17.00 | 39.00 |
| Afternoon | 41.00 | 32.00 | 14.00 | 32.00 |
| Night skiing | 24.00 | 22.00 | 12.00 | 22.00 |
| Last hour | 15.00 | 15.00 | 10.00 | 15.00 |

**Hourly (not upgradeable – valid from time of purchase or until closing)**

| Categories | Adult 18+ | Youth/Student | Child 6–12 | Senior 55+ |
|---|---|---|---|---|
| 2 hours | 29.00 | 25.00 | 11.00 | 25.00 |
| 2.5 hours | 32.00 | 27.00 | 12.00 | 27.00 |
| 3 hours | 35.00 | 30.00 | 13.00 | 30.00 |
| 3.5 hours | 38.00 | 33.00 | 14.00 | 33.00 |
| 4 hours | 41.00 | 35.00 | 15.00 | 35.00 |
| 4.5 hours | 44.00 | 38.00 | 16.00 | 38.00 |
| 5 hours | 47.00 | 40.00 | 17.00 | 40.00 |

**Multi-day (must be used on consecutive days)**

| Categories | Adult 18+ | Youth/Student | Child 6–12 |
|---|---|---|---|
| 2 days | 98.00 | 76.00 | 31.00 |
| 3 days | 138.00 | 108.00 | 44.00 |
| 4 days | 184.00 | 144.00 | 58.00 |
| 5 days | 230.00 | 180.00 | 73.00 |

*Source*: Banff Mount Norquay Lift Ticket Prices (2007)  Retrieved 15 April, 2007, from www/banffnorquay.com.

---

**PRICE SPREAD**

a range of products and prices that will suit the budget of all target markets

---

**Price points** are the number of 'stops' along the way between the lowest-priced item and the highest-priced item. Price points vary among industry sectors and types of business. In a restaurant, it is possible to create a menu with a wide range of dishes and to allot a different price to each dish. Restaurants will generally pick several price points and group dishes around those prices. There may be several dishes priced at £10–£13, then several priced around £19–£20, then others at £23–£28. The idea here is to simplify costing and menu planning, and to create points of comparison for the consumer.

---

**PRICE POINTS**

the number of 'stops' along the way between the lowest-priced item and the highest-priced item

Some tourism organizations, notably from the transportation sector, have been accused of having convoluted systems of fare categories, termed 'confusiology' by one author (Adams, 1997).[6] The rail companies in the UK, for example, have come under fire for confusing passengers with their fare systems in order to charge more. In 2006, travellers had the option of 34 different fares for the same route between London and Manchester, from a £6 advance fare to a £317 business return (Macfarlane, 2006).[7] In response, a report by the all-party Transportation Select Committee suggested that the railways should develop a simple, user-friendly and affordable structure of train fares that apply across the network to give passengers a fair deal. First Great Western reacted to the report by withdrawing SuperSaver, Advance, Super-Advance, Apex and First Apex fares and replacing them with 'leisure' and 'business' class tickets.

## Global Spotlight

### 'Save Time, Save Money': Ski by the Hour at Banff Mount Norquay

'Save time, save money'. This is the slogan used by Alberta ski area Banff Mount Norquay to promote its skiing-by-the-hour concept. In 1995, the resort introduced the concept of hourly skiing, which has ultimately proved to be an extremely successful long-term pricing strategy. The resort decided to test the waters in 1995 by selling a mid-week-only, two-hour ticket called a 'flex-time' ticket, targeted at the local market. Reaction to the flex-time ticket was extremely positive – skiers who had never been to Norquay were turning up for a couple of hours of skiing and then going back to work. Hourly skiing opened up a new market, so after two seasons Norquay decided to expand the idea by introducing two-, three-, four-, and five-hour tickets, seven days a week. 'We found it was not abused, and it did not cannibalize existing business,' says Robert Coté, Norquay's director of marketing. 'People bought a two-hour ticket because they only wanted to ski for two hours – they wouldn't normally have bought a day ticket, and they wouldn't have bought a season's pass because they didn't ski enough to make it worthwhile.'

According to Coté, hourly skiing takes down all the barriers to skiing that would normally prevent people from coming. 'We knew everyone liked Norquay, but it wasn't accessible from a customer's point of view. If someone wanted to ski for the morning they had to buy a whole day's lift ticket, and if they wanted a half day, they had to wait until midday. This meant Norquay was imposing its timetable on customers. Now we have put customers in control of their own day.'

Competitors have not followed Norquay's lead on hourly tickets, mainly because they are not as close to Banff or Calgary, and also because the layout of their resorts is not conducive to hourly skiing. For hourly skiing to succeed, a close proximity to the client base is necessary. Norquay's proximity to Banff allows visitors to the city to snatch a few hours of skiing on arrival or departure day, or to put in a half-day of skiing before an afternoon at the hot springs or shopping. Locals can also come up just for a short period. 'The way the lifts are laid out here, you can do a lot of skiing in two hours,' explains Coté. 'At other resorts it may not work because they are bigger and more spread out.'

For Coté, the most significant advantage to skiing by the hour is that skiers now feel they are getting value for money. 'There is a general perception that the sport of skiing is expensive. I don't think it is the actual money spent – I think it is a whole-value equation. Normally, if you don't make it by 9 am for the first lift, you are not going to get full value for your lift ticket. You are going to leave with an unused portion and leave with the feeling of being ripped off. Our slogan is 'save time, save money'.' Coté adds, 'The biggest thing here is saving time. In today's society with all the time demands placed on people, time is the most valuable commodity out there. People want to ski, but they don't necessarily want to commit so much time to it. Unfortunately, the full-day/half-day scenario of purchasing lift tickets just doesn't allow for that. It all of a sudden puts a high demand on people's time.' The hourly tickets have also led to fewer queues, as skier numbers are spread throughout the day, and this puts less stress on the customers. Yield is also higher as it is proportionately more expensive to ski by the hour than by the day.

In 2002–2003, in response to customer demand for even more flexibility, Norquay decided to offer half-hourly increments as well as hourly ones. The resort's ski-by-the-hour ticket options are shown in Table 6.1. The 2001–2002 season was the first winter in which gross sales from the different hourly tickets exceeded sales from full-day tickets – the three-hour ticket being the most popular, followed by two-hour and four-hour tickets. But full-day sales have remained steady, so hourly tickets have not adversely affected sales of full-day tickets. And skiing by the hour has become so popular at Norquay that Coté tags the skiing-by-the-hour concept onto many of its resort promotions. 'After six years of it, people are really catching on to it, and it is becoming associated with us,' he says.

*Source*: R. Coté, director of marketing, Mount Norquay, personal communication 15 February 2003 and 5 January 2006.

## Discriminatory Pricing

Organizations often alter prices to suit different customers, products, locations, and times. This **discriminatory pricing** allows the organization to sell a product or service at two or more prices, despite the fact that the product costs are the same. For example, many restaurants charge higher prices in the evening than they do at lunchtime, even if the food is identical, because of demand differences. Ski resorts may charge more for a weekend ski pass than a week-day one if the majority of their customers drive up on a Saturday or Sunday.

---

**DISCRIMINATORY PRICING**
selling a product at two or more prices, despite the fact that the product costs are the same

---

These are examples of 'time-based' discriminatory pricing, but a market may also be segmented to encourage increased participation from special groups, such as senior citizens or students. In this case, the groups are offered special concessions, as seen in Banff Mount Norquay's cheaper prices for children, students and seniors (see Table 6.1). The market must be capable of being segmented if discriminatory pricing is going to be an effective strategy. Segments will have highly distinct sensitivities, and being able to price differently to each is key to success in maximizing profits (Hiemstra, 1998).[8] Care should also be taken to ensure that the strategy is legal and that it does not lead to customer resentment.

## Discounting

From time to time, most businesses need to consider discounting their standard prices. Many tourism organizations engage in **volume discounting** – offering special rates to attract customers who agree to major purchases. Hotels and airlines for example, offer special prices (or upgrades) to corporate clients to encourage volume business, and loyalty programmes frequently offer discounts to ensure that travellers use a particular brand. The discount will often reflect the level of overall demand. Airlines and hotels traditionally discount during slow periods and low seasons. A discounted price is only a wise move if it increases demand, brings new users, or increases consumption by regular users. Organizations that discount key products but don't lower costs to offset the discount are taking an economic risk unless the discount is only for a very short period, or is designed to overcome a very specific problem. There is also the risk that discounting may not lead to increased demand.

---

**VOLUME DISCOUNTING**
offering special prices to attract customers who agree to major purchases

---

## Yield Management

**Yield** is the profit that is made on the sales of goods and services; the calculation is based on the number of customers, how much they spend, and the number of products they buy. **Yield management** is the practice of developing strategies to maximize sales of an organization's perishable products, such as airline seats, hotel rooms and tour seats, and therefore improving its long-term viability. More simply, it has been defined as 'lowering the price... according to expected demand, and relying heavily on computers and modelling techniques'(Lundberg et al., 1995).[9] It was initiated by the airline industry in the 1980s as a way to increase revenue from existing routes and aircraft. Computer technology made it possible for airlines to predict the number of seats that would be sold on a given flight, called the load factor. By analyzing costs, and also determining the price sensitivity of various types of airfares, airlines discovered that by offering seats at a variety of special fares they could boost load and revenues.

> **YIELD**
> the profit that is made on the sales of goods and services; calculation is based on the number of customers, how much they spend, and the number of products they buy

> **YIELD MANAGEMENT**
> developing strategies to maximize sales of an organization's perishable products, such as airline seats, hotel rooms and tour seats, and therefore improving its long-term viability

Many have argued in favour of yield-management techniques, using price to balance the market conditions of supply and demand. Duadel and Vialle (1994), for example, distinguished between 'spoilage', the under-utilization of resources, and 'spill', selling too cheaply early, with the result that later, higher-yielding demand has to be denied.[10] The practice of yield management is now common in other sectors of tourism, from hotels to ski resorts. Different rates are offered for certain groups of customers, and restrictions are placed on the use of these rates by other groups. Even theatres use yield management techniques to maximize revenue. The Snapshot below shows how the Cherry Blossom Festival in Kyoto uses a simple three-tier approach to pricing tickets.

## Snapshot

### Pricing at a Cherry Blossom Festival in Japan

The recent Hollywood blockbuster, *Memoirs of a Geisha*, may have attracted an increased number of tourists to the Gion area of Kyoto, Japan's historic 'flower town'. But for many years, Japanese tourists have been flocking to the Miyako Odori Festival, held each April in the Koubu Kaburenjo theatre.

The Miyako Odori, or Cherry Blossom Festival, takes place over the whole of April, with four afternoon hour-long performances each day. Busloads of tourists arrive from all over Japan, as well as from international destinations, for the chance to see geishas and maiko perform. Visitors anxious for photos tour the narrow, winding streets hoping to bump into a fully dressed and made-up geisha on her way to the festival or the many tea shops. Also, hundreds of Japanese spectators take the opportunity to wear traditional kimonos; the audience for the dancing show can often be half full of authentically-clad women.

The Miyako Odori dates back to an exposition held in 1872 when Kyoto was reinforcing its 1,000-year-old dignity as the former capital of Japan. The capital had just been transferred to Tokyo and the city introduced the Cherry Blossom Dance as a classic Kyoto stage production, with its geisha and maiko troupes and musicians specializing in the *shamisen*, an ancient Japanese string instrument. Every year, the Gion area is inundated with tourists anxious to see the dance as well as tour the religious and historical icons of the city with the famous cherry trees in full bloom. Nowadays you can even rent a geisha outfit, complete with wooden sandals, wig, kimono and make-up, by the hour.

The theatre uses a simple three-tier approach to pricing tickets for the festival. Creating pricing tiers is a traditional aspect of theatre attendance world over. The premium-priced tickets, at Y4,300 in 2006 (around £20) enable viewers to sit on reserved seats on the first floor or the front of the second floor. They are also invited to attend a geisha tea ceremony 40 minutes before the performance. This includes green tea in exquisite cups with Japanese cake, and guests can keep a souvenir dish. They also have the opportunity to walk around the authentic Japanese-style garden.

First-class tickets, at Y3,800, give patrons reserved seats – either on the second floor or on the designated seating area without chairs at the sides of this floor. They get a close-up appreciation of the dancers and musicians and a clear view for photos. The cheapest, second-class tickets, at Y1,900, are for the free seating area without chairs on the third floor. Here viewers either kneel barefoot on cushions on raised deck areas or perch on narrow wooden benches.

*Sources*: Aitken, W. (17 December 2005). 'Glimpsing geisha in Gion', *The Globe and Mail*, Travel, T3; Miyako Odori '06 brochure, Gion Koubu Kaburenjo, Hanamikoyi, Gion, Higashiyama-ku, Kyoto.

## Strategic and Tactical Pricing

Organizations in the tourism and hospitality industries operate pricing policies at strategic and tactical levels. In **strategic pricing**, prices are determined early on in the planning of the marketing strategy; the nature of the business means that they have to be set a long way in advance so that brochures and guides can be published. These pricing decisions are based on the long-term view of corporate strategy, product positioning, and value for money in the marketplace.

---

**STRATEGIC PRICING**
setting prices early, in accordance with the long-term view of corporate strategy, product positioning, and value for money in the marketplace

---

While strategic pricing is concerned with the overall plans for the implementation of pricing policy, **tactical pricing** relates to day-to-day techniques in pricing, which can be rapidly altered to suit changing conditions in the marketplace. Thus, a strategy of discriminatory pricing that involves the setting of different prices for different market groups (e.g., business travellers and leisure travellers) may be introduced, but the actual prices to be charged and

**Table 6.2**   The Most Expensive Cities in the World

| Mercer Human Resource Consulting Cost of Living Survey – Worldwide Ranking 2007 (including housing) | | | | | |
|---|---|---|---|---|---|
| **Base city: New York, USA (= 100)** | | | | | |
| **Rankings** | | | | **Cost of Living index** | |
| **March 2007** | **March 2006** | **City** | **Country** | **March 2007** | **March 2006** |
| 1 | 1 | Moscow | Russia | **134.4** | 123.9 |
| 2 | 5 | London | United Kingdom | **126.3** | 110.6 |
| 3 | 2 | Seoul | South Korea | **122.4** | 121.7 |
| 4 | 3 | Tokyo | Japan | **122.1** | 119.1 |
| 5 | 4 | Hong Kong | Hong Kong | **119.4** | 116.3 |
| 6 | 8 | Copenhagen | Denmark | **110.2** | 101.1 |
| 7 | 7 | Geneva | Switzerland | **109.8** | 103 |
| 8 | 6 | Osaka | Japan | **108.4** | 108.3 |
| 9 | 9 | Zurich | Switzerland | **107.6** | 100.8 |
| 10 | 10 | Oslo | Norway | **105.8** | 100 |

*Source*: 2007 Cost of Living Survey: Mercer Human Resource Consulting

the ways in which these fares will be adjusted require tactical decisions. The fact that organizations cannot stock services means that if the planned supply exceeds demand in the marketplace for whatever reason, the organization must sell excess capacity. This often means resorting to tactical strategies, in the form of promotional pricing or discounting, for example. Hotels have become skilled at using last-minute tactical pricing methods to fill unoccupied rooms. Customers can often negotiate a substantial reduction on the rack rate if they phone the hotel during the evening on which they want a room.

---

**TACTICAL PRICING**
making short-term pricing decisions in response to changes in the marketing environment

---

One of the strategic decisions that must be taken is whether to price differently in different geographic areas. Should the price set be common to all customers, or should it vary to reflect different market demand in various countries? It may be more costly to sell a package tour to the Japanese than to Americans, because of higher costs in Japan; elsewhere it may be necessary to boost agents' commission levels to secure their support. According to the 2007 Cost of Living Survey from Mercer Human Resource Consulting, Moscow London and Seoul are the most expensive cities in the world (see Table 6.2). Tourism players who operate in an international market have to be aware of such statistics when setting prices.

**Figure 6.5**   Club Med Print Advertisement, 2006

Other popular strategies include **all-in pricing** or **all-inclusive pricing**. This type of pricing was used originally in holiday camps in the UK, where customers were provided access to every entertainment facility in the camp for a single price. The strategy proved highly successful, and Club Med built on this model for its chain of holiday resorts around the world. Club Med now advertises 'total all-inclusive' holidays, so that consumers pay for no extras whatsoever (see Figure 6.5). Today, tourists are very familiar with booking all-inclusive holidays in resorts like the Caribbean and Mexico. Theme parks also normally adopt the all-inclusive strategy by charging just one fee for the use of all their attractions.

> **ALL-IN PRICING (ALL-INCLUSIVE PRICING)**
> charging consumers a single price for the various products or services on offer

A contrasting strategy involves charging a low basic entrance fee and recouping profits through add-ons, which require that customers pay for each individual attraction. Organizers at the Calgary Stampede (see Global Spotlight in Chapter 12) have used this strategy for the funfair set in the middle of the Stampede grounds. Guests pay a small entrance fee but then have to pay for all of the rides. This is similar to **off-set pricing** or **bait pricing**, in which an operator such as an attraction will set a very low entry charge, possibly even a 'loss leader' at below cost, in order to attract visitors who then find themselves facing extra charges for every event. Casino hotels provide an example of bait pricing. Prices are often extremely reasonable for rooms, food and drink because profits are reaped through gambling on the premises.

> **OFF-SET PRICING (BAIT PRICING)**
> charging a low basic price and charging for extra services

## Tourism and Hospitality Characteristics That Affect Pricing Policy

Although some of the following points have already been referred to in this chapter, a separate discussion of the particular features of the tourism and hospitality industry that affect pricing is warranted here.

### High Level of Segmentation in the Industry

The tourism industry is highly segmented, with varying elasticities of demand in the segments. These demand segments may be associated with different income levels, age groupings, seasonality, and types of pleasure or business. Groups are also not homogeneous in their demands. Some may be business travellers with expense accounts and others may be pleasure travellers spending their own funds.

### Variability of Demand

Different products also face much variability in level of demand depending on the day of the week, holidays, different seasons of the year, and fluctuations in local personal or business situations. For hotels, this variability makes it difficult to forecast normal room demands for an individual property, and requires that each day of the year be projected and priced differently.

## Perishable Nature of the Product

The tourism product is perishable, i.e., it cannot be stored and sold at a later date. In addition, suppliers may not wish the surplus to be sold through the same channel as the standard product, as this may affect future demand and pricing. This is why outlets exist that allow the supplier to remain anonymous. For example, the internet provides an outlet for tour operators and airlines to offload surplus holidays or flights at reduced margins without changing their main brochures.

## High Fixed Costs

High fixed costs in major tourism sectors exacerbate the perishable nature of selling holidays, seats or hotel rooms. This means that an organization saves little by not filling to capacity. In the hospitality sector, for example, variable costs associated with the rooms department account for only a quarter of total room department income, while fixed costs associated primarily with paying for the building and overhead expenses account for a large share of the remaining revenue. This feature gives strong incentive to rent rooms at relatively low rates rather than leaving them vacant.

## Cost Fluctuations

For many operators in the tourism industry, there is a high probability of unpredictable but major short-term fluctuations in cost elements, such as oil prices and currency exchange rates. A tour operator running packages to various European and South American destinations may, according to exchange rates and the general climate of tourism in each country, have to vary its prices. High oil prices in 2006 forced many airlines to cut costs. One Chinese airline, China Southern, calculated that it takes a litre of fuel to flush a toilet at 30,000 feet, so urged passengers to go to the toilet before they boarded.[11]

## Vulnerability to Demand Changes

The industry is vulnerable to demand changes resulting from unforeseen economic and political events. Tourism worldwide suffered a downtrend between 2001 and 2004 due to terrorism, the Iraq war, low economies and the SARS outbreaks. Since 11 September 2001 there have been more than 3,000 major terrorism attacks worldwide, most of which have impacted the tourism industry.

## High Level of Customers' Psychological Involvement

Customers display a particularly high level of psychological involvement in choosing vacation products, in which price may be a symbol of status as well as value (Laws, 1998).[12] They are therefore likely to invest considerable care in their choice. In the packaged holiday market, where the tour operators or travel agents emphasize prices rather than destination attributes in their promotions, the customers' attention is likely to be focused on comparing prices rather than on what each destination offers, potentially resulting in a reduced commitment to the resort visited. Under these conditions, there is more likely to be a mismatch between the tourists' holiday expectations and their destination experiences, resulting in dissatisfaction and complaint.

## Seasonal Demand

One of the most common ways of setting holiday price differentials is the seasonal banding that is typical of tour operators' brochures – and familiar to all who purchase inclusive holidays – in the form of price and departure date matrices. Seasonality of demand leads to differing price expectations. Commercial business demand for some hotels often declines in high summer. This leads to domestic consumers anticipating lower rates and higher availability mid-week. Conversely, many tour operators and airlines are able to increase prices in high summer when demand is at its peak. An interesting pricing strategy was set by the Eden Roc Resort & Spa in Miami in the 1990s. The resort charged guests the same figure in dollars as the day's highest temperature. The idea was to give guests no cause for complaint even in the event of a cold snap!

## Tactical Price Cutting and Price Wars

If supply exceeds demand, there is near certainty of price-cutting by major competitors. This leads to the high possibility of price wars being provoked in sectors such as transport, accommodation, tour operating and travel agencies, in which short-term profitability may disappear.

## Low Prices

Price competition in many sectors has led to an industry characterized by low prices. Low prices have not only stimulated demand for holidays currently on offer, but have also altered the timing of demand – for example, by extending the holiday season – and have changed the demographic profile of holidaymakers to include all age groups and most socioeconomic groups of society. A lower price provides increased access to the product, bringing it to a new group of potential purchasers that have different behavioural characteristics. One example of this is that cruise holidays are now promoted to a broader market on the basis of reduced prices.

## Fixed Capacity

Even though demand may be highly variable and unpredictable, in many sectors of the industry supply tends to be relatively fixed. For a hotel, for example, it takes a long time to expand a building or to build a new one. Adding part-time or seasonal labour may be useful in better serving guests during periods of peak occupancy, but it can add little to available room inventory. As a result, pricing policies are largely restricted to allocating existing supplies among competing demands. This restriction adds importance to effective no-show policies.

## The Customer's Total Purchases

Some sectors of the industry have to consider the customer's total purchases when considering prices and profits. Hotels should not consider room rates and restaurant prices separately. Selling a room cheaply to a guest who will use the restaurant and bars extensively may be more profitable than selling it to someone who pays full rate for the room but purchases nothing else. For example, mixed-offering destinations like those owned by Intrawest (see Case Study in Chapter 5) do not have to concern themselves too much with visitors not skiing, as they can earn huge profits from selling other on-snow activities, as well as earn revenue from the restaurants and retail units. Destinations are keen to attract medical tourists (see Case Study below) because of the total purchases such a tourist will make both before and after surgery.

## Increased Use of the Internet

Many travel consumers are 'empowering' themselves by learning the routines of internet research and transacting for airfares. They are also increasingly aware of their ability to exercise more control over their purchases, and a large percentage of hotel customers attempt to negotiate lower prices for their rooms. In general, consumers have become more self-reliant; and the most adventurous are building their own holidays, many of them encouraged to make online purchases with internet-only discount rates (Davis, 2002).[13]

## Late Booking

Price reductions for late booking are a widespread holiday industry response to its unsold capacity, and are typically promoted by travel agents and tour operators shortly before departure. However, operators are increasingly using website pricing options to accommodate late bookers. It wasn't long ago that most businesses made only non-discounted rates available through the web. Today, pricing is more complex, and many travel websites now have a whole menu of pricing options online. It is now typical to see last-minute discounts; web-only offers; discounted pricing for groups; incentive rates for travel agents, tour operators and reservation agents; and a variety of packages at different price points, including such add-ons as meals, activities and transportation (Hudson and Larg, 2002).[14]

## Chapter Summary

The key factors determining pricing decisions are marketing objectives, costs, other mix variables, channel member expectations, buyer perceptions, competition, and legal and regulatory restrictions.

The analysis of buyers' reactions to price change uses the concept of 'elasticity of demand'. If demand increases in line with price cuts, the product is said to be elastic. But if demand remains relatively unaltered by price changes, the product is said to be inelastic.

Generally, companies use pricing as part of their positioning of a product, employing one of three strategic approaches: premium pricing, value-for-money pricing and undercut pricing.

Basic approaches to pricing fall into three main categories: cost-based methods, demand-based methods and competition-oriented pricing.

Three strategies commonly used for the introduction of new products are prestige pricing, market skimming and penetration pricing. Other pricing techniques include promotional pricing, product-bundle pricing, price spread and price points, discriminatory pricing, discounting, and yield management.

Particular features of the tourism and hospitality industry that affect pricing include the high level of segmentation within the industry; variability of demand; the perishable nature of the product; high fixed costs; cost fluctuations; vulnerability to demand changes; the high level of customers' psychological involvement; seasonal demand; tactical price-cutting and price wars; low prices; fixed capacity; the customer's total purchases; increased use of the internet; and late booking.

## Key Terms

all-in pricing (all-inclusive pricing), p. 205
break-even analysis, p. 191
buyer-based pricing (sensitivity pricing), p. 192
competition-oriented pricing (going-rate pricing), p. 193
cost-based pricing, p. 190
cost-plus pricing, p. 191
discriminatory pricing, p. 199
elasticity of demand, p. 184
fixed costs, p. 191
market share, p. 181
market skimming, p. 195
monopoly, p. 188
negotiating, p. 193
off-set pricing (bait pricing), p. 205

## Discussion Questions and Exercises

1. What are the benefits and costs to a tourism operator in providing discounts?
2. When would a new restaurant introduce a new product with premium pricing? When might it use undercut pricing?
3. What pricing strategy is Virgin Galactic using for space tourists? How could the company find out about price sensitivity for its proposed space flights?
4. Collect advertisements for hotels in your area and find examples of product-bundle pricing. Explain how they work. Try to calculate the savings that the bundle offers.
5. Explain the differences between prestige pricing, market skimming and penetration pricing, using examples from a sector of tourism and hospitality other than hotels.
6. What type of pricing strategy is Banff Mount Norquay following? Can you see any disadvantages to this strategy?

## Safari and a Facelift: The Rise of Medical Tourism

Medical tourism, whereby patients travel to a different country for either urgent or elective surgery, is fast becoming a worldwide, multi-billion-dollar industry. Time, money and anonymity are three reasons driving international medical queue-jumping. The rapid rise in this new industry is attributable to the exorbitant costs of medical care in developed countries, in conjunction with the comparative ease and afford-ability nowadays of international travel, rapidly improving technology and standards of care worldwide, and the proven safety records of medical care in many develop-ing countries around the world.

Surgery wait times, in particular, can lead patients to seek alternative venues. North Americans are finding that trips abroad combined with surgery can cost between four and ten times less than medical procedures at home. Also, by mixing surgery with pleasure, less time away from work is required. And, for everyone, for-eign travel can disguise the primary purpose of the vacation so that friends and col-leagues attribute their newly refreshed, youthful appearance to the benign effects of the holiday rather than the cosmetic surgeon's scalpel.

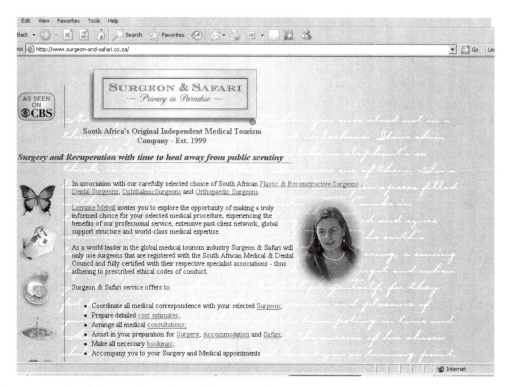

Homepage for Johannesburg-based Surgeon & Safari

As far back as the times of ancient Greece, pilgrims and patients travelled throughout the Mediterranean to the sanctuary of the healing god, Asklepios, at Epidarus. The healing waters at Bath, first established in Roman Britain, have been a shrine for more than 2,000 years. Baden Baden in Germany was another traditional watering-hole for rich European patients seeking alleviation of arthritis and other debilitating ailments. Now, in the 21st century, cheap airfares and increasingly high standards of medical facilities and expertise worldwide have opened up 'medical tourism' to a growing middle class market.

Countries that actively promote medical tourism include Cuba, Costa Rica, Hungary, India, Israel, Jordan, Lithuania, Malaysia and Thailand. India is currently considered the leading country to promote this phenomenon, and has been encouraging its expatriates from all over the world to return for cheaper and quicker access to medical attention for the past decade. Government and private sector studies there estimate that medical tourism, with a growth rate of 30 per cent annually, could bring between US$1 billion and $2 billion into the country by 2012. Apollo Hospital Enterprises is the largest of the outsourcing medical corporations in India, having treated about 60,000 patients between 2001 and spring 2004.

Even South Africa, where medical advertising is still illegal, is joining in with medical safaris, dubbed 'beauty and beast tours'. South Africa is particularly attractive to cosmetic surgery patients because of its high-quality surgeons and its prices, which are cheap as a result of the ailing currency rate rather than any deficiency in facilities or expertise. Surgeon and Safari is one Johannesburg-based company capitalizing on this growing demand, and has consultants located online and in South Africa, Britain and the United States. Set up in 1999 by Lorraine Melvill, it circumvents advertising restrictions by providing a middleman-type service between patients and doctors. Melvill, a marketing executive, saw that she could exploit the unusual synergy between the demand for tourism on one hand and for cosmetic surgery that is affordable, high quality and offers the client anonymity on the other.

Clients are informed via the website about the medical and tourism aspects of their trip. Melvill makes all the arrangements for transportation, surgery, recuperation, hotels and safari plans, meeting all her clients right off the plane. She attributes her success to this personal, hands-on, reassuring business approach. She even sits by her clients' side during the lead-up to surgery. On offer are a range of cosmetic and reconstructive surgeries including plastic, ophthalmic, orthopedic; dentistry, hair transplants and sports medicine are also offered, as well as non-surgical Botox and restalyne treatments. Almost half of the clients are from the UK and they opt mainly for reconstructive procedures. The other half, from the US, arrive with a shopping list of mainly cosmetic requests.

Costs vary according to the type of operation and the length of recuperation required. A seven-day package, including two surgical procedures (e.g. liposuction and tummy tuck), accommodation in a luxury resort as well as some meals would cost approximately US$3,800. If you tack a safari onto that package, the overall cost equals the price of having the surgery alone done back in the US. A facelift in the States costs around $9,000 compared to $4,400 in South Africa. And Melvill

**Table 6.3**   Plastic Surgery and Safari Tally (in US dollars)

| | |
|---|---|
| Round-trip flight to South Africa | $979 |
| Safari/whale watching | $215 |
| Room and meals | $1,173 |
| Tummy tuck and lipo | $3,333 |
| Private nurse and driver | $519 |
| TOTAL | **$6,219** |
| Average price of just surgery in the US. | **$11,000** |

*Source*: *People Magazine*, 2006

assures her customers that the cost differential is purely due to the country's weak currency and represents value for money rather than low standards.

As with any surgery, there are risks associated with surgery abroad. The American Society for Aesthetic Plastic Surgery warns about the risks of sitting in the sun post-surgery, inconsistent follow-up care, drinking alcohol when on strong medications, flying too soon after surgery with the potential for deep vein thrombosis, and the possibility of insufficient credentials among foreign surgeons. Melvill counters all these criticisms, claiming that the South African surgeons are of the highest quality and expertly trained. The hospital's blood supply is screened for HIV, patients are tested for blood clots in their legs, and surgeons refuse to operate on the mentally unstable, anorexic or obese.

The future of medical tourism seems strong in light of the potential baby boomer market of over 220 million people throughout the US, Canada, Western Europe, Australia and New Zealand. It capitalizes upon the fascination with vanity, agelessness and beauty at any cost among an increasingly older population, as well as the globalization of tourism and medicine. 'Come for the surgery, stay for the scenery' is a website advertising slogan attracting many people to South Africa to combine their elective surgeries with safaris, sightseeing and even a round of golf. Table 6.3 shows the price of medical tourism for one American customer who travelled to South Africa to have excess skin removed, followed by a safari and a whale-watching trip.

*Sources*: Marcelo, R. (2 July 2003) 'India fosters growing "medical Tourism" 'sector', *Financial Times*; Souter, E. and Rubin, C. (27 March 2006) 'Beauty and the beast', *People Magazine*.

## Questions

1.  Is demand for medical tourism price-elastic or inelastic? Explain your answer.
2.  How would a developed country, such as the UK or the US, argue that medical tourism in a developing country like India, involves a price–quality trade-off?
3.  What kind of pricing strategy is Lorraine Melvill following?
4.  Account for the increase in demand for medical tourism. Where will the growth come from in the future for this particular sector of tourism?
5.  What other tourism products could be 'bundled' into the package detailed in Table 6.3?

## Websites

| | |
|---|---|
| www.surgeon-and-safari.co.za | Surgeon and Safari |
| www.banffnorquay.com | Banff Mount Norquay Resort |
| www.spaceadventures.com | Space Adventures |
| www.burjalarab-hotel-dubai.com | The Burj Al Arab Hotel, Dubai |
| www.easycruise.com | EasyCruise |
| www.ryanair.com | Ryanair |

## References

1   Ungoed-Thomas, J. (20 August 2006) 'Tourists tell Britain: you're a rip-off', *The Sunday Times*, 9.

2   Dickman, S. (1999) *Tourism & Hospitality Marketing*. Oxford: Oxford University Press.

3   Anon. (5 November 2005) 'A cool $1 million to ski at Aspen', *Calgary Herald*, G1.

4   Teather, D., Kundnami, H. and Clark, A. ( 23 June 2006) 'BA price-fixing turmoil: offices raided, executives suspended', *The Guardian*, 1–2.

5   Carmin, J. and Norkus, G. (1990) 'Pricing strategies for menus: magic or myth?', *Cornell Hotel and Restaurant Administration Quarterly*, 31(3), 50.

6   Adams, S. (1997) *The DilbertTM Future: Thriving on Business Stupidities in the 21st Century*. New York: Harper Business, 160.

7   Macfarlane, J. (20 May 2006) 'Rail bosses holding you to ransom,' *Daily Express*, 8.

8   Hiemstra, S. J. (1998) 'Economic pricing strategies for hotels', in T. Baum and R. Mudambi (eds), *Economic and Management Methods for Tourism and Hospitality Research*. New York: Wiley, 215–232.

9   Lundberg, D. E., Krishnamoorthy, M. and Stavenga, M. H. (1995) *Tourism Economics*. New York: Wiley, 106.

10   Duadel, S. and Vialle, G. (1994) *Yield Management: Applications to Air Transport and Other Service Industries*. Paris: Institut du Transport Aerien.

11   Anon. (1 December 2006) 'Chinese airline urges passengers to go to the bathroom before they board to save fuel', *National Post*, A3.

12   Laws, E. (1998) 'Package holiday pricing: cause of the IT industry's success, or cause for concern?', in T. Baum and R. Mudambi (eds), *Economic and Management Methods for Tourism and Hospitality Research*. New York: Wiley, 197–214.

13   Davis, T. (2002) 'Ski operators meet in Whistler to review "extraordinary" 2001', retrieved from www.canadatourism.com/en/ctc/ctx/ctx-news/search/newsbydateform.cfm.

14   Hudson, S. and Lang, N. (2002) 'A destination case study of marketing tourism online: Banff, Canada', *Journal of Vacation Marketing*, 8(2), 155–165.

# 7

# DISTRIBUTION

## Making Alliances in South Africa's Game Reserves

The spirit of co-operation is thriving in South Africa's Greater Kruger National Park conservation area. The Kruger itself has pulled down fences delineating its lands, allowing animals freedom to roam in and out of the national park and the bordering private reserves. This open-fence policy is also extending to its borders with Mozambique where an ambitious multi-national conservation programme is opening up ancient wildlife trails, providing limitless grazing for large herds and thereby reducing devastation to vegetation in order to protect vital ecosystems.

At Motswari Private Game Reserve, one of six camps in the Timbavati area just west of the Kruger, co-operative marketing is also in vogue. The 'White Lions of the Timbavati' originally made the area famous and Motswari (meaning to 'keep and conserve') was established in 1976 as a new, luxurious destination for tourists to view wildlife and witness the captive breeding programme established there. The four-star operation is linking with its neighbours in a concerted marketing effort to attract international and domestic tourists. The accommodations at Timbavati are very varied, including a top-notch five-star lodge, where 'dressing for dinner' is de rigueur and, at the other end of the scale, M'bali, a basic tented operation that offers safaris in the raw.

Motswari was set up in a climate of political unrest and social and economic upheaval. These days it is fraught with the problems of increased competition in the Kruger area and throughout Southern Africa, a volatile tourist market, floods, and also anxiety over burgeoning elephant populations. The open-fence policy with Mozambique as well as a trans-border relocation programme is intended to help ease the elephant problem. Co-operation in marketing initiatives is also coupled with a co-operative approach to game spotting. All guides within the Timbavati area alert the others about animal sightings, kills and activities, making their successes available to everyone.

The INDABA conference, held annually in Durban, is where Motswari marketers promote their lodge, safaris and conference facilities. Over four days, the company entertains local agents as well as overseas clients, planting promotional

Tourists photograph a leopard at Motswari private game reserve

'seeds' which often take up to a year to flourish in terms of bookings, according to Zalene, the reservations manager. She explains the co-operative marketing policy: 'We market exclusivity for the whole area in co-operation with the other lodges. They all offer something intrinsically different, such as specialized packages that include hot-air ballooning or township visits.' Manager Kathy Bergs confirms this marketing practice, saying that with such distinct offerings in terms of facilities and activities, the Timbavati lodges all recognized the validity of pooling their resources in order to compete with well-known safari rivals in the area. Some of these competitors have become too 'commodified', she says, and have developed into larger hotel operations, taking away the original, exclusive feel of the safari. In response, Motswari is promoting its small size and one-to-one, attentive, personal service as its marketing differential.

'Arrive as a visitor, leave as a friend' epitomizes Motswari's attitude towards personalized, high-quality service. Every member of the team, from housekeepers and cooks to guides, spotters and the management, welcomes and interacts with the guests, imbuing the luxurious but laid-back compound with a friendly, homey ambiance.

Via a website, newsletter, videos and high-quality promotional written material, Motswari is targeting mainly Northern Europe, utilizing the intermediary services of Welcome Tours (South Africa-based), Kuoni (Swiss) and African Pride (British). They are also trying to attract Australian tourists via the tour operator African Outpost. Domestic tourists make up the largest percentage of South Africa's tourists and Motswari is appealing to these short-haul tourists with its lower-cost sister companies, which offer self-catering accommodations within Timbavati as well as shorter-stay safaris.

Growth in safari tourism in South Africa has been largely driven by foreign tour operators who homed in on the country after 1994, when Nelson Mandela became President, promising political stability for the future. SATOA (Southern African Tourist Organizers' Association) is a UK-based promotional group for all aspects of tourism in southern Africa and the Indian Ocean islands. It now encompasses more than 60 members including tour operators, ground handlers, car hire companies, hotel groups, national boards, airlines and shipping companies. It also provides statistics and information regarding travel and tourism for both travel agents and the public. With more and more tourism facilities and data available, it is reliable groups such as this which help promote South Africa as a safe and achievable destination for European travellers.

*Sources*: Horner, S. and Swarbrooke, J. (2004) *International Cases in Tourism Management*. London: Elsevier, 198–211; Interviews with Kathy Bergs, Frankie La Grange and Zalene at Motswari Private Game Reserve, 17–18 February 2006.

## OBJECTIVES

On completion of this chapter, you should understand:

▶ the two main types of distribution channels used in tourism and hospitality;

▶ the key intermediaries involved in the tourism and hospitality distribution system;

▶ the main forms of channel conflict in tourism and hospitality;

▶ the two main types of channel organization in tourism and hospitality;

▶ the two major forms of vertically integrated marketing systems – alliances and franchises; and

▶ how a company designs its distribution system and how it ensures the effective execution of the distribution strategy.

## Introduction

The Opening Vignette provides examples of one form of distribution in tourism: the formation of alliances. This chapter examines the various ways in which tourism and hospitality products are distributed. It begins by looking at the nature and types of distribution channels and the different functions of a distribution system. The key intermediaries involved in the tourism distribution system are then discussed, including travel agents, tour operators, convention and meeting planners, and travel specialists; the increasing use of the internet as part of the distribution channel is also analysed. The next section of the chapter is concerned with channel conflict and organization; it explores the two main forms of channel conflict – horizontal and vertical conflict – and the two main types of channel organization – the conventional marketing system and the vertical marketing system. Two major forms of vertically integrated marketing systems are alliances and franchises. Both have advantages and disadvantages, which are considered in detail and illustrated with several examples from the tourism industry. Finally, attention is given to how a company designs its distribution system and how it ensures the effective execution of the distribution strategy.

An organization's **distribution system** is centred on the 'place' aspect of a company's marketing mix. Its purpose is to provide an adequate framework for making a company's product or service available to the consumer; in the tourism industry, distribution systems are often used to move the customer to the product. The true rationale behind a company's distribution system can be traced back to its specific needs and wants. Figure 7.1 shows that each distinct distribution participant has a unique set of needs and wants. The motivation for developing an effective distribution network, therefore, is to help the different members meet their individual needs. By choosing to combine the activities of the various members, participants in the distribution system can work together to identify opportunities to fulfil each other's needs.

---

**DISTRIBUTION SYSTEM**
the 'place' aspect of a company's marketing mix; its purpose is to provide an adequate framework for making a company's product or service available to the consumer

---

## The Nature and Types of Distribution Channels

A **distribution channel** is a method of delivery used by a supplier, carrier or destination marketing organization. There are two different types of distribution channels that a firm can use to deliver its product. The first and most simple form of distribution is a **direct distribution channel**, a channel through which a company delivers its product to the consumer without the outside assistance of any independent intermediaries. In such a case, the service provider is solely responsible for the delivery of its product. Most bed and

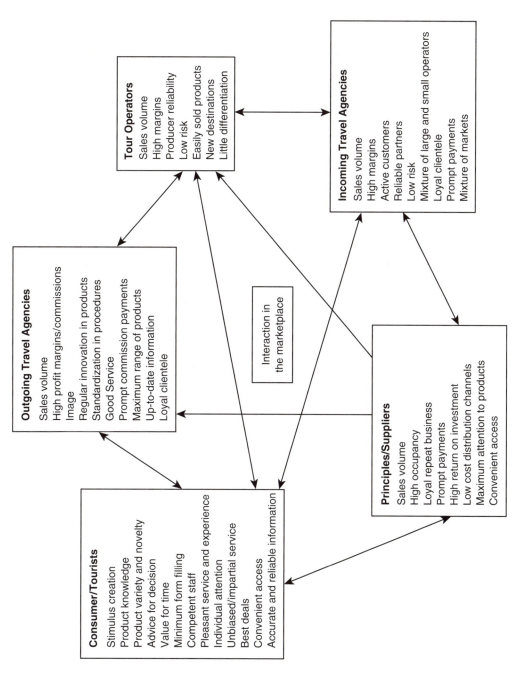

**Figure 7.1** Needs and Wants of Tourism Distribution Channel Members

*Source:* Buhalis, D. and Laws, E. (2001) *Tourism Distribution Channels: Practices, Issues and Transformations.* New York: Continuum

breakfasts use a direct distribution channel to market products to potential customers. They perform all the necessary channel functions on their own, without relying on any assistance from outside intermediaries.

---

**DISTRIBUTION CHANNEL**
a direct or indirect delivery arrangement used by a supplier, carrier or destination marketing organization

---

**DIRECT DISTRIBUTION CHANNEL**
a channel through which a company delivers its product to the consumer without the outside assistance of any independent intermediaries

---

The second type of distribution channel used to deliver a product is an **indirect channel**. In this case, the service provider makes use of independent intermediaries to help facilitate the distribution of its product. Outside intermediaries such as travel agents, tour operators and other tourism specialists assist the supplying company by helping to attract consumers to the product or destination. In the Opening Vignette, Motswari uses both methods of distribution to sell its safaris. The company targets consumers directly through a website, newsletter, videos and promotional written material, but it also uses intermediaries – in the form of selected tour operators around the world – to attract customers.

---

**INDIRECT DISTRIBUTION CHANNEL**
a channel through which a company distributes its product with the assistance of independent intermediaries

---

## Functions of the Distribution System

In order for a company's distribution system to operate effectively, members must perform several key functions. One member can carry out these functions alone, or they can be executed by a number of different channel participants. The functions are listed below; tasks should be assigned to those members that are best equipped to carry each of them out.

1. **Acquiring information**. The purpose of this task is to gain access to relevant, complete, accurate and timely information, thus enabling the company to assess its marketing environment. Information can be acquired through both primary and secondary research, using both qualitative and quantitative techniques (see Chapter 4).
2. **Promotion**. The purpose of promotion is to communicate the benefits of the destination's product to the consumer. This can be achieved through a variety of means, including the use of brochures, videos, magazine advertisements and websites (see Chapters 8, 9, and 10).

3. **Contact**. Making contact with potential customers is critical to a company's success. It is important that the company establishes contact with its target market in order to be able to communicate effectively the benefits of its product.
4. **Negotiation**. The negotiation of high-quality arrangements and contracts is key to any business relationship. In the case of a tourism distribution system, it is important for the member to negotiate agreements with regard to price, operating procedures and other issues that may arise among the system's participants.
5. **Physical distribution**. Obviously, a distribution system cannot be effective if there are no means of actually delivering the service to the consumer. The service provider is responsible for ensuring the successful distribution of its product at this stage.
6. **Financing**. An important task for every member of the distribution channel is to acquire the necessary resources to pursue its activities. Without funds in place, it may be impossible for the company to distribute its product.

## Distribution and Physical Location

It is important to acknowledge that distribution as a marketing term can also refer to the physical location, as this is a prerequisite of consumption of the core service. Operational requirements may set tight constraints for the distribution of some tourism services. Airports, for example, are often inconveniently located relative to travellers' homes, offices or destinations. Because of space, noise and environmental factors, finding suitable sites for the construction of new airports is a complex task. The need for economies of scale may be another restriction on location. Also, many tourism services require a fixed geographic location that severely restricts distribution. By definition, ocean beach resorts have to be on the coast and ski resorts have to be in the mountains. The Snapshot below highlights the importance of physical location for the ski industry. In the US, for example, 67 per cent of resorts are within 74 miles or easy commuting distance to major metropolitan areas.

## Snapshot

Travel Flows in the Ski Industry

The current ski market is estimated at some 70 million worldwide. Of that number, 77 per cent are alpine skiers, 16 per cent are snowboarders, while the remainder prefer cross-country skiing. Europe accounts for approximately 30 million skiers, the US and Canada between them generate an estimated 20 million skiers or boarders, and Japan 14 million. Today, there are approximately 6,000 ski areas in 78 countries, although data exists for only 5,665 of these. Of the recorded ski areas, about 4,000 are in Europe, less than a 1,000 each are found in North America and Asia, and about 100 are in the southern hemisphere, mostly in Argentina, Chile, Australia and New Zealand. The skiing market is mature in Europe as well as in America, but is evolving faster in other areas of the world such as Eastern Europe, Korea and Southeast Asia.

Ski resorts can be broken into three categories. Firstly, there are national resorts that generally attract people from within a state, province, or region. Secondly, there are regional resorts, those that skiers will travel several hundred miles to reach. In Europe, these resorts entice skiers across one or several countries. Examples are skiers travelling from the UK to Austria or from New York to the Canadian Rockies. Lastly, there are top-class international resorts (around 400) that attract skiers from all over the world, such as Whistler in Canada, Vail in Colorado and Zermatt in Switzerland. In the first few decades of ski area development, most people did not ski beyond their own ski hills. But that has changed as people travel more and as ski companies become multinationals. Thousands of North Americans now flood the European Alps every year, with an even greater influx of Europeans to North America. In fact, without European skiers, Canadian resorts would be showing negative growth.

In North America the largest number of ski areas are in the northeast. The northeast is the most densely populated area of the US, and home to a large number of professionals who can afford to ski during weekends and holidays. These ski resorts are easily accessible from major gateways such as New York, Boston and Philadelphia. For most Americans, travel time and cost are critical variables when deciding to ski; 67 per cent of resorts are within 74 miles or easy commuting distance to major metropolitan areas. A high proportion of weekend resort areas require two or more hours of driving time, while vacation destinations are typically in more remote locations where snow conditions are more consistent. Because of the need for snow, appropriate terrain and climate, resort areas tend to be clustered and therefore offer skiers several choices when they reach the mountains. This is also the case in Canada, where most of the ski area facilities are clustered around the eastern, most populated provinces, Ontario and Quebec, which are close to the American border. However, the most popular resorts, particularly among overseas visitors, are in western Canada. About half of all international visitors head for British Columbia and 23 per cent visit Alberta, the neighbouring province.

In Europe, vacation skiers from northern countries such as Germany, Benelux, the UK and Scandinavia, represent half the skier market for European Alpine countries. Austria is in the top position for the European winter vacation market, receiving 47 per cent of European winter sports enthusiasts (largely from Germany and the UK), while 14 per cent travel to France (mainly from the UK) and about 11 per cent visit both Switzerland and Italy. Accessibility to the latter two countries has improved with a new regional airport serving the Engadin region of Switzerland, with St. Moritz at its heart, and with the opening of the new international airport at Turin in Italy. However, British skiers are increasingly favouring France as a destination, using low-cost airlines and high-speed rail and road links via the Channel Tunnel. The policy of developing the world's biggest ski areas at snow-sure altitudes has paid dividends for the French, who boast over 56 million skiers' visits, and the country continues to invest in better road and rail links in the mountains. Andorra, located between France and Spain, has benefited from easy access from Barcelona. With over 2.3 million skier visits, the main problem now is finding road space and lodging to fit everyone. Large numbers of Russians travel to Andorra each winter, attracted as much by the low prices in the shops as by the skiing.

In other parts of the world, access is always an important consideration in ski area development. In China, for example, where skiing is growing faster than anywhere else in the world, numerous studies have been made to determine the best locations within easy reach of the major populated cities. To date, the best option for the Chinese capital Beijing is Saibei, a rather basic resort created within 170 miles (272 kms) of the capital. Alongside Jilin province, Heilongjiang in the northeastern corner of China appears to be the country's major boom area for resort development, especially around the city of Harbin, which has seen heavy investment in a modern airport and road network. The provincial government has announced plans to open up 250 new ski centres in that province alone in the next decade. This would place it alongside Austria's Tyrol and Canada's Quebec as one of the few 'regions' in the world to boast in excess of 100 ski centres.

*Source*: Hudson, S. (2003) 'Travel flows and spatial distribution in the ski industry', in Higham, J. and Hinch, T. (eds) *Sport Tourism Development*. Clevedon, England: Channel View Publications, 95–98.

## Marketing Intermediaries

**Marketing intermediaries** are channels of distribution that include travel agents, tour operators, travel specialists and the internet. Their purpose is to help the service provider complete the six different functions listed earlier. Through the use of channel intermediaries, a company is able to expand the strength of its distribution network and to reach a much larger portion of its target market. As a result, the combined marketing efforts of the entire distribution network will lead to an increase in the number of customers using the service, thus boosting overall revenues.

---

**MARKETING INTERMEDIARIES**
channels of distribution that include travel agents, tour operators, travel specialists and the internet

---

### Travel Agents

**Travel agents** offer the tourism customer a variety of services, including everything from transportation plans and tour packages to insurance services and accommodation. They are the most widely used marketing intermediaries in the tourism industry. An agency will earn a commission for each sale, the amount depending on the type of product sold. The modern tradition of holiday packages started with the Industrial Revolution and the railways. In July 1841, a Baptist cabinet-maker called Thomas Cook booked a party of 500 on a train from Leicester to a temperance rally in Loughborough. The future travel agent negotiated a price that included entertainment in local private gardens.

---

**TRAVEL AGENTS**
marketing intermediaries that offer the tourism customer a variety of services, including everything from transportation plans and tour packages to insurance services and accommodation

---

Today, the travel agency market is very competitive. Barriers to entry are low and as a result there are many new entrants, which is especially true of the rapidly growing segment of online agents. Independent travel agents are under pressure not only from e-agents but also from direct selling by tour operators. They therefore seek to differentiate themselves, and add value to the product in order to justify their role in the value chain and retain market share. Travel agencies perform four distinct functions that pertain to a company's distribution system:

1. **Distribution and sales network**. Travel agents are a key player in the distribution and sale of a company's product under an indirect distribution system. Travel agents essentially act as tour brokers that bring the buyers and sellers of travel products together. The agents have access to an extensive network of suppliers and customers and are able to help facilitate interaction between the two by identifying the particular needs of each group.
2. **Reservations and ticketing**. Making reservations and issuing tickets are two of the more traditional roles of travel agents. Through the use of a global distribution system (GDS) such as Galileo, Abacus or Sabre, travel agents can place reservations in numerous locations throughout the world. However, with the arrival of ticketless travel systems in the 1990s, the role of travel agents in issuing tickets (particularly airline tickets) is slowly diminishing.
3. **Information provision and travel counselling**. Travel agents have a wealth of information at their disposal. They possess an extensive knowledge of tourism destinations and are well equipped to offer advice to the inexperienced traveller. Whether a customer is looking for a quick flight across the country or planning a major expedition around the world, travel agents can provide valuable assistance.
4. **Design of individual itineraries**. The person-to-person nature of the travel agent business allows the travel agent to gain an in-depth understanding of customers' travel needs. By identifying what a customer's specific needs are, the agent can put together a personalized itinerary. Travel agents can arrange transportation, accommodation, insurance, activities and tours, all with the intent of satisfying the traveller's particular needs and expectations.

Despite the benefits that travel agents can provide to a company's distribution system, the emergence of new and cheaper distribution tools such as the internet has placed the future role of travel agents in doubt. For this reason, a large number of travel agencies are seeking new positioning strategies to maintain their foothold in the tourism market. In the last decade, most airline carriers have eliminated base commissions for travel agents, so many agents are charging service fees to customers. Agents used to earn up to 10 per cent on all airline tickets sold; approximately one-third of agency business came from the sale of scheduled airline tickets. Apart from charging fees to customers, agencies are now looking at other ways to make up for the loss of airline commissions, including selling more package tours and cruises and focusing on selling their expertise.

While traditional agents have lost market share to online purchasing, expert advice from travel advisors is likely to remain a vital service in the tourism marketplace. Travel agents are especially valuable to marketers of luxury travel. Nearly three out of ten (28 per cent) affluent leisure travellers reported using a travel agent to gather information or book a leisure trip in 2005. Among these, the majority reported using an agent to book a hotel or resort and/or an airline reservation. One-third used the services of an agent to book a cruise, and a slightly lower percentage used an agent to book a vacation package or tour (2006).[1] Business travellers are also major uses of travel agents, although a recent survey of 4,000 business travellers in the UK found that the use of travel agents for booking business was down from 31 per cent in 2005 to 28 per cent in 2006, as the use of the internet has increased (2007).[2]

**Table 7.1**   Tourism Turnover in Million euro by the Largest European Tour Operators

| | | | Tourism turnover | |
| | | | 2002 | Change in % (2001/2002) |
| Rank | Enterprise/Group | Country | | |
|---|---|---|---|---|
| 1 | TUI | Germany | 12,461 | −2.7 |
| 2 | Thomas Cook | Germany | 8,063 | 3.2 |
| 3 | My Travel Group | UK | 7,017 | −13.1 |
| 4 | Rewe Group | Germany | 4,660 | −6.9 |
| 5 | First Choice | UK | 3,471 | −8.0 |
| 6 | Kuoni | Switzerland | 2,543 | −8.0 |
| 7 | Grupo Iberostar | Spain | 2,027 | 10.4 |
| 8 | Club Méditerranée | Spain | 1,744 | −12.1 |
| 9 | Hotelplan | Switzerland | 1,435 | −7.8 |
| 10 | Alltours | Germany | 1,115 | 4.2 |

*Source*: FVW documentation, Germany, 'European operators 2002,' No 13, p. 9, supplement to the edition FVW International No 13, 5.6. 2003.

## Tour Operators

**Tour operators** are organizations that offer packaged vacation tours to the general public. These packages can include everything from transportation, accommodation and activities to entertainment, meals and drinks. Tour operators typically focus their marketing efforts on the leisure market, which represents the dominant buying group. The tour operating sector has become increasingly concentrated. In Europe, for example, about 70 per cent of the market is cornered by the five largest companies, which all have their corporate seats in either Germany or the UK (see Table 7.1). In the 1990s these tour operators followed a strategy of vertical integration. By controlling the value chain from sales and packaging through to transportation and hotels, tour operators sought to strategically secure their market share and shore up low profit margins in their core business with more profitable activities in downstream areas of the value chain. But a slowing and changing tourism market has exposed the lack of flexibility in this model. The 'de-packaging' of travel – with customers building their own trips piece by piece on internet platforms – has struck a blow at the heart of traditional tour operator products.

---

**TOUR OPERATORS**
organizations that offer packaged vacation tours to the general public

---

This has led to even further consolidation. In 2007, the four premier league package tour companies re-formed into two Anglo-German leviathans accounting for almost half the UK market. Manchester-based MyTravel merged with German-owned Thomas Cook, while Crawley-based First Choice merged with TUI to form TUI Travel. The new TUI Travel group comprises 200 brands worldwide, 30 million customers from at least 20 source markets, a fleet of 155 aircraft and nearly 3,600 retail shops.

Tour operators have the ability to bring in large volumes of customers. They receive discounted rates from various service providers in exchange for providing a large number of guaranteed visitors. Tour operators make their profits by providing low-margin travel packages to a large number of consumers. Typically, organizations that offer travel packages must sell between 75 and 85 per cent of the packages available in order to break even. The majority of tour operators distribute their travel packages through travel agencies. Each travel agency represents an average of four tour operators, and has traditionally been an important player in the distribution of tour operator products. However, tour operators are increasingly selling their packages direct to customers, cutting out the intermediary, by using their own outlets or web pages.

With the rising use of the internet as a distribution mechanism, a large number of tour operators are choosing to restrict their offerings to only a select number of specialized travel packages. Companies profiled in this book such as G.A.P Adventures in Toronto, Canadian Mountain Holidays in Banff and Atlantic Tours Gray Line in Halifax specialize in offering unique tour packages to different markets. G.A.P Adventures has chosen to target young, adventurous individuals interested in purchasing travel packages to the developing world, while CMH focuses on offering up-market heli-skiing packages in the Canadian Rockies. Atlantic Tours, on the other hand, specializes in escorted sightseeing tours throughout the Canadian Atlantic provinces. By reducing the scope of their operations, these companies have managed to differentiate themselves in their respective areas, and have thus been able to focus their efforts on appealing to niche markets. The Snapshot below profiles a company, weekendtrips.com, which sells specialized short-term getaway packages via the internet.

## Snapshot

### Weekendtrips.com

Travellers are turning in increasing numbers to the internet to help them plan and book their travel. A parallel trend is that people lack the time for frequent, extensive holidays. The amount of time they spend working has been increasing steadily since the '90s fast-paced work environments that place intense demands on individuals are now the norm. People are often too busy to dedicate the time, energy and imagination necessary to arrange all the elements of a comprehensive weekend getaway.

Responding to these trends is weekendtrips.com, a Toronto-based travel and leisure company that focuses on designing short-term getaways and selling them via the internet. Building on its network of partners in the travel, hospitality and recreation industries, the company uses its resources to package and market weekend experiences. In Canada, the development and marketing of weekend getaways is led primarily by hotels and inns, small leisure activity operators, and tourist trade associations. For the most part, these operators act independently, often with limited marketing resources. While a number of informative resource guides were already available to consumers, until weekendtrips.com came along there was no company that offered a comprehensive selection of pre-arranged weekend experiences.

**Table 7.2**   Examples of Packages Offered by weekendtrips.com (as of March 2007)

| Day Trips | Weekend Trips |
| --- | --- |
| Good Earth Cooking – $135 | One Starry Night in Elora – $95 |
| Cave Exploration – $ 110 | Wine Country Getaway – $299 |
| Introduction to Ice Climbing – $160 | Sail & Stay – $240 |
| Zipline Extreme – $150 | Retail Therapy Package – From $260 |
| Interactive Dinner Party – From $75 | Spontaneous Country Getaway – from $149 per person per night |
| Tea at the Royal York – $25 | Wine & Food Pairing – $135 |
| Wrangler's Day – $139 | Weekend Culinary Retreat – $299 |
| Cycle and Winery Tour – $89 | The 'New' Bachelorette Party – $375 per person with 4 – 6 guests |
| Superhero Rappelling – $110 | Stay & Play at Blue Mountain – from $418 |
| Sail Escapes! – $189 | Georgian Bay Getaway – from $280 |

The company was founded by two friends, Francesco Contini and Marawan El-Asfahani, who were sitting in Toronto commenting on how uneventful their weekend had been and, for that matter, how routine every weekend had become. Both agreed that their lives were so hectic that it was hard to find the time to plan something eventful for the weekend. So they created weekendtrips.com, and now El-Asfahani, who has an extensive background in the hospitality industry and is a co-founder of Oxygen Design + Communications, runs the company on his own.

Weekendtrips.com offers a diverse range of weekend programmes: multi-day cultural getaways in vibrant urban centres; adventurous canoeing excursions along remote northern rivers; guided nature appreciation day trips for children at conservation areas, and more (see Table 7.2). The variety of travel packages suits singles, couples and families – people of all ages, interests and budgets. The trips are as diverse as gliding over Southern Ontario or taking a four-day culinary spree in Bologna, Italy's gastronomic capital. Other ideas include sailing in Ontario's Prince Edward County, cycling tours in Mennonite country, photography workshops, cave exploration, gardening seminars and off-road motorcycling, to name just a few. 'We recognize that our clients are busy, so we want to make it as simple as possible for them to take off for the weekend. For instance, when we develop a trip, not only do we provide accommodation and travel arrangements, but we also take care of any necessary gear and equipment,' says El-Asfahani.

The advent of the internet has brought many new opportunities, and by allowing weekendtrips.com to deliver frequently changing product information to a mass market in a cost-effective way, it has dramatically increased the economic viability of the weekendtrips.com business model. Each week, consumers can browse the weekendtrips.com website and select from a variety of offers. By centralizing the fragmented resources and expertise of its partners, the website becomes a point of reference, a reliable source of ideas for the weekend. By simplifying the decision-making process, the company encourages weekend travel and leisure, thereby creating new market opportunities for weekendtrips.com and all its partners.

At the beginning of 2007, the company had booked over 4,000 packages and had amassed a database of 36,000 customers.

*Sources*: 'Canadians logging on to destination websites', (2000), retrieved from http://tourism together.com/tourismweb/news/buzz/sep; F. Contini, general manager, weekendtrips.com, personal communication, 14 April 2003; Hudson, S. and Lang, N. (2002) 'A destination case study of marketing tourism online: Banff, Canada', *Journal of Vacation Marketing*, 8(2), 155–165; www.weekendtrips.com.

## Convention / Meeting Planners and Corporate Travel Managers

Convention and meeting planners plan and co-ordinate their organizations' external meeting events. These planners work for associations, corporations, large non-profit organizations, government agencies and educational institutions. Some combine the task of convention planning with that of corporate travel management, whereas other organizations split up the tasks. The private sector is also involved in the marketing of conventions and exhibitions. An example is Reed Exhibitions, one of the world's leading organizers of trade and consumer events. Every year the company runs over 460 events in 38 countries, bringing together over 90,000 suppliers and more than 5.5 million buyers. With 2,300 employees in 33 offices around the globe, Reed serves 52 industries worldwide. Reed say that the company is not just about organizing trade shows. Its role is that of a relationship broker – identifying, targeting, attracting and matching the needs of buyers and suppliers. The company can assist in everything from sightseeing tours and ground transportation to entertainment, event co-ordination and team-building exercises. On the incentive side, Reed can arrange for travel packages, reward evenings and dinners, spa weekends, gift certificates and merchandise rewards.

## Travel Specialists

**Travel specialists** are intermediaries that specialize in performing one or more functions of a company's distribution system. Hotel representatives, for example, specialize in providing contact with a hotel's customers in order to identify their specific accommodation needs. Advertising agencies can also act as specialists, performing the promotional aspect of a company's distribution system. By using travel specialists, a company can designate particular functions to the intermediaries that are best equipped to perform them. Focusing on one specific operation within the distribution channel allows the travel specialist to perform the function at hand in the best possible way.

> **TRAVEL SPECIALISTS**
> intermediaries that specialize in performing one or more functions of a company's distribution system

An example of a travel specialist is Travelcare Sports, part of the Co-operative Group in the UK. Travelcare Sports manages the travel requirements of football clubs such as Manchester

United – for players, players' families, club staff, press and supporters. Over 15 years, the company has arranged official travel packages for over 100,000 fans. In 2003 for instance, Travelcare Sports was appointed as the official ground operator for the Champions League final held in Manchester, and booked over 30 hotels across the northwest of England for UEFA officials, sponsors, and both sets of fans. Through the website www.travelcaresports.com, fans can book packages to see their favourite teams. In 2006 it was possible to book a Dream Break Manchester United package that included a match ticket, one night's accommodation, museum and stadium tour, match programme and discount vouchers for various merchandisers. For many fans, this would be the only way of obtaining tickets for a match.

Other examples of specialist intermediaries are tour brokers, motivational houses and junket representatives. **Tour brokers** sell coach tours, which are attractive to a variety of markets. Such tours are important to hotels en route as well as to the attractions themselves. **Motivational houses** provide incentive travel, offered to employees or distributors as a reward for their efforts. Incentive trips usually involve staying in high-class accommodation in resort areas, but not necessarily in warm destinations: winter sports incentives are becoming increasingly popular in North America.

---

**TOUR BROKERS**

companies that sell coach tours, which are attractive to a variety of markets

---

**MOTIVATIONAL HOUSES**

companies that provide incentive travel, offered to employees or distributors as a reward for their efforts

---

Finally, **junket representatives** serve the casino industry as intermediaries for premium players. Junket reps maintain lists of gamblers who like to visit certain gaming areas such as Las Vegas, Reno or Atlantic City, and they work for one or two casinos rather than the whole industry. Junket reps are paid a commission on the amount the casino earns from the players or, in some cases, on a per-player basis.

---

**JUNKET REPRESENTATIVES**

companies that serve the casino industry as intermediaries for premium players

---

## The Internet

Tourists are turning in increasing numbers to the internet to help them plan and book their travel. Some stakeholders in the travel industry, such as airlines, car rental companies and international hotel chains, have been quick to grasp the potential for marketing and selling their services online. They have recognized an opportunity to bypass intermediaries and to sell their basic products and services directly to the customer. Many hotels have developed web-based booking tools for both leisure and group sales. Increasingly, package holiday tour operators are including direct sales via the internet in their sales strategy, thus bypassing the travel agent. These travel companies are adopting both organic (internal) and acquisitive growth strategies. Many traditional companies have developed their own websites and interactive divisions, while others are acquiring internet companies. Others are setting up business and selling exclusively online. Examples are weekendtrips.com (see Snapshot above), and VocationVacations, profiled in the Global Spotlight below.

However, some critics have suggested that the tourism industry has traditionally been relatively slow on the uptake of new information technologies, particularly in the travel agency sector (Christian, 2001).[3] Many researchers have focused on the impact of the internet on travel agents and on the role of electronic intermediaries in the travel business (Reinders and Baker, 1998).[4] Since the internet encourages direct and immediate contact between suppliers and customers, together with a decrease in transaction and commission costs, there is a strong case for the elimination of intermediaries entirely. However, the last decade has witnessed the emergence of electronic brokers, an electronic version of the traditional model, whose role is that of aggregating and disseminating travel information to customers. Examples are Travelocity and Expedia, which offer information and reservations for flights, hotels and car rental.

In contrast to the commercial sector, destination marketing organizations (DMOs) have been slow to adopt information technology (IT) in their operations. Most DMOs did not start considering electronic distribution until public awareness of the internet increased in the mid-1990s, and a key issue that DMOs have had about web development has been whether to field enquiries themselves or pass them on through links to member websites. Only a few DMOs have designed and developed their internet sites to enable customers to move quickly and easily from travel planning to reservations. An increasing amount of research is focused on the challenges faced by DMOs in keeping pace with the evolution of new technologies. One study conducted by the World Tourism Organization (WTO), which evaluated the websites of 25 DMOs, found great variations in sophistication and quality (1999).[5] One DMO that has made a concerted effort to attract customers via the web is New York. In an effort to become a one-stop resource for travellers seeking information on America's largest city, NTY & Company, the city's official tourism marketing organization, has expanded its accommodations section to include an online hotel reservation system that provides instant access to more than 160 hotels. Users can access property details, up-to-date information on pricing and special packages. They can also book rooms online. The site features a comprehensive calendar of events, suggested itineraries, traveller's tips and maps of all five boroughs.

Figure 7.2 shows a model of online distribution applicable to many destinations, and illustrates the various ways customers can reach individual websites. In the diagram, the browser window is depicted below the customer because it can have an impact on the ultimate message delivery, usability, and pathway to the operator websites. The most common means of navigating through the online maze from customers to operator is typically for the customers to select the search engine or index service of their preference. For example, if they are looking for a hotel in the Paris area, they will type in, or funnel down through search categories to something like 'Paris France' or 'Paris France Hotels'. Alternatively, they may go through an index structure by

**Figure 7.2**   Intermediaries Involved in the Online Distribution of Destination Tourism Products and Services

geography (Europe, France, Paris), by service type, or through a topical index that includes entries such as 'Travel', 'Accommodations' and 'Hotels'. The other route they may take is to click on a link from a search engine to a destination travel guide or an electronic broker.

The diagram also indicates that some customers may book travel through a corporately managed website. These are sites operated by national companies, such as Howard Johnson, Sheraton, Marriott, Best Western and Fairmont that distribute hotel room reservations for the area via their corporate reservation systems. Customers may also book directly, through the various destination travel guides. An important part of the diagram in Figure 7.2 is the cross-link marketing, whereby complementary services supply each other with links to each other's websites. In this case, the user may stumble on a transportation website, explore the links to a hotel and to an attraction, and end up purchasing a hotel reservation and a sight-seeing trip via the online systems on those other websites.

Obviously, individual operators would prefer to reach the customer directly, but the majority, especially the smaller operators, have to rely on electronic intermediaries to direct customers their way, in much the same way as they used to rely on travel agents. And while the internet may be one of the most effective marketing channels for tourism companies, its costs are rising sharply. It is important, therefore, that operators keep track of the impact of websites on the bottom line. Michael Porter (2001), a marketing strategy specialist, has recently suggested that the internet is not necessarily a blessing and that it tends to alter industry structures in ways that dampen over-all profitability.[6] He predicts that many of the companies that succeed will be the ones that use the internet as a complement to traditional ways of competing. Porter has also suggested that average profitability is under pressure in most industries that are influenced by the internet, a comment backed up by Alford (2000), who estimates that 80 per cent of online travel businesses currently trading will not exist in two to three years' time.[7] Porter says that to gain competitive advantage in such a climate, individual companies will have to set themselves apart from the pack: 'As buyers' initial curiosity with the web wanes and subsidies end, companies offering products and services online will be forced to demonstrate that they provide real benefits.'

## Global Spotlight

### VocationVacations

Mixing business with pleasure is usually the ultimate 'no-no', especially when it comes to precious holiday time. However, one US career change company has turned this time-honoured cliché into an opportunity to make dreams come true, by giving tourists the chance to experience first-hand the business or career they have always hankered after.

The first of its kind, VocationVacations was set up in 2004 in Portland, Oregon, by Brian Kurth. The company offers its customers experiences in the United States that combine travel with their dream job, via a choice of over 225 mentorships with experts in jobs as diverse as artist, cheese-maker, vintner, fashion designer, comedian and television producer.

It is more than just job shadowing; it's the chance to test-drive a career without financial risk or endangering a current form of employment. Kurth generally chooses smaller companies, where owners tend to be particularly passionate about their specialization. 'People who love what they do are more willing to share it,' he explains. From this initial taste of the new career, 'vocationers' can then decide, with some experience as well as expert guidance, if they want to change their life or retreat to the safety of their chosen job.

The job choices, from horse trainer to pastry chef, are realistic options – 'Dream jobs, jobs anyone can learn to do with a little initiative,' says Kurth. 'Not fantasy jobs, such as rock star. You may not be qualified to be a rock star.'

Inquiries are made via the company's website or by calling its toll-free number. The VocationVacations site includes extensive lists of media reviews as well as 'vocationer' testimonials. Many journalists from TV, radio and print have test-driven careers with VocationVacations in order to write about their real-life experiences. Packages range from US$399 for a basic day to US$1,999 for a three-day dream job experience with a Grand Am racing pit crew or a Wedding Planner VocationVacation with a celebrity wedding planner in Los Angeles. The company is partnered with credit card and hotel loyalty programmes offering, for example, two-day Music Producer holidays for 150,000 points.

After being laid off in 2001 by a dot.com company, Kurth set up in this innovative new business following six months of travel around the US. The statistics are in VocationVacations' favour, with 55 per cent of American workers disliking their jobs, 42 per cent burned out and 33 per cent stuck in dead-end careers. These were the results of a survey of 7,718 US workers carried out by Harris Interactive Inc. in 2004. Kurth realizes that the market is huge for his unique concept. He is finalizing a book on the Vocationing process for Warner Business Books and has signed with Al Roker Productions to create a career-change TV series based on VocationVacations.

'Work can be much, much more than just a four-letter word,' claims Kurth; he works on the theory that people are ready for different experiences during their holidays, which he calls 'adventures'. The chance to learn something new was rated as 'very important' by 64 per cent of people polled in the 2004 RoperReports NOP survey. This survey tracks vacation trends and found that relaxation was down slightly as a major motivation for holidaymakers, whereas the urge to learn was up from 51 per cent the previous year.

Kurth rates VocationVacations in the culinary, fashion, entertainment, hospitality, animal-related and sports fields as the most popular to date. But he counsels that people should see 'beyond the glamour' and experience the job 'warts and all'.

*Sources:* Kurth, B. (17 March 2007) personal interview with author; Davis, A. (January 2006) 'Dream a little dream job', *Westjet.com Inflight Magazine*; Frazier, J. B. (June 2004) 'Vocation vacations: try out a "dream job" without leaving the one you have', retrieved from www.post-gazette.com; 'Test-drive your dream job', retrieved from http://www.vocationvacations.com.

## Channel Conflict and Organization

### Channel Conflict

In order for companies within a distribution channel to be successful, it is necessary that they work together. When every member in the value chain co-operates, it allows the channel to combine its resources to perform in a more efficient and effective manner. The success of the entire channel will in turn benefit all the individual members. Unfortunately, many companies in the tourism and hospitality industry tend to focus on their own, individual performance rather than on that of the entire chain. They frequently disagree about the roles each should play or who should do what for which rewards. Thus a co-operative marketing system is often difficult to achieve, and a common occurrence is **channel conflict**, in which one member perceives another to be engaged in behaviour that prevents or hinders the first member from achieving its goals.

---

**CHANNEL CONFLICT**
conflict that occurs when one member of a distribution channel perceives another to be engaged in behaviour that prevents or hinders the first member from achieving its goals

---

There are two main forms of channel conflict: horizontal conflict and vertical conflict. **Horizontal conflict** takes place between organizations at the same level of the distribution channel. An example is a conflict over territory between two Best Western franchises. Due to the rapid growth of this company, it is common for two separate franchises to compete for the same market segment of customers. **Vertical conflict** occurs between organizations at different levels of the same channel, and it is more common. An example is the argument between travel agents and airlines over the latter's cutting of base commissions for the former.

---

**HORIZONTAL CONFLICT**
conflict between organizations at the same level of the distribution channel

---

**VERTICAL CONFLICT**
conflict between organizations at different levels of the same distribution channel

---

In the UK in the late 1990s, independent travel agents complained to the government about the practice of **directional selling**, which is a vertically integrated travel agent's sale, or attempted sale, of the foreign package holidays of its linked tour operator in preference to the holidays of other operators. The practice was facilitated by the lack of transparency of ownership links (see Opening Vignette in Chapter 4). It caused considerable conflict both between the large tour operators and between travel agents and tour operators (Hudson et al., 2001).[8]

---

**DIRECTIONAL SELLING**
a vertically integrated travel agent's sale, or attempted sale, of the foreign package holidays of its linked tour operator in preference to the holiday of other operators

---

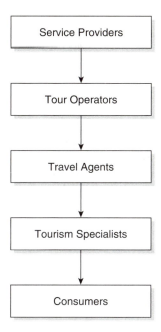

**Figure 7.3** The Conventional Marketing System

Conflicts may be caused by simple misunderstandings. For franchisees, for example, understanding the decisions made by the franchiser can sometimes be difficult. Dennis Murray, a Thrifty car rental franchisee says, 'It can be exceptionally challenging when a decision made by the franchiser seems undesirable to a franchisee's particular location, but it is better for the entire system in the end.' Co-operating to achieve overall channel goals sometimes means giving up individual company goals.

## Channel Organization

There are two main types of channel organization: the conventional marketing system and the vertical marketing system.

**The conventional marketing system** is the traditional system that organizations used to adopt because the conventional hierarchical structure was consistent with the structure within individual organizations. This distribution system consists of a loose collection of independent organizations, each of which tries to maximize its own success (see Figure 7.3). For example, many small hotels pay a commission to travel agents, but no formal contract is signed between the hotel and the agent. The hotel simply communicates its policy and can, if it wishes, make rooms unavailable to travel agents on a temporary basis. Although this system has worked in the past, trends of globalization and technological advancement have forced many tourism organizations to reorganize their distribution channel into a vertical marketing system in order to remain competitive.

**CONVENTIONAL MARKETING SYSTEM**
a distribution system that consists of a loose collection of independent organizations, each of which tries to maximize its own success

**In the vertical marketing system,** all members of the distribution channel work together as a unified whole (see Figure 7.4). They become vertically integrated so that they can all work together to achieve a common goal. Usually, one member dominates, and leads the entire channel toward its shared goal by reducing conflict within the system. This leader may be appointed either formally or informally. Formal leadership can be obtained through ownership control over the other members (e.g., TUI's ownership of Lunn Poly travel agents) or by forming contractual agreements with the other members in the channel (e.g., Thomas Cook's deal with Avis for specially priced car rentals). Informal control is usually given to the channel member with the most brand ownership or financial strength, or is simply designated on the basis of the role that the leader plays within the system.

**VERTICAL MARKETING SYSTEM**
a system in which all members of the distribution channel work together as a unified whole

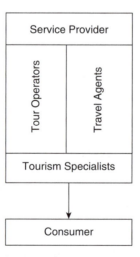

**Figure 7.4** The Vertically Integrated Marketing System

The vertical marketing system has five main advantages over the conventional marketing system. It:

1. **allows economies of scale**. The entire chain is able to produce goods or services less expensively than competitors due to economies of scale (i.e., declines in unit costs of production as the volume of production increases), thus giving all channel members a competitive advantage;
2. **makes managing conflict easier**. With just one member dominating the channel, this leader has the authority to punish those channel members that are creating conflict, as well as to implement solutions to resolve such situations;
3. **eliminates duplication**. The vertical integration of the distribution channel allows all duplicated duties to be eliminated. This increases the efficiency of the chain;
4. **levers bargaining power**. The vertical integration of the channel gives the system and its members more power to bargain than when channel members work individually;
5. **creates shared goals**. The system allows for all the members of the channel to benefit from an achieved goal, rather than only one specific member benefiting.

There are two main forms of the vertical marketing system: alliances and franchises. Both carry with them advantages and disadvantages; which form an organization chooses depends on which one best matches that company's specific goals.

### Alliances

An **alliance** is a partnership formed when two or more organizations combine resources through a contractual agreement that allows them to combat each other's weaknesses and benefit from each other's strengths. In this form of distribution channel, each organization shares everything from information to resources to strategies, but the key advantage is in increased distribution. Members of the alliance will enjoy access to new markets through new and diversified sales locations. The Opening Vignette provides an in-depth analysis of marketing alliances in South Africa's game reserves. Other examples referred to in this book include the BestCities Alliance, the world's only convention bureau global alliance, which includes Puerto Rico, Cape Town, Copenhagen, Dubai, Edinburgh, Melbourne, Singapore and Vancouver (see Case Study on Puerto Rico Convention Centre in Chapter 9) and the Adventure Collection (see Case Study on CMH below), a group of nine adventure companies that have joined together to form an alliance. The alliance prints a collective brochure that is sent to guests of all nine companies, and the companies jointly promote each other's trips. They also combine itineraries to create new trips in order to give travellers more choices.

---

**ALLIANCE**
partnership formed when two or more organizations combine resources through a contractual agreement that allows them to combat each other's weaknesses and benefit from each other's strengths

---

### Franchises

**Franchises** are businesses in which a franchiser grants a franchisee the right to engage in offering, selling, or distributing its goods or services under its marketing format. Franchising has become increasingly popular in tourism and hospitality, particularly in the hotel and restaurant sector. The Snapshot below focuses on the Hard Rock franchise and shows how the American Indian Seminole Tribe has expanded its commercial operation overseas by buying the British-owned chain of Hard Rock Café restaurants and casinos. Most investors in hotels today require some type of chain affiliation before they will consider becoming involved in a hotel project. They believe that the benefits of having an established brand image, a central reservations system, co-ordinated marketing and a frequent traveller programme are worth the cost of associating with a hotel chain. Hotel companies that have an established brand give independent lodging owners the right to use their brand logo, reservations system and other programmes by either granting a franchise or actually taking over the property's management through a management contract. Globally, franchising has become the most popular method of obtaining brand identity because the hotel owner does not have to relinquish operational control. Normally the franchisee will pay a fee to purchase a full-service franchise, as well as paying an annual percentage of sales. For example, in the car rental business, Thrifty Car Rental franchisees pay a monthly fee of 5 per cent of their gross revenue from rental and parking activities, which helps pay for headquarters support and for select programmes for franchises. There is also an advertising fee, but many services are provided to franchisees for free. Many people in the world of franchising claim that the relationship between franchiser and franchisee is one of the most important and challenging aspects of the business. Some of the advantages and disadvantages to both franchiser and franchisee are outlined below.

---

**FRANCHISES**

businesses in which a franchiser grants a franchisee the right to engage in offering, selling, or distributing its goods or services under its marketing format

---

### Franchiser Benefits

1. The main benefit to the franchiser is the increased distribution coverage, as franchises usually service markets nationally or globally. This global coverage is becoming increasingly important in the face of globalization.
2. Increased revenue through obtaining a percentage of the franchisees' sales.
3. Expansion of the brand, allowing access to new market segments.
4. Increased bargaining power with suppliers.
5. The creation of economies of scale in areas such as purchasing and advertising.

### Franchiser Costs

1. Increased expenditure due to the need to monitor all franchisees' activities.
2. Limitation of the franchising organization's ability to expand other methods of distribution (like alliances) due to territorial conflict.
3. Increased number of decision-makers within the system leading to a higher likelihood of conflict.
4. Limitation of options for changing current operations because changes must occur throughout the entire franchise.

## Franchisee Benefits

1. Brand name recognition reduces risk by ensuring consumer awareness of the company. Thrifty franchisees, for example, benefit from worldwide brand recognition and widespread advertising, as well as frequency-based programmes linked with internationally and nationally recognized airlines, hotels and other organizations.
2. Methods of operation are already decided, reducing the amount of time and money needed to start the company. This includes everything from the franchise layout and equipment to the entire marketing plan.
3. Costs are reduced due to economies of scale in areas such as advertising and purchasing. One of the major benefits for Thrifty franchisees, for example, is help with buying cars, as car manufacturers will provide incentives for purchases when a company is part of a bigger system.
4. Free consulting on business issues.
5. Assistance with financing.

## Franchisee Costs

1. The new organization must continually pay fees and royalties for the benefits that it receives, such as the use of brand name and advertising.
2. Decision-making is limited because of the amount of planning already done by the franchiser.
3. If one company in the organization performs badly, every company in the franchise is affected.

Overall, although there are costs to franchising, choosing this method of distribution has benefits to both franchiser and franchisee. A study of franchising in the hotel sector found that the total cost of a hotel affiliation ranges from 2.3 per cent of rooms' revenue for Best Western to 11.3 per cent for a Marriott hotel. Most hotel brands cost between 8 per cent and 10 per cent of rooms' revenue, the median being 8.3 per cent. Other organizations achieving low percentages include Master Host Inns at 4.4 per cent, Guesthouse Inns at 5.3 per cent and Key West Inns at 5.4 per cent (Rushmore, 2001).[9] Hotel franchise affiliations usually entail several types of fees. They start with an initial fee, typically based on a dollar amount per room. Ongoing fees usually include a royalty fee for the use of the trade name and service marks, an advertising or marketing contribution fee, reservation expenses, and frequent traveller programme costs. Other fees include computer software, training programmes, global distribution systems and equipment rentals. The total of all these fees and expenses is used in calculating the percentage of rooms' revenue to be paid to the franchiser. The total ten-year cost for a Best Western hotel, for example, would be more than $1 million, although the chain does have the lowest percentage of rooms' revenue (2.3 percent). HVS International recommends that owners carefully evaluate the price/value relationship of all the potential hotel brands before signing a long-term franchise agreement. Unlike most franchise agreements that require five-, ten-, or even 20-year commitments, Best Western memberships are renewed annually, with no long-term lock-in and no management fees, making this company very attractive to potential franchisees.

## Snapshot

### Expanding Overseas: Native Tribe Buys Hard Rock Café Chain

The Native American Seminole Tribe boldly expanded its highly successful commercial operation overseas in 2006 by buying the British-owned chain of Hard Rock Café restaurants and casinos for just under US$1billion from Rank Group PLC. The Florida tribe was the first native band in the casino business to expand internationally on such a large scale. The tribe had already partnered successfully with Hard Rock in hotel, gambling and entertainment complexes in Tampa and Hollywood, Florida.

The chain, Hard Rock International Inc., includes 124 cafés in the US, Europe, Australia and Puerto Rico, four hotels, two casino hotels, two concert venues and a British casino and hotel company. Pre-tax profits for 2005 were US$493 million. The tribe also acquired reputedly the world's largest collection of rock 'n roll memorabilia. Comprising around 70,000 pieces, it includes guitars formerly owned by Bob Dylan, Eric Clapton, Jimi Hendrix and Chuck Berry as well as clothing from Madonna and Elton John. However, the deal excluded Hard Rock's Las Vegas casino as well as the Morgans Hotel Group's intellectual rights in Australia, Brazil, Israel, Venezuela and some areas of the US.

'This is a proud moment for the Seminole Tribe of Florida and for all Indian tribes,' said Mitchell Cypress, chairman of the elected Tribal Council. 'It is also an opportunity for the Seminole Tribe to diversify its business operations and help a very successful company to achieve even greater growth.'

The tribe planned to continue work on existing growth plans in conjunction with current Hard Rock International management teams, according to Cypress and Seminole Gaming Chief Executive James Allen.

The Florida Seminoles had subsisted on cattle ranching and farming citrus fruits, backed by federal loans, until the late 1970s. Known as 'the Unconquered' because of their refusal to sign a treaty with the US government, the Seminoles were the first native group to enter the gambling world commercially with the opening, in 1979, of their first bingo hall and tax-free tobacco store in Florida. Aggressive expansion followed throughout Florida and Oklahoma with gaming the main focus. The tribe has been a pace-setter for tribal gaming, which is now worth more than US$22 billion in annual revenues, according to US government figures.

'The Seminoles were in the forefront of those who did it right and did it successfully, so I'm sure they can take what they learned there and put it into other areas of entertainment and hospitality,' said Phil Hogan, chairman of the National Indian Gaming Commission, a US federal agency which oversees tribal gambling.

Echoing a national trend of tribal casinos partnering with large corporations or expanding to other states, the Florida tribe is setting the pace for other native groups. For example, the Mashantucket Pequot tribe, which operates Foxwoods Resort Casino in Connecticut, planned to lease the MGM Grand name from MGM Mirage. The $700 million hotel and casino expansion would be called MGM Grand but would be run by Foxwoods' employees.

*Sources*: Morton, P. (7 December 2006). 'Seminoles snap up Hard Rock Café', *National Post*, FP7; Anon. (2006) 'Seminole Tribe buying Hard Rock Café business for $965 million', retrieved from www.wsvn.com/news.

## Designing the Distribution System

Tourism organizations must decide how to make their services available to their selected target market by choosing their distribution mix strategy. This can be a complex decision. They must select a mix that will provide them with the maximum amount of exposure to potential travellers as well as ensure that the chosen strategy aligns with the company or destination image. In addition, the strategy should maximize control over sales and reservations and should work within the organization's budget.

An organization can consider three broad distribution strategies:

1. **Intensive distribution**. In this case the organization maximizes the exposure of its travel services by distributing through all available outlets or intermediaries. This strategy is most useful for an organization that is trying to obtain high market coverage. An example of a tourism organization that uses this strategy is Thomson Holidays in the UK.
2. **Exclusive distribution**. Here the organization deliberately restricts the number of channels that it uses to distribute its product or service to its customers. Because only a limited number of intermediaries are given the right to distribute the product, the result is often a strengthening of the company's image and an increase in the status of those who purchase the product. This strategy is an effective method for prestige tourism products and is used by companies like Canadian Mountain Holidays, profiled in the Case Study at the end of this chapter.
3. **Selective distribution**. In this strategy between intensive and exclusive distribution, a company uses more than one but less than all of the possible distribution channels. The Rocky Mountaineer, profiled in Chapter 9, employs selective distribution, using sales representation in 18 countries to sell over half a million tours each year.

---

**INTENSIVE DISTRIBUTION**
strategy in which an organization maximizes the exposure of its travel services by distributing through all available outlets or intermediaries

---

**EXCLUSIVE DISTRIBUTION**
strategy in which an organization deliberately restricts the number of channels that it uses to distribute its product or service to its customers; an effective method for marketing prestige products

---

**SELECTIVE DISTRIBUTION**
strategy between intensive and exclusive distribution, in which a company uses more than one but less than all of the possible distribution channels

---

Before an organization begins to design its distribution strategy, it must consider the following five factors:

1. **Market coverage**. The amount of market coverage should be considered in co-ordination with the organization's goals and objectives, as this factor will directly impact the particular distribution mix that is best for the company.
2. **Costs**. Only the most cost-effective distribution methods should be implemented, and they should make effective use of the organization's budget.
3. **Positioning and image**. The distribution strategy chosen should be consistent with the position and image that the company wants to achieve and maintain.
4. **Motivation of intermediaries**. Intermediaries should be provided with appropriate incentives in order to motivate them to sell the product or service to consumers. The Quebec City Convention Bureau, for example, hosts about 700 tour operators and 400 meeting planners on custom itineraries each year. These trips provide an excellent promotional forum for giving intermediaries a first-hand appreciation of the facilities and services being offered.
5. **Characteristics of the tourism organization**. Each organization has unique characteristics and needs that are specific to its operations. These needs must be considered when designing the distribution strategy. For example, if an organization operates in a manner that requires it to communicate directly with the consumer in order to be successful, then it must develop its distribution strategy to meet those needs.

The Case Study on Canadian Mountain Holidays at the end of the chapter shows how an exclusive distribution strategy worked well for the adventure tourism company. Cruise lines, too, have a carefully planned distribution strategy. These companies have traditionally used exclusive distribution, but are gradually moving toward selective distribution. Roughly 90 per cent of cruises are sold through traditional travel agencies, and, in today's economy, suppliers are reluctant to jeopardize these firmly established, reliable relationships, despite the agency commissions involved. However, even though only 10 per cent of cruises are predicted to be sold online by 2005, the internet is now an important part of the equation, as many consumers will make their travel decisions online, even if they ultimately purchase offline. Cruise lines work with online travel agencies to sell discount and last-minute inventories, but they use their own websites for marketing purposes rather for than direct sales. Many companies don't even feature consumer booking engines on their sites.

## Distribution Channel Management

Once the tourism organization has decided on its distribution mix strategy, it must implement and manage the chosen distribution channel. **Channel management** includes selecting and motivating individual channel members and evaluating their performance over time.

> **CHANNEL MANAGEMENT**
> a process that includes selecting and motivating individual channel members and evaluating their performance over time

## Selecting Channel Members

Tourism organizations must share information and work closely with the members of their distribution system. It is critical, therefore, that an organization selects the best suited channel members in order to ensure an effective distribution system. In the Opening Vignette, Motswari had selected certain tour operators to distribute its safari packages, based on their geographic position and their ability to reach key international markets. When selecting channel members, the service provider should determine the characteristics that distinguish the most valuable marketing intermediaries from the others. Evaluation criteria may include such aspects as a channel member's number of years in business, the services and products it already carries, its past growth and financial history, its level of co-operativeness, and its reputation and image.

## Motivating Channel Members

After an organization has selected its distribution channel members, it must continually motivate these members to perform their best. Three incentives are commonly used to motivate a company's intermediaries. The first one is financial, and includes commissions and bonuses. The second is the provision of educational trips for intermediary staff, during which they can experience the supplier's product for themselves. Such 'familiarization trips' are common in the travel agency sector. Canadian Mountain Holidays (see Case Study) uses both these methods to motivate international agents. Another incentive, again quite common in travel agencies, is to provide intermediaries with reduced-price holidays. This gives them greater knowledge of the product and enthusiasm for selling it to consumers.

## Evaluating Channel Members

Tourism organizations must constantly monitor each channel member's performance in order to ensure the success of the channel as a whole. Performance can be measured through the generation of sales, customer delivery time, and/or the success of combined promotional efforts among intermediaries. Channel members who perform well should be recognized and rewarded, and assistance should be provided to those who are struggling to meet the company's goals and objectives. The organization should also 're-qualify' its channel members periodically, replacing the weaker members that harm the overall effectiveness of the distribution system. Best Western likes to renew contracts annually so that it can maintain control over the distribution channel. The company has also implemented a 'quality assurance process', whereby a quality inspection team uses the same criteria to review every one of the member hotels around the world. Finally, the Best Western website gives customers the opportunity to provide online feedback regarding service quality.

## Chapter Summary

There are two different distribution channels that the service provider or principal can pursue: direct or indirect. In a direct channel, a company delivers its product to the consumer without the outside assistance of any independent intermediaries. In an indirect channel, the supplier makes use of several marketing intermediaries in order to help distribute its product.

These intermediaries are independent associations that are not under the company's control, and include travel agents, tour operators, convention and meeting planners, travel specialists and internet sites.

The conventional marketing system consists of a loose collection of organizations, each of which tries to maximize the benefits of the channel for its own best interests. However, under a vertical marketing system, organizations work together to achieve group objectives established by the channel as a whole, resulting in benefits for each independent party.

There are two main forms of vertical marketing system: alliances and franchises. Alliances are partnerships formed when two or more organizations combine resources through a contractual agreement that allows them to combat each other's weaknesses and benefit from one another's strengths. Franchises are formed when a franchiser grants a franchisee the right to engage in offering, selling, or distributing the franchiser's goods or services under its marketing format.

When designing its distribution system, a company can choose among three different types of strategy: intensive distribution, exclusive distribution and selective distribution.

Before an organization begins to design its distribution strategy, it is important that it consider the following five factors: market coverage, costs, positioning and image, motivation of intermediaries, and the characteristics of the tourism organization itself.

In order for the company to ensure the effective execution of its distribution strategy, it must select individual channel members, motivate these members, and monitor their performance over time.

## Key Terms

## Discussion Questions and Exercises

1. How does the tourism and hospitality industry's distribution system differ from that of other industries?
2. Explain the difference between the structure of a conventional marketing system and that of a vertical marketing system. Can you think of two companies in the tourism industry that use these two different strategies?
3. Choose a company within the tourism industry of your country and explain how it uses its distribution strategy to attract customers to its product. Do you think that the company is using the most effective distribution channel available to it? What do you recommend that the company do to improve its distribution system?
4. Considering two different tourism franchise organizations in your country, compare the different distribution strategies used by each franchise. Which franchise do you think is more effective in distributing its product or service to consumers?
5. What are the two different types of channel conflict that can arise in a distribution system? Give one example for each type from the tourism industry. How can these conflicts be resolved?
6. How would you evaluate the performance of a channel member as the manager of a large hotel franchise?

## Profiting from Fun: Canadian Mountain Holidays

Canadian Mountain Holidays (CMH), a helicopter tourism pioneer, was founded in 1965 and operates in 12 mountain areas of southeastern British Columbia. The Banff-based company has annual revenues of about CDN$70 million and claims an 80 per cent repeat-booking figure in the winter. CMH has the leasehold rights from

**Case Study**

A CMH Helicopter prepares to take skiers into the wilderness

the B.C. government to 15,765 square kilometres of remote territory in the Purcell, Cariboo, Selkirk and Monashee mountain ranges. Boasting several times the number of heli-ski visits carried out by its nearest competitor, CMH has 21 helicopters and eight remote lodges – many accessible in winter only by helicopter. Lodges have been designed specifically to meet the needs of heli-tourists. Each lodge has a dining room and a fully stocked lounge, and each is equipped with a sauna and a Jacuzzi. There is even a resident qualified massage practitioner who can rejuvenate skiers' tired muscles. The company divides its business into three strands: heli-skiing, heli-hiking and mountaineering.

According to Chief Marketing Officer Marty von Neudegg, 'CMH is just a bunch of mountain guides taking people into the mountains to have fun, and the company philosophy reflects this attitude.' But is having fun a good enough foundation for a successful business model? It was the late Hans Gmoser who founded the company. In 1965, after several years working as a mountain guide, he took a few friends up in a helicopter to go skiing in untracked powder. It didn't take long to catch on. 'Demand literally exploded,' he said in an interview in 2005. 'Suddenly there were no four- to five-hour walks and areas became so accessible. I was driven because I had such a good time myself, but it was infectious, and it rubbed off on the guests.'

Since its inception, CMH has hosted more than 135,000 skier weeks. Each winter CMH sells 7,000 holidays and actually has a waiting list of 3,000. About 50 per cent of customers are from the United States and 40 per cent from Europe. A seven-day package costs between $6,000 and $9,000 and includes 100,000 vertical feet of skiing, and accommodation and food for seven nights. CMH invented heli-hiking (an abbreviation of helicopter-assisted hiking) in 1978, and from June to September it runs excursions that depart from five mountain lodges. All-inclusive packages range from family adventures and photography workshops to alpine ecology. Stays can be at one or a combination of five lodges, and three-night heli-hiking packages cost approximately $2,000. Helicopters transport guests to remote wilderness areas around B.C., where participants can decide from day to day whether they want to be mountaineers scaling steep ridges or to stroll leisurely along the glaciers and flower-filled meadows.

Marketing at CMH is different. 'We are often considered insular or aloof but we are deliberately unique. We don't want to follow traditional promotional or distribution paths – we position ourselves distinctly because we are distinct and unique,' says Walter Bruns, president of the company. The company's greatest marketing vehicle is 'encouraged word of mouth' and CMH does very little advertising. Marty von Neudegg says that the company has three marketing areas: sales, advertising and service. However, 90 per cent of the marketing budget is spent on service, in order to encourage customer loyalty. CMH produces colourful brochures for each of its three activity strands (winter brochures being produced in six languages), expensive videos are made for all three activities in up to six languages, and a website exists for each activity.

CMH also hosts marketing events called 'An Evening with CMH' throughout North America, Europe, Japan, and Australia. These are invitation-only evenings at which CMH staff and guides entertain and provide information to past guests and their friends. These events are very successful, generating conversion rates in excess of 75 per cent of all participants.

When CMH began marketing in Europe during the late 1960s and early 1970s, Europeans had no knowledge of Canadian heli-skiing opportunities. Rather than following the normal route of mass-media advertising, CMH chose to place no advertisements at all. Instead, the company found one person in each nation to be the CMH agent, and this person had to know the product and its market intimately. They sold heli-skiing to one person at a time. This took place many years before the term 'one-to-one' marketing had been coined. Although the distribution system has become more sophisticated over the years, these 12 agents still work in Europe and bring in 40 per cent of the business. For the US and Canadian markets CMH employs its own travel agency, based in Banff. 'The referral from a happy client to a new client is critical for CMH,' says Bruns. 'These relationships have evolved organically right from the beginning of the company – and our agents are seen as part of the family.'

CMH is also part of the 'Adventure Collection', a group of nine adventure companies that have formed an alliance based on the principle that each company is deeply committed to the environment and culture through which it takes its guests. The alliance prints a collective brochure that is sent to guests of all nine companies, and the companies jointly promote each other's trips. They also combine itineraries to create new trips, giving travellers more choices.

**Case Study**

Case Study

Although the company may not have changed much in culture over the years, the ownership structure has. Gmoser himself found the only way he could detach himself emotionally from the company was to sell it to Alpine Helicopters in 1995. Two years later, Intrawest Corp. of Vancouver purchased a 45 per cent stake in Alpine, and in November 2005 bought the remaining 55 per cent. Involved in 15 mountain resorts in North America and Europe, Intrawest invests heavily in real estate developments and tourism infra-structure, adding retail, lodging and restaurants to attract people to its resorts and keep them there. 'The Intrawest deal concerns me as I cannot see why they bought CMH', said Gmoser. 'If they tinker with it they are making a big mistake. The loyalty the company has built is very fragile. You can't be too hard-nosed in the business sense.'

*Source*: Hudson, S. (ed.) (2003) *Sport and Adventure Tourism*. Binghamton, NY: Haworth.

## Questions

1. What particular distribution strategy is CMH following to sell its heli-skiing trips?
2. Should the company follow the same strategy for summer (heli-hiking) business?
3. Why is CMH able to distribute its heli-skiing holidays without using intermediaries like travel agents or tour operators?
4. What are the advantages and disadvantages of relying on word of mouth to sell heli-skiing holidays?
5. What will be the advantages and disadvantages to CMH of being purchased by Intrawest?

## Websites

| | |
|---|---|
| www.adventurecollection.com | The Adventure Collection |
| www.bestwestern.com | Best Western hotels |
| www.cmhski.com | Canadian Mountain Holidays |
| www.expedia.com | Expedia.ca (online travel agency) |
| www.hoteldiscounts.com | hoteldiscount.com (online hotel agency) |
| www.hedna.org | Hotel Electronic Distribution Network Association |
| www.iata.org | International Air Transport Association |
| www.thrifty.ca | Thrifty Car Rental |
| www.travelocity.com | Travelocity.ca (online travel agency) |
| www.whitespot.ca | White Spot Restaurants |
| www.travelcaresports.com | Travelcare Sports |
| www.reedexpo.com | Reed Exhibitions |
| www.vocationvacations.com | VocationVacations |
| www.weekendtrips.com | Weekendtrips.com |
| www.hardrock.com | Hard Rock cafés and casinos |
| www.motswari.co.az | Motswari Game Lodge |

# References

1  Anon. (2006) 'Travel agents: Do they still matter?', *Travelweek*, 34(47), 1–2.
2  Anon. (2007) 'Internet eating further into business travel bookings', retrieved from www.travelmole.com.
3  Christian, R. (2001) 'Developing an online access strategy: issues facing small to medium-sized tourism and hospitality enterprises', *Journal of Vacation Marketing*, 7(2), 170–178.
4  Reinders, J. and Baker, M. (1998) 'The future for direct retailing of travel and tourism products: the influence of information technology', *Progress in Tourism and Hospitality Research*, 4, 1–15.
5  World Trade Organization Business Council. (1999) *Marketing Tourism Destinations Online. Strategies for the Information Age.* Madrid: World Trade Organization.
6  Porter, M. E. (2001) 'Strategy and the Internet', *Harvard Business Review*, 79(3), 63–78.
7  Alford, P. (2000) 'E-business models in the travel industry', *Travel & Tourism Analyst*, 3, 67–86.
8  Hudson, S., Snaith, T., Miller, G.A. and Hudson, P. (2001) 'Distribution channels in the travel industry: using mystery shoppers to understand the influence of travel agency recommendations', *Journal of Travel Research*, 40(2), 148–154.
9  Rushmore, S. (June 2001) 'What do hotel franchises actually cost?' *Hotels*, 35(6); Membership makes the difference. (2002). Best Western membership document, Phoenix Arizona, 1–10.

# 8

# MARKETING COMMUNICATIONS: THE ROLE OF ADVERTISING AND SALES PROMOTIONS

## 'What Happens in Vegas, Stays in Vegas'

The highly successful advertising campaign based around this slogan has succeeded in re-branding Las Vegas as 'Sin City' again after a failed attempt to reposition it as a family destination. The slogan, used extensively by Mayor Oscar Goodman, was coined by two advertising copywriters who were brainstorming for a new concept for Las Vegas in 2002. Jason Hoff and Jeff Candido have since developed a series of innovative television ads that do not dwell on the typical images of neon, showgirls and gambling, but rather create an updated concept of Vegas as the place to realize your dreams, secret ambitions and fantasies with no comeback.

Between 2001 and 2004 the two market researchers conducted a brand planning exercise. This involved qualitative research to understand consumer behaviour, including observational research and 'tag-alongs' (following visitors around from the moment they arrive until the moment they leave). They used projection techniques, such as asking consumers questions like 'If Las Vegas was an animal what would it be?' or 'If Las Vegas was a person what type of person would it be?' (visitors often talked about themselves). They used other innovative research techniques such as asking people to write an obituary for Las Vegas. A sextant system was then used to segment guests. The sextant takes 40,000 people nationally, examines their psyches and behaviour, and neatly classifies them into 12 'tribes', such as Embittered Conservatives, Disaffected Escapists and Gilded Gamesmen. It attributes 13 'glyphs' – symbols that convey attitude or appearance such as 'trendy', 'shocking', 'flirtatious' and 'cool and hip' – to the tribes. Researchers then looked for one message that could resonate with the target tribes – one that had the Las Vegas brand personality: exciting, sexy, safely dangerous.

The following US$60 million advertising campaign, launched by the Las Vegas Convention and Visitors Authority (LVCVA) to increase tourism in the famous

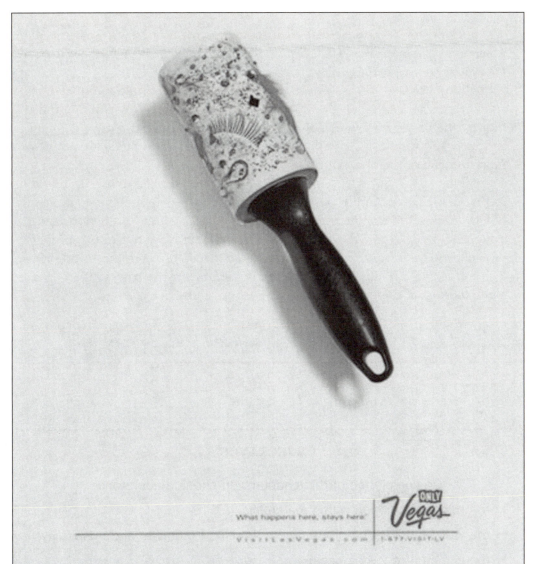

What happens here, stays here®

*Vegas*

ONLY LV

VisitLasVegas.com | 1-877-VISIT-LV

A print ad from the 'What happens in Vegas stays in Vegas' campaign

casino city, resulted in visitor numbers increasing from 35 million in 2000 to a record-breaking 37 million by 2004. By 2005 there were 135,000 hotel rooms in Vegas, compared to 71,000 in 1955, and plans were being developed for 155,000 rooms as well as 14,000 timeshare and condo hotel units in the near future. *USA Today* voted the television ads the most likeable ads in 2004. Sexually suggestive and humorous, they appealed to both men and women and a variety of age-groups, and were aired during episodes of *Las Vegas* and *CSI*, both filmed in the city, heightening links between the advertising message and the product.

The slogan's success was such that media outlets such as *The Tonight Show with Jay Leno*, *Saturday Night Live* and *The Simpsons* exploited the concept, further increasing awareness for Las Vegas.

In alignment with the re-imaging of Vegas via its food, shopping facilities and entertainment, the ads drew attention to staying out late, spending more money, and eating well with none of the inhibitions or restraints of daily life at home. The website is provided at the end of each ad to facilitate access to more information and easy bookings.

Previous to the 'Sin City' re-imaging, Las Vegas had tried unsuccessfully to re-brand itself as a family destination, providing pirate and circus themed hotels, funfairs, rides, amusement and games arcades, animal attractions and a dose of Disney at the MGM Grand. With the extra blow to visitor numbers provided by the fallout from 9/11, marketers decided to recapture the original, raunchy glamour of Vegas and the decadence of the past with a veritable explosion of topless shows and after-hours clubs.

*Sources*: Banks, K. (November 2005) 'Vegas Baby', *Westworld Alberta*, 49–55; Farhi, P. (24 December 2004) 'What Happens in Vegas, Stays in Vegas', *Calgary Herald*, K4.

### OBJECTIVES

On completion of this chapter, you should understand:

▶ the role of promotion within marketing;

▶ the various marketing promotion tools used in tourism and hospitality;

▶ the communication process;

▶ the importance of integrated marketing communications (IMC);

▶ the stages involved in an integrated marketing communications campaign plan;

▶ the role of advertising in the promotional mix;

▶ sales promotion objectives and techniques used in tourism and hospitality; and

▶ types of joint promotions.

## Introduction

Effective communication with target customers is carried out by a variety of methods, referred to as 'marketing communications'. The Opening Vignette offers an example of the successful implementation of one promotional technique: advertising. The next three chapters look at the various promotional techniques used by tourism and hospitality providers. Chapter 8 begins with an introduction of the role and types of promotional tools used in tourism and hospitality. A section follows that focuses on the communication process. The chapter then discusses the rise of integrated marketing communications (IMC) as a result of the recognition that advertising can no longer be crafted and executed in isolation from other promotional mix elements. Consideration is then given to the communication techniques of advertising and sales promotion.

In many people's perception, marketing is promotion, for promotion is the highly visible, public face of marketing. However, promotion is only one element of the marketing mix, its role being to convince potential customers of the benefits of purchasing or using the products and services of a particular organization. Organizations use marketing communications – promotional tools used to communicate effectively with customers – for many reasons other than simply launching new products. They may, for example, be trying to encourage potential customers to try their product at the same time as encouraging their existing customers to purchase or use the same product again. Together with marketing, marketing communications dramatically increased in importance in the 1980s and 1990s, to the extent that effective, sustained communication with customers is now seen as critical to the success of any organization, whether in the private, public or not-for-profit sector, from international airlines to tourism destinations and attractions.

## Marketing Promotion Tools

Promotions decisions will be determined by the overall marketing plan, as illustrated in Figure 8.1. Chapter 3 explains how marketing objectives are derived from the strategic tools of targeting and positioning. The marketing mix is then used to achieve these objectives, and promotions are just one part of this marketing mix.

The blend of promotional elements outlined in Table 8.1 is known as the **promotional mix**, and promotional management involves co-ordinating all the elements, setting objectives and budgets, designing programmes, evaluating performance and taking corrective action. Promotion can be a short-term activity, but considered at a strategic level it is a mid- and long-term investment aimed at building up a consistent and credible corporate or destination identity. Promotion, when used effectively, builds and creates an identity for the product or the organization. Brochures, advertisements, in-store merchandising, sales promotions and so on, create the identity of the company in the mind of the consumer, and all aspects of the promotional effort should therefore project the same image.

---

**PROMOTIONAL MIX**
a company's total marketing communications programme

---

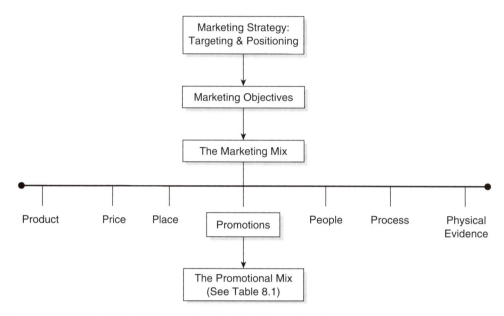

**Figure 8.1** The Role of Promotions in the Marketing Strategy

This chapter discusses the first two tools listed in Table 8.1 – advertising and sales promotion – and Chapters 9 and 10 discuss the remaining five promotional tools.

It is worth clarifying that promotion management deals explicitly with the promotional mix. In contrast, **marketing communications** is an all-encompassing term (and activity) that includes communication via any and all of the marketing mix elements. How a product is packaged, priced and distributed communicates an image to a customer just as much as how the product is promoted.

---

**MARKETING COMMUNICATIONS**
an all-encompassing term (and activity) that includes communication via any and all of the marketing mix elements

---

## The Communication Process

The communication process that takes place between the sender and receiver of a message is outlined in Figure 8.2. The diagram presents a scenario in which the message is prepared in a symbolic form by the sender (a cruise line for example) for the prospective audience, perhaps as a visual representation. This process is referred to as 'encoding'. The message is then transmitted by way of a suitable medium such as a television advertising campaign. The

**Table 8.1**    The Promotional Mix Used in Tourism and Hospitality

| Promotional Tool | Tourism and Hospitality Application |
|---|---|
| Advertising | Television, newspapers, magazines, billboards, internet, brochures, guidebooks |
| Sales promotion | Short-term incentives to induce purchase. Aimed at salespeople, distributors such as travel agents and consumers. Can be joint promotions. Include merchandising and familiarization trips. |
| Public relations | All non-paid media exposure appearing as editorial coverage. Includes sponsorship of events and causes. |
| Personal selling | Meetings and workshops for intermediaries; telephone contact and travel agents for consumers. |
| Word of mouth | Promotion by previous consumers to their social and professional contacts. Often perceived by consumers to be the most credible form of promotion. |
| Direct marketing | Direct mail, telemarketing and travel exhibitions |
| Internet marketing | Direct email marketing, internet advertising, customer service, and selling and market research |

receiver sees the message and decodes it; 'decoding' is the method by which the message is filtered or internalized. The major concern of the sender at this stage is that the message is not distorted in the process by what is termed 'noise'. For example, a television advertisement promoting a cruise holiday following a news item about a cruise ship being attacked by pirates (as happened off the coast of Africa in 2005) would fail to convey a convincing message. Likewise, the message might be distorted by clutter, which means the audience may see an excessive number of commercial messages that just get in the way of the advertiser's intended message.

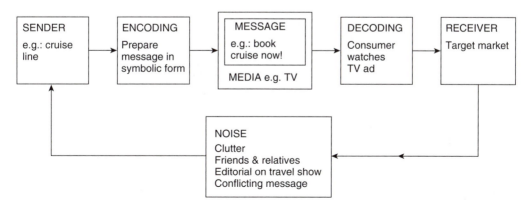

**Figure 8.2**    The Communication Process

**Figure 8.3**   Print Advertisement for Newfoundland and Labrador

## How Communication Works

There are a number of models that show how communication works, particularly in advertising. The models developed invariably assume that customers follow a number of pre-determined stages, commencing with awareness and progressing to purchase. The most commonly cited model is that first proposed by Strong (1925),[1] called the **AIDA model** (**a**ttention, **i**nterest, **d**esire, and **a**ction). The idea of this model is that communication should first attract the receiver's attention, then engage the receiver's interest, then create in the receiver a desire for the product or service, and then inspire action in the receiver. For example, in the print advertisement for Newfoundland and Labrador, Canada, in Figure 8.3, the tail of a humpback whale with a giant iceberg in the background grabs the reader's attention. This visual image works with the print copy to gain the reader's interest and to provoke the desire in him or her to travel to that part of Canada. The website and 1-800 number are included in the ad to inspire action.

---

**AIDA MODEL**
a memorable and useful checklist of the aims of advertising, standing for attention, interest, desire, and action

---

**Table 8.2**    Hierarchies of Effects Models

| Type of Effect | Strong (1925) | Lavidge & Steiner (1961) | Rogers (1962) | Broadbent & Jacobs (1984) | Colley (1961) | Wells et al. (2003) |
|---|---|---|---|---|---|---|
| Cognitive | Attention | Awareness | Awareness | Problem Recognition | Awareness | Perception |
|  |  | Knowledge |  | Information Search | Comprehension | Learning |
| Affective | Interest | Liking Preference | Interest | Attitude | Conviction | Persuasion |
|  | Desire | Conviction | Evaluation | Intention |  |  |
| Behavioural | Action | Purchase | Trial | Behaviour Adoption | Action | Behaviour |

Though undoubtedly over-simplistic, the AIDA model is a memorable and useful checklist of the aims of advertising, and it provides a framework for other, more complex theories. All of the models of communication that have been developed are known as 'hierarchies of effects models', as they assume a progression from one stage to the next (see Table 8.2).

All the hierarchies of effects models have as their basis the assumption that an effective advertisement makes the receiver think about the product, feel positively towards it, and do something to purchase it. Lavidge and Steiner (1961) label these the cognitive, affective, and conative stages of the response.[2] The cognitive stage involves the rational, conscious part of the brain; the affective stage involves the emotions; and the conative stage involves a resulting change in behaviour. Rogers (1962) argues that the effect of advertising is to interest the consumer enough to evaluate the merits of the product and then to give it a trial before adopting it.[3] Broadbent and Jacobs (1985) go further in saying that it is often the trial and not the advertisement that convinces the customer to change an attitude toward a product.[4] Colley (1961) presents the DAGMAR model (**d**efining **a**dvertising **g**oals for **m**easured **a**dvertising **r**esults), which begins with awareness, moves to comprehension, then to conviction, and ends with action.[5] Finally, Wells et al. (2003) suggest that there is a set of categories of typical effects that advertisers hope to achieve.[6] The first category is perception, which means the advertiser hopes the ad will be noticed and remembered. Then there are two categories of effects that are focused either on learning, which means the audience will understand the message and make the correct associations, or on persuasion, which means the advertiser hopes to create or change attitudes or touch emotions. The last major category of effects is behaviour: getting the audience to try or buy the product or perform some other action.

## Integrated Marketing Communications (IMC) in Tourism

Perhaps one of the most important advances in marketing in recent decades has been the rise of **integrated marketing communications (IMC)** – the unification of all marketing communications tools, as well as corporate and brand messages, so they send a consistent, persuasive message to target audiences. This approach recognizes that advertising can no longer be crafted and executed in isolation from other promotional mix elements. As tourism markets and the media have grown more complex and fragmented, consumers find themselves in an ever more confusing marketing environment. Tourism marketers must address this situation by conveying a consistent, unified message in all their promotional activities. IMC programmes co-ordinate all communication messages and sources of an organization. An IMC campaign includes traditional marketing communication tools, such as advertising or sales promotion, but recognizes that other areas of the marketing mix are also used in communications. Planning and managing these elements so they work together helps to build a consistent brand or company image.

---

**INTEGRATED MARKETING COMMUNICATIONS (IMC)**
the unification of all marketing communications tools, as well as corporate and brand messages, so they send a consistent, persuasive message to target audiences

---

Table 8.3 outlines an IMC communications campaign plan, and it can be seen that such a plan considers a variety of communications tools – not just advertising. Two cases in this chapter highlight how both VisitBritain and Carnival Cruises used a number of promotional

**Table 8.3**   An IMC Campaign Plan

| Steps in the campaign | Details |
| --- | --- |
| 1. Situation analysis | Product and company research <br> Consumer and stakeholder research <br> Industry and market analysis <br> Competitive analysis |
| 2. SWOT (strengths, weaknesses, opportunities, and threats) analysis | Internal strengths and weaknesses <br> External opportunities and threats <br> Problem identification |
| 3. Campaign strategy | Objectives <br> Targeting <br> Positioning |
| 4. Message strategy | Message development research <br> The creative theme <br> Tactics and executions |
| 5. Media plan | Media mix <br> Scheduling and timing |
| 6. Other marketing communications activities | Sales promotion <br> Direct marketing <br> Public relations |
| 7. Appropriation and budget | Based on the cost of reaching the target market |
| 8. Campaign evaluation | Measure the effectiveness of stated objectives |

techniques to achieve their promotional objectives. Carnival, for example, in an effort to promote the concept of giving cruise vacations as holiday gifts, used television and print ads, banner ads, point-of-purchase promotional items, postcards, flyers and e-cards. The end-of-chapter Case Study is another example of a company integrating different promotional tools as part of its marketing strategy. Saatchi and Saatchi were given the task in 2004 of eradicating sex and drink from Club 18–30's promotional material in order to change its image. The famous ad agency came up with an 'underground' campaign based on teaser advertising techniques, which banished the company logo from all marketing material and from the resorts themselves. Cryptic advertisements with no mention of Club 18–30 directed viewers to a website, and the new up-market, trendy image was disseminated via posters, magazines, and radio as well as the viral email advertising. The Global Spotlight below highlights how Visit Britain used an integrated marketing strategy to leverage the fact that the Harry Potter movies were made in Britain.

# Global Spotlight

## VisitBritain Leverages Pottermania

The phenomenon of Harry Potter – or 'Pottermania' – has had huge domestic and international repercussions for the author, her readers, for the British film industry and also for tourism in the UK. Pottermania has been thoroughly and successfully exploited by VisitBritain to rescue the country's ailing tourism industry hit by the 9/11 terrorism in 2001 and then the foot-and-mouth crisis. In an integrated marketing strategy, VisitBritain has utilized the books and the films for their promotional potential, increasing tourist visits throughout Britain and, in particular, to destinations featured in the books and movies.

Harry Potter has boosted British filmmaking globally as well as created jobs locally for crew and post-production technicians. There has also been a trickle-down benefit for hotels, restaurants, taxis and so on in the areas where the movies are shot. With allied tourism promotions, films can create major interest in international tourism markets in ways that traditional advertising and marketing cannot afford to do. When this is specifically targeted, film-tourism marketing can now be more successful than the more hackneyed conventional marketing. In a world fascinated with celebrities and their lifestyles, films can act as the vehicles by which viewers are transported to the world of their famous idols. Tourism can jump on the bandwagon by directing visitors and fans to recreated scenes from the movies in the locations where they were actually shot (or, sometimes, perceived to have been shot). Thus, readers and viewers alike affected with Pottermania have been flocking to Britain to recreate the magic of the stories for themselves, spurred on by their children.

VisitBritain, supported by Warner Bros. which permitted it to utilize the logo and license for a year, created a film tourism destination experience associated with the first Harry Potter film. By creating a web-based movie map, it was able to direct tourists to the main locations of the book and film, regenerating interest in such varied destinations as Alnwick Castle, the Bodleian Library, Lacock Abbey, the Cathedral of Gloucester, the city of Oxford, London's Kings' Cross Station, Goathland Station and London Zoo. Visitor numbers at Alnwick Castle, for example, were up fourfold – from 50,000 to 200,000 by 2004 – with a marked increase in younger visitors. Package tours were also created to target different market segments with specific combinations of destinations. With each new book and film release, VisitBritain produced an updated movie map for reproduction throughout the media to encourage both domestic and international visitors and continue the advertising momentum along with the development of the series.

Learning from the New Zealand government's exploitation of *The Lord of the Rings* trilogy for tourism regeneration, both government and tourism agencies in Britain collaborated more closely with film commissions than ever before in order to develop film tourism's huge potential via Pottermania. Beyond the traditional merchandising, the internet has been utilized to spread the word, linking the films with travel opportunities. Film commissions now insist that locations are listed in the film credits.

*Sources*: Edge, S. (17/06/2003). As the fifth instalment of the young wizard's adventures is released, Simon Edge looks at how the magic has spread far beyond the pages of the book; how Harry Potter changed the world. *The Express*, 23; Grihault, N. (2003). Film tourism – the global picture. *Travel and Tourism Analyst*, No. 5, 1 – 22; Tooke, N. and Baker, M. (1996). Seeing is believing: The effect of film on visitor numbers to screened locations. *Tourism Management*, Vol. 17, No. 3.

## Push and Pull Promotional Strategies

One final factor to consider in the promotional strategy is the position of the organization in the distribution channel. For example, does a retailer (i.e., the travel agent or the venue) carry out its own promotion for the travel product? Or does the producer (i.e., the tour operator or destination organization) have to promote the product in order to bring the public into the travel agency to buy it? This is known as the choice between push and pull promotional strategies. A **push strategy** uses the sales force and trade promotion to push the product forward; the producer promotes the product to wholesalers, the wholesalers promote to retailers, and the retailers to consumers. In contrast, a **pull strategy** calls for spending a large amount on advertising and consumer promotion to build up consumer demand; if successful, consumers will ask their retailers for the product, the retailers will ask the wholesalers, and the wholesalers will ask the producers. The two strategies are contrasted in Figure 8.4.

**PUSH STRATEGY**
a promotion strategy that uses the sales force and trade promotion to push the product forward; the producer promotes the product to wholesalers, the wholesalers promote to retailers, and the retailers to consumers

**PULL STRATEGY**

a promotion strategy in which a large amount is spent on advertising and consumer promotion to build up consumer demand; if successful, consumers will ask their retailers for the product, the retailers will ask the wholesalers, and the wholesalers will ask the producers

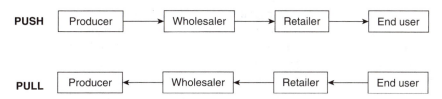

**PUSH**  Producer → Wholesaler → Retailer → End user

**PULL**  Producer ← Wholesaler ← Retailer ← End user

**Figure 8.4**  Push and Pull Promotional Strategies

The choice of strategy depends on the degree of influence each member of the distribution channel has on the consumer's decision process, and on the relative power of the producer's and the retailer's brand names. In most cases, a combination of the two strategies are used, with each player in the channel marketing itself to the others and providing support for joint promotions. In the Snapshot on Carnival Cruise below, a pull strategy was used to entice consumers to purchase cruise vouchers as gifts using advertising and promotion, whereas a push strategy was used to promote the idea using virtual sales kits for travel agents, which were available on the cruise line's travel agent internet portal.

## Snapshot

### Carnival Cruise's Holiday Gift Marketing Campaign

Capitalizing on recent consumer trends towards purchasing unique, experiential items as holiday gifts, Carnival Cruises launched an innovative integrated marketing campaign in 2005 to promote the concept of giving the line's 'Fun Ship' vacations as holiday gifts. Created by Carnival's advertising agency, Cooper DDB, the multi-million dollar campaign debuted in October and encompassed television commercials and consumer and trade print placements. The fully integrated campaign also included splash pages and banner ads on Carnival's website, carnival.com, and point-of-purchase promotional items for gift shops on board the ships. A variety of other collateral materials tied to the campaign, including postcards, flyers and e-cards, were created, while a virtual sales kit for travel agents was available on the line's travel agent internet portal, bookccl.com.

Launching the campaign, Carnival president and CEO Bob Dickinson said that the campaign served to suggest the purchase of a cruise vacation to consumers in a manner they may not have considered previously. 'This innovative, thought-provoking ad campaign, which is designed to pique the interest of first-time cruisers and reinforce the Carnival brand to experienced guests, emphasizes family bonding while promoting the uniqueness of giving a 'Fun Ship' cruise as a holiday gift,' he said.

The three-second television commercial was an adaptation of the line's *Beyond the Sea* campaign, with the song modified to include sleigh bells and other traditional holiday musical accompaniments. It opens with images of shoppers carrying large boxes of foil-wrapped Fun Ships, recognizable by the line's winged funnel, along a bustling main street during the holiday season. The commercial then cuts to a family window-shopping, but instead of traditional holiday gifts, a replica of a Carnival Fun Ship is shown behind the glass. The spot ends with the family driving away with the gift-wrapped Fun Ship tied atop their car, in much the same way that Christmas trees are transported home during the holidays.

The gift theme was also present in the consumer print campaign, which included a shot of a foil-wrapped Carnival ship encircled with a giant red ribbon and bow. Running across the top of the ad were the words 'Give them a holiday to remember'. Along the bottom of the ad, the copy read: 'How do you wrap togetherness? Can you put a bow on fun? It's easy when you give a Carnival Cruise. Nothing creates family togetherness and lasting memories like a Carnival vacation. It's a gift of fun everyone will treasure.'

*Sources*: Anon. (20 October 2005) 'New "holiday gift marketing campaign" launched by Carnival', *Travelweek*, 6.

## Tourism Advertising

Advertising has emerged as a key marketing tool in the tourism and hospitality industries. These industries require potential customers to base buying decisions upon mental images of product offerings, since they are not able to sample alternatives physically. As a result, advertising is a critical variable in the tourism marketing mix, and it covers a wide range of activities and agencies. Its role reflects that of promotion in general, which is to influence the attitudes and behaviour of audiences in three main ways: confirming and reinforcing, creating new patterns of behaviours, or changing attitudes and behaviour. Thus tourism and hospitality companies use images to portray their products in brochures, posters and media advertising. Destinations do the same, attempting to construct an image of a destination that will force it into the potential tourist's list of options, leading ultimately to a purchase. Whatever the tourism or hospitality product, its identity is the public face of how it is marketed, and the importance of advertising in tourism marketing should therefore not be underestimated.

### Defining Advertising

**Advertising** can be defined as paid non-personal presentation and promotion of ideas, goods, or services by an identified sponsor, using mass media to persuade or influence an audience. This standard definition of advertising has six elements. First, advertising is a paid form of communication, although some forms of advertising, such as public service announcements,

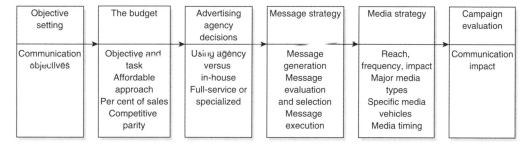

**Figure 8.5**  Developing an Advertising Programme

use donated space and time. Second, not only is the space paid for, but the sponsor is identified. Third, most advertising tries to persuade or influence the consumer to do something, although in some cases the point of the message is simply to make consumers aware of the product or company. Fourth, the message is conveyed through many different kinds of mass media, and fifth, advertising reaches an audience of potential consumers. Finally, because advertising is a form of mass communication, it is also non-personal.

---

**ADVERTISING**

any paid form of non-personal presentation and promotion of ideas, goods, or services by an identified sponsor, using mass media to persuade or influence an audience

---

## Developing an Advertising Programme

The process of developing an advertising programme includes six important stages. These are illustrated in Figure 8.5 and discussed below.

### Setting the Objectives

In planning and managing advertising, a key factor is the setting of objectives. An **advertising objective** can be defined as a specific communication task designed to reach a specific target audience during a specific period of time. In general terms, advertising has four major tasks: informing, persuading, reminding, and selling. However, advertising in tourism and hospitality can have many uses. These might include creating awareness; informing about new products; expanding the market to new buyers; announcing a modification to a service; announcing a price change; making a special offer; selling directly; educating consumers; reminding consumers; challenging competition; reversing negative sales trends; pleasing intermediaries; recruiting staff; attracting investors; announcing trading results; influencing a destination image; creating a corporate image; soliciting customer information; improving employee morale; and contributing to co-operative/partnership advertising ventures.

---

**ADVERTISING OBJECTIVE**
a specific communication task designed to reach a specific target audience during a specific period of time

---

In the Opening Vignette, the objective of the 'What Happens in Vegas Stays in Vegas' advertising campaign was to assist in re-branding Las Vegas as 'Sin City' after a failed attempt to reposition it as a family destination. In the end-of-chapter Case Study, Club 18–30's advertising objective was to change the perception of the company and create a new up-market, trendy image. However, the Snapshot on Brazil later in this chapter describes how the Brazilian tourism industry used prevention ads to discourage unwanted behaviours – rather the opposite of the normal behavioural responses sought through advertising.

### Setting the Budget

Ideally, the advertising budget should be calculated on the basis of the objectives set in the first stage of the process. The media plan must reach sufficient numbers in the target market to produce the size of response that will achieve the sales target. Several methods can be used to set the advertising budget. The **objective and task method** involves developing the promotion budget by (1) defining specific objectives, (2) determining the tasks that must be performed to achieve these objectives, and (3) estimating the costs of performing these tasks. Using this method requires considerable experience of response rates and media costs, as well as confidence in the accuracy of predictions. Cautious managers prefer to base the advertising budget on what they know, from previous experience, they can afford to spend. This is often referred to as the **affordable method**. The **percentage of sales method** involves setting the promotion budget at a certain percentage of current or forecasted sales or as a percentage of sales price. In tourism and hospitality, the percentage of gross sales generally set aside for marketing is somewhere between 4 and 12 per cent, advertising being allocated about a quarter of this amount. Cheddar Caves & Gorge in the UK, for example (see Snapshot below), spend about 10 per cent of gross turnover on marketing and publicity. The actual percentage will vary according to the product's position on the product life cycle (see Chapter 5). For example, new products will require more advertising to launch them into the market. The budget size for communications can have a tremendous range. For example the Las Vegas Convention and Visitors Authority spent US$60 million on their 'What Happens in Vegas Stays in Vegas' advertising campaign (see Opening Vignette), whereas at the other end of the scale, Club 18–30 had only £1.5 million to spend on their promotional campaign (see Case Study).

---

**OBJECTIVE AND TASK METHOD**
developing the promotion budget by (1) defining specific objectives, (2) determining the tasks that must be performed to achieve these objectives, and (3) estimating the costs of performing these tasks

---

**AFFORDABLE METHOD**
setting the promotion budget according to what management thinks the company can afford

**PERCENTAGE OF SALES METHOD**
setting the promotion budget at a certain percentage of current or forecasted sales, or as a percentage of sales price

Another way of setting the budget is the **competitive parity method**, which sets the promotion budget at the level needed to achieve parity or 'equal share of voice' with competitors. It may seem unwise to spend significantly less than competitors if you are aiming for a similar share of the same market. In the hotel business the advertising expenditure for the average hotel is 1 per cent of sales, but for limited-service hotels, advertising expenditure is higher, representing 2 per cent of sales.

**COMPETITIVE PARITY METHOD**
setting the promotion budget to match competitors' outlay

*Advertising Agency Decisions*
Since advertising is usually considered the most important tool in the marketing communications mix, companies must decide carefully whether they are going to do the work themselves or hire an outside agency. Only very small businesses, such as guesthouses or local visitor attractions, are likely to undertake their own advertising without professional help. At the very least, advertising agencies can help with the purchase of advertising space at discounted rates. Most advertising agencies enjoy working on tourism and hospitality accounts as they involve intrinsically interesting products, and may welcome the account as a stimulating break from their usual subject matter.

The best advertising agencies create value for their clients, as seen in the Club 18–30 example (see Case Study). An agency can clearly interpret what the customer wants and then communicate information about the client's product so meaningfully, so uniquely, and so consistently that customers reward that product with their loyalty. An agency can add perceived value to the product by giving it a personality, by communicating in a manner that shapes basic understanding of the product, by creating an image or memorable picture of the product, and by setting the product apart from its competitors.

There are two main types of advertising agency: the full-service agency and the specialized agency. In advertising, a **full-service agency** is one that provides the four major staff functions: account management, creative services, media planning and buying, and account planning (which is also known as research). A full-service advertising agency will also have its own accounting department, a traffic department to handle internal tracking on completion of projects, a department for broadcast and print production, and a human resources department. However, tourism and hospitality organizations often use the services of a **specialized agency**. This type of agency will specialize in certain functions (e.g., writing copy, producing art, media buying), audiences (e.g., minority, youth), or industries (e.g., health care, computers, leisure), or in certain marketing communication areas, such as direct marketing, sales promotion, public relations, events and sports marketing, and packaging and point-of-sale.

---

**FULL-SERVICE AGENCY**
an advertising agency that provides the four major staff functions: account management, creative services, media planning and buying, and account planning

---

**SPECIALIZED AGENCY**
an advertising agency that specializes in certain functions (e.g., writing copy, producing art, media buying), audiences (e.g., minority, youth), or industries (e.g., health care, computers, leisure)

---

*Message Strategy*
The message strategy is the fourth stage in the process of developing an advertising programme. Studies have shown that creative advertising messages can be more important than the number of dollars spent on the message. Creative strategy plays an increasingly important role in advertising success. Developing a creative strategy requires three message steps: generation, evaluation and selection, and execution.

Providers of tourism and hospitality products face an inherent barrier to effective communication with their customers: the intangibility of the product. A hotel or airline flight is experienced only at or after the time of purchase. This characteristic of services in general poses genuine challenges for message generation. Advertisers need to make tangible an intangible product, using emotion and experience. An example of a very creative and successful print ad produced on a low budget is the Dog & Sock ad for Calgary Zoo (see Figure 8.6). It was developed through the zoo's advertising agency (Parallel Strategies which is now Trigger Communications). Strategically the zoo wanted something that would convey a very simple message but have a strong, funny, visual appeal to both young and old and work in all mediums. The budget was low at only $35,000 for the entire campaign, including creative design, fees, production, photography and media buys. However, the campaign was so successful the zoo continued it for another three years and now has 17 'No Substitute for the Zoo' ad executions. The campaign has won several awards including the Trans-Canada Agency Network Award for Best in Show (2003), Extra Award of Merit (Certificate of

**Figure 8.6**    Calgary Zoo Dog and Sock Ad

Excellence) in 2004, Ad Rodeo Anvil 2004, International Association of Amusement Parks & Attractions (IAAPA) Brass Ring for Best Outdoor and Best of Show for the same in 2004.

Although advertisers may create many possible messages, only a few will be used in the campaign, and the second step in developing a creative strategy – evaluation and selection – will determine the final message to be used. According to Kotler et al., (2003) the advertiser must evaluate possible ads on the basis of three characteristics.[7] First, messages should be meaningful and should point out benefits that make the product more desirable or interesting to consumers. Second, messages should be distinctive. They should tell the consumer how the product is better than competing brands. Finally, messages must be believable. This goal is difficult to achieve, as many consumers doubt the truth of advertising.

In the third step of developing a creative strategy execution, the creative staff must find a style, tone, words and format for executing the message. Any message can be presented in a variety of styles. The following are commonly used in tourism and hospitality:

1. **Slice of life**. This style shows people using the product in a normal setting. An example is the print ad in Figure 8.8 for Club 18–30 (see Case Study) that shows a normal office setting.
2. **Fantasy**. This style creates a wonder-world around the product or its use. The human psyche is receptive to fantasy, so companies like Disney have capitalized on this type of advertising, which is particularly effective in an industry that appeals to one's desire to escape.
3. **Mood or image**. This style builds a mood or image around the product or service, such as beauty, love or serenity. Destination marketers often attempt to create an emotional relationship between the destination and potential visitors. In this type of advertising, branding activities concentrate on communicating the essence or the spirit of a destination via a few key attributes and associations. The print ad for Newfoundland and Labrador in Figure 8.3 is such an example.

4. **Lifestyle**. This style shows how a product fits with a lifestyle. For example, British Airways, advertising its business class, featured a businessman sitting in an upholstered chair in the living room, having a drink and enjoying the paper. The other side of the ad featured the same person in the same relaxed position with a drink and a paper in one of the airline's business-class seats.

5. **Musical**. This style shows one or more people or cartoon characters singing a song about a product. Almost 30 years ago, Coca-Cola wanted to 'teach the world to sing in perfect harmony', and the pattern was set for an important ingredient in successful advertising. Airlines have used music to good effect. Delta Airlines used music effectively in its 'We Love to Fly' campaign, as did British Airways in its 'World Images' campaign. The association various destinations have with music is often used in advertising campaigns. For instance, the haunting strains of Irish music are the background sounds in an ad for Ireland.

6. **Testimonial evidence**. In this style, celebrities we admire, created characters (McDonald's Ronald McDonald, for example), experts we respect, or people 'just like us' whose advice we might seek out, speak on behalf of the product to build credibility. An example is a print ad that appeared extensively in travel magazines in 2006 for Samsonite luggage, in which Richard Branson, Chairman of Virgin, endorses the products. In 2005 Elton John appeared on 20 AirTran jets in a move to promote the Florida-based airline's launch of satellite radio at each passenger seat. In return John was given a $50,000 cheque for the Elton John AIDS Foundation.

7. **Technical expertise**. In this style of advertisement, the company shows its expertise. Hotels, for example, may use this style in advertising to meeting and convention planners, to show that they have the technical ability to support them. Airlines also sometimes make use of expertise to reassure the consumer about the technical qualities of their pilots and mechanics.

## Snapshot

### Advertising to Tourists You Don't Want: Sex Tourism in Brazil

Most marketing programmes are directed towards sales or positive actions of some kind. *Prevention* ads, however, discourage unwanted behaviours, so are seeking the opposite of normal behavioural responses to advertising. Deterring actions or behaviours is a complicated process that involves presenting negative messages about unwanted behaviour and creating the proper incentives to stimulate desired behaviour. Over the last few years, the Brazilian government has been using prevention ads to deter sex tourists from visiting the country. After the 2004 tsunami, Brazil unwillingly replaced Thailand as the number one sex tourism destination. In response, Embratur, the agency responsible for marketing Brazil abroad, and the Brazil Ministry of Tourism, worked together to develop marketing programmes to deter sex tourism. The Sustainable Tourism and Childhood Programme was created to combat sexual exploitation via tourism in Brazil. Tactics included television 'prevention' ads that were shown in Brazil and on certain airlines within the country. An example is a television ad that begins with the usual pictures of beautiful beaches and spectacular Brazilian icons such as the Amazon and Iguassu Falls. However, the closing shot is of the rear view of

**Figure 8.7**    Brazilian Sex Tourism Prevention Ad

a little girl, swinging happily in a playground while the narrator talks about the prison sentences for child sex abuse. The ads highlighted the campaign to eradicate sexual abuses of children and adults, which was inaugurated during carnival season in March 2005 to create maximum impact.

Print ads (see Figure 8.7) were also used in the campaign, placed in selected magazines and newspapers throughout Brazil, and distributed through travel operators and federal police officials at Brazilian air and sea ports. With an emphasis on improving the international image, postcards of scantily-dressed women were banned; retailers reported that sales were not affected, as tourists continued to buy more scenic postcards instead. In a press statement, Tourism Secretary Sergio Ricardo said, 'Postcards that exploit photos of women in skimpy wear suggest sex tourism, a practice that stigmatizes us with undignified labels.' Traditionally, Brazil has sold millions of postcards of scantily-clad women, usually baring their almost naked buttocks in tiny bikinis. The World Tourism Organization (WTO) was also involved in this collaborative project, and details of the campaign were easily accessible on the WTO website.

In a country where the minimum wage is US$135 per month and millions live under the poverty line, particularly in the rural areas, sex tourism is a growing concern. Uneducated and poverty-stricken parents in the Amazon region and northwest Brazil are even selling children into the trade via well-established child-trafficking routes. Both sexes are exploited, though the vast majority of victims are female. According to the Centre of Reference Studies on Children and Adolescents (CECRIA), Brazil was one of the major exporters of women for prostitution in the world in 2005, with around 70,000 15–25-year-old women being sent abroad annually, via 131 trafficking routes, to other South American countries. There are also travel services available internationally to organize child sex tourism to Brazil. In Italy in 2004 authorities arrested four people in a crackdown on travel agents engaged in selling sex tourism to Brazil. They were allegedly sending tourists to bars, discos and hotels in Fortaleza where child prostitution was practised.

*Sources*: Vincent, I. (December 2005) 'No More Itsy-Bitsy', *Maclean's*, Vol. 118, Issue 50, 30; Finger, C. (5 April 2003) 'Brazil pledges to eliminate sexual exploitation of children', *Lancet*, Vol. 361, Issue 9364, 1196; Chesshyre, T. (18 December 2004) 'Sex tourism crackdown', *The Times*, Travel, 2.

### Media Strategy

The media plan section in an advertising plan includes media objectives (reach and frequency), media strategies (targeting, continuity and timing), media selection (the specific vehicles), geographic strategies, schedules and the media budget. The range of advertising media available to today's advertiser is increasingly bewildering and is becoming ever more fragmented. While these changes offer the prospect of greater targeting, they also make the job of the media planner more difficult. Table 8.4 provides a reference guide to the main advertising media and lists their major advantages and disadvantages. In the Carnival Cruise campaign, the media plan included TV, radio, newspapers, trade magazines and other promotional vehicles to stimulate people to purchase cruise holiday gift vouchers. All these media outlets are referred to as the **media mix** – created by media planners by selecting the best combination of traditional media vehicles (print, broadcast, etc.), non-traditional media (internet, cell phones, unexpected places like the floors of stores), and marketing communication tools such as public relations, direct marketing and sales promotion to reach the targeted stakeholder audiences.

---

**MEDIA MIX**

a combination of traditional media vehicles (print, broadcast, etc.), non–traditional media (electronic media, unexpected places like the floors of stores), and marketing communication tools such as public relations, direct marketing and sales promotion, used to reach the target audiences

**Table 8.4**    The Advantages and Disadvantages of the Major Advertising Media

| Media Type | Advantages | Disadvantages |
|---|---|---|
| **Print Media** | | |
| Local press | High market coverage<br>Short lead time<br>Easily laid out<br>Frequency/immediacy<br>Relatively inexpensive<br>Allows for repetition of ads<br>Creates local image | Audience reads<br>  selectively<br>Short life span<br>Low attention<br>Media clutter<br>Poor reproduction<br>  quality |
| National press | Large circulation<br>Many creative options for layout<br>Appeals to all income levels<br>Relatively cheap for national coverage<br>Frequency allows repetition<br>Allows audience/geographical selectivity | Audience reads<br>  selectively<br>Short life span<br>Poor reproduction<br>Low attention<br>Clutter |
| Consumer magazines | Large circulation<br>High pass on readership<br>High-quality reproduction and colour<br>Relatively long life and read in leisurely<br>  fashion<br>Well-segmented audience<br>High information content<br>Allows sales promotion inserts | Expensive<br>Distant copy dates<br>Clutter |
| Specialist trade journals | Well-segmented audience<br>Short lead times<br>Potential for high information content ads | Clutter<br>Competitors' ads may<br>  be featured |
| Circulars | Low production and distribution costs<br>Blanket coverage in target areas | Poor image<br>Distribution abuse<br>Short attention span |
| Inserts in free press and magazines | Relatively cheap<br>Good for direct response ads | Short life span<br>May be seen as<br>  having a poor image |
| Posters | Cheap<br>Target specific areas/groups<br>Longevity (especially on public<br>  transport – buses, etc.) | Short exposure time<br>Poor image<br>Clutter<br>Audience segmentation<br>  difficult |
| **Broadcast Media** | | |
| Television | Opportunity for high creativity and<br>  impact (sound, visual, etc.)<br>Good for image | Relatively high<br>  production and<br>  airtime costs<br>Short life span |

*(Continued)*

**Table 8.4**   *(Continued)*

| Media Type | Advantages | Disadvantages |
|---|---|---|
| | Appeals to all income levels<br>Relatively cheap for national coverage<br>Frequency allows repetition<br>Allows audience/geographical selectivity<br>High attention gaining | Clutter<br>Fleeting attention |
| Commercial radio | Large localized audience<br>Gains local recognition<br>Flexible deadlines<br>Well-segmented audience<br>Allows repeat messages | Production can be expensive<br>Allows audio message only<br>Clutter<br>Short life span<br>Fleeting message<br>Low attention; audience distraction high |
| Cinema | Possibility to segment audience or mass market<br>Allows frequent exposure<br>Potential for high creative impact of colour and visuals – large screen and sound | Relatively high production and air time costs<br>Competitors' ads may be featured<br>Fleeting message<br>Difficult to establish audience profile |
| **Out of Home**<br>Billboards | High impact<br>Low cost and large readership<br>Longevity<br>Ability to create awareness | Brief exposure<br>Limited message – unsuitable for complex ads<br>Needs large-scale distribution<br>Creativity needed for impact |
| Transit | Can be targeted to specific audiences with high frequency<br>Allows for creativity<br>Can provide detailed information at a low cost | Brief exposure<br>Image factors |
| **Other Media**<br>Direct mail | Allows tracking<br>Prepared mailing lists<br>Allows audience/geographical selectivity<br>High information content | Relatively high production costs of creating and maintaining databases<br>Potential for poor image |
| Exhibitions/ trade fairs and shows | Large target audience<br>Reach large numbers of customers simultaneously<br>Good for attracting new, maintaining existing customers | Costs of set-up and staffing can be expensive<br>Clutter |

*(Continued)*

**Table 8.4**   *(Continued)*

| Media Type | Advantages | Disadvantages |
|---|---|---|
| Sponsorship and events | Possibility to reach attractive segments or mass market<br>Allows company to build credibility and benefit from reflected success<br>Potential for unusual, attention-grabbing activity<br><br>Builds company recognition | Relatively costly<br>Transience of celebrity and lack of control over others' actions<br>Time-consuming to build relationships and links with partners<br>Difficult to evaluate impact |
| Point-of-sale displays, in-store merchandising | Relatively inexpensive<br>Reinforces ad message<br>Incentive for trade location to stock product | Reaches customers already likely to purchase |
| **Ambient media** | Good coverage<br>Good segmentation potential<br>Many creative options | Creativity a constant challenge<br>Targeting can be difficult<br>Impact wears off quickly |
| **Internet** | Global impact<br>Immediacy<br>Many creative options for design<br>Possibility of direct response and audience profiling | Short life span<br>Creativity and web design costs<br>Low attention<br>Targeting can be difficult |

Given cost constraints, media planners usually select the media that will expose the product to the largest target audience for the lowest possible cost. The process of measuring this ratio is called efficiency – or **cost per thousand (CPM)**. To calculate the CPM, two figures are needed: the costs of the unit (e.g., time on TV or space in a magazine) and the estimated target audience. The cost of the unit is divided by the target audience's gross impressions to determine the advertising dollars needed to expose the product to 1,000 members of the target.

$$CPM = \frac{\text{cost of message unit}}{\text{gross impressions}} \times 1000$$

---

**COST PER THOUSAND (CPM)**

a measurement of the media that will expose the product to the largest target audience for the lowest possible cost ('M' is the Roman numeral for 1000)

---

For example, if the show *Pilot Guides* has 92,000 target viewers, and the cost of a 30-second announcement during the show is $850, the CPM will be $9.42 (CPM = $850/92 000 × 1000 = $9.24).

There are many components to the media mix, and how an organization blends them depends on a number of factors, particularly the nature of the product or service and the target audience. For example, tour operators and major destinations rely heavily on television advertising, but niche players such as special interest operators tend to focus their advertising in specialist publications. Decisions also have to be made about reach and frequency. Marketers for Cheddar Caves & Gorge have decided that printing 1.5 million leaflets and distributing them within a 50-mile radius of the attraction is the best way of spending the bulk of their promotional budget (see Snapshot below).

While tourism and hospitality advertising makes use of all of the main media, the key vehicles are print and electronic media advertisements and brochures. In fact, the most popular medium used by tourism advertisers is undoubtedly the travel brochure. For many organizations, the design, production and distribution of their annual tourism brochure is the single most important and most expensive item in the marketing budget. However, the position of the brochure as a major travel medium is being threatened by new technology, such as CD-ROMs, videos and the internet (see Chapter 10).

One of the fastest growing sectors of media is **ambient advertising**. This approach includes place-based advertising and uses new, unexpected ways of getting messages across. Examples of ambient advertising include ads on the back of grocery receipts, on gas pumps, in elevators, on ATM screens, on shop floors, on washroom walls, on toilet paper, on pizza boxes, on welcome mats and on tickets. Such tactics might involve live advertising. Golden Palace Casino has been advertising on the back of professional boxers for many years using large tattoos. Sony Ericsson Mobile Communications Ltd. hired actors to create buzz about a new mobile phone that was also a digital camera. The actors pretended to be tourists who wanted their picture taken, thus persuading consumers to try the product. The use of hyper-tag technology by Whistler and its partner in the UK, Neilson, referred to later in this chapter, is an example of ambient advertising. Another is the 'talking urinal' developed by Wizmark that uses a sensor to detect someone approaching, which then activates an attention-grabbing display of lights flashing in a pre-programmed pattern. This draws the eye to the graphics incorporated within the waterproof 9 cm viewing screen at the base of the urinal. After a period of animation, the display automatically resets itself in anticipation of the next viewer.

---

**AMBIENT ADVERTISING**
advertising that uses new, unexpected ways of getting messages across

---

In 1999, Virgin Atlantic made innovative use of ambient media in the tourism sector when it painted the traditionally green and white Hong Kong harbour's Star Ferry bright red with its own logo. A further use of ambient advertising is the use of airfields as a context in which to view ads cut into crop fields. An example of such an attempt to capture the interest of the business traveller occurred at Munich airport, where arriving passengers saw a giant ad for Swissair growing in the fields below. A 250-metre-long aircraft, grown in green barley against a background of brown straw, depicted the red and white Swissair logo, the colours created by using pigments.

*Campaign Evaluation*

Managers of advertising programmes should regularly evaluate the communication and sales objectives of advertising. The campaign evaluation stage is often the most difficult in the advertising cycle, largely because while it is relatively easy to establish certain advertising measures (such as consumers' awareness of a brand before and after the campaign), it is much harder to establish shifts in consumer attitudes or brand perception. Despite such uncertainties, the evaluation stage is significant not only because it establishes what a campaign has achieved but also because it will provide guidance as to how future campaigns could be improved and developed.

There are many evaluative research techniques available to marketers to measure advertising effectiveness. Memory tests are often used, and are based on the assumption that a communication leaves a mental residue with the person who has been exposed to it. Memory tests fall into two major groups: recall tests and recognition tests. In a traditional **recall test**, a commercial is run on a television network and the next evening interviewers ask viewers if they remember seeing it. This type of test, in which the specific brand is mentioned, is called aided recall. Alternatively, the interviewers may ask consumers what particular ads they remembered from the previous day; this is known as unaided recall. If the commercial fails to establish a tight connection between the brand name and the selling message, the commercial will not receive a high recall score. Another method of measuring memory, called a **recognition test**, involves showing the advertisement to people and asking them whether they remember having seen it before.

---

**RECALL TEST**

a test that evaluates the memorability of an advertisement by contacting members of the audience and asking what they remember about it

---

**RECOGNITION TEST**

a test that evaluates the memorability of an advertisement by contacting members of the audience, showing them the ad, and then asking whether they remember having seen it before

---

The **persuasion test** is another evaluative research technique used to measure effectiveness after execution of a campaign. In this technique, consumers are first asked how likely they are to buy a particular brand. Next, they are exposed to an advertisement for the brand.

After exposure, researchers again ask them what they intend to purchase. The researcher analyses the results to determine whether intention to buy has increased as a result of exposure to the advertisement. Persuasion tests are expensive and have problems associated with audience composition, the environment and brand familiarity. However, persuasion is a key objective for many advertisers, so even a rough estimate of an advertisement's persuasive power is useful.

---

**PERSUASION TEST**
a test that evaluates the effectiveness of an advertisement by measuring whether the ad affects consumers' intentions to buy a brand

---

## Snapshot

### Promoting Cheddar Caves & Gorge

Cheddar Caves & Gorge is one of Britain's oldest and most popular tourist attractions; a honeypot operating within a fragile and scientifically important natural environment. The attraction is an L-shaped 300-acre landholding comprising the whole of the south side of Cheddar Gorge, about 50 caves (including two Showcaves which are Scheduled Ancient Monuments), Britain's highest inland limestone cliffs, a grassland plateau of great ecological significance, and various car parks, buildings and man-made attractions. The 300 acres are owned by the Marquis of Bath's family trust, which also owns Longleat House, and are operated through a private limited company, Longleat Enterprises Ltd. While activities have to be self-financing, the main objective is to protect the fragile environment rather than to make money.

More than 500,000 visitors a year spend time in Cheddar Gorge, and of these between 300,000 and 400,000 buy a ticket to visit the Showcaves. According to Marketing Manager Bob Smart, visitor numbers have not risen significantly since the mid-1970s, due to overseas holiday-taking and an increasing supply of British attractions. 'Most of our customers are on holiday or visiting other places within 30 miles of Cheddar,' he says. Visitors tend to be from those social classes with least disposable income and are couples aged 25 to 44 years, with or without children. School groups account for 10 per cent of the total number of visitors. Most visitors come during the summer months, with peaks at bank holiday weekends. Plans are in hand to encourage wealthier visitors, winter visitors, repeat visitors, older and younger visitors and local residents.

'All the attractions in Cheddar Gorge are run by the same company and can be visited with a single ticket,' says Smart, 'a fact that most of our visitors don't realize.' Ticket prices in 2006 were £11.50 per adult, £8.50 for children, and £31.50 for a family of four. Ticket sales amounted to £2,500,000 in 2005. 'Until 1992 we operated a very complicated ticketing system, with over twenty different ticket prices. We have now converted to a 'pay one price' system (POP) which has eliminated much confusion and resentment.' The ticket admits visitors into a variety of attractions, including the cathedral-like caverns of Gough's Cave where Explorer Audioguides allow visitors to tour at their own pace and select the information they wish to hear. The latest attraction is the 'Cheddar Man and the Cannibals' Museum which vividly brings to life Stone Age survival and the prehistoric world of our cannibal ancestors.

Promoting Cheddar Caves & Gorge is the responsibility of Smart who admits that it is challenging trying to attract visitors to such a mature attraction. Spending on marketing and publicity tends to be about 10 per cent of gross turnover. In the past they have tried, and have now rejected, television advertising, newspaper advertising (except for events and special promotions), local radio advertising, adverts in trade magazines and specialized guide books. 'We no longer employ an advertising agency, and our publicity material is produced by a designer working closely with our marketing department,' says Smart. 'We do a limited amount of promotion with consortium leaflets, door-to-door deliveries, open-topped buses painted to look like our leaflets, and out-of-season events.'

The bulk of promotion spending goes into producing a single promotional leaflet. Each year 1.5 million copies are printed and distributed in all the shops, pubs and cafes within a 50-mile radius. 'Almost all our visitors live, or are staying, within this core area,' says Smart. 'Producing a leaflet, which potential customers select, carry round, read closely and then pass on to someone else, is the best way of encouraging a considered purchase of this type.'

*Sources*: Personal interview with Bob Smart, Marketing Manager Longleat Enterprises Ltd, 13 July 2007; Cheddar Caves & Gorge Fact Sheet 2006.

### International Advertising and the Global versus Local Debate

In 2006, global expenditure on advertising worldwide was about US$450 billion and is expected to rise to $511 billion by 2009. Of all the elements of the marketing mix, decisions involving advertising are those most often affected by cultural differences among country markets. Consumers respond in terms of their culture, value systems, attitudes, beliefs and perceptions. Because advertising's function is to interpret or translate the qualities of products and services in terms of consumer needs, wants, desires, and aspirations, the emotional appeals, symbols, persuasive approaches, and other characteristics of an advertisement must coincide with cultural norms if the ad is to be effective. In Chapter 10, the end-of-chapter Case Study looks at the success of Australia's 'Where the Bloody Hell Are You?' campaign. The television ads resonated with consumers in Japan, UK, USA, Germany, China, New Zealand and South Korea, even with subtitles. The phrase 'bloody hell' was expressed in English by an Australian but caught the attention of all those cultures, while the local translation in subtitles, in colloquial language, conveyed the same sentiment and meaning.

Reconciling an international advertising campaign with the cultural uniqueness of markets is the challenge confronting the global marketer. A classic *Harvard Business Review* article by Theodore Levitt ignited a debate over how to conduct global marketing. He argued that companies should operate as if there were only one global market. He believed that differences among nations and cultures were not only diminishing but should be ignored, because people throughout the world are motivated by the same desires and wants. Other scholars like Philip Kotler disagreed, pointing to companies like Coca-Cola, PepsiCo and McDonalds, and arguing that they did not offer the same product everywhere.

The outcome of this debate has been three schools of thought on advertising in another country:

1. **Standardization**. This school of thought contends, like Levitt, that differences between countries are a matter of degree, so advertisers should focus on the similarities of consumers around the world.
2. **Localization**. The localization or adaptation school of thought argues that advertisers must consider differences between countries, including local culture, stage of economic and industrial development, stage of life cycle, media availability and legal restrictions.
3. **Combination**. The belief here is that a combination of standardization and localization may produce the most effective advertising. Some elements of brand identity or strategy, for example, may be standardized, but advertising executions may need to be adapted to the local culture.

The reality of global advertising suggests that a combination approach will work best, and most companies tend to use this or even lean towards localization. Starbucks, for example, offers more tea in the Far East, stronger coffees in Europe and gourmet coffees in the US. The company has standardized its product name, logo, and packaging to maintain brand consistency even though there is variation in its product line.

## Sales Promotions

Whenever a marketer increases the value of its product by offering an extra incentive to purchase it, it is creating a **sales promotion**. In most cases, the objective of a sales promotion is to encourage action, although it can also help to build brand identity and awareness. Like advertising, sales promotion is a type of marketing communication. Although advertising is designed to build long-term brand awareness, sales promotions are primarily focused on creating immediate action. Simply put, sales promotions offer an extra incentive for consumers, sales reps, and trade members to act. Although this extra incentive usually takes the form of a price reduction, it may also be additional amounts of the product, cash, prizes and gifts, premiums, special events and so on. It may also be a fun brand experience. Furthermore, a sales promotion usually has specified limits, such as an expiry date or a limited quantity of the merchandise.

---

**SALES PROMOTION**
a technique used by a company to increase the value of its product by offering an extra incentive to purchase it

---

The use of sales promotion is growing rapidly for many reasons: it offers the manager short-term bottom-line results; it is accountable; it is less expensive than advertising; it speaks to the current needs of the consumer to receive more value from products; and it

**Table 8.5**   Sales Promotion Objectives and Techniques Used in Tourism and Hospitality

|  | Objectives | Techniques |
|---|---|---|
| Customer | Sell excess capacity – especially as the delivery date approaches<br>Shift the timing of product purchases/peaks and troughs<br>Attract and reward regular/loyal customers<br>Promote trial of products (new users)<br>Generate higher consumption per capita<br>Increase market share<br>Defeat/pre-empt competitors' promotions | Price cuts/sale offers including internet<br>Discount vouchers/coupons<br>Disguised price cuts<br>Extra product<br>Additional services<br>Gifts<br>Competitions<br>Passport schemes for regular customers<br>Prize draws<br>Point-of-purchase displays and merchandising materials<br>Contests, sweepstakes and games |
| Distribution channels | Secure dealer support and recommendations<br>Achieve brochure display and maintain stocks<br>Support for merchandising initiatives<br>Improve dealer awareness of products<br>Build room value<br>Increase room rate | Extra commission and overrides<br>Prize draws<br>Competitions<br>Parties/receptions<br>Trade and travel show exhibits<br>Educational seminars<br>Recognition programmes<br>Flexible booking policies |
| Sales force | Improve volume of sales through incentives<br>Improve display in distribution outlets<br>Achieve sales 'blitz' targets among main corporate accounts<br>Reward special efforts | Bonuses and other money incentives<br>Gift incentives<br>Travel incentives<br>Prize draws<br>Visual aids |

responds to marketplace changes. Sales promotions can also be extremely flexible. They can be used at any stage in a product's life cycle and can be very useful in supporting other promotional activities. In a recent survey of marketers in North America, 82 per cent said sales promotion was a part of the integrated effort and 31 per cent of those marketers said it was the core component (Wells et al., 2006).[8]

Tactical promotional techniques designed to stimulate customers to buy have three main targets: individual consumers, distribution channels and the sales force. Table 8.5 highlights the sales promotion objectives for each target market, along with typical techniques used to achieve these objectives in the tourism and hospitality industry. As the table shows, many tools can be used to accomplish sales promotion objectives. Some of the main tools used are discussed below, including samples, coupons, gift certificates, premiums and point-of purchase displays (often referred to as merchandising), patronage rewards, contests, sweepstakes and games.

An important dimension of sales promotion effectiveness is payout planning. There are many examples of poorly designed or performing promotions, and such failures hurt companies' reputations, waste money, and sometimes even hurt consumers. In Chapter 1, the Opening Vignette showed how Hong Kong Disneyland suffered from poor payout planning. The overwhelming success of a discount-ticket promotion in 2006, in conjunction with the Chinese Lunar New Year, led to huge numbers of mainland families being turned away at the gates despite having valid tickets. This resulted in a large amount of negative publicity for the newly opened attraction.

## Samples

**Sampling** involves giving away free samples of a product to encourage sales, or arranging for people to try all or part of a service. As many tourism and hospitality services are intangible, sampling is not always a straightforward process. However, restaurants and bars often give customers free samples of menu items or beverages. Sampling for the travel trade often comes in the form of familiarization trips. A familiarization trip (commonly referred to as a 'fam trip') is a popular method used to expose a product to intermediaries in the channel of distribution. For example, a hotel might have a group of travel agents visit the facility to familiarize them with its features and benefits. If travel agents are impressed with a facility during a fam trip, they will convey their enthusiasm to customers, and bookings will increase. The trips are free or reduced in price and can be given to intermediaries by suppliers, carriers, or destination marketing groups.

---

**SAMPLING**
giving away free samples of a product to encourage sales, or arranging for people to try all or part of a service

---

## Coupons

**Coupons** are vouchers or certificates that entitle customers or intermediaries to a reduced price on a good or service. In the US, the national coupon industry is estimated at more than US$6 billion a year. Major companies like Procter & Gamble, S.C. Johnson, General Mills and Kraft continue to rely on traditional paper coupons, despite the increasing importance of the internet and online coupons. Companies issue coupons to encourage people to sample new products, to make impulse purchases and to foster brand loyalty. Coupons are used extensively in the tourism and hospitality industries, especially among restaurants, hotels, rental car companies, tourist attractions and cruise lines. Besides stimulating sales of a mature product, coupons are also effective in promoting early trial of a new product. But many marketing professionals feel that too much promotional use of coupons creates a commodity out of a differentiated product. Overuse has also led to coupon wars and other forms of price discounting, all the while detracting from the intrinsic value of a company's product or service.

> **COUPONS**
> vouchers or certificates that entitle customers or intermediaries to a reduced price on a good or service

## Gift Certificates

**Gift certificates** are vouchers or cheques that are either selectively given away by the sponsor or sold to customers, who in turn give them to others as gifts. The Snapshot on Carnival Cruises showed how the company promoted the sale of gift vouchers for cruise vacations over the Christmas period.

> **GIFT CERTIFICATES**
> vouchers or cheques that are either selectively given away by the sponsor or sold to customers, who in turn give them to others as gifts

## Premiums

**Premiums** are goods offered either for free or at low cost as an incentive to buy a product. There are several varieties of premiums, including self-liquidators (sold at a price to recover the sponsor's cost) and free premiums (distributed by mail, in or on packages). Most marketing professionals agree that, to be effective, premiums must be of an appropriate quality and durability, be appealing, and have high perceived value to certain customer groups. The danger of such promotions is that they can be expensive and – far from creating loyalty – they encourage consumers to switch brands constantly.

> **PREMIUMS**
> goods offered either for free or at low cost as an incentive to buy a product

## Point-of-Purchase Displays

**Point-of-purchase merchandising** is a technique used to promote a product at locations where it is being sold. The value of point-of-purchase merchandising has long been recognized in retailing and is making rapid inroads in restaurants, hotels, car rental companies and travel agencies. In the food and beverage industry, menus and wine and drink lists are the key tools. In fact, many restaurants now put their menus on the web for customers to view; most wineries now offer free tasting in order to entice customers to purchase; and hotels also use a wide variety of merchandising techniques, including in-room guest directories, room-service menus, elevator and lobby displays and brochure racks. In the travel agency business, brochures, posters, and window and stand-up displays are fairly common forms of sales promotion. A few years ago, Club Med designed a floor display for travel agents that featured a beach chair with a surfboard on one side and a pair of skis on the other to show that Club Med has both snow and sun destinations.

---

**POINT-OF-PURCHASE MERCHANDISING**
a technique used to promote a product at locations where it is being sold

---

## Patronage Rewards

Patronage rewards are cash or other prizes given to customers for their regular use of a company's products or services. The intent of such rewards is to encourage loyalty and to create a positive change in the behaviour of the consumer. Examples are the frequent flyer plans that award points for miles travelled. Many hotel chains also have frequent stay programmes, and some restaurants have frequent diner programmes. These will be discussed in more detail in Chapter 11.

## Contests, Sweepstakes and Games

**Contests** are sales promotions in which entrants win prizes based on some required skill that they are asked to demonstrate. **Sweepstakes** are sales promotions that require entrants to submit their names and addresses. Winners are chosen on the basis of chance, not skill. **Games** are similar to sweepstakes, but they involve using game pieces, such as scratch-and-win cards. The use of contests, games and sweepstakes has been shown to increase advertising readership. These promotional tools can be useful in communicating key benefits and unique selling points, and can be targeted at both consumers and members of the trade.

---

**CONTESTS**
sales promotions in which entrants can win prizes based on some required skill that they are asked to demonstrate

---

**SWEEPSTAKES**
sales promotions that require entrants to submit their names and addresses; winners are chosen on the basis of chance, not skill

---

---

**GAMES**
sales promotions similar to sweepstakes but involving the use of game pieces, such as scratch-and-win cards

---

As mentioned above, promotional techniques designed to stimulate sales often target the trade. In 2005 the Dubai-based hotel Jumeirah launched the World's Most Luxurious Competition, offering travel agents worldwide the chance to win a stay at Jumeirah over the next ten years. The competition was designed to promote the group's new private label GDS code. Travel agents using a GDS to process hotel reservations could register to participate by visiting a dedicated website. The first phase of the competition was an online memory game.[9]

## Joint Promotions

In a **joint promotion**, two or more organizations that have similar target markets combine their resources to their mutual advantage. This collaboration can reduce the cost of the incentives offered, and it may be a one-off joint promotion or a long-term campaign such as a trade association campaign using an 'umbrella' brand name. For example in 2006, the Guam Visitors Bureau partnered with JCB, an international credit card brand, to promote tourism and spending in Guam.[10] During the campaign, JCB card members received a chance to win prizes for every US$200 they spent on Guam using their JCB card. Prizes included a free trip to Guam for 40 winners and $50 Duty Free Shop gift certificates for 200 winners. Japanese travellers were the target market, as approximately 950,000 Japanese visit Guam each year, and each one spends an average of $675 during their stay. JCB card members' spending power is higher than that of the average tourist to Guam. As a result of the 'True Guam Campaign', JCB expected 10,000 more JCB card members than the previous year to visit the island. The name of the campaign echoed the Guam Visitors' Bureau catchphrase for 2006, 'Do You Know True Guam?', and the promotion was developed to assist the Bureau in achieving their goal of one million inbound visitors that year, a 10 per cent increase on 2005.

---

**JOINT PROMOTION**
a promotion in which two or more organizations that have similar target markets combine their resources to their mutual advantage

---

Another example of a joint promotion was a partnership between Whistler ski resort and UK tour operator Neilson. In 2006, Tourism Whistler used hypertag technology in a UK outdoor advertising campaign in attempt to bring more skiers to the Canadian resort. Hypertag is a new way of allowing people to access relevant information and content on a mobile phone or PDA (e.g. Palm Pilots or Pocket PCs) directly from objects such as advertising panels, marketing or exhibition displays. In the Whistler-Neilson campaign, the hypertag ads were placed in 25 key areas of central London. Interested consumers could use their PDAs to interact with the hypertag chip imbedded in the poster to download Whistler content directly. Tourism Whistler used contests (Win Your Dream Vacation to Whistler and daily prize contests) to encourage the user to interact. People were able to win instant prizes (such as Whistler backpacks, jackets, T-shirts etc.) whereby they got a 'You're a Winner!' message on their PDA. All users (winners and losers) were given instructions to visit a website, www.dreamskivacation.com to enter a contest for the grand prize.

The campaign achieved 2,601 downloads. In each interaction, a person stopped, read the poster, chose to devote time to downloading the Whistler message and went away with a successful interaction. The download rate increased as the campaign progressed – by the end of the campaign the network was consistently achieving over 100 downloads a day.

---

**Chapter Summary**

In marketing communications, the blend of promotional elements is known as the promotional mix; this includes advertising, sales promotions, public relations, personal selling, word of mouth, direct marketing and internet marketing.

Perhaps one of the most important advances in marketing in recent decades has been the rise of integrated marketing communications (IMC) – the recognition that advertising can no longer be crafted and executed in isolation from other promotional mix elements.

Advertising can be defined as any paid form of non-personal presentation and promotion of ideas, goods, or services by an identified sponsor, using mass media to persuade or influence an audience. There are six important stages in developing an advertising programme: setting the objectives, setting the budget, advertising agency decisions, message strategy, media strategy and campaign evaluation.

The use of sales promotions is increasing rapidly for many reasons: it offers the manager short-term bottom-line results; it is accountable; it is less expensive than advertising; it speaks to the current needs of the consumer to receive more value from products; and it responds to marketplace changes. Many tools can be used to accomplish sales promotion objectives. These include samples, coupons, gift certificates, premiums and point-of-purchase displays, patronage rewards, contests, sweepstakes and games.

---

## Key Terms

## Discussion Questions and Exercises

1. Find an example of an advertisement from a tourism or hospitality organization. What execution style is it using? How effective is the ad, and what changes would you make to improve its effectiveness?
2. What are the main factors that determine an airline's choice of advertising media? If possible, obtain details or examples of advertising from specific airlines to support your answer.
3. Which do you think is an effective advertisement: one that creates an emotional bond with consumers or one that is designed to inform consumers about the product's unique benefit? Or do you have another definition and explanation?
4. How can sales promotions be used to support other elements of the marketing communications mix? Give examples to support your answer.
5. Do you think sales promotions create loyalty or encourage switching to competitors' products? Use examples from your own experience.

## Club 18-30 Growing Up

In 2003, Thomas Cook had a crisis of confidence over its Club 18–30 brand that sold overseas holidays to young people, due to dwindling bookings, bad press and the daunting task of trying to reinvent the brand. However, by summer 2005 numbers were up 25 per cent and a new 'grown-up' image was gradually being established in the public forum, thanks to a radical change of direction in communications.

Club 18–30 was first launched in the 1960s and targeted affluent youth, but by the mid-1980s was increasingly associated with cutting-edge licentiousness – sex, sex and more sex. Bad publicity was as good as any publicity when its outrageous ads, as well as the much-publicized bad behaviour of both its clients and some of its overseas staff, engendered endless debate and criticism in the media. By the mid-1990s, Club 18–30 was thriving thanks to headline-grabbing advertising campaigns featuring such double entendre slogans as 'Beaver Espana', 'Summer of 69' and 'Wake up at the crack of Dawn'. However, by 2003 the high profile, self-styled sex-on-the-beach tour company had been undermined by its own risqué image. What had once been tongue in cheek had now become dirty. The ITV reality series *Club Reps* that documented the drunken antics and promiscuity of young Brits abroad, regular detrimental press reports of both tourists and Club reps being arrested in various Mediterranean resorts in a widespread police crackdown against lewd and rowdy British tourists, and negative reactions to 'soft porn' ads all finally contributed to turning youth away from the travel company.

The Club 18–30 management team decided to reinvigorate the brand and reinvent it through advertising, a review of its core overseas offering and promotions. Women, in particular, were targeted as a key element in re-branding the company in an effort to attract a different type of customer. The gaudy, high-profile logo was replaced by a softer, sleek, monochrome design, banners were removed from destinations, and company literature was upgraded to resemble a lifestyle magazine rather than the traditional brochures which had always featured scantily clad young people on the beach and in night clubs. Bar crawls and beach parties featuring lewd drinking games were stopped and nocturnal club and bar nights were supplemented with shopping trips, scuba diving, golf, spas, cultural visits and, in particular, an emphasis on music events and the up-market club scene. Kate Stanners, creative director of the campaign, said, 'The club scene, fashion and the holiday scene have become more and more sophisticated, so Club 18–30 has responded accordingly.'

Overseas, Club 18–30 clients are now being directed in their choice of holiday activities by Club 18–30 representatives rather than 'Clubreps' who used to be the ringmasters of alcohol-fuelled debauchery. 'We are attempting to change the perception of the type of holiday we offer,' said Ian Ailles, managing director of specialist business for parent company, Thomas Cook. The ratio of men to women has now improved to almost 50:50 thanks to the well-publicized image clean-up and change of focus. The number of bookings was up by around 25 per cent to 73,000 for 2005, after a fall in 2004 from 100,000 (in 2000) to only 59,000. The average age of clients has also risen from 20 to 21. Also, the company is expanding into new areas such as Bulgaria and Turkey, with Egypt being a future potential destination. And clients

Club 18–30 print ad

are being wooed for long weekends and more flexible holiday durations rather than the traditional seven- or 14-day trips.

How has this shift actually been achieved? In 2004, Saatchi and Saatchi were given the seemingly impossible task of eradicating sex and drink from Club 18–30's ads. The famous ad agency came up with an 'underground' campaign based on teaser advertising techniques, which banished the company logo from all marketing material and from the resorts themselves (see above). Paul Little, the Club's overseas director, said, 'We have worked really hard on keeping it low key. We have avoided the press through our underground policy and it's working well.' Cryptic advertisements with no mention of Club 18–30 have directed viewers to a website, www.beonthelist.co.uk. The crux of this £1.5 million campaign is the new slogans 'be on the list' and 'not on the list' which suggest an exclusive club only accessible to cool, sophisticated young people. The new up-market, trendy image is being disseminated via posters, magazines, and radio as well as the viral email advertising.

*Sources*: Walsh, C. (August, 2003) 'Club 18–30 thrives on a bad rep', *Guardian,* Business & Media, retrieved from http://web.lexis-nexis.com; Ciar Byrne Media Correspondent. (2005) 'It's no longer sex, sex, sex as Club 18–30 goes upmarket', *The Independent,* News, 15, retrieved from http://web.lexis-nexis.com; Swarbrick, S. (2005) 'Club 18–30 crawls up market', *The Herald* (Glasgow), Travel, 4, retrieved from http://web.lexis-nexis.com; Davies, C, (2005) 'No sex please as Club 18–30 throws off its boozy image', *The Daily Telegraph* News, 10, retrieved from http://web.lexis-nexis.com.

## Questions

1. Do you think publicity for outrageous or unethical ads generally helps or hinders the sale of a product? Think of some examples to support your answer.
2. Do you think Club 18–30 was taking a risk by attempting to change its image? What could have been (and still could be) the negative consequences of such a strategy?
3. Why do you think it took consumers nearly 40 years to boycott the company because of its reputation? Is this a reflection of changing travel habits in general?
4. Take a look at the Club 18–30 website. What does it tell you about the company's current advertising strategy?

## Websites

| | |
|---|---|
| www.cheddarcaves.co.uk | Cheddar Caves & Gorge |
| www.club18-20.com | Club 18–30 |
| www.braziltour.com | Brazil Ministry of Tourism |
| www.carnival.com | Carnival Cruises |
| www.visitbritain.com | VisitBritain |
| www.visitguam.org | Guam Visitors Bureau |
| www.visitlasvegas.com | Las Vegas Visitors' Convention Bureau |

## References

1  Strong, E. K. (1925) *The Psychology of Selling*. New York: McGraw-Hill.
2  Lavidge, R. C. and Steiner, G. A. (1961) 'A model for predictive measurement of advertising effectiveness', *Journal of Marketing*, October, 59–62.
3  Rogers, E. M. (1962) *The Diffusion of Innovations*. New York: Free Press.
4  Broadbent, S. and Jacobs, B. (1985) *Spending Advertising Money*. London: Business Books.
5  Colley, R. H. (1961) *Defining Advertising Goals for Measuring Advertising Results*. New York: Association of National Advertisers.
6  Wells, W., Burnett, B. and Moriarty, S. (2003) *Advertising Principles and Practice*. Englewood Cliffs, NJ: Prentice Hall.
7  Kotler, P., Bowen, J. and Makens, J. (2003) *Marketing for Hospitality and Tourism*. Upper Saddle River, NJ: Prentice Hall.
8  Wells, W., Burnett, B. and Moriarty, S. (2006) *Advertising Principles and Practice*. Englewood Cliffs, NJ: Prentice Hall, 470.
9  Anon. (1 December 2005). GDS code promotion. *Travelweek*, 26.
10  Anon. (22 December 2006) 'JCB launches promotion with Guam visitors bureau: true Guam campaign', *JCN Newswire – Japan Corporate News Network*, 1.

# 9

# MARKETING COMMUNICATIONS: PUBLIC RELATIONS, PERSONAL SELLING, DIRECT MARKETING, AND WORD OF MOUTH

## Marketing the Most Spectacular Train Trip in the World

CANADA

A FEAST FOR THE EYES AND SOUL

Discover the Canadian Rockies onboard
the Rocky Mountaineer®, recently awarded
*World's Leading Travel Experience by Train.*
Visit your travel agent or call 1-800-665-7245.

ROCKY MOUNTAINEER *Vacations*

*Experience*
"The Most Spectacular Train Trips in the World."®

rockymountaineer.com

A 2007 Rocky Mountaineer Print Ad

Imagine a trip, by train, through the heart of the spectacular Canadian Rockies, specifically scheduled so that the breathtaking mountain scenery can be enjoyed entirely by daylight. Some of the most beautiful places in Canada are seen from the country's oldest form of mass transportation – passenger rail. This should be an ideal tourism product, one that would be easy to promote and easy to sell. Nevertheless, in the spring of 1990, the newly privatized Rocky Mountaineer passenger train service was facing many challenges, not the least of which was marketing this wonderful product on a minuscule budget.

The new company was headed by Peter Armstrong, who had previously turned Vancouver's Gray Line tour-bus business into a profitable operation. The marketing of the Rocky Mountaineer would be crucial, so Armstrong recruited the help of skilled marketers. Rick Antonson, formerly of the Edmonton Convention & Tourism Association, became the vice-president of sales and marketing. Murray Atherton, who had worked for Armstrong at Gray Line and had his own hospitality consulting firm, was brought in to reach the overseas tour companies, particularly those in the United Kingdom. Finally, Mike Leone, who had handled media relations in the United States for Expo 86, was entrusted with the company's public relations.

The company's first trip was for the Pacific Asia Travel Association (PATA), from which the company benefited in a number of ways. First, Tourism Canada (CTC's precursor) had filmed portions of the trip for their own promotions and the company was able to get a couple of hundred copies of this video into circulation. Second, the PATA trip provided the company with first-hand knowledge provided by overseas tour operators on the best ways to sell travel products in their home markets. Finally, the then minister of external affairs for the federal government, Joe Clark, remarked during the trip that it was 'the most spectacular train trip in the world'. The company registered that quotation as a trademark and uses it in promotional materials.

A huge obstacle for the fledgling company was the media reports on the 'demise' of passenger rail in Canada. This was particularly troublesome in the United States, where a PBS special and the evening news reported the end of passenger rail between Vancouver and Toronto. With such a limited marketing budget, it would be difficult to bring all the pertinent media on board for familiarization tours to promote the Rocky Mountaineer. Mike Leone's skill at public relations brought press coverage and feature write-ups in the United States, all in an effort to overcome the public mindset that rail travel had disappeared.

The most important marketing task for that first year was to obtain bookings to fill the trains. Given the financial constraints, very few dollars were available for marketing and the company had to make every one count. Few tour operator contacts were passed on by VIA, leaving only the very shell of an operator network. Murray Atherton was getting up at 2 am to contact tour companies in the United Kingdom, trying to 'paint the dream, paint the picture' for the tour operators. This personal selling was crucial, as the new company was building its tour contacts from scratch.

Marketing the next season was complicated by the fact that the company was well into the first before it could confirm the schedule for the second year. It was also trying to develop offerings and contracts that would suit the needs of diverse markets, including Europe and Southeast Asia. Moreover, the company had had no capacity at the time to arrange travel packages beyond its two-day service, and had referred that business to other tour companies.

During a trip to London with Tourism Canada in September, a company representative discovered that a Canadian tour operator had just cancelled a luxury train trip across Canada that had been arranged with Thomas Cook, and the cancelled trip was featured in a publication that had already gone to print. The company scrambled to have a Rocky Mountaineer brochure sent overnight to Thomas Cook for insertion into the publication. Its ability to capitalize on this opportunity led to a $10,000 deal and an eight-page feature in the Thomas Cook travel magazine.

For all their challenges, the people behind the Rocky Mountaineer knew they had a winning product to sell, and the company has gone from strength to strength. Today, media public relations plays a significant role in marketing the Rocky Mountaineer and Whistler Mountaineer, which debuted in 2006. Rocky Mountaineer Vacations employs two full-time travel media specialists to focus on attracting travel writers to travel on and write about their experiences aboard the trains. These travel media specialists are supported by public relations companies located in the United States, England and Australia who spend countless hours promoting the Rocky Mountaineer and Whistler Mountaineer to leading travel publications and media outlets. In 2006 this strategy paid big dividends, with over 200 travel writers from around the world travelling onboard and writing about both trains. This resulted in a media value of several million dollars.

The popularity of the Rocky Mountaineer is evidenced by its continued growth as well as its international recognition. The Rocky Mountaineer has been named one of the '20 Best Rail Experiences in the World' three times by *The International Railway Traveller* magazine and was voted 'Best Attraction' by the North American Association of Travel Writers in 1998. The future looks very bright indeed for 'The Most Spectacular Train Trip in the World®'.

*Source*: Grescoe, P. (2000) *Trip of a Lifetime: The Making of the Rocky Mountaineer*. Vancouver: Hurricane; Personal communication with Ian Robertson, executive director, Corporate Communications and Public Affairs, 2 April 2007.

## Introduction

The Opening Vignette highlights how the Rocky Mountaineer used public relations (PR) as a key part of its communications programme. This chapter begins by examining the roles and functions of public relations and the main public relations techniques used in tourism and hospitality. Personal selling is the focus of the next section of the chapter, which discusses the roles and objectives of personal selling, the sales process, and the roles of a sales manager. The key advantages of direct marketing are discussed in the following section, as are the major direct marketing tools. The chapter then concludes with a section on word-of-mouth communication – an important but often misunderstood form of promotion in tourism.

**Public relations (PR)** includes all the activities that a tourism or hospitality organization uses to maintain or improve its relationship with other organizations or individuals. Although public relations has a distinguished tradition, people often mistake it for **publicity**, which refers to attention received through news media coverage. Public relations is broader in scope than

---

**PUBLIC RELATIONS (PR)**
the activities that a tourism or hospitality organization uses to maintain or improve its relationship with other organizations or individuals

---

publicity, its goal being for an organization to achieve positive relationships with various audiences (publics) in order to manage the organization's image and reputation effectively. Its publics may be external (customers, the news media, the investment community, the general public, government bodies) and internal (shareholders, employees). Figure 9.1 shows the

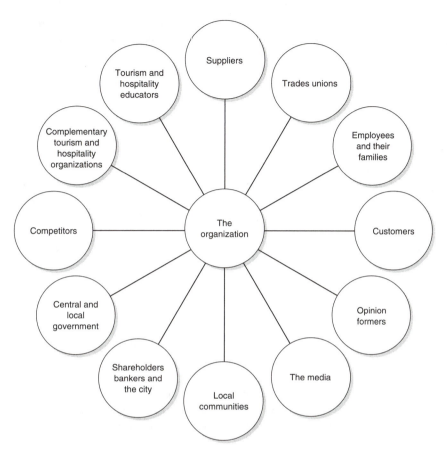

**Figure 9.1**    Various Publics in the Tourism and Hospitality Industry

different publics who may have an influence over the organization. Managing the relationships and communications with each and every public is essential to effective public relations.

**PUBLICITY**
attention received through news media coverage

## Roles and Functions of Public Relations

The three most important roles of public relations and publicity in tourism and hospitality are maintaining a positive public presence, handling negative publicity, and enhancing the effectiveness of other promotional mix elements (Morrison, 2002).[1] In this third role, public relations paves the way for advertising, sales promotions and personal selling by making customers more receptive to their persuasive messages. Ultimately, the difference between advertising and public relations is that public relations takes a longer, broader view of the importance of image and reputation as a corporate competitive asset and addresses more target audiences. The functions of the PR department include the following:

## Establishing Corporate Identity

The objectives of establishing a corporate identity are similar to those of branding: to create an image of consistency, reliability and professionalism that is easily recognized by the public. Everything that the organization owns or produces must project the same image. Richard Branson has created a clear corporate identity for the Virgin group. Over the past 25 years, he has diversified his Virgin brand into a far-reaching empire, encompassing mobile phone services, a rail service, and even wedding dresses as well as his original record label and discount airline. His personal image is one of unconventionality, youthful energy and enthusiasm, entrepreneurial spirit and thinking big, and he imbues all his products with this brand distinction (see Chapter 11).

## Government Relations

The organization's business may be affected by changes in the law or in government policy, and a company may wish to ensure that politicians are aware of the impact their decisions will have. Lobbying can be done by individual companies, professional bodies or specially formed groups. The Snapshot below describes how, in the face of travel advisories that were crippling the Kenyan tourism industry, the Kenyans lobbied the British government in an attempt to get them reviewed. These travel advisories were imposed by many countries following outbreaks of terrorism.

## Crisis Management

When a serious incident occurs, it is the PR department's job to take the pressure off operational managers by handling media enquiries and ensuring that the organization's version of events is presented. The organization needs to be seen to be acting swiftly, efficiently and responsibly to deal with the problem, and must have a crisis management plan in place before an incident occurs. In November 2005, a cruise ship – the *Seabourn Spirit* – was attacked by pirates off the coast of Somalia. The ship's crew managed to prevent the hijackers from getting on board by increasing speed and changing course. Miami-based Seabourn Cruise Lines was quick to respond to the crisis. It gave the passengers vouchers for a free cruise in the future and quickly organized a day of activity in the Seychelles to buoy the tourists' spirits.

## Internal Communications

Since staff play an important role in creating the image of the company and the quality of the customer's experience, it is important that they are kept fully informed and made to feel part of the team. The PR function often includes producing staff newsletters and briefing presentations. Other employee relations techniques include employee recognition programmes, cards or gifts that mark important dates such as birthdays, incentive programmes, and promotions.

## Customer Relations

Customers are the lifeblood of every organization, and techniques that improve relationships with them are very important to an organization's long-term survival. For example, answering customer complaints and claims promptly and fairly can limit the bad word-of-mouth publicity that dissatisfied customers can spread. The Sheraton Suites in Calgary (see Chapter 11) produces a newsletter for customers, which includes profiles on top-performing employees, a schedule of events in and around Calgary, and the procedure for giving customer feedback.

## Marketing Publicity

Marketing publicity is part of the wider PR function and is therefore part of the promotional mix. Its objective is to secure editorial space to achieve marketing goals. Editorial space in a newspaper (or even a television show) can be extremely effective, as was highlighted in the Opening Vignette. In June 2006, the Royal Shakespeare Company promoted its Complete Works Festival summer season by commissioning a flotilla of hot-air balloons to drift over the town of Stratford-upon-Avon, serenading residents with ambient music and readings from Shakespeare. The stunt generated a considerable amount of publicity, including a half-page feature in a major daily newspaper (Britten, 2006).[2]

## Snapshot

### Kenya's Efforts to Recover from a Crisis

Between 1998 and 2002, terrorism attacks, threats of further attacks and travel advisories against Kenya caused an unforeseen and abrupt decline in the country's tourism arrivals. The 1998 simultaneous bombings of the American embassies in Nairobi and Dar es Salaam, Tanzania, put Kenya on the map as a target for terrorism. In 2002, terrorists struck again, this time bombing a beach-front hotel at Kikambala, north of Mombassa. In both incidents, Kenyan citizens suffered loss of life and property although the attacks were targeting foreign interests and nationals.

The American and British governments issued travel advisories warning their citizens against travel to Kenya, and other European countries followed with similar warnings. At the same time, the British department of transport advised British airlines to suspend all flights to and from Kenya, a decision that received a lot of media coverage in the US and Europe. Historically, the British are regarded as experts on Kenya and their actions immediately sent a worldwide message that Kenya was indeed not safe; as a result, tourists from other markets started cancelling flights and hotel bookings.

The travel warnings and flight suspensions had disastrous effects on the country's tourism. The Somak group, one of the largest tour operators in Kenya, reported losses of between US$500,000 and $700,000 in revenue due to cancellations by more than 500 would-be tourists. 'Every day, we receive emails and telephone calls either suspending or postponing travel,' lamented Suresh Raman, the group's director. At the coast, many hotels were forced to close or radically reduce services, resulting in the laying off of at least 10,000 local staff. Also affected were the independent local restaurants and residents who relied on tourism for their livelihood. Suppliers of goods and services to tourists were severely hit.

Official government figures estimated the loss due to the ban and the travel warnings at US$1 million per week. A report by Raitt Orr & Associates, a London-based public relations firm for the Kenyan Government, estimated the loss at about 2 per cent of the country's gross domestic product in 2003. In an attempt to lobby for a review of the flight ban, the Kenyan government presented the report to the British government. While acknowledging that travellers have the right to be informed, some Kenyans thought that the advisories were insulting, while other officials believed the warnings to be extremely subjective. 'I think it is about perception. When I went to London a few years ago I was worried about safety – same in the New York subway,' said Mr Raphael Tuju, Kenya's acting tourism minister. 'There is no cause for alarm. Kenya is still a safe destination to visit. All our systems are on high alert and ready to respond to any threat, real or imagined.'

Meanwhile, the industry was turning to domestic tourists. Beach resorts in Mombassa were wooing conference tourists to fill their empty rooms. Conferences now provided about 80 per cent of bookings along the coast. However, hoteliers were unhappy as, unlike overseas tourists, conference-goers do not want to lie on the beach or spend money at the bar. Other than being a 'survival kit for hotels', the 'new customers' provided less added value. With little hope of full recovery, most investors were forced to cut costs to break even. As a result, the necessary hotel refurbishment programmes, needed to maintain facilities at internationally acceptable standards, were not implemented in many of the resorts.

As the crisis deepened, the Kenya Tourist Board took proactive steps to market the destination and maintain presence in the American market. The organization, together with five major US tour operators (African Travel, Big Five, Classic Escapes, Micato and Somak Safaris), hosted a group of 160 top American travel agents in a familiarization trip, the first of its kind for Kenya. The trip was geared to help educate travel agents about travelling to the country, and even included a welcome reception at the US Ambassador's residence.

As a result of these efforts, Kenya's tourism started to recover. Following an aggressive US$6.6 million marketing campaign in Europe, tourist arrivals to Kenya rose by 28 per cent in 2004, while revenues rose by 66 per cent to more than 42 billion shillings. 'For 2005, we are projecting a continued increase at somewhere around 25 per cent higher than 2004; assuming everything stays normal and there are no external factors beyond our control,' said Jake Grieves-Cook, the chairman of Kenya Tourism Board, referring to numbers of tourists arriving in the country. However, it was precisely 'external factors' that precipitated the previous crisis! Were valuable lessons missed?

*Sources*: Yobesia, M.N. (2006) 'Kenya's tourism bumpy recovery from effects of terrorism', Project for Master in Tourism and Environmental Economics, UIB, Palma, Mallorca.

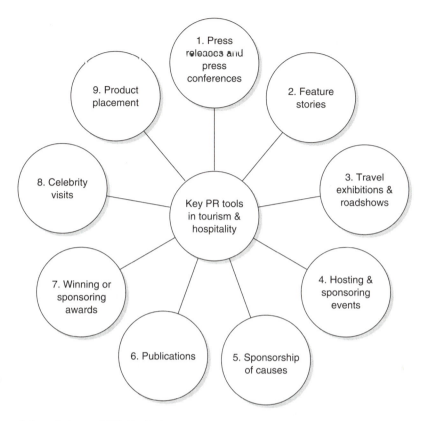

**Figure 9.2**    Selected PR Techniques Available to Tourism and Hospitality Organizations

## Public Relations Techniques

A variety of PR techniques are available to tourism and hospitality organizations. Nine of the key techniques are highlighted in Figure 9.2 and discussed below.

### Press Releases and Press Conferences

A **press release** or **news release** is a short article about an organization or an event that is written in an attempt to attract media attention, which will then hopefully lead to media coverage. Preparing press releases is probably the most popular and widespread public relations activity. To be effective, the release must be as carefully targeted as an advertising media schedule. It should be sent to the right publications and be written in a style that those publications would use. The headline should give a clear idea of the subject. The release should then open with a paragraph that summarizes the main points of the news story by stating who did what, when, why and where. The style should be that of a news report, and the story must be genuinely interesting to the publication's readers. Ideally, it should tell them something new that is happening and should contain a strong human angle. Other useful contents of a press release include a photograph and quotations, and it is essential to provide a contact name and telephone number in case journalists require further information. Just as press releases can be effective media attention-grabbers, so can special press conferences. A press conference is a meeting at which a prepared presentation is made to invited media people.

---

**PRESS RELEASE (NEWS RELEASE)**
a short article about an organization or an event that is written in an attempt to attract media attention, which will then hopefully lead to media coverage

---

## Feature Stories

**Feature stories** or features are articles of human interest that entertain, inform or educate readers, viewers or listeners. They are longer and have less immediate news value than press releases. However, such features can be extremely effective, and organizations in the tourism and hospitality sectors often encourage journalists to write stories about their products. The Opening Vignette describes how Rocky Mountaineer Vacations employs two full-time travel media specialists to focus on attracting travel writers to travel on and write about their experiences aboard the trains. In 2006 over 200 travel writers from around the world travelled onboard and wrote about both trains, resulting in a media value of several million dollars.

---

**FEATURE STORIES**
articles of human interest that entertain, inform or educate readers, viewers or listeners

---

## Travel Exhibitions and Roadshows

Many hospitality and travel organizations exhibit at travel trade shows, exhibitions or conventions. Generally, these occasions bring all parts of the industry (suppliers, carriers, intermediaries and destination marketing organizations) together. Exhibiting at a trade show is similar to putting together a small promotional mix. Some exhibitors send out direct mail pieces (advertising) to intermediaries, inviting them to visit their booths. The booth displays (merchandising) portray the available services and may be tied in with recent advertising campaigns. Representatives working the booth hand out brochures and business cards and try to develop sales leads (personal selling). They may also give away free samples or vouchers (sales promotions). When the trade show is over, exhibitors often follow up with personalized mailings (direct mail) or telephone calls (telemarketing). The Case Study at the end of the chapter shows how for marketers at the Puerto Rico Convention Centre, trade shows are an important tool in spreading the word.

## Hosting and Sponsoring Events

**Event sponsorship** is the financial support of an event (e.g., a car race, a theatre performance or a marathon road race) by a sponsor in return for advertising privileges associated with the event. Sponsorships are usually offered by the organizer of the event on a tiered basis, which means that a lead sponsor pays a maximum amount and receives maximum privileges, whereas other sponsors pay less and receive fewer privileges. Investment in sponsorships is mainly divided into three areas: sports, entertainment and cultural events. Sporting events attract the lion's share of sponsorship revenue. For example, the London 2012 Olympics are expected to attract over £100 million from just the top four to six sponsors.[3]

---

**EVENT SPONSORSHIP**

the financial support of an event (e.g., a car race, a theatre performance or a marathon road race) by a sponsor in return for advertising privileges associated with the event

---

Events are occurrences staged to communicate messages to target audiences. Public relations departments arrange press conferences, grand openings, public tours and other events to create opportunities to communicate with specific audiences. Tourism and hospitality companies can draw attention to themselves by arranging or sponsoring special events. The Empire State Building in New York, for example, has two annual events that generate large amounts of publicity for the 75-year-old attraction, which draws more than 3.8 million visitors each year (Perri, 2006).[4] Valentine's Day weddings are the first event; fourteen couples are chosen each year, on the basis of their strong attachment to the building. Then there is the Empire State Building Run-Up, when more than 100 runners from around the world race up 1,576 steps to the 86th floor.

The sponsorship of events is also an effective way of gaining publicity, as it allows the sponsor to invite and host suppliers, journalists, distributors and customers, as well as bring repeated attention to the company's name and products. Companies should be careful, however, in choosing the events that they sponsor. In 2005 there was some controversy over the decision by Eos, a luxury firm running business-class flights, to sponsor a performance by Sting in New York. The partnership was seen by some as incongruous, as Sting is a self-proclaimed environmentalist, and Friends of the Earth have labelled Eos 'the world's worst' when it comes to pollution.[5]

## The Sponsorship of Causes

The sponsorship of causes is part of the wider activity of **cause-related marketing**, a technique whereby companies contribute to the well-being of society and associate themselves with a positive cause that will reflect well on their corporate image. Cause-related marketing is a rapidly expanding public relations trend, and is covered in more detail in Chapter 13.

---

**CAUSE-RELATED MARKETING**
a technique whereby companies contribute to the well-being of society and associate themselves with a positive cause that will reflect well on their corporate image

---

## Publications

Companies rely extensively on communication materials to reach and influence their target markets. **Publications** such as annual reports, brochures and company newsletters and magazines can draw attention to a company and its products, and can help build the company's image and convey important news to target markets. Audio-visual materials, such as films, videocassettes and DVDs are coming into increasing use as promotional tools. Many destination marketing organizations use CDs or DVDs to promote their destinations, and large companies such as Disney send promotional CDs directly to consumers as well as to members of the travel trade. Smaller companies, such as Canadian Mountain Holidays (see Case Study in Chapter 7), produce CDs (CMH, for example, makes CDs for heli-skiing, heli-hiking and mountaineering in up to six languages) and then show them to intermediaries or targeted audiences.

---

**PUBLICATIONS**
annual reports, brochures and company newsletters and magazines that draw attention to a company and its products, and help build the company's image and convey important news to target markets

---

### Winning or Sponsoring Awards

In many industries, such as the car industry, it has become common practice for companies to promote their achievements. Automotive awards presented in magazines such as *Motor Trends* have long been known to carry clout with potential car buyers. The winning of awards has become increasingly important in tourism and hospitality sectors as well. For individual operators, the winning of an award is a campaign opportunity, a fact recognized by award-winning organizations such as Virgin Atlantic and Whistler Resorts. These organizations use the third-party endorsements in their advertising to build credibility and attract customers. Most of the awards in tourism and hospitality promote best performance and are often an indication of quality. They can therefore provide excellent publicity for winners.

### Celebrity Visits

Encouraging celebrities to use tourism and hospitality products can result in considerable media coverage, and can therefore help to promote that particular product. For example, Richard

Branson built Virgin Atlantic Airways with the help of a strong public relations campaign that included inviting as many rock stars as possible to fly on his airline. Destinations, too, can benefit from celebrity visits. The ski resorts at Whistler, BC, have a reputation for attracting high-profile film and music stars, like Arnold Schwarzenegger, Kevin Costner and British singer Seal, as well as business magnates like Microsoft's Bill Gates. Many consider the 1998 visit to Whistler by Prince Charles and his sons, Princes William and Harry, as the biggest thing to have happened on the Whistler celebrity scene. The Snapshot below shows how the Atlantis Resort has generated publicity by attracting movie, music and television celebrities from all over the world.

## Snapshot

### Celebrity Power at Atlantis Resort

The Bahamas' luxury resort Atlantis is a success story of suitably mythic proportions, which has developed its Las Vegas-style theme to its fullest potential via a playful celebration of the legends of the lost city of Atlantis. With its aquatic and tropical decorated rooms costing up to US$700 per night, its fashionable Ocean Club facilities and the $25,000 per day Bridge Suite, it attracts movie, music and television celebrities from all over the world. An episode of Jessica Simpson's *Newlyweds* was filmed there. Both Christina Aguilera and Gloria Estefan have staged concerts there and Michael Jordan, who favours the Bridge Suite, regularly hosts his own celebrity golf tournaments at the island's onsite golf course. With its celebrity connections, Atlantis marketers have naturally turned to product placement in films as a focus of advertising strategy. In the hit film *Meet The Parents* a poster advertising the Atlantis is clearly visible in the background of airport scenes.

In 1994 South African mega-millionaire Sol Kerzner began construction of the $250 million resort by refurbishing two existing high-rise hotels on Paradise Island, former haunts of Howard Hughes and the Shah of Iran, who both frequented its beautiful palm-fringed white sandy beaches. He also rebuilt the elite Ocean Club Inn and constructed a chain of lagoons to create the world's largest aquarium. Always associating the hotel with the grandeur and glitz of international celebrities, he threw a $7 million party in 1998 for the newest addition, the Royal Towers hotel, inviting Oprah Winfrey, Michael Jackson, Julia Roberts, Natalie Cole and Quincy Jones. The setting was incomparably grand with its 20-metre domed and gilded rotunda, massive columns and marble floors plus huge picture windows revealing underwater views of the half-hectare Waterscape. The Lost Continent of Atlantis was depicted with sharks swimming through ancient-looking fallen columns and stones carved like Mayan art.

By 1998 the massive resort comprised 38 restaurants and bars, 11 swimming pools with waterslides, rides, waterfalls, fountains, a luxury spa, extensive conference facilities with themed meeting services for groups of up to 2,000, a ten-acre marina for yachts of up to 60 metres, plus the largest 24-hour casino and largest ballroom in the Caribbean. It is a Vegas-style mega-resort intended as a destination in its own right, attractive to families with its various facilities and programmes for different ages, who never need to set foot off the sprawling property during their vacation – thus concentrating all their spending power on the resort, which charges individually for everything from its $24-per-head breakfast buffet to its $79-per-day kids' club (2006 prices). The Atlantis beats rival tropical gardens hands-down with its world-beating collection of open-air marine habitats, dramatically backlit with fibre optics, each aesthetically stunning for both the snorkellers and swimmers who can explore a five-storey replica of a Mayan temple with 18-foot waterslides, as well as the spectators who view it all from catwalks or glassed-in underwater viewing tunnels. Day trippers, especially from visiting cruise ships, flock to the Atlantis in their thousands to see the spectacle of more than 200 species of fish in 11 distinctly different exhibition lagoons.

*Sources*: Lee, G. (2005) 'Lack of creature comforts sinks expensive Atlantis Resort', *Bahamas Tourist News*, retrieved from www.bahamasb2b.com; Snyder, L. (2005) *Atlantis, Paradise Island: a resort destination like no other in the world fact sheet*, Kerzner International Bahamas Ltd.; Blackerby, C. (1 December 2005) 'Atlantis keeps spending – and celebs keep coming', *The Globe and Mail*, Travel, T5.

## Product Placement

**Product placement** is the insertion of brand logos or branded merchandise into movies and television shows, and it is another tactic for generating publicity. Since television viewers have a tendency – and now the technology – to zip through or avoid commercials, product placement has become increasingly popular with many companies. Tourism and hospitality companies have been quick to take advantage of this growing trend. British Airways was one of the first companies to be endorsed by James Bond in his movies, and Virgin paid a large amount for a promotional tie-in with the 1999 film *Austin Powers: The Spy Who Shagged Me*. The movie contained a huge plug for 'Virgin Shaglantic', and star and writer Mike Myers promoted the film in the United States by appearing on posters for Virgin Atlantic with the headline 'There's only one virgin on this poster, baby'. Hotels have also got in on the act. The Snapshot above showed how Atlantis marketers have turned to product placement in films as a focus of advertising strategy. In the hit film *Meet The Parents* a poster advertising the Atlantis is clearly visible in the background of airport scenes. The Plaza Hotel in New York was heavily featured in *Home Alone II: Lost in New York*. In the same movie, the family spent considerable time discussing an Avis car rental.

---

**PRODUCT PLACEMENT**
the insertion of brand logos or branded merchandise into movies and television shows

---

Destinations, too, have begun to see product placement as an opportunity to gain exposure. Many are keen to persuade producers to make films, television series or commercials in their country or province. Destination Marketing Organizations (DMO) in Britain, Kansas and Singapore are examples. VisitBritain has been targeting Indian film producers for some time in the belief that they can be persuaded to use British locations for Bollywood films, and, thereby generate significant economic benefits for Britain's tourism industry. In the US, Kansas's Travel and Tourism Development Division spends US$1.2m annually on tourism and film promotion. And the Singapore Tourism Board announced a three-year US$7m scheme in 2004 to lure leading international film-makers and broadcasters to produce their work there. Approved screen projects that showcase Singapore's appeal receive special help with resources and work permits. Some destinations appoint public relations specialists to 'place' their regions in films. One of the Snapshots in Chapter 13 shows how the Bahamas has been proactive in attracting film-makers to the islands.

## Personal Selling

**Personal selling** is a personalized form of communication in which a seller presents the features and benefits of a product to a buyer for the purpose of making a sale. The high degree of personalization that personal selling involves usually comes at a much greater cost per contact than mass communication techniques. Marketers must decide whether this added expense can be justified, or whether marketing objectives can be achieved by communicating with potential customers in groups. Some tourism and hospitality organizations favour personal selling far more than others, as for them the potential benefits outweigh the extra costs. In this age of evolving technology and ubiquitous electronic communication, one element hasn't changed in the meetings and convention business: the industry is still driven by personal relationships. For the Puerto Rico Convention Centre (see-end-of chapter Case Study) personal sales are an important part of its communications strategy.

---

**PERSONAL SELLING**
a personalized form of communication in which a seller presents the features and benefits of a product to a buyer for the purpose of making a sale

---

### Roles of Personal Selling

While the salesperson's job is to make a sale, his or her role goes well beyond this. Personal selling has a number of important functions in the tourism and hospitality industry, six of which are discussed below.

#### Gathering Marketing Intelligence
The salesperson must be alert to trends in the industry and to what competitors are doing. Competitive knowledge is important when the salesperson faces questions involving product comparisons, and information on competitor's promotions can be very useful for the marketing department. Data collected by the salesperson is often reported electronically to the company's head office, where managers can retrieve it and use it appropriately at a later date.

#### Locating and Maintaining Customers
Salespeople who locate new customers play a key role in a company's growth. They can identify qualified buyers (those most likely to purchase travel services), key decision-makers

(those who have the final say in travel decisions), and the steps involved in making travel decisions. This important information can be gathered effectively through inquiries and from sales calls to an organization.

### Promoting to the Travel Trade

Many organizations find personal selling to be the most effective communication tool in promoting to key travel decision-makers and influencers in the travel trade, such as corporate travel managers, convention or meeting planners, tour operators and retail travel agents. The purchasing power of these groups is impressive, and there are relatively few of them, which justifies the added expense of personal selling.

### Generating Sales at Point of Purchase

Personal selling can significantly increase the likelihood of purchase and the amount spent by customers at the point of purchase. Reservations staff at hotels and car rental desks have a great opportunity to up-sell (sell upgraded accommodations or cars), and staff in restaurants and travel agencies can have a major influence on the purchase decision of the customer. Increased sales are a result of the proper training of service and reservations staff in personal selling techniques.

### Using Relationship Marketing

Sales representatives provide various services to customers: consulting on their problems, rendering technical assistance, arranging finance and expediting delivery. These representatives are very important for building relationships with customers and maintaining their loyalty. Careful attention to individual needs and requirements is a powerful form of marketing for tourism and hospitality organizations. Key customers really appreciate the personal attention they receive from professional sales representatives and reservations staff. This appreciation normally results in increased sales and repeat use, and the focus is on creating and keeping long-term customers. This is just one part of a process that has become known as 'customer relationship management' (CRM).

### Providing Detailed and Up-to-Date Information
### to the Travel Trade

Personal selling allows an organization to pass on detailed information to the travel trade and provides an opportunity to deal immediately with a prospect's concerns and questions. This is especially important for an organization that relies on travel trade intermediaries for part or all of its business. Tour operators, for example, should have regular contact with travel agents in order to update them on changes in the marketing environment.

## Objectives of Personal Selling

Although sales objectives are custom-designed for specific situations, there are general objectives that are commonly employed throughout the tourism and hospitality industry.

*Sales Volume*

Occupancy, passenger seats or miles, and total covers (restaurant seats) are common measures of sales volume within the industry. An emphasis on volume alone, however, leads to price discounting, the attraction of undesirable market segments, cost cutting and employee dissatisfaction. Some sectors, such as exclusive resorts, unique adventure holidays and upper-end cruises, restrict prospecting to highly selective segments, believing that price and profits will take care of themselves. Others may establish sales volume objectives by product lines to ensure a desired gross profit. This system is the basis for yield management (see Chapter 6).

*Cross-Selling, Up-Selling, and Second-Chance Selling*

**Cross-selling** occurs when a seller offers a buyer the opportunity to purchase allied products as well as the obvious core products. Cross-selling is now integral to virtually every segment of the travel industry, travel insurance being one of the most profitable cross-sells in the industry. Good opportunities exist for tourism companies, such as hotels and resorts, to upgrade price and profit margins by selling higher-priced products (such as suites) through **up-selling**. A related concept is **second-chance selling**, in which a salesperson may contact a client who has already booked an event such as a three-day meeting. The salesperson may try to sell additional services such as airport limousine pick-up, or try to upgrade rooms or food and beverage services.

---

**CROSS-SELLING**

offering a customer the opportunity to purchase allied products as well as the obvious core products

---

**UP-SELLING**

upgrading price and profit margins by selling higher-priced products

---

**SECOND-CHANCE SELLING**

trying to sell additional services to a customer who has already booked services

---

*Market Share*

Some sectors of the tourism industry are more concerned with market share than others. Airlines, cruise lines, major fast-food chains and rental car companies, for example, are often more focused on market share than are restaurants, hotels and resorts. As a consequence, salespeople are sometimes required to measure market share or market penetration and are held accountable for a predetermined level of either or both.

*Product-Specific Objectives*

Occasionally, a sales force will be charged with the specific responsibility of improving sales volume for specific product lines. This objective may be associated with up-selling and second-chance selling, but may also be part of the regular sales duties of the sales force. Such objectives might be to sell more hotel suites, holiday packages to Mexico, honeymoon packages, or more premium car rentals. A common approach used to encourage the sale of specific products is to set objectives and to reward performance with bonuses or other incentives.

## The Sales Process

The sales process consists of the following seven steps (see Figure 9.3).

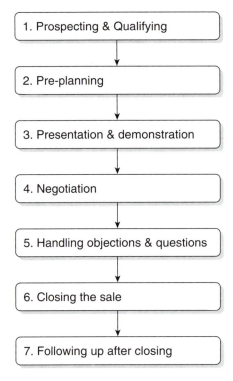

**Figure 9.3**   The Sales Process

*Prospecting and Qualifying*

**Prospecting** is the process of searching for new accounts. It has been said that there are three truisms about prospecting: most salespeople don't like to prospect; most salespeople do not know how to prospect; and most companies are inept at teaching or training salespeople to prospect. There are two key elements to successful prospecting. The first is to determine positioning strategy, i.e., to whom you should prospect. The second is implementing a process to find and ultimately contact those prospects on a one-to-one basis.

---

**PROSPECTING**
the process of searching for new accounts

---

*Pre-planning*
A successful sales call, made either by telephone or in the field, requires careful pre-planning and preparation. There are two elements to pre-planning a sales call: the pre-approach and the approach. In the pre-approach stage, a salesperson needs to learn as much as possible about the prospect in order to be able to establish a rapport during the sales call and to have the foundation on which to build the sales presentation itself. For example, sales people at The Westin Edmonton (see Snapshot below) put pictures up of prospective buyers everywhere back-of-house prior to the visit, so that all members of staff can give the buyer personal attention. The approach then follows and involves all the activities that lead to the sales presentation. These include arranging the appointments with prospects, establishing rapport and confidence at the start of a sales call, and checking preliminary details prior to the sales presentation. Sales representatives have three principal objectives in their approaches: to build rapport with the prospect, to capture a person's full attention, and to generate interest in the product.

*Presentation and Demonstration*
The salesperson now tells the product 'story' to the buyer, often following the AIDA formula of gaining attention, holding interest, arousing desire, and inspiring action. Companies have developed three different styles of sales presentation. The oldest is the canned approach, which uses memorized sales talk that covers the main points. The formulated approach identifies the buyer's needs and buying styles early on, and then uses an approach formulated for this type of buyer. It is not canned but follows a general plan. The need/satisfaction approach starts with a search for customers' real needs by encouraging them to do most of the talking. This approach calls for good listening and problem-solving skills.

According to experts, there are certain words that make listeners take notice. According to Brooks (2002), the 15 most persuasive sales words are: discover, money, guaranteed, love, proven, safe, own, best, good, easy, health, new, results, save and free.[6] Farber (2001) suggested that a salesperson needs to introduce a 'wow' factor: an intangible element that causes an emotional response in potential buyers, making them take a second look, draw in breath, and say, 'Wow, I have to buy that!'[7] There are two ways to create the wow factor. The first is by introducing a product that is unique. More often than not, this is impossible, so the second way is to generate enthusiasm, and deliver what is promised.

*Negotiation*
Much selling to the travel trade involves negotiation skills. For meeting planners and hotel groups, for example, the two parties need to reach agreement on the price and

other terms of the sale. The hotel salesperson will be seeking to win the order without making deep concessions that will hurt profitability. Although price is the most frequently negotiated issue, other factors may be taken into account, and numerous bargaining tools exist. Sales force members should be taught to negotiate using services or bundled services as the primary negotiating tool rather than price. For the hotel salesperson, negotiations should begin with rack rates, and price concessions should be given only when absolutely essential. Other negotiating tools, such as upgrades, airport pick-up, champagne in rooms, etc., should be employed. A hotel might package these amenities into bundles of services and brand them with names such as the Prestige Package, in order to entice buyers into making a booking. In the Snapshot below, food and beverage are an important part of the negotiation process, and sales managers are encouraged to get buyers to commit to a certain amount of food and beverage sales even if the event is three years away.

### Handling Objections and Questions

When most sales presentations are completed, prospects ask questions and raise one or more objections. Objections come in all forms, even through body language. Resistance can be psychological (e.g. preference for an established hotel) or logical (e.g. price). There are several effective ways to handle objections. One is to restate the objection and to prove diplomatically that it is not as important as it seems. Another is the 'agree and neutralize' tactic or the 'yes, but' approach. In this approach, sales representatives initially agree that a problem exists, but go on to show that the problem is not relevant or accurate. No matter which approach is used, objection must be met head-on.

### Closing the Sale

Closing means getting a sales prospect to agree with the objectives of the sales call, which normally implies making a definite purchase or reservation. Closing the sale can be the most important stage of the sales process, but many salespeople are not comfortable about asking for the order or do not recognize the opportune moment to wrap things up. A sales call without a close is unsuccessful, and every salesperson must ask for the business or at least some commitment to continue the dialogue. Knowing when and how to close are the keys to success. As with objections, this again requires careful attention to the prospect's words and body language. Closing techniques include actually asking for the order, offering to help the secretary write up the order, asking whether the buyer wants A or B, asking how the buyer would like to pay, or by indicating what the buyer will lose if the order is not placed immediately.

### Following Up after Closing

A salesperson's work is not finished until all the required steps and arrangements are made to deliver the promised services. In some cases, such as the organization of major association conventions or the planning of incentive travel trips, this 'delivery' work is extensive.

However, the follow-up is essential if the salesperson wants to ensure customer satisfaction and repeat business. 'Follow up or foul-up' is the slogan of many successful salespeople. It is often advisable to give buyers some kind of reassurance that they have made the right decision. This reduces their level of **cognitive dissonance** – a state of mind that many customers experience after making a purchase, in which they are unsure whether they have made a good or bad decision. An important part of post-sale activity also involves immediate follow-up after prospects or their clients have actually used the services. Many travel agents use this effectively by telephoning clients soon after their trips to find out what they liked and did not like.

---

**COGNITIVE DISSONANCE**
a state of mind that customers experience after making a purchase, in which they are unsure whether they have made a good or bad decision

---

## Snapshot

### Selling Beds at The Westin Edmonton

The Westin Edmonton is part of Starwood Hotels & Resorts. The 4.5-star hotel has 416 guest rooms and suites as well as 24,000 square feet of meeting and banquet space, and selling to groups and business travellers is the main focus of the sales team. 'Due to the strong economy in Alberta, we are experiencing a marked increase in leisure and business travel. We are also able to garner higher rates based on demand and our newly renovated guestrooms,' says JoAnn Kirkland, director of sales and marketing.

Site visits are an important part of the sales process. When a buyer visits the hotel, the team does everything possible to impress. For example, they may put pictures up of the prospective buyers everywhere back-of-house prior to the visit, so that all members of staff can give the buyer personal attention. Preparation for the site inspection is very important. By finding out beforehand everything they can about the company, exactly who they are and exactly what their needs are, the Westin sales team can then tailor the site inspection to those needs. However, not all selling takes place at the hotel. Sales managers travel three to four times a year to major Canadian cities for sales purposes, and occasionally to cities outside of Canada.

Sales planning is a key part of Kirkland's job. 'What we do is forecast the entire year, based on existing bookings and historical data, and then plot a grid for our sales managers. We then work out a minimum target for each period, and the sales managers will be armed with this knowledge when they meet with a buyer.' If a buyer or meeting planner is not prepared to pay the target room rate, then the sales personnel may negotiate by offering services such as free parking. Each sales manager has a room–night target and a revenue target. Food and beverage sales are also very important, and sales managers are encouraged to get buyers to commit to a certain amount of food and beverage even if the event is three years away.

Most of the training for the Westin sales team is web-based; it is live and interactive and contains about six different modules covering topics such as negotiating, handling objections and making presentations. Salespeople can take them on their own, and each module takes about two and a half hours. Kirkland can see how well they have performed on each module, so if she sees that one salesperson has not done well with presentations, she can offer extra training. Turnover is high among salespeople in the hotel industry, so the Starwood philosophy is to 'pay for performance' to try to keep high-quality salespeople. Sales managers can also win incentive trips to luxury resorts by meeting pre-determined targets. Other incentives used by Kirkland include team-building exercises outside the hotel (such as a game of golf), reward points and extra holidays. She also offers small cash incentives for good performance on the Starwood Mystery Shopping programme. In this programme, telephone calls are made by third-party researchers to various Starwood Hotels as well as to key competitors, and sales managers are scored on factors such as greeting, qualification of needs, presentation, handling of objections, attempts to close and professionalism.

To encourage repeat business there is a loyalty programme in place for meeting and event planners, called Starwood Preferred Planner®. This allows planners to earn one Starpoint® for every US$3 group revenue spent. These points can be redeemed and put toward future hotel room nights, as a credit toward their group master bill.

*Source*: JoAnn Kirkland, director of sales and marketing, the Westin Edmonton email communication, 24 November 2006.

## Sales Management

**Sales management** is the management of the sales force and personal selling efforts to achieve desired sales objectives. A sales manager has five key roles to play: recruiting salespeople, training them, motivating and rewarding them, sales planning and sales performance evaluation.

---

**SALES MANAGEMENT**
the management of the sales force and personal selling efforts to achieve desired sales
objectives

---

### Recruiting Salespeople

A sales manager's first job is to hire competent people to fill available positions. In tourism and hospitality, it is uncommon for field sales representatives to be hired without sales experience. The more established practice is for entry-level people to be order takers, who are eventually promoted to sales representative positions. Hiring salespeople from competitors and related outside organizations is also common. Research has shown that no one set of physical characteristics, mental abilities, and personality traits predicts sales success in every situation. Salespeople's success depends more on the actual tasks assigned to them and the environment in which they operate. Most customers say they want salespeople to be honest, reliable, knowledgeable and helpful. Companies should look for these traits when selecting candidates. Another approach is to look for traits common to the most successful salespeople in the company. A study of super-achievers found that super-sales performers exhibited the following traits: they were risk-taking, had a powerful sense of mission, had a problem-solving bent, cared about the customer, and engaged in careful planning (Garfield, 1986).[8]

### Training Salespeople

Sales training programmes are very important to the continuation of success in personal selling. In the Snapshot above, most of the sales training takes place via the internet, and many other companies are now offering their training online. Cunard Line, for example, created an online course in 2007 for travel agents to learn more about its upcoming ship, the *Queen Victoria*, through its Cunard Academy online sales training website. The course featured a detailed overview of the new ship, and then a short quiz.

### Motivating and Rewarding Salespeople

The majority of salespeople require encouragement and special incentives to work at their best level. This is especially true of field selling, which can be frustrating: sales reps usually work alone, their hours are irregular, and they are often away from home. Even without these factors, most people operate below capacity in the absence of special incentives, such as financial gain or social recognition. Sales managers therefore need to understand motivation theories and to provide financial and non-monetary incentives to keep sales-force motivation at its peak.

Financial incentives include salary and commissions, or fringe benefits such as paid vacations, insurance programmes and medical programmes. Often bonuses are given when predetermined volumes of sales and profits, or sales quotas, are achieved. In the tourism industry, free travel is a very important fringe benefit, especially for travel agency and airline staff. Non-monetary compensation and motivators are reward/recognition programmes and job advancement opportunities. Sales promotions can also be used to motivate a sales force. However, they tend to work best in achieving short-term objectives and are not advisable over the long term. In the Snapshot above, sales managers at the Westin Edmonton can win incentive trips to luxury resorts by meeting pre-determined targets. Other incentives used by the hotel include team-building exercises outside the hotel, reward points and extra holidays.

### Sales Planning

The heart of sales planning is the sales plan, usually prepared annually and containing a detailed description of personal selling objectives, sales activities and the sales budget (as in the Snapshot above). These selling objectives are frequently set as forecasts of unit or sales volumes or some other financial target derived from expected sales levels. This sales forecast is very useful to others outside the sales department and is a key planning tool for the entire organization. Expected sales levels influence the allocation of personnel and financial resources in many other departments. But the selling objectives may also be non-financial, such as the number of sales calls, new sales prospects converted to customers, or the number of inquiries answered successfully.

The sales department budgets are another part of the sales plan. Typically these will include the sales forecast, the selling expense budget, the sales administration budget, and the advertising and promotion budget. Given the relatively high cost of personal selling, this budget plays a key role in planning and controlling the sales effort. Finally, the sales plan will include the assignment of sales territories and quotas. **Sales quotas** are performance targets set periodically for individual sales representatives, branch offices or regions. They help sales managers motivate, supervise, control and evaluate sales personnel. The sales manager is likely to use a combination of past territory performance and market indices to allocate quotas for each territory.

---

**SALES QUOTAS**

performance targets set periodically for individual sales representatives, branch offices or regions

---

*Evaluating Sales Performance*

The final function of sales management is the measurement and evaluation of sales performance. 'Sales analysis' is the term used most frequently for the evaluation of performance. This analysis can be done by considering total sales volume or by looking at sales by territory or customer groups. One of the most important methods of evaluation is to judge actual results against sales forecasts and budgets.

## Direct Marketing and Direct Response Advertising

**Direct marketing** is a marketing system, fully controlled by the marketer, that develops products, promotes them directly to the final consumer through a variety of media options, accepts direct orders from customers, and distributes products directly to the consumer. It is rapidly becoming a vital component of the integrated marketing communications mix. In the UK, for example, direct marketing grew 15.3 per cent in 2005 to be worth £17.17 billion (Direct Marketing Report, 2006).[9] Direct marketing has increased in popularity as businesses have come to place more importance on customer satisfaction and repeat purchase. It makes use of databases, which allow precision targeting and personalization, thus helping companies to build continuing and enriching relationships with customers. There are eight key advantages of direct marketing, which are listed in Table 9.1.

---

**DIRECT MARKETING**

a marketing system, fully controlled by the marketer, that develops products, promotes them directly to the final consumer through a variety of media options, accepts direct orders from customers, and distributes products directly to the consumer

---

**Table 9.1**  The Key Advantages of Direct Marketing

| | | |
|---|---|---|
| 1. | Precision targeting | Direct marketing is aimed at a specific individual. It provides opportunities to target not only general groups of potential buyers but specific buyers individually. |
| 2. | Personalization | Direct marketing provides an opportunity to personalize messages and build stronger links between the company and the consumer. It enables the sender to use names, and thus to target promotions to the individual. |
| 3. | Flexibility | Not only can the contents of each direct marketing message be changed to suit the specific requirements of each participant, but the message can also be delivered to specific geographic locations. |
| 4. | Privacy | Offers made by direct marketing methods are not readily visible to competitors. Direct marketing does not broadcast an organization's competitive strategy as widely as mass communication advertising. |
| 5. | Measurability | A major advantage of direct marketing is the ability it gives a company to measure the effectiveness of various response fulfilment packages sent out to prospects, in terms of converting inquiries into sales, costs per booking, response by market segments, and so on. |
| 6. | Low cost | Direct marketing has the advantage of generally lower costs per transaction than other forms of communication. |
| 7. | Detailed knowledge | Direct marketing methods allow the gathering of valuable consumer information – not only names and addresses, but also lifestyle information and purchasing behaviour. |
| 8. | Fast or immediate | Because of the format of direct marketing, offers can be made quickly – and can be quickly accepted. This has become more applicable recently with the advent of the internet. |

These advantages of direct marketing are fundamental in their implications for achieving more cost-effective marketing. They are especially useful to businesses that are too small to engage in large-scale advertising or to achieve cost-effective access through retail distribution channels. It is worth emphasizing that many of the benefits derive from the use of new information technology that was not available to earlier generations of marketing managers. Bearing in mind that most large tourism and hospitality businesses, such as hotels, car rental companies and scheduled airlines, have a large proportion of frequent-repeat customers that are vital to their profitability, the advantages of direct marketing in this industry cannot be underestimated. It is no coincidence that hotel groups and airlines have been competing ever more strenuously in recent years to bind their loyal customers to them with a wide variety of membership or club schemes, frequent traveller rewards, and other 'special relationship' arrangements for their key accounts.

**Direct response advertising** is one segment of the direct-marketing industry, and it plays a major role in influencing consumer purchase patterns. It can be defined as advertising through any medium, designed to generate a response by any means that is measurable (e.g. mail, television, telephone, fax or internet). If traditional mass media are used, the message will include a toll-free telephone number, mailing address or website address where more information can be obtained. The major forms of direct response advertising are direct mail, telemarketing, the internet and direct response television (DRTV). Figure 9.4 presents some of the communication strategies of the four main forms of direct response advertising, discussed below.

---

**DIRECT RESPONSE ADVERTISING**

advertising through any medium, designed to generate a response by any means that is measurable (e.g., mail, television, telephone, fax or internet)

---

## Direct Mail

**Direct mail**, in which an offer is sent to a prospective customer by mail, is by far the most common form of direct response advertising. The use of mail is widespread because it is possible to personalize the message (the name can be included in the mailing), it can convey lengthy messages (printed sales messages can be sent with reply cards or contracts that can be returned by prospects), and can provide a high degree of geographic coverage economically (the mailing can be distributed to designated postal codes). There are numerous options available to companies wishing to use direct mail – examples include sales letters, leaflets and flyers, folders, brochures, DVDs and CD-ROMs.

---

**DIRECT MAIL**

a type of direct response advertising in which an offer is sent to a prospective customer by mail

---

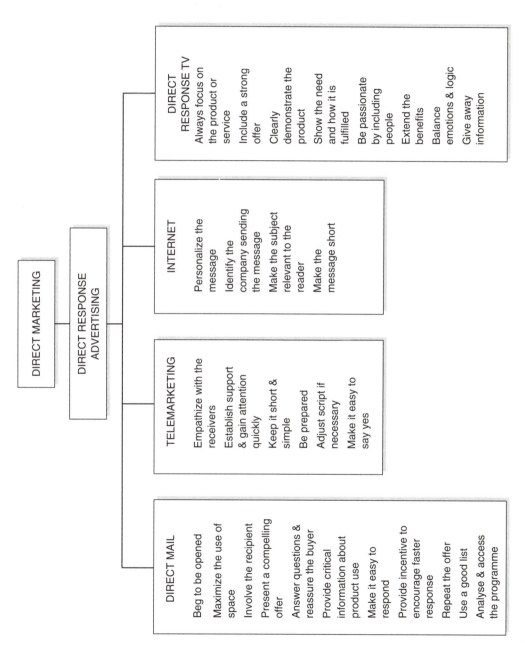

**Figure 9.4** Strategic Considerations for the Major Forms of Direct Response Advertising

Essentially, an organization has the option of using **solo direct mail** – delivering a mail piece by itself and absorbing the costs associated with such a mailing (as in the postcard campaign highlighted in the Global Spotlight), or **co-operative direct mail** – delivering an offer as part of a package that includes offers from other companies.

---

**SOLO DIRECT MAIL**
a direct mail piece delivered by a single company

---

**CO-OPERATIVE DIRECT MAIL**
a direct mail offer delivered as part of a package that includes offers from other companies

---

The three basic steps involved in direct mail marketing are obtaining a proper prospect list, conceiving and producing the mail piece, and distributing the final version. However, the first step is the backbone of the entire campaign. Both the accuracy and definition of the list can have a significant bearing on the success or failure of a campaign. Companies recognize that it costs five to seven times as much to acquire a new customer as it does to keep an existing one, so they compile databases to keep track of existing customers and form relationships with them through mail and by electronic means.

Lists are secured from internal and external sources. There is no better prospect than a current customer, so a company's internal database must be monitored and updated routinely. In direct mail terms, an internal customer list is referred to as a 'house list'. As an alternative, companies can take steps to form lists of potential customers. Such customers are referred to as 'prospects'. A list broker can assist in finding these prospects – those that perhaps mirror the demographic and psychographic profile of existing customers. The use that many hotels and airlines make, for example, of American Express or other credit card company membership databases illustrates the value of third-party address lists. Such lists can usually be accessed at a cost per 1,000 names. A company can also purchase a response list, which is a list of proven mail-order buyers, or a circulation list, which is a magazine subscription list. The Global Spotlight below describes a particularly innovative direct mail campaign that proved to be extremely successful for one Canadian tour operator.

## Global Spotlight

### Dennis Campbell's Postcard Campaign

At the age of 18, Dennis Campbell believed he could build a successful tourism business based on Nova Scotia's Scottish history and heritage. To do this he registered a company in 1987 called Halifax City Guide Services and tagged it 'The Company With The Kilts'. By 1995, the company – now called Ambassatours Gray Line – was grossing

$3.5 million and had become the number one tour operator in Atlantic Canada after merging with Atlantic Tours. These days, the Atlantic Tours product is the company's main revenue generator, selling the four Atlantic Provinces as a coach destination to customers all over the world. To do this, Campbell, who is president of the company, markets through direct mail, the trade and aggressive web marketing, aims primarily at clients in Canada, the United States, the UK, Germany, Australia and New Zealand, and has a marketing budget of $400,000.

However, in building his business in the early days, Campbell's best idea was the least expensive one. Called the 'postcard campaign' by Campbell, it was simple, creative, and possessed the boldness that only someone with nothing to lose would dare. Campbell was trying to attract the attention of his 'dream client list'. A dream client was a Holland America, a Carnival Cruise Line, a Cunard Cruise Line, a Tauck Tours – 'Someone who has the potential to give us a couple hundred thousand dollars' worth of business,' said Campbell. These companies were at the conventions, but Campbell was aware that 'they were practically a fortress. They don't want to talk to you because they get bombarded – our dream client is everyone's dream client.' He realized that mailing or phoning was not going to work, so he decided to start sending them postcards until he had their attention. 'I sent one every month, and I wrote out for each month what the message would be.'

He started with the cruise lines. He obtained the list of these lines and started writing postcards. Using Paul Stouffer at Holland America, for example, his first postcard read, 'Dear Paul, We are a shore excursion company that provides kilted guides, bagpipers, step dancers and all kinds of neat things.' The next month's read 'Dear Paul, Hope you got our postcard last month. We would like you to consider using us.' The third month's read, 'Dear Paul, We're not going to stop sending you postcards until we have your business.' The next postcard read, 'Dear Paul. Don't mean to sound pushy like the last postcard, but we really want your business.'

After bombarding Holland America's Seattle offices with postcards, Campbell finally encountered his target – Paul Stouffer, the head of shore excursions for the cruise lines – at a Miami trade show. When he found him, he approached him and said, 'Paul Stouffer? Dennis Campbell. Would you like a postcard?' Apparently, Paul laughed and said, 'Dennis Campbell! Dennis, listen, I'll make you a deal. Stop sending me those damn postcards and I'll give you our business.' The same thing happened with Cunard Cruise Lines. When Campbell called Cunard Cruise Lines and said, 'It's Dennis Campbell, I'm going to be down in New York, can I meet with you?' The response of the woman on the phone was, 'Dennis Campbell, I'd like anything more than a postcard! I'd love to meet with you!'

The postcard mailing worked with Carnival, Cunard, Holland America, Clipper, Renaissance and Silver Seas. In the summer cruise seasons of 1994–1995, the unique campaign, which used about 200 nine-cent handwritten postcards and stamps, brought in $600,000 in sales from some of the world's leading cruise lines! The value of this simple but persistent campaign over many years has generated literally many millions of dollars in sales. A key part of the campaign was Campbell's insistence that each card be handwritten with a short, simple but consistent message so as not to lose its effect. He even asked his mother to write them, as she had much nicer handwriting than he did!

Ambassatours Gray Line now owns the following group of companies: Atlantic Tours Limited, Nova Tours, Absolute Charters, Gray Line of Nova Scotia, Gray Line of New Brunswick and Gray Line of Prince Edward Island. It is now not only the largest tour operator in Atlantic Canada but also the largest coach tour operator, having grown from owning 14 buses in 2003 to 53 buses in 2007. In 2006, the company had 45 year-round staff and just over 200 seasonal staff, with revenues in excess of $10.5 million. The company still uses postcard campaigns today as one of its most effective ways to get incremental business.

The company is now using technology to build on this persistent targeted approach by sending custom-designed, personalized handwritten cards and postcards through the web with www.sendoutcards.com. Ambassatours Gray Line now sends through the web a personalized thank you card to each and every customer who has travelled on one of their multi-day tour packages. This personal touch is paying off. According to Dennis Campbell, 'It's cheap, very cool and it works – awesome! Personalized direct marketing at its finest.'

*Source*: Lynch, A. (1996) 'Ambassatours: heritage drag pays off', in A. Lynch (Ed.) *Sweat Equity: Atlantic Canada's New Entrepreneurs*. 181–194. Halifax: Nimbus; Dennis Campbell, personal communication on 12 March 2007.

## Telemarketing

A form of direct marketing that combines aspects of advertising, marketing research and personal sales, **telemarketing** uses the telephone to reach customers or prospective customers. Telemarketing developed massively in the 1990s through the combination of technology-led development of consumer databases, telephone communications and the creation of call centres. A **call centre** is a central operation from which a company operates its inbound and outbound telemarketing programmes. Inbound telemarketing refers to the reception of calls by the order desk, customer inquiry and direct response calls often generated through the use of toll-free numbers. Outbound telemarketing, on the other hand, refers to calls that a company makes to customers to develop new accounts, generate sales leads and even close a sale.

> **TELEMARKETING**
> using the telephone to reach customers or prospective customers

> **CALL CENTRE**
> a central operation from which a company operates its inbound and outbound telemarketing programmes

The primary advantage of telemarketing is that it is much cheaper to complete a sale this way than via techniques as face-to-face sales calls or mass advertising. However, for this method to be effective, proper training and preparation of telemarketing representatives needs to be as comprehensive as it is for personal selling. Planning the message is as important as the medium itself. A drawback to telemarketing is the fact that consumers react negatively to it. The majority of the public consider telemarketing calls unwelcome and intrusive, and they are ranked as one of the least desirable sales techniques. Despite this, organizations believe that its advantages, such as call reach and frequency and cost efficiency, outweigh the disadvantages.

## Internet

The role of the internet in direct response advertising is discussed in Chapter 10. Needless to say, direct email marketing, often eliciting direct email response, is one of the most promising applications of online advertising. The Global Spotlight above showed how Atlantic Tours is using technology to build on its persistent targeted approach by sending custom-designed, personalized handwritten cards and postcards through the web.

## Direct Response Television

Direct response television is one of the fastest-growing segments of the direct response industry. Advertisers are attracted to this medium because it allows them to track response rates. Today, savvy advertisers like American Express do very little advertising without a built-in response mechanism that allows them to judge results. There are essentially three forms of direct response television: 60-second (or longer) commercials that typically appear on cable channels, infomercials, and direct-home shopping channels. In all cases, the use of toll-free telephone numbers and credit cards make the purchase more convenient for the viewer.

Cable television lends itself to direct response because the medium is more tightly targeted to particular interests. The Shopping Channel (TSC), for example, has annual sales of US$150 million, reaching millions of households. Direct response television also makes good use of the infomercial format. An **infomercial** is a commercial, usually 30 minutes long, that presents in great detail the benefits of a product or service. Criticized in the past for being exclusively 'get-rich-quick' concepts, infomercials are now being created that are highly informative and well produced, although tourism and hospitality organizations have been slow to adopt this form of direct response advertising.

---

**INFOMERCIAL**
a commercial, usually 30 minutes long, that presents in great detail the benefits of a product or service on the television

---

Digital television is likely to have a huge impact on the sale of tourism products and services, even though interactive television sets with computer capabilities are still a novelty. Digital television offers consumers travel services via digital travel agents or online tour operators, allowing them to make an immediate booking for the destination or tour featured on the television screen. This is an exceptionally effective sales tool. Many travel agents believe that digital television will be a greater threat to business than the internet, precisely because it is an incredibly interactive medium facilitated by a very familiar tool – the television remote control. In 2004, tourist body VisitLondon launched a 24-hour digital TV channel to promote the capital as a tourist destination. London TV appears on SkyDigital and provides reports and features on topics such as film, theatre, shopping and tourist sites. Digital specialist Enteraction TV, the company behind Thomas Cook TV, runs the channel and produces content. Martine Ainsworth-Wells, general manager for marketing at VisitLondon, said the decision to launch the channel was made because it was more cost effective than ploughing money into advertising (Sweney, 2004).[10]

## Word of Mouth

**Word of mouth** is communication about products and services between people who are perceived to have no vested interest in promoting them (Silverman, 2001).[11] It is a communication tool that works particularly well for the tourism and hospitality industry, and is worthy of special attention. Recommendations or advice from friends, relatives, peers and influential persons are without doubt one of the most powerful communications media. Word of mouth can be controlled only to a degree, but it must nevertheless be a priority for tourism businesses, and it is indeed used in a variety of sectors of tourism.

> **WORD OF MOUTH**
> communication about products and services between people who are perceived to have no vested interest in promoting them

Word-of-mouth communications can be conversations or just one-way testimonials. They can be live or canned. They can be conveyed in person, by telephone, by email, via a listserv group, or by any other means of communication. They can be one to one, one to many (broadcasts), or group discussions. The essential element is that they are from or among people who are perceived to have little commercial vested interest in persuading someone else to use a particular product and therefore no incentive to distort the truth in favour of it. In contrast, advertising is the communication of a message that is chosen, designed and worded by the seller of the product, in a medium that is owned or rented. A sales message is a 'company line' delivered by a representative of the company. On the other hand, word of mouth is originated by a third party and transmitted spontaneously in a way that is independent of the producer or seller, and can therefore have a high level of credibility.

Word of mouth is a communication tool that works well for the tourism and hospitality industry. In his recent book, *The Anatomy of Buzz*, Emanuel Rosen (2000) takes a substantive look at creating word-of-mouth excitement about a product.[12] Rosen suggests that the best starting points are 'hubs', also known as influencers and opinion leaders. Some hubs are obvious, such as regional and national media outlets. For instance, if a local talk-show host discusses a restaurant on Monday, it will probably be full on Tuesday. Oprah Winfrey's 'book club' is an example of this phenomenon. Other hubs are less obvious. They include fashion leaders in junior high schools (social leaders who made skinny scooters popular), gurus on college campuses (technical leaders who spread the word via the internet), and people on the boards of local charities (community leaders who attend many social functions). The best hubs also span networks, in addition to influencing people in their own network. The leapfrogging of word of mouth from one network to another accelerates the rate of beneficial buzz.

Often generated within the hive of the internet, 'buzz' has become essential to a product's success in today's fast-paced business environment. As Rosen (a former marketing executive for Niles Software) explains, in pre-internet days a new product would appear in stores, consumers would buy it or not, and the company would then take however long it wished to evaluate the launch. Today, however, consumers immediately voice their views – on blogs, message boards, review sites, company sites, complaint sites, via email, or on their own websites – and so have a strong and immediate influence on whether a launch succeeds.

Rosen points out that hubs are where you find them. Sometimes they come to you. People who attend specialized conferences are often hubs for their organizations. Other times, you have to seek them out. People who are looked up to by others as experts and who talk to a lot of people are good prospects. People who are known by friends and colleagues as being interested in cuisine and fine wine are considered experts whose opinions are sought when a new restaurant opens. Certain tourist segments can be more influential than others. For example, gay tourists, who attend events like the Gay Games, are a minority of consumers, but they tend to be 'hyperconsumers' who not only consume more but also influence the purchases of their gay and straight friends and colleagues, thus providing vital word-of-mouth endorsements for destinations, products, brands and companies (Pritchard et al., 1998).[13] Word of mouth is also considered to be the main force of influence in the backpacker market (Australian Tourist Commission, 2003).[14]

Silverman (2001) suggests that word of mouth is powerful for ten key reasons.[15]

1. **It has independent credibility.** A decision-maker is more likely to get the whole, undistorted truth from an independent third party than from someone who has a vested interest in promoting the company's point of view. It is this unique credibility that gives word of mouth much of its power. So if you are thinking about backpacking around Australia, you are more likely to take advice from friends who have been there than from a travel agent.
2. **It delivers experience.** Lack of positive experience with a product or service is usually the single greatest factor holding it back from greater and faster acceptance. Again, hearing about other backpackers' experiences will act as the accelerator or the brake on booking your backpacking holiday.
3. **It is more relevant and complete.** Word of mouth is 'live', not canned like most company communication. When your friend tells you about a country she thinks you would like, she is telling you because she thinks that you – not some anonymous stranger – would like it. She wouldn't tell you about it if she thought you weren't interested in going.
4. **It is the most honest medium.** Because it is custom-tailored, and because people participating in it are independent of the company, it is the most honest medium. And

customers know it. Advertising and salespeople can be biased and not fully truthful. The inherent honesty of word of mouth further adds to its credibility.

5.  **It is customer-driven.** Closely related to the two reasons given above, word of mouth is the most customer-driven of all communications channels. Customers determine whom they will talk to, what they will ask, and whether they will continue to listen or politely change the subject.

6.  **It feeds on itself.** Word of mouth tends to breed and is self-generating. If ten people have ten experiences each while backpacking around Australia, that's one hundred direct experiences. If they each tell ten people, that's an additional 1,000 (indirect) experiences, which can be just as powerful as the direct ones. It doesn't take long for everyone to hear about the wonders of Australia, often several times each, which provides additional confirmation (e.g. 'everybody's talking about it').

7.  **It has expert power.** The 'hubs' referred to earlier have one overriding attribute that gives them their influence: trust. People trust them to filter, distil, and objectively evaluate an overwhelming amount of information, make sense of it, and present it in a recommendation that is most likely to be right. Tiers of experts and influencers tend to initiate word of mouth, sustain it, give it even more credibility, and supply the initial 'bang' that can start the chain reaction of word of mouth.

8.  **Influencers like to influence.** One of the reasons that the initial stages of word of mouth are sustained and can spread so rapidly is that influencers like to influence. That's one of the reasons that they are influencers. If they didn't enjoy the process, they would keep their mouths shut and their keyboards still.

9.  **It saves time and money.** Another attribute of word of mouth is that it can be extremely efficient. If you want to visit a destination that you don't know too much about, the best way is often to find a few people who have either been there or collected information about the place, and learn from them what they have found out.

10. **It is an illusory force.** Word of mouth is an invisible, illusory force (sometimes even called 'underground' communication, or 'the grapevine', as well as 'the buzz'). A company can gain competitive advantage by making competitors think that increased sales are due to active promotional efforts, so the illusion is that the advertising, or the sales message, or the mailing caused the effects. In fact, many products or services succeed despite the marketing supporting them, for reasons other than the positioning of the product or the most emphasized benefits.

## Chapter Summary

Public relations includes all the activities that a tourism or hospitality organization uses to maintain or improve its relationship with other organizations or individuals.

The functions of the PR department include establishing corporate identity, government relations, crisis management, internal communications, customer relations and marketing publicity.

The main techniques used in public relations are press releases and press conferences, feature stories, travel exhibitions and road shows, hosting and sponsoring events, sponsoring causes, publications, winning or sponsoring awards, celebrity visits and product placement.

Personal selling is a personalized form of communication that involves a seller presenting the features and benefits of a product or a service to a buyer for the purpose of making a sale.

In the tourism and hospitality industry, personal selling plays a number of important roles: gathering marketing intelligence, locating and maintaining customers, promoting to the travel trade, generating sales at point of purchase, relationship marketing, and providing detailed and up-to-date information to the travel trade.

Objectives of personal selling include achieving sales volume, up-selling and second-chance selling, market share or market penetration, and product-specific objectives.

The sales process consists of seven steps: prospecting and qualifying, pre-planning, presentation and demonstration, negotiation, handling objections and questions, closing the sale and following up after closing.

A sales manager has three key roles to play. The first is to recruit salespeople, the second is to train them, and the third is to motivate and reward them.

There are eight key advantages of direct marketing: precision targeting, personalization, flexibility, privacy, measurability, low cost, detailed knowledge of consumers, and fast or immediate response.

Direct response advertising is one segment of the direct-marketing industry, and it plays a major role in influencing consumer purchase patterns. It can be defined as advertising through any medium, designed to generate a response by any means that is measurable (e.g. mail, television, telephone, fax or internet).

Word of mouth is communication about products and services between people who are perceived to have no vested interest in promoting them, in a medium perceived to be independent of the relevant companies.

## Key Terms

call centre, p. 318
cause-related marketing, p. 300
cognitive dissonance, p. 309
co-operative direct mail, p. 316
cross-selling, p. 305
direct mail, p. 314
direct marketing, p. 312
direct response advertising, p. 314

## Discussion Questions and Exercises

1. How important are public relations and publicity to tourism and hospitality organizations? Give examples to support your answer.
2. You have just won a tourism award and would like to publicize your achievements. Write a press release for the local newspaper in an attempt to get them to run a story relating to your win.
3. Which do you think is the most important step in the sales process? Explain your answer.
4. Think of some recent examples when someone has attempted to up-sell or cross-sell a product to you. Explain why they succeeded or failed. What are the disadvantages of these selling techniques?
5. Which direct response advertising technique do you think would be most effective for a growing ski resort attempting to attract new skiers?
6. The chapter talks mainly about the advantages of direct marketing. But what, in your opinion, are the disadvantages of the various tools mentioned?
7. Why is it, do you think, that word of mouth is the most neglected promotional tool in the marketplace?

# Puerto Rico Targets Business Travellers

Puerto Rico convention centre

An aggressive, international integrated marketing campaign culminated in 2005 in the grand opening of the US $415m Puerto Rico Convention Centre. The marketing plan was created and implemented by the Convention Bureau, a non-profit, partially government-funded body, with an association of members from the hotel, property and tourism services industries. Its mandate was to promote and package the huge convention centre in conjunction with the resort facilities of Puerto Rico as a world class business tourism destination.

Gloribel Wachtel, Marketing Director for the Convention Bureau, deems printed brochures her best marketing tool and the Bureau spends much time, money and creative thought on its leaflets, annual fiscal reports, presentation material, ads and promotional postcards. Tactics over the past three years have included a dedicated website (www.meetpuertorico.com), direct mail, e-marketing, trade shows, site inspections, sales calls, special events including golf tournaments, client functions, orientations and reviews, publications, e-newsletters as well as printed news bulletins, media relations and catalogues. The Bureau has been responsible for inaugurating data mining and strategic research with the aid of professional consultants and for setting up strategic partnerships within the industry and the community at large. It also has a destination feedback programme to monitor service quality and has set up various sponsorships to help encourage groups that are more financially challenged.

However, the Puerto Rico Convention Centre is not positioning itself cheaply. Ms Wachtel explains, 'One of the main challenges we face as a meetings destination is that it can be more costly to meet here than many other US mainland and Caribbean destinations. The truth is that we are comparable in cost to many large US cities. We offer a world-class meeting destination with top hotel brand names, a high level of service and a full-range of amenities sought out by business travellers. In addition, we have a modern communications infrastructure, where cell phones work, high-speed Internet and wireless access is easily accessible, and business travellers can count on being able to stay in touch with the home office in a seamless fashion. In that way, you can't compare us to other destinations in the region.' Higher prices are also offset by the ease of travel to and from the US, since Americans don't require visas or passports to visit Puerto Rico. The Bureau is also working closely with air services to develop more regular direct flights from all over North America. Plus, of course, having English as the second language and the US dollar as currency can be a plus for Americans. The Bureau uses all these selling features in its promotional material – even the voltage is used to encourage visitors.

In January 2004 the Convention Bureau was accepted as a permanent member of the BestCities Alliance, the world's first (and only) convention bureau global alliance, which includes Cape Town, Copenhagen, Dubai, Edinburgh, Melbourne, Singapore and Vancouver. The Puerto Rico Bureau differentiates itself from its competition with a combination of reliable good weather, high technological standards, a packaged tourism/business service and a colourful, ethnically rich culture and history: 'Our main selling feature is the weather because basically you can come here year round. Then, with the beautiful beaches, and having regular good weather, you can do events outside. We have the 400-year-old fortified city here so that's something very different from other destinations. And we are technologically advanced; we provide more infrastructure than many other islands in the Caribbean. There are upper-level facilities here that are as good as at your own house or your own city. So, we package it that way. Good transportation helps, too, and we have also some major attractions on the island to visit alongside a business trip, like the caves and the rainforest which are a little bit different than other cities or destinations,' says Ms Wachtel.

Strategic priorities for the 2005–06 fiscal year included branding of the Puerto Rico Convention Bureau and also developing an integrated high-tech team with employee retention and motivation being top of the list. Ms Wachtel outlines, 'Right now our objective is to continue spreading the word that the centre is finally open, because it is something we have been talking about for ten years. Two dedicated salespersons from the Bureau are trying to sell it and get it full. But we all sell it because part of our contract is to include the centre in everything that the Bureau is doing. So pretty much every time we make a presentation we mention the centre. The complete Bureau has around 45 to 48 employees. And also the government does its part; it has its economic development company which is in charge of the convention centre. It is also mentioned at the airports and other government-run institutions. We have a very close working relationship with not only the Puerto Rico Tourism Company, but with the Convention Center District Authority and the Puerto Rico Hotel & Tourism Association, as we are all part of the destination team to sell and market Puerto Rico from our different perspectives. There is, of course, some variation in our efforts and marketing investment.'

Trade shows are an important tool in spreading the word about the vast new Convention Centre, which covers 580,000 gross square feet of prime real estate in the downtown area of Isla Grande in San Juan. The Bureau attended the Chicago trade fair in September 2005 where numerous potential clients were interested in revisiting Puerto Rico now that it has such an upbeat facility. Conventions tend to move location regularly in order to maintain interest amongst delegates, but after five or six years or so, event planners can be attracted back to a destination – especially if it has improved facilities and infrastructure.

Hosting meeting planners, attending trade shows, and advertising in news and industry media has been backed up by client events. So far pharmaceutical and medical companies plus insurance and banking have been the main groups attracted to the Convention Centre. But sports and music are both markets which the Bureau intends to corner. Wachtel says, 'We are trying to educate people that the convention centre is suitable for sporting events, both amateur and professional. There's one actual trade show for these sporting events called TEAM that we are participating in for promoting destinations and we want to bring it here. Last year they did it in Fort Lauderdale in October. We also do entertainment; for example the music awards, MTV etc.'

Once a group or event planner has decided to hold a conference or show at the Convention Centre, the Bureau provides an array of free services. It will co-ordinate hotels and suppliers and provide links with its 500 local association members for all back-up services. It also updates planners on local attractions, events, festivals and entertainments. It will educate the planners and their clients in person by scheduling, accompanying and transporting personnel to meeting sites and areas and providing property inspections. The Bureau will also offer creative ideas, marketing expertise and its professionally produced promotional materials to help market the event. Plus the Bureau has a broad regional sales network with offices throughout America and Canada and one in Madrid.

*Source*: Personal interview with Gloribel Wachtel, marketing director, Puerto Rico Convention Bureau.

**Case Study**

## Questions

1.  What particular challenges face the marketers of convention centres (as opposed to marketing direct to consumers)?
2.  How would you describe the target market of the Puerto Rico Convention Bureau?

3. Critically analyse the marketing mix currently used by the Puerto Rico Convention Bureau. Are there some communications tools you would put more or less emphasis on?
4. Take a look at the websites of both the Convention Bureau and Puerto Rico Tourism Company. Would you say that they are positioning themselves as a world-class business tourism destination?

## Websites

| | |
|---|---|
| www.atlantictours.com | Atlantic Tours |
| www.rockymountaineer.com | Rocky Mountaineer |
| www.meetpuertorico.com | Puerto Rico Convention Bureau |
| www.magicalkenya.com | Kenyan Tourism Board official website |
| www.atlantis.com | Atlantis Resort |
| www.thewestinedmonton.com | The Westin Edmonton |
| www.gotopuertorico.com | Puerto Rico Tourism Company |
| www.ambassatours.com | Ambassatours Gray line |

## References

1  Morrison, A. M. (2002) *Hospitality and Travel Marketing* (3rd ed.). Albany, NY: Delmar Thomson Learning.
2  Britten, N. (2006) 'Is it a bard? Is it a plane? No, it's Shakespeare's flying circus', *The Daily Telegraph*, 3.
3  Anon. (8 August 2006) 'London 2012 organizers expect record sponsorship', *Guardian Sport*, 2.
4  Perri, L. (28 April 2006) 'Celebrating 75 years on top', *USA Today*, 4D.
5  Anon. (3 November 2005) 'Tree-hugger Sting takes "worst" polluting airline's sponsorship', *The Independent*, 10.
6  Brooks, B. (June 2002) 'Prospecting: how to stay in the mind of your prospect and win', *Home Business*, 40, 42.
7  Farber, B. (2001) 'That's a shocker', *HSMM Marketing Review*, Fall/Winter, 85–86.
8  Garfield, C. (1986) *Peak Performers: The New Heroes of American Business*. New York: Avon.
9  Direct Marketing Report (1 October 2006) Key Note Publications, retrieved from www.marketresearch.com.
10  Sweney, M. (11 March 2004) 'VisitLondon plans digital TV channel', *Marketing*, 6.
11  Silverman, G. (September 2001) 'The power of word of mouth', *Direct Marketing*, 64(5), 47–63.
12  Rosen, E. (2000). *The Anatomy of Buzz: How to Create Word of Mouth Marketing*. New York: Doubleday Currency.
13  Pritchard, A., Morgan, N. J., Sedgley, D. and Jenkins, A. (1998) 'Reaching out to the gay tourist', *Tourism Management*, 19(3), 273–282.
14  Australian Tourist Commission. (2003) 'Australia a popular destination for backpackers', retrieved from www.australia.com.
15  Silverman, G. (September 2001) 'The power of word of mouth', *Direct Marketing*, 64(5), 47–63.

# 10

## INTERNET MARKETING

### Travel Blogs

Forget the brochures, and even destination websites. The latest, most up-to-date travel tips, stories and experiences are now available as travel 'blogs' (a corruption of the phrase web logs). Blogs are part of the latest trend in travel and destination decision-making, giving the consumer a credible guide to tourism 'dos' and 'don'ts' without the consumer having to worry about advertising exaggerations. Created by travellers, blogs are helping the tourist to become informed before travelling, taking the anxiety out of booking independent trips and also aiding with planning itineraries, booking accommodation and transportation options. They can also be very detailed – for example, even directing the consumer to the right meal choices in specific restaurants on the best nights – and are frequently modified and updated. The authors, or bloggers, are becoming *de facto* watchdogs and self-proclaimed experts in specific fields.

Websites such as MySpace, LinkedIn and Friendster have inspired wild popularity amongst millions of internet users who use them to find friends, professional contacts and also as a forum for their own unvarnished opinions. With the new travel blogs, tourists can quickly access information, up-to-date prices, weather reports, etc., tapping into the combined experiences of the travelling public free of charge and at any time of the night or day, rather than having to sift through advertising material and sort the truth from the promotional chaff. Tripadvisor (www.tripadvisor.com) is a site that collects user testimonials on hotels and attractions worldwide, gearing itself towards vacationers rather than backpackers, and providing both glowing and scathing reports arbitrarily. The number of travel-oriented sites is growing, ranging from Hotel.chatter.com which focuses specifically on boutique hotels and CruiseDiva.com which reports on the cruise industry, to more narrow focuses such as pesticide.hu which calls itself 'the daily dish of cosmopolitan Budapest'.

Carnival Connections, a blog platform created for passengers by Carnival Cruises

Already, sites are becoming more adventurous, linking photo albums to written pieces and also connecting bloggers to one another based on compatible travel interests and destinations. In theory one blog surfer could actually meet up with an assiduous blog writer during a trip, having exchanged notes on their similar travel experiences. Real Travel (realtravel.com) and TravelPod (travelpod.com) both fulfil this social purpose, catering primarily to adventure travellers. Also 43places.com links like-minded tourists by asking them to list the 43 places they would most like to visit.

Blogs inspire much dialogue on the internet, as opinions rarely go unanswered. Criticisms from readers are often levelled at authors regarding reliability of information, alternative experiences, spelling, grammar and writing ability. The author can then choose whether the comments are included alongside the original. Many of the blogging websites are relatively ad-free and the only guideline for contributors is that their work should be original. Newspaper travel guides are even giving editorial space to updated, recent blogs as a credible form of travel journalism.

Prompted by the success and popularity of blogs, some tourism operations have jumped on the internet bandwagon, eschewing conventional advertising for this more modern marketing tool. Carnival Cruise Lines created CarnivalConnections.com in early 2006 to provide a platform for cruise passengers to hook up with former shipmates, plan future sea trips together and share experiences and opinions on cruise destinations and facilities. By mid-2006 this site had attracted 13,000 registered users, of which 2,000 had already planned further trips with Carnival's 22 ships. These consumers were predicted to bring in around US$1.6 million in revenue, which makes the relatively small investment a very high-yielding marketing strategy for Carnival. According to the Miami-based cruise company's director of internet and database marketing, Diana Rodriguez-Velasquez, there is no editing of subscribers' articles – 'It doesn't have the make-up brush that the company would put on copy.' Although initially this made marketers nervous regarding adverse comments, it seems that for every negative experience or opinion, there are many more positive reports in reply, giving an all-round favourable flavour to this indirect form of advertising. Moreover, it provides valuable consumer opinion, giving marketers immediate market research and feedback for free.

Wikitravel (www.wikitravel.org) is a website dedicated to amassing the collective wisdom of world travellers, one article at a time, with *carte blanche* as to content. Wayfaring (www.wayfaring.com) has taken Google maps a stage further by allowing subscribers to add anything from national guides to neighbourhood tours to their favourite watering holes. Also, Expedia and Yahoo! Travel have employed blogs to publicize their travel companies. Expedia is allowing consumers to compile itineraries of local attractions with personal reviews to complement its flights, hotels and car rental facilities. It is cashing in on this by selling tickets in advance to recommended attractions alongside its regular travel services. Yahoo has gone a step further by allowing travellers to draw upon fellow users' suggestions in planning their tourism itineraries down to the smallest detail. It even allows details of *free* attractions and experiences, listing them in order of reader popularity, and is not in the business of booking tickets. It is, however, a smart strategy to gain consumers' confidence in a world where there are increasing alternatives to regular advertising and tour information.

*Sources*: Personal interview with Mason, M. 20 April 2006; Tossell, I. (1 April 2006) 'Pack your blogs', *Globe & Mail*, R12; Fass, Allison. (8 May 2006) 'TheirSpace.com', *Forbes*, 122–124; Anon. (4 January 2006) 'Wikis let travelers create content from scratch', *Globe & Mail*, R12-13.

## Introduction

The Opening Vignette highlights a relatively new way of communicating and obtaining travel information online – via travel blogs. Blogs are just one way in which the internet is changing the marketing landscape and this chapter looks at an important and growing area of tourism and hospitality marketing: internet marketing. It describes the growth of the internet generally and how it has affected the marketing of tourism. It then discusses how the tourism and hospitality industry is using the internet to perform six key marketing functions: direct email marketing, advertising, distribution and sales, providing information, customer service and relationship marketing, and marketing research.

The world is going online in huge numbers. In 2005, 200 million Americans were internet users representing over two-thirds of the population; of these, 84 per cent are travellers. In the UK, the average internet user spends the equivalent of more than 50 days a year online, according to a new survey that backs up claims that the net is replacing television as the public's medium of choice (Johnson, 2006).[1] The study shows that internet usage has risen dramatically over the past few years, with surfers spending an average of 23 hours a week online. In fact, in spite of the failure of some very high-profile companies over the past decade or so, the internet is thriving, and transforming the tourism industry. The impact of e-marketing can be felt across all sectors in the industry, from large hotel chains to small outfitters. The advantage of this business model is that it is based on a sound foundation – consumer demand. Customers are looking to the internet to research, plan, and even book their trips in greater numbers every year. The Opening Vignette describes how travel blogs are increasingly being used by consumers as a source of travel information. The Snapshot below also shows how the brochure is slowly becoming redundant, to be replaced by travel pods that use internet access and colour printers to give customers a streamlined hard copy of their travel options.

The internet is also changing the behaviour of consumers when they arrive at a destination, with many now demanding free internet use. Wireless – or Wi-Fi – provision is becoming quite common in bars, hotels and airports. Wi-Fi technology is no less secure than a regular (wire) internet connection, and transmits a signal over a limited space that can be accessed only by people within that space and with a Wi-Fi enabled machine. Many Starbucks outlets around the world offer free Wi-Fi access, and some destinations like Dubai have internet access pretty much everywhere – even in petrol stations. In the US, Philadelphia has recently become the country's first completely wireless major city. Hotels tend to charge for wireless access in Europe, whereas in North America it is often free. Marriott's UK properties charge about £15 a day, whereas Marriott's Courtyard hotels in the US do not charge because the service is cheaper to provide in the US, and there is more competition. However, a few hotels in the UK are offering Wi-Fi on a free-for-all basis – not just for guests, but for anyone who wanders into the lobby or on to the terraces with a laptop. The City Inn chain, whose flagship hotel is in Westminster, estimates that 100,000 people used the service in 2005 (Taylor, 2006).[2]

Internet technology is also being used by travellers as a replacement for printed maps and guidebooks when they arrive at destinations. Consumers are using PDAs – small hand-held computers – to access digital maps or for satellite navigation. Podcasts are also widely available, whereby tourists can download digital guides to attractions onto their iPods, rather than having to be led by an audio guide. Podscrolls can also be downloaded onto iPods and these are lists of restaurant reviews stored as photographs. Internet postcards are also commonly available on destination websites; consumers can send an email postcard to friends or family with a choice of pictures that usually promote the destination. The internet is also allowing travellers to watch their home TVs from anywhere in the world. Slingboxes, as they are called, are chocolate bar-sized devices that sit on the top of a cable box and pump home TV signals across the internet. By plugging it into a high-speed modem and connecting it to the cable box's audio and video ports, you can watch and control your TV from anywhere in the world, as long as you can get online.

The impact of the internet does have some negative effects on travel consumers. There has been an increase in the number of individuals and firms who buy up tickets for events or festivals in bulk and then sell them on websites such as eBay at vastly inflated prices. In the UK, there is growing concern about the behaviour of online agencies such as the now-defunct Getmetickets.net, and the use of internet auction sites to sell overpriced and fake tickets. When tickets for the 2007 'T in the Park' festival in Scotland went on sale in July 2006, the entire advanced allocation of 35,000 was snapped up in just over an hour. Within five minutes of going on sale, they were on offer on eBay for up to five times face value. Officials are currently attempting to alleviate the problem, including recommending the set-up of a website by the Consumer Promoters Association where people can exchange tickets at face value (Jones, 2006).[3]

## Snapshot

### The End of the Brochure as We Know It?

Browsing through the new season's holiday brochures used to be a favourite pastime for travellers – leafing through the pages until the perfect holiday caught the eye. However, the days of the travel brochure as we know it may well be numbered. In the UK in July 2006 the country's first 'travel pods' – the brainchild of high-street travel retailer First Choice – went on trial. Demonstration pods appeared in six of the company's supermarket concessions, four in Asda stores in Sheffield, Basildon, Milton Keynes and Manchester, and an additional two in First Choice 'Travel Centres' at Sainsbury's stores in Torquay and Liverpool.

Occupying less than half the area of a standard concession, each travel pod is entirely brochure-free, using Internet access and colour printers to give customers a streamlined hard copy of their travel options. 'The idea arose because supermarkets like the rent that concessions provide, but don't like giving up the shelf-space that brochures need,' explained Cheryl Powell, managing director of First Choice Retail. Powell, who developed the idea after visiting a nail bar in her local shopping centre, believes that her new idea will benefit the environment as well as sales. 'The travel industry faces a huge problem with brochure wastage. With tons of brochures dumped every year, it is a genuine environmental issue.'

First Choice is not the only company revisiting its marketing strategies with a view to preparing itself for a time when digital formats could render brochures obsolete. British Airways Holidays, for example, has developed a range of destination-specific brochures that contain no prices, instead referring customers to dedicated online micro-sites that run 'live pricing', regularly updating flight and package costs. 'A problem with traditional hotel-led brochures is that the prices are out of date almost as soon as they hit the shelves,' said Tracy Long from British Airways. BA is now moving towards 'lifestyle brochures', A5-size booklets offering attractive content on a destination's various attractions. 'On the accompanying micro-site for each destination prices are continually revised to reflect market forces, such as changes in exchange rates,' said Long. 'If people still want to talk to a human being, we also provide a call-centre number.'

The technology behind recreating entire brochures online is relatively simple and is becoming more sophisticated. Downloading a brochure in digital format takes just a few seconds and there is an increase in rich media that allows more dynamic content. Like many other sectors, travel websites are exploiting this technology, and the prevalence of broadband means most people can download video footage of a destination quite easily. However, a recent survey by Transversal, a company that helps businesses to communicate online with customers, found that travel companies have the least user-friendly websites of any service industry, at least in the UK. The research found that sites owned by Britain's most popular tour operators and airlines failed to answer even the most basic queries. For example, travel sites were emailed the question: 'Will I get a refund if a natural disaster affects my destination?' First Choice (and it was not the slowest!) took 43 hours to respond. Perhaps the travel industry has some work to do before the printed brochure can be ditched once and for all.

*Sources*: Mackenzie, M. (30 July 2006) 'Bin the brochure', *The Independent on Sunday*, 19; Skidmore, J. (17 June 2006) 'Shocking online services', *The Daily Telegraph Travel*, 4.

## The Use of the Internet in Tourism and Hospitality

The internet is being used by the tourism and hospitality industry to perform six key functions: direct email marketing, advertising, providing information, distribution and sales, customer service and relationship marketing and marketing research.

### Direct Email Marketing

One of the most promising applications in online advertising is **direct email marketing**, in which a user chooses to receive messages from a particular advertiser. In 2004, over 36 million online travellers in the US signed up with travel suppliers to receive email offers and promotions. Of these, 11 million said they booked trips based solely on an emailed travel promotion.[4] This form of advertising is relatively inexpensive, has high response rates and is easy to measure, and is targeted at people who want information about certain goods and services. Unlike banner advertising in its various forms, sending sales messages by email seems quite acceptable to internet users, since they agree to accept the message.

---

**DIRECT EMAIL MARKETING**
marketing in which a user chooses to receive messages from a particular advertiser via the internet

---

The success of an email campaign – like that of a direct mail campaign – depends on the quality of the list, which can be created in-house or be rented from a list broker. Typically, these lists include opt-in names and addresses. 'Opt-in' means that the people on the list have agreed to receive direct email. Email advertisements sent to lists that are not opt-in are called **spam**. Spam refers to the inappropriate use of a mailing list or other networked communications facility as a broadcast medium. It is unsolicited 'junk' email. One of the problems with email is its low cost, which results in users receiving an increasing number of unwanted messages. The consequence is that more and more email goes unopened, and gaining permission to send someone a message is becoming more important.

---

**SPAM**
email advertisements sent to lists of recipients who have not agreed to receive them

---

Establishing first contact is the toughest goal of any email marketer. The most obvious place to find prospects is via other websites, newsgroups and mailing lists. This can work, but many mailing lists and newsgroups have settled on their own set of experts. It is harder to penetrate market share this way. Email marketing is still in its infancy online, and many of the so-called lists are not tested or even targeted. The best means of survival is still endorsed mailing to a group of interested customers, which is why it is important to allow people to remove themselves from lists.

The goal is to have customers make first contact, and then have the marketer follow up. This can be encouraged by giving customers something of real value, such as a good special report or newsletter. Yukon Tourism in Canada had major success in 2006 reaching brand new audiences with an email campaign promoting the 'Yukon Alaska Ultimate Adventure Contest'. Yukon Tourism rented two types of lists: one owned and operated by TELUS, made up of Canadians who had previously requested other types of travel information, and the second a Forge Marketing database of people who had already indicated an interest in Yukon travel. The 'click thru' rate (those who viewed the messages) was almost 19 per cent, and 69 per cent of people on the second list asked for more information.

## Advertising

These days, the internet is an important part of the media mix, and internet advertising is seen by some as the convergence of traditional advertising and direct response marketing. Online advertising holds four distinct advantages:

1. **Targetability**. Online advertisers can focus on users from specific companies, geographical locations and nations, as well as categorize them by time of day, computer platform and browser. They can target using databases, a tool that serves as the backbone of direct marketing. They can even target using a person's personal preferences and actual behaviour.
2. **Tracking**. Marketers can track how users interact with their brands and learn what is of interest to their current and prospective customers. Advertisers can also measure the response to an ad (by noting the number of times an ad is clicked on, the number of purchases or leads an ad generated, etc.). This is difficult to do with traditional television, print, and outdoor advertising.
3. **Deliverability and flexibility**. Online, an ad is deliverable 24 hours a day, 7 days a week, 365 days of the year. Furthermore, an ad campaign can be launched, updated or cancelled immediately. This is very different from print or television advertising.
4. **Interactivity**. An advertiser's goal is to engage the prospect with a brand or a product. This can be done more effectively online, where consumers can interact with the product, test it, and, if they choose, buy it.

Online marketers can advertise via email (as discussed earlier) and by sponsoring discussion lists and email newsletters. But a common form of advertising on the internet is the **banner ad** – an advertisement placed as a narrow band across the top of a web page. In terms of appearance and design, banner ads are often compared to outdoor posters. The content of the ad is minimal. Its purpose is to stir interest, so that the viewer clicks the ad for more information. Once the banner ad is clicked, the viewer sees the advertisement in its entirety, usually via a link to the advertiser's home page. The design characteristics of the ad are critical, since the goal is to encourage clicking. The website the ad links to must be interesting, or the surfer will quickly return to the previous page. A recent study of internet strategies used by resorts showed that well-placed and appropriate use of banner ads can be highly effective.[5]

---

**BANNER AD**

an advertisement placed as a narrow band across the top of a web page; the most common form of advertising on the internet

---

Advertising money is also increasingly being spent on search-engine advertising, which allows companies to target consumers as they research a holiday. The growth of search engine use for online travel research or booking is staggering, and has been facilitated by the introduction of newer 'travel-specific' search engines such as Kayak, Sidestep and Yahoo's Farechase. In Britain, seven out of ten people use Google when they trawl the internet for flights, for instance. The search engine delivers the results and alongside them displays about a dozen 'sponsored links' from companies that have paid to appear on the page. Each time a consumer clicks on one of these links, Google gets a fee.

Marketers are also using the internet to place ads that may or may not be shown on television at a later date, taking advantage of internet users' insatiable appetite for online content. The

Case Study at the end of this chapter shows how an ad created by Tourism Australia was downloaded by over 100,000 people in the UK alone before being aired on television. BMW expanded the boundaries of advertising formats on the web with its short films featuring BMW automobiles, which were an attraction in themselves, rather than an advertising distraction. The company launched its first round of films online in the summer of 2001 and the short film *The Hire,* featuring its Z4 and X5 models, also spawned its own comic book collection.

Advertising in online virtual worlds is another opportunity for marketers. An example is Second Life, an online world with a million registered users and a thriving virtual economy (see Opening Vignette in Chapter 13). Second Life allows its users to create a new, and improved, digital version of themselves. 'Residents' can buy land, build structures and start businesses. The service is fast becoming a three-dimensional test bed for corporate marketers, including Sony BMG Music Entertainment, Sun Microsystems, Nissan, Adidas, Toyota and Starwood Hotels. Retailers have set up shops to sell digital as well as real-world versions of their products, and even musicians can promote their albums with virtual appearances. In October 2006, performer Ben Folds promoted a new album playing at the opening party for Aloft, an elaborate digital prototype for a new chain of hotels planned by Starwood Hotels and Resorts. Projects like Aloft are designed to promote the venture but also to give its designers feedback from prospective guests before the first real hotel opens in 2008.

Table 10.1 offers ten tips for a better website. According to marketing experts, the success factors for marketing tourism on the web include the following: attracting users, engaging users' interest and participation, retaining users and ensuring that they return, learning about user preferences, and relating back to users to provide customized interactions (Parsons et al., 1998).[6] Learning about user preferences would appear to be the most important element of this model, as it affects the remaining elements, and yet very few studies have attempted to understand the behaviour of tourists online. Although statistical measures can be obtained through log files, it is difficult to ascertain the meaning behind the results (e.g. whether clicking on a link was an accident or an intended behaviour). Surveying visitors might be a better way to understand consumer preferences and to establish the effectiveness of a site.

Research that has looked at content of web pages suggests that it is crucial that content is accurate, attractive and easily searchable (Beirne and Curry, 1999).[7] Interactivity is also an imperative, as the behaviour of consumers changes when they log onto the internet: they not only search for information but also expect interaction and entertainment (Schwartz, 1998).[8] A positive experience on the website increases the time spent there, and therefore increases the dollar amount spent (Hoffman and Novak, 1996).[9] Offering virtual tours is one way of providing interactivity, and many destinations offer these for an extensive selection of places. Virtual tours of hotels on the corporate website have proven to be a major sales asset for some hotel chains. Live video is another way of allowing visitors to interact with websites. For example, the Wavehouse website (www.wavehouse.com) allows users to view live video of surfers using the San Diego attraction.

It is also important for tourism operators and destinations to consider the language of their online visitors. It was mentioned in Chapter 3 that the New York tourism bureau had added Chinese language pages to its website in order to take advantage of the growing Chinese market. Outrigger Hotels and Resorts has also recognized that it holds an international presence

**Table 10.1**   Ten Tips for a Better Website

| | | |
|---|---|---|
| 1. | Navigation | Keep it simple (KIS), and make sure it's consistent from page to page. No matter where you place your menu bar – either at the top or down the side – always include a small text menu at the bottom of every page. Make your domain name short, catchy and memorable. |
| 2. | Privacy policy | With all the concern over privacy on the web, if you collect any type of information from your visitors (even if it's just an email address), you need to include a privacy policy. There are many online templates that will help you to create one easily. Once made, post a link to it on every page of your site. |
| 3. | Contact | Post your contact information at the bottom of every page of your site. Don't make the viewer fill out a whole form when he or she just wants to send a simple comment. Include your email address, hotlinked and ready to go. |
| 4. | Logos and graphics | Please keep your graphics down to a reasonable size. No one wants to wait two minutes while your huge, beautiful logo loads onto the screen. |
| 5. | Fonts | Stick to standards. Remember, if you stray from using the standard fonts that everyone has installed on their computers (such as Arial, Verdana, and Times New Roman), the viewer won't see your fonts as intended. |
| 6. | Make it sticky | Include interactive features if possible, such as live news feeds. Use chat rooms, discussion boards, etc. You want to create a sense of community – a place to which people will want to return. |
| 7. | Newsletter | If you're going to have a website, you need to offer an email newsletter, even if it's strictly going to be about sale items, specials or site updates. You need to start collecting a list of your visitors' email addresses so you can keep in touch with them. |
| 8. | Browsers | Make sure you take a peek at your site in both Netscape and Internet Explorer. Recent statistics show that Internet Explorer has about 80 per cent of the market share, but you'll still want to make sure that the other 20 per cent can view your site without any problems. |
| 9. | Screen | This is a highly debatable subject. The norm these days seems to be 800 × 600 resolution although there are still a small number of people limping along in 640 × 480. |
| 10. | Index page | On the very first page of your site (the homepage), the first paragraph should answer the '5 Ws', basically telling visitors who you are and what you're offering. Surfers are a very impatient group. Stop them before they click away. Make sure you keep your website current. Nothing is more irksome than finding the site was updated a year ago. |

*Source*: Anon (17 March 2005) 'Eight steps to a better website', *The Globe & Mail*, C5; '10 tips for a better website', (2003), retrieved from http://main.tourismtogether.com/inforesources.

and needs to disseminate information about its properties in several languages. Its locations in the Pacific and South Pacific receive a lot of business from Korea and Japan, so the company has built portals to address these markets.

In recent years, there has been much discussion of Web 2.0. The phrase Web 2.0 was first coined in 2005 by Tim O'Reilly, a web pioneer, as a way to mark a turning point in web development. It takes into account a fundamentally different point of view, where a website is built around a rich user experience, not a product or service. Customer-centric 2.0 websites require that a company puts itself in the shoes of a website visitor and sees its organization as it appears through that. A recent study of ski area websites concluded that those that take the time to design their site with the needs of their customers as the primary focus will not only be rewarded with more visitors on the web, but on the slopes too (Rufo, 2006).[10] The survey found the most user-friendly ski area websites had four things in common:

1. They provided current information in a simple, clear, and attractive way;
2. They gave visitors a good reason to come back again (in technical web terms, they have 'stickiness');
3. They involved the visitor. Not only did they provide interactive tools, they openly encouraged guests to contribute comments, content or images to their site;
4. They made sure the website matched other branding materials such as brochures and ads.

A major challenge for tourism organizations selling via the internet is converting surfers into buyers. A 2006 study of North American consumers found that the top three reasons for those who research but hesitate to continue with an online booking are concern over credit card security, website performance issues and limits on the actions that can be taken online, and frustration with website performance. Interestingly, and worryingly from an internet marketing point of view, the number of consumers concerned with submitting their credit card information nearly doubled from 9 percent in 2005 to 16 percent in 2006 (Wilkening, 2007).[11] The Snapshot below provides some advice to tourism marketers on how to convert hits into sales.

## Snapshot

### How to Convert Website Hits into Sales

One of the common questions asked by website owners is, 'I'm getting plenty of hits but no sales – what is going on?' Kevin Sinclair, author of two free e-books, *Success Secrets* and *How to Choose a Home Based Business*, offers some tips on how to address this issue.

### Your Product

The first area to review is the product or service that you are offering. Does a market exist for it? To answer this question you need to find out whether similar products are being sold on the internet successfully. If not, you may need to rethink your internet strategy. If others *are* selling a similar product successfully, then this would tend to confirm that there is a market for your product. Next, look at the strategy and pricing being adopted by your competitors. How do you compare? Why should your visitors buy from you rather than from one of your competitors? Answering these questions will provide you with valuable information that you can use to improve your situation and generate more sales. Also, take a critical look at your product quality. Does it live up to the claims you are making on your web pages? If not, improve your product so that it does, or modify your website to be more truthful about it.

## Provide Solutions

Your visitors are looking for a solution to a problem. Do you know what problems your visitors are looking for solutions to? Does your website show how your product will solve your visitors' problem? You will need to put yourself into your visitors' shoes to understand what they are seeking, so that you can provide the solution they need. One way to understand your visitors better is to monitor how they are getting to your site. If they are coming from search engines, knowing what search terms they are using can provide some clues. This means you may need to invest in some sort of statistical package for tracking. You may find some surprises when you review the statistics about your site. Once you understand your visitors' problem, revise your website to show that your product will provide the solution they need.

## Site Design

Your site needs to look like a commercial website rather than an amateur one. The design needs to be consistent from page to page, and the site needs to be easy to navigate. Contact details including physical address, phone numbers and email address need to be shown. Graphics need to be minimized to ensure that your homepage downloads quickly. Also, ensure that your web host provides a fast connection to the internet. Most people will not wait for a page that takes a long time to download. They will just move on to your competitor. Also, make it easy to order. A large number of people abandon a website in the middle of the ordering process, often because the ordering process is too time-consuming and complicated. Make yours simple and quick and you will lose fewer sales.

## Testimonials and Guarantees

Testimonials and guarantees can have a huge impact on your level of sales. On the web, a key priority is to build credibility. The common methods used are having a privacy statement, publishing a newsletter, publishing testimonials from satisfied customers, and providing a strong guarantee. Take every opportunity to gather comments from your customers about how your product has helped them. A way of getting comments is a customer feedback survey. This can be used for the purpose of gaining testimonials as well as seeking ways to improve your product or develop additional products your customers may need. A strong guarantee will provide your visitor with greater confidence. Try to make it simple and without too many conditions, and always honour it without question or delay. According to consumer reports, online travel services that are likely to secure return visits are those that offer 'best rate guarantees'.

*Source*: Sinclair, K. (2006) 'How to convert hits into sales', retrieved from http://ksinclair.com/Article68.htm

## Providing Information

Online users are often divided between those that plan and those that book. In the US, some 78 per cent of travellers can be described as online travel planners, since they consulted the internet to get travel and destination information. The most popular sources of travel information in 2005 for the Americans were online travel agencies such as Expedia and Yahoo (67 per cent); search engine sites (64 per cent); travel company sites (54 per cent) and destination sites (46 per cent). One in three online planners checked websites and then called a supplier's toll-free number (Pollock, 2006).[12] The most popular planning activities conducted on the internet are: searching for maps and driving directions (50.6 million), searching for airfares (49 million) and looking for places to stay (48 million). The internet is also the preferred method of obtaining travel information amongst internet users in the UK, with some 65 per cent of UK internet users in 2005 using the web to research travel. A major trend affecting web usage for travel planning in the UK is the arrival of such meta-search engines as www.kayak.com and www.allcheckin.com, which enable customers to compare instantly details for flights, hotels and rental cars.

The internet is also an important source of information for tourism practitioners. A new international tourism portal set up for the travel trade is Tourism-Review.com. Launched in 2006, this website provides daily, weekly and monthly tourism news as well as an online TV newscast that communicates relevant information between professional organizations and industry practitioners worldwide. Several synoptic directories list festivals, conferences and travel destinations, as well as travel trade companies and organizations. 'With so much information overloading travel trade professionals, there is a demand for more relevant and focused sourcing,' said the site's project head, Igor Fes. 'Our final target is providing the users with customized information in all rich media formats available with the latest developing technology.'[13] Another online source of information for the travel trade, travel media or researchers is WorldTourismDirectory.com. The site has detailed information on countries and territories listed and organized by the following categories: Government Tourism Agencies; Tourism Schools & Institutes; Travel Associations & Services; Transport; Outdoor & Recreational Activities; Publications & Information Sources; Immigration & Foreign Affairs; Chambers of Commerce; Regional & Local Tourist Information Offices; Miscellaneous Information Offices; Information Offices Abroad; and Embassies/Consulates. Besides the comprehensive country directory there is also a visitor's guide, country profile and a country map.

Another trend is the importance of **travel blogs** in gathering travel information. Rather than passively viewing a collection of static pages, today's internet user is becoming an active participant and, as the Opening Vignette highlighted, there is a growth in social networking – the creation and sharing of free content made by individual users. It is changing the way people consume media. For example, home video nights have been replaced by YouTube.com, and flipping through photo albums is now done via Flickr.com. Ease of use is the biggest factor driving this trend, both for users and creators. Jupiter Research in New York tracked a dramatic growth of internet users who read blogs, from 11 per cent in 2005 to 23 per cent in 2006 (Rocha, 2006).[14] In September 2006, YouTube was recording 100 million views a day, and receiving 60,000 new videos a day. One of the major reasons for the success of Australia's 'Where the bloody hell are you?' advertising campaign was the number of people viewing the ads on YouTube (see Case Study at the end of the chapter).

---

**TRAVEL BLOGS**
Travel blogs are web-based pieces of travel information created by travellers, which give the consumer a credible guide to tourism 'dos' and 'don'ts'

---

## Distribution and Sales

In 2005, the share of online travel planners who also book online continued to grow worldwide. The purchase of airline tickets continues to dominate the booking activity, closely followed by accommodation reservations. Ticket sales for all kinds of events and attractions are also showing steady growth. In the US, while the major online travel agencies attracted the most online bookers (29.6 million Americans used either Expedia, Travelocity and Priceline at least once in 2005), search engine sites experienced the fastest growth (from 11.6 million bookers in 2004 to 18.7 million in 2005) closely followed by destination sites – up to 12.6 million bookers (Pollock, 2006).[15] In Europe, the enthusiasm for the internet in the UK made it the largest online travel market in 2004, accounting for 36 per cent of the European travel market (Pollock, 2006).[16] It is believed that one of the reasons for this is the high volume of airline tickets purchased online via UK low-cost carriers, which lifts internet usage overall.

In Europe, fragmentation in the online travel agency market is high compared to the US. Of the European online travel agency market, 60 per cent is in the hands of the top five agencies, whereas in the US, the three companies referred to above serve 93 per cent of the online agency market. One growing competitor for these agencies is Orbitz.com, created when five airlines – American, Continental, Delta, Northwest and United – came together to develop a state-of-the-art travel website. Orbitz is now one of the largest online travel companies in the world, selling airfares, lodging, car rentals, cruises and vacation packages. Orbitz's inventory includes 455 airlines, 500,000 lodging properties, 25 car rentals, 30 vacation package providers and 18 airlines.

Hotels, in particular, are turning to the internet to increase sales. High-tech investments in websites and other facilities already have paid off for many participants in the hospitality industry. A survey of hotels in 2005 found that online sales represented 44 per cent of business for those questioned (Green and Warner, 2006).[17] Their average spend on online marketing was US$50,000 per year, and respondents rated their own website as more effective than any other online channel of distribution. The greatest challenge for hotels was setting prices of optimized revenue and having consistency between prices in different distribution channels. Online agencies and non-hotel sites have also been building up their hotel business as a way to diversify from low-margin air sales. Southwest, for example, launched a hotel reservations service in 2001 using the Galileo global distribution system. Expedia is also having tremendous success online. In March 2001, it announced that it had sold more than one million room nights in less than three months. In comparison, it took the company three years to sell its first million room nights. Through its Travelscape division, which operates on the merchant model, Expedia contracts for special room blocks to resell to consumers at a margin, thus guaranteeing revenue for the hotel. Hotels can sign on to become an 'Expedia Special Rate Hotel' through Travelscape, to help fill unsold inventory. Travelscape helps hotels maximize revenue during peak, shoulder and off-peak travel periods; it also offers hotels an Extranet tool that allows them to manage inventory and rates online. However, tensions between hotels and online agencies have led to some hotels pulling inventory from websites. For example, InterContinental Hotels pulled its 3,500 hotels from Expedia and hotels.com in 2004. IHG said the online agencies would not comply with business guidelines it had issued, and sought to have more control over how its rooms were sold.

Many companies are forming online partnerships in order to distribute their travel products or services. An example is Luxurylink.com. Following the lead of auction sites such as Priceline (see Global Spotlight below), Luxurylink.com is an alliance of tourism companies around the world that lets visitors bid on sumptuous accommodation and vacation packages. Properties are sorted into nine geographic sections – such as the Caribbean or Europe – and can be accessed by browsing or by conducting a customizable search based on destination. Listings include photos and a thorough description of the package; pricing and auction details such as 'retail value'; the minimum bid for the package; the start and close dates of the auction; and the smallest bid increments that the listing accepts. Before visitors can bid on listings that pique their interest, they must first register at the site. Winning bidders receive notification by email, followed by a personal phone call within 20 minutes to collect payment information.

The Global Spotlight below highlights a customer-driven pricing strategy for travel that has increased in popularity due to the internet – the reverse auction. Priceline is one of a number of companies that act as intermediaries between prospective buyers, who request quotations for a product or service, and multiple suppliers who quote the best price they are willing to offer. Buyers can then review the offers and select the supplier that best meets their needs.

## Global Spotlight

### Shatner Still Flying: the Priceline Model

In May 2006, with gross bookings of US$747 million reflecting a 33 per cent growth rate for the year, Priceline.com declared its mission 'to be the leading online travel business for value-conscious leisure travellers in North America' with similar goals for 'unmanaged business travel' too. Priceline.com is the 'Name Your Own Price' internet service that specializes in booking online airline tickets, hotel rooms and rental cars. It has also had rather more limited success with its subsidiary interests in finance (home mortgages, refinancing and home equity), cars, online groceries and long-distance phone calls. It was originally launched in early 1998 with a unique purchasing concept whereby prospective customers chose their merchandise via their own price, and the service then offered possibilities within the price framework, enabling customers to bid for the products.

In February 2002, Priceline.com amalgamated with eBay to create a new travel booking service for eBay Travel, thus combining the strengths and reputations of these two major online travel booking services. For booking airlines, hotels, cars, cruises, timeshares and vacation packages, consumers compete in an auction style or 'Buy It Now' format. Priceline.com is responsible for the technology, development, transaction processing infrastructure and ongoing support of the booking service. Recent research at eBay had shown that 42 per cent of eBay users had purchased online travel in the previous year, representing around US$8.4 billion in gross merchandise sales.

In research results revealed in its 7th Annual Internet Conference in May 2006, Priceline.com noted that 61 per cent of purchasers considered price to be key when choosing a travel website, compared to 52 per cent in 2005. Moreover, 51 per cent claimed that lower prices would be the primary reason for choosing to purchase travel merchandise by methods other than online. In order to capitalize on this 'bottom line' attitude, the Priceline.com website is littered with slogans such as 'More Ways to Save', 'Best Deal', 'Package and Save' and, of course, 'Name Your Own Price'. Its success has also been partly due to an aggressive and expensive ad campaign featuring a series of high-profile television commercials starring *Star Trek*'s 'Captain Kirk', aka William Shatner. Mr Shatner's self-mockery and unique mixture of classical interpretations with today's lifestyle have attained cult status for him and, in turn, Priceline. In 2002, around US$40 million was spent on advertising the company via Hill, Holliday, Connors and Cosmopulos, who had been directing the Shatner ad campaigns for the previous three years. However, since then, Priceline has decided to dispense with the high-cost service and produce its own radio and television commercials internally, retaining Shatner as the figurehead.

The 'Name Your Own Price' model seems to work well in the travel industry because accurate, timely information about travel prices is otherwise inaccessible to independent purchasers. Airlines' complex yield-management systems, designed to fill as many seats as possible at the highest prices, mean that seat prices fluctuate from minute to minute. Priceline helps consumers obtain the best information possible which hitherto had only been available to industry insiders. It appears that Priceline lacks that edge in other markets. Despite its obvious travel market successes, it has had its share of failure and criticism since its launch. Its foray into the grocery business, whereby customers were able to shop and bid online for lowest price foods and gasoline, ended in 2000 after just two years. Plans to enter the life insurance and mobile telephone businesses were abandoned in 2000 as well.

*Sources*: Mullaney, T. J. (2000) 'Priceline should buy Priceline', retrieved from www.businessweek.com/2000/00; Carter, B. and Rutenberg, J. (15 May 2002) 'Priceline cuts ties with Hill, Holliday', retrieved from http://query.nytimes.com; Jones, A. (13 December 2000) 'Can Priceline cling on to Captain Kirk?', retrieved from http://web.lexis.com; Priluck, R. (2001) 'The impact of Priceline.com on the grocery industry', *International Journal of Retail & Distribution Management*, Vol. 29, No. 3, 127–134, retrieved from www.emeraldinsight.com.

## Customer Service and Relationship Marketing

The internet is moving marketers much closer to one-to-one marketing. The web not only offers merchants the ability to communicate instantly with each customer, but it also allows the customer to talk back, and that makes it possible for companies to customize offers and services. It is now relatively easy for customers to check on the status of their bookings or their frequent flyer/visitor programmes at any time of the day. The Snapshot below presents the key motivating factors behind consumers' planning and booking travel online. The main reason consumers have adopted the internet is that it enables them to shop 24/7 in the comfort of their home. Ease of navigation is then the primary reason for variations in purchase decisions between different online products.

Many consumers, too, are looking to build relationships on the web. Godin introduced the concept of **permission marketing**, in which online consumers volunteer to be marketed to in return for some kind of reward. This type of marketing uses the interactivity offered by the web to engage customers in a dialogue and, as a consequence, in a long-term interactive relationship (Godin, 1999).[18] Permission marketing is based on the premise that the attention of the consumer is a scarce commodity that needs to be managed carefully. Its emphasis is on building relationships with consumers instead of interrupting their lives with mass-marketing messages. About two-thirds of hotels are using their online channels to collect information on their customers, and then use that information to drive marketing campaigns (Green and Warner, 2006).[19]

---

**PERMISSION MARKETING**
online marketing in which consumers volunteer to be marketed to in return for some kind of reward

---

Selective marketing, whereby consumers are shown advertising and promotions related to their browsing interests, is also on the increase. For example, the use of online coupons is rising rapidly, by more than 50 per cent a year, as internet giant Google, joins companies like ValPak and CoolSavings to bring new technology to the business of marketing national or local coupons over the internet. Digital coupons typically must be printed and physically turned in at a store so there is still some paper handling. The next stage, according to marketing experts, will come with the spread of digital cell phones with location tracking and automatic short-range communication technology. Electronic coupons will be delivered to cell phone owners on demand and redeemed by whisking the phone past a cash register, eliminating all the paper (Lohr, 2006).[20]

## Snapshot

### Why Do Travellers Purchase Online?

Holidaymakers are increasingly turning their noses up at traditional package holidays purchased through a travel agent, in favour of a holiday bought online. In 2005, the share of online travel planners who also book travel continued to grow, with 82 per cent of planners making a reservation or purchase. But what is it that motivates the traveller to purchase online? According to experts, the main reason consumers have adopted the internet is that it enables them to shop 24/7 in the comfort of their home. Ease of navigation is then the primary reason for variations in purchase decisions between different online products. In an attempt to simplify navigation, many sites have become 'content aggregators' that offer one-stop shopping. This strategy has been extremely successful for such agencies as Travelocity and Expedia. Dynamic packaging, whereby web users create their own package while retaining a certain degree of flexibility, has added a new twist to the tourism landscape. Silvia Bartels, a travel and leisure analyst for market research company Mintel, says that people increasingly want their holidays to have a 'sense of adventure', preferring to devise their own rather than be tied down by traditional packages. 'The internet plays a big role, as people have so much information to hand at the touch of a button. It is almost too easy to book a flight and hotel, and to be flexible', she says. 'Five years ago people would book around four months ahead. Now they book online one month ahead, getting the cheapest flight they can find, then choosing a hotel separately.'

One study of North American travellers examined the top six factors that motivate consumers to make online purchases. The first motivation factor was the opportunity to earn points through a customer loyalty programme. Some sites have even set up a special page for members to track their reward points (marriottrewards.com for example). The second reason was the availability of the desired product, with the third being clear, detailed information that enables the user to make an informed decision. A simple reservation process is the fourth key factor in the online purchase decision, especially in the case of more complex travel products. The reputation of the company or site's banner is also important as this reassures the purchaser and may positively influence the outcome of the transaction. Finally, consumers are more sensitive to the price of online products than they are to conventionally purchased products. This is partly due to aggressive advertising campaigns that have gradually led consumers to expect discounts.

Behaviour online varies according to travel sector, but, regardless of the amount of web user experience, a user-friendly interface is a key factor in the decision to buy any kind of online travel product, leading experts to conclude that all consumers want a simple reservation process. Competitive prices play a greater role in the purchase of less complex products, such as airline tickets, packages or car rental. The quality and accuracy of the site's information was a deciding factor for travellers looking for activities, events, tours, attractions and accommodation. Company reputation was less important to those making 'simple' transactions – such as renting a car – compared to those purchasing more complex products. Finally, customer loyalty programmes constitute a greater draw for expert users and mainly affect purchase of airline tickets, car rental and attractions.

Another study, by JupiterResearch in the US, found that best-rate guarantees would motivate the majority of online consumers to make more purchases online. Consumers are highly interested in the ability to fix mistakes without penalty and cancel or change reservations on the website where travel was booked. Approximately one in four consumers suggest that they would be more inclined to purchase travel online if websites offered clearer wording regarding penalties and fees. Unlike their European counterparts, US consumers are not as receptive to the idea of buying bundled products online, largely because they prefer to shop around. 'Online travel consumers continue to be price-sensitive and increasingly demanding,' says Diane Clarkson, online travel analyst at JupiterResearch. 'Best-rate guarantees have begun to benefit suppliers in increasing direct online bookings. If airfare prices are equal, consumers are more likely to use an airline site than any other type of site to book their travel,' she adds.

*Sources*: Peloquin, C. (2005) 'Why purchase online?' *Tourism*, September/October, 5; Behan, R. (31 July 2004) 'Invent your own adventure', *Telegraph Travel*, 4; Anon (9 September 2004) Best-rate guarantees by travel suppliers help boost online bookings', *Travelweek*, 4.

## Marketing Research

The internet has introduced some exciting new ways of conducting surveys. The two main alternatives are using either email or the web to deliver and receive questionnaires. Many hospitality and travel organizations have placed HTML questionnaires on their websites to collect information from site visitors. For example, resort company Intrawest runs regular surveys on its website to collect data from past and prospective customers. Others may poll email subscribers to gather information. In 2006, the British Columbia Automobile Association (BCAA) received a 12 per cent response rate in an email campaign designed to understand the views of its membership. With the information gathered through the survey, the BCAA was planning highly targeted email direct mailings to its members in the future, based on their stated preferences.

Researchers are still experimenting with online surveys, and there are no conclusive guidelines about their strengths and weaknesses. However, their relative speed and flexibility are seen to be two major advantages. Additionally, there is the potential of reaching a large and growing audience of people. Internet software is available to take a written survey and convert it into email or web-compatible formats, to email or administer it, and then automatically collect responses, enter them into a database, and calculate descriptive statistics. By using this software on a busy website, it is possible to collect hundreds of responses in a short time period. However, Tierney (2000) has suggested that it may be increasingly difficult to get potential web surfers to become survey respondents.[21] Since they must click on the link to find the survey, an incentive is often necessary to get them to do so. But the use of incentives with internet surveys has been shown to cause at least three methodological concerns. response bias, multiple entry and unwanted entries.

## Chapter Summary

In spite of the failure of some very high-profile companies over the past decade or so, the internet is transforming the tourism industry. The impact of e-marketing can be felt across all sectors of the industry, from large hotel chains to small outfitters. The advantage of this business model is that it is based on a sound foundation – consumer demand. Customers are looking to the internet to research, plan, and even book their trips at rates that are increasing every year.

The internet is being used by the tourism and hospitality industry to perform six key functions: direct email marketing, providing information, advertising, distribution and sales, customer service and relationship marketing, and marketing research.

## Key Terms

banner ad, p. 336
direct email marketing, p. 335
permission marketing, p. 345
spam, p. 335
travel blogs, p. 342

## Discussion Questions and Exercises

1. After reading this chapter, explain how the internet is impacting the marketing of tourism and hospitality products and services.
3. Explain how direct marketing and internet marketing are related.
4. What are the main advantages and disadvantages of internet marketing?
5. The internet is being used by the tourism and hospitality industry in six key areas. In which area do you foresee the greatest future potential?
6. Take a look at an existing website for a particular tourism or hospitality organization. Referring to Table 10.1, make a list of the strengths and weaknesses of the website. How would you improve it?

**Case Study**

### Where the bloody hell are you? Australia ad creates 'global online traffic jam'

In late February 2006, the Hon. Fran Bailey, Australia's Minister for Small Business and Tourism, unveiled the US$180 million 'Where the bloody hell are you?' marketing campaign in markets around the world. The campaign was developed specifically for

Print ad from the 'So where the bloody hell are you?' campaign to promote Australia

international markets with the intention of showcasing the tourism assets of the entire country. Australia is well known for its personality and character, and this campaign was developed to extend an invitation to motivate people to visit Australia *now*. In an increasingly competitive and tough commercial environment, Tourism Australia feels its advertising must be 'bold, aggressive and distinctive' to grab consumer attention. But it must do this while remaining authentic and distinctively Australian. Tourism is very important to Australia. In 2005, it generated more than 500,000 jobs across the country and delivered more than AUS$17 billion to the national economy, from inbound tourists alone.

The adverts, created by the Sydney office of the London headquartered advertising agency M&C Saatchi, featured images of Australians 'preparing' for visitors to their country. The television ad begins in an outback pub with the barkeeper saying, 'We've poured you a beer'. Further imagery to a similar effect is then shown, including a young boy on the beach saying, 'We've got the sharks out of the pool,' and partygoers watching Sydney harbour fireworks saying, 'We've turned on the lights'. The advert ends with bikini-clad model Lara Bingle stepping out of the sea and asking, 'So where the bloody hell are you?'

Almost immediately the advertising was met with concern and criticism from consumers and media outlets alike; complaints ranged from the use of the words 'bloody hell' to worries about age-appropriateness and a scene in which one actor is taking a swill of beer. However, not only was Tourism Australia prepared for the backlash; it frankly welcomed it. 'According to Tourism Australia the campaign created a "talkability" that marketers can usually only dream about. More than 180 destinations advertised on UK television in 2005 to attract tourists and only one of them, Australia, was now gaining cut-through. Even British Prime Minister Tony Blair asked, 'Where the bloody hell am I?' when speaking in the Australian Parliament and suffering from jet lag. The advertising also caused a stir in Canada, with the Canadian Broadcasting Corporation expressing concern over the TV-spots. The CBC later opted to allow the ads, choosing instead to limit them to certain time slots. Regulators in Canada were not so much concerned about the language – it was more the implication of 'unbranded alcohol consumption' by the opening line, '*We've bought you a beer.*'

In regards to the UK market specifically, the British Advertising Clearance Centre initially chose to ban the TV-spots. They would not allow the word 'bloody' to be used in television versions of the commercial. This ban was seen as particularly pointless because accompanying print ads and cinema commercials for the campaign would not have been censored. Following lobbying by the Australia Tourism Commission, including a visit to the UK by Australia's Tourism Minister Fran Bailey and Sydney model Lara Bingle, who appears in the ad, the ban was subsequently lifted. The controversy did, however, gain much media interest. Tourism Australia maintained that they had always factored in the prospect of such a decision in the UK. They decided to press ahead knowing that a ban would only increase interest in the campaign and give them the public relations equivalent of 'a free kick in front of an open goal.' The destination marketing organization was careful to ensure that less 'bloody' versions were prepared should they be required. Tourism Australia said that the tagline for the new campaign, 'So where the bloody hell are you?' had been thoroughly tested in all of the major markets, in particular Japan, UK, USA, Germany, China, New Zealand and South Korea, and was given the green light by their customers.

In the meantime Tourism Australia made the most of the opportunity created by the controversy. UK traffic to the campaign website quadrupled in the week following the BACC ban. According to Tourism Australia the response to their new campaign was unprecedented, creating a global online traffic jam. Even before its official television debut the campaign was picking up momentum, with over 100,000 people in the UK having viewed the ad online. A similar effect was achieved in the Canadian market. The campaign was soon viewed in nearly every country in the world and generated record levels of worldwide online traffic. A dedicated website was created by Tourism Australia – www.wherethebloodyhellareyou.com – whereby consumers could log on, view the ad, send a postcard, or download specific pictures from the ads. Despite only being launched in five countries (including Australia), the uncut advertisement was downloaded by around 700,000 people in nearly 20 countries and Tourism Australia reported that consumer and trade support in their top seven markets was 'phenomenal'. In the meantime, Tourism Australia's Managing Director joked in a press release: 'We thank the UK authorities for the extra free publicity and invite them to have a "bloody" good holiday in Australia. To show there are no hard feelings we are happy to extend them an invitation.'

For Tourism Australia, there was a simple reason why the commercial had such impact. 'It cuts through the clutter and conveys a distinct message that people find appealing and authentic.' It was also no accident that the ad resonated with the target market. Tourism Australia invested AUS$6.2 million profiling the target audience for the campaign, known as 'Experience Seekers', to ensure the campaign worked. This audience is high-yielding travellers, who typically come from households that have higher than average income and are well educated. Tourism Australia constructed their message and tested it on them in their top seven markets and they gave it the thumbs up – saying it cuts through, they got it and it delivers a uniquely Australian invitation. According to Tourism Australia, the commercial is all about the tone, the personality, the images and messages. 'They all combine together to convey a feeling – in this case a warm, distinctive and authentically Australian invitation that says we want you to come and get involved now. This in turn makes them more inclined to take the all-important next step to come to Australia, rather than put it off for ever.'

*Sources*: Anon (2006) 'Tourism Australia extends a warm welcome', www.canadatourism.com; www.wherethebloodyhellareyou.com; Morrison, S. (2006) 'It's a bloody tourism ad, and a good one!', www.tourism.australia.com.

**Case Study**

## Questions

1. Account for the success of the 'Where the bloody hell are you?' advertising campaign.
2. Some people believe that the future of advertising lies in consumers being able to pick the ads they want to watch on television or on the internet. Do you agree?
3. It would be very cost effective for a destination to advertise solely on the internet. What would be the disadvantages of such a strategy?
4. Surf the net and find three examples of tourism advertisements that can be viewed online. Briefly explain each ad.

## Websites

| | |
|---|---|
| www.tourism.australia.com | Tourism Australia |
| www.ksinclair.com | Kevin Sinclair's website |
| www.luxurylinks.com | Auction site for luxury holidays |
| www.tripadvisor.com | Tripadvisor – a site that collects user testimonials on hotels and attractions worldwide |
| www.CruiseDiva.com | Travel blog that reports on the cruise industry |
| www.realtravel.com | Real Travel blog catering primarily to adventure travellers |
| www.travelpod.com | TravelPod blog catering primarily to adventure travellers |
| www.CarnivalConnections.com | Carnival Cruise Lines social networking platform for cruise passengers |
| www.wikitravel.org | Wikitravel travel blog |
| www.wayfaring.com | Wayfaring travel blog |
| www.kayak.com | Travel search engine |
| www.allcheckin.com | Travel search engine |
| www.priceline.com | PriceLine |

| | |
|---|---|
| www.outrigger.com | Outrigger Hotels and Resorts |
| www.Tourism-Review.com. | Provides daily, weekly and monthly tourism news |
| www.WorldTourismDirectory.com | Information for the travel trade, travel media or researchers |
| www.secondlife.com | Second Life online service |

## References

1  Johnson, B. (8 August 2006) 'British internet users spend 50 days a year surfing web', *The Guardian*, 13.

2  Taylor, R. (30 June 2006) 'Check in, log on, fork out', *Guardian Travel*, 6.

3  Jones, R. (22 July 2006) 'New move to pull the plug on concert ticket touts', *Guardian Money*, 4.

4  Anon. (2006) 'Internet marketing and distribution strategy for resorts', *Hospitality Sales & Marketing Association International*, 23(1), A1–12.

5  Ibid.

6  Parsons, A. M., Zeisser, M. and Waitman, R. (1998) 'Organizing today for the digital marketing of tomorrow', *Journal of Interactive Marketing, 12*(1), 31–46; Gretzel, U., Yuan, Y. L. and Fesenmaier, D. R. (2000) 'Preparing for the new economy: advertising strategies and change in destination marketing organizations', *Journal of Travel Research, 39*(2), 146–156.

7  Beirne, E. and Curry, P. (1999) 'The impact of the Internet on the information search process and tourism decision-making', in D. Buhalis and W. Schertler (eds), *Information and Communication Technologies in Tourism*. Wien, Austria: Springer-Verlag, 88–97.

8  Schwartz, E. I. (1998) *Webonomics: Nine Essential Principles for Growing your Business on the World Wide Web*. New York: Broadway.

9  Hoffman, D. L. and Novak, T. P. (1996) 'Marketing in hypermedia computer-mediated environments: conceptual foundations', *Journal of Marketing*, 60(July), 50–68.

10  Rufo, S. (2006) '10 Things your website should have (but probably doesn't)', *Ski Area Management*, 45(4), 31–35.

11  Wilkening, D. (2007) 'Why consumers don't book online travel', retrieved from www.travelmole.com.

12  Pollock, A. (2006) 'Reaching travelers online', *Tourism*, 10(2), 5.

13  Anon. (19 October 2006) 'Newly launched international tourism portal focuses on travel trade professionals', retrieved from www.worldtourismdirectory.com.

14  Rocha, R. (23 September 2006) 'Internet's second coming gets users more involved', *Calgary Herald*, A14.

15  Pollock, A. (2006) 'Reaching travelers online', *Tourism*, 10(2), 5.

16  Pollock, A. (2006) 'Reaching travelers online: Part II', *Tourism*, 10(3), 5.

17  Green, C.E. and Warner, M.M. (2006) 'Hospitality approach to online marketing: survey of attitudes and approaches', HSMAI Foundation, NYU, TIG Global Survey.

18  Godin, S. (1999) *Permission Marketing*. New York: Simon & Schuster.

19  Green, C.E. and Warner, M.M. (2006) 'Hospitality approach to online marketing: Survey of attitudes and approaches', HSMAI Foundation, NYU, TIG Global Survey.

20  Lohr, S. (5 September 2006) 'Still holding value', *Financial Post*, FP10.

21  Tierney, P. (2000) 'Internet-based evaluation of tourism website effectiveness: methodological issues and survey results', *Journal of Travel Research*, 39, 212–219.

# 11

# PROVIDING SERVICE QUALITY THROUGH INTERNAL MARKETING

## Beyond the Call of Duty

In order to provide customer satisfaction and build loyalty in a highly competitive climate, tourism providers are going beyond the call of duty to wow their guests. The Fairmont Chateau Lake Louise in Canada, for example, recently sent a private car on a four-hour round trip to pick up a passport and ski pass left behind at a car hire desk. The Fairmont chain is also famous for providing a fire truck so that a young firefighter guest could propose to his girlfriend. There have been similar stories from many of the international hotel groups. In Britain, a Four Seasons Hotel concierge went the extra mile by becoming a private eye and tracking down a guest's long-lost friend on his day off work and reuniting the couple.

Hotels are not just relying on one-off incidents of exceptional service. Intercontinental Hotels are concentrating on making their guests' night's sleep more comfortable by providing extra pillows, both feather-filled and hypo-allergenic, according to preference. They took this initiative even further by hiring a doctor to design a sleep programme for jet-lagged guests. As a result, many of the rooms come equipped with drape clips to ensure darkness, CDs offering tips for good sleep, ear plugs, eye shades, scented oils and a night light to make the bathroom easily accessible. Wake-up calls are also guaranteed by offering the guest free accommodation if the call doesn't actually come.

An innovative provision is the 'Recovery Concierge' at Loews New Orleans Hotel. The concierge is head of a hangover cure programme for guests who overindulge in the city's excesses of alcohol and rich food, but need to bounce back in time for morning business meetings. After extensive research with nutritionists and experts, rooms now come complete with foot creams, face mists, Alka Seltzer, ginger tea, vitamins to replace electrolytes, painkillers and soft rolls and smoothies to help settle upset stomachs. The Recovery Concierge also offers prevention ideas such as drinking water to avoid hangovers, or what

'Pets can stay' travel services, targeting people who travel with pets

shoes to wear while touring the French Quarter to prevent sore feet. The idea is not new (the Ritz-Carlton has a make-your-own Bloody Mary bar in the spa for example) but Loews has taken the concept one step further to differentiate its appreciation of guest needs and its pampering services.

Special treatment is not just dished out to two-legged customers. Delta is chasing families by encouraging them to bring along the family dog. At the Halifax property in Canada, for example, dogs get a registration kit including a food bowl, place mat and treats. Other hotel chains, including Best Western, Howard Johnson Canada and Loews Hotels also allow guests to bring along their pets. Loews, in particular, treats pets as honoured guests, calling them 'VIPs' (Very Important Pets). At check in, guests are provided with a welcome letter for their pets outlining rules as well as local vet facilities, pet stores and dog-walking routes. The chains' pet perks include a toy-filled bag, specialized bedding and even gourmet room service with meals designed by chefs and approved by vets. Cats have a choice of salmon or tuna, dogs choose from 'bow wow' burgers, chicken with rice or grilled fillet and there is even a vegetarian dish especially for jetlag. In the rooms, there are special place mats, water bowls and toys for pets plus treats in the mini bar.

These examples are all part of a new super-service ethos that is extending to other sectors of the tourism industry, with companies like Enterprise Rent-A-Car trying to make a difference to their service quality by offering 'Good Samaritan' awards backed by financial prizes. Airlines, too, are improving service to woo customers. Family travel, in particular, is being encouraged by concentrating marketing tactics on the children. In order to reduce the rigours of travelling with kids, airlines are providing travel perks for the children, considering them 'the consumers of tomorrow'. Air Canada, for example, introduced a range of meals designed for children's appetites and tastes, including many healthy options as well as souvenirs all wrapped up in a brightly coloured box. Also, flight attendants distribute games and reading materials geared to different ages during the journey. British Airways provides family-oriented in-flight entertainment as well as giving kids a backpack or shoulder bag full of age-related goodies. Children can purchase an airline log book to record their travels, which the captain will sign and certify.

*Sources*: Anon. (20 September 2004) 'Airlines, hotels woo "consumers of tomorrow"', *Globe and Mail*, Travel Rewards II, E5; Anon. (20 September 2004) 'Pet project', *Globe and Mail*, Travel Rewards II, E7; Brieger, P. (3 May 2005) 'Hotels get personal with their perks', *National Post*, FW8.

## OBJECTIVES

On completion of this chapter, you should understand:

▶ the internal marketing process;

▶ the link between service quality and customer satisfaction;

▶ the measurement tools and the behavioural consequences of service quality;

▶ the link between customer satisfaction and loyalty;

▶ relationship marketing strategies; and

▶ the importance of service recovery.

## Introduction

The Opening Vignette shows how tourism organizations are differentiating on service in order to attract and retain loyal customers. Having a service culture is one part of internal marketing and is the focus of this chapter. The chapter begins by defining internal marketing and examining the four key steps in the internal marketing process. The next section focuses on delivering service quality, and includes discussions of the 'gaps model' of service quality, the measurement of service quality, and the behavioural consequences of service quality. The third main section discusses loyalty and relationship marketing. Various customer retention strategies are introduced, as are the benefits of relationship marketing to both company and customer. The final part of the chapter analyses service recovery and offers guidelines for tracking and handling complaints.

**Internal marketing** was introduced in Chapter 1 as an integral part of the services marketing triangle (see Figure 1.5), and can be defined as marketing aimed internally, at a company's own employees. Internal marketing takes place through the fulfilling of promises. Promises are easy to make, but unless providers are recruited, trained, equipped with tools and appropriate internal systems, and rewarded for good service, the promises may not be kept. Internal marketing was first proposed by Berry et al. in the 1970s[1] as a way to deliver consistently high service quality, but despite the rapidly growing literature on the subject, very few organizations actually apply the concept in practice. One of the main problems is that a single unified concept of what is meant by internal marketing does not exist. Lack of investment in internal marketing may also be the result of corporate distraction. Companies that are busy trying to boost revenues and cut costs may not see why they should spend money on employees, thus missing the point that these are the very people who ultimately deliver the brand promises the company makes.

---

**INTERNAL MARKETING**
marketing aimed internally, at a company's own employees

---

However, there is growing awareness that an effective internal marketing programme has a positive effect on service quality, customer satisfaction and loyalty, and eventually profits. Figure 11.1 illustrates the link between internal marketing and profits.

## The Internal Marketing Process

The main objective of internal marketing is to enable employees to deliver satisfying products to guests. This takes place through a four-step process.

### Establishment of a Service Culture

Organizational culture refers to the unwritten policies and guidelines, both in relation to what has been formally decreed, and to what actually takes place in a company. It is the pattern of

**Figure 11.1**    The Link Between Internal Marketing and Profits

shared values and beliefs that helps individuals understand organizational functioning and thus provides them with norms for behaviour in the business. In the past few decades, researchers have begun to analyse the linkage between culture and the marketing of services. Due to the unique characteristics of services (i.e. intangibility, inseparability of production and consumption, perishability and heterogeneity), the nature of the culture of a service organization is particularly important and worthy of attention.

Marketing culture refers to the unwritten policies and guidelines that provide employees with behavioural norms, both in relation to the importance the organization as a whole places on the marketing function, and to the manner in which marketing activities are executed. Since service quality is one dimension of marketing culture, it follows that the kind of marketing culture an organization has would be particularly important for a service organization, as the simultaneous delivery and receipt of services brings the provider and customer physically and psychologically close. Research has shown a strong positive relationship between the kind of marketing culture a service organization has and its profitability and degree of marketing effectiveness (Webster, 1995).[2]

A **service culture** is a culture that supports customer service through policies, procedures, reward systems and actions. An internal marketing programme flows out of a service culture. A services marketing programme is doomed to failure if its organizational culture does not support servicing the customer. Such a programme requires a strong commitment from management. If management expects employees to have a positive attitude toward customers, management must have a positive attitude toward both the customer and the employees. The Global Spotlight on p. 368 shows how service culture at the Sheraton Suites Calgary Eau Claire in Calgary is driven by top management. Similarly, the Case Study at the end of this chapter shows how Virgin's service culture is driven by CEO Richard Branson. The change to a customer-oriented system may require changes in hiring, training, reward systems and customer complaint resolution, as well as empowerment of employees. It requires that managers spend time talking to both customers and customer-contact employees.

**SERVICE CULTURE**
a culture that supports customer service through policies, procedures, reward systems and actions

Turning potentially dissatisfied guests into satisfied ones is a major challenge for tourism and hospitality organizations, and empowering employees to go the extra mile in satisfying guests is recognized as one of the most powerful tools available to a service organization. **Empowerment** is the act of giving employees the authority to identify and solve guest problems or complaints on the spot, and to make improvements in the work processes when necessary. Often this will mean decentralizing decision-making and flattening organization charts in order to give more power to the front-line employees who directly serve customers. It also means that managers must have greater levels of trust in their subordinates and must respect their judgement.

---

**EMPOWERMENT**

the act of giving employees the authority to identify and solve guest problems or complaints on the spot, and to make improvements in the work processes when necessary

---

Empowerment is regarded as an essential aspect of internal marketing, and vital for the operationalization of Gronroos's interactive marketing concept, a part of the services marketing triangle introduced in Chapter 1. In order for interactive marketing to occur, front-line employees need to be empowered. However, the degree of empowerment is contingent on the complexity and variability of customer needs and the degree of task complexity. Also, empowerment does not suit all employees because of the extra responsibility that it inevitably entails. The Snapshot below highlights how WestJet staff are empowered to think outside the box and go the extra mile to provide customers with exceptional service.

## Snapshot

### The Airline with a Sense of Humour: WestJet Airlines

WestJet Airlines is a company that has, so far, beaten the odds to become a favourite of both travel agents and consumers in Canada. It is, after all, the airline that boards passengers by sock colour or zodiac sign; concocts promotions that enable passengers with names like 'Love' and 'Heart' to fly free on Valentine's Day; and has seen gate agents bring out flutes to entertain stranded passengers during an ice storm. And compared to rigid, often humourless Air Canada, WestJet earns raves from the travel trade. 'They'll do almost anything for you,' one Ontario agent gushed to *Canadian Travel Press*. In fact, WestJet recently placed first in 'Canada's Most Admired Corporate Cultures' for the second year in a row.

Bob Cummings, Executive Vice-President, Guest Experience and Marketing for WestJet, says the formula is simple: 'We foster a caring culture.' While company employees earn industry averages, they also take part in profit sharing and share purchase plans which has WestJet matching 100% of WestJetter's contributions for share purchase on up to 20% percent of their salary. This evokes 'a strong sense of ownership' in every WestJetter in the company, says Cummings. 'When someone picks up the phone, they're an owner. The person at the gate is an owner.' Another key ingredient of WestJet's success is its underlying philosophy to emulate and 'Canadianize' the model of successful US discount carrier, Southwest Airlines.

WestJet has evolved to become more of a hybrid model within the airline industry. It is moving away from the no-frills, discount airline reputation with the addition of live seat-back satellite television at every seat and pay-per-view movies as well as buy-on-board services. WestJet also has the most modern fleet of jet aircraft in North America with the average age of its fleet being only 2.5 years. 'What won't go away is our focus on the guest and on our people. The way we interact with our guests is really what sets us apart,' says Cummings. And after a decade, this core strategy of a focus on people has been wildly successful. In an industry that has seen the majority of airlines fail in Canada, WestJet has been consistently profitable. Apart from a small loss in 2004, WestJet has been profitable every year and led North American airlines in percentage operating margin and percentage net earnings in the third quarter of 2006. People want to be a part of this success – WestJet receives more than 1,000 unsolicited CVs each week.

Clive Beddoe, president and CEO of WestJet, was one of Canada's Entrepreneurs of the Year in 2000 because of his willingness to take risks. He was already a wealthy and successful businessperson (in plastics), but was willing to risk everything to move into an industry in which the failure rate is extremely high. WestJet's entry into the marketplace in early 1996 was a watershed in the Canadian airline industry, as it was the first true low-cost, low-fare, short-haul scheduled carrier. What has enabled this airline to make money for its owners in each year of its existence while many others fight to simply survive? Some suggest it is the fact that WestJet operates an airline in a non-traditional manner and achieves non-traditional results. WestJet has been praised by guests for its service and light-hearted humour, which starts from the first booking call. If you're put on hold, you will hear a message full of corny jokes, as well as helpful information. In the airport, passengers may be boarded by the colour of their hair or shoes. At other times the pilot may sing, or attendants will offer prizes for the passenger with the most lipstick in her purse or the one with the biggest hole in his socks. Invariably, a WestJet guest leaves the aircraft with a smile. As WestJet spokesperson Richard Bartrem says, 'We take our job seriously, but not ourselves'.

WestJet says empowerment is more than a buzzword because it wants its front-line staff to be able to make the right decision in a given situation. The idea is that the goodwill generated by resolving a complaint will translate into repeat business. WestJet's executive vice-president of culture, Don Bell, often sends handwritten notes to recognize top-performing employees. These sometimes include small rewards such as a movie pass or a $10 gift certificate. Praise is also made public. WestJet issues a monthly newsletter called Kudos Corner, containing a selection of ten or so letters from passengers giving praise for good service.

But the airline industry is extremely vulnerable to changes in the environment. In 2001, as a result of September 11, air traffic fell off as much as 50 percent. International air carriers like Swissair, Sabena of Belgium, and Canada 3000 crumbled. Airlines across North America called for government bailouts and compensation packages as 100,000 people lost jobs in the industry. The domestic airline industry in Canada went through a consolidation process with only two players – WestJet and Air Canada – left standing. Despite the drop in passenger numbers and fares around the world after September 11, WestJet managed to continue growing by adding new destinations and airlines to its fleet, and was well positioned to fill the competitive void left by the grounding of Canada 3000. 'We just continued to do what we'd set out to do from the beginning of the year. We had a plan for the year and we sustained it' said Beddoe. 'We felt confident that travel would come back. We saw what happened after the Gulf War in the early 1990s. It was short-lived, but there was a catastrophic reaction within the industry when people stopped travelling.'

Beddoe says it was WestJet's culture that brought the airline through tough times after September 11. 'We were the first airline in North America to be fully operational, with every one of our scheduled flights flying,' he said. 'On the 12th of September we were given the rules by which we were going to operate and our people worked through the night to figure how we were going to apply those rules and how to disseminate those operating procedures and standards out to all of our bases. By four o'clock in the morning we were able to be up and operational and ready to go.' The display of excellence in leadership, corporate performance, innovation, focus on customer relationships, and human resource practices was truly evident around this single catastrophic event. 'It was probably the most extreme example of how well this culture of teamwork can work and how it can be applied to create extraordinary results,' says Beddoe.

However, Beddoe is aware that additional terrorist attacks, the fear of such attacks, or increased hostilities could further impact the airline industry and WestJet, and could cause a decrease in travel and an increase in costs to airlines and airline travellers. In the aftermath of the terrorist attacks, the availability of insurance for airlines has decreased and the costs of such insurance have increased. In the event that the Canadian government does not renew its indemnity regarding war and terrorism insurance, it is possible that such insurance will not be available to the Canadian airline industry, including WestJet.

Industry watchers argue that WestJet's expansive growth will make it difficult for the company to keep its distinctive culture alive. Beddoe argues that Southwest Airlines, on which WestJet has been based, has kept its culture alive for 25 years even as its work force has swelled to 30,000. Having said this, Beddoe realizes that protecting the culture is essential. 'It's focus number one. Our risk, in my view, is internal, not external. And that's why we put so much emphasis on it.' However, Beddoe is cautious about becoming too arrogant and conceited. 'It's not me who made all this happen; it's 6,000 people here that make it happen. The focus is on the teamwork and that no matter how good we are at what we're doing, we can always be better.'

*Sources*: Jang, B. and Grant, T. (17 October 2006) 'Fuller planes, cost cuts propel airlines', *Globe & Mail*, B12; Baginski, M. (2002) 'WestJet celebrates sixth anniversary', retrieved from www.canadatourism.com/en/ctc/ctx/ctx-news/search/newsbydateform.cfm; Fitzpatrick, P. (16 October 2001) 'Wacky WestJet's winning ways', *National Post*, C1; Quinn, P. (12 September 2001) 'Success stories: flying in the face of adversity', *Financial Post*, E1; Welner, C. and Briggs, D. (2002) 'Reaching for the skies', *Alberta Venture*, 6(5), 26–27; WestJet annual information form, 20 March 2002.

## Development of a Marketing Approach to Human Resource Management

A marketing approach to human resources management (HRM) involves the use of marketing techniques to attract and retain employees. EasyJet, the UK-based low-cost airline, recently added a 'come and work for us' plea to the address that greets passengers boarding its planes. The airline employs over 2,000 cabin crew across Europe, and this was an attempt to recruit staff by saving money on advertising. Taking a marketing approach to

HRM also means using marketing research techniques to understand the employee market. Different employee segments look for different benefits, and it is important to understand what benefits will attract who. Advertising for staff can then be developed with prospective employees in mind, building a positive image of the company for present and future employees and customers.

Such a marketing approach to developing positions and benefits helps to attract and retain good employees. Companies should ensure that they recruit employees who are highly motivated, customer oriented and sales minded, because changing employee attitudes and behaviours is more difficult and costly once they have been recruited. Employees also need the right type and level of training to perform their jobs. This can help to reduce ambiguity surrounding their role and can help them to meet the needs of customers more effectively.

More and more managers are trying to tap into the psyche of employees as the continuous turnover of staff takes its toll on the industry. Employee turnover in the hospitality industry is often ten times that of other industries. Turnover in easyJet, for example, is about 18–20 per cent annually. Some managers are finding that giving increased responsibility is improving retention and performance, a strategy that has proved successful for both WestJet and Fairmont, companies profiled in this chapter. Fairmont also offers employee exchange programmes to boost staff loyalty (see Snapshot below). It is not, however, just entry-level positions that are difficult to keep filled. Turnover among hospitality industry sales and marketing professionals is at almost 25 per cent. A National Restaurant Association poll of more than 400 food service managers also found that about a quarter of the respondents intended to leave their positions in the near future, with at least half of those planning to depart the food service business entirely (Sutherland, 2002).[3]

According to Jon Katzenbach, author of *Why Pride Matters More Than Money* (2003), feelings of pride can motivate people to excel far more effectively than money or position.[4] He says that institutions such as Southwest Airlines and Marriott International, which manage to sustain the emotional commitment of a large proportion of their employees over good times and bad, seldom rely on monetary incentives. Instead, they find ways to instil institution-building pride in what people do, in why and how they do it, and in those with whom they do it. Pride-builders accomplish this by (a) setting aspirations that touch emotions, (b) pursuing a meaningful purpose, (c) cultivating personal relationships of respect, (d) becoming a person of high character, and (d) injecting humour along the way. For the Sheraton Suites Calgary Eau Claire (see Global Spotlight), instilling pride in employees is a key motivator.

Continuous training can also help improve employee morale and reduce turnover of employees, as is the case at Fairmont Hotels & Resorts (see Snapshot below). In Singapore, an unusual training programme for taxi drivers is improving the service offered to tourists. Hundreds of taxi drivers have qualified as tourist guides, having spent more than 80 hours training over a three-month period. After sitting a written exam and taking practical assessments, drivers who make the grade are awarded a special Taxi Tourist Guide License.[5] Seok Chin Poh of the Singapore Tourism Board, which helped set up the scheme, said: 'We are seeing a growth in independent travellers from Europe visiting Singapore who want to explore at their own pace but still benefit from the knowledge of a guide. The scheme offers visitors a refreshing and interesting alternative to touring Singapore.'

## Snapshot

### Internal Marketing at Fairmont Hotels & Resorts

Fairmont Hotels & Resorts is a good example of a company that aims its marketing efforts towards its employees. Fairmont is the largest luxury hotel management company in North America and has achieved great success since it opened in 1914. The company now operates 77 hotels with about 30,000 rooms and employs 28,000 people. The company sees internal marketing as critical in achieving guest satisfaction, and consequently Fairmont is world-renowned for its excellent guest service. The company measures the success or failure of its internal marketing programmes through employee turnover rate – currently running at about 20 per cent, with hotel industry averages five or six times higher. Staff loyalty in turn encourages customer loyalty; repeat guests make up 60 per cent of Fairmont's business.

Fairmont knows that it is important to segment the employee market as well as the guest market, and to develop a marketing mix to attract the best staff for its company. Attracting self-motivated, results-oriented staff for Fairmont is key to its employee marketing mix, which is why it has an extensive recruiting and hiring process to select the best employees to interact with its guests. Once hired, the employee participates in a mandatory two-day orientation offered by the Fairmont Learning Organization (FLO). New recruits learn Fairmont's service culture (policies, procedures, reward systems and actions) and organizational culture (mission, vision, values and history of the company).

Empowerment is about turning the traditional organizational structure upside down, with the customers and employees at the top of the structure and management at the bottom. Management and employees now work to serve the guest, versus serving the CEO or 'boss'. Focusing on the needs and wants of the customer and granting employees the power to achieve the ultimate guest service creates an atmosphere in which employees are not afraid to tell supervisors of a mistake in order to rectify it. The company-wide emphasis is on giving each employee – at both the corporate and the property levels – the tools, training, authority and support they need in order to make informed decisions and take appropriate actions to deliver the highest level of service excellence to Fairmont guests. The goal is to empower employees to create customized experiences that make lifetime memories for guests – what Fairmont calls 'wow' experiences.

Employee reward and recognition programmes are an important part of the process of internal marketing. Once Fairmont has attracted and recruited the right employees, attention is focused on keeping them satisfied and motivated to impress the guests. Benefits and perks are important factors. Substantial discounts of up to 50 per cent off food, beverages and hotel rates are offered as employee incentives to encourage them to use these products/services, thus facilitating first-hand knowledge. Employees are part of the product, and encouraging them to be excited about Fairmont hotels and services will in turn make the customer more excited. Fairmont also has a number of recognition awards that are presented throughout the year. These benefits and awards market the company to the employees and install a positive attitude within the workplace. Internal communication at Fairmont is also taken seriously. A bi-monthly newsletter is distributed in each specific hotel, and a company-wide newsletter, 'The Dialogue', keeps staff up to date on new company procedures.

*Sources*: Cohen, S. (2001) 'Concierges go the extra mile to make visitors' stays memorable', *The Business Journal*, Kansas City, 19(50), 24; Liddle, A. J. (28 January 2002) 'Regional powerhouse chains', *Nations Restaurant News*, 36(4), 100–102; Mueller, S. (2000) 'How do you set your hotel apart from others?' *The Business Journal*, Kansas City, 17(51), 44; The Fairmont Learning Organization (September 2001) MyFairmont Serviceplus Training Binder.

## Dissemination of Marketing Information to Employees

Managers need to pay significant attention to the communication of marketing (and other organizational) strategies and objectives to employees, so that they understand their own role and importance in the implementation of the strategies and in the achievement of the objectives. Research evidence suggests that the frequency, quality and accuracy of downward communication moderates employee role ambiguity and hence increases job satisfaction. Such communication mechanisms may come in the form of company meetings, training sessions, newsletters, emails, annual reports or videotapes. In the Snapshot above, Fairmont distributed a bi-monthly newsletter in each hotel as well as a company-wide newsletter to keep staff up to date on new company procedures.

Unfortunately, many companies exclude customer-contact employees from the communication cycle. The director of marketing may tell managers and supervisors about upcoming promotional campaigns, but some managers may feel that employees do not need to have this information. However, it is important that staff are informed. They should hear about promotions and new products from management, not from external advertisements meant for customers. Changes in the service delivery process should also be communicated. In fact, all action steps in the marketing plan should include internal marketing. If company advertising and other promises are developed without input from operations, contact personnel may not be able to deliver service that matches the image portrayed in marketing efforts.

## Implementation of a Reward and Recognition System

For employees to perform effectively, it is important that they know how they are doing, so communication must be designed to give them feedback on their performance. The Global Spotlight on the Sheraton Suites Eau Claire later in this chapter shows how every effort is made to recognize the achievement of employees and to ensure that they are happy and proud of their jobs. In order to feed an employee's energy level and overall desire to perform, organizations need to communicate performance objectives clearly, as well as provide relevant training, feedback and recognition in the form of non-cash rewards. However, the rewards should be tailored to the interests of the employees they are designed to motivate. Group excursions are popular with employees in the 18–29 age groups, while older employees prefer personal trips. More men than women, for some reason, appreciate getting company-logo merchandise as a reward. For some, the ideal reward is the gift of a personal chef for the evening, and for others time off with pay is perfect. Sometimes, recognition and regular feedback alone is enough.

## Delivering Service Quality

Service quality has been increasingly identified as a key factor in differentiating service products and building a competitive advantage in tourism. The process by which customers evaluate a purchase, thereby determining satisfaction and likelihood of repurchase, is important to all marketers, but especially to services marketers because, unlike their manufacturing counterparts, they have fewer objective measures of quality by which to judge their production. **Service quality** can be defined as customers' perceptions of the service component of a product, and these perceptions are said to be based on five dimensions: reliability, assurance, empathy, responsiveness and tangibles (Parasuraman et al. 1988).[6]

---

**SERVICE QUALITY**

customers' perceptions of the service component of a product

---

Many researchers believe that an outgrowth of service quality is **customer satisfaction**, measured as the difference between the service that a customer expects and the perceived quality of what is actually delivered (Cronin and Taylor, 1994).[7] Satisfying customers has always been a key component of the tourism industry, but never before has it been so critical. In these uncertain times, and with increased competition, knowing how to win and keep customers is the single most important business skill that anyone can learn. Customer satisfaction and loyalty are the keys to long-term profitability, and keeping the customer happy is everybody's business. Becoming customer-centred and exceeding customer expectations are requirements for business success.

---

**CUSTOMER SATISFACTION**

the difference between the service that a customer expects and the perceived quality of what is actually delivered

---

Well-publicized research shows that companies can increase profits from 25 to 85 per cent by retaining just 5 per cent more of their customers (Reichheld and Sasser, 1990),[8] but the newest research indicates that merely 'satisfying' customers is no longer enough to ensure loyalty (Heskett et al., 1997).[9] There is little or no correlation between satisfied (versus highly satisfied) customers and customer retention. This means that it is not enough just to please customers. Each customer should become so pleased with all elements of their association with an organization that buying from someone else is unthinkable.

The issue of understanding needs and expectations is an important part of the quest for customer satisfaction. The 'gaps model' of service quality (see Figure 11.2) provides a method of graphically illustrating these needs and expectations (Parasuraman et al., 1985).[10] This conceptual model enables a structured thought process for evaluating and 'designing

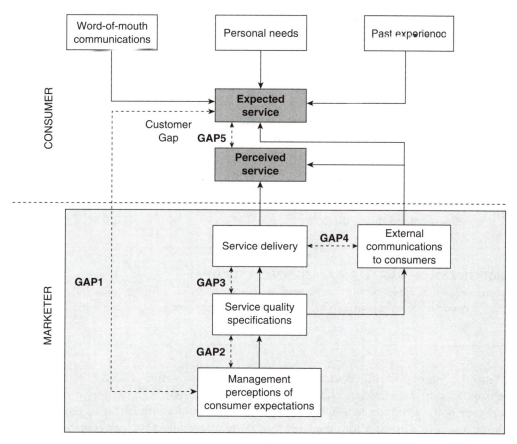

**Figure 11.2**    The Gaps Model of Service Quality

*Source*: Parasuraman, A., Zeithaml, V. A. and Berry, L. L. (1985) 'A conceptual model of service quality and its implications for future research', *Journal of Marketing*, 49(4), 40.

in' customer satisfaction. The model begins with expected service as viewed by the customer. Every customer has certain expectations about a service, which may come from word of mouth, personal needs, group needs, past experience, and/or external communications. When the service is delivered and the customers' expectations are exceeded, the customers perceive the quality as relatively high. When their expectations have not been met, they perceive the quality as relatively low. Thus, as stated above, customer satisfaction can be defined as the difference between what the customer expects and the perceived quality of what is actually delivered. Often there is a gap between expected service and the actual service as perceived by the customer, and in the model, this is gap 5. The magnitude of this gap is driven by four other possible gaps, each of which denotes failure in some aspect of service delivery.

## Measuring Service Quality

The two main research instruments that have been developed over the years to analyse the concepts of quality and consumer satisfaction in the service industry are importance–performance analysis (IPA) and SERVQUAL. **Importance–performance analysis (IPA)** is a procedure that shows both the relative *importance* of various attributes and the *performance* of the company, product, or destination under study in providing these attributes. Its use has important marketing and management implications for decision-makers, and one of the major benefits of using IPA is the identification of areas for service quality improvements. Results are displayed graphically on a two-dimensional grid, and through a simple visual analysis of this matrix, policy-makers can identify areas where the resources and pro- grammes need to be concentrated. Introduced over 20 years ago (Martilla and James 1977),[11] IPA is well documented in the literature.

---

**IMPORTANCE–PERFORMANCE ANALYSIS (IPA)**

a procedure that shows both the relative importance of various attributes and the performance of the company, product or destination under study in providing these attributes

---

Figure 11.3 shows the importance and performance mean scores of ski destination attrib- utes from a study in Switzerland (Hudson and Shephard, 1998).[12] The action grid identifies where each of the attributes falls in terms of the four quadrants, with examples pinpointed in each quadrant. In this variation, the largest number of attributes (42 per cent) was plotted into the 'Concentrate Here' area of the action grid. Respondents rated these attributes high in importance but low in performance. These attributes included the majority of services on the ski slopes, comfortable beds, value for money in bars and restaurants, and the prices in the ski shops.

**SERVQUAL** is an instrument developed by Parasuraman, Zeithaml and Berry (1985),[13] which is used to measure the difference between consumers' expectations and perceptions of service quality. Exploratory research conducted in 1985 showed that consumers judge service quality by using the same general criteria, regardless of the type of service. Parasuraman et al. capture these criteria using a scale composed of 22 items designed to load on five dimensions reflect- ing service quality. The dimensions are: assurance, empathy, reliability, responsiveness and tangibles. Each item is used twice: first, to determine customers' expectations about compa- nies in general, within the service category being investigated; second, to measure perceptions

---

**SERVQUAL**

an instrument used to measure the difference between consumers' expectations and perceptions of service quality

---

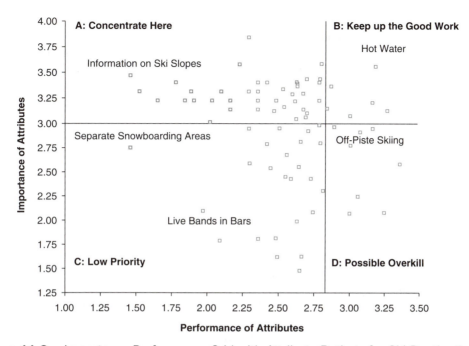

**Figure 11.3**   Importance-Performance Grid with Attribute Ratings for Ski Destination

*Source*: Hudson, S. and Shephard, G. (1998) 'Measuring service quality at tourist destinations: an application of Importance–Performance Analysis to an Alpine ski resort', *Journal of Travel and Tourism Marketing*, 7(3), 69.

of performance of a particular company, within this same service category. These evaluations are collected using a seven-point Likert scale. According to the authors, the service quality is determined as the difference between customers' expectations and perceptions.

Other researchers have suggested that the mere fact of asking respondents to mark their perceptions of performance already leads them to compare mentally their perceptions and their expectations. In other words, the estimation of perceptions might already include a 'perception minus expectation' mental process. They suggest that performance on its own, or SERVPERF (which stands for 'service performance'), is the measure that best explains total quality. However, although the perceptions format offers the most predictive power – a finding that has consistently emerged in the literature – it offers little diagnostic potential and, indeed, may result in inappropriate priorities being established. From a managerial perspective, it would seem important to track the extent to which expectations are met over time as well as trends in performance. The use of difference scores gives managers a better understanding of whether increasing expectations or diminishing performance might be responsible for declining service quality and customer satisfaction. An examination of minimum expectations may also be fruitful. Similarly, disregarding importance may mean losing useful insights. Without considering attribute importance, one has no indication of the relative importance that respondents attach to particular aspects of service performance. The Case Study in Chapter 4 expands on this discussion.

Measuring service quality, and hence guest satisfaction, is very important for many tourism and hospitality organizations. The Global Spotlight below describes how the Sheraton Suites Eau Claire in Canada continually scores highly in terms of guest satisfaction relative to other Sheraton properties.

# Global Spotlight

## 'It's Our Pleasure!' – Service Excellence at the Sheraton Suites Calgary Eau Claire

The Sheraton Suites Calgary Eau Claire has a reputation for service excellence. The hotel was awarded the Sheraton Brand Highest Guest Satisfaction from 2001 straight through to 2006 continuously. This Sheraton award recognizes exceptional levels of hospitality, service and attention to detail, as well as upscale facilities and variety of amenities. The Sheraton Suites was also the winner of the Alberta Tourism Award (ALTO) for Service Excellence in 2002 and 2005. This particular award honours an organization in the tourism industry that demonstrates a commitment to service excellence, delivering outstanding customer service to their visitors, employees, suppliers and other stakeholders.

But exactly what does it take to win awards like this?

Randy Zupanski, was the hotel general manager from its opening and led this great team to terrific results, instilling a service culture and customer service focus for all the associates. In 2005 Ross Meredith was appointed general manager and in that year the hotel was awarded the Sheraton Hotel of the Year Award Worldwide, from Starwood Hotels and Resorts. Meredith says there are two key reasons why the Sheraton Suites Calgary Eau Claire is so different from its competitors: customer loyalty and quality employees. First, a focus on customer loyalty is driven by the 'It's Our Pleasure' programme – a recognition and reward programme for guests. On every fifth stay, each guest receives a gift, one that is meaningful to that guest, and the value of the gift increases the longer a customer remains loyal. For example, on the fifth stay a guest may receive a bottle of wine in his or her room, and by the twenty-fifth stay, a personalized bathrobe will be given as a loyalty gift. Meanwhile, the hotel collects valuable data on the personal preferences of customers and stores this in a database. For example, if a guest likes extra towels and feather pillows, then these will be waiting in the room when the guest arrives, with a note saying 'It's our pleasure to provide you with these items….'.

Meredith suggests that the majority of hotels put in the customer service effort *after* the guest arrives, whereas the Sheraton Eau Claire takes care of preferences *before* arrival. A guest relations officer is employed for the sole purpose of co-ordinating the 'It's Our Pleasure' programme, and a room is not ready for a guest until this officer has ensured all preferences are taken care of.

Perhaps the most important reason that the Sheraton Eau Claire is an award winner is the quality of its employees. The hotel hires 'nice people with great attitudes' and takes training very seriously. Training programmes include a two-day hotel orientation, a full day spent on the 'It's Our Pleasure' programme, and brand specific 'Building World Class Brands' an extensive Starwood training programme that supports both the service delivery culture in each building and across the brand. Training programmes use role-playing to emphasize the meaning and importance of employee empowerment, employees are trained in the art of service recovery and are taught the importance of customer contact. Energy is put into 'key contact area', so that before a guest reaches his or her room, there has been plenty of opportunity for personal contact from the valet, bellman, reception staff, or the general manager him- or herself. For Meredith, pride is the key, and every effort is made to recognize the achievement of employees and to ensure that they are happy and proud of their jobs. Loss of employees to other competitive set hotels is extremely low, he says, and if employees do leave, it is to go into other industries.

Sheraton Eau Claire's success has been a fascination and curiosity to a number of service companies and the hotel leadership team has been providing them with best practices and programs that supports service delivery. These include employee empowerment, celebrating success, managing key measurements and the benefits of goal setting, actions plans and follow up.

The results of these efforts are not just manifested in the winning of awards. The hotel has occupancy rates 10 per cent higher and room rates $40–50 above the competitive set hotels. Since opening, the Sheraton Suites Eau Claire has led the market with an overall market share on revenue per available room (RevPAR) of 130–140 per cent. Its competitive set includes the Hyatt, Fairmont, Westin, Delta and Marriott brands. This lengthy period of successful financial and guest service results clearly positions the Sheraton Suites Calgary Eau Claire as the market leader and service delivery leader. The challenge will be to maintain this position in a highly competitive downtown hotel market. In the meantime, the Sheraton Suites Calgary Eau Claire provides an excellent example of the value of internal marketing.

*Source*: R. Meredith, general manager, Sheraton Suites Calgary Eau Claire, personal communication, 13 July, 2007.

## The Behavioural Consequences of Service Quality

In the Global Spotlight above, the internal marketing efforts of the Sheraton Suites Eau Claire resulted in high occupancy rates, high room rates and a very high overall market share on revenue available. The issue of highest priority today involves understanding the impact of service quality on profit and other financial outcomes. Executives of many companies in the 1980s were willing to trust their intuitive sense that better service would lead to improved financial success. They therefore committed resources to improving service prior to having documentation of the financial payoff. Some of these companies, such as Four Seasons and

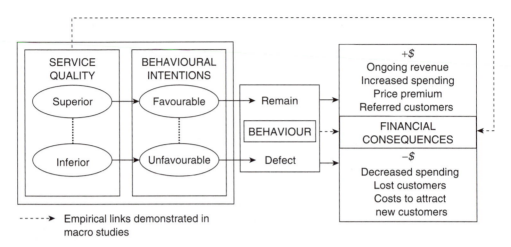

**Figure 11.4** A Model of the Behavioural and Financial Consequences of Service Quality

*Source*: Zeithaml, V. A., Berry, L. L. and Parasuraman, A. (1996) 'The behavioural consequences of service quality', *Journal of Marketing*, 60, 31–46.

Ritz-Carlton, have been richly rewarded for their efforts. But executives in other companies have been reluctant to invest in service improvements without solid evidence of their financial soundness. However, research on the relationship between service quality and profits has begun to accumulate. Findings from these studies show that companies offering superior service achieve higher-than-normal market share growth (Buzzell and Gale, 1987);[14] that the mechanisms by which service quality influences profits include increased market share and premium prices (Phillips et al., 1983);[15] and that businesses in the top quintile of relative service quality realize on average an 8 per cent higher price than their competitors (Gale, 1992).[16]

Another fruitful area of research is that which examines the relationship between service quality and behavioural intentions. Zeithaml, Berry and Parasuraman (1996) have developed a conceptual model that depicts the behavioural consequences of service quality as intervening variables between service quality and the financial gains or losses from retention or defection (see Figure 11.4).[17] The left portion of the model is at the level of the individual customer and proposes that service quality and behavioural intentions are related and, therefore, that service quality is a determinant of whether a customer ultimately remains with or defects from a company.

By integrating research findings and anecdotal evidence, a list of specific indicators of customers' favourable behavioural intentions can be compiled. These include saying positive things about the company to others, recommending the company or service to others, paying a price premium to the company, and remaining loyal to the company. Loyalty may be manifested in a variety of ways – for example, by expressing a preference for a company over others, by continuing to purchase from it, or by increasing business with it in the future. Customers perceiving service performance to be inferior are likely to exhibit behaviours signalling that they are poised to leave the company or spend less money with it. These behaviours include complaining, which is defined by many researchers as a variety of negative responses that stem from dissatisfaction and predict or accompany defection.

After testing this model, the authors found strong empirical support for the intuitive notion that improving service quality can increase favourable behavioural intentions and decrease unfavourable ones. The findings demonstrate the importance of strategies that can steer behavioural intentions in the right directions, including (1) striving to meet customers' 'desired-service' levels (rather than merely performing at their 'adequate-service' levels), (2) emphasizing the prevention of service problems, and (3) effectively resolving problems that do occur. However, multiple findings suggest that companies wanting to improve service, especially beyond the desired-service level, should do so in a cost-effective manner.

## Loyalty and Relationship Marketing

### The Link between Satisfaction and Loyalty

As Figure 11.1 shows, customer satisfaction is a requisite for loyalty. Customer satisfaction is a measure of how well a customer's expectations are met. **Customer loyalty**, on the other hand, is a measure of how likely customers are to return to an organization, and of their willingness to build relationships with the organization. Customer expectations must be met or exceeded to build loyalty. Research has shown that there is an important relationship between customer satisfaction and loyalty (Heskett et al., 1997).[18] The relationship is particularly strong when customers are very satisfied. Thus, businesses that simply aim to satisfy customers may not be doing enough to engender loyalty. They must instead aim to more than satisfy – or even delight – their customers.

---

**CUSTOMER LOYALTY**
a measure of how likely customers are to return to an organization, and of their willingness to build relationships with the organization

---

However, it is important to understand that there are several reasons why satisfied customers may not become loyal customers in the tourism industry. First, many travellers prefer to visit different places and may not return to the same destination or hotel even if they are extremely satisfied. Second, some travellers are very price-sensitive and shop for the best deal, regardless of satisfaction measures. Finally, customers expect to be satisfied with their purchase, so satisfaction ratings are often inflated. This underscores the need to have extremely satisfied customers in order to encourage loyalty.

Loyal customers are therefore more valuable than satisfied customers. A satisfied customer who does not return and does not spread positive word of mouth has no value to the company. On the other hand, a loyal customer who returns and spreads positive word of mouth has a very high value, and it is therefore important that companies identify those patrons who are likely to become loyal customers. Over the last few decades, loyalty reward programmes have burgeoned as companies seek to retain customers in an increasingly competitive market. Loyalty programmes are popular because they are easy to enrol in, and the consumer has the potential to earn rewards for products and services they already use. Loyalty programmes have expanded to the extent that points can be earned in every consumer category, from groceries, to books, to car rentals and even phone bill payments. Travel rewards are the most prized rewards amongst consumers, and the Snapshot below looks at these in more detail.

## Snapshot

### Travel Rewards Still a Hot Ticket

More than 25 years after frequent flyer miles sparked the current obsession with loyalty programmes, public interest in travel rewards shows no signs of waning. In 2006, there were about 89 million participants worldwide in airline frequent flyer programmes, and travel rewards – flights and accommodation – continue to be the most prized rewards amongst consumers, with cash rebates and merchandise running second and third. However, travel reward redemptions have moved from simple air flights to include vacation packages, hotel accommodation anywhere in the world, car rentals, cruises, train trips, bus tickets, attraction passes and dining options for travellers once they reach their destination. For loyal business travellers, travel redemptions can be payback to their families for all the time they spend on the road.

Experiential rewards – rewards that involve creating an experience instead of handing over cash or a piece of merchandise – are part of a trend in the reward industry to keep consumer interest engaged in loyalty programmes. 'Travel is the ultimate experiential reward. It allows customers to dream,' says Kelly Hlavinka, director of Colloquy, a US-based loyalty programme research firm. Of course, consumer satisfaction is only one half of the equation. Travel rewards for loyalty shown are also a big benefit to the travel industry, particularly in an era when the marketplace has become so competitive and soaring oil and insurance prices as well as terrorism threats have made the industry volatile.

As well as cultivating loyalty amongst consumers, loyalty programmes provide detailed information about what these customers are looking for in services and give them a very direct means of communication – through email newsletters and promotions, for example. With growing competition to attract and retain customers throughout the tourism industry, loyalty programmes are increasingly trying to outdo each other, offering more opportunities to build points, more ways to redeem them and also a variety of rewards geared to personal preferences. Partnerships between travel, retail and credit card companies are increasing the scope and sophistication of loyalty schemes in an attempt to persuade consumers that they can benefit from the system.

Car rental companies, for example, are differentiating their redemption options to cater for particular needs. Customers can choose between bonus miles, greater comfort and upgrades or savings and free days, with an increasing number of deals attached to online bookings. Restaurants are also jumping on the bandwagon with points being gained by consumers eating in a particular venue and then paying the bill with a VISA card. Cinemas and golf courses are joining schemes to give a wider scope for point or mile redemption. Hotel rewards schemes have recently been adapted to erase the differences between business and leisure travellers, promoting the interchangeability of points gained in both forms of travel and also in redemption of the points. In response to customer complaints that while points are easy to gain, they are very difficult to redeem, the Holiday Inn chain now has no expiration dates for points and also no blackout periods for redemptions. Also, Days Inn offers redemption on hotel stays, car rental and retail uses in order to make its scheme attractive to both leisure and business travellers. Hotels are getting increased bookings from these schemes and are also tapping into a rich vein of data on their customers' preferences, which is vital for the marketing strategies.

*Sources*: Collis, R. (10 March 2006) 'Earning miles: Is it worth it?', *International Herald Tribune*, retrieved from www.iht.com; Schachter, H. (30 November 2005) 'Loyalty myths shredded like old air-miles statement', *Globe & Mail*, C 5; Anon. (20 September 2004) 'Rewarding experience; loyalty programs expanding opportunities to earn points', *Globe & Mail*, Travel Rewards II; Anon. (20 September 2006) 'Business, leisure lines blurred in today's hotels', *Globe & Mail*, Travel Rewards II; Anon (19 September 2006) 'Travel rewards still a hot ticket', *National Post*, JV2.

## Relationship Marketing

As mentioned in the Snapshot above, as well as cultivating loyalty amongst consumers, loyalty programmes provide detailed information about what these customers are looking for and give them a very direct means of communication. Once a company has identified potential loyal customers, the next stage is to create a relationship with them that will eventually lead to customer loyalty. This is called **relationship marketing**, a form of marketing that attracts customers, retains them, and enhances their satisfaction (Berry, 1983).[19] In the past, tourism and hospitality marketers have tended to put more emphasis on attracting new customers. More recently, the idea of nurturing the individual relationships with current and past customers has received greater attention. Most marketers now accept that it is less expensive to attract repeat customers than to create new ones, and this is the basic concept behind relationship marketing. The key outcome of all relationship marketing efforts is to make individual customers feel unique and to make them believe that the organization has singled them out for special attention.

---

**RELATIONSHIP MARKETING**
marketing that attracts customers, retains them, and enhances their satisfaction

---

## Retention Strategies

There are four different levels of retention strategies that encourage relationship marketing: financial bonds, social bonds, customization bonds and structural bonds (Zeithaml and Bitner, 2000).[20] These are illustrated in Figure 11.5.

**Figure 11.5** Levels of Retention Strategies for Relationship Marketing

*Source*: Zeithaml, V. A. and Bitner, M. J. (2000) *Services Marketing: Integrating Customer Focus Across the Firm*. New York: McGraw-Hill, 153. Reproduced with permission of the McGraw-Hill Companies.

At level 1, the customer is tied to the organization primarily through financial incentives – often in the form of lower prices for greater volume purchases or lower prices for customers who have been with the company for a long time. Frequent flyer programmes (see Snapshot above) are a good example of such retention strategies. In other cases, firms aim to retain customers by simply offering loyal customers the assurance of stable prices, or at least smaller price increases than those paid by new customers. Other types of retention strategies that depend primarily on financial rewards are focused on bundling and cross-selling of services.

Level 2 strategies bind customers to the business through more than just financial incentives. Marketers using this retention strategy build long-term relationships through social and interpersonal as well as financial bonds. Services are customized to fit individual needs, and marketers find ways of staying in touch with their customers, thereby developing social bonds with them. Interpersonal bonds are common among professional service providers and their clients, as well as among personal care providers and clients. Sometimes relationships are formed with the organization due to the social relationships that develop among customers, rather than between customers and the service provider. For example, people who vacation at the same place during the same weeks every year build bonds with others who vacation there at the same time.

Level 3 strategies involve more than social ties and financial incentives, and two commonly used terms fit within the customization bonds approach: mass customization and customer intimacy. Both of these strategies suggest that customer loyalty can be encouraged through intimate knowledge of individual customers and through the development of one-to-one solutions that fit the individual customer's needs. The Ritz-Carlton, for example, maintains a computerized guest history profile of thousands of individual repeat guests. When guests visit any Ritz-Carlton, members of staff already know about their likes and dislikes. Casinos also maintain sophisticated databases of guest preferences, as well as their wagering habits. The Global Spotlight profiling the Sheraton Suites Eau Claire showed how the hotel takes care of preferences before the guest arrives. A guest relations officer is employed for the sole purpose of co-ordinating the 'It's Our Pleasure' programme, and a room is not ready for a guest until this officer has ensured all preferences are taken care of.

Level 4 strategies are the most difficult to imitate and involve structural as well as financial, social, and customization bonds between the customer and the firm. Often structural bonds are created by providing the client with customized services that are technology-based and that serve to make the customer more productive. An example would be a reservations system installed in a travel agency by a tour operator. The agent is therefore structurally bound to that operator.

## Benefits of Relationship Marketing

Both parties in the customer–company relationship can benefit from customer retention. It is not only in the best interest of the organization to build and maintain a loyal customer base; customers themselves also benefit from long-term associations. Table 11.1 summarizes the various benefits of relationship marketing for both the company and the customer. Assuming they have a choice, customers will remain loyal to a company when they receive greater value relative to what they expect from competing organizations. Value represents a trade-off for the consumer between what they give and what they get. Consumers are more likely to stay in a relationship when the 'gets' (quality, satisfaction, specific benefits) exceed the 'gives' (monetary and non-monetary costs). When companies can consistently deliver what the customer considers to be value, the customer clearly benefits and has an incentive to stay in the relationship.

The benefits to an organization of maintaining and developing a loyal customer base are numerous, but they are linked directly to the bottom line. Among service organizations, reducing customer defections by just 5 per cent can boost profits by 25 to 85 per cent (Reichheld and Sasser, 1990).[21] Retained customers are much more profitable than new ones because they purchase more and they purchase more frequently, often at a price premium, while at the same time requiring lower operating costs. They also make referrals that cost the business nothing. And, of course, their acquisition cost is nothing, which is significant because it costs a company five to seven times more to prospect for new customers than it does to maintain the current ones (Zeithaml and Bitner, 2000).[22]

**Table 11.1** Benefits of Relationship Marketing to the Company and the Customer

| Benefits to the company | Benefits to the customer |
| --- | --- |
| Increased purchases | Social benefits |
| Lower costs | Confidence and trust |
| Employee retention | Special treatment |
| Increased profits | Reduced risk |
| Less customer defection | Increased value |
| Free advertising through word of mouth | Customized services |

To understand the financial value of building long-term relationships with customers, companies sometimes calculate lifetime values. The **lifetime value of a customer** is a calculation that considers customers from the point of view of their potential lifetime revenue and profitability contributions to a company. This value is influenced by the length of an average lifetime, the average revenues generated in that time period, sales of additional products and services over time, and referrals generated by the customer. For example, Snowsports Industries America have estimated that each skier beginning at the age of ten has a lifetime value to the industry of $52,024. But is not just the lifetime value of consumers that is important to tourism providers. In the Bahamas, where diving is a multi-million dollar industry, and sharks are an ever increasing draw, experts (Holland, 2007) have calculated that a single shark in a healthy habitat is worth as much as $200,000 in tourism revenue over its lifetime![23]

> **LIFETIME VALUE OF A CUSTOMER**
> a calculation that considers customers from the point of view of their potential lifetime revenue and profitability contributions to a company

## Focusing on the 'Right Customers'

The idea of targeting the 'right customers' for relationship marketing has emerged in the literature and in practice over the last few decades. Reichheld (1990), for example, stresses that companies aspiring to relationship marketing should make formal efforts to identify those customers who are most likely to remain loyal, and should develop their overall strategy around delivering superior value to these customers.[24] Targeting profitable customers for relationship marketing involves studying and analysing loyalty- and defection-prone customers, searching for distinguishing patterns in why they stay or leave, what creates value for them, and who they are.

Innovative service companies today are beginning to recognize that not all customers are worth attracting and keeping. Many customers are too costly to do business with and have little potential to become profitable, even in the long term. To build and improve

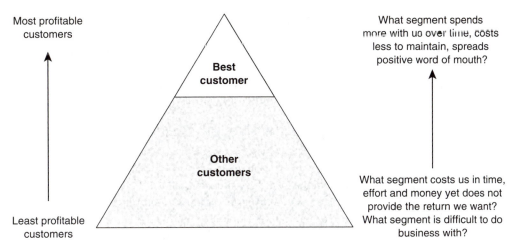

**Figure 11.6** The 80/20 Customer Pyramid

*Source*: Zeithhaml, V. A. and Bitnen, M. J. (2000) *Services Marketing: Integrating Customer Focus Across the Firm.* New York: McGraw-Hill, 470. Reproduced with permission of the McGraw-Hill Companies.

upon traditional segmentation, companies are now trying to identify segments that differ in current and/or future profitability to the organization. After identifying profitability bands, the company offers services and service levels in line with the identified segments. Virtually all companies are aware at some level that their customers differ in profitability – in particular that a minority of their customers account for the highest proportion of sales or profits. This has often been called the 80/20 rule: 20 per cent of customers produce 80 per cent of sales or profits. This 80/20 customer pyramid is shown in Figure 11.6.

A few years ago, Thomas Cook Travel divided its customers into As (those who bring in US$750 or more in annual revenues), Bs (those who bring in US$250–$749), and Cs (those who bring in less than US$250). The company found that 80 per cent of its customers were Cs. By focusing on the more profitable customers (As and Bs), and by charging Cs for their time-consuming demands (a $25 deposit was taken for researching any trip), the company increased its profits considerably. The growth of the company's A- and B-level clients also increased by 20 per cent (Rasmusson, 1999).[25]

However, customers' unprofitability may not be the only reason a company chooses to refuse or terminate a relationship with them. For various reasons, the belief that 'the customer is always right' does not always apply in service industries. It would not be beneficial to either the company or the customer to establish a relationship in which the company cannot meet the customer's needs. Every server in the restaurant business has met the 'customer from hell', a paying guest whose behaviour is beyond rude and who seems determined to ruin the evening for everyone concerned. These disruptive customers have even been segmented in some research articles, into classifications like 'Egocentric Edgars', 'Freeloading Fredas', and 'Dictatorial Dicks' (Withiam, 1998 and Zemke, 1990).[26] Such customers are often impossible to satisfy, and may place too much stress on employees and the organization.

Similarly, it is not always wise to forge relationships simultaneously with incompatible market segments. In many tourism businesses, customers experience the service together and can influence each other's perceptions about the value received. For example, a conference hotel may find that mixing executives in town for a serious training programme with students in town for a sporting event is not a good idea. If the student group is a key long-term customer, the hotel may choose to pass up the executive group in the interest of retaining the students' business.

Although the idea of firing customers is catching on in the West, it appears that in Asia, service providers are still doing all they can to satisfy their awkward customers. One bar in China is allowing its stressed patrons to unleash pent-up anger by allowing them to attack staff, smash glasses, and generally make a ruckus (Reuters, 2006).[27] The Rising Sun Anger Release Bar in Nanjing, capital of the eastern province of Jiangsu, employs 20 muscled young men as 'models' to punch and scream at. Since it opened in April 2006, most of the patrons have been women, especially those working in karaoke bars and massage parlours.

## Service Recovery

Service delivery failure is likely to occur at some point within organizations in the service industry. Though it is unlikely that businesses can eliminate all service failures, they can learn to respond effectively once they occur. This response is often referred to as **service recovery**, defined as the process by which a company attempts to rectify a service delivery failure. An effective recovery will retain customer loyalty regardless of the type of failure. In one study, customer retention exceeded 70 per cent for those customers who perceived effective recovery efforts (Kelley et al., 1993).[28] Another study reported that customers who experienced a service failure told nine or ten individuals about it, whereas satisfied customers told only four or five (Collier, 1995).[29] Therefore, an effective recovery process may lead to positive word of mouth, or at least diminish the negative word of mouth typically associated with poor recovery efforts. The companies profiled in this chapter, Fairmont Hotels & Resort, WestJet, Sheraton Suites Eau Claire and Virgin, all have effective service recovery programmes. In the Opening Vignette, an example was given of exceptional service recovery, when staff at the Fairmont Chateau Lake Louise in Canada sent a private car on a four-hour round trip to pick up a passport and ski pass left behind at a car hire desk.

---

**SERVICE RECOVERY**
the process by which a company attempts to rectify a service delivery failure

---

The clear advantages of effective service recovery display the importance of these efforts in satisfying current customers and reducing defections. The average business does not hear from 95 per cent of dissatisfied customers; every complaining customer represents 20 dissatisfied but non-complaining customers. As was mentioned above, reducing customer defections can boost profits. In addition, retained customers are much more profitable than new ones because they purchase more and they purchase more frequently, while at the same time requiring lower operating costs. It is critical that companies attempt to reduce customer defections, and therefore must take a strategic look at customer complaints.

The events that actually wind up irritated and frustrated customers are the end points of a process that needs to be fixed immediately. Airlines around the world are often criticized for poor service and tend to receive more complaints than most sectors of the travel industry. In a 2005 survey of airline complaints, delays, cancellations and waiting were the top irritants for air travellers, followed by cramped seating and crowding. According to a *Guardian* report, complaints about airlines jumped 50 per cent in 2005, but the industry ignored many of those complaints and refuses to compensate passengers, despite regulations protecting rights (Brignall, 2006).[30]

Harari (1997) offers eight guidelines for tracking and handling complaints:[31]

1. **Make It Easy for Customers to Complain**. Create survey cards that are easy to fill out and that have return postage. Include these with all products, at all sites, and with invoices or other correspondence. Position suggestion boxes in as many sites as possible. Establish electronic accessibility to central terminals. Make sure that home phone numbers are on all business cards. Proactively solicit complaints. Call customers and ex-customers with a list of specific questions. Carefully probe what didn't work, what didn't go well, or what could have been done better. Every manager should be responsible for making at least five calls per month. Hold regular small focus groups; solicit specific, even 'minor', sources of hassle and irritation. Every manager should be a part of at least one focus group per month. The Sheraton Suites Calgary Eau Claire (see Global Spotlight) hosts a weekly cocktail party at the hotel, which gives guests the opportunity to offer suggestions as to how service could be improved.

2. **Respond Quickly to Each and Every Complaint**. This is where empowerment comes in. If production workers, clerks, salespeople, service representatives, account representatives, dealers, accountants, engineers, and all other employees of an organization are not given the information and authority (including spending authority) to resolve problems quickly, then the organization's concern about complaints is not commitment, but rather lip service. Empowerment implies responsibility. Somebody in the organization has to 'own' each complainer – that is, see that the problem is fixed, follow up to ensure customer satisfaction, and champion appropriate changes in the organization. Every manager's job description should include being such a 'somebody' regularly, if not frequently.

3. **Educate Employees**. Teach employees about the strategic and financial value of complaints, about the need for urgency in responding, and perhaps most important, teach them that everyone owns the problem – not just the 'customer service' people. This can be done in orientation, in management development sessions, in memos and briefings, and in meetings and speeches.

4. **Approach Complaints as Operational Problems and Strategic Opportunities**. Approaching complaints as opportunities means putting complaints in the category of

research and information, not of personal attacks. It means replacing blame analysis with problem analysis. It means viewing complaints in the Renaissance tradition, in which the critic was an ally who helped the object of the criticism to focus better on reality.

5. **Make Complaints and Complainers Visible**. Post quantitative complaint data publicly (for employees and for customers). Post raw, unedited letters and phone call transcripts on bulletin boards. Reprint them in newsletters. Read and discuss them in meetings. Publicize responses to the complaints. Identify and applaud the employees who did the responding. Invite complainers to address people in the organization and to work with them on improvements. Pay them if necessary. Include a 'customer panel' in every management retreat.

6. **Adjust Quality Measures, Performance Reviews, and Compensation Accordingly**. What gets measured and rewarded gets done. Quality measures should always incorporate pervasive customer complaints. Key questions for managers' performance evaluation and pay might include the following: How many complaints have you solicited? How many 'firefighting' teams have you been on? How have you used the input of complainers to improve this organization? Rewarding managers for discovering and acting on complaints should be encouraged. Winners of the Nova Scotia Pineapple Awards for service excellence in Canada, for example, are often employees whose service recovery goes above and beyond what is expected to enrich a visitor's stay in Nova Scotia.

7. **Reward Complainers**. Complainers can help a business prosper, and their advice is often priceless. Visible displays of gratitude not only make good common sense but also send a signal to complainers and to the organization. Consider thank-you notes and phone calls, small cash rewards, plaques and certificates, gifts, 'consultant of the month' awards, feature stories in company newsletters, and periodic celebrations with complainers as guests of honour.

8. **Stop Calling Them 'Complainers'**! Or 'difficult customers' or 'jerks'. They are critics, allies, consultants or guests of honor. Call them anything as long as it reflects their contribution to the success of the organization.

---

## Chapter Summary

Internal marketing can be defined as marketing aimed internally at a company's own employees. The main objective of internal marketing in the service industry is to enable employees to deliver satisfying products to guests. It is a process that involves four steps: the establishment of a service culture, the development of a marketing approach to human resource management, the dissemination of marketing information to employees, and the implementation of a reward and recognition system.

A solid internal marketing programme will lead to good service quality, defined as the customer's perception of the service component of a product. Such perceptions are said to be based on five dimensions: reliability, assurance, empathy, responsiveness and tangibles.

An outgrowth of service quality is customer satisfaction. The issue of understanding needs and expectations is an important part of the quest to achieve customer satisfaction. The 'gaps model' of service quality provides a method of graphically illustrating these needs and expectations, and this conceptual model enables a structured thought process for evaluating and 'designing in' customer satisfaction. The two main research instruments that have been developed over the years to analyse the concepts of service quality and consumer satisfaction in the service industry are importance–performance analysis (IPA) and SERVQUAL.

An issue of high priority today involves understanding the impact of service quality on profit and other financial outcomes of the organization. This has led in turn to a focus on customer loyalty and relationship marketing, which involves attracting customers, retaining them and enhancing their satisfaction. It has been suggested that there are four different retention strategies that encourage relationship marketing: financial bonds, social bonds, customization bonds and structural bonds.

Finally, service failure is apt to occur at some point for businesses in the service industry. Though it is unlikely that companies can eliminate all service failures, they can learn to respond effectively once they occur. This response is often referred to as service recovery, defined as the process by which a firm attempts to rectify a service delivery failure. Harari offers eight guidelines for tracking and handling complaints: make it easy for customers to complain; respond quickly to each and every complaint; educate employees; approach complaints as operational problems and strategic opportunities; make complaints and complainers visible; adjust quality measures, performance reviews, and compensation accordingly; reward complainers; and stop calling them complainers.

## Key Terms

## Discussion Questions and Exercises

1. Apart from those companies discussed in the chapter, name a tourism or hospitality organization that has an outstanding service culture. What is the evidence of this culture?
2. If you were the manager of a hotel and wanted to apply the gaps model to improve service, which gap would you start with? Why? In what order would you proceed to close the other gaps?
3. Think about a service organization that retains you as a loyal customer. Why are you loyal to this provider? What would it take for you to switch?
4. With regard to the same organization, what are the benefits to the firm of keeping you as a customer? Calculate your 'lifetime value' to the organization.
5. Why is it important for a tourism organization to have a strong service recovery strategy? Think of a time when you received poor service from a tourism or hospitality company. Was any recovery effort made? What should or could have been done differently?

**Case Study**

### Richard Branson: Driving Service Quality From the Top

A service culture is often driven by personalities within a business. It comes from the top and trickles down throughout the company. Sir Richard Branson, billionaire and self-styled world champion of adventure capitalism, personifies the best of everything. Through his personal 'live life to the full' ethos, he drives industry in every area he expands, from his Virgin record business to airlines, phones and more recently space tourism with Virgin Galactic. However, despite his jet-setting lifestyle and purchase of his own island, he does not fly on a private plane. He tries to remain 'grounded' in reality and stays in touch with his customers by travelling on his own airline, spending six hours each flight at the bar, mixing with the passengers and valuing their feedback. In 2004, Virgin became the first airline to introduce double beds on board its planes. When Branson first floated the idea in 1999, he said: 'The legitimate mile-high club is finally aboard.'

Over the past 25 years, Branson has diversified his Virgin brand into a far-reaching empire, encompassing mobile phone services, a rail service and even wedding dresses, as well as his original record label and discount airline. His personal image is one of unconventionality, youthful energy and enthusiasm, entrepreneurial spirit and thinking big and he imbues all his products with this brand distinction, In 2005 *Forbes* estimated his worth at over $4 billion despite many financial ups and downs over the previous decade. He now controls over 200 mostly private companies and employs thousands of people worldwide. Branson equates entrepreneurialism with being 'in the jungle learning

Richard Branson. Driving service quality from the top

the hard way, learning from your mistakes, learning your good points and learning the art of survival'. His own career was launched at the age of 16 when he created a national magazine, *Student*.

Despite his personal riches, Branson has retained an 'everyman' persona, marked by his casual dress, modest manner and disrespect for convention. He understands the concerns and needs of his customers and his employees and acts as a conduit for fulfilling those needs. He may appear to plunge into new businesses just for fun, but there is much more calculation to it than that. 'The time to go into a business is when it is abysmally run by other people,' he says, and when he feels Virgin can provide a significantly better customer experience. For example before moving into cell phones, he realized that many young people couldn't afford the expensive monthly charges the big players were asking for. Instead, he envisioned a pay-as-you-go approach, so teenagers wouldn't need to lock themselves into yearlong contracts or pay for airtime they didn't use.

The romantic, financial and promotional promise of commercial space flight has most recently fuelled Branson's thirst for adventure and pioneering. Virgin Galactic, formed in 1991 and later partnered with Kurt Rutan of SpaceShipOne, the Ansari X Prize winner, is constructing five seven-seater spacecraft for launch by 2008. According to Branson, it is his 'final frontier'. In competition with Planetspace Corp, an offshoot from the Canadian Arrow team, he is racing to mount the first space tourism operation at a cost of over a billion dollars, which will give 200 $236,000 ticket holders around

30 minutes of weightlessness in space during a three-hour trip. He has also negotiated construction of the first ever private commercial space port with authorities in New Mexico and has 40,000 people registered for future flights.

Always flamboyant and with an eye to exploiting his escapades for their advertising value, Branson's trademark is outlandish publicity stunts. In March 2005, he arrived at an outdoor downtown Toronto press conference wearing a superhero costume and rappelled down a four-storey building into a group of models dressed as nurses. This was part of a promotion to introduce Virgin Mobile's phone service in Canada. Virgin Mobile earned $49 million in 2004 on revenue of over $1 billion. The Toronto stunt celebrated the acquisition of a half interest for him in Virgin Mobile Canada in partnership with Bell Mobility. He reinforces such obvious publicity stunts with regular appearances on television shows. *The Rebel Billionaire* is an adventure-reality show, watched by six million viewers in England, in which Branson participates in outlandish adventure challenges alongside the contestants, consolidating his hands-on spirit. He explains his adventures as another facet of his entrepreneurship which has always led him to take on challenges, risks and new projects which he calls 'brand stretching' – for example Virgin Cola which specializes in cornering the market in countries where Pepsi and Coke have difficulties. He considers his dare-devil activities 'a double duty', serving as both personal achievements and effective, relatively cheap advertising.

Branson also inaugurated the ultimate loyalty scheme for Virgin Atlantic's frequent flyers in December 2005. He has offered *free* space flights in 2008 for Flying Club members who can save the requisite two million flying club miles to be redeemed against a trip into space with Virgin Galactic. He also intends to put money earned in the early flights back into the venture in order to bring prices down for the future, opening space tourism up to the masses. His goal: 'A company that will enable dreams to come true and, at the same time it will help put the Virgin brand on the map on a global basis.'

In September 2006 Branson joined a growing list of billionaires contributing huge amounts to worthy causes by committing to spending all the profits from his airline and rail business – an estimated $3.5 billion over the next ten years – on combating global warming. He said the money would be spent on renewable energy initiatives within his company and on investments in bio-fuel research, development, production and distribution, as well as projects to tackle emissions. 'I really do believe the world is facing a catastrophe and there are scientists who say we are already too late, but I don't believe that is the case,' he said. Branson's fuel bill for Virgin Airlines rose $l-billion between 2003 and 2006. The first investment project of Virgin Fuels will be in a California company called Cilion, which is carrying out research on new kinds of ethanol production.

*Sources*: Restivo, K. (2 March 2005) 'Virgin Mobile serves industry wake-up call', *Financial Post*; Evans, M. (2 March 2005) 'Sir Entrepreneur', *Financial Post*; McCarthy, S. (17 December 2005) 'Can Branson trump the Donald?' *Globe and Mail*, B4; Reuters. (7 December 2005) 'Virgin Atlantic offers its frequent flyers chance to soar into outer space', *Financial Post*, FP4; Banks, B. (August 2005) 'Life wish', *National Post,* Business, 30–40; Branson, R. (August 2005) 'My final frontier', *National Post, Business, 33*; Reiss, S. (May 2006) 'The original adventure capitalist', *Men's Journal*.

## Questions

1. The Case Study highlights several reasons for Branson's success. In your opinion, which one is the most important?
2. Is the culture at Virgin critically important to the success of the organization?
3. How serious is the threat from competitors that want to imitate the Virgin culture? What does it take to imitate organizational culture?
4. How does Virgin's culture affect customer service?
5. In your opinion, what are the motives behind Branson's efforts to combat global warming?

## Websites

| | |
|---|---|
| www.fairmont.com | Fairmont Hotels & Resorts |
| www.sheratonsuites.com | Sheraton Suites Calgary Eau Claire |
| www.westjet.com | WestJet Airlines |
| www.virgin.com | Virgin |
| www.virgin-atlantic.com | Virgin Atlantic |
| www.loewshotels.com | Loews Hotels |

## References

1 Berry, L. L., Hensel, J. S. and Burke, M.C. (1976) 'Improving retailer capability for effective consumerism response', *Journal of Retailing,* 52(3), 3–14.
2 Webster, C. (1995) 'Marketing culture and marketing effectiveness in service firms', *The Journal of Services Marketing,* 9(2), 6–22.
3 Sutherland, S. (2002) 'Hospitality trends', *Alberta Venture,* 6(4), 49–53.
4 Katzenbach, J. (2003) *Why Pride Matters More Than Money.* New York: Crown Business.
5 Anon. (31 July 2004) 'Singapore cabbies wheel out the knowledge', *Telegraph Travel,* 4.
6 Parasuraman, A., Zeithaml, V. A. and Berry, L. L. (1988) 'SERVQUAL: A multiple item scale for measuring consumer perceptions of service quality', *Journal of Retailing,* 64, 12–20.
7 Cronin, J. and Taylor, S. (1994) 'SERVPERF versus SERVQUAL: Reconciling performance-based and perception-minus-expectations measurements of service quality', *Journal of Marketing,* 58(1), 125–131.
8 Reichheld, F. F. and Sasser, W. S., Jr. (1990) 'Zero defections: quality comes to services', *Harvard Business Review,* 68, 105–111.
9 Heskett, J. L., Sasser, W. E., Jr. and Schlesinger, L. A. (1997) *The Service Profit Chain: How Leading Companies Link Profit and Growth to Loyalty, Satisfaction, and Value.* New York: Free Press, 83.
10 Parasuraman, A., Zeithaml, V. A. and Berry, L. L. (1985) 'A conceptual model of service quality and its implications for future research', *Journal of Marketing,* 49(4), 41–50.
11 Martilla, J. A. and James, J. C. (1977) 'Importance–Performance Analysis', *Journal of Marketing,* 41(1), 13–17.
12 Hudson, S. and Shephard, G. (1998) 'Measuring service quality at tourist destinations: an application of Importance–Performance Analysis to an Alpine ski resort', *Journal of Travel and Tourism Marketing,* 7(3), 61–77.

13 Parasuraman, A., Zeithaml, V. A. and Berry, L.L. (1985) 'A conceptual model of service quality and its implications for future research', *Journal of Marketing,* 49(4), 41–50.

14 Buzzell, D. and Gale B. T. (1987) *The PIMS Principles.* New York: Free Press.

15 Phillips, L. D., Chang, D. R. and Buzzell, R. (1983) 'Product quality, cost position and business performance: a test of some key hypotheses', *Journal of Marketing,* 47(Spring), 26–43.

16 Gale, B. (1992) 'Monitoring customer satisfaction and market-perceived quality', *American Marketing Association Worth Repeating Series,* Number 922CSO I. Chicago: American Marketing Association.

17 Zeithaml, V. A., Berry, L. L. and Parasuraman, A. (1996) 'The behavioral consequences of service quality', *Journal of Marketing,* 60, 31–46.

18 Heskett, J. L., Sasser, W. E., Jr. and Schlesinger, L. A. (1997) *The Service Profit Chain: How Leading Companies Link Profit and Growth to Loyalty, Satisfaction, and Value.* New York: Free Press, 83.

19 Berry, L. L. (1983) 'Relationship marketing', in Berry L.L., Shostack G.L. and Upah G. (eds), *Emerging Perspectives on Services Marketing.* Chicago: American Marketing Association, 25–28.

20 Zeithaml, V. A. and Bitner, M. J. (2000) *Services Marketing: Integrating Customer Focus across the Firm.* New York: McGraw-Hill.

21 Reichheld, F. F. and Sasser, W. S., Jr. (1990) 'Zero defections: quality comes to services', *Harvard Business Review,* 68, 105–111.

22 Zeithaml, V. A. and Bitner, M. J. (2000) *Services marketing: integrating customer focus across the firm.* New York: McGraw-Hill.

23 Holland, J.S. (2007) 'An Eden for sharks', *National Geographic,* 211(3), 116–137.

24 Reichheld, F. F. and Sasser, W. S., Jr. (1990) 'Zero defections: quality comes to services', *Harvard Business Review,* 68, 105–111.

25 Rasmusson, E. (1999) 'Wanted: profitable customers', *Sales and Marketing Management,* 151(5), 28–34.

26 Witham, G. (1998) 'Customers from hell', *Cornell Hotel and Restaurant Administration Quarterly,* 39(5), 11; Zemke, R. and Anderson, K. (1990) 'Customers from hell', *Training, 27*(2), 25–33.

27 Reuters. (8 August 2006) 'Bar aims for smash hit by letting customers run riot', *The Guardian,* 16.

28 Kelley, S. W., Hoffman, K. D. and Davis, M. A. (1993) 'A typology of retail failures and recoveries', *Journal of Retailing,* 69(4), 429–452.

29 Collier, D. A. (1995) 'Modeling the relationships between process quality errors and overall service process performance', *Journal of Service Industry Management,* 64(4), 4–19.

30 Brignall, M. (29 July 2006) 'Airlines cleared for rip-off', *Guardian Money,* 3.

31 Harari, O. (1997) 'Thank heavens for complainers', *Management Review,* 86(3), 25–29.

# 12

## DESTINATION MARKETING

---

### From Prison Cell to Tourist Attraction: Robben Island, Cape Town, South Africa

Turning something associated with pain, suffering and evil into an 'attraction' for tourists without modifying and sanitizing it – can it be done? Well, according to former inmate, political activist and critic Dennis Brutus, it is not possible. He thinks Robben Island, with its guided tours of the political prison where Nelson Mandela was incarcerated for 18 years, has been beautified and altered with flower gardens and murals to transform it from an 'island of hell' in an attempt to 'rewrite history'. However, another former inmate, poet and prison guide Modise Phekonyane, claims that while ex-prisoners and former guards are still available to guide and educate the eager tourists flocking to the island near Cape Town, the prison will remain an educational symbol of hope and unity for the future of South Africa.

Over the past 400 years, Robben Island has had a remarkably varied history, serving as a post office, fishing base, whaling station, hospital, mental asylum, military base, leper colony and most infamously as a brutal penal colony and symbol of political oppression during Apartheid in South Africa. Since the prison and island were opened to the public in January 1997 as the Robben Island Museum by Nelson Mandela himself, the number of annual visitors has risen from 100,000 in the first year to over 400,000 in 2005. At peak times of the year, 2,000 tourists a day take a three-and-a-half hour tour that includes a catamaran ride, a bus trip and a guided tour of the prison. The bus ride encompasses famous sites such as political activist Robert Sobukwe's isolated house, the limestone quarry where Mandela and fellow prisoners slaved to cut stone to build prison facilities (ruining their eyesight in the glaring reflection), the lepers' church and graveyard, wardens' village and the habitat of the island's penguins, antelopes and other magnificent wildlife. The highlight of the prison tour is interaction with an ex-political prisoner and sometimes a prison guard as well as a view and photograph of the tiny, ill-equipped cell where Mandela spent 18 years of his 27-year prison term, secretly writing and smuggling out

Robben Island in South Africa. Once a prison and now a major tourist attraction

illicit books and inspiring his fellow inmates in the revolutionary movement against Apartheid.

There are many examples of prisons open to public view throughout the world. However, Robben Island differentiates its experience by offering an up-close and personal look at the suffering of its political prisoners by introducing the visitors to the actual prisoners themselves, who have now elected to be guides among an eclectic team of staff including artists, historians, environmentalists and even ex-wardens. Robben Island, therefore, is not a museum of relics and photographs but an interactive, experiential, emotional and educational facility that is striving to promote brotherhood, racial equity and peace with its example of reconciliation and forgiveness. Its promotional brochure explains the philosophy behind the unique facility: 'Those imprisoned on the island succeeded on a psychological and political level in turning a prison "hell hole" into a symbol of freedom and personal liberation. Robben Island came to symbolize, not only for South Africa and the African continent, but also for the entire world, the triumph of the human spirit over enormous hardship and adversity.'

Robben Island Museum is thus offering a memorable experience rather than a monument or product to attract tourists. With its poignant history and its designation as a World Heritage Site in 1999, together with its environmental attributes, such as the beautiful backdrop of prosperous Cape Town, a full view of Table Mountain, the colourful international harbour and its abundant wildlife, it will always remain an important tourist destination as well as a tangible symbol of South Africa's divided history. The primary challenge for the future, however, will be to find ways to keep the museum original and vital as the main attraction of its unique staff passes on. Many of the current guides met and associated with Mandela himself as well as other famous political activists, making them a living part of history which could never be replicated with more remote guides, actors or even recorded walkman-style commentaries.

*Sources*: Robben Island Museum brochure (2006); Personal interviews with Dennis Brutus and Modise Phekonyane at Robben Island 14 February 2006; *Lonely Planet South Africa* (2005), 100–101.

## OBJECTIVES

On completion of this chapter, you should understand:

▶ the principles of destination marketing;

▶ the role of destination marketing organizations (DMOs);

▶ the principles of destination branding;

▶ strategies used to promote destinations;

▶ the marketing of events and conferences; and

▶ the marketing of all-inclusive resorts.

## Introduction

The Opening Vignette provides an example of an international tourist attraction, one that is helping establish Cape Town as one of the most popular destinations in the world. As tourism expands around the globe, it brings new opportunities for destination marketers, such as the high levels of interest in new, experiential attractions like Robben Island. But at the same time, this globalization leads to a dilution of established destination identities and to increased competition among emergent tourism destinations. This chapter looks at both the opportunities and challenges inherent in marketing destinations. It begins by discussing the principles of destination marketing and defining, characterizing, and classifying destinations. A small section also examines the scope of visitor attractions. A summary of the objectives and benefits of destination marketing is followed by a more in-depth look at the role of destination marketing organizations (DMOs). The next two sections focus on destination branding and destination promotion. Finally, the chapter looks at the marketing of two particularly important sectors for destinations: events and conferences, and all-inclusive resorts.

To understand the principles of destination marketing it is important to comprehend what is meant in the tourism industry by the term 'destination'. **Destinations** are places that have some form of actual or perceived boundary, such as the physical boundary of an island, political boundaries, or even market-created boundaries. The tourism destination can comprise a wide range of elements that combine to attract visitors to stay for a holiday or day visit, but there are four core elements that make up the destination product: prime attractors, built environment, supporting supply services, and socio-cultural dimensions such as atmosphere or ambience (see Table 12.1).

---

**DESTINATIONS**
places that have some form of actual or perceived boundary, such as the physical boundary of an island, political boundaries, or even market–created boundaries

---

## Classifications of Destinations

Kotler, Bowen, and Makens (2003) distinguish between macro-destinations such as the United States and micro-destinations such as the states, regions, and cities within the US.[1] However, there are many different types of destinations, including those listed in Table 12.2.

There is an increasing grey area in the distinction between attractions and destinations. Some human-made attractions such as Disney World in Florida, while technically attractions, appear to have more in common with destinations than with most other attractions. In terms of the area they cover and their visitor numbers, as well as the fact that they have on-site accommodation, for example, they appear to be more like destinations. However, the fact that they are usually single-ownership rather than multiple-ownership operations confirms that they are not like other destinations, as does the fact that they usually have a single core product or theme.

## International Attractions

Attractions are one of the most important components in the tourism system, often being the main motivator for a trip to a destination. There is a strong link between destination and attractions, and it is usually the existence of a major attraction that stimulates the development of a destination, whether the attraction is a beach, a religious temple or a theme park.

**Table 12.1**  Characteristics of a Destination

| Characteristics | Description | Examples |
|---|---|---|
| Prime attractors | The main attractors that appeal to visitors and that differentiate one destination from another | Great Wall of China; pyramids in Egypt; Niagara Falls in the US and Canada; Angkor Wat Temples in Cambodia |
| Built environment | The physical layout of a destination, including waterfronts, promenades, historic quarters and commercial zones. Major elements of infrastructure such as road and rail networks, plus open spaces and commercial facilities | London Docklands in the United Kingdom; Venetian canals in Italy; Bullet train in Japan; Peace Memorial Museum in Hiroshima |
| Supporting supply services | Essential facilitating services such as accommodation, communications, transport, refreshment and catering, entertainment, and amenities | Essential at most destinations |
| Socio-cultural dimensions | Cultural attributes: bridges between past and present, the mood or atmosphere – ranging from sleepy to vibrant. The degree of friendliness and cohesion between the host community and visitors | The friendliness of Canadians; chaotic transport in China; the music in Ireland; the laid-back attitude of Fijians |

*Source*: Adapted from Lumsdon, L. (1997) *Tourism Marketing*. Oxford: Thomson Business Press.

As with other sectors of the tourism industry, attractions are increasingly polarized between a few large attractions and thousands of micro-sized enterprises.

Tourist attractions can also be classified as natural or human-made. An example of a popular natural attraction is the Volcano National Park on the Big Island of Hawaii, which is Hawaii's number one attraction. However, it was mentioned in Chapter 1 that increasingly tourists are drawn to human-made attractions that offer entertainment and education, and a good example is Vulcania in France. Set amid the extinct volcanoes of the Auvergne in central France, this is a theme park built three-quarters underground. Costing €110 million, Vulcania is based on an idea by vulcanologists Maurice and Katia Krafft, who died in 1991 in the eruption of Japan's Mt Unzen; they had wanted to open a museum in the Auvergne national park. The 14-acre park contains state-of-the-art technology. In one of its cinemas, footage of volcanoes covers a screen the size of an Olympic swimming pool. The second cinema shows films in 3-D, featuring a computer-generated mammoth that appears to stick its trunk right out into the audience. In an adjoining room, visitors are transported, virtually, to the slopes of a volcano, while another room hosts a synthesized landscape of mud pools bubbling like cauldrons and steam spurting from fissures in the ground, in an attempt to recreate the scene from Mt St Helens' eruption in 1980.

There are a number of key factors that influence the marketing of visitor attractions (Swarbrooke, 1995).[2] Foremost are the marketing objectives, which may vary considerably. For private attractions, like most theme parks, the objectives are often profit, market share or

**Table 12.2** Classifications of Destinations

| Destination type | Description |
|---|---|
| Major international destinations | Destinations on 'must-see' lists. Examples are places such as Paris, New York, London and Vancouver, which have mass appeal to large numbers of international travellers. |
| Classic destinations | Destinations where the natural, cultural or historical appeal encourages long-stay holidays. Examples are Saint-Tropez or Lourdes in France, or Banff National Park in Canada. |
| Human-made destination resorts | Destinations where visitors view the resort as the destination itself and rarely venture outside the perimeters. Examples are the all-inclusive resorts in the Caribbean or Mexico, or the Hilton Hawaiian Village in Honolulu. |
| Natural landscape or wildlife | Destinations that have high natural appeal and are habitats of rare species of flora or fauna. Examples are the Galapagos Islands in Ecuador, the Serengeti wildlife reserve in East Africa, and the Queen Charlotte Islands in B.C. |
| Alternative destinations | More contemporary destinations such as cruises, theme parks, massive shopping centres like West Edmonton Mall in Canada and time-share properties. |
| Business tourism destinations | Destinations where retailing and entertainment sectors encourage longer stays by business executives and partners. This is often accompanied by a thriving hospitality sector and a desire to heighten the destination's image through events marketing. |
| Stopover destinations | Destinations that are situated between generating areas and holiday destinations. Often characterized by having a wide-ranging budget accommodation sector and a strong mix of restaurants and cafés. |
| Short break destinations | Destinations that have national appeal – and often international appeal if suitable attractions exist. Niagara Falls is a classic example. |
| Day trip destinations | Destinations that attract primarily regional, day-visitor demand; the most common of all destinations. They range from seaside ports to major retailing centres in all parts of the world. |

achieving a satisfactory return on investment. Public sector attractions, on the other hand, may have wider and less financial objectives, such as encouraging participation from people who are socially disadvantaged. In the Opening Vignette, the objective for Robben Island was to symbolize the triumph of the human spirit over enormous hardship and adversity. The Opening Vignette in Chapter 1 explained the objectives of the Hong Kong government when investing in Disneyland Hong Kong. It was seeking to reposition the island as a tourism leader in Asia, enhancing its international image and creating a stronger leisure tourism destination in line with its established success in business tourism. Other goals were to add quality to the life of residents, to provide a model for staff training and human resource management for fellow tourism organizations, and to fill a gap in its tourism product.

Another important factor is that attractions are often marketed by other agencies as well as by themselves. Using the example above, inbound tour operators in Hong Kong use Disneyland in their brochures to encourage tourists to take their packages, while the government promotes the theme park to persuade people to visit the country. The level of competition also varies drastically between different types of attraction. For example, the theme park and seaside amusement arcade business in the UK is highly competitive in its bid to outdo all other genres of attractions. However, local authority museums may simply be competing with other council-run museums. The Association of Leading Visitor Attractions reported in 2005 that the most visited attraction in the UK was Blackpool Pleasure Beach (5.9 million visitors), followed by the British Museum (4.5 m), the National Gallery (4.2 m) and the Tate Modern (3.9 m). However, many theme parks did not disclose their arrivals figures.

The attraction market is particularly volatile and fashion-led, with many factors in the visitor experience being outside the control of attraction operators. The Global Spotlight in Chapter 4 showed how Disney's entry into Paris was thwarted by factors outside of the company's control, such as domestic economic recession and the Gulf War of 1991. Visitor usage also varies dramatically, from occasional purchases, perhaps just once in a lifetime, to multiple visits by those who visit the same attraction time and time again. Attractions often create and promote special exhibitions to increase visitor numbers during the off-peak seasons. For example, the Rock and Roll Hall of Fame and Museum in Cleveland, US, opened an exhibit in November 2006 to honour The Clash, an English punk band from the 1970s. Revolution Rock: The Story of the Clash was open to the public until 15 April 2007.

Finally, marketers need to be sensitive to the fact that some attractions are extremely fragile and therefore need to be protected and not exploited. The UNESCO World Heritage List consists of sites considered to be of global importance either because of their natural qualities or their significant man-made contribution to world culture. An example of a listed cultural site is the Parque Nacional Rapu Nui Easter Island, home of the famous Easter Island Statues (the *moai*), which date back some 1,000 years. Each year, between 20-40,000 travellers visit Easter Island, most coming to see these massive stone statues that are spread across the Chilean island. Each of the statues is unique, differing in expression, height or weight, representing carved images of ancestors. In 2005, a major conservation project effort began to restore the statues. Made of pressed volcanic ash, the stones are particularly susceptible to erosion, a process that threatens to erase clues to their origins and endanger the local tourism industry; but some are also under threat from the tourists themselves. Apparently booming tourism is having a catastrophic effect on Egypt's antiquities, too, with the number of people visiting famed sites like the Valley of the Kings causing serious damage in a way that centuries of weather has failed to do.[3] Chapter 13 looks at the relationship between tourism and environmental damage in more detail, but the Snapshot below shows how one Brazilian community has succeeded as a tourist destination by preserving what used to be destroyed – turtles.

## Snapshot

### Targeting Turtle-lovers: Praia do Forte in Brazil

Historically, when a type of rural subsistence (agriculture, mining, fishing, for example) becomes obsolete in the modern world, communities collapse and towns dwindle as the work force moves elsewhere. However, there are some cases where preserving what used to be destroyed can actually regenerate a community way beyond its origins. Praia do Forte, on the northeast coast of Brazil, is such a case. Turtle eggs, meat and shells used to be the mainstay of the village economy via a significant fishing industry. The same items are still prized commodities today, but now they must be in their original pristine condition – i.e. alive and thriving – in order to satisfy environmental concerns about endangered species and the needs of tourism.

With international pressure from turtle conservationists having developed through the 1970s, a two-year survey launched in 1980 identified the crucial situation regarding sea turtles along the Brazilian coastline. The Tamar Project was established in the Bahia village of Praia do Forte, along with other bases in Espirito Santo and Sergipe, to learn vital turtle nesting and reproductive habits from residents and fishermen, to educate the locals environmentally, and to hire fishermen to protect their former prey. The empirical knowledge of the locals, together with the science of the researchers, created today's conservationism whereby thousands of baby turtles are released each year and the females are able to complete their reproductive cycles without harm.

Despite initial suspicion, alarm and distrust from local populations, the Tamar Project has led to a fruitful partnership and alliance between conservationists and locals in saving the sea turtles in Brazil as well as creating new ways of subsistence, preserving local culture and offering jobs. Nationwide, the Tamar Project has 20 stations, with visitor centres, shops selling themed merchandise and on-site restaurants, providing 1,200 jobs, 85 per cent of which are filled by fishermen and their relatives. It is administered by IBAMA in partnership with the Pro-Tamar Foundation, monitoring 1,000 kilometres of beach across eight Brazilian states. Tamar also supports cultural activities to preserve village traditions and values, providing an ongoing educational programme and promoting information services to further job creation and alternative sources of income.

Tamar staff live in the village centres year round, reflecting their status as pivotal members of the local communities. Integrating the project and its personnel into the everyday life of the regions has been intrinsic to its success both in conservation efforts and in improving the lives of local residents. Community outreach projects, such as school presentations of videos and slides, hatchling release ceremonies (popular among locals and tourists) and festivals, all help in allying preservation of the healthy marine ecosystem with more personal materialistic goals.

Praia do Forte, just 72 kilometres from Salvador, has become the eco-friendly tourist resort most favoured by Bahian weekenders and the local tourist market as well as an international tourism destination. Today the 'Projecto Tamar' is the resort's biggest attraction, resulting in a burgeoning beach resort of quaint 'pousadas' (small inns), eclectic restaurants, stylish boutiques and lively bars all lining the three main cobbled streets. Boasting a beautiful sandy coconut palm-lined beach with great swimming and snorkeling in the warm azure waters, Praia do Forte is now a source of far greater levels of income than in its previous incarnation as a fishing hamlet.

The turtle sanctuary at Praia do Forte is set right on the sand with a large shop, several themed restaurants and a visitor information centre. Tourists can view between 15 and 30 turtles of various species in different stages of maturity for a small fee. There is a hatchery, video information and a 'Mini Guide' programme providing environmental education and experience for the young people of the village. Alongside the turtle preservation schemes, the resort has the 'Reserva De Sapiranga' where rare orchids and bromeliads are protected within 1,482 acres of secondary Atlantic forest. This is also a sanctuary for endangered animals, with more than 187 species of native birds, as well as various indigenous monkeys. Limited jeep, raft and canoe tours are permitted in the nature reserve.

*Sources*: Marcovaldi, M.A. and Marcovaldi, G. G. (1999) 'Marine turtles of Brazil: the history and structure of Projecto TAMAR-IBAMA', *Biological Conservation* 91, 35–41.

## Objectives and Benefits of Destination Marketing

A fair proportion of destination marketing tends to be carried out by public sector bodies, and hence it is quite complicated. These public bodies are often involved in destination marketing for a wide range of reasons other than just attracting tourists.

These objectives might include:

1. improving the image of an area in the hope that this will encourage industrialists to relocate their factories and offices to the area;
2. providing jobs for local residents;
3. increasing the range of facilities that are available for the local community;
4. giving local residents more pride in their local area, which can happen when people see that tourists want to visit their region;
5. providing a rationale and funding for improvements to the local environment; and
6. trying to make the destination politically more acceptable.

However, public sector bodies can earn income from tourism in a number of ways, so economic benefits are just as important. Revenue may come in the form of sales taxes or hotel room taxes, and from admissions to publicly owned attractions. A large tourism benefit comes from the multiplier effect, as tourist expenditures are recycled through the local economy. The Snapshot below shows how the Singapore government is promoting gambling in its country for the first time because of its economic benefits. Governments use economic impact models to estimate overall employment gains in goods and services consumption resulting from tourism multipliers. Tourism is often used to shift the burden of taxes to non-residents. Taxation of tourists has in fact become very popular, and it includes taxes on airline tickets, hotel taxes, and other user fees. Many in the tourism industry have suggested that these taxes should go back into promoting tourism and developing the infrastructure to support it.

Not all tourism marketing campaigns are directed at potential tourists. In some cases, DMOs need to convince residents that tourism is an important sector and worth supporting. For example, in 2007, the Kenai Peninsula Tourism Marketing Council (KPTMC) in Alaska developed a print advertisement that ran in a special section of the local paper that focuses on the peninsula's three biggest industries: oil and gas, commercial fishing and tourism (see Figure 12.1).

**Figure 12.1** KPTMC Print Advertisement

KPTMC is a non-profit membership-based organization that receives partial funding from local government, the Kenai Peninsula Borough. As is the case with many Alaskan communities, tourism is very important to the local economy. Of licensed businesses on the peninsula, 25 per cent are tourism related, and a conservative estimate is that 30 per cent of sales tax revenue is directly related to the visitor industry. 'Unfortunately, many of our residents believe that our visitors are a nuisance and the dollars they bring to the area only benefit a small group of people. Many also take issue with our resource allocation,' said Shanon Hamrick, executive director of KPTMC. 'Residents don't want outsiders catching all of their fish and crowding the rivers; commercial fisherman feel like they are unfairly restricted because of the sport fisheries. A favourite debate is the value of a salmon caught in a commercial net versus one caught at the end of a fishing line by a visitor.'

The advertisement generated a lot of interest. 'We had several people contact us and congratulate us on taking such a "bold stance" in support of tourism,' said Hamrick. 'As we are a tourism marketing organization, I didn't feel like our statement was all that bold, but I think our tourism business owners are tired of being treated as unimportant and were pleased to see someone make a public statement in support of the industry. We will continue running similar ads throughout the year. I will stick with the theme of businesses who aren't considered a tourism business and how they benefit from the industry. My ultimate goal is to make people understand that tourism is an important renewable resource that generates money for our local economy and improves our quality of life. If by doing that we have an easier time getting increased funding for marketing each year, I have really done my job.'

## Snapshot

### Singapore Gambling on the Future

Singapore has always frowned on gambling. Thomas Stamford Raffles forbade it when he founded the city in 1819. As patriarch of independent Singapore, Lee Kuan Yew cracked down on illegal gambling dens, although he approved state-sponsored lotteries and horse-race betting. But Singapore has now joined the rush in Southeast Asia to build casinos as it competes with neighbours to attract tourists. Global consumer spending on all gambling was estimated at US$244 billion in 2004 and is expected to grow to $295 billion by 2010 with the introduction of new casinos. At least 50 of those will be built in Asia.

Singapore had to weigh up its options carefully regarding opening the island to casinos. Amid media, government and public concern over vice, crime and social degeneration, parliament finally gave the go-ahead for construction of two casinos in March 2005, in a bid to boost the economy and rebrand Singapore as a tourism destination. One casino was planned for Sentosa Island as part of a resort with other tourist attractions, and the second was projected for Marina Bay on the main island. Both sites, costing a total of Singapore $5 billion, would be five minutes' drive from the central business district. Analysts have estimated the casino venture could be worth more than $1 billion in annual revenue.

Singapore has traditionally been a regular stop-over point for travellers between Australia and Europe. It already allows betting on racehorses, sports events, lotteries and in slot machine parlours. More than a fifth of visitors to Kuala Lumpur's mountaintop casino resort, owned by Genting, are from Singapore, confirming the existence of a strong domestic market, too. Visitor numbers are predicted to double within the next decade due to the new casino resorts, and visitor spending is hoped to triple.

Singapore's main competitors in the tourism market are Malaysia, Thailand and Hong Kong, all of which are considering allowing casinos in the near future. Macau, a Chinese city close to Hong Kong, already has 15 casinos. Asia's gambling market was expected to generate US$19 billion by 2006, increasing from $13 billion in 2004. Las Vegas gambling giants Sands Corp., Harrah's Entertainment Inc. and MGM Mirage, among others, are all vying for a piece of the action. Sands Macau was the first Las Vegas-style casino in Asia, opening in May 2004, costing US$265 million and grossing $1.37 million on average per day – an unprecedented return on investment, according to gambling analyst Jonathon Galaviz. Sands Corp. is now trying to raise $350 million in an initial share sale to expand in Asia. As well as having ripe domestic markets, lower building costs in Asia are an economic draw for US based hotel-casino magnates. In Las Vegas it costs around $2 million to build a high quality resort compared to only $1 million in Asian countries where labour, materials, land and taxes are often cheaper.

Singapore still plans to restrict gambling for local residents. The government intends to impose a daily entry fee of about $70 for citizens and permanent residents. For visitors, though, there will finally be some bright lights and adult-rated activities. In fact, in 2006, the Singapore private sector pumped more than $60 million into the city to spice up its nightlife. A city that once banned *Cosmopolitan* because it was too racy, and chewing gum because it was too messy, Singapore is now aiming to be the life of the Asian party.

*Sources:* Burton, J. (29 May 2004) 'Singapore finds temptation of roulette hard to resist in battle for tourists', *Financial Times*, 2; Nowak, P. (7 October 2006) 'Cashing in on betting fever', *Financial Post*, FP5; Stokes, D. (1 July 2006) 'Out with the old and in with the new', *Calgary Herald*, H1.

## The Role of Destination Marketing Organizations (DMOs)

The role of national tourist boards in proactively marketing and advertising destinations that they represent has changed substantially in the last few decades (Gauldie, 2000).[4] A major development of the 1980s and 1990s was the appearance of private–public sector **destination marketing organizations (DMOs)** or National Tourist Organizations (NTOs), complementing

> **DESTINATION MARKETING ORGANIZATIONS (DMOs)**
> government agencies, convention and visitors bureaus, travel associations and other bodies that market travel to their respective destination areas

and sometimes replacing the advertising and marketing activities of conventional, fully state-funded tourism offices. DMOs are government agencies, convention and visitors' bureaus, travel associations and other bodies that market travel to their respective destination areas. This trend is being reinforced by the very rapid expansion of the internet as a medium that gives the tourism industry the ability to market, promote, advertise, sell, provide information and accept reservations. The appearance of regional tourist boards with an agenda to promote and advertise only their own attractions in foreign markets is another trend that is likely to develop. Meanwhile, the world's leading names in travel have moved pronouncedly to the use of advertising and promotions that create brand awareness.

The growth in tourism has lured many government agencies and other groups into marketing their destinations to pleasure and business travellers. Nearly every state, province, and territory now has a separate body that is responsible for marketing. Nationally, organizations such as the Australian Tourist Commission, the British Tourist Authority, and the Canadian Tourism Commission are investing millions of dollars in tourism marketing and development. At a state or province level, marketing agencies also spend millions of dollars promoting tourism. Their marketing programmes target both individual travellers and travel trade intermediaries. Often they enter into co-operative marketing with suppliers, carriers, intermediaries and other destination marketing organizations. Many agencies also provide seed money to other DMOs for their individual marketing programmes.

In North America, at a regional or city level, **convention and visitor bureaus (CVBs)** have been created to be responsible for destination marketing. In the US, nearly every community with a resident population of more than 50,000 now has a CVB. Approximately 500 of the larger bureaus belong to **DMAI – Destination Marketing Association International**, which provides educational resources and networking opportunities to its members and distributes information on the CVB industry to the public. The individual bureaus divide their attention between the travel trade – particularly convention/meeting planners and tour operators – and individual travellers. Their goal is to bring more conventions, meetings and leisure travellers to their communities. These bureaus represent a broad group of suppliers in their destination areas and are often funded through local accommodation and restaurant taxes.

---

**CONVENTION AND VISITOR BUREAUS (CVBS)**
regional or city-level organizations responsible for marketing a specific destination

---

**DMAI – Destination Marketing Association International**
an organization that provides educational resources and networking opportunities to its members and distributes information on the CVB industry to the public

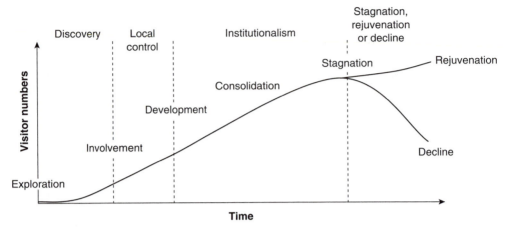

**Figure 12.2** Hypothetical Tourist Area Life Cycle

*Source*: Adapted from Butler, R. W. (1980) 'A tourism area cycle of evolution,' *The Canadian Geographer*, 14(1), 7.

## Tourism Development

The tourism marketer is likely to be involved in the process of developing a destination, in terms of either building new resorts or rejuvenating old ones. Part of the process involves estimating future demand, as in a feasibility study, but increasing emphasis is being placed upon evaluating the likely impacts – such as direct or indirect economic impact – of any development. These issues are discussed in more detail in the next chapter.

It has been argued that the nature of the marketing strategy adopted by a destination is often dictated by the tourism destination life cycle, also known as the **tourism area life cycle** **(TALC)** (Butler, 1980).[5] Like the product life cycle (see Chapter 5), the tourism area (or destination) life cycle follows a pattern as outlined in Figure 12.2, moving from exploration to involvement to development to consolidation to stagnation to rejuvenation or decline. The assumption is that at each stage the tourism marketer will plan the marketing effort to fit the next predicted phase of development, or possibly, in the later stages, to suit the resort's ultimate decline.

---

**TOURISM AREA LIFE CYCLE (TALC)**
the stages a destination goes through, from exploration to involvement to development to consolidation to stagnation to rejuvenation or decline (also known as the 'tourism destination life cycle')

---

The life cycle also suggests that the destination will appeal to different markets as it matures. This fits with consumer typology framework set out by Plog (1974), introduced in Chapter 2, which suggests that the adventurous, outgoing visitors (venturers) seek unfamiliar and unspoiled destinations.[6] Those who are more passive and like the familiar (dependables) prefer mature destinations. Midcentrics (a mixture of the two extremes) head for resorts that are more developed, or are becoming mature.

Many Chinese destinations would be considered to be in the development stage of the tourism area lifecycle. According to the World Tourism Organization, China will become the world's most popular destination by 2010. Inbound tourist arrivals are forecast to grow to 210 million by 2020, with foreign tourist revenue set to reach US$58 billion. China is widely seen as an exotic new destination, and both domestic and inbound tourism are growing at unprecedented rates. Currently about 75 per cent of all Chinese travellers go to Hong Kong or Macao, the earliest beneficiaries of a still-evolving policy to permit Chinese from certain areas to travel on their own. However, with the rise of low-cost airlines, people with relatively low income levels are able to travel by air for the first time, and they are setting their sights on more exotic locations in China. An example is Hainan Island off the south coast of mainland China. Known as China's 'Hawaii', Hainan is a tropical island. Its capital, Haikou, with streets lined with palm trees, is the main port and business centre. Hainan Province has also been a Special Economic Zone since 1988 and has as such become a magnet for investment and tourism development. The total number of domestic visitors increased by 7.4 per cent in 2005 to 14.7 million.

## Destination Branding

The subject of **destination branding** has received increased attention over the last few decades. In an increasingly competitive global marketplace, the need for destinations to create a unique identity – to differentiate themselves from competitors – has become more critical than ever. The Case Study at the end of this chapter focuses on New Zealand's efforts to brand itself as 'Middle Earth'. As suggested in Chapter 5, a brand in the modern marketing sense offers the consumer relevant added value, a superior proposition that is distinctive from competitors', and imparts meaning above and beyond the functional aspects. Today, most resorts claim to have luxury accommodation, superb attractions, friendly people and a unique culture and heritage. However, these factors are no longer differentiators, and successful destination branding lies in its potential to reduce substitutability.

> **DESTINATION BRANDING**
> creating a superior proposition that is distinctive from competitors' and imparts meaning above and beyond the functional aspects of the destination

Destinations will often 're-brand' or reinvent themselves to broaden their appeal. Hong Kong, for example, having established itself as a mecca for shopping, great food and other adult pleasures, is pursuing the family market. Building on the success of its 'Live it. Love it' campaign, the Hong Kong Tourism Board launched 'Discover Hong Kong Year' in 2006. Three new attractions headlined this campaign, all of which targeted the family market: Hong Kong Disneyland, Hong Kong Wetland Park and the Ngong Ping historic village. India is also heading in a new direction – away from back-packers and towards well-heeled tourists. With five-star hotels and resorts spreading throughout the country, some built from former maharajas' palaces, India is moving up-market. Finally, Taiwan declared 2004 the 'Visit Taiwan Year' as part of its efforts to boost tourism. Often seen as a manufacturing hub and a place under constant military threat from neighbouring China, Taiwan is trying to change its image. The government is seeking to attract five million tourists by 2008, double the numbers of 2004. The plan is to bring people to the less-populated, hard-to-reach areas that comprise 80 per cent of the island by promoting attractions such as the 17-year-old theme park called the Formosan Aboriginal Culture Village and the Taroko Gorge, a 19-kilometre-long canyon with deep gorges and long trails for hikers.

## Challenges of Destination Branding

But destination branding has its challenges. Morgan and Pritchard (2002), in a recent book on destination branding, suggest that there are five key challenges faced by destination marketers.[7]

### Limited Budgets

The first challenge facing destination marketers is their extremely limited budgets by comparison with those of marketers of many consumer goods and services. Combine this problem with evidence that tourism promotion does not persuade uncommitted vacationers (but rather acts to confirm the intentions of those already predisposed to visit), and destination marketers have genuine cause for concern. As a result, they have to outsmart rather than outspend the competition – and that means creating innovative, attention-grabbing advertising on a budget and maximizing the amount spent on media. In Uganda, due to a pitiful marketing budget, high-school students were recruited to help choose the African country's first-ever slogan, 'Gifted by Nature'. In Bangladesh, tourism officials are attempting to re-brand the country with a budget of just US$71,000. Inspired by India's success with the 'Incredible India' campaign (see Snapshot below), they dropped the decades-old 'Visit Bangladesh Before the Tourists Come' in 2004, and are now promoting 'Bangladesh – Beautiful Surprise'. However, lack of funding means that the slogan is unlikely to be very successful. 'Until and unless we have an aggressive marketing plan, the slogan doesn't really matter,' said Mahfuzul Haque, chairman of the Bangladesh Tourism Organization (Stanley, 2006).[8]

### Politics

Public sector destination marketers are hampered by a variety of political pressures; they have to reconcile a range of local and regional interests and promote an identity acceptable to a range of constituencies. Destination brand-building is frequently undermined by the short-term mindset of the tourism organization's political masters. It was not until 2002 that India's decision-makers began to take tourism seriously and invest money in promoting the country (see Snapshot below). Effective advertising can also be confounded by bureaucratic red tape. For example, political considerations within a province or country can often dictate the range of photographs that are included in a campaign. Politics in other countries can also affect the success of a branding campaign. Singapore, for example, refused to air the edgy Australian 'Where the bloody hell are you?' ads (see Case Study in Chapter 10), and even British regulators objected to the word 'bloody'.

### External Environment

It has become evident at the beginning of the 21st century that destinations are particularly vulnerable to external forces such as international politics, economics, terrorism and environmental disasters. The war in Iraq, 11 September 2001 and the outbreak of severe acute respiratory syndrome (SARS) were just some of the crises that have derailed destination promotional planning in the past few years. Even the best branding effort can unravel because of political unrest, rampant crime or disease. The deadly SARS virus, which caused fever and respiratory distress, brought Hong Kong's economy to a virtual standstill in 2003, striking just after the city had launched a tourism campaign under the slogan, 'Hong Kong Will Take Your Breath Away'. Similarly, Israel's new 2006 branding campaign called 'Who Knew?' fell on deaf ears when the country began hostilities with Lebanon.

### Destination Product

The tourism destination combines a number of elements that attract visitors to stay for a holiday or day visit. These elements include accommodation and catering establishments; tourist attractions; arts, entertainment, and cultural venues; and the natural environment. Destination marketers have relatively little control over these different aspects of their product, and a diverse range of agencies and companies are partners in the task of crafting brand identities. While packaged goods normally have an obvious core – so that their advertisements can anchor themselves to product performance and attributes – with destinations the situation is much less clear. Many destination branding efforts have foundered for lack of focus. The Philippines has branded itself many times over the past 30 years, with slogans ranging from 'Pride of the Orient' to 'Fiesta Islands' to 'Philippines: The Last Bargain in Asia'. Its most recent slogan, 'WOW Philippines', was intended as much to instil national pride as to attract overseas visitors.

### Creating Differentiation

The final challenge of destination branding is that of creating differentiation in spite of the pressures on destination marketing. Countries often promote their history, their culture and their beautiful scenery in their marketing, but most destinations have these attributes, and it is critical to build a brand on something that uniquely connects a destination to the consumer now, or has the potential to do so in the future. Australia's US$180 million 'Where the bloody hell are you?' campaign (see Case Study in Chapter 10) had an incredible impact, cutting through the clutter and conveying a distinct message that people found appealing and authentic. According to the creators, the commercials were all about the tone, the personality, the images and messages. 'They all combine together to convey a feeling – in this case a warm, distinctive and authentically Australian invitation that says we want you to come and get involved now. This in turn makes them more inclined to take the all-important next step to come to Australia, rather than put it off for ever,' said Scott Morrison, managing director of Tourism Australia. Other suggestive or in-your-face slogans have broken out before. Las Vegas, for example, has succeeded with 'What Happens in Vegas Stays in Vegas' (see Opening Vignette in Chapter 8).

## Brand Building

Morgan and Pritchard (2002) suggest that there are five stages in the process of building a destination brand.[9]

*Market Investigation, Analysis, and Strategic Recommendations*
The first stage is to establish the core values of the destination and its brand. This stage should consider how contemporary or relevant the brand is to today's tourism consumer and how it compares with key competitors. Destinations tend to retool their messages more frequently than in the past. Australia's 'See Australia in a Different Light' was only a few years old, before Tourism Australia hired M&C Saatchi to come up with something different that would resonate with the target market. After conducting focus groups for six months, what they found was that people liked Australia not so much for Australia but for the Australians. The recommendation was to come up with a campaign that would capture the real Australia and who the people really are. The result was the 'Where the bloody hell are you?' campaign that proved so successful. The objective behind the Discover Hong Kong Year in 2006 was to show off the island's hidden treasures, and so the campaign highlighted the contrast between the urban centre of the city and the green space found on nearby islands.

*Brand Identity Development*
Once this market investigation is complete, the next stage is to develop the brand identity. Of importance here is the brand benefit pyramid (see Figure 12.3). Critical to the success of any destination brand is the extent to which the destination's brand personality interacts with the target market. A brand's personality has both a head and a heart: its 'head' is its logical features, while its 'heart' is its emotional benefits and associations. Brand propositions and communications can be based around either. Brand benefit pyramids sum up consumers' relationships with a brand and are frequently established during the consumer research process, in which consumers are usually asked to describe what features a destination offers and what the place means to them. Using their answers, it should then be relatively easy to understand what particular benefit pyramids consumers associate with the destination in question. In 2007, Canada re-branded itself with the slogan 'Canada. Keep Exploring'. The campaign attempted to look beyond Canada's clichéd brand attributes of mountains, Mounties and moose to depict a more vibrant tourist destination. One ad used intersecting lines labelled 'midnight' and 'mischief' to highlight discarded clothes by a pool. The ad suggests a more risqué tourism destination than previous ads. 'Overall, the brand positioning is designed to bridge the gap between the consumers' historical perspectives of what Canada is – a place of beautiful geography – and connect that with our emerging international reputation of being a more progressive, welcoming society,' said Michele McKenzie, president and CEO of the Canadian Tourism Commission.[10]

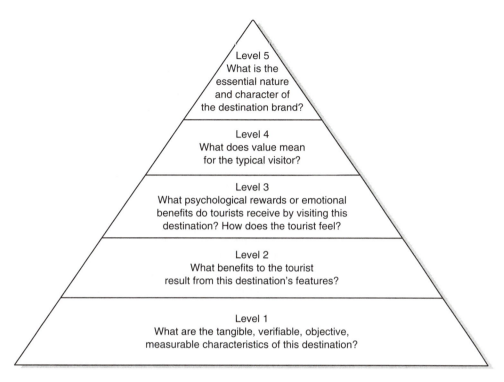

**Figure 12.3** The Destination Brand Benefit Pyramid

*Source*: Morgan, N. and Pritchard, A. (2002) 'Contextualizing destination branding', in Morgan, N., Pritchard, A. and Pride, R (eds), *Destination Branding*. Oxford: Butterworth-Heinemann, 31.

*Brand Launch and Introduction*

The third stage in brand building is to communicate the vision and launch the brand. This may be done through a single announcement or as a part of huge international advertising campaign. For the 'Where the bloody hell are you?' campaign, a dedicated website was created by Tourism Australia whereby consumers could view the ad, and this created tremendous publicity for the ads before they appeared on television and in print. Australia's Tourism Ministry planned to spend about US$135 million over a two year period promoting their fresh tagline in commercials aired all over the world. In 2006, the Tourist Authority of Thailand (TAT) presented its new marketing slogan 'Thailand Unforgettable' as a key component of a strategy to achieve a target of 13.8 million arrivals in 2006 and 15 million in 2007. TAT also set a target of 82 million domestic trips for 2007. The branding strategy was decided upon after extensive consultation with the private sector and launched at the annual marketing meeting in August 2006.

*Brand Implementation*

The implementation stage involves translating the brand personality and proposition into deliverable messages. A logotype or brand signature and a design style guide, which ensures consistency of message and approach, should also reinforce the brand values. The vision should be expressed in the brand's core values that are consistently reinforced through the product and in all marketing communications. Every execution in all media contributes to maintaining brand presence. When Canada re-branded itself with the slogan 'Canada. Keep Exploring', the slogan appeared not only on televisions and print ads around the world, but also on coffee sleeves, branded bakery bags and in the London Underground. When Israel introduced the 'Who Knew?' campaign, tourism ads appeared in a number of North American newspapers while the trade was encouraged to attend educational seminars and offered FAM trips to the country. The answer to the question behind the new slogan was that Israel had more to offer than religious tours and walking in the footsteps of Jesus. So the new ads promoted beaches, ski slopes and a thriving night life. Finally, the Snapshot below describes how the 'Incredible India' campaign was rolled out all over the world using print and television, and outdoor ads.

*Monitoring, Evaluation and Review*
The final stage is to evaluate the brand's performance in the marketplace. Continuous monitoring and evaluation of the communications is the key here, as are open-mindedness and a willingness to embrace change on the part of the brand managers. Any change must be managed with the overall consistency of the brand in mind. The secret is to evolve continually and enrich the original brand personality, building on the initial strengths to increase their appeal and broaden the market. The Snapshot below describes how the 'Incredible India' campaign has developed a number of themes such as spirituality, festivals and wildlife.

## Snapshot

### The Incredible India Campaign

Until the end of 2002, India was being promoted differently in different countries. Tourism was not promoted in an organized fashion and the wealth of historic sites that India has to offer were not made known to potential tourists. In comparison, countries like Thailand, Malaysia, China and Singapore were attracting increasing numbers of tourists. However, in 2002 the Indian government's attitude to tourism changed, and a new advertising campaign, launched in December of that year, focused on showing the numerous facets of India's cultural heritage and geographical diversity, all under the umbrella tagline of 'Incredible India'.

The following year, $5.9 million was spent on the campaign, in print and television, targeting Southeast Asia, Australia, Britain, France, Italy and Germany. Promoting a kaleidoscope of experiences including yoga, wildlife and festivals, the 'Incredible India' campaign also placed ads outdoors, choosing popular sites such as Times Square in New York, and international airports. The campaign focused on various themes, but one successful print campaign focused on the popular spiritual amenities that the country offered. 'Body, mind and soul are a big thing for tourists opting for India as a destination,' said V. Sunil, of Ogilvy and Mather. 'In Singapore the focus is on shopping, fun and entertainment. Similarly, most

**Figure 12.4**    Incredible India print advertisement

people come to India for spiritual reasons. That is the big differentiator for India, in comparison with other countries.'

In 2003, India's tourism inflow rose 15.3 per cent, mostly because of this campaign, with foreign-exchange earnings through tourist arrivals rising as much as 20 per cent. Foreign tourist arrivals increased a further 25 per cent in 2004. The campaign continues to be successful. In 2006, advertising agency Grey Worldwide India won a bronze Euro Effies award for its 'Incredible India' campaign that ran from December 2005 to March 2006 across most big European markets. Since the beginning of 'Incredible India', as many as ten ad agencies have worked on the campaign. While the original print campaign was created by Ogilvy and Mather, Delhi, the television commercials were created by Enterprise Nexus, Mumbai. 'We focused on the fact that India has plenty to offer. India is one country with thousands of places worth visiting and is a country of tremendous contrasts,' said Enterprise Nexus executive director Anil Sanjeevan.

The internet has also been used as a platform for the 'Incredible India' campaign. In 2002 the first online campaign was launched, with the communication objective 'to project India as a unique opportunity for physical invigoration, mental rejuvenation, cultural enrichment and spiritual elevation'. The existing website – www.tourismindia.com – was revamped to make it attractive, functional and resourceful to help a user plan a trip to India. Over 100 different creatives were designed for the campaign across twelve themes, and innovations such as contests were used to increase user interaction. The campaign resulted in more than 13 million hits to the website per month. Since then, the website has been relaunched as www.incredibleindia.org with the new website designed to be a showcase of all good things in India – colours, technology, vastness, diversity and depth. By April 2005, the website was receiving more than 25 million page views per month.

The 'Incredible India' campaign continues to attract tourists to India. In 2005–06 the campaign was given a kitsch look and was targeted at more affluent tourists who saw the country as a destination suited to their thirst for interests such as yoga, spirituality and wildlife. Responsibility for the 2007 campaign was handed to A Advertising and creative director V. Sunil who has moved from Ogilvy. He said, 'The new campaign will again be a visual campaign, and thus a reflection of India. However, this time the focus will also be on creating an unapologetic, confident and growing India. Thus it combines spectacular images of India with a wry, self-assured tone – a far cry from the bowing and scraping of the past.' The media mix will include print and outdoor executions, the two media that 'Incredible India' have used extensively in the past. Some of the major international publications where the campaign will be released are *National Geographic, New York Times, Conde Nest Traveller, Time Magazine* and the *Wall Street Journal*. Outdoor locations will include Times Square in New York and airports in London, Paris, Singapore and Dubai.

*Sources*: Vats, R. (2007) 'Incredible India Global Account Goes to A Advertising'. *Agencyfaqs!*, retrieved from http://agencyfaqs.com; Neelakantan, S. (22 January 2004). *Far Eastern Economic Review*, 167(3), 44; Indiatelevision.com (2003) 'Tourism Ministry sells Incredible India with generous dose of spirituality', retrieved from www.indiatelevision.com.

## Destination Promotion

### Identifying Target Markets

Chapter 3 discusses in detail the importance of segmentation and targeting, and a lengthy discussion on this subject is therefore unnecessary here. However, it is worth underlining the importance of understanding what motivates tourists, how they make their decisions, and how they evaluate and perceive destinations. Having gained such understanding, destinations must then segment the market – whether it is into sub-categories such as business travellers, conference and convention delegates, incentive travellers, and tourists, or into classifications such as the typologies proposed by Plog (1974).[11] There are also growing tourism markets that destinations need to court, such as the baby-boomer, gay, senior and family markets. But there are also others, such as those travellers interested in sport tourism, film tourism (see end of chapter Case Study on New Zealand) and those looking for environmentally friendly tourism. One of the Snapshots in this chapter profiled a Brazilian seaside resort targeting 'turtle-lovers'.

A destination can identify its natural target market in two ways. The first is to collect detailed information about its current visitors. The second is to audit the destination's attractions and select segments that might logically have an interest in these attractions. Marketers should not, however, make the assumption that current visitors reflect all of the potentially interested groups. After a destination has identified its natural target markets, tourism planners should conduct research to determine where these tourists are found. If many segments are identified, the relative potential profit from each should be evaluated. The potential profit of a target tourist segment is the difference between the amount the tourist segment is likely to spend and the cost of attracting and serving it. Ultimately, potential tourist segments should be ranked and selected in order of their profitability.

Whatever tourist segments a destination seeks, it needs to be very specific in its targeting. A ski area attracts skiers, yet even with such givens, potential visitors must be segmented by additional characteristics. For example, Lake Louise in Banff National Park appeals to image-conscious, upper-income and professional skiers, whereas Norquay, just an hour away, attracts a more price-conscious family market. Marketing organizations need to be aware of these subtle differences. Likewise, destinations need to monitor the relative popularity of their various attractions closely, by determining the number and type of tourists attracted to each. Information should be collected continuously on the changing needs and wants of existing markets, emerging markets, and potential target markets. The research conducted by Tourism Whistler, for example, has contributed considerably to the unprecedented growth and rising stature of Whistler as a world-class year-round destination. By identifying and targeting potential target markets such as British and South American skiers, Whistler has become North America's most acclaimed recreational destination. Tourism Whistler regularly conducts customer surveys to gauge satisfaction levels, to identify areas that need improvement and to formulate strategies.

## Destination Promotion Strategy

A destination's **promotion strategy** is concerned with reaching prospective visitors via expenditure on a promotional mix intended to achieve destination awareness and influence prospective customers' attitudes and purchasing behaviour (Middleton and Clarke, 2001).[12] The promotional campaigns of most DMOs fall into three main categories: traditional image or brand-building campaigns, which aim to build or/and maintain awareness of the destination; strategic campaigns, aimed, for example, at attracting visitors in the shoulder season; and 'damage control' campaigns typified by Thailand's promotional campaign that followed the tsunami in 2004 (see Case Study in Chapter 13). Media investment in attracting tourists has grown rapidly in recent years, and most destination marketing organizations are involved in a range of promotional activities. These include the following six types.

---

**PROMOTION STRATEGY**
reaching prospective visitors via expenditure on a promotional mix intended to achieve destination awareness and influence prospective customers' attitudes and purchasing behaviour; a traditional approach to destination marketing

---

*Brochures*
Brochures are produced for both promotional and informational purposes, although both functions may be served by a single brochure. As well as a general brochure covering the whole destination, a range of others may also be offered. These may cover smaller geographical entities within the overall region. Alternatively, they may be targeted at specific market segments. An example is the magazine launched by Tourism Montreal in 2001 to attract the gay market. *Gay Destination Montreal* is distributed to gay industry decision-makers in North America and contains articles on the various pride events, nightlife, fashion and the gay village in Montreal. Canada is perceived as a gay-friendly destination, with the top three cities for the gay traveller being Montreal, Toronto and Vancouver. Each city has developed, supported and marketed its gay spaces and events to great success.

*Advertisements*
Due to the challenge of limited budgets referred to earlier in the chapter, most destinations' ads are placed in print media rather than on the more expensive, but more effective, medium of television. Most resort advertising is seasonal and takes place when it is thought potential visitors will be making their holiday decisions. The majority of ads seek to encourage potential consumers to request a copy of the destination's brochure, although more recently ads have been created to drive the audience to a destination website or to combat tourism crises. For example, in June 2003 the Tourism Authority of Thailand offered a US$100,000 SARS-free guarantee in all its print ads, saying, 'Any tourist who enters and stays in Thailand legally

between May 20 and Nov 19, 2003, and contracts SARS within the kingdom is eligible to receive $100,000 if death results within 90 days of the entrance date. Up to US$10,000 for hospitalization.' Presumably, the authority undertook a risk assessment, but this is a good example of the use of monetary incentives to combat tourism crises.

### The Press and Public Relations

The press and public relations play a significant role in the marketing of destinations, and Chapter 9 provides many examples of destinations using familiarization trips, celebrity visits, press releases, product placement and television broadcasts to attract attention and improve their image with the general public. For agencies that have limited budgets, this low-cost form of promotion is particularly attractive. Promotional videos are often used as a sales tool by destinations. In 2005, the Big Cat Press from the UK was commissioned by the Kenya Tourist Board to film Kenya's rich attractions and wildlife. The promotional video was sponsored in part by industry players in Kenya, including Nairobi's Holiday Inn and Heritage Hotels and Safari Link. Targeted mainly to potential travellers in the UK, the objective of the video was to promote the diversity of the country.

### Personal Selling

Relatively little personal selling is carried out by destination marketing agencies. However, some destinations find personal selling to be the most effective communication tool in promoting to key travel decision-makers and influencers in the travel trade, such as corporate travel managers, convention or meeting planners, tour operators and retail travel agents. The purchasing power of these groups is impressive, and there are relatively few of them, which justifies the added expense of personal selling. In 2005, the Kenya Tourist Board launched the Fall 2005 Roadshow in order to increase awareness of the destination across the US. Along with 20 tour operators from Kenya, members of the tourist board visited travel agents in Arizona, Florida, Los Angeles, New York and Texas, in order to educate them on the virtues of travelling to Kenya. At the same time, an extensive network of newly appointed global market representatives were employed in Kenya's key markets in Europe, the US and Asia. Their role was to raise the profile of Kenya among trade representatives and consumers by emphasizing the quality and diversity of the country.

### Sales Promotions

Due to the lack of control over the destination product and pricing, sales promotions are used relatively little in destination marketing. However, 'added value' promotional offers may be made available, featuring elements of the destination product over which the destination marketing agency does have control. In Chapter 8, we saw how Guam Visitors' Bureau partnered with credit card company JCB in a promotion to attract higher-spending Japanese tourists to the island in 2006. Card members received incentives for spending more while they were on holiday, so that both the country and the credit company would benefit from the promotion. Another example of a destination using sales promotion comes from the UK, where VisitBritain partnered with Columbia Pictures in 2006 to plan a series of events that capitalized on the film *The Da Vinci Code.* Promotional campaigns relied heavily on an online code-breaking competition to tie in with the book's plot and locations in

London and Scotland. VisitBritain also provided incentives for tourists to write blogs about their experiences for its website.

*Trade Fairs and Exhibitions*
Many DMOs exhibit at travel trade shows, fairs, exhibitions or conventions. Generally these occasions bring all parts of the industry together. Such events may be annual, or used as a short-term tactic to boost tourism interest. In October 2006, Zimbabwe opened an international tourism fair to promote its once booming resorts, largely deserted because of President Robert Mugabe's controversial politics. The southern African country's tourism revenues had collapsed in the face of a crumbling economy, chronic fuel shortages and Mugabe's standoff with Britain and other Western nations. Although the country has some of Africa's most popular tourism destinations, including the famous Victoria Falls and some of the continent's largest game reserves, promoters have found it hard to sell Zimbabwe overseas.

## Marketing Co-operation

Considering the fact that DMO budgets for marketing purposes are equivalent to an average of 0.5 per cent or less of tourism expenditure, as well as the fact that most DMOs cannot influence more than around 10 per cent of all prospective visitors, the question of how effective their marketing campaigns are in practice is a valid one. DMOs therefore often co-operate with other members of the tourism industry. These co-operative strategies create marketing bridges between a DMO and individual operators in the tourism industry, and between 'umbrella' campaigns and industry marketing expenditure. One of these strategies is the participation in joint marketing schemes. Many destinations have formed partnerships with travel, recreational and communication businesses on joint promotional efforts. They advertise in national magazines and travel publications and do vertical marketing with business travel promotions to link to the business–leisure segment of the travelling public; and they target intermediaries such as travel agents.

The Case Study at the end of the chapter shows how different agencies in New Zealand worked together on a co-ordinated strategy to leverage *The Lord of the Rings* for tourism purposes. The government invested up to US$18.6 million on projects to promote New Zealand in the wake of the film, even appointing a *The Lord of the Rings* minister to assist in the process. The promotional campaign included a huge international media programme with numerous events leveraging off the three films, featuring, for example, food and wine. Tourist maps were produced listing 35 filming locations; the films were promoted on the tourist board's website; and links to film tours by local operators were set up including everything from half-day tours to 22-day trips.

Another effective way to attract potential travellers is to offer them convenient packages that not only include the basic necessities but also contain visits to the icon attractions in the destination. Packaging destinations either for the general mass tourism market or for niche specialist markets can significantly increase a destination's appeal. Inbound operators are usually responsible for packaging the destinations, putting together the combination of stopovers, attractions, accommodations and tours; deciding the best transportation to use along the way; and allocating the amount of time to be spent at each destination. These operators, working with DMOs and provincial tourism offices, as well as with regional tourism groups and individual suppliers, create tours and promotional materials that will help to win business in the highly competitive international marketplace.

An example of successful destination packaging comes from the Stellenbosch Wine Route in South Africa. Sponsored by American Express, the wine route of over 200 wineries offers travellers what they call a 'wine experience'. Most of the wineries work with restaurants, attractions and accommodations to package this wine tourism experience. For example, visitors to the Spier winery can take advantage of a four-star hotel, five restaurants, a wine centre, a golf course, lakefront picnic facilities, horseback riding, art festivals and a conference centre. In the past few years Spier has developed a lavish Summer Wine Festival that runs from November through March.

## Marketing Events, Festivals and Conferences

For business and leisure travellers, events and conferences often play a key role in bringing people to destinations. These can vary from conventions and exhibitions for the business market to huge sporting events like the Olympics or the soccer World Cup, which attract millions of sport tourists. From the destination's perspective, event tourism is the development and marketing of events to obtain economic and community benefits. To the consumer, it is travel for the purpose of participating in or viewing an event.

### Events

Events are often introduced to cope with seasonality and to boost tourism receipts during normally quiet times of year. For example, in 1995, Whistler held its first World Ski and Snowboard Festival in April in order to increase occupancy rates at the end of the winter season. Now the event is North America's largest snow-sport and music event, attracting thousands of enthusiasts from all over the world. Hotel rooms are fully booked during the event, which spans two weekends in order to maximize occupancy rates. In addition to ski and snowboard competitions, film events, parades and a lively club scene at night, more than 50 acts are booked for the Outdoor Concert Series. The concerts usually attract audiences of up to 10,000 revellers. According to an independent research study commissioned by the festival organizers, the 2006 festival resulted in a CDN$37.7 million impact on the province, including nearly $21.3 million for the resort. The staging of major events in Whistler is not a new experience, and although the destination lost the World Cup skiing competition to Lake Louise, it was successful in its bid to be the host city for the 2010 Olympic Winter Games. The estimated cost of the joint Vancouver/Whistler Olympic bid was about $20 million, but hosting the games is expected to generate $1.3 billion in revenue from ticket sales, sponsorships and television rights.

Whistler is not alone in aggressively marketing sporting events. There is an increasing popularity for hosting sporting events in order to increase future visitation, improve the image of the city or country, or to disperse tourism activities in a wider region (Hudson et al., 2004).[13] Destinations are also becoming more skilled at leveraging impacts from an event. The success of previous sporting events such as the Barcelona Olympic Games has drawn attention to the strategic value of events. For example, in the Bahamas, an events management company has been given the task of developing events that show the natural beauty of the islands. Australian tourism organizations implemented a series of strategies and tactics designed to leverage tourism benefits from the 2000 Olympic Games. The Australian events sector now has a very high profile as it is seen to be of national, strategic importance for developing tourism in the country. In 2006, the Irish government spent £10 million to stage and market the Ryder Cup golf tournament, in an effort to reverse a five-year decline in North American visitors (Cole, 2006).[14] Television ads appeared on US channels such as CBS and the Golf Channel. The Ryder Cup was expected to generate about £50 million in business through TV rights, merchandise, tickets and sponsorship.

Events do not necessarily have to involve sport. To commemorate the best-known date in British history, 1066, when the Norman William the Conqueror defeated the Anglo-Saxon King Harold, the re-enactment of the Battle of Hastings is held every year at Battle Abbey in Battle, East Sussex. The event typically attracts up to 7,000 spectators, but 21,000 people turned up in 2006. The reason for this was a specially extended script that attempted to imitate the original battle as closely as possible. More than 3,000 fighters massed in full battle dress for the event. Men marched from Yorkshire and Kent, and from Cambridge and Leicester. But in a revisionist twist, the ranks of the Norman, Breton, Flemish and Saxon armies were swelled on the 1040th anniversary by 'actors' from 18 countries worldwide. Performances took place on both Saturday and Sunday, and 30,000 people attended the fireworks display in Hastings that followed Saturday's re-enactment.

The Global Spotlight describes the Calgary Stampede, an annual ten-day celebration of Western culture and heritage.

## Global Spotlight

### The Greatest Outdoor Show on Earth –
### The Calgary Stampede

The Calgary Stampede started from humble beginnings as an agricultural fair in 1882, with attractions and attendance growing each year, until the first rodeo was added in 1912. Nowadays, over 1.2 million people attend annually, including some 300,000 foreign tourists, helping to generate around CDN$150 million in direct revenue, amounting to 15 per cent of Calgary's yearly tourism earnings. Visitors also spend another $50 million at other local attractions during their stay, for example Calgary Zoo, Calgary Science Centre and Spruce Meadows.

Dubbed back in 1912 'The Greatest Outdoor Show on Earth', the Stampede has now become an intrinsic part of the city's identity, an international symbol even, just like Mardi Gras in New Orleans and Carnival in Rio de Janeiro. Calgary has branded itself (no pun intended) as Cowtown. The Stampede organizers are committed to preserving and promoting Western heritage and values while ensuring that the event remains relevant to the community. According to president Don Wilson, these core values include 'honesty, true values, a handshake's a deal, respect for your fellow man'. The cowboy hat is the major icon associated with the event and also the city in general. It is almost a crime against society *not* to wear one during the whole of the ten-day summer fair and cowboy boots, jeans and other appropriate apparel and paraphernalia proliferate amongst audiences, competitors and vendors.

The Stampede Parade starts the festivities off each year with around 400,000 spectators lining the downtown area to watch 55 appropriately themed floats, 750 horses, 1,000 band members, celebrity rodeo clowns, street sweepers dressed as 'critters' and an oxen train. There is no entry fee for floats, but there is heavy competition to attain one of the coveted spots. Local celebrities and families of former pioneers are also honoured at these occasions. By this time, visitors will probably have experienced their first 'Stampede Breakfast'. These began in 1923 when a chuckwagon driver decided to cook up breakfast in his wagon in the core of the downtown area. Since then the theme has developed to encompass all major corporations, church groups, schools, community associations, city attractions, retail and restaurant outlets, car lots, as well as the Stampede ground itself. These breakfasts are traditionally free for all comers and are used to promote businesses.

Another cultural spin-off from the Stampede phenomenon is the Young Canadians School of Performing Arts, a music, dance and drama facility for students aged 8–22. Scholarships worth $7,500 each were established to provide free training in music performance, all forms of dance and gymnastics to create a yearly line-up for the Stampede Grandstand Show. Nowadays, there is even training in a Cirque de Soleil-style circus programme and hip-hop, in keeping with contemporary trends. With audiences of 20,000 each night, the 500 cast members produce a visual spectacular in 1,200 specially designed costumes and a variety of elaborate sets. The show culminates in a dazzling firework display.

The Stampede ground houses multiple stages and marquees for 'Nashville' style music as well as more modern singers and bands. There is also an extensive funfair in the 'Midway', many restaurants as well as kiosks selling food, a native Indian camp with daily shows, farm animal enclosures with entertainments and competitions, on top of all the rodeo and chuckwagon events. Many local businesses use it as a team-building corporate opportunity, hosting hospitality events among the festivities. The whole of Calgary traditionally dresses up shop fronts with old straw bales and rickety pieces of wood to simulate old-style pioneer buildings; restaurants, bars and nightclubs all theme themselves accordingly and host Stampede events with internationally famous Country and Western singers and bands as well as more mainstream stars. Doing the rounds of these nightspots is now called 'Stampeding' and many locals save up all year to be able to throw themselves into the 'Stampeding' spirit with a vengeance.

*Sources:* McGinnis, S. (4 July 2003) 'Stampede brings boom', *Calgary Herald*, B1; Toneguzzi, M. (4 July 2003) 'New Stampede president driven by western values', *Calgary Herald*, SE5; MacGregor, R. (5 July 2005) 'The Greatest Outdoor Show on Earth', *Globe & Mail*, A2; Partridge, J. (7 August 2005) 'A great big birthday bash', *Calgary Herald,* AA4; Knapp, S. (8 July 2005) 'Pioneer's progeny part of centennial salute', *Calgary Herald*, AA4.

## Festivals

Festivals, like events, also attract tourists to destinations. Some destinations may be known for just one festival. In the north of China, for example, Harbin is well known for its International Ice Festival held every January. Being one of the few tourism attractions in the city – an otherwise bleak industrial city of four million people where temperatures drop below – 30°C during winter – even an environmental disaster in 2005 did not deter the organizers from hosting the event. Water supplies were cut for over a week when toxic chemicals poured through the city's water supplies. The event went ahead as scheduled. Tens of thousands of visitors from around the country and the world travel to Harbin for the month-long festival, which is famous for its dazzling array of ice sculptures, which include replicas of world historical monuments such as the Eiffel Tower, the Great Wall and Egyptian pyramids.

Hong Kong has positioned itself as a destination of high-quality festivals, hosting a number of traditional festivals throughout the year. Hong Kong has 20 public holidays per year, many linked to Chinese festivals and each with its own identity. These religious, mythical and historical celebrations are open to non-Chinese locals and tourists. Examples include the Dragon Boat Festival at Stanley Beach, which is an annual event attracting large crowds to watch the fierce competition amongst teams of rowers, kept in rhythm by pounding drums, in sleek dragon-prowed racing boats. The Bun Festival on the Cheung Chau waterfront features a procession of colourfully dressed children on carnival floats along with 16-metre-high bun-studded bamboo towers traditionally erected for the occasion. The island's population triples during this cultural event. As the luxury retail capital of Asia, Hong Kong naturally has to host a 'Shopping Festival' during the summer months when sales, late shopping hours and special restaurant menus encourage consumers to adopt the 'shop til you drop' culture. Sporting events attracting international audiences include the Champions Challenge tennis tournament in January, the Hong Kong Marathon in February, and the most famous event of them all, the Hong Kong Sevens. This is a rugby tournament, celebrating its 30th anniversary in 2007, which is a magnet for rugby fans from all over the world but particularly from Australia, New Zealand, South Africa and Britain.

## Conferences

The convention and exhibition market, another lucrative market for destinations, has experienced unparalleled growth during the past 20 years. However, the period between 2000 and 2002 saw significant declines in demand for convention centres. During that time, several technology events associated with the 'dot.com' era ceased to exist and many others downsized as a result of general economic conditions and the reduction of travel following 9/11. The market has now recovered, and convention centre events experienced an increase of over 2 per cent from 2005 to 2006, following a significantly higher increase of 16 per cent the year before. Convention and trade show occupancy rates at the largest halls were strong in 2006, at 44.9 per cent, topping the previous year's 43.9 per cent, with other size centres also showing improvement.[15]

High-quality convention and exhibition centres can be found in virtually every city around the world, although when it comes to numbers of international meetings, the US remains in first place, according to the International Congress & Convention Association (ICCA). The

Case Study in Chapter 9 showed how Puerto Rico is attempting to position itself as a world class business tourism destination. An aggressive, international integrated marketing campaign culminated in 2005 in the grand opening of the US$415m Puerto Rico Convention Centre. Puerto Rico is a member of the BestCities Alliance, a convention bureau global alliance, which includes Cape Town, Copenhagen, Dubai, Edinburgh, Melbourne, Singapore and Vancouver. Other countries, like Jordan, are also positioning themselves as convention-friendly destinations. In 2006, the Jordan Tourism Board (JTB), the kingdom's official marketing organization, launched a sales drive and communications campaign to promote Jordan as a business and Meetings, Incentives, Conventions and Exhibitions (MICE) destination for Gulf Co-operation Council (GCC) members.

## Marketing All-inclusive resorts

The concept of all-inclusive resorts is not new. As mentioned in Chapter 6, this type of holiday originated in holiday camps in the UK over 50 years ago. However, over the past few decades, there has been a huge increase in the development of new all-inclusive resorts, as well as an adaptation of a number of older traditional hotels into all-inclusive properties. All-inclusive packages were originally designed for resorts situated in isolated tourist destinations where the absence of infrastructure and the insufficient supply of services limited tourists' consumption possibilities. The concept became popular, as it decreased uncertainty about the total amount of money needed for a holiday. It also offered value, as it normally involved the sale of different products as a unique package at a price lower than the total price of its separate components. 'All-inclusives' normally supply a room, three meals daily, unlimited beverages, sports and entertainment for one fixed price. Sol Melia is the world's largest resort operator, running more than 300 hotels with 80,000 rooms, mostly located in Europe and the Caribbean. 2006 profits were expected to be about €112 million, a gain of 24 per cent on the previous year. All-inclusives are very popular with honeymoon couples, but another trend is 'Au Naturel' resorts. SuperClubs Hedonism II was so popular in Negril, Jamaica, that Hedonism III was opened in Ocho Rios.

The market for this type of holiday has grown steadily over the last few decades, and has also become increasingly competitive. Resorts are not just competing on price, and continue to add new services and components to provide more choices. Today, it is hard to find an all-inclusive resort that has only buffet meals; most resorts now have à-la-carte restaurants. Resorts are also improving facilities and services. Royal service at Sol Melia's Paradisus Riveria Cancun, for example, includes private check-in and check-out, access to a private lounge for club members, a private buffet, private beach club, a pool butler service, and free internet access. Like golf, spas are very popular, and more all-inclusive resorts are adding them. For example, Sandals Resorts have full-service, state-of-the-art European spas offering a variety of both rejuvenating and fitness services. Some resorts like SuperClubs are providing 'No Hurricane Guarantees' year-round. Should a hurricane happen to strike, the resort will issue a voucher for the same number of disrupted nights for a stay during the same month of the following year. The same applies with the 'Jamaica Sunshine Guarantee' should one encounter a sunless day – a rare occurrence in Jamaica.

Despite the success of all-inclusives, they have been criticized on a number of fronts in terms of their social, economic and environmental impacts (Horner and Swarbrooke, 2004).[16] Socially, they are accused of creating ghettos, segregating tourists and locals and discouraging the mixing of the two. Economically, they often provide little income for the local communities. Many all-inclusives are internationally owned and much of the money spent in the resorts leaks out of the country where the resort is situated. In Majorca, for example, where all-inclusive accommodation grew sharply from 9.6 per cent in 2002 to 16.3 per cent in 2004, some representatives of the government have complained that such hotels do not generate significant revenues for the island. Finally, all-inclusives are accused of negatively impacting the local environments as they are often complexes on a very large scale. As well as harming the visual amenity of sites, they often use valuable water and damage wildlife habitats. In a video titled 'Thailand for Sale' produced in the 1980s, Club Mediterranean were strongly criticized for the negative environmental and social impacts of their developments. In terms of the future, all-inclusive resorts could be a permanent feature, or they may prove to be part of a transition phase which new destinations go through until their local infrastructure has developed to the point where facilities and quality are on a par with the all-inclusive resort.

## Chapter Summary

Destinations are places that have some form of actual or perceived boundary, such as the physical boundary of an island, political boundaries, or even market-created boundaries. There are many different types of destination, including major international destinations, classic destinations, human-made destination resorts, natural landscape or wildlife tourism destinations, alternative destinations, business tourism destinations, stopover destinations, short break destinations, and day trip destinations.

There is a strong link between destinations and attractions, and it is usually the existence of a major attraction that stimulates the development of destinations, whether a beach, a religious temple or a theme park. As with other sectors of the tourism industry, attractions are increasingly polarized between a few large attractions and thousands of small, micro-sized enterprises. Tourist attractions can also be classified as natural or human-made.

Destination brand-builders face five key challenges: limited budgets, politics, the external environment, the destination product and creating differentiation. The destination brand-building process comprises five stages: market investigation; analysis and strategic recommendations; brand identity development; brand launch and introduction; brand implementation; and monitoring, evaluation and review.

For business and leisure travellers, events and conferences often play a key role in bringing people to destinations. From the destination's perspective, event tourism is the development and marketing of events to obtain economic and community benefits. To the consumer, it is travel for the purpose of participating in or viewing an event. Events are often introduced to cope with seasonality and to boost tourism receipts during normally quiet times of year. The convention and exhibition market is another lucrative market for destinations, and has experienced unparalleled growth during the past 20 years.

Over the past few decades, there has been a huge increase in the development of new all-inclusive resorts, as well as an adaptation of a number of older traditional hotels into all-inclusive properties. All-inclusive resorts could be a permanent feature, or they may prove to be part of a transition phase which new destinations go through until their local infrastructure has developed to the point where facilities and quality are on a par with the all-inclusive resort.

## Key Terms

convention and visitor bureaus (CVBs), p. 399
destination branding, p. 401
destination marketing organizations (DMOs), p. 398
Destination Marketing Association International (DMAI), p. 399
destinations, p. 390
promotion strategy, p. 410
tourism area life cycle (TALC), p. 400

### Discussion Questions and Exercises

1. Considering the characteristics and classifications of destinations, do you think Disneyland Florida is an attraction or a destination?
2. Research the marketing activities of a local destination marketing organization. What promotional tools is it using?
3. Apply the tourism area life cycle to a destination you are familiar with. What does its position on the life cycle tell you about its target market?.
4. Apply the Destination Brand Benefit Pyramid (Figure 12.3) to a local destination. What does the exercise tell you about the destination's brand?
5. Find an example of a destination that is attempting to attract tourists through events and festivals. Is such a marketing strategy sustainable?

## Branding New Zealand as Middle Earth

In 2001, the first of *The Lord of the Rings* trilogy was released on 10,000 cinema screens worldwide. It provided tourism marketers in New Zealand with the perfect opportunity to re-brand the destination. In fact, the whole country was branded as Tolkien's Middle Earth through forward thinking, calculated risk-taking, quick reaction to public demand, best

**Case Study**

Milford Sound, New Zealand. One of the main locations used in the *Lord of the Rings* films.

marketing practices, thorough research and sustained management of media opportunities, as well as speedy but controlled tourism development in all locations used.

Film director Peter Jackson used 150 sites across New Zealand, showcasing the country's dramatic, diverse and extreme landscape, featuring Wellington, Queenstown, Matamata, Tongariro National Park and Poolburn. In the media, most reports maintained that the film was being shot in New Zealand, linking the film and location right from the start. The long production time and the staggered release of each film made for a longevity for New Zealand tourism, and the subsequent Academy Awards helped to sustain exposure. Also, the stars provided endorsement on everything from the scenery to the fashion and the cafés. The 2003 annual survey of visitors found that almost 90 per cent of all tourists knew that *The Lord of the Rings* series was made in that country, and the outstanding scenery in the films was one of the main reasons people travelled there.

When the first of the three films was released in 2001 the New Zealand Tourism board looked at the film as the equivalent of a promotional piece and worked out what the exposure would have cost to access commercially. Based on attendances and making a range of assumptions, they estimated the exposure was worth over US$41 million. By 2002, international visitor numbers had risen by 7 per cent in New Zealand, compared to a global rise of only 3 per cent, and contrary to a general expectation of falling numbers in the wake of 9/11. After the 2002 Academy Awards and a series of ads announcing New Zealand as 'Best Supporting Country', the nation's tourism website had more than a billion hits. Even now the home page of the website has a direct link to an interactive *New Zealand, Home of Middle Earth* section. This section has pictures and clips from the film, recorded testimonials from the actors, guides to destinations used in the film, and links to *The Lord of the Rings* themed tour operators.

The government invested up to US$18.6 million on projects to promote New Zealand in the wake of the film. The prime minister, Helen Clark, personally endorsed the 'branding' of New Zealand as the home of *The Lord of the Rings*, acknowledging the opportunity to showcase the country worldwide through film. She even appointed a *The Lord of the Rings* minister to assist in the process of leveraging the trilogy. The promotional campaign, co-coordinated by Investment New Zealand, included a huge international media programme with numerous events leveraging off the three films, featuring, for example, food and wine. Because it was a trilogy with a year's gap between each release, there was sufficient time to organize appropriate promotions to coincide with each release and promote different sectors of tourism. Tourist maps were produced listing 35 filming locations; the films were promoted on the tourist board's website; and links to film tours by local operators were set up, including everything from half-day tours to 22-day trips.

Countless tourism entrepreneurs have capitalized on the success of the films. Called the 'Frodo economy' by some locals, the films have provided a much-needed injection of confidence into small rural towns. *The Lord of the Rings Guidebook*, by Ian Brodie, sold 70,000 copies in the first 7 weeks after the film's release in 2001. There are also a number of *Lord of the Rings* related tours such as a '*Lord of the Rings* Flight' with Nelson Helicopters, and a drive around *Lord of the Rings* country with Nomad Safaris. The owners of the farm that hosted the film set for 'Hobbiton' had pulled in CDN$350,000 from Tolkien fans by November 2003 – more than 20 times the average annual income on the farm. The town of 'Hobbiton' is actually a farm in the small, hitherto unknown, town of Matamata which has transformed itself into a thriving tourism centre. Town signs emphasize 'Hobbiton' rather than Matamata; there's Hobbiton Nursery, the Hobbit Hole internet centre, Hobbiton tour buses named Bilbo and Frodo, and, of course, the farm itself where most of the filming took place. It has changed from a sheep farm to a tourist destination hosting three tours daily at around $40 per person. Interestingly, the original agreement with the production company was for them to dismantle the set. This procedure was disrupted by rains and when time came for the dismantling, the family pleaded to keep it, as they had already been inundated with unexpected visitors.

These additional services and businesses created through film tourism have extended the traditional tourist seasons in New Zealand. The film also benefited destinations that had little to do with the location of film production. Popular areas of Birmingham in the UK, immortalized by Tolkien in *The Lord of the Rings* adventure, including Moseley Bog and Sarehole Mill, experienced renewed interest following the films.

After the furore of the first film's release, a report on 'Scoping the Lasting Effects of *The Lord of the Rings*' was sponsored by the New Zealand Film Commission with the NZ

**Case Study**

Institute of Economic Research. This 2002 report advocates product placement, whereby advertising messages are embedded in films and TV programmes. Feature films are a valuable vehicle, it states, 'for specific product placement and a catalyst for destination-specific tourism when the film's message is memorable and durable'. It goes on to stress that getting on board right from the outset of a film production is crucial: 'The ability to recognize promotional opportunities and to act in anticipation of demand is critical to maximizing benefits.' This also requires that associated destination-related entrepreneurial activity (such as tour organization) has to complement the possible motivation factors of tourists to allow film enthusiasts to carry through on their inclinations.

The report pointed out potential negative impacts on local people's lives, such as inflated house prices, increased labour costs, adverse environmental impacts on fragile ecosystems within the agricultural areas and congestion in cities; but it concludes that the economic advantages would far outweigh the negative concerns and that 'the cumulative effect cannot be ignored'. It suggested broadening and deepening film-related infrastructure and contributing to a more user-friendly regulatory environment. Since then, New Zealand has announced a 12.5 per cent recoup of production costs for film-makers to encourage future production. This has apparently worked already as several big productions have been attracted there, including *The Last Samurai, King Arthur* and a new *King Kong* movie.

*Sources*: Croy, W.G. and Walker, R.D. (2003) 'Rural tourism and film – issues for strategic regional development', *New Directions in Rural Tourism*. Aldershot, UK: Ashgate Publishing Ltd; Grihault, N. (2003) 'Film tourism – the global picture', *Travel & Tourism Analyst*, 5: 1–22; Kim, H. and Richardson, S.L. (2003) 'Motion picture impacts on destination images', *Annals of Tourism Research*, 30(1): 216–237; New Zealand Institute of Economic Research (April 2002) 'Scoping the lasting effects of *The Lord of the Rings*', A Report to the New Zealand Film Commission; Zukowski, H. (2003) 'Outtakes from Middle-Earth', *Westworld*, November, 50–53.

## Questions

1. Do you think the marketing of New Zealand as 'Middle Earth' is sustainable?
2. What other factors could have accounted for the rise in visitor numbers in 2002?
3. Based on attendances and making a range of assumptions, New Zealand estimated the exposure from the first film was worth over US$41 million. What do you think is meant by this, and how do you think this figure was arrived at?
4. Make a list of the advantages and disadvantages of the impacts of the films on New Zealand. Do you agree with the report's suggestion that the advantages far outweigh the negative concerns?

## Websites

www.resortsmarketing.org      Resort Marketing Organization
www.rockhall.com      Rock and Roll Hall of Fame and Museum, Cleveland

www.incredibleindia.org      Incredible India website
www.vulcania.com      Vulcania Theme Park
www.calgarystampede.com      Calgary Stampede
www.visitsingapore.com      Singapore destination website
www.newzealand.com      New Zealand destination website
www.destinationmarketing.org      DMAI – Destination Marketing Association International

## References

1  Kotler, P., Bowen, J.and Makens, J. (2003) *Marketing for Hospitality and Tourism*. Upper Saddle River, NJ: Prentice Hall.
2  Swarbrooke, J. (1995) *The Development and Management of Visitor Attractions*. Butterworth Heinemann: Oxford, UK.
3  Anon. (2 November 2006) 'Booming tourism taking terrible toll on Egyptian antiquities, experts say', *National Post*, A14.
4  Gauldie, R. (2000) 'Advertising and promotion in the travel industry', *Travel & Tourist Analyst*, 4, 71–84.
5  Butler, R. W. (1980) 'The concept of a tourist area life cycle of evolution: implications for management of resources', *Canadian Geographer*, 24(1), 5.
6  Plog, S. C. (1974) 'Why destination areas rise and fall in popularity', *Cornell Hotel and Restaurant Quarterly*, 14(4), 55–58.
7  Morgan, N. and Pritchard, A. (2002) 'Contextualizing destination branding', in N. Morgan, A. Pritchard and R. Pride (eds), *Destination Branding*. Oxford: Butterworth-Heinemann, 11–41.
8  Stanley, B. (10 March 2006) 'Australia throws another tourism advertising slogan on the barbie'. *Wall Street Journal*, B1.
9  Morgan, N. and Pritchard, A. (2002) 'Contextualizing destination branding', in N. Morgan, A. Pritchard and R. Pride, (eds), *Destination Branding*. Oxford: Butterworth-Heinemann, 11–41.
10  Anon. (15 November 2005) 'Rebranding campaign unveils a new, more risqué Canada', *The Globe & Mail*, B13.
11  Plog, S. C. (1974) 'Why destination areas rise and fall in popularity', *Cornell Hotel and Restaurant Quarterly*, 14(4), 55–58.
12  Middleton, V. T. C. and Clarke, J. (2001) *Marketing in Travel and Tourism*. Oxford: Butterworth-Heinemann.
13  Hudson, S., Getz, D., Miller, G.A. and Brown, G. (2004) 'The future role of sporting events: evaluating the impacts on tourism', in Weiermair, K. and Mathies, C. (eds) *The Tourism and Leisure Industry – Shaping the Future*. The Haworth Press Inc: Binghampton, NY, 237–251.
14  Cole, C. (20 September 2006) 'Ireland has never been greener', *National Post*, B8.
15  Anon. (25 October 2006) 'PriceWaterhouseCoopers reports increase in demand for convention centers', retrieved from http://www.hsmai.org
16  Horner, S and Swarbrooke, J. (2004) *International Cases in Tourism Management: All-Inclusive Resorts* Elsevier Butterworth-Heinemann: Oxford, UK, 226–232.

# 13

# CONTEMPORARY ISSUES IN TOURISM AND HOSPITALITY MARKETING

### Second Life and the Virtual Hotel

It is October 2006, and performer Ben Folds is promoting his new album by playing at the opening party for Aloft, a new Starwood hotel. People wander in, sit down and discuss the music. Everything seems normal, but the whole scene exists only on the internet. The audience is made up of virtual representations of real people. The real people are sitting at their computer screens around the world, living their lives through avatars, the characters that appear on the screen. Ben Folds is real but he is selling his music in a virtual world, his music company believing that releasing his album to this 'virtual listening party' is the marketing strategy of the future.

Welcome to Second Life, an online world with millions of registered users and a thriving virtual economy. Second Life allows its users to create a new, and improved, digital version of themselves. They then guide their avatar wherever they choose: down streets, into nightclubs and into stores. When they meet another avatar they can start a conversation, develop friendships, love affairs and entire subcultures. 'Residents' can buy land, build structures and start businesses, and the service is fast becoming a three-dimensional test bed for corporate marketers, including Sony BMG Music Entertainment, Sun Microsystems, Nissan, Adidas, and Toyota. Retailers have set up shops to sell digital as well as real-world versions of their products, and even musicians can promote their albums with virtual appearances.

The demographics of Second Life users are interesting. The average age is 33, half of the users are women, and a very large number have not played online games before. 'It's the best combination of social networking, chat rooms and a 3D experience,' said Justin Bovington, chief executive of Rivers Run Red, a London branding agency helping to shape Second Life. 'It's such an immersive experience that people get it quicker than anything else. We'd been looking for the broadband killer application, and Second Life is it.'

The Aloft Hotel in Second Life

Linden Labs, the San Francisco company that operates Second Life, makes most of its money leasing 'land' to tenants. A company like Nissan or its advertising agency could buy an 'island' for a one-time fee of about US$1,250 and a monthly rate of about $195. Programmers could then be hired to create a driving course and design digital cars that people 'in world' could drive, as well as some billboards and other promotional spots through-out the virtual world that would encourage people to visit Nissan Island.

Starwood Hotels is the first real-world hospitality company to open in Second Life, featuring its new line of moderately priced, loft-style hotels called Aloft. Projects like Aloft are designed to promote the venture but also to give its designers feedback from prospective guests before the first real hotel opens in 2008. Starwood will observe how people move through the space, what areas and types of furniture they gravitate towards, and what they ignore. Consumers are encouraged to post comments about the hotel on a blog, which features regular updates on the virtual hotel's design, along with detailed screenshots. The ultimate goal is to attract trendy, youthful, tech-savvy customers to the Aloft brand, and the plan is to keep the virtual hotel as an interactive marketing tool, even after the real-world buildings open.

The prototype being built in Second Life is based on a physical prototype under construction in a warehouse in New York. Starwood hired two New York-based companies to build the digital model and then to market it within Second Life and beyond: marketing firm Electric Artists, and the Electric Sheep Company, which specializes in designing goods for sale within Second Life. Both sites feature clean architectural lines, high ceilings, and minimalist couches, tables, and beds that characterize the Aloft brand as efficient yet stylish. This is the first time the company has created a complete mock hotel, and it is unusual for the industry. Hotel prototypes usually don't amount to more than a single-room model that might be shown at a trade show. But the company says that both prototypes made financial sense. 'We're saving money,' said Starwood vice-president Brian McGuiness. 'If we find that significant numbers of people don't like a certain feature, we don't have to actually build it.' Starwood predicts that by 2012, there will be 500 Aloft properties worldwide.

Whether or not this innovative approach to marketing lures Second Lifers, and more importantly, real-life guests, toward the Aloft brand, remains to be seen. Meanwhile, why not check into the hotel and see for yourself?

*Sources*: Jana, R. (23 August 2006) 'Starwood Hotels explore Second Life first', BusinessWeek Online, retrieved from www.businessweek.com; Siklos, R. (16 October 2006) 'A virtual world but real money', *New York Times*, C1.

## OBJECTIVES

On completion of this chapter, you should understand:

▶ trends in tourism and hospitality marketing;

▶ how tourism should be marketed in the experiential economy;

▶ the growing importance of responsible marketing;

▶ the application of cause-related marketing in tourism;

▶ the marketing of sport and adventure tourism; and

▶ the marketing of tourism at times of crisis.

## Introduction

The Opening Vignette is an example of an innovative new way to present and promote a hospitality product, and it is future trends that this chapter is mainly concerned with. An analysis of tourism marketing trends is followed by a discussion about tourism marketing in the experiential economy. The next section looks at the responsible marketing of tourism, and then examples of cause-related marketing in tourism are outlined. The final two sections of the chapter look at the marketing of sport and adventure tourism, and marketing tourism in times of crisis.

Tourism is expected to grow 4.3 per cent annually between 2008 and 2017, with the World Travel & Tourism Council (WTTC) predicting that, by 2017, that will amount to a market of more than US$13 trillion. By 2020, according to the World Tourism Organization (UNWTO), an army of 100 million Chinese will fan out across the globe replacing Americans, Japanese and Germans as the world's most numerous travellers. China will soon be the most popular destination as well, with 130 million arrivals in 2020. Also, by 2020, 50 million Indians are expected to tour overseas. Business travel from, and among, developing countries, will grow much more rapidly than the business market in general, as industries migrate from countries with a shrinking, expensive labour force to those where more skilled personnel are available at lower cost. Two obvious growth areas are China and India.

Certain sectors of the tourism industry will grow faster than others. The world's airlines were expected to report a profit in 2007 for the first time in six years, but they will remain constrained by the rising costs of fuel, government taxes and airport service fees. Cruises, a favourite vacation for older travellers, have grown by 50 per cent in recent years; they now attract some eight million travellers each year, and growing numbers of business meetings occur on board cruise ships. The ships themselves are also expected to get larger. Royal Caribbean International's *Freedom of the Seas*, for example, is longer than three football fields and 15 storeys high with a pool area featuring a stationary 'wave' big enough to surf on for its 4,370 guests. Most Caribbean island docks are not vast enough to accommodate it so it has to anchor offshore and send passengers to land in smaller boats. Even the Chinese cruise industry is looking towards the future. A new 'love boat for millionaires' is inviting China's growing number of eligible male millionaires to join a matchmaking boat cruise that promises 'good-looking and desirable' women. The love boat service was launched in Shanghai in November 2006, and takes place along Shanghai's Huangpu River. Organizer Xu Tianli said that the men had to be worth at least 2 million Yuan ($250,000; £130,000), and only women 'who were attractive in every category' could participate.

Unfortunately, the growth of the tourism industry does have some pitfalls. Increased international exposure includes a greater risk of terrorist attack. Since 11 September 2001, American-owned hotels have experienced several major bomb attacks, in part because American government facilities overseas have been effectively hardened against terrorist assault. Such attacks may well continue, as terrorist activity in the world is likely to increase in the next 10 years. The *World of Travel in 2020* study, commissioned by Cendant Travel Distribution Services (2006), suggests that the perception of danger that is generated by our culture of fear has created two contrasting consumer groups with very different attitudes and purchasing behaviour.[1] They are New Puritans, who let their worries prevent them from living a full life, and Hyperlifers, whose response to fear is to try and live life to the full to avoid acknowledging risks. These groups represent opposite ends of the behavioural spectrum,

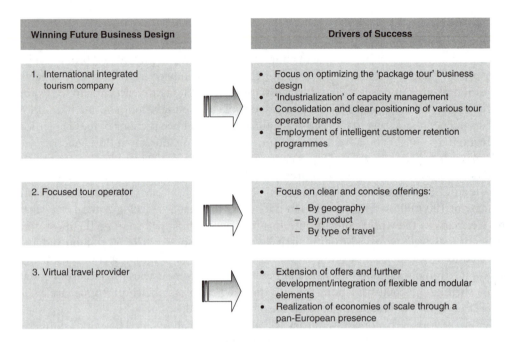

**Figure 13.1**  Potential Winning Business Designs in Tourism

*Source*: Schneiderbauer, D. and Döring, F. (2004) 'Surviving the crisis in European tourism', *Mercer on Travel and Transport*, with permission from Mercer Management Consulting (www.mercermc.com).

whereas in reality, most people fall somewhere in between, or change groups depending on the circumstances.

As for the structure of the tourism industry, it is predicted that there will be increased competition, and many more mergers among hotel chains, cruise lines, and other segments (Cetron, 2005).[2] The greatest activity may come in Europe, particularly in the tour operating sector. A recent Mercer study determined that three business designs offer the greatest potential for success for European tour operators (see Figure 13.1):

1. The international, integrated tour operator, with a strong presence in all major European tourism markets, along with complete vertical integration and the broadest possible coverage of all travel destinations, different kinds of leisure trips and customer segments.
2. The focused tour operator, with a clearly differentiated competitive position, that concentrates on defined target customer segments and/or service offerings.
3. The virtual tour operator, specializing in the simple, low-cost distribution of standard products (such as flights, hotels, rental cars), enabling the customer to pick and choose among individual travel components, even from different providers, to build individual travel packages (Schneiderbauer and Döring, 2004).[3]

The Mercer study says that travel providers that do not aggressively pursue one of the above business designs are likely to find the future hard going. It also says that whether large or small,

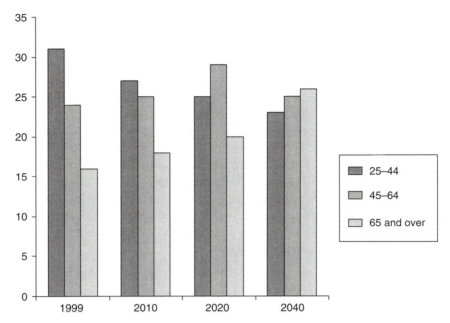

**Figure 13.2**    Forecast Changes in the Demographic Structure of the EU
(age classes in percentage of total population)

*Source:* Eurostat (NewCronos), Theme 3; demo, dpop + dpro, own calculation.

all tourism participants must face up to a world in which they will be challenged to adapt faster and more flexibly than ever before to an increasingly diverse array of customer desires.

## Demographic Trends

In terms of demographics, the world population is forecast to reach 8.9 billion people by 2050 with the most populous nations being India, China, Pakistan, Indonesia and Nigeria. Although this population growth will be driven by Asia and Africa, over the next 20 years the key markets for outbound travel will remain Europe, Asia and the Americas. One of the most significant implications of demographic change in this century is the ageing of the world's population. The world median age is projected to rise from 26 years in 2000 to 44 years by 2100.

Figure 13.2 shows the forecast changes in the demographic structure of the European Union. The figure indicates the rise in the retirement-age population. In Germany, for example, this segment will climb from under 16 per cent of the population in 2000 to nearly 19 per cent in 2010 and 31 per cent in 2050. In Europe, as well as in the US and Japan, the aged also form the wealthiest segment of society, and this will have a positive impact on the travel industry. Off-season tourism by seniors will help to smooth out the annual cycle in cash flow for hotels, motels, resorts and other travel businesses. However, this segment will also require special amenities, such as extra help with transportation and baggage, faucet handles that can be operated by arthritic hands and larger signs with easier-to-read type.

An aging population does not mean that tourism marketers should ignore other cohorts. According to the World Youth Student & Educational Travel Confederation (WYSE), young travellers are the travel industry's fastest growing sector, representing over 20 per cent of all international visitors. WYSE say that these adventurous young backpackers stay longer, spend more, seek out alternative destinations and enjoy a wider mix of travel experiences compared with average tourists. In 2007, WYSE launched a partnership with the World Tourism Organization (UNWTO) to promote and develop this multi-million dollar industry by encouraging governments to actively support and develop youth tourism products and services.

Changing family structures will also have an effect on tourism products and cost structure. Over the next 15 years there will be more flexible travel formats and cost structures to suit different family compositions. However, family travel (adults with children) is expected to grow at a faster rate than all forms of leisure travel, as both parents and grandparents continue to look at travel as one way in which to 'reunite' families in a contemporary world that is increasingly dominated by the demands of work.

## Behavioural Trends

The desire for experiences has been referred to in Chapter 2 and expanded on in a separate section in this chapter. But, in addition to collecting experiences, individuals are showing an increasing desire to convert them into images and stories, which in return enable them to engage others – whether to please, convince or gain status. This has been termed **life caching**. Rapid improvements in technology are allowing consumers to capture, store, collect and display their holiday experiences to friends or family – or even the entire world. 'Digital Scrapbooking' (see www.digitalscrapbookplace.com) is one way that consumers can capture moments, create layouts and art that transforms experiences into memories.

---

**LIFE CACHING**
desire of individuals to convert experiences into images and stories

---

Technology is also affecting the way travel is purchased. As the internet grows internationally, so will its use by the tourism industry. By 2011, 38 per cent of travel revenue sold in the US will be done online, according to a report by JupiterResearch – 'US Travel Forecast, 2006 to 2011'.[4] The company predicts that US$128 billion in travel will be sold online in the US in 2011, growing from $85 billion in 2006. Factors that will spur online spending are greater consumer discretionary income, increasingly sophisticated products available online and improved online compliance in business travel. Higher fares and an increase in people flying have driven total air revenue to $138 billion in 2006, with $49 billion of that sold online. JupiterResearch predicts that this figure will grow to $72 billion in 2011. Online bookings for hotels will also rise. In 2005, internet sales represented 18 per cent of Best Western's total business, and that percentage can only grow in the years ahead (Cetron, 2005).[5]

The *World of Travel in 2020* study, referred to earlier, gives some insight into the consumer of the future. It suggests that the 'one size fits all' approach will no longer work, and in their pursuit for individualism, consumers will look for new experiences such as controlled danger, unusual environments and cultures, personal or physical improvement and emotional development. They will not wish to revisit the same place. Loyalty to a travel supplier will be driven by an intermediary's ability to deliver a fresh stream of one-off experiential vacations. The twin goals of individualism and experience will present some interesting challenges for the global travel industry. Marketers can expect to see growing demand from European and North American consumers for increasingly specialized holidays that combine unusual experiences and the potential for personal development. For example, a visit to a Russian Gulag, described in the Snapshot below, will be typical of the niche offers that experience-seeking travellers will be purchasing.

The study points to a trend towards inconspicuous consumption in the developed world with a desire by people to express their identity in more subtle ways than in the past. Visible expressions of status are becoming less important and instead, a more fluid and less elitist concept of luxury is emerging that is driven by consumer concerns about authenticity, experience and individualism. Increasingly, luxury is about the pursuit of authentic and exotic experiences and services, rather than scarcely available, high value goods. Intangibles such as time and experience will therefore define the luxury holiday of the future, creating challenges for companies who presently offer more traditional luxury holidays that focus on exclusivity and price.

Hand in hand with the shift towards inconspicuous consumption is a greater awareness of issues such as sustainable development, ecotourism and ethical consumption. It is expected that ethical initiatives will enter the mainstream and take on a different dimension as consumers demand more responsible behaviour from tour operators and airlines. In the coming decades, the world needs to develop and adopt new, low-emission and low-carbon energy resources. Transport and accommodation account for a significant proportion of energy consumption by the tourism industry. As a result, it is likely that we will see some innovative alternative-energy solutions for tourism beginning to appear in the world's more environmentally minded countries, like Sweden and Germany. Belgium's transport minister has even proposed banning the shortest domestic flights in his country to lessen the burden on the environment. Other sectors are likely to adopt green policies in an effort to operate in an environmentally friendly manner. In 2006, Starwood Capital announced plans to develop a new hotel chain called *1*. Hotels will be designed from the inside out to be as eco-friendly as available technology can make them. Destinations will also become more responsible. The Global Spotlight in this chapter shows how Machu Picchu in Peru is limiting access to preserve the environment, and more destinations are likely to follow suit. The Kenya Tourism Board for example, has launched a programme to curb visitor numbers and preserve the fragile environment of the Masai Mara game park. A section on responsible marketing of tourism follows later in this chapter.

Finally, the report suggests that streamlining the travel process to minimize travel stress will hold much higher appeal to the time-poor traveller of 2020. Consumers of the future will demand more time-convenient flights, the ability to check in and have a boarding pass before getting to the airport, better connections, online visas and either a waiting private car transfer or a 'good to go' rental car. The study also suggests that personal service will increasingly outweigh price as the key differentiator.

## Snapshot

### Torture Tourism? Visit a Gulag in Russia

The mayor of a remote Arctic city that hosted some of the most feared Soviet prison camps plans to build a replica of a forced labour camp, charging tourists hundreds of dollars for a few nights of incarceration. 'I want to make a camp like those that existed in the times of the gulag,' Igor Shpektor, mayor of Vortuka, said. 'The same regime will be followed as it was in those camps.' The watchtowers, barbed wire, guard dogs and gruel that Shpektor envisions may appeal to history buffs, students of Alexander Solzhenitsyn's book, *Gulag Archipelago* – or to just plain masochists.

Vorkuta, a city built by gulag labour in the tundra 1,200 miles northeast of Moscow and 100 miles above the Arctic Circle, is slowly dying – and many of those who remain cannot afford to leave. The most significant foreign investment in the city since the collapse of the Soviet Union has been a programme by the World Bank to relocate people, encouraging them to abandon the far North for better prospects elsewhere. Coal mining first attracted the gulag's architects in the 1930s and resulted in forced labour from two million prisoners before the camps shut down in 1950s. The mines, however, are closing.

Shpektor has cited one of the abandoned settlements as a prime spot for his gulag. It is called Uzhny, which means simply 'southern', and was one of 132 camps that existed in and around Vorkuta at the gulags' peak. At the proposed gulag, tourists will be able to eat turnip gruel and sleep in wooden barracks in a faux camp surrounded by barbed wire and guard towers, patrolled by soldiers and dogs. 'Americans can stay here,' Shpektor said. 'We will give them a chance to escape. The guards will shoot them,' – with paint balls, naturally, not bullets.

Gulag camps have been largely demolished or abandoned, and public recognition of them is far lower profile than for the Nazi concentration camps, such as Auschwitz and Buchenwald which have been turned into museums. However, gulag tourism is not a new phenomenon. For over 20 years, American tourists have been visiting the gulag network in Siberia, originally established by Stalin. One travel company, Dula Tours, offers a 12-day package for 'dark tourists' wishing to understand what life was like for Soviet political prisoners at first hand.

Shpektor is currently seeking investors and believes that £500,000 should cover the initial phase. He is convinced there are plenty of 'extreme tourists' who will be willing to fork out at least £250 for a three-day stay. He casts the idea as a way to remember the city's tragic past while pulling Vorkuta out of its post-Soviet slump which saw it lose some 80,000 residents in a decade. Shpektor's proposal doesn't stop with the recreated camp: he also suggests building a five-star hotel where those who suffer through the camp can be pampered afterwards.

The gulag is not Mr. Shpektor's first outlandish proposal. In 2001, he created a stir with a proposal to open Russia's first legal brothel. Political opposition to prostitution – and a failure to attract investors – doomed the idea. His new idea is attracting many critics, including survivors of the camps, but with the mines privately owned and managed and not sustained by the state, the need to diversify Vorkuta's economy is indisputable. Perhaps the time is ripe for gulag tourism in Vorkuta.

*Sources*: Trolanovski, A. (16 August 2006) 'Russian mayor plans to promote gulag tourism', *Western Star*, 11; Myers, S.L. (6 June 2005) 'Above the Arctic Circle, a gulag nightmare for tourists?', *New York Times*, A4; Osborn, A. (4 April 2006) 'Club gulag: tourists are offered prison camp experience', *The Independent*, 25

## Tourism Marketing in the Experiential Economy

According to many marketing experts, marketing in the 21st century is all about delivering the customer experience. Future generations of consumers will have more discretionary income, less time and more choices, and will display wholly new spending patterns, depending on age, geography and wealth. Customers will be looking for an experience, not just a product. The *World of Travel in 2020* study predicts that travellers of the future will seek, on average, up to four very different experiences a year. A passion for 'doing' rather than 'having' will double the number of consumers flying by 2020.

This book contains many examples of such experience-driven travel, such as war tourism in Vietnam, volunteer tourism, space tourism, nostalgia tourism, gulag tourism in Russia, VocationVacations, and film tourism in New Zealand. Another example comes from Cape Town, South Africa, where township tourism has increased hugely in popularity since South Africa's multiracial elections of 1994. More than 80 per cent of Cape Town's 250 licensed tour operators take tourists into the sprawling settlements set up by the old apartheid government, which are still home to the majority of the population. In 2006, 320,000 people went on a township tour for the 'cultural experience'.

In a recent survey of 362 firms by Bain & Company, 80 per cent believed they delivered a 'superior experience' to their customers. When customers were asked, it was a very different story: they said that only 8 per cent of companies were really delivering (Allen and Markey, 2006).[6] To close that gap, companies need to put customers at the heart of the organization, and engage in **experiential marketing**. Experiential marketing comprises marketing initiatives that offer consumers in-depth, tangible experiences, in order to provide them with sufficient information to make a purchase decision (Williams, 2006).[7] It is widely argued that, as the science of marketing evolves, experiential marketing will become the dominant tool of the future. The difference between traditional and experiential marketing can be highlighted in a number of ways. Firstly, the focus is on customer experiences and lifestyles, which provide sensory, emotional, cognitive and relational values to the consumer. Chapter 2 described how companies like Walt Disney are explicitly designing and promoting experiences. Secondly, there is a focus on creating synergies between meaning, perception, consumption and brand loyalty. Thirdly, it is argued that customers are not rational decision-makers, but rather driven by a combination of rationality and emotion. Finally, it is argued that experiential marketing requires a more diverse set of research methods in order to understand consumers.

---

**EXPERIENTIAL MARKETING**
marketing initiatives that offer consumers in-depth, tangible experiences, in order to provide them with sufficient information to make a purchase decision

---

In order to promote tourism experiences, tourism marketers will have to think beyond traditional advertising techniques. Promoting experiences via the internet, through channels such as Second Life (see Opening Vignette), is one new way tourism providers can introduce products to consumers. Product placement (see Chapter 9) is another promotional tool growing in significance for tourism and hospitality providers. The Snapshot below shows how the Bahamas' Ministry of Tourism fully supports filming in the Bahamas as part of its publicity and as an effective communications tool to attract tourists.

One emerging variation on product placement is **tryadvertising**. Tryadvertising is the practice of making consumers familiar with products by getting them to actually try them out.[8] It involves integrating goods and services into the daily life of consumers in a relevant way, so that they can make up their minds based on their experience, not a commercial message. Hotels, for example, are partnering with luxury car-makers to offer high-end model test drives to guests during their stay. The Ritz Carlton offers a *Key to Luxury* programme in co-operation with Mercedes Benz. Hotels are also making deals with furniture companies. Swedish IKEA have partnered with French ETAP hotels to equip all 60 ETAP budget hotels in Germany with an IKEA room and a public quiet space. One company that has responded to this growth area is Vacations Connections which offers an organized approach to in-room placement of samples targeted at vacationers. Carnival Cruises is one of their clients.

---

**TRYADVERTISING**

integrating goods and services into the daily life of consumers in a relevant way, so that they can make up their minds based on their experience, not a commercial message

---

Experience advertising requires more creative expression on the part of advertisers. Campaigns of the past were built on bricks and mortar, whereas today advertisers are trying to touch emotions and get into the consumer psyche. Advertising now is more about reasons why people do things and less about the pragmatic factors that go into their decision-making. An example was given in Chapter 8 with Las Vegas promising 'What Happens in Vegas Stays in Vegas', but another comes from Hilton Hotels, which won a 'Best of Show' award in the 2006 HSMAI Adrian Awards Competition for its 'Travel Should Take You Places' ad campaign. Instead of trying to entice guests through rational product attributes, Hilton decided to engage them at an emotional level, winning their hearts rather than their heads. The big idea was that the very nature of travel is transformative, and that transformation should be an enriching experience, changing you for the better. The ads (see example in Figure 13.3) remind the consumer that travel is more than A to B if we open our eyes to travel's possibilities. The campaign resulted in increased brand differentiation and brand energy, and translated into concrete business results.

Beyond creative expression, other influences have altered the course of tourism advertising. The 1980s was all about broadcast and mass advertising, and the 1990s was the decade of the internet. However, in today's age of iPods, PDAs, digital recorders, remote controls, podcasts, blogs, wikis, mo-blogs and VOD, the audiences are narrower and fragmented, and tune in or out as they please. Advertising has to capture an audience in mere seconds, or it is gone. One hotel label that has experienced success with podcasts (downloadable audio recordings) is Desires Hotels operated by Tecton Hospitality. About 70 per cent of guests at Desires Hotels

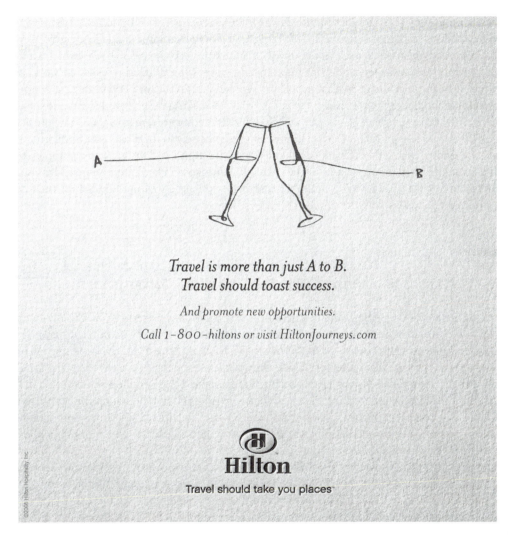

**Figure 13.3**   Hilton Print Advertisement

are Generation X demographically, and executives noticed that they were tuned into a new wave of social media, or social networking, via the internet on sites like MySpace and TripAdvisor. Desires properties in Miami, San Juan and Atlanta began to record a podcast each week about that week's upcoming events – the nightlife, restaurants and concerts. In the three-month period following the start of the podcasts, over 100,000 people visited the podcasts' section of the websites and the click-through rate to the reservations booking engine from the podcasts was a healthy 5 per cent (Schneider, 2006).[9]

As for the future, perhaps the movie *Minority Report* (set in 2054), provides a glimpse of advertising to look out for in the not-too-distant future. Projecting out from today's marketing and media technologies – web cookies, GPS devices, Bluetooth-enabled cell phones, TiVo personal video recorders, and barcode scanners – the Steven Spielberg film gives shape to an advertising-saturated society where billboards call out to you on a first-name basis, cereal boxes broadcast animated commercials, newspapers deliver news instantly over a broadband wireless network, and holographic hosts greet you at retail stores where biometric retina scans deduct the cost of goods from your bank account. So tourists of the future may be walking past a travel agent and a radio frequency identification (RFID) scanner will check their credit cards, link to their travel history, and text-message, or even call out, an invitation tailored precisely to their interests. Similarly, people may be driving near a theme park or other tourist attractions, and the car's navigation system will light up with an offer for discount tickets. Already, Chicago's O'Hare International Airport has interactive billboards where people can touch a screen to obtain a weather forecast for their destination city or get up-to-date news.

## Snapshot

### Promoting Destinations Through Film: The Case of The Bahamas

Placing a destination in a film is the ultimate in tourism product placement, and the Bahamas' Ministry of Tourism fully supports the use of film locations as part of its publicity and as an effective communications tool to attract tourists. The Bahamas realized the potential of promoting tourism through films after the Beatles filmed *Help* there in 1964. Now the Ministry gets actively involved immediately it receives a script. For example, US$16 million was invested in the recent film *After the Sunset*, starring Pierce Brosnan, in order to ensure maximum exposure for the island. 'We consider tourism as our main business and we hold it up as our core industry. Filming is part of the communication and publicity drive and tourism is the engine that powers it all,' explains Basil Smith, communications director for the Ministry.

'2004 was a great year for the film industry in the Bahamas,' says Craig Woods, Bahamas' film commissioner. 'We had three movies back to back; *After the Sunset, Into the Blue* and *Pirates of the Caribbean II*.' Woods is keen to land television series as well as films. A weekly TV show means longer commitments than are typical in movie productions, which are usually one-shot deals.

A number of attractions exist on the islands for film tourists to visit. For example, the Hilton in Nassau boasts a 'Double-O' Suite, stocked with James Bond movies, soundtracks, posters, movie stills, and memorabilia from the filming. There are also Bond books, a special bathrobe and, of course, Martini. The hotel has a 'Live and Let Dive' package, which includes dive visits to the 120-foot freighter that was sunk for the movie *Never Say Never Again* and the Valkin Bomber airplane from *Thunderball*.

In fact, dive sites are the most popular film tourism attractions in the Bahamas. Stuart Cove, who is a regular stunt diver for the Bond movies, takes 50,000 divers and snorkellers every year to his diving/film location on the south coast of New Providence Island. He says, 'Production of film, TV and commercials is a very important part of our business, and very important for marketing. We emphasize the connection to film and television in all of our marketing material – in the brochures and on the website. Divers just love the connection to the James

Bond movie sites, and our monthly news releases consistently refer to films and TV programmes being made here.'

Stuart Cove attempts to keep movie locations and memorabilia to attract more tourists and also to add to the quality and differentiation of their diving experience. The film *Flipper* was based at his site and he manages to keep his dock much as it was in the movie: 'We have learned our lesson with the movie sets. The producers destroyed the set for *For Your Eyes Only* but since then we have tried to negotiate right from the start to keep any sets used in movies.' Photographer Claudia Pellarini says that 80–90 per cent of divers purchase photographs and some spend hundreds of dollars. 'Some of the most popular photographs are those of divers in the film sets. For example, they just love having their photo taken on the *Thunderball* set.' The photo shop itself turns over US$430,000 a year.

Movie producers were attracted to the Bahamas initially for various economic reasons and environmental exigencies. Cove claims, 'The main reason is that we have the perfect location. The natural beauty of the islands is a terrific pull – the Bahamas sells itself – and we are very close to the mainland. There is also a beneficial tax situation, and we can supply labour very easily and very cheaply. In fact, the producers can get much better value all round by coming here than they could on mainland US.' The Atlantis Resort gives free rooms in exchange for exposure in films. An example was *After the Sunset* where the resort gave three months of rooms to the crew in exchange for very favourable shots in the film.

Most of the film and television business is generated through word of mouth, according to Cove, and these days there is normally no charge for his assistance: 'We are very aware that the exposure these films and TV programmes give Stuart Cove is critical for our business.' Morgan O'Sullivan, film commission consultant, says that the Ministry of Tourism is now looking at the possibility of producing movie maps related to locations, particularly in relation to *Pirates of The Caribbean*, and also movie tours. The *James Bond* genre, especially, draws large numbers of tourists to the Bahamas, so a *Bond* tour would be the first one to be launched.

*Sources*: Personal interviews with: Basil Smith, director of communications, Bahamas Ministry of Tourism (11 January 2006); Craig Woods, film commissioner, Bahamas Film & Television Commission (11 January 2006); Stuart Cove, Stuart Cove's Dive Bahamas (13 January 2006); Claudia Pellarini, Stuart Cove's Dive Bahamas (13 January 2006); Opal Gibson, director of business development, British Colonial Hilton; Morgan O'Sullivan, co-managing director, World 2000 Entertainment Ltd. (11 January 2006).

## Responsible Marketing of Tourism

The tourism marketer is likely to be involved in the process of developing an attraction or a destination, in terms of either building new resorts or rejuvenating old ones. Part of the process involves estimating future demand, as in a feasibility study, but increasing emphasis is being placed upon evaluating the likely impacts – such as direct or indirect economic impact – of any development. Techniques have also been developed to monitor other impacts, such as the environmental and social impacts of development. Common analytical frameworks include an environmental audit, environmental impact analysis, carrying capacity, and community assessment techniques. It is beyond the scope of this book to cover these techniques in detail, but the tourism marketer needs to have knowledge of the most current models and techniques applied to the evaluation of environmental and social impacts.

A tourism marketer must also have an understanding of the principles of **sustainable tourism**. Butler (1993) describes sustainable tourism development as 'tourism which is developed and maintained in an area in such a manner and at such a scale that it remains viable over an indefinite period and does not degrade or alter the environment (human and physical) in which it exists to such a degree that it prohibits the successful development and well-being of other activities and processes'. He defined sustainable tourism as 'tourism which can maintain its viability in an area for an indefinite period of time'.[10] The Global Spotlight below shows how officials in Peru are taking measures to ensure that tourism at Machu Picchu is sustainable.

---

**SUSTAINABLE TOURISM**
tourism which can maintain its viability in an area for an indefinite period of time

---

The theory of sustainable tourism emphasizes the critical importance of environmental stewardship. Similarly, a common thread running through all the existing literature on competitiveness suggests that to be competitive, an organization must be sustainable from an environmental perspective. However, most tourism organizations and destinations are still inexperienced in handling environmental issues creatively. A substantial fraction of environmental spending relates to the regulatory struggle itself and not to improving the environment, particularly in the tourism sector. But corporate managers in certain industry sectors have begun to consider environmental management as a critical component for sustaining competitive advantage, and in the tourism industry it is time for managers to start recognizing environmental improvement as an economic and competitive opportunity, rather than an annoying cost or inevitable threat.

If environmental improvement is to provide a competitive opportunity, an organization must consider **responsible environmental marketing**, which is the balancing of environmental initiatives and environmental communication in order to achieve sustainable competitive advantage. Unfortunately, there has been no consistent approach to environmental marketing practices in tourism. Some companies neglect their environmental obligations, perhaps because of a lack of guidelines and examples of best practice, or perhaps because they don't understand the benefits. Others exploit environmental communication for short-term gains or fail to tell visitors about their environmental initiatives. Many studies indicate that environmental considerations are now a significant element of travellers' destination-choosing process, and much of what first-time visitors learn about a destination's environmental qualities depends on the effectiveness of information and the motivation stimulated by commercial brochures or websites.

---

**RESPONSIBLE ENVIRONMENTAL MARKETING**
the balancing of environmental initiatives and environmental communication in order to achieve sustainable competitive advantage

---

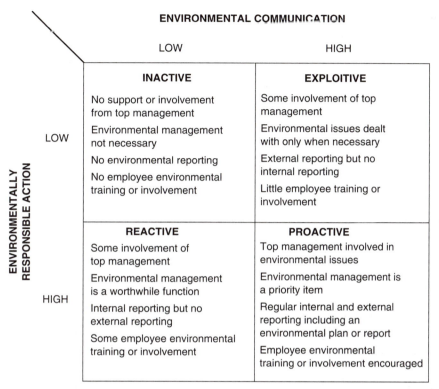

**Figure 13.4** A Model of Responsible Marketing

Figure 13.4 is model of responsible marketing that managers in the tourism industry can use to improve their environmental marketing practices. The model is based on previous literature in marketing and in strategic and environmental management, and it adopts the view that an organization or destination can be plotted on a two-by-two matrix to identify its position regarding responsible marketing. The vertical axis represents environmental action and the horizontal axis represents communication of these activities. Organizations can take up one of four theoretical positions within the model. They can be classified as *inactive* when they tend not to see the benefits of allocating any resources toward environmental activities and when they have a low level of commitment to both environmental improvement and communication of environmental activities. Those that see the benefits of environmental action (perhaps for regulatory purposes) but fail to communicate these efforts are *reactive*. Organizations that exploit consumer interests in environmentally friendly products without considering resource characteristics, environmental ethics, or a long-term perspective are seen as *exploitive*. The position in the model most likely to remain sustainable (and competitive) is that in which both environmental action and environmental communication of this action are high, and these organizations are labelled as *proactive*. In the proactive position, products and services are developed sensitively, with regard to their long-term future, and consumers are aware (both before purchase and during the visit) of the concern for the resources involved.

It is important to recognize that an organization's position in the model may only be temporary, as it may be in transit between one place and the next. Further, there is likely to be a variety of contingency factors that will affect the position. Previous research suggests that these influences include the level of environmental pressures from stakeholders, managerial interpretations of environmental issues, the level of environmental regulations, and the size and the financial position of the company.

## Global Spotlight

### Machu Picchu in Peru Limits Access to Tourists

Over-popularity as a tourism attraction can often lead to a destination becoming the environmentally unsustainable victim of its own success. Machu Picchu, Peru, an Inca site rediscovered in 1911, is fast seeing the detrimental impacts caused by its international popularity. The Peruvian government is keen to market the UNESCO World Heritage site in order to generate tourist dollars. However, if the destination is to remain intact and therefore viable for the future, the government needs to look at sustainability, which involves limiting access.

Back in 1992 only 9,000 tourists visited the ruins all year but by 2002 the figure had risen to 150,000, and had reached around 400,000 by 2005. There was little restriction on either access or visitor behaviour within the sacred sites, which reportedly generates US$47 million annually for the Peruvian economy. Aguas Calientes, the village at the base of Machu Picchu, mushroomed in size, rubbish lined the banks of the nearby Urubamba River and the Inca Trail had deteriorated due to many years of unrestricted over-use. Overcrowding, erosion and the exploitation of local people as guides and porters were all endemic before January 2001 when the government finally intervened and initiated a system of regulations and permits.

Increasing pressure from UNESCO, the World Tourism Organization (UNWTO) and numerous non-government agencies has encouraged a limit on the number of visitors to the ancient Inca ruins. Laws limit numbers on the trail to 500 per day, and visitors must join guided tours with registered companies to ensure adherence to conservation regulations. In 2000 the World Monuments Fund (WMF), a New York conservationist group, numbered the ruins amongst the 100 most endangered sites, but removed them from the list when the Peruvian government regulated the Inca Trail. UNESCO continually threatens to put Machu Picchu on its list of World Heritage in Danger sites, a designation meant to encourage immediate corrective action. Archaeologists and preservationists alike regularly bemoan the deterioration caused by over-use.

Since the 2001 regulations were introduced, conditions are better for trekkers, porters and the Inca Trail itself despite the continued rise in numbers. As a result of lobbies from the NGO Inka Porter Project, wages for porters have increased and work conditions, first aid provision and language tuition have all improved. Moreover, tour operators must use assigned campsites with proper toilet facilities, remove all rubbish, use only propane for fuel, maintain a ratio of one guide per seven tourists, and limit weight loads to 25 kilos per porter. To promote continued sustainability in the area, the tourists themselves have to shoulder some responsibility as well as the government and the tourism industry. Prices are rising – general admission is now US$30 per person and the Inca Trail permit has gone up from US$17 to US$60 in order to pay for trail maintenance, monitoring of regulations and better facilities.

Machu Picchu is promoted by Peruvians as an intrinsic part of Peru via the official destination website and its link to Go2Peru.com. Responsible tour operators, such as G.A.P Adventures and Trek Holidays, include tours to Peru's most famous destination. G.A.P promotes Machu Picchu by appealing to travellers who are aware of ecotourism and sustainability. Published literature plays a key role in promoting Machu Picchu as a tourist destination. Non-fiction literature about the ruins also encourages visitors, as well as films, such as Alberto Granado's screenplay *The Motorcycle Diaries* which eulogized Machu Picchu and the land of the Incas and has a huge and continuing impact on international visitor numbers. A 2003 music video for Gloria Estefan's song, 'Wrapped' is such a good advertisement for both Machu Picchu and Peru as a whole that it appears, mistakenly, to be a PromPeru or government-sponsored project. The site is also projected positively in many documentaries and educational videos focusing on its history and its dramatic rediscovery.

However, even filming can further the deterioration of the ancient ruins while at the same time promoting tourism success. The making of commercials and music videos has helped boost tourist numbers, but during actual filming of a Cusquena beer commercial in 2001, a sacred sundial was damaged accidentally, resulting in criminal charges against the production company for using a prohibited crane.

*Sources*: Rachowiecki and Beech (January 2004) *Lonely Planet: Peru*, 5th edition, 209; Leffel, T. 'Saving Machu Picchu – responsible tourism is a 3-way deal', retrieved from www.transitionsabroad.com; Roach, J. (2002) 'Machu Picchu under threat from pressures of tourism', *National Geographic News*, retrieved from news.nationalgeographic.com.

## Cause-related Marketing in Tourism

**Cause-related marketing (CRM)**, said to be 'corporate philanthropy organized to increase the bottom line', (Barnes and Fitzgibbons, (1991),[11] is a rapidly expanding trend in marketing communications, and is growing at a time when the public is increasingly cynical about big

---

**CAUSE-RELATED MARKETING (CRM)**
corporate philanthropy organized to increase the bottom line

**Table 13.1**   Branding Approaches to CRM

| Features | Autonomously Branded | Co-Branded | House Branded | Industry Branded |
|---|---|---|---|---|
| **Charity reputation** | Established/ independent of company | Tied to company and charity | Company dependent | Established/ independent of industry |
| **Firm's involvement in charity administration** | None | Partial to jointly administered | Company controlled | None |
| **Company control over charity use of funds raised by CRM Program** | Limited | Some influence | Complete | Limited |
| **Strategic opportunity** | Leverage external brand | Leverage brand congruence | Support existing company/product brand | Leverage industry brand |
| **CRM promotional objective** | Demonstrate firm – charity congruence where not obvious | Demonstrate firm – charity brand congruence | Promote firm's commitment | Promote industry's commitment |

business. It is basically a marketing programme that strives to achieve two objectives – improve corporate performance and help worthy causes – by linking fundraising for the benefit of a cause to the purchase of the firm's products and/or services.

It was an American Express campaign that signified the inception of CRM in 1981. American Express joined with a non-profit group to promote fine arts in San Francisco. Profits from increased use of American Express cards were donated to the organization. The success of this campaign led to the first national CRM campaign in 1983 between American Express and the Statue of Liberty–Ellis Island Foundation. The results were US$1.7 million donated to the foundation and an increase in American Express card usage of 28 per cent. American Express called its link with charity 'cause-related marketing' and registered the term as a service mark with the US Patent Office.

CRM has spread rapidly over the last 20 years and is not only used by product-oriented corporations. Other industries such as education, health care, human services and community and civic affairs are becoming active users of CRM. Companies use CRM to contribute to the well-being of society and to associate themselves with a respected cause that will reflect positively on their corporate image. Companies, and their brands, can benefit from strategic alignments with causes or with not-for-profit organizations. It is hoped the emotional attributes associated with cause-linked brands differentiate them from their rivals (sometimes referred to as 'cause branding').

CRM efforts can be categorized into **autonomously branded, co-branded, house branded, and industry branded** approaches, the distinctive features of each being summarized in Table 13.1.

## Autonomously Branded CRM Initiatives

Autonomously branded philanthropic collaborations are characterized by an arm's length relationship between the corporate sponsor's brand and the brand of the charity/cause that it supports. These are the quickest and easiest kind of relationships to arrange and are the dominant form of philanthropic activity. An example is the American Express initiative described above. Generally those companies in the tourism industry embracing autonomous CRM are those offering a wide range of destinations to their clients. In recent years there have been an increasing number of travel companies that collect funds to distribute to established charitable concerns. These include Abercrombie and Kent, Bales Worldwide, Intrepid Travel and Ultimate Travel – the later adding a 'voluntary £10 contribution' to each customer booking that has resulted in an 85 per cent take-up. With some of these philanthropic programmes there is a link, if only a subtle one, between the programme and the purchase of holidays. The Galapagos Conservation Fund created by Lindblad Expeditions provides guests with a direct solicitation envelope the night before landing, and they are offered a discount coupon of US$250 on future Lindblad excursions in return for charitable contributions of US$250 or more. Since 1997, guests have contributed close to US$1 million.

## Co-branded CRM Initiatives

In co-branded collaborations, the company and the charity form a new brand co-sponsored and marketed by both organizations. An example of this type of branding approach is Avon's sponsorship of the *Race for the Cure* in partnership with the Breast Cancer Coalition. Collaborations of this type are more strategic than autonomously branded programmes because the company can differentiate itself by becoming the sole sponsor of an event or cause, and because co-ownership implies increased commitment and effort. In its simplest form co-branded CRM initiatives might best be demonstrated where a tour operator and a charity jointly market a holiday in a chosen project area, with a proportion of the money generated being used to fund the project. Wildlife conservation projects on Kenya's Masai Mara, in the Galapagos Islands and at Ranthambhore Tiger Park, India, have benefited from holidays jointly marketed with tour operators. Similar arrangements are in place elsewhere between Save the Rhino and the UK tour operator Discovery Initiatives. The relationship between Born Free and Kuoni benefits from both partner organizations being located in the same town, thereby aiding local links and marketing.

## House Branded CRM Initiatives

With the house branded approach, 'the firm takes ownership of a cause and develops an entirely new organization to deliver benefits associated with the cause' (Hoeffler and Keller, 2002).[12] Similar to private label products, house branded charities are by definition differentiated from other charities, and in the increasingly crowded marketplace for philanthropic programme partners, the firm has unfettered access to its own charity. The number one quick-service restaurant in the US, McDonald's, has a house branded charity benefiting children – Ronald McDonald House – achieving true charitable status in the minds of consumers.

Examples of tourism companies establishing a programme that works independently of partners are less easy to identify. For the travel industry, taking full responsibility for the continuing success of initiatives, usually abroad, is a significant commitment. However, examples do exist. In general the companies using this strategy are well established and have a mission focused around the cause they support. Ad Terrae Gloriam (ATG), Oxford, is a UK tour operator founded in 1979 on principles of conservation and sustainable tourism 'long before these concepts became fashionable'.[13] Of ATG's pre-tax profits, 10 per cent are donated to their own ATG Trust. The ATG Trust works with local communities to identify, develop and complete conservation projects in areas where ATG clients travel.

## Industry Branded CRM Initiatives

Finally, industry branded initiatives are those that involve contributions to a cause from the industry as a whole, rather than separate corporations. As with house branded CRM initiatives, few examples exist in tourism, but the Travel Foundation in the UK fits this typology. The Travel Foundation was established in 2004 as a partnership between government, NGOs and the travel industry to acknowledge that tour operators have a responsibility to help protect the places that tourists visit and ensure that the benefits of tourism reach the local communities. The Travel Foundation is largely funded by the commercial industry which, as such, forms part of its various CRM programmes, but is firmly the industry's charity. It was mentioned above that a disadvantage of industry dependent brands is that the public relations benefits are shared and more difficult to leverage for the individual firm. This may explain why the number of tour operators actively committed to the Travel Foundation is relatively small – many preferring their CRM to be directed by the interests of their own staff and clients rather than by the Foundation.

## The Future for CRM in tourism

Despite the examples above, and research which shows that travel companies can gain competitive advantage by adopting ethical policies, the use of CRM in the tourism industry is not widespread and is still in its infancy. However, there is evidence that tourism organizations are beginning to wake up to the threat of legislative intervention should the industry fail to address its negative impacts. Players in the industry are also starting to recognize that taking, and then promoting, an ethical stance can be good for business as it potentially enhances profits, management effectiveness, public image and employee relations. The tourism industry also affords an excellent example of brand fit where the charitable causes supported often bring direct benefits to the company and its travelling clients.

One weakness of CRM is that it is often short term, opportunistic, and seen by some as self-serving and exploitive. It is therefore important that tourism companies adopt a cause and make it an important part of the company's business by integrating a non-commercial, socially redeeming value system into the company's business plan and operations. Considerable attention also needs to be paid to the role of 'fit' between the firm and the charity in philanthropic efforts. Which CRM approach a company adopts will often depend on the size of the company and resources available. Whilst the autonomous branded programmes can be effective for specialist operators, co-branded approaches to CRM offer an opportunity for firms to move away from just making donations and towards a more collaborative partnership with charitable organization partners. Industry branded initiatives have the advantage of benefiting the industry as a whole (as well as the cause), but not individual companies. For players in the tourism industry, the house branded philanthropic initiative may be the most strategic of the four branding approaches because its development, promotion and administration is entirely within the control of the corporate sponsor.

## Marketing Sport and Adventure Tourism

### Sport Tourism

One of the fastest growth areas in the tourism sector is sport tourism, and many destinations are seeking to capitalize on this growth. Although sport tourism is a relatively new concept in contemporary vernacular, its scope of activity is far from a recent phenomenon. The notion of people travelling to participate and watch sport dates back to the ancient Olympic Games, and the practice of stimulating tourism through sport has existed for over a century. Within the last few decades, however, destinations have begun to recognize the significant potential of **sport tourism**, and they are now aggressively pursuing this market niche. Broadly defined, sport tourism includes travel away from a person's primary residence to participate in a sporting activity for recreation or competition; travel to observe sport at grass roots or elite level; and travel to visit a sport attraction such as a sports' hall of fame or a water park. Five major areas of sport tourism have been identified: attractions, resorts, cruises, tours and events, each of which is discussed below.

---

**SPORT TOURISM**
travel away from a person's primary residence to participate in a sporting activity for recreation or competition; travel to observe sport at grass roots or elite level; and travel to visit a sport attraction

---

#### Sport Tourism Attractions
Sport tourism attractions are destinations that provide the tourist with things to see and do related to sport. Attractions could be natural (parks, mountains, wildlife) or human-made (museums, stadiums, stores). This core area of sport tourism also includes visits to (a) state-of-the-art sports facilities and/or unique sports facilities that generally house sports events,

such as stadiums, arenas, and domes; (b) sport museums and halls/walls of fame dedicated to sport heritage and to honouring sport heroes and leaders; (c) sport theme parks, including water slides, summer ski jumps and bungee jumping; (d) hiking trails developed for exploring nature; and (e) sport retail stores. An example of a sport tourism attraction is the World Golf Hall of Fame, situated in the World Golf Village in Florida. With a blend of conventional museum-style exhibits and cutting-edge video presentations, the 2,973-square-metre exhibition space offers hundreds of artifacts and displays from the sport's early days through to the modern game.

### Sport Tourism Resorts

Sport tourism resorts are well-planned and integrated resort complexes that have sport or health as their primary focus and marketing strategy. In many situations, these vacation centres have high-standard facilities and services available to the sport tourist. The sport tourism resort category includes amenity and destination spas, golf and tennis resorts, water and snow sport resorts, as well as nature retreats offering outdoor adventure and exploration. Generally speaking, these resorts have state-of-the-art sport equipment and facilities and offer visitors various levels of activity opportunities, along with educational programmes led by instructors who have a great deal of expertise and personal visibility. These resorts do vary in their focus, however, ranging from those that have high-level international standards and specialize in specific and highly developed skills, to campground services specializing in recreational sporting activities.

### Sport Tourism Cruises

The sport tourism cruise category incorporates all boat-related trips that use sports or sporting activities as their principal market strategy. Many ships built today resemble hotels and resorts and have unique sport installations. They also use guest sport celebrities as a marketing tool. To satisfy the sport tourist even further, cruise ships often provide guests with opportunities to participate in activities such as snorkelling and water skiing in unique and varied water environments. Other planned activities include provision of onboard sport competitions and/or modified games (e.g. a golf driving range on deck) and special presentations or clinics from invited sport celebrities. 'Cruise-and-drive' programmes allow tourists to board their own vehicles to facilitate transportation to desired sport destinations. Private yachts may also be chartered, which may be sailed directly to the sport destination of the sailor's choice. The use of watercraft for sporting activities (e.g. recreational and competitive sailing or jet skiing) is also an important dimension to this category.

### Sport Tourism Tours

Sport tourism tours take visitors to their favourite sport events, facilities, or destinations around the world. These tours may be self-guided or organized, depending upon access, location and nature of the activity. For example, many ski tour packages provide air travel, accommodation, local transportation and ski-lift tickets with no special guide or amenities. At a more organized level, some companies specialize in travel packages that fly fans to a sports event – such as a football match – in another city, put them up in a hotel for a couple of nights, provide tickets to the game, arrange for a cocktail party and pre-game briefing with media as well as a post-game reception with players and coaches, and then return them safely home. This type of tour is especially appealing to sport aficionados who want to follow their team on the road or take in a major event such as the Super Bowl or Indianapolis 500, and for those whose dream is to walk the fairways of Augusta National during the Masters golf tournament. An example of a travel specialist catering to this market is Travelcare Sports, referred to in Chapter 7. The company arranges packages in Europe for football fans to see their favourite teams.

*Sport Tourism Events*

Finally, sport tourism events are sport activities that attract a sizable number of visiting participants and/or spectators. The type of visitor depends on the event: some are obviously more spectator-driven than others (e.g. the Olympic Games versus the National Amateur Shuffleboard Championship). Furthermore, they have the potential to attract non-resident media and technical personnel such as coaches and other sports officials. High-profile sport events such as the Super Bowl, Olympic Games or World Cup are often referred to in the literature as 'tourism hallmark events' or 'mega events'. Of the five categories of sport tourism, the sport event category has the most significant economic impact on host destinations. It is increasingly common for organizers to calculate the amount of new dollars or hotel room nights that are generated by an event. Events designed to attract large numbers of spectators can bring thousands, or even millions, of dollars into a local economy. However, smaller participatory events, such as tournaments or marathons, can also bring benefits, particularly to smaller cities or less populated regions. Since participatory events often make use of existing infrastructure and volunteer labour, they can be relatively inexpensive to host, thereby yielding high benefit-to-cost ratios. Further, participatory sport events have been shown to be an effective way to attract new visitors and to generate return visits.

The Snapshot below shows how destination marathoners have become a huge draw around the world. New races are starting up, and even successful, long-established marathons are diversifying into new options such as shorter runs, concerts by big-name musical acts, elaborate fitness expos and hotel discounts.

## Snapshot

### Destination Marathoners

The image of the long-distance runner has been overhauled and remade in the image of modern society. In the past, marathon winners hailed from the traditions of the great long-distance runners from small African villages. The majority of participants these days are white middle-aged urban professionals, and are often given the label of destination marathoners. Destination marathoners are runners who combine the physical and spiritual rush of completing a 42-kilometre (26.2-mile) road race with the pleasures of a vacation. Every one of the 50 US states now caters to these travellers who follow their passion – whether it is to Alaska's Midnight Sun Marathon, New York City's beloved five-borough block party, or races at Disney World, Mount Rushmore, and in Nashville (where country music bands play at each

**Table 13.2**  Marathon Calendar from around the World

| Month | Marathon |
| --- | --- |
| January | Walt Disney World Marathon, Orlando, Florida; Las Vegas Marathon |
| February | Tahiti Nui Sunrise Marathon, Moorea |
| March | Napa Valley Marathon, California; Rome Marathon; Thailand Temple Run, Bangkok |
| April | Country Music Marathon, Nashville, Tennessee; Paris International Marathon; London Marathon |
| May | Great Wall Marathon, Tianjen Province, Republic of China |
| June | Mayor's Midnight Sun Marathon, Anchorage, Alaska; Safaricom Marathon, Lewa Wildlife Conservancy, Kenya; Edinburgh Marathon |
| July | Nova Scotia Marathon, Barrington |
| August | Quebec City Marathon; Marathon by the Sea, Saint John, New Brunswick |
| September | Maui Marathon, Hawaii; Berlin Marathon |
| October | Melbourne Marathon |
| November | New York City Marathon; Athens Marathon |
| December | Honolulu Marathon, Hawaii |

mile along the race course). London, Berlin, Athens and Paris play host to a few of Europe's top races, and even the Great Wall of China has its own marathon, held each May. Table 13.2 provides a sample of some of the marathons from around the world.

The marathon is one of the most storied races of all time, dating back to the ancient Greeks. But once the exclusive domain of Olympic athletes and hard-core fitness fiends, today's marathon is geared towards people who compete not to win, but to finish. In the US alone in 2005, an estimated 382,000 runners finished marathons, with the average age of runners being 40.5 for males and 36.1 for females. New races are springing up all around the world, and even successful, long-established marathons are diversifying to offer new options such as shorter runs, concerts by big-name musical acts, elaborate fitness expos and hotel discounts. Even though Mbarak Hussein of Kenya won the 2002 Honolulu Marathon in 2 hours and 12 minutes, the course stayed open for another 8 hours to see over 26,000 racers pass the finishing post. To cater to these marathon travellers, Honolulu puts on a luau with guest musicians such as Brian Wilson and Van Morrison, and on race day holds a 10-kilometre walk for runners' families and friends.

There are some concerns over the number of participants who have given their lives in the quest for the 42.2-kilometre grail. For example, four men, aged 36 to 54, have died in the Toronto marathon over the past five years. 'Back in the '70s and '80s, people who ran marathons were people who were very, very fit,' said Dr James Edwards, a Toronto coroner. 'Over the last 10 or 15 years, it has become an event that more average-type people participate in. There is the danger that people who should not be participating in marathons may be doing so.'

*Sources*: Cummings, S. (2002) 'Sport Planner of the Year Award, Saint John', retrieved from www. canadatourism.com/en/ctc/ctx/ctx-news/search/newsbydateform.cfm; MarathonGuide.com website: www.marathonguide.com; Mate, S. (4 September 2002) 'The marathon tourist', *The Globe and Mail*, R10; Wluik, M. (2003) 'Going the distance', *Travel + Leisure*, 33(4), 124–128; Blackwell, T. (14 October 2006) 'The new opiate of the middle-class masses', *National Post*, A14.

## Adventure Tourism

Adventure tourism brings together travel, sport and outdoor recreation, and, like sport tourism, is one of the fastest-growing segments of the tourism industry. The Adventure Travel Society classifies adventure tourism according to activity, distinguishing between 'hard' and 'soft' activities. Mountaineering is classified as a hard adventure activity, along with activities like white-water rafting, scuba diving and mountain biking. Soft adventure activities include camping, hiking, biking, animal watching, horseback riding, canoeing and water skiing.

---

**ADVENTURE TOURISM**
a combination of travel, sport and outdoor recreation

---

The Travel Industry Association of America estimates that 10 per cent of North Americans have taken an adventure travel vacation, and that the market is growing by 10 per cent a year (Jackson, 2005).[14] According to the first annual 2006 *Adventure Travel Industry Survey, Practices and Trends*, released in 2007 by the Adventure Travel Trade Association (ATTA), women comprise the majority of adventure travellers worldwide (52 per cent). The highest participating age group are 41–60 year olds, and South America ranks highest in terms of increasing destination interest among consumers.[15]

As the adventure tourism bug has spread to the masses, adventure companies are attracting a growing number of people who are not necessarily passionate about one particular activity, and there is a strong trend in the industry toward multi-activity soft adventure tourism packages in nature-based environments. In fact, what is sold as the ultimate multi-sport adventure is the 'Survivor' tour. The incredible success of the TV series of the same name has encouraged companies to launch Survivor-themed trips that offer participants multiple challenges.

Adventure tourism companies tread a careful line between selling adventure as an idea and delivering adventure as an experience. In this respect, adventure is socially constructed and has been subjected to a process of commodification. Three key factors have facilitated this commodification: a deferring of control to experts; a proliferation of promotional media; and the application of technology in adventurous settings (Beedie and Hudson, 2003).[16] These factors have combined to create a cushioning zone between the normal home (often urban) location of everyday life and the extraordinary experience of an adventure holiday.

To explain the rise of this commodification, consider Spirit of the West Adventures, a Vancouver Island outfitter that takes small groups of guests on camping and kayaking trips to see the killer whales in B.C.'s Johnstone Strait. The company provides a wilderness camping experience without the inconvenience of having to 'rough it'. Each couple is housed in a four-person tent kept high and dry on cedar platforms. Guides and cooks prepare snacks and meals such as barbequed sockeye salmon and prawn shish kebab, followed by wine and chocolate-dipped fruit. 'We sometimes jokingly call it "float-and-boat", an eating trip with some kayaking thrown in between meals,' says Spirit of the West owner John Waibel. 'What out guests want is a chance to have an outdoor adventure without the risk of being uncomfortable.'

Waibel's customers are among a growing number of aging North Americans that many in the outdoor recreation business are referring to as 'bobos': bourgeois bohemians. They are looking for an escape to nature from their stressed-out urban lives, but the catch is that they want the experience without the hassle of hauling a lot of gear into the backcountry, sleeping on lumpy ground, and hunting for kindling to cook smoky, second-rate meals. Alberta-based Pure West Lifestyles & Adventures is another company catering to 'bobos'. It offers camping adventures along the foothills of the Rocky Mountains 'without the hassles of packing in tents and equipment'. In fact, participants don't even have to walk much. The company's website promises access by all-terrain vehicles 'so you and your family can enjoy the remote wilderness without the exhausting long hikes on foot usually required to get to such secluded and pristine backcountry locations'.

## Marketing Tourism in Times of Crisis

### Destination Crisis

**A destination crisis** is normally the result of external factors impacting negatively on the appeal and marketability of the destination concerned, beyond the direct managerial control of destination authorities (Beirman, 2003).[17] Such factors may be acts of terrorism, national disasters, health issues, crime or international conflict. Since 11 September 2001, there have been more than 3,000 major terrorist attacks, most of which have impacted on the tourism industry. Although terrorism is not a new phenomenon, what is new is its use to attain political ends and global media coverage. The continuous publication by the media of the horror of terrorist attacks and their subsequent results are often enough to sway many international travellers towards reconsidering their vacation plans.

---

**DESTINATION CRISIS**
the result of external factors impacting negatively on the appeal and marketability of the destination concerned, beyond the direct managerial control of destination authorities

---

Nepal exemplifies this situation, a country where global terrorism, coupled with the ongoing domestic Maoist war, wrecked its image as a popular adventure tourism destination between 2000 and 2003. Security concerns sapped the vitality of the country as a desirable destination, especially for those from the West, as they seemed to be the target of terrorist acts in international hubs (Bhattari et al., 2004).[18] In Turkey too, terrorists have made a point of targeting tourism. In 2006, after bombings in two Turkish resort towns, Kurdish militants warned tourists not to come to Turkey as it was not safe. Worth nearly $US20 billion in 2005, tourism is Turkey's second most lucrative sector. In other parts of the world, terrorism and conflict continues to have a negative impact on tourism. In the wake of the military coup in Bangkok in 2006, and a series of deadly bomb blasts in tourism hotspots, thousands of travellers cancelled holidays to Thailand.

Natural disasters can also have a devastating impact on tourism. The Case Study at the end of this chapter focuses on the impact of the 2004 tsunami on Thailand. In 2005 New Orleans in the US was hit by Hurricane Katrina, which devastated the city, damaging 80 per cent of it and killing 1,836 people. Prior to Katrina, New Orleans received about ten million visitors a year, but a year after the disaster, hotel bookings were still down by 26 per cent. In response to the threat of hurricanes, hurricane guarantees are now offered by many tour operators and travel agents. In 2005, resorts like Beaches, Sandals, SuperClubs and Club Med were promoting policies that allowed travellers to rebook for another time without penalty if a hurricane ruins their vacation.

## Responding to Crisis

It has been suggested that there are three steps to the marketing management of a destination crisis (Beirman, 2003).[19]

### Establishing a crisis management team

The first step is to establish a crisis management team and assign key roles, such as media and public relations, relations with the travel industry in source markets, and destination response co-ordination with the local tourism industry. In theory, the middle of a crisis is not a good time to formulate a strategy for managing image or reputation, but for many organizations it is precisely when the conservation begins. Businesses and destinations that are serious about their reputation need to manage risk as an ongoing issue, and plan for unfortunate events. In 2006, the Caribbean Tourism Organization (CTO) and the Caribbean Disaster Emergency Response Agency (CDERA) agreed to develop a disaster risk management strategy for the tourism sector that would help minimize negative impact from any crisis in the region. Under the agreement, CDERA will make an immediate and co-ordinated response to any disastrous event as required by participating CTO members.

### Promoting the destination during and after the crisis

Promotional campaigns following a crisis are often the only way a destination can persuade visitors to travel there. Initiatives can include offering incentives to restore the market, and ensuring that opinion leaders in source markets visit the destination to see that recovery is in place. After 11 September 2001, the challenge for many tourism organizations was to encourage people to travel again with creative marketing campaigns. An example was Choice Hotels, who saw the challenge as twofold: to persuade people to travel again while appearing compassionate and selfless; and to provide travellers with a compelling reason to stay at a Choice Hotel property. The promotional strategy came together with the central idea 'Thanks for Travelling', which was emblazed on 15,000 banners outside Choice Hotel properties and along highways, bridges, and tollbooths. A fully integrated ad campaign followed the use of banners using TV, print, out-of-home, interactive, point-of-purchase and collateral, direct response, event marketing, and international communications. The campaign was effective and the slogan 'Thanks for Travelling' became a rallying cry for the entire travel and tourism industry, generating a value of over US$5 million in consumer and trade public relations. Choice Hotels' CEO Chuck Ledsinger was invited to appear on Capitol Hill in support of new tourism legislation, and the White House invited Ledsinger to attend the signing of the Airport Security Bill. The success established Choice as the industry leader without making the company appear opportunistic.

For countries with an image problem, such as Israel in 2006, promoting to the trade, media and consumers is often more effective within a regional framework than if they choose to market their destinations alone (Beirman, 2001).[20] Regional organizations also serve as a cost effective umbrella under which to continue marketing a destination. An example is the Eastern Mediterranean Marketing Association (EMTA) that markets the entire region (Italy through Jordan) to Australia. The formation of EMTA was based on the realistic perspective that travellers from long-haul source markets such as Australia and New Zealand are likely to combine several destinations in the Eastern Mediterranean, and consequently a joint marketing exercise (especially to the trade but also to consumers and the media) would be more cost-effective and attractive to sellers and consumers than single-destination marketing exercises.

Destinations can also seek marketing support from the public sector. In 2006, the United Nations World Tourism Organization worked closely with the Lebanese Government to help restore the country's tourism industry following the conflict with Israel. UNWTO offered marketing, branding and media support, with a particular focus on trade fairs. UNWTO also assisted Indonesia in recovering from the earthquakes that damaged the country's tourism industry that same year.

*Monitoring recovery and analysing the crisis experience*
The final stage for marketing in times of crisis involves monitoring statistical trends and the duration of both the crisis and recovery process. Analysis of source markets, which under- or over-performed during the crisis, assists the destination marketers in determining the allocation of marketing resources to each market. Market research will gauge the effectiveness of marketing campaigns on source markets and segments within those markets.

---

## Chapter Summary

Trends in tourism marketing include a general growth in tourism, with certain sectors, like cruise lines, growing faster than others. It is predicted that there will be increased competition, and many more mergers among hotel chains, cruise lines and other segments. One of the most significant implications of demographic change in this century is the ageing of the world's population. The world median age is projected to rise from 26 years in 2000 to 44 years by 2100.

The consumer of the future is likely to be seeking experiences, and there is an increasing desire of individuals to convert them into images and stories. In their pursuit for individualism, consumers will look for new experiences; loyalty to a travel supplier will be driven by an intermediary's ability to deliver a fresh stream of one-off experiential vacations. There will be a shift towards inconspicuous consumption and a greater awareness of issues such as sustainable development, ecotourism and ethical consumption. Consumers of the future will also demand more convenience, and personal service will increasingly outweigh price as the key differentiator.

If environmental improvement is to provide a competitive opportunity, an organization must consider responsible marketing, which is the balancing of environmental initiatives and environmental communication in order to achieve sustainable competitive advantage. Cause-related marketing is also a rapidly expanding trend in marketing communications, and is being adopted by some players in the tourism industry. CRM efforts can be categorized into autonomously branded, co-branded, house branded and industry branded approaches.

Once a destination has identified and acknowledged it is facing a crisis, it has been suggested that there are three steps to its marketing management: establishing a crisis management team, promotion of the destination during and after the crisis, and monitoring recovery and analysing the crisis experience.

## Key Terms

adventure tourism p. 449
cause-related marketing (CRM)p. 441
destination crisis p. 450
experiential marketing p. 433
life caching p. 430
responsible environmental marketing p. 438
sport tourism p. 445
sustainable tourism p. 438
tryadvertising p. 434

### Discussion Questions and Exercises

1. The text states that one of the most significant implications of demographic change in this century is the ageing of the world's population. What are the implications for the tourism industry?
2. The text suggests that marketers can expect to see growing demand for increasingly specialized holidays that combine unusual experiences and the potential for personal development. Do some research and find some vacations on offer today that would fulfil these criteria.

3. Apply the model for responsible marketing to a tourism organization or destination you are familiar with. What position does the organization take, and how could it become more sustainable?
4. Find a current example of a tourism or hospitality organization that is engaged in cause–related marketing activities. Which of the four approaches to CRM discussed in the text is the company following?
5. Find an example of a destination that is attempting to attract sport tourists. Which of the five areas of sport tourism discussed in the chapter is the destination focusing on?

## Marketing After a Crisis: Recovering From the Tsunami in Thailand

Warning came too late or not all on 26 December 2004, when an earthquake off the coast of Sumatra triggered a tsunami that struck more than a dozen countries throughout the Indian Ocean. The tsunami had an overwhelming human and physical impact. A total of 223,492 people lost their lives, a further 43,320 are still missing, some 400,000 homes were reduced to rubble, 1.4 million people lost their livelihoods, and more than 3,000 miles of roads and 118,000 fishing boats were damaged or destroyed. The disaster caused US$10 billion in damages in barely 24 hours. The world responded to the plight of the tsunami's victims on a massive scale and with unprecedented generosity. In the weeks following the disaster, multi-agency assessment teams calculated that approximately $10 billion would be needed to reconstruct the destroyed communities. In response, official and private pledges reached $13.6 billion.

Before the tsunami, tourism in Thailand was at an all-time high, continuing its strong growth with a 20 per cent rise from the previous year with visitor numbers reaching 12 million. However, the tsunami had devastating affects on Thailand's Andaman coast, leaving more than 8,000 people – about half of them foreign tourists – dead or missing. Damages and losses were close to $2.2 billion, hitting the tourism sector particularly hard. On Ko Phi Phi island, for example, the tsunami killed more than a 1,000 people, wiped out many restaurants and rooms, shattered coral reefs and moved white sand beaches into coconut groves. For Phuket, tourism is a very important source of income and employment. The industry employs about 300,000 people, many from other Thai provinces.

However, while the United Nations said the tsunami affected more than 500 Thai villages in six provinces, many popular beaches were relatively unscathed or have been quick to recover their natural beauty, if not their usual number of visitors. 'People watched TV news and thought that everything was damaged. But that wasn't true,' said Suwalai Pinpradab, Tourism Authority of Thailand's (TAT) southern regional director. But

Phuket shortly after the tsunami in 2004

Thailand needed to get the word out that it was open for business. Potential tourists were cancelling their bookings because they assumed that all the hotels had been destroyed, and this was not the case. For example, only 12 per cent of Phuket's hotel rooms were damaged.

To combat the problem, tourism experts representing 42 countries, the private sector and several international organizations, drew up the *Phuket Action Plan* which spelled out a comprehensive series of activities intended to restart the region's economically vital tourism industry, which had stalled after the tsunami. The main objective was to restore travel confidence in the region, with marketing and communications playing a key role. Marketing campaigns began to attract tourists back to Thailand. Phuket's hotel occupancy rates, which dipped below 10 per cent in January, rose to 40 per cent in February, helped by the first planeloads of package tourists from Scandinavia, which landed in Phuket on 2 February to much local media fanfare. In 2005 Phuket received 2.5 million visitors, compared with 4.2 million in 2004. Pinpradab said that because there were fewer tourists, everybody wanted to serve those who came. 'We've realized that tourism is very important for us. So we treat tourists much better than before.'

To combat the loss of tourism at a local level, Phuket's tourism board partnered with local businesses to offer lower airfares, two-for-one deals and extra meals included in the price of hotel rooms. Laguna Phuket, a company that owns five hotel properties in and around Phuket, cut hotel rates by 50 per cent to entice tourists to return. Managing director James Batt said, 'We are trying to position Phuket as a summer destination for the British. In addition to offering special packages and lower room rates, we have launched a $208,000 campaign with UK operators to revive business.'

At an international level, the Thai cabinet approved a $125 million project to rebuild and market the tourism industry in Thailand. The Thai government partnered with Thai Airways International (TAI) and others to promote its 'Best Offer' – three days and two nights at any of 11 different resorts for as little as $80 for the whole stay. In addition, a highly publicized series of events was planned, beginning with a religious ceremony where monks and priests 'freed' the souls of those lost during the tsunami and gave permission for the tourists to return to southern Thailand. This took place on the first anniversary of the tsunami. The TAT even found something positive to say about the effects of the tsunami. Juthamas Siriwan, governor of TAT, said that environmental studies showed that the tsunami actually cleansed the water and beaches, improving quality and helping the ecosystem. The TAT planned to capitalize on this by restoring and improving tourist hot spots.

TAT also partnered with TAI and the Tourism Council of Thailand (TCT) to organize two 'Mega' familiarization trips to the south of Thailand. The second trip, which took place in July 2005, hosted 270 tour operators and travel journalists from visitor-generating countries in Northeast Asia and the Middle East, while the first trip was targeted at the remaining international market. These trips were part of the Andaman Recovery plan to promote Thailand as a safe and beautiful destination, and designed to show tour operators that it was open for business. TAT also contacted corporations to offer incentives to stage conferences in Phuket. TAT was hoping that business travellers from Thailand and nearby Singapore, China and Japan would occupy beaches and pools vacated by Westerners. This strategy of focusing on regional tourism helped Bali recover from the 2002 bombing, which killed more than 100 foreigners and emptied resorts for months.

Longer-term recovery efforts are still underway, but the tourism sector suffered revenue losses of about $1.4 billion, and the rebound in arrivals has been slower than expected. The government continues to support measures to speed up the recovery with packages and incentives to encourage tourists to return to the affected areas. The government has also invested in the establishment of an early warning system and in disaster preparedness planning.

*Sources*: Johnson, C. (26 March 2005) 'Thai beaches bounce back – but where are the tourists?' *The Globe and Mail*, T6; Anon. (2005) 'Tourism sector hopeful about tsunami recovery', *WTO News*, Issue 4, 1, 3; Anon. (2005) 'Solidarity overcomes competition', *WTO News* Issue 1, 1,3,7; United Nations (2006) 'Tsunami recovery: taking stock after 12 months', United Nations, Office of the Secretary-General's Special Envoy for Tsunami Recovery.

## Questions

1.  Overall, would you say that the tourism authorities in Thailand responded well to the tsunami and its impact on tourism?
2.  What more could have been done to promote Thailand after the tsunami?
3.  Restoring travel confidence is often the major marketing challenge for a destination after a crisis. How did tourism officials in Thailand cope with this challenge? Is there more they could have done to restore consumer confidence?
4.  Tourism in Thailand has more recently been impacted by political instability and terrorism. How should (or how did) the Tourism Authority of Thailand (TAT) respond to the latest crisis?

## Websites

| | |
|---|---|
| www.perusinfo/perueng.asp | Peru Tourism |
| www.machupicchu.org | Machu Picchu Library |
| www.wgf.com | World Golf Hall of Fame in Florida |
| www.bahamas.com | Official Bahamas tourism website |
| www.tourismthailand.org | Tourism Authority of Thailand |
| www.kayak-adventures.com | Spirit of the West Adventures |
| www.secondlife.com | Second Life |
| www.adventuretravel.biz/ | Adventure Travel Trade Association (ATTA) |
| www.marathonguide.com | A guide to marathons around the world |

## References

1   Future Foundation. (2006) 'Travel and tourism in 2020', commissioned by Cendant Travel Distribution Services.
2   Cetron, M. (2005) 'An updated report on ten trends impacting the hospitality industry', *HSMAI Marketing Review*, 22(2), 19–25.
3   Schneiderbauer, D. and Döring, F. (2004) 'Surviving the crisis in European tourism', *Mercer on Travel and Transport*, retrieved from www.mercermc.com, 32–38.
4   Anon. (2006) 'JupiterResearch forecasts online travel spending to reach US$128b in 2001', *Travelweek*, 34(46), 2.
5   Cetron, M. (2005) 'An updated report on ten trends impacting the hospitality industry', *HSMAI Marketing Review*, 22(2), 19–25.
6   Allen, J. and Markey, R. (2006) 'Seven things you need to know about marketing in the 21st century', *World Business*, May, 81.
7   Williams, A. (2006) 'Tourism and hospitality marketing: fantasy, feeling and fun', *International Journal of Contemporary Hospitality Management*, 18(6), 482–495.
8   Anon. (2006) 'Tryadvertising', retrieved from www.trendwatching.com.

9 Schneider, T. (2006) 'Travel advertising today', *HSMAI Marketing Review*, 23(3), 25–26.

10 Butler, R. (1993) 'Tourism – an evolutionary perspective', in Butler, R.W., Nelson, J.G. and Wall, G. (eds) *Tourism and Sustainable Development: Monitoring, Planning, Managing.* Department of Geography Publication 37, University of Waterloo, Waterloo, 29.

11 Barnes, N. G. and Fitzgibbons, D. (1991) 'Is cause-related marketing in your future?' *Business Forum*, 16(4), 20.

12 Hoeffler, S. and Keller, K.L. (2002) 'Building brand equity through corporate societal marketing', *Journal of Public Policy & Marketing*, 21(1), 84.

13 ATG Oxford (2006) www.atg-oxford.co.uk.

14 Jackson, K. (20 May 2005) 'Going semi-wild on adventure tours', *Seattle Times*.

15 Adventure Travel Trade Association (2006) *Adventure Travel Industry Survey, Practices and Trends*, Adventure Travel Trade Association, Seattle.

16 Beedie, P. and Hudson, S. (2003) 'The commodification of mountaineering through tourism', *Annals of Tourism Research*, 30(3), 625–643.

17 Beirman, D. (2003) *Restoring Destinations in Crisis: A Strategic Marketing Approach.* Wallingford: CABI International.

18 Bhattari, K., Conway, D. and Shresta, N. (2004) 'Tourism, terrorism and turmoil in Nepal', *Annals of Tourism Research*, 32(3), 669–688.

19 Beirman, D. (2003) *Restoring Destinations in Crisis: A Strategic Marketing Approach.* Wallingford: CABI International, 23.

20 Beirman, D. (2001) 'Marketing of tourism destinations during a prolonged crisis: Israel and the Middle East', *Journal of Vacation Marketing*, 8(2), 167–176.

# INDEX

# CREDITS

## Chapter 1

Figures 1.1 and 1.2 reprinted with permission from the United Nations World Tourism Organization.

Table 1.1 reprinted with permission from 'Marketing strategies and organizational structures for service firms', *Marketing Services*, published by the American Marketing Association, B.H. Booms and M.J. Bitner, 1981, p. 47–51.

Figure 1. 4 reprinted from *Marketing in Travel and Tourism*, p. 11. Oxford: Butterworth-Heinemann. Copyright 2001, with permission from Elsevier.

## Chapter 2

Vacations from the Heart Opening Vignette reprinted with permission from Responsible Travel.

Figure 2.3 reprinted from *Agricultural Economics*, 48(1), U.R. Orth and J. Tureckova, 'Segmenting the tourism market using perceptual and attitudinal mapping', p.41. Copyright 2002, with permission from Elsevier.

## Chapter 3

Bruce Poon Tip Opening Vignette photo reprinted with permission from G.A.P. Adventures.

Figure 3.3 reprinted with permission from Oliver Wyman (formerly Mercer Management Consulting).

The Failure of Roots Air Case Study photo provided by Trevor Ogle.

## Chapter 4

Figure 4.1 reprinted with permission from the Context-Based Research Group.

Figure 4.3 reprinted from *International Journal of Hospitality Management*, 21(2), D.C. Rutherford and W.H. Samenfink, 'Out for the count: A response', pp. 111–117. Copyright 2002, with permission from Elsevier.

Table 4.4 reprinted from *International Journal of Hospitality Management*, 21(2), D.C. N. Johns and R.Pine, 'Consumer behaviour in the food service industry: A review', pp. 119–134. Copyright 2002, with permission from Elsevier.

Table 4.8 reprinted with permission from SAGE.

Table 4.9 reprinted with permission from SAGE.

**Chapter 5**

Concorde Opening Vignette photo reprinted with permission from British Airways.

Figure 5.1 reprinted from *The Development and Management of Visitor Attractions*, J. Sawrbrooke, Copyright 1995, with permission from Elsevier.

Creating an Alpine Winter Experience Case Study photo reprinted with permission from Tourism Whister.

**Chapter 6**

Space Tourism Opening Vignette reprinted with permission of Space Advetures Ltd.

Figure 6.1 Copyright © 1994 by Houghton Mifflin Company. Used with permission.

Table 6.2 reprinted with permission from  Mercer Human Resource Consulting.

Table 6.3 reprinted with permission from *People* magazine.

Figure 6.5 Club Med Print Advertisement, 2006 reprinted with permission.

Safari and a Facelift Case Study, Surgeon and Safari webpage reprinted with permission by Surgeon and Safari.

**Chapter 7**

Profiting from Fun Case Study photo provided by Canadian Mountain Holidays (CMH).

Figure 7.1 reproduced by kind permission of Continuum International Publishing Group.

**Chapter 8**

What Happens in Vegas, Stays in Vegas Opening Vignette photo provided with thanks to the Las Vegas Visitor and Convention Bureau.

Figure 8.3 Print Advertisement for Newfoundland and Labrador reprinted with permission from Newfoundland Labrador Tourism.

Table 8.3 reprinted with permission from Prentice Hall.

Figure 8.6 Calgary Zoo Dog and Sock ad reprinted with thanks to Calgary Zoo.

Figure 8.7 Brazilian Sex Tourism Prevention ad reprinted with permission from the Brazilian Ministry of Tourism.

Club18-30 Growing Up Case Study photo provided with thanks to Club Med.

**Chapter 9**

A 2007 Rocky Mountaineer Print Ad Opening Vignette provided with thanks to Rocky Mountaineer Vacations.

Puerto Rico convention centre Case Study photo provided with thanks to the Puerto Rico Convention Centre.

**Chapter 10**

Travel Blogs Opening Vignette, Carnival Connections webpage reprinted with permission from Carnival Connections.

'Where the bloody hell are you?' Case Study photo provided with thanks to Tourism Australia.

**Chapter 11**

Pets can stay Opening Vignette webpage reprinted with permission from Pets Can Stay Inc.

Figure 11.2 reprinted with permission from 'A conceptual model of service quality and its implications for future research', *Journal of Marketing*, published by the American Marketing Association, A. Parasuraman, V.A. Zeithmal, and L.L. Berry, 1985, 49(4), p. 40.

Figure 11.3 reprinted with permission from SAGE.

Figure 11.4 reprinted with permission from 'The behavioural consequences of service quality', *Journal of Marketing*, published by the American Marketing Association, V.A. Zeithmal, L.L. Berry and A. Parasuraman, 1996, 60, pp. 31–46.

Richard Branson Case Study photo provided with thanks to Virgin.

**Chapter 12**

Figure 12.1 provided by the Kenai Peninsula Tourism Marketing Council (KPTMC).

Figure 12.3 reprinted from 'Contextulaising destination branding', in N. Morgan, A. Pritchard and R.Pride (eds), *Destination Branding*, p. 31. Copyright 2002, with permission from Elsevier.

Figure 12.4 provided by the the India Tourism Office (UK).

**Chapter 13**

The Aloft Hotel in Second Life Opening Vignette image provided with thanks to Electric Artists Inc.

Figure 13.2 © European Communities [2004], Source: Eurostat.

Figure 13.3 reprinted with permission from the Hilton Hotels Corporation (HHC).

Phuket case study photo reprinted with thanks to Sebastian Bordage.